'Festschrifts usually suffer from lack of cohesion and variable quality. This work doesn't, and in fact provides an excellent introduction to the Reformed Heritage especially for readers who are not a part of that tradition. The articles combine to offer the reader an outstanding historical overview of the Reformed Heritage while sustaining a focus on the church and her mission in the world. From its roots in the past to the place of Presbyterian Theology in America, the articles consistently demonstrate the implications of this theology for church life and for personal discipleship. The articles are significant and engaging and they all contribute to the central theme of church life and practice as well as personal discipleship. Combining the historical, the theological and the practical is not only a fitting tribute to Dr. D. Clair Davis, but it represents the character of his teaching.'

James Grier,
Academic Dean,
Grand Rapids Baptist Seminary, Michigan

'Although 'The Practical Calvinist' may seem a contradiction to the prejudiced or uninformed, such a misconception will be dispelled by this volume in honor of D Clair Davis. In these pages is a feast, both appetizing & satisfying, of contemporary reflection on the Presbyterian & Reformed heritage. Articles from a galaxy of scholars lead us into matters historical, theological, homiletical & pastoral. In the very nature of a work which draws from such a wide range of contributors, one will find views which he cannot endorse. But while, for example, I am not 'Drawn Eastward', I am grateful to Christian Focus for providing such a range of stimulating & valuable material.'

Edward Donnelly
Professor of New Testament,
Reformed Theological College, Belfast

'The Practical Calvinist is an appropriate tribute to a highly regarded teacher of the history of Christianity. Anyone concerned to understand and to maintain the heritage of conservative Reformed Christianity will find many engaging essays that fit their interests.'

George M. Marsden
Francis A. McAnaney Professor of History,
University of Notre Dame, Indiana
Author, 'Fundamentalism and American Culture',
and 'The Soul of the American University'

'A marvelous collection of superb essays by some of the leading scholars of the Reformed tradition. Here is scholarship and pastoral theology at its best — both done in the service of the church.'

Timothy George,
Dean of Beeson Divinity School, Samford University,
Executive editor of Christianity Today

Contributors

Dr. Jay E. Adams,
Mr. Robert Anderson,
Dr. Will Barker,
Dr. Joel Beeke,
Dr. Edmund Clowney,
Rev. David F. Coffin Jr.,
Mr. Erik V. Davis,
Dr. William Edgar,
Dr. Sinclair B. Ferguson,
Dr. Richard B. Gaffin Jr.,
Dr. Richard Gamble,
Dr. W. Robert Godfrey,
Dr. John Hannah,
Dr. Darryl G. Hart,

Dr. Frank A. James III,
Dr. Peter A. Lillback,
Dr. Samuel T.Logan Jr.,
Dr. Ronald E. Lutz,
Dr. Dan G. McCartney,
Dr. K. Scott Oliphint,
Dr. James R. Payton Jr.,
Dr. Joseph A. Pipa Jr.,
Dr. David Powlison,
Dr. Vern S. Poythress,
Dr. Philip Graham Ryken,
Dr. Douglas H. Shantz,
Dr. Carl Trueman,
Dr. John V. Yenchko

THE PRACTICAL CALVINIST:

An Introduction
to the
Presbyterian & Reformed Heritage

In Honor of

Dr. D. Clair Davis

On the Occasion of His Seventieth Birthday

And to Acknowledge His
More Than Thirty Years of Teaching

At
Westminster Theological Seminary in Philadelphia

Edited by Dr. Peter A. Lillback

Mentor

ISBN 1 85792 814 8

© Peter Lillback

Published in 2002

by

Christian Focus Publications
Geanies House, Fearn, Ross-shire,
IV20 1TW, Great Britain
www.christianfocus.com

Cover Design by Alister MacInnes

Printed and bound by WS Bookwell, Finland

Contents

PART 1
THE PRACTICAL IMPLICATIONS OF THE
FIVE POINTS OF CALVINISM

Cont..

PART II
ESSAYS IN PRACTICAL CALVINISM:
THE REFORMED HERITAGE THROUGHOUT
CHURCH HISTORY

A. The Reformed Heritage from the Ancient Church to Protestant Liberalism

Cont.

PART III
ANECDOTES FROM THE MINISTRY AND
TEACHING CAREER OF DR. DAVIS

PART IV
REPRESENTATIVE BIBLIOGRAPHY
OF DR. DAVIS' PUBLISHED ARTICLES
527

Indices

Appendix

CONTRIBUTORS

Dr. Jay Adams
Past Professor of Practical Theology at both Westminster Seminary in Philadelphia and California. Instrumental in the founding of the Christian Counseling and Educational Foundation of Laverock, Pennsylvania.

Mr. Robert Anderson
Vice President for Development, Westminster Theological Seminary, Philadelphia.

Dr. Will Barker
Former President of Covenant Theological Seminary, St. Louis, Missouri. Professor Emeritus of Church History and Academic Dean of Westminster Theological Seminary, Philadelphia. Past Moderator of the General Assembly of the Presbyterian Church in America.

Dr. Joel Beeke
President and Professor of Systematic Theology and Homiletics at Puritan Reformed Theological Seminary, Grand Rapids, Michigan. Pastor of the Heritage Netherlands Reformed Congregation in Grand Rapids, Michigan.

Dr. Edmund Clowney
Retired Professor of Practical Theology and first President of Westminster Theological Seminary, Philadelphia. Past Theologian in Residence, Trinity Presbyterian Church, Charlottesville, Virginia.

Rev. David F. Coffin, Jr.
Senior Pastor, New Hope Presbyterian Church, Fairfax, Virginia. Ph.D. candidate at Westminster Theological Seminary, Philadelphia

Mr. Eric Davis
Comptroller of Westminster Theological Seminary, Philadelphia.

Dr. William Edgar
Professor of Apologetics, Westminster Theological Seminary, Philadelphia. President, The Huguenot Fellowship, Glenside, Pennsylvania.

Dr. Sinclair Ferguson
Pastor of St. George's Tron Church, Glasgow, Scotland, and was formerly Charles Krahe Professor of Systematic Theology at Westminster Theological Seminary, Philadelphia.

Dr. Richard Gaffin, Jr.
Professor of Biblical and Systematic Theology, Westminster Theological Seminary, Philadelphia. Current occupant of the Charles Krahe Chair of Systematic Theology.

Dr. Richard Gamble
Professor of Systematic Theology at Reformed Theological Seminary in Orlando, Florida. Past Director of the Calvin Meeter Center at Calvin Theological Seminary.

Dr. W. Robert Godfrey
President and Professor of Church History at Westminster Theological Seminary, California.

Dr. John Hannah
Chair and Distinguished Professor of Historical Theology, Dallas Theological Seminary, Dallas, Texas.

Dr. Darryl Hart
Past Librarian at Westminster Theological Seminary, Philadelphia. Currently Professor of Church History and Academic Dean at Westminster Theological Seminary, California.

Dr. Frank A. James, III
Associate Professor of Historical and Systematic Theology at Reformed Theological Seminary in Orlando, Florida, and annual lecturer at Keble College, Oxford University.

Dr. Peter A. Lillback
Adjunct Professor of Historical Theology at Westminster Theological Seminary, Philadelphia. Senior Pastor at Proclamation Presbyterian Church in Bryn Mawr, Pennsylvania. Executive Director of The Providence Forum, Bryn Mawr, Pennsylvania.

Dr. Sam Logan
President and Professor of Church History, Westminster Theological Seminary, Philadelphia.

Dr. Ronald Lutz
Senior Pastor New Life Presbyterian Church of Fort Washington, Pennsylvania. Has served on the Boards of World Harvest Mission and the Christian Counseling and Educational Foundation.

Dr. Dan McCartney
Professor of New Testament, Westminster Theological Seminary, Philadelphia.

Dr. Scott Oliphint
Associate Professor of Apologetics Westminster Theological Seminary, Philadelphia.

Dr. James Payton, Jr.
Professor of History at Redeemer University College, Ancaster, Ontario.

Dr. Joseph Pipa, Jr.
President and Professor of Historical and Systematic Theology at Greenville Presbyterian Theological Seminary in Taylors, South Carolina.

Dr. David Powlison
Lecturer in Practical Theology at Westminster Theological Seminary, Philadelphia. Counselor, Christian Counseling and Educational Foundation.

Dr. Vern Poythress
Professor of New Testament, Westminster Theological Seminary, Philadelphia.

Dr. Phil Ryken
Senior Pastor at Tenth Presbyterian Church in Philadelphia, Pennsylvania.

Dr. Douglas H. Shantz
Associate Professor of Christian Thought at the University of Calgary, holding the Endowed Chair of Christian Thought.

Dr. Carl Trueman
Associate Professor of Church History and Historical Theology, Westminster Theological Seminary, Philadelphia.

Dr. John Yenchko
Senior Pastor, New Life Presbyterian Church of Glenside, Glenside, Pennsylvania. Adjunct Professor of Practical Theology, Westminster Theological Seminary, Philadelphia.

FOREWORD

Edmund Clowney

The humble and unassuming demeanor of Clair Davis was matched by his intellectual brilliance. He regularly reduced complicated issues to a few words. I had the privilege of having him in class early in my own teaching years at Westminster Seminary. Only one other student of mine ever matched him in the brevity of a final exam. Clair simply answered the question – directly, using no more words than necessary. He was asked to bring greetings from the Orthodox Presbyterian Church to the second General Assembly of the Presbyterian Church in America. The OPC was concerned about the theological direction of the PCA in its earliest days. Clair began his brief remarks: 'The Orthodox Presbyterian Church loves you and has a wonderful plan for your life!'

Often with humor, and always salted with insight, Clair's teaching caught the meaning of history. His lectures were vivid, sketching episodes from the lives of the fathers, reformers, and heretics to catch the excitement of the new in the setting of the old.

Sometimes the velocity of his thought lost a student or two on the curves. He was likened to a goat crossing a mountain range by leaping from peak to peak. He rightly felt that getting the direction and movement of the happenings was the key to meaning. He was convinced that history, too, is a revelation of God's work – the ordering of his providence. Wisdom combines the truths of revelation with reflective grasp of changing events and personalities. Clair's gifts of wisdom did not match Solomon's in classifying plants and animals, or in compiling ancient Near Eastern wisdom literature. Yet his wisdom enables him not only to see both sides of a question but to appreciate the concerns of both. When he dealt with the views of theonomists, he appreciated their presenting so much information about civil law in the Old Testament. At the same time he wanted to show how the great shift in the nature of the kingdom in the New Covenant affected the relations of church and state.

Clair's teaching of history has always held to the touchstone of the gospel of Christ. He kept the Bible open in his evaluation of every period. At the same time, he clearly recognized the periods that separated the apostolic church from the early catholic church and the Middle Ages. He did not deal with these periods as givens, but helped students to see the processes of change that produced them.

No doubt his experience as a teacher of history heightened his own probing of the processes of declension and renewal. As a master teacher, he took the time to make Martin Luther a real person for students, and requires their reading from what Luther wrote. But Clair was also at pains to present Abelard, Aquinas, Calvin, Knox, and Jonathan Edwards. He traced the lives of the teachers of the church, and so presented their writings, to better understand both. He was also ready to reflect on Billy Graham and Bill Bright of Campus Crusade or the latest charismatic newsmaker.

In a magisterial chapter on the reformed Church of Germany Clair notes that Calvin's 'finishing the Reformation' answered Renaissance humanism as well as Roman Catholicism.[1] He goes on to show how the division of Germany into feudal governing units provided areas where Reformed ecclesiastical polity could find fuller expression in relation to Lutheranism as well as to Rome. The influence of the Reformed minority in doctrine is seen, for example, in the Tetrapolitan Confession drawn up by Bucer and Capito. The German Reformed churches emphasized the continuing relationship of Christ to his people, not just his eternal election and bringing the individual to faith at the time of his conversion. The German church also went beyond the Augsburg Confession in stressing the need for biblical support for all aspects of worship.

John Laski in the Frisian Church of northwest Germany

developed the place and importance of the local elder. The presbytery had been recognized as a city-wide governing body of ministers and elders. Davis remarks, 'a presbytery without sessions!' Laski coordinated the relation of presbyteries to sessions and congregations. As always, Dr. Davis clarifies this history to benefit current discussions of Presbyterian polity, including the relation of teaching to ruling elders.

Church assemblies of Reformed people, devoted to doing all things decently and in order, keep Roberts Rules of Order at the Moderator's table, often with a parliamentarian charged to unsnarl tangles, and to save face for the moderator when possible. One could hope for committed students of Dr. Davis to leaven church debates with wisdom from the past – especially if they could add a touch of salt from the Davis cupboard.

We who know Clair Davis are delighted by this festschrift in his honor, and grateful to Dr. Peter Lillback for editing it. We could wish for another blessing, a collection of his writings. We could then read an article Clair wrote on 'The Love of God and Evangelism' in the *Messenger* of the Presbyterian Church in America:

> What can the Lord do with people like us? What He has always done – disarm us with His love. What He said to the older brother, He says to you too: 'You're with me always. All I have is yours. But I want you at My party too.'
>
> You need a clearer perspective of the Lord's love. Otherwise you can't enjoy the Gospel party. That is what got the Pharisees and Galatians all bent out of shape. They did not want people saved unless they were worth saving. The only way they could stand God loving anybody was if they were lovable – like themselves. Martin Luther said all the Germans he knew were Galatians.[2]

Contributors to this volume will reflect Clair's vision of God's hand in history. They may also show the touch of his seasoning with salt.

NOTES

1. W. Stanford Reid, ed., *John Calvin: His Influence on the Western World* (Grand Rapids, MI, Zondervan, 1892) pp. 123-137.

2. PCA *Messenger*, vol. 13, no. 5 (May 1989), p. 8.

INTRODUCTION

Peter A. Lillback

The word 'festschrift' is not an everyday word. But that is not surprising when one understands that what prompts the creation of a festschrift is not an everyday occurrence. A festschrift, or 'birthday book' or 'celebration book' as the German word means when literally translated, is a way that students and scholars honor a special friend, teacher and colleague for an unusual and significant impact on their lives and thought.

The purpose of *The Practical Calvinist* is to honor a unique teacher at his 70th birthday and in recognition of 30 years of teaching at Westminster Theological Seminary. As the anecdotes at the end of the book reflect, Clair has indeed made a unique and lasting impact on his students and colleagues.

In preparing this volume, effort has been made to capture a theme of his ministry – the timeless relevance of Reformed theology throughout church history. The emphasis here falls on the practice of the living church in all ages, or what we might call 'practical Calvinism'. Indeed, Clair himself wrote a series in the *Presbyterian Journal* entitled *Practical Calvinism*. Some of those articles are reproduced here in Part I.

Because of the vast relevance of the practical implications of the Calvinist faith throughout history, this book also has the happy benefit of providing an introductory survey of the Reformed and Presbyterian heritage. Herein are topics that are relevant to the Church as well as the church historian. In fact, many of these topics have been considered in Dr. Davis' teaching as well.

Each contributor has attempted to present an article written with scholarly precision, yet with a length and practical focus that will be useful not only to scholars, but will also be helpful to the lay leadership in the church. Special effort has been made to create a work that is accessible to ruling elders, beginning seminarians, or those readers who might be new to the Presbyterian tradition.

Surely Clair's legacy, and Westminster Seminary's influence, can be seen in the accomplishments of the contributors to this volume:

- They have been students, colleagues or both students and colleagues of Dr. Davis.
- They represent different nations: U.S.; Canada; Scotland, England.
- They represent several ecclesiastical denominations.
- They represent some ten different seminaries and colleges.
- They include Presidents past and present of Seminaries in the Presbyterian and Reformed tradition.
- Most are teaching or have taught full-time in seminaries or colleges, and several are currently serving primarily as pastors.
- Many have had books published. Collectively they have published over 100 books, and countless articles.

In presenting this study to the reader, I wish to express my sincere thanks to Westminster Seminary for allowing me to pursue this project. I also thank each of the contributors for their excellent work and cooperation, which has enabled this fine volume to come to the reader.

In particular I wish to thank Dr. Will Barker, Mr. Bob Anderson, and Mrs. Alexandra Thompson for their invaluable wisdom and support in its development. My abiding gratitude is also affirmed to the Congregation of Proclamation Presbyterian Church in Bryn Mawr, PA for allowing me the privilege of serving both as a pastor and as a teacher and writer. I also thank God for my family's love and constant support. My sincere appreciation is expressed to all of the directors and publishing staff of Christian Focus for their willingness to publish this project and to do so with a consistent commitment to quality and excellence in honor of Christ.

Finally, it is my prayer that this volume will bring glory to God by increasing our love for Him and our Reformed heritage. May the Lord be pleased to use this book to remind us of the great impact a life lived for Christ can have on so many. Thank you Clair!

BIOGRAPHY OF D. CLAIR DAVIS

Erik V. Davis

Daniel Clair Davis was born in Washington, Iowa on March 25, 1933. His parents, Harvey Davis and Kathryne (Daniel) Davis, were third-generation Americans of Welsh descent who did not learn English until they attended elementary school. They were proud of their rich Welsh heritage and pleased to live in southeastern Iowa, where many families of Welsh descent lived. Clair was proud that he could count to ten and summon the family dog in Welsh. It was not uncommon to encounter such names as John Jones, Evan Evans, Hugh Hughes, and Robert Roberts. Clair's mother came from a family of farmers and preachers over several generations in Wales. She was a college graduate who taught high-school German and Latin in North Dakota prior to meeting her husband. Clair's father had an eighth-grade education and was a hog farmer until 1942, when severe asthma forced him to retire. Clair graduated from high school in 1950 as the valedictorian of Washington High School.

Clair was an only child. He developed a love of learning and reading at an early age and found reading to be his favorite pastime. Some of his favorite books were *Tom Sawyer*, *Huckleberry Finn*, and *Robin Hood*. He was known as the neighborhood checkers champion and as 'Uncle Clair', the teenager who narrated plays held at the band concerts at the local park during the summer months. Later in life, Clair was proud to have hailed from Iowa, 'where the tall corn grows'.

Clair became a Christian at the age of 12 and grew in his Christian faith in his high school years through the discipleship ministry of David Livingston. (David and Clair became reacquainted in the early 1970s when both of them lived in the Philadelphia area. They served as elders together and remain good friends.) Through this relationship with David, Clair became familiar with Wheaton College in Illinois and eventually attended Wheaton, majoring in philosophy. During his Wheaton years, Clair's interest in philosophy and theology developed, and he became convinced of the truths of the historic Reformed faith. He discovered the writings of Dr. J. Gresham Machen, one of the founders of Westminster Theological Seminary in Philadelphia, which led him to consider continuing his studies at Westminster. Clair received a B.A. from Wheaton in 1953 and enrolled as a student at Westminster later that year.

During Clair's Westminster years, his love for Reformed theology continued to grow. He was especially influenced by the teachings of Dr. Paul Woolley in church history and Dr. Edmund Clowney in homiletics. Of particular interest was Clowney's emphasis on biblical theology, the centrality of Christ in all of Scripture, and his teaching on the doctrine of the church. Clair had the privilege of being mentored by Dr. Woolley, who encouraged him to consider a teaching ministry. Clair enjoyed a special bond with Dr. Woolley and appreciated his breadth of knowledge in areas beyond church history and the Reformed/Presbyterian tradition of Christendom. He also enjoyed listening to Dr. Woolley's anecdotal accounts of matters of mutual interest.

Clair graduated with a B.D. (Bachelor of Divinity) from Westminster in 1956. That same year he received an M.A. from the Wheaton Graduate School of Theology, where his advisor and mentor was Dr. Merrill C. Tenney, Professor of Bible and Theology and Dean of the Graduate School. Clair's master's thesis was entitled *The New Testament's Doctrine of Assurance*.

Inspired by his growth at Westminster and Wheaton, Clair began to consider a call to the Gospel ministry. He was interested in becoming an army chaplain during the Korean conflict or teaching systematic theology, combining the theoretical and the practical aspects of the Christian faith. He spent six months at the University of Edinburgh to study systematic theology under Dr. Thomas F. Torrance. Following his time at Edinburgh, he began doctoral studies at the Georgia Augusta Universitaet in

Goettingen, Germany, receiving his Dr. Theol. in June 1960. Clair was positively influenced by his advisor at Goettingen, Dr. Otto Weber. The subject of his dissertation was *The Hermeneutics of Ernst Wilhelm Hengstenberg: Edifying Value as Exegetical Standard.*

Of particular interest is the fact that Clair knew very little of the German language prior to enrolling at Goettingen. He quickly learned German by attending American movies that were dubbed in German and by reading German newspapers. It was during his time in Europe that Clair met his future wife, Goentje 'Lynn' Davis, at the 1958 World's Fair in Brussels. They were married in the rural village of Posteholz, home of her mother, near the city of Hameln. The couple moved to the United States during the summer of 1960.

Clair taught philosophy and religion at Olivet College from 1960–1963 and theology at the Wheaton Graduate School of Theology from 1963–1966. While at Wheaton, Clair received an invitation to teach church history at Westminster, filling the large shoes of Dr. Paul Woolley, his mentor and friend. Clair gladly accepted the invitation to 'carry the baton' of one of the original Westminster Faculty and considered it a high privilege to teach at Westminster 'in the tradition of Woolley'.

During Clair's tenure at Westminster, there have been several developments in the life of the seminary: the inauguration of Ed Clowney as its first president; the inception of the M.A.R., Ph.D. and other programs of study; the increased number of international and female students; the beginning of Westminster Theological Seminary in California as well as satellite campuses in Dallas, New York and Seoul; and the growth of biblical counseling and its part in Westminster's curriculum.

Clair has been greatly influenced by his personal friendships with two Westminster colleagues, Dr. Jay Adams and the late Dr. C. John 'Jack' Miller, and their respective ministries. The founding of the Christian Counseling and Educational Foundation (CCEF) and New Life Presbyterian Church (Jenkintown, Pennsylvania) in the early 1970s were of particular significance in Clair's life. Clair saw these institutions as vital ways in which the doctrines of grace were brought to bear on the local church and on the body of believers. His relationships with the CCEF faculty have been a blessing to him personally and professionally. Clair has also enjoyed his service as elder/

associate pastor at New Life Churches in Jenkintown and Fort Washington, Pennsylvania, as well as his role on the Board of Mission to the World.

During his early years on Westminster's faculty, Clair continued to enjoy a warm relationship with Paul Woolley. Clair's other colleagues in the church history department were Drs. Philip Hughes, Robert Godfrey, Richard Gamble, Samuel Logan, William Barker, and Peter Lillback.

In addition to his responsibilities in the church history department, Clair had the privilege of teaching systematic theology courses (such as the 'Doctrine of Man' course) for several years. He also served as moderator of the faculty for much of his Westminster career.

Clair's pedagogical style may defy description, as his lectures tend to weave storytelling and humor (often unintended) with the profound and serious themes being discussed. It is well-known that Clair does not rely on written notes during his lectures. His teaching is enriched by strong underpinnings of philosophical thought of any given era as well as the practical outworking of theological convictions into social theory and action.

In 1997 Clair was diagnosed with colon cancer and had a particularly challenging recovery following surgery and chemotherapy. It was an opportunity for him to grow in his own faith and to experience the love and support of the Westminster community and others around the world.

Clair and Lynn are the parents of four children (Erik, Jessica, Emily, and Marc) and have five grandchildren.

NOTES

Please see the Photo Section at the end of the book for some pictures that reflect the life and career of Dr. Davis.

PART 1

THE PRACTICAL IMPLICATIONS OF THE FIVE POINTS OF CALVINISM

Selections from Dr. Clair Davis' series entitled, '*Practical Calvinism*', originally published in *The Presbyterian Journal*

SPECIAL SALVATION

D. Clair Davis
Presbyterian Journal, June 18, 1986

What makes you special? Can you recognize a song from just three notes? Can you figure your own taxes? Can you tell when a child is naughty and when he's sick? Can you tell when someone is hurting?

Is there something special about you as far as the Lord is concerned? He made you special, so there should be. But just because you're musical doesn't mean you sing praises. Just because you're mathematical doesn't mean you count your blessings. Just because you're a good judge of character doesn't mean you do a good job judging your own character. Just because you're sensitive doesn't mean you're sensitive to the Lord.

Just because you're special doesn't mean you're using your distinctives for the Lord. You might be using it against him, as a reason to be independent and proud. It's easy to twist a good gift from the Lord and become arrogant about it. And it's easy to think that whatever you're good at is what the Lord loves the most, and whatever you're not good at isn't important to him. You might even believe what you have is so special that you don't need the Lord to show you how to use it.

The Totality of Your Fall

That's why you need to remember that *every* side of you fell in Adam, and every bit of you was under God's curse and Satan's bondage. Maybe you weren't dominated by obvious things like greed and lust. After all, you were brought up to be a lady! But if your mind was so good at controlling your desires, why were you so proud about it? Your aesthetic spirit and cultured mind didn't bring you to Christ, did they? Your problem wasn't that you had an inferior side to your personality that you hadn't quite outgrown. It wasn't just part of you that was something to be ashamed of. Right at your heart you were stubborn and rebellious.

Looking back, you know there wasn't some holy beachhead in your life where the Lord could get a friendly welcome before saving the rest of you. Everywhere within you there was so much dullness and resistance that only the powerful love of the Lord could change you – *without* any help from anything within you. Even the special things about you needed to be turned around by the Lord's grace. Your rebellion wasn't half-hearted or superficial. You were a comprehensive, skilled sinner. Read again Romans 1:29-32: 'Filled with all manner of wickedness … They not only do them but approve those who practice them,' and then read 3:10-19. Paul was right – hearing that is enough to shut any mouth.

Why does the Lord tell you this? Is it so you'll be depressed? No, he wants you to start to understand the greatness of his love. Maybe you could imagine dying for a good man. 'But God demonstrates his own love for us in this: While we were still sinners, Christ died for us.' Why should the Lord love you so much? The more you see how unlovely you are, the more you see how enormously and incredibly he loves you.

The Lord doesn't talk about your sin so you'll think you're trash. He talks about it just because you're not. He talks about it because he made you in his own image, with an infinitely higher and brighter plan for you than the one you chose for yourself. He loves you so much that nothing but his best for you is good enough – nothing less than your complete forgiveness and cleansing. The Lord is reshaping your mind to think straight about priorities. He's turning around your will to do the right thing and not just think about it. He's setting your emotions free to resonate with his praise. For your good and his glory, he's re-making every facet of you so it will sparkle forever!

So don't slip into thinking that all Jesus did for you was to take care of your forgiveness, and now it's up to you. Don't think you have to grow up on your own into the maturity of Christ. Of course, you should *respond* with a life of gratitude for all he's done for you. But since when did gratitude come so easily for you? For that too you need the Lord's grace.

The Totality of His Grace

So focus on the depth and totality of his grace, just as you did on the depth and totality of your sin. It's confusing to *guess* about where you're going to get the Lord's mercy for living. It's just as confusing as guessing about how you can be forgiven. You don't dare guess about it. You have to see it clearly.

To see it you have to look at Jesus Christ – at him *crucified*. You need his redemption and liberation. You need freedom from the bondage of sin, the foolishness of doubt, the oppression of fear, the crippling of pride. By his death, he gave you that freedom, freedom for you to use today.

You need the propitiation of his blood. The Lord's wrath wasn't just against your sins. It was against you personally. Because you knew that, you were afraid of him and stayed away from him. But when he poured out his anger not on you but on his Son, he gave you boldness to come to him in your need. Again and again today you find that confidence as you look to Jesus Christ crucified.

You need fellowship with Jesus and his people. His work of reconciliation brought down the barrier that kept you from him and his family. You need him to work out his reconciling work in your life. You need him as you destroy the walls that stunt your growth and hold you back from real living in the Lord's family.

How special you are! What a special salvation Jesus Christ has accomplished for you. What a special future is ahead for you. And what a special day this is today, for you to look at your crucified Savior and receive from him again all you need for body and soul, for time and eternity.

PERSONAL SALVATION

D. Clair Davis
Presbyterian Journal, July 30, 1986

My name could be either a woman's or a man's. It used to cheer me up a lot that Claire Chennault was head of the *Flying Tigers*. Mail is the worst. It used to come addressed to Mrs. It's some improvement that now it says 'Ms.'. But while those letters keep telling me where I live and what my name is, when they keep on calling me 'Ms.' they lose their punch. It's hard to believe they know me as well as their computer lets on. Getting my name right is crucial. Is it that way with you?

Do you think there's more to you than the computer says? Do you amount to more than your credit rating and the number of points in your driving record? Do you think Freud must be wrong, and that there's more to you than childhood sexuality? Do you think Marx must be wrong, and that you're more than cannon-fodder in the class struggle? Do you keep thinking you're a *person*?

Then you're agreeing with the Lord. He takes you totally seriously as an individual. He treats you as a person, not as a result. He holds you responsible for what you do and for what you become. Don't be misled by that talk about how the Lord hates sin, but loves the sinner. It's people he gets angry with and sends to Hell, not boxes full of sin.

That's why you need a personal Savior. Christians say that all the time. What we mean is that everyone must make his own peace with the Lord. Growing up in a good home doesn't do it. Being able to wear white at your wedding doesn't do it. Only Jesus Christ crucified can save you. If you don't have that straight, you don't have anything straight. Unless you build on that foundation, nothing else matters. But you do need to build on it. You need to start with Christ – and then go on with him. You need everything the Lord has for you.

You need to lay hold of all Jesus did for *you personally* on the cross. You need his propitiation. He did more than take away your sin. He took upon himself his Father's anger against you. 'My God, my God, why have you forsaken me?' Jesus really said that. He had to say that. For ages he had lived in fellowship with his Father. Here on earth he had grown in favor with God. He had tasted in his own life the Lord's love for the righteous. But then that was over. Then he experienced in his own soul and body the wrath of God against a rebel. Then the beloved of the Father knew personal rejection and abandonment. There on Golgotha your savior drank to the bottom the cup of the Lord's judgment and wrath – in your place. There he underwent the outraged anger of a Holy God.

But Jesus had set his face to go to that cross. No one took his life from him, but he laid it down. So his atoning work was personal too. He gave his life not for sin, but for sinners. He died for *you*. His atoning death was for his *people*. Presbyterians may call it limited or definite, but personal is what they mean. Jesus didn't die to open the door. He didn't die to give you some help. He didn't die to stir you up to make something of yourself. He did a lot more than that. He *saved* you from your sins. He set you free from your foolish unbelief, so that now you see him in his glory.

While you wrestle with temptation and suffering, you know that nothing can separate you from his love (Romans 7–8). You're sure of that since you know he's still completing his plan for you. Since he died for you, he will go on to raise you from the dead. Since he justified you, he will keep on sanctifying you. Jesus didn't die for you, and then leave you to take it from there. He didn't lay down his life for you and then sit back to watch you slide off into confusion. Jesus has begun a good work in you, and he will carry it out faithfully to the end.

So you live out of bold faith and triumphant hope. Not that your faith never waivers, but you know Jesus doesn't. Not that you never feel as if you're being bounced around in a meaningless game, but that you know the Lord's purpose for you in Jesus is jealously personal. He's not giving you some stock treatment. He's carrying out the plan with your name on it.

That plan hurts sometimes. That's because it's so personal. The Father chastens only his children. It's not like when you're in church surrounded with crying babies and know you're not responsible for any of them. But the Lord takes the trouble to deal with his sons and daughters. He cares for you so much that he'll do anything he has to do to see you grow up into the full maturity of Jesus Christ.

Of course the Lord knows better than you do what you're growing up to be. He enjoys telling his children what their real names are. You there, you're not really just ordinary Sarai, but Princess Sarah. And you're not just father Abram, but Abraham the Father of Many. Simon, you're Peter my Rock. The rest of you will have to find out what your real names are. But soon you'll see them written down in the Lamb's book of life.

You'll enjoy finding out who you really are. You'll marvel more and more at your Father's custom design for you alone. So what if the computer doesn't care a bit about who you really are. So what if your wife is sometimes right when she says she really can't understand you. Not to mention Freud and Marx. The Lord calls you by name.

UNCONDITIONAL   SALVATION

D. Clair Davis
Presbyterian Journal, August 20, 1986

While you're waiting for the bride to finally cut the cake, you can always play, 'What on earth can she see in him?' You don't need to be catty about it. Just figure out what she *does* see in him. In her whole life she's never done anything really dumb, so there must be more to him than there seems. He doesn't say much, but he must be deep. He's a shrimp, but that must have made him aggressive. He's entry-level, but he must be fast-track.

It's not dumb to commit your life to someone who doesn't look like much, just so long as he's going places. It's his potential that's important. Don't you believe that's what the Lord thinks too? Maybe there aren't any great personalities in his church, but at least they're not killing themselves with cocaine. Maybe Christians don't look so impressive, but the Lord knows what he's doing. He knows how to get in on the ground floor with a winner. After all, he knows how to size you up better than your neighbors do, doesn't he? When he picked you out, he really knew what he was doing.

That's the way people are. When good things happen to you, you're not surprised. You think it just makes sense, considering how hard you work and how flat you keep your stomach. When bad things come to others, that makes sense too. And when the Lord sets his personal saving love upon you, that makes the most sense of all.

Only the Lord doesn't talk that way. Israel, do you think I chose you because you amount to something? Well, it's the other way around – I picked you so the whole world could see I love losers. Paul says the same thing. The reason there aren't many wise or influential or important people in the church is so no one can boast about being a believer. The Lord's mercy is the only reason that *anyone* is in Jesus Christ. So 'let him who boasts boast in the Lord!' (1 Cor. 1:26-31).

It's hard to accept the Lord's *mercy*, isn't it? It just humbles you to the ground to grasp how his kindness works. It's hard to admit that his love doesn't have anything to do with who you are or what you've done or what you're planning to do.

That's hard, but it's glorious too. The Lord loves unconditionally, not just to make some things clear to you but because that's the way he is. The way he is, the way love really is. It's not that you love him, but that he loves you. It's that God loved the world so much that he gave his only son. It's that he loved you when there was nothing lovable about you.

He knows about your future, and that without him in it there's nothing there but gloom and horror. But he loves you enough to change you and make you what you should be. Wait till you get to heaven and look back at how puny your hopes and dreams were, compared to the reality of what he did in you. Wait till next month and do the same thing. But you'll never look back and say, 'Look what I did without the Lord, look how I earned his love'.

So when the Lord tells you about this unconditional love, then you're learning how high and long and wide and deep it really is. It's just incredible. Why should he give *you* the unspeakable gift of his only son? "Who has ever given to God, that God should repay him?" (Rom. 11:35). He has mercy upon whom he has mercy. He's teaching you about *believing* in his love to you (1 John 3:16). He teaching you about basking in his grace, rich and free. More and more he's showing you your salvation rooted only in your savior's righteousness and faithfulness.

Paul knew it isn't easy to choose between what's better for you and what's necessary for others. He knew all about being bone-weary. He knew all about how you never finish meeting other people's needs. But he was still sure he'd do what was necessary and keep on being a servant (Phil. 1:23-25). You can be sure about that too. In the midst of your weariness you know the Lord will finish in you the good work he's begun (1:6).

So you can stop looking for people who appreciate you, and look for the ones who need you. You can come into the room and see your friends on one side and someone looking lost on the other and know which way to go. You can love your wife when she's tired and unresponsive to your wit and wisdom. You can tell your children with a smile that you'll love them even if they drop out of school or marry Yankees.

You can stop trying to convince yourself how outstanding you are. Just be content with sitting down at the foot of the Lords' bountiful table, and be astonished when he calls you up to the head, into his own arms.

IRRESISTIBLE SALVATION

D. Clair Davis
Presbyterian Journal, October 1, 1986

How do people come to believe in Jesus? Usually they need some help from their Christian friends. Usually a man comes to Christ because a friend talked to him.

You can learn what to say. You can invite people to church or a Bible study. You can learn how to talk naturally about what the Lord did for you when your baby died. You can tell about how you became a believer. You can learn how to use the New Life booklet.[1]

Your pastor has learned some skills and can pass them on. Others can help too. Encourage your church to get in touch with Bill Vermeulen at the POC or Kennedy Smartt at the PCA's Mission to North America and see what they do. Let the PCAs call Bill and OPs call Kennedy!

You can take some initiative yourself. Start thinking as soon as you see the SOLD sign going up across the street. How can you welcome these folks? Talk it over with your wife. Take over some tomatoes. Borrow his chainsaw.

You know that's what the Lord wants you to do. You're convinced. But something still intimidates you. Tips on sharing your faith aren't much good when you feel that way. Maybe you could learn how to wrestle alligators too, but you're in no hurry to sign up. Maybe you could learn how to talk about Jesus, but why even try when nobody's going to listen?

That you know from experience. You once told your best friend what the Lord meant to you. He listened politely and said he was glad religion was such a help to you. Then he said it wasn't for him. When you go to a funeral, everyone tells you that George is going to heaven if anyone is because of all he did for the community. They don't understand at all. So you just stand there and try not to nod. Nobody has to tell you how hard it is to talk about what the Lord has done for you.

See what the Lord has taught you already? For you to have a plan for sharing your faith is one thing. For rebellious sinners to turn to Jesus is another. It's not just that people are complicated and you can't program the way they'll respond. It's more serious than that. The Lord says people don't believe because they don't want to. They won't come to the light because it will show how evil they are. And Satan isn't about to let them go either, not without a fight. What that means is devastating. No strategy is clever enough to break Satan's chains. No presentation is plain enough to get through to a sin-clouded mind. No amount of conviction can open glazed eyes wide enough to see Jesus. No amount of love can break down a defiant heart.

So there's no way *you* can bring men and women to Jesus Christ. But you know the Lord can. What's impossible for you is what the Lord does all the time! That's what makes Presbyterians so joyful about the powerful, triumphant, *irresistible* grace of God. You don't have to be intimidated by the problems your friends have with the gospel. You can glory in the saving power of Jesus Christ.

To do that, it helps to understand what's holding you back. Jesus talked about that in John 6. He said he was the bread from heaven, and that if you eat of him you'll live. He said 'If you want to see the Lord's salvation, look at me.' But the people responded, 'How can we believe that? We all know Joseph, and he's just his son. How can we make sense out of this talk about eating his flesh? How can we make use of what he says in a way that fits our religious orientation?' Jesus called that *grumbling*. He said, 'If you want to know how you can believe, I'll tell you. This is how: All that the Father gives me will come to me. No one can come to me unless the Father draws him. This is why I told you that no one can come to me unless the Father has enabled him' (vv. 37, 44, 65).

That's how Jesus spoke to people playing games with the Lord's grace. They sounded like adolescents giggling about love while not knowing a thing about it. They would rather talk about their fascinating religious experience than trust God's son from heaven! People like that need a sharp reminder. They need to hear about their *unbelief*. They need to hear that they're not in charge of evaluating Jesus. They need to hear again that it's the Father who sent him, and that it's the Father who brings people to his Son. They need to hear again that it's the Father who brings people to his Son. They need to hear again that *salvation is of the Lord.*

But why did the Lord put his rebuke of grumblers in a gospel for believers? Why does he want *you* to listen in? He wants you to know about the danger of grumbling over how hard it is for your friends to believe. It's easy for you to be afraid of their problems instead of being bold and confident in the Lord. You learned that a long time ago about your own faith. You don't spend any time now thinking about how hard it was for *you* to believe. Instead you're still marveling at how much *Jesus* did when he died for you. You're still marveling at his grace greater than all your sin. So why theorize about what's wrong with people today, when you could be trusting the Lord's triumphant, invincible grace? Why be so sure that the Lord *can't* save your neighbor or your neighborhood? Why not talk to your friends about Jesus in *faith*?

Now it's time to ask your pastor for some direction, and then to wash off the tomatoes before you take them over. But pray first. 'Lord, show yourself again in mercy and in power. May your mighty hand turn my friend and my city and the world to Jesus, the Savior from heaven.' Pray that yourself right now. Tomorrow too.

NOTES

1. Available from Presbyterian Evangelistic Fellowship, P. O. Box 1890, Decatur, GA 30031.

PERSEVERING SALVATION

D. Clair Davis
Presbyterian Journal, October 22, 1986

It's good to get something over and done with. Don't you feel great when you finally get those taxes off in the mail? But then in ten minutes you start thinking about being audited. After a woman has carried her baby overtime and then gone through a long labor, isn't she ecstatic to know it's all over? But then she sees it's another boy and she knows she has to try again.

Isn't it wonderful to come to Christ and know your sins are forgiven? But then too many things go wrong and you wonder why the Lord doesn't notice. You've been passed over at work once too often. Your marriage is stale and getting staler. What the preacher says sounds flat. God must be more bored with your prayers than you are.

You can't say the Lord didn't warn you. He told you that you're here to run a race with weary knees and feeble arms. He doesn't mean a fast 50-yard dash either, where it's all over before you can think about it. Even a marathon is only three hours. But the strait and narrow path you're on just keeps getting steeper and rougher. After you stagger up Heartbreak Hill, straight up in front of you is Peril Peak. Just behind that you see Agony Alp filling up the sky.

The world smirks at you that truth is fuzzy, that nothing will ever change, and that you're a fool if you don't take what you can get. Maybe you can remember when temptation wasn't so blatant, but now it's just a finger-touch away on your TV control. It's getting worse too. 'Those will be days of distress unequaled from the beginning, when God created the world, until now – and never to be equaled again. If the Lord had not cut short those days, no one would survive' (Mark 13:19-20).

And what you can see is nothing compared to what's actually there. You're actually fighting with Satan, the liar hungry for your soul. It doesn't just happen that you're hemmed in by groaning and complainers. It doesn't just happen that you feel like quitting. When you're already confused, then Satan spits lies at you. When you're already in deep trouble because of old sinful habits, then he tells you Jesus doesn't love you.

It isn't easy to walk in faith when your life is hard. The Bible is full of people who said to the Lord, 'Why am I hurting when the wrong people are doing just fine? Are you sure, Lord, that you mean what you say?' If you start reacting like that, you'll really be in trouble. Malachi knew people who said, 'It is futile to serve God. What did we gain by carrying out his requirements and going about like mourners before the Lord Almighty? But now we call the arrogant blessed. Certainly the evildoers prosper, and even those who challenge God escape' (3:14-15). What they thought they acted upon. They thought sacrificing to the Lord was a burden, so they brought him just the culls of the herd and held back their tithes (1:6-14, 3:6-12). When you don't know how to handle trouble, you're on the way to half-hearted worship. Then you're about to tune the Lord out entirely. You're over the chasm of unbelief.

But you need to see more than the dangers ahead. You need to see how the Lord is *protecting* you. In 2 Kings 6, Elisha's servant was terrified by the enemy army all around them. But then the Lord answered Elisha's prayer and opened his servant's eyes. He saw who was really all around them – it was the Lord with his chariots of fire! He learned that 'those who are with us are more than those who are with them'. But you see much more than that. You see the 'one who is in you is greater than the one who is in the world' (1 John 4:4).

You know how much you want to quit. But you know too that on the cross Jesus said, 'It is finished.' After finishing 'he sat down'. The last time you saw the Lord do that was on the Seventh Day of creation, when he had finished making everything there was. Now he's done all that needs to be done for your salvation, right through to the end. After telling you that, the Lord encourages you to pray with confidence now, since Jesus has opened the way. He asks you to find out how you can spur each other on to love and good deeds. He calls you to keep on encouraging each other (Heb. 10:1-25).

Jesus finished your *complete* salvation. He laid down his life for his sheep, for you, to give you *eternal* life. 'They shall *never* perish. No one can snatch them out of my hand. My Father, who has given them to me, is greater than all; no one can snatch them out of my Father's hand' (John 10:28-30).

And he prayed for you: 'Holy Father, protect them by the power of your name – the name you gave me – so that they may be one as we are one. While I was with them, I protected them and kept them safe by that name you gave me' (John 17:11-12). He prays that way for you today. He knows what you need. Once Satan came to him and said, 'You're hungry, so make some bread. You can have the world if you worship me.' And at the end Jesus cried out, 'Let this cup pass from me.' Three times. He knows how hard faithful persevering obedience is. He knows what to ask for you. The Father hears his prayers.

'Be not weary in well-doing.' That's your calling from the Lord for the rest of your life. It's a hard calling. You'll be stretched to the limits of your strength and courage, and beyond. But you'll never be beyond the reach of his eternal love.

WHAT'S SO GOOD ABOUT BEING A CALVINIST?

D. Clair Davis
Presbyterian Journal, December 3, 1986

What's so good about being a Calvinist? Well, it's good for nostalgia. If your people came from Scotland, then you can put on your tartan bathrobe, play a bagpipe record, and say the first question of the Catechism. But then you're only playing a game. You're not a Scot, you're a Tarheel. Grits beats oatmeal anytime.

It gives you something special to do while everyone else is into Halloween. You can have a Reformation Day slide show of the pastor's wife in front of the John Calvin statue, which does brighten it up! Back in college we used to bring out a history prof to talk about Luther with a Norwegian catch in his voice. Then he disappeared for another year. He was the only Lutheran we had and we treasured him. Calvinists are rare too, but are you ready to be a prized antique?

You can hear really far-out sermons on the Five Points of Calvinism, like my last five articles (June 18, July 30, Aug. 20, Oct. 1 and 22). But basically the Five Points tell you how God saves people, and you've been saved for years. What you need to know is how to be a better wife and mother. You need to know how to get ready for your next mid-life crisis. You need to know how to pray when the pain gets sharper. How does being a Calvinist help then?

It helps because underneath all those questions about *how* to live is a much bigger, much more essential one: *Why bother?* How do you know the Lord really cares?

You don't ask that one out loud in your Sunday-school class. But you know you're eaten up with worry. You've gotten used to being bored with the Bible. You can't identify with the things the other Christians talk about. You need a fresh start with the Lord. But where do you begin?

Now that's where Calvinism really comes through for you. It applies the Bible where you need it the most. Think through the basics. Jesus died for you personally (Personal Atonement). He loves you, not what he can get out of you (Unconditional Election). He pours out his love on every bit of you, not just on what you think is your sweeter and nicer side (Total Depravity). His love is stronger than all your doubt and foolishness and fear put together (Irresistible Grace). He keeps on loving you, all the way through to the end (Perseverance of the Saints). That's the Five Points of your Father's love!

When you've digested how much the Lord has done for you, then you'll know what you're doing. That's why the Lord kept telling his people, 'Remember the Exodus!' In the middle of the clutter and snarls in your life, keep in mind the Lord's mighty, loving arm that lifted you out of slavery into the Land of Promise. 'He who did not spare his own Son, but gave him up for us all – how will he not also, along with him, graciously give us all things?' (Rom. 8:31-32).

Pondering the five points of God's grace isn't a nostalgia trip. When you're alert about your salvation, then you know what life is all about. When you see how your salvation comes only from the Lord and not a bit from yourself, then you understand a lot of other things too. You know what's really important, and what to do next.

In Philippians 3:3-7 the Lord spells it out for you. Don't put any confidence in the flesh, don't rely on anything you've ever accomplished. Paul has a list of what he could be proud of, but you could make one a lot longer without even trying. Why is it so easy to think of all the things you've ever done right, and so hard to remember all the rest? But did beating up the big kid in third grade really make you a winner in life? Did swinging the biggest deal of the month really lay up treasure in heaven? Are you really looking forward to having a two-column obituary? Make the list as long as you can, but the bottom line is still the same. Before the Lord no flesh shall glory.

But don't stop there. Orthodox Presbyterian minister Henry Coray once told his congregation to turn 360 degrees from sin, and it took them five minutes to figure out where that would take them. But your problem isn't in going too far, but in not going far enough. After turning away from glorying in yourself, be sure to start glorying in Jesus Christ. If you stop half-way, all you have left is apathy. But the Lord has called you to *enjoy* him forever. You do that by looking at Philippians 2 and doing some solid thinking about what Jesus gave up for you. Weigh what it meant for him to be a servant. Consider his obedience all the way to death. Try to grasp Jesus Christ crucified, crying out, 'My God, my God, why have you abandoned me!' Now you're ready to start telling yourself and the Lord how wonderful and glorious Jesus Christ is.

And then worship him in the Spirit. Only the Holy Spirit can turn your foolish heart away from that list of achievements to the cross of Christ. Only the Spirit can show you Jesus in his glory. Only the Spirit can focus your whole heart and life and hope upon your Savior.

That's what so good about being a Calvinist. You have a way to apply the splendor of God's love to the nitty-gritty of your life. Go on taking the Lord seriously, in all his grace and mercy. Go on living before his face with joy.

PART II

ESSAYS IN PRACTICAL CALVINISM: THE REFORMED HERITAGE THROUGHOUT CHURCH HISTORY

A. The Reformed Heritage from the Ancient Church to Protestant Liberalism

DRAWN EASTWARD

The Attraction of Eastern Orthodoxy for Western Christians

James R. Payton, Jr.

Since the 1980s, interest in Eastern Orthodoxy has mushroomed in the West. Many scholars, journalistic pundits, and ecclesiastical leaders were surprised by the continued vigor of a group of churches that had weathered the worst atheistic storms of repressive Communism.[1] The influence of Orthodox churches in Serbia, Romania, Bulgaria, Ukraine, and Russia on politics and national self-understanding has become obvious–sometimes devastatingly so in ethnic rivalries and hostilities,[2] at other times in helping positively to form policies and attitudes in their nations, but always in startling contradistinction to Western Christian churches which find themselves more ignored than reckoned with on the national and political scenes.[3] Few people in the West were prepared to discover the strength of Orthodoxy in much of Eastern Europe.

Perhaps even more surprising to Western Christians has been an influence exercised by Orthodoxy much closer to home – indeed, in our own ecclesiastical backyards, as it were. Over the last two decades or so, many Western Christians have been attracted by Eastern Orthodoxy. That some found it a fascinating area of study is understandable: Orthodoxy offers a distinctly different approach to the Christian faith from what Western Christians are familiar with, an approach that offers much to enrich our appreciation of the Christian faith and its practice.[4] Beyond that, though, some Western Christians have embraced Orthodoxy as their own faith, converting from Roman Catholicism, Anglicanism, Lutheranism, the various strands of the Reformed tradition, and the welter of evangelical and free church groups.[5] Some of these converts to Orthodoxy have written about their turn eastward[6] – all of them write in obvious gratitude for what they have found in Orthodoxy[7]; some write with acerbic criticism of the Western Christianity they have left.[8]

What has happened demands some kind of response from us. But what should our response be? Too often within Reformed circles, we have dealt with criticisms or allegations of failures by mounting the barricades and loading our polemical cannon for holy war. Sometimes that may be necessary; in cases like those of converts from 'our side' to Orthodoxy, though, perhaps the part of wisdom is to listen for what these brothers and sisters in Christ have found wanting in us. Some of their assessments may be flawed, some of their analyses unfair, and some of their language may be untempered. But we should recognize that they found something lacking among us, something serious enough that they could leave our folds for pastures they found more spiritually nourishing.

As we listen, we may not agree with their evaluations, and we might even strongly disagree with some of what they find attractive in their turn to Eastern Orthodoxy, to be sure; in all likelihood, though, we will hear the expression of deep Christian yearning for something we were not providing them. If so, does that not call us to seek ways to enhance our practice of the faith that will allow us to give an even fuller manifestation of the Lord's presence among us than at present? If we genuinely believe the slogan we use to describe our Reformed self-understanding, *ecclesia refomata et semper reformanda* ('the church, reformed and always reforming'), must we not be open to what other Christians – especially those who weighed us in the balances and found us wanting – have found elsewhere? And if we can catch a glimpse of what has attracted them, is it not possible – indeed, even necessary – for us to try to engage in further reform so that we can more closely approximate that ecclesiastical bride 'without spot or wrinkle or anything of the kind' which the Lord has betrothed to himself?

I have spent much of the last quarter-century studying Eastern Orthodoxy. That has not been wasted time, for there is much that is intriguing and compelling in it: for example, Orthodoxy's perspective on what is going on in worship is striking[9]; its endorsement of icons and understanding of their significance for the Orthodox faithful is challenging[10]; and its simple but profound way of involving the whole person in worship is fascinating.[11] None of these, interesting as they may otherwise be, intersect with our Reformed practices in a way that would facilitate easy listening. However, there are reasons offered by these erstwhile Western Christians for their conversion to Eastern Orthodoxy which do intersect with our practices. In the rest of this article I want to set forth some of what these converts say has actually drawn them eastward. Instead of offering some statistical survey of such reasons, though, I will present three foundational emphases of Eastern Orthodoxy which come up regularly among these reasons; all these reasons intersect with how we view the Christian faith and teach it. Perhaps they may challenge us in the Reformed tradition today in ways that will enrich us and thereby stimulate us to reform our own cherished tradition.[12]

I. Ancient Heritage

One of the significant attractions of Eastern Orthodoxy for Western Christians is Orthodoxy's ancient heritage. Struck by Christ's promise to remain with the Church throughout the age until the consummation (cf. Matt. 28:20), some of these converts became uneasy with our seeming Protestant indifference toward the continuity of the Church. Eastern Orthodoxy offered them a sharp contrast in this regard: rooted in the ancient Church, Orthodoxy has continued through all the intervening centuries in the liturgy, teaching, and practice which marked ancient Christianity. Two aspects of this antiquity are worth noting.

In the first place, Eastern Orthodoxy deliberately roots its teaching in the Church fathers. Orthodox theologians live in continuous dialogue with Clement of Rome, Justin Martyr, Irenaeus, Athanasius, the Desert Fathers, Basil the Great, Gregory Nazianzen, Gregory of Nyssa, and John of Damascus (to name no others). In Orthodoxy, these giants of Christian antiquity are not merely faint predecessors of the later (Protestant?) stalwarts upon whom we rely; rather, for Orthodoxy, the Church fathers are the mother lode of true doctrine.[13] The Church fathers faithfully passed on what they had received from their forebears, all the way back to the apostles themselves, all before the unfortunate division of Christendom into rival western and eastern segments.

We in the Protestant traditions typically know little of and read less in patristic works. Even so, with all of Christianity we rely on the Church fathers for the articulation and defence of the doctrines of the Trinity and of Christology, and for the leadership of the Church in the days from the apostles down to the medieval period. We believe, indeed, that Christ has been with the Church through the ages, down to our time (and not just from the Reformation onwards); and we believe that, as Christ promised (cf. John 16:13), the Holy Spirit has continued to guide the Church through the ages, down to our time (and not just from the Reformation onwards). But does that profession manifest itself in any recognizable way in our teaching and practice? If it does not, we should be neither surprised nor defensive when some of those who read the dominical promises look for evidence, and not just the claim, that we are standing with the Church of all ages and building on the rock of patristic teaching.[14]

We can get a dim but overwhelming sense of the difference between us and the Orthodox in this regard by considering a second way in which Orthodoxy manifests its stalwart adherence to Christian antiquity. Among the Orthodox, the liturgy used in almost every worship service throughout the year is the St. John Chrysostom liturgy.[15] That remarkable pastor[16] had polished and modified the liturgy common throughout the Greek-speaking Church in antiquity; the liturgy that bears his name is a spiritually compelling one, moving back and forth among praise for God, acknowledgement of human frailty and sin, repentance, assurance of pardon and grace, concern for church and state, and prayer for God to glorify himself in this world and the one to come. This liturgy has been in continuous use in the 1700 years since his time (he died in 407). That means that the St. John Chrysostom liturgy – the one used almost always in Eastern Orthodox worship services – has been celebrated for over 88,000 weeks running! Nothing we do in the Protestant or Reformed tradition can begin to claim such historical standing, all the way back to Christian antiquity.

For some of us in the Reformed tradition today, this will hardly faze us. Can we claim our attitude is faithful to the promises of Christ cited above, though? Have we really wrestled with the significance of the Lord's promises to be with and to guide the

Church through the ages? Does not our lack of concern for this manifest just how much we have been shaped in this regard by our North American culture, rather than by Christ's words? Given the cavalier indifference to historical connections common in North America, it may not be surprising that we Calvinists in this hemisphere have shown little interest in our connections to Christian antiquity – but while that betrays our participation in our culture, it hardly marks us as alert to the promises of the Lord about the history of the Church.

It is virtually unthinkable that any contemporary Reformed congregation would adopt the St. John Chrysostom liturgy, even in a greatly shortened form, as its own; and even if we did, we could not begin to play 'catch-up' to the Orthodox faithfulness to this sterling worship exemplar from antiquity. Perhaps, though, we could begin to read patristic literature and become familiar with the bracing and insightful presentations the Church fathers offer of the Christian faith and its impact on life. If so, this would start to manifest itself in our teaching, from time to time, and in our attitude toward the Church through the ages, all the way back to antiquity. We in the Reformed tradition could do worse than become familiar with the Church fathers.[17]

II. Sense of Mystery

A second aspect of Orthodoxy frequently cited by Western Christian converts for turning eastward is the rich Eastern Orthodox sense of mystery, as evidenced in liturgy, spirituality, and faith. From antiquity, Orthodoxy has reveled in the mystery which they discern and respect at every point of Christian teaching and practice. While the Orthodox use the term 'mysteries' to refer especially to the sacraments, the Orthodox see the sacraments in continuity with the rest of the Christian faith, and not as ritual exceptions to it.

Of course, we Western Christians acknowledge mystery in the Christian faith, too – even if some of us in the Protestant (and especially we of the Reformed) tradition tend to be suspicious of the mysticism which follows hard on a sense of mystery. A number of those who have turned eastward have sensed our fundamental unease with mystery, even in the sacraments[18]; in contrast, these converts to Eastern Orthodoxy have learned to appreciate mystery in their Christian experience. Eastern Orthodoxy has a far richer sense of mystery than we Reformed Protestants do–and the Orthodox allow it to be a much more constitutive element of their teaching and practice than we have so far allowed it to be.

In much of Protestant teaching – and certainly among us who are Reformed–mystery is what we encounter when we get to the end of doctrinal explanation.[19] Our challenging seminary training and our emphasis on teaching and proclamation have bred among many of us a confidence in our ability to set forth the Christian faith well. We acknowledge, of course, that since the faith comes to us by way of revelation and deals with God's relationship to fallen human beings, an element of mystery is inescapable. But how much do we allow mystery to pervade our sense even of that which we think we are setting forth clearly? We manifest – if not in explicit declaration, nevertheless by our approach and emphases – considerable confidence in our theological ability to set forth capably 'the truth, the whole truth, and nothing but the truth'; at least, that is what many of those who have converted to Eastern Orthodoxy have sensed. Where did they get the idea, if not from our bearing and attitudes? Are we aware of the mystery that is, from an Orthodox perspective, inescapable in anything and everything having to do with life and our relationship to God?

Eastern Orthodoxy has emphasized that mystery undergirds and wraps itself around the divine/human relationship from beginning to end; Orthodoxy learned this from the Greek Church fathers. Gregory of Nyssa urged, 'Even if I were capable of grasping all that Scripture says, yet that which is signified is more.'[20] For his part, the Desert father Macarius said, 'Since the wisdom of God is infinite and incomprehensible, it brings about the manifold dispensations of grace toward the human race in an incomprehensible and unsearchable manner.'[21] To communicate this graciousness toward us, Pseudo-Dionysius affirmed, 'The Word of God uses poetic imagery ..., not for the sake of art, but as a concession to the nature of our mind'[22]; on this, Gregory of Nyssa taught, 'The inspired book teaches us in metaphors' and 'God communicates the divine mysteries by words intelligible to us and uses expressions such as are within the range of human life and circumstances.'[23] John of Damascus encapsulated the Greek patristic appreciation for the mystery that enfolds all God's dealings with humanity when he declared, 'All the things of God are above the natural order and beyond speech and understanding.'[24]

If we in Western Christianity step back somewhat from our confidence in our doctrinal systems and our ability to articulate them, and if we then reflect on what we are talking about, perhaps we can be drawn ourselves to a greater appreciation for mystery. After all, the whole Christian faith is permeated by mystery: it begins with the ineffable and incomprehensible God who is Triune, proceeds through the incarnation in which the Son of God was made flesh, and culminates in the resurrection of the dead and the renewal of all things. Surely, any preacher, no matter how learned and articulate, who thinks or speaks as if he has mastered any of that is at once spiritually illiterate and intellectually arrogant – a deadly pastoral combination. Many of us in Western Christianity need to open ourselves anew to humility and wonder before the unfathomable depths of God's gracious dealings with us; such a response is near of kin to that apostolic wonder before 'the depth of the riches and wisdom and knowledge of God, whose judgments are unsearchable and whose ways are inscrutable' (cf. Rom. 11:33).

III. Suspicion of Reason

Closely related to Orthodoxy's profound appreciation for mystery is its suspicion of human reason when it begins to talk about God; this caution about human rationality has proven attractive to a number of Western Christian converts to Eastern Orthodoxy. Ever since the ancient period, Eastern Christianity has shown serious reservations about the capabilities of the human mind – no matter how intellectually gifted, doctrinally instructed, and spirit-led – adequately to speak the truth about God and his works. Orthodoxy recognizes that talking about God is a risky venture, even with the best of intentions.

According to Orthodoxy, speaking about God *can* be done, because God himself has communicated to human beings in human language; but he has done so in human language, not in a divine one. Speaking about God *must* be done, because God calls his people to tell others about him; but our proclamation is not thereby assured to be either faithful or full. Eastern Orthodoxy knows that human language must always fail to express God and his works fully, since human language can rise no higher than its created capacities, which are incommensurate with the one being discussed. God must ever remain above and beyond our best human efforts to express him in words – but human hubris too often speaks as if it can capture him in the nets of our reason. A more appropriate stance for us, according to Orthodoxy, is to become silent before the divine majesty and his works. Our words may often fail; our worship probably will not. Awe and contemplation will not be inadequate; verbiage must inevitably be.[25]

Eastern Orthodoxy stresses, indeed, that we can know God, but this knowledge is not particularly something to be intellectually grasped; rather, consonant with scriptural emphases, such knowledge is wrapped up in intimacy and love. The affirmation that 'the man [Adam] *knew* his wife Eve, and she conceived and bore Cain' (Gen. 4:1) intended something more than intellectual acquaintance: it indicated the intimacy of marital union. God's declaration to Israel, 'You only have I *known* of all the families of the earth' (Amos 3:2), implied no ignorance on God's part, but focused on the special and intimate relationship he had granted of old only to the descendants of Abraham, Isaac, and Jacob. And Jesus Christ confessed in prayer to his Father in heaven, 'This is eternal life, ... [to] *know* you, and Jesus Christ whom you have sent' (John 17:3). In biblical teaching, knowledge of God and his truth is never merely an intellectual accomplishment. It is always rooted much deeper within us than that; it is a knowledge that reaches into and fills the innermost recesses of the center of our beings – our hearts. Reflecting this rich biblical background, in Eastern Orthodoxy *knowing* God means having intimate communion with him, not just mastering a wealth of information about him.

Knowing God in this sense is, for Eastern Orthodoxy, the prerequisite to all teaching about God and his works. Knowing God in this sense means far more – and yet, paradoxically, much less – than intellectual expertise in revelatory, doctrinal, and confessional data about God. Knowing God in this sense means communion with him in a life of openness toward and wonder before him. Knowledge of God involves a fellowship between the Creator and the creature that does not bridge the chasm between them and yet brings them together in intimacy. Not mastery of but submission to data marks this knowledge – and yet the submission is not to data but to the divine persons. Knowing God in this sense means *loving* God without reservation. Such knowledge of God reaches far beyond thought to the innermost recesses of the one who would *know* God.

In the practices of Eastern Orthodoxy, from antiquity to the present, meditation before and contemplation of God are the ways to *know* him. Of course, divine revelation is foundational to such meditation and contemplation. Even so, what God has made known about himself and his ways toward humanity is not so much to be analyzed as to be imbibed; one needs to be saturated with it through wonder, rather than to connect its elements in intellectual curiosity. In the history of Eastern Orthodoxy, those who have been respected for their understanding of God and his ways have not been the academically trained, but those who have devoted themselves to meditation and contemplation: such a lifestyle was both the root and the evidence of knowing God. Living in mystical devotion to God is the only way to knowing God, and knowing God in this sense is necessary for any acceptable speech about him. Gregory of Nyssa, one of the Cappadocian fathers (so influential in Eastern Orthodoxy), stated this perspective memorably, in an epigram often cited within Eastern Orthodoxy: 'If you are a theologian, you will pray truly. And if you pray truly, you are a theologian.' No mention is made of specifically academic learning of data about God, although such learning is not proscribed; open communion with him is the prerequisite and authentication of a theologian.

In Western Christianity, such a cautious attitude about human intellection has not been entirely unknown, but the results to be found among us suggest that it has been displaced in favor of other concerns. Over the centuries, we have manifested an overweening confidence in thought and argument to lay out the truth about God and his works. If we reflect for a moment on the numerous doctrinal systems developed within Western Christianity; the unending stream of books on doctrine; our penchant for arguments over ever more arcane points of doctrinal disagreement; and our confidence that others would come to agree with us if only they would consider the evidence honestly and read the Scriptures fairly – all these indicate that we in Western Christianity have great confidence in human rationality and language to 'speak the truth, the whole truth, and nothing but the truth' as we pronounce on God and his works.

Yet, as each of us has discovered, some recalcitrants just don't seem to get it. Despite our best efforts to lay out the truth clearly and present the arguments for our doctrinal understanding persuasively, many of our partners in conversation and argument remain unconvinced. In the face of our common Western Christian confidence in thought and argument, this is disappointing. Given this common experience, though, can we really be surprised that we have so many divergent systems of doctrine and differences in perspective?

Significantly, while Eastern Orthodoxy has emphasized

communicating truth faithfully – it is called 'Orthodoxy', after all – it has diligently warned its people against too much confidence in human capacities for articulating the ways of God to humankind. Theology flourishes within Eastern Orthodoxy, indeed; but it is, as one of its noted practitioners has emphasized, a *mystical* theology,[26] one more attuned to wonder and silence than system and conclusion, a doctrinal approach steeped in awe and bounded by silence before the mystery of the divine/human encounter in all its variety. This may well sound strange to us; it certainly is not the way we in Western Christianity instinctively and commonly approach doctrine.

Orthodoxy has placed much less confidence in human ability to elaborate Christian doctrine than we in Western Christianity typically have. In most regards, differences in regard to doctrine are what divide us in the Christian West. Many of us have, at times, despaired over the way in which we in the Protestant tradition have cut ourselves off from other Christians over particular doctrinal issues. I do not wish to minimize the importance of doctrine, to be sure; but what can justify our propensity to separate from each other over so many points of doctrine? An organization that manages to keep track of such dreary statistics informed its readers that as of the year 2000 there were over 25,000 Protestant denominations.

Since the days of Christian antiquity, Eastern Orthodoxy has stressed that human capacities in the exposition of Christian truth are limited, and that we 'do' theology better with praise than with argument. When we consider that our Western Christian confidence in human intellection to speak of God and his works, with its concomitant predilection for doctrinal argument, has led – preeminently, among other reasons – to so many divisions within Western Christianity, although Christ himself prayed for the unity of the Church; and when we further consider that this desultory process had resulted, as the third millennium dawned, in more than 25,000 Protestant variants within Western Christianity; then we may well pause to consider whether we might have something significant to learn from Eastern Orthodoxy's suspicion of human intellection in dealing with God and his works. Maybe – without entirely ditching our concern to understand – we in Western Christianity could learn from our brothers and sisters in Eastern Orthodoxy a little more intellectual humility than usually has marked us, and a greater caution about the ultimate veracity of our particular package of teaching.

Conclusion

Eastern Orthodoxy offers us Western Christians much to consider. Her faithful continuity with Christian antiquity challenges us to reflect on how much we believe and, believing, are shaped by the Lord's promises regarding the history of the Church. As he uttered those promises, that history lay in the future; for us, much of it is now in the past. But what kind of past is it for us? Is it – indeed, dare it be – a dead past for us? Or are we building appreciatively on it? How we deal with the ancient heritage of the Church is our real exegesis of Christ's promises. Eastern Orthodoxy encourages us to do better than we have so far in this regard.

As well, Eastern Orthodoxy invites us to embrace the mystery that surrounds and undergirds the Christian faith from beginning to end. In the glorious privilege of relationship with God, initiated by his love, mystery envelopes us at every turn. At times, we Western Christians have lost sight of that mystery, or we have relegated it to the fringes of our faith and practice. In that regard, we in the Reformed tradition are perhaps especially culpable: why, though, do we shrink from mystery, when that mystery is the depths of divine love for us? We acknowledge, and even revel, in the awesome mystery involved in the divine decree of election in Christ. If that predestinating love is the foundation of all our privilege, then must not mystery be welcome at every point in our proclamation and practice? The Eastern Orthodox show us that we could do better.

Eastern Orthodoxy also calls us to caution regarding our ability to set forth the truth in its fullness and purity. Western Christians have carefully articulated doctrinal systems of considerable sophistication; we in the Reformed tradition have offered pristine service in this regard. How much, though, do we acknowledge that these are, at best, only feeble attempts to set forth what is beyond comprehension? Eastern Orthodoxy stands as a continual reminder of our human limitations in this venture. According to Orthodoxy, knowledge of God does not flow from arduous application of intellectual ability to all the available data in Scripture, confessions, and doctrinal textbooks: genuine knowledge of God comes from living in utter openness to him. Any supposed knowledge of God that does not begin and continually return to that point is only 'a noisy gong or a clanging cymbal'. Eastern Orthodoxy can help us remember that.

For centuries, we in Western Christianity have known little about Eastern Orthodoxy. In the last couple of decades, that has changed dramatically. The last few years have shown us that, whatever weaknesses Orthodoxy has and problems with which it wrestles, it has much to offer in the present day. Not the least of what it offers is the opportunity for Western Christians to reevaluate their approaches to faith and practice by learning about the faith and practice of Eastern Orthodoxy. In this article, we have considered some of what others raised in Western Christianity have found compelling in Eastern Orthodoxy. The points we have considered call Western Christians – yes, and us, too, in the Reformed tradition – to hear emphases which have become muted among us. We could do worse than listen to and learn from our brothers and sisters in Eastern Orthodoxy.

NOTES

1. For a discussion of the impact the collapse of the Communist bloc is having for the study of the history of Eastern Europe (which necessarily includes the role of Orthodoxy [and other churches] in that history), see my 'Revisioning the Historiography of Eastern Europe', *Fides & Historia* 31 (1999):77-89; for an evaluation of Christian scholarship's contribution to that history, and of what such scholarship should seek to offer in the wake of the collapse of the Soviet empire, see my 'Bypassing the History of Eastern Europe: A Failure of Twentieth-Century Christian Scholarship', *Christian Scholar's Review* 29 (2000):713-730.
2. For an insightful treatment of the role of religion in the conflict in the former Yugoslavia during the 1990s, see Paul Mojzes, *Yugoslavian Inferno: Ethnoreligious Warfare in the Balkans* (New York: Continuum, 1994); further to this, see also the volume he edited, *Religion and the War in Bosnia* (Atlanta: Scholars Press, 1998).
3. For an introduction to this, see my 'Religion and the Historiography of Eastern Europe', in *Religion in Eastern Europe* 21 (2001, No. 2):1-16, and the literature there adduced; the six yearly issues of *Religion in Eastern Europe* offer a sustained and extensive scholarly treatment of the role of religious faith and practice (including Orthodoxy) in the region.
4. I have found it so myself. During my studies at Westminster Theological Seminary in Philadelphia, while pursuing a Th.M. in Church History, I discovered a course in the seminary catalogue on Eastern Orthodoxy. It had not been offered in a number of years, but I asked to take it. The honoree of this festschrift, D. Clair Davis, took on the responsibilities of guiding me through an independent study course on Eastern Orthodoxy. I had already studied the various segments of Church History – ancient, medieval, Reformation, and modern age – closely, and I thought I knew Church History pretty well. The course on Eastern Orthodoxy opened my eyes to a host of approaches to and elements in the Christian faith which had not formed our Western Christian heritage, but which had been foundational to the Eastern Orthodox tradition. Over the last quarter-century, I have continued to study Eastern Orthodoxy with great intellectual, spiritual, and personal profit: while remaining firmly committed to the Reformed faith, I have regularly taught a course on Eastern Orthodoxy, have developed numerous close friendships with Orthodox priests and faithful, and have lectured on Orthodoxy in Canada,

England, Ukraine, and Russia. For the initial stimulation in this direction, I am indebted to D. Clair Davis.

5. Peter E. Gillquist recounts the fascinating story of how a group of parachurch leaders, concerned to develop a genuine church, embarked on a study of Christian antiquity and actually ended up 'reinventing' Orthodoxy; in due course, they became aware of the continued existence of Orthodoxy and sought and received welcome into it: see his *Becoming Orthodox: A Journey to the Ancient Christian Faith* (Brentwood, Tennessee: Wohlgemuth & Hyatt, 1989). He edited a further volume, provocatively entitled, *Coming Home: Why Protestant Clergy are Becoming Orthodox*, 2d ed. (Ben Lomond, California: Conciliar Press, 1995); this volume offers the stories of eighteen former Protestant pastors and church leaders who converted to Eastern Orthodoxy, with each of the stories indicating the rationales for turning from whatever branch of Protestantism had formerly been embraced to Eastern Orthodoxy. A similar book is Thomas Doulis, ed., *Journeys to Orthodoxy: A Collection of Essays by Converts to Orthodox Christianity* (Minneapolis: Light and Life Publishing Company, 1986).

6. The works of the English convert to Eastern Orthodoxy, Timothy (now, Bishop Kallistos) Ware, stand as classic presentations of Orthodoxy: his *The Orthodox Church*, 2d rev. ed. (New York: Penguin Books, 1993) is widely recognized as the best one-volume introduction to the history, teaching, and worship of Orthodoxy; his *The Orthodox Way*, rev. ed. (Crestwood, New York: St. Vladimir's Seminary Press, 1995) offers a warm and inviting presentation of Orthodoxy's mystical approach to faith and practice.

7. Two of the most winsome presentations of this journey are by Frederica Mathewes-Green: her *Facing East: A Pilgrim's Journey into the Mysteries of Orthodoxy* (San Francisco: HarperSanFrancisco, 1997) takes the reader along on her bumpy and questioning trek into Eastern Orthodoxy; her *At the Corner of East and Now: A Modern Life in Ancient Christian Orthodoxy* (New York: Jeremy P. Tarcher/Putnam, 1999) allows the reader to follow her through her further exploration of and life within Orthodoxy.

8. The most biting work in this genre of testimonies of Western Christian converts to Eastern Orthodoxy is by Frank Schaeffer in his *Dancing Alone: The Quest for Orthodox Faith in the Age of False Religion* (Brookline, Massachusetts: Holy Cross Orthodox Press, 1994); in this volume, the son of the well-known Presbyterian intellectual and founder of L'Abri presents a harsh assessment of Western Christianity, and especially of the Reformed tradition in which he was raised. He has picked up on some elements in the broader and the narrower traditions which warrant criticism, to be sure: his zeal is not without knowledge, if without restraint. The caricature he offers of the Augustinian tradition might cause those familiar with the history of Western Christian thought to toss the book aside, but such a reaction – otherwise warranted, in view of the straw man he erects and torches – would be regrettable, for it would prevent the reader from encountering Frank Schaeffer's sympathetic presentation of what he has found so attractive in Eastern Orthodoxy. (For those readers of wounded Western Christian sensibilities, and especially the Calvinists whom he so harshly denounces, it may be coldly comforting to know that he offers a similarly biting presentation of contemporary Orthodoxy's failures in his *Letters to Father Aristotle: A Journey through Contemporary American Orthodoxy* [Salisbury, Massachusetts: Regina Orthodox Press, 1995].)

9. In summary, the Orthodox understand that a congregation joins in the ongoing worship offered continually in God's presence by the entire community of heaven,

including the angels and the faithful departed (cf. Heb. 12: 22-24); this shapes what is accepted in Orthodox worship: *e.g.*, praying to the saints is not, on this basis, seeking out superhuman intercessors, but is petitioning for the loving concern of brothers and sisters in Christ, living in God's presence, who are also right now living members of the Church.

10. I have summarized the main arguments of the defenders of icons and considered John Calvin's response to the iconoclastic controversy's conclusion in 'Calvin and the Legitimation of Icons: His Treatment of the Seventh Ecumenical Council', *Archiv für Reformationsgeschichte* 84 (1993):222-241; for a fuller presentation of the arguments offered by the iconodules, see the outstanding treatment by Jaroslav Pelikan, *Imago Dei: The Byzantine Apologia for Icons*, The A. W. Mellon Lectures in the Fine Arts, 1987 (Princeton, New Jersey: Princeton University Press, 1990); for additional or specialized treatments, see his bibliography (pp. 183-193).

11. Simply stated, any Orthodox worship service involves all five senses; as Fr. Anthony Ugolnik put it in addressing the 1993 'Christians in the Visual Arts' conference, 'If you can't touch it, taste it, hear it, smell it, and above all else see it, it's not Orthodox' (cited from *CIVA Newsletter* 6).

12. To serve this end, I have produced a manuscript, *Light from the Christian East*, which I am currently shopping to publishers. The manuscript presents the distinctives of Eastern Orthodoxy in a way that enables Western Christians to understand and benefit from them.

13. This can be seen in the fact that ever since the eighth century, down to the most recent generation, the textbook used among the Orthodox to study theology has been John of Damascus' *The Orthodox Faith*. The Damascene's brilliant synthesis of the prior Greek patristic tradition served as a convenient presentation of the faith received from the Church fathers and to be transmitted to subsequent generations of the Church. Within the last generation, though, works by the Greek Orthodox theologian Christos Yannaris and the Romanian Orthodox theologian Dumitru Staniloae have become commonly used; the Damascene's outstanding work is still widely read and studied, however.

14. In the last few years, a remarkable development has taken place in this regard in the evangelical and Reformed world: a number of scholars have encouraged a return to the patristic sources. Thomas C. Oden, a professor at Drew University, has been perhaps the most vocal proponent of this move, but numerous others have urged it, as well; among them, D. H. Williams, an ordained Baptist minister who is also a professor of patristics at a Roman Catholic university, has authored a monograph, *Retrieving the Tradition and Renewing Evangelicalism: A Primer for Suspicious Protestants* (Grand Rapids, Michigan: Wm. B. Eerdmans Publishing Company, 1999), in which he urges his free church confreres to reconsider their views on the patristic era and on the continuity of the church's teaching through history. A further sign of this movement is that some young Reformed scholars have pursued doctoral studies in patristics (as, *e.g.*, David Rylaarsdam, a professor at Calvin Theological Seminary in Grand Rapids, Michigan). Beyond all this, InterVarsity Press and Eerdmans have both initiated publishing ventures in which they are producing multi-volume studies of patristic exegesis and teaching.

15. On certain special days of the church year, the Orthodox use the St. Basil liturgy; it is largely the same as the St. John Chrysostom liturgy, but with some expansions and slight modifications.

16. As with the other Reformers of the sixteenth century, John Calvin quoted Church fathers to authenticate what he was presenting as true. In this regard, he cited John Chrysostom more frequently than any other Church father except Augustine.

17. I have produced a manuscript which, I hope, will help in this regard. Over the course of the past fifteen years or so, I have been engaged in an extensive reading program in patristic literature; from those readings, I have culled out segments which manifest keen insights or offer thought-provoking treatments on a wide range of questions and issues. I have collected them and written an introduction for the collection; the result is a manuscript tentatively entitled *A Patristic Treasury: Readings in the Church Fathers*, which I hope to see published soon.

18. This is witnessed by the widespread acceptance of a merely symbolical or memorial view of the sacraments among Reformed people and their pastors; however, this perspective – no matter how common it has become – is at variance with the viewpoints presented in all the Reformed confessions and catechisms, as even a casual reading of those doctrinal standards reveals (cf., *e.g.*, the Westminster Confession of Faith, Chs. 27-29; the Westminster Larger Catechism, Qus. 161-174; the Westminster Shorter Catechism, Qus. 92-97; the Heidelberg Catechism, Qus. 69-82; and the Belgic Confession, Arts. 33-35).

19. In the controversy between Cornelius Van Til and Gordon Clark, the question of divine incomprehensibility played a major role; significantly, Van Til posited that divine incomprehensibility pervaded everything we may say or think about God, but Clark relegated incomprehensibility to the realm beyond the reach of reason and explanation. Thus, the common attitude abroad among many of us Reformed is – even if unreflectively – in agreement with Clark rather than Van Til; for a treatment of the controversy, see Fred H. Klooster, *The Incomprehensibility of God in the Orthodox Presbyterian Conflict* (Franeker: T. Wever, 1951).

20. Gregory of Nyssa, *The Beatitudes*, Sermon 7.

21. Macarius, *The Fifty Spiritual Homilies*, 29:1.

22. Pseudo-Dionysius, *The Celestial Hierarchy*, 2:1.

23. Both citations are from Gregory of Nyssa, *The Beatitudes*, Sermon 2.

24. John of Damascus, *The Orthodox Faith*, 4:11.

25. Cf. the following sampling of patristic affirmations, fundamental to Eastern Orthodoxy's perspectives: 'God cannot be measured by the heart, and he is incomprehensible by the mind' (Irenaeus, *Against Heresies*, 4:19,3); '[God's power in creating is] a power as incomprehensible to human reason as it is unutterable by human voice' (Basil the Great, *In Hexaemeron*, 2:2); 'It is not the continual remembrance of God that I would hinder, but only the talking about God' (Gregory Nazianzen, *The Theological Orations*, 1:5); 'He who transcends the universe must surely transcend speech' (Gregory of Nyssa, *Commentary on Ecclesiastes*, Sermon 7); "Human language and comparisons cannot offer a satisfactory explanation for the things of God .... We necessarily have to speak about what we think and understand in accordance with our own environment and in our own words' (Hilary, *The Trinity* 4:2); 'The sacred incarnation of Jesus for our sakes is something which cannot be enclosed in words nor grasped by any mind" (Pseudo-Dionysius, *The Divine Names*, 2:9); 'It is necessary that the one who seeks after God in a religious way never hold fast to the letter, lest that one mistakenly understand things said about God for God himself' (Maximus Confessor, *Chapters on Knowledge*, 2:73); 'One must always bear in mind that the ways of God's providence are many, and that they can neither be explained in words nor grasped by the mind' (John of Damascus, *The Orthodox Faith*, 4:11).

26. Cf. the work by Vladimir Lossky, *The Mystical Theology of the Eastern Church* (Crestwood, New York: St. Vladimir's Seminary Press, 1976).

THEOLOGICAL LIGHT FROM THE MEDIEVAL ERA?

Anselm and the Logic of the Atonement[1]

Peter A. Lillback

The presuppositions of historians are sometimes suggested by the titles that they give to the epochs of history. For example, The Medieval Period of church history spans a vast time beginning around AD 600 and concluding shortly after AD 1500. But just what exactly makes this period the 'middle ages' as implied by the epithet 'Medieval'? Is it because it comes between the vast learning of the classical Greek and Roman world and the renewal of classical studies in the Renaissance? Or is it because it comes between the high water mark of Patristic Theology and the renewal of original biblical language studies that marked the humanists of the Reformation Age?

At other times historiographical presuppositions are openly unveiled by the choice of descriptive labels. Thus those in the Reformation and Enlightenment traditions have sometimes denominated the Medieval Era with a term of opprobrium – 'The Dark Ages'. Certainly with the collapse of the Roman Empire in the West, and the resulting hegemony of barbarian tribes, social order and scholarly pursuits were deeply imperiled. And what became of the light of the apostolic gospel of grace as the Medieval system of merit developed? What happened to true religion as the cult of the saints evolved and then blended into a syncretistic worship that seemingly baptized the old pagan gods and gave them Christian names? But even if we acknowledge that this pejorative phrase is appropriate for a time of spiritual, cultural and intellectual decline, we must remember that shining lights of substantial glory can illumine midnight skies.

Indeed, Anselm, Archbishop of Canterbury (1033–1109), is one such luminary in the benighted medieval firmament. As the most influential theologian between Augustine and Thomas Aquinas,[2] a fact evidenced by his creative and substantive writings,[3] many of Anselm's theological insights still shine into contemporary philosophical and theological discussion.[4] While it is seemingly contradictory to suggest that a Medieval theologian could make a lasting impact upon both Christian theology and philosophical thought, the work of Anselm, however, belies this almost reflexive wholesale negative assessment of the Medieval Era.

On the other hand, the fact that Anselm is but only one of many bright lights that form the theological constellations of the Medieval Era argues that there must be a better descriptor for the Medieval Era than the 'Dark Ages'. Some in the Christian tradition view this period of history as 'Christendom' – a contraction of 'Christ's Kingdom' – a time when the unifying worldview of all aspects of Western European life and culture was self-consciously Christian and allegedly under the rule of Christ. Moreover, the Eastern or Greek part of the Christianized Roman Empire, often designated as the Byzantine Empire, never experienced an intellectual and cultural collapse, as did the West. The Eastern Empire flourished until the 1400's when the Ottoman Turks, with their clashing swords of conquest brandished in the name of the Muslim faith, finally conquered it.

Moreover, can an era spanning nearly a millennium even be characterized by a single conception? Rather than compressing this remarkable period of the Church's life into a one-size-fits-all description, it is surely more accurate to recognize this middle millennium as an aggregate of smaller eras, each centuries long with their own distinctive characteristics and concerns. However one resolves the debate implicit in the selection of a compelling historical title, the Medieval Era, the title with which I will content myself, ought not to be considered exclusively as a time of slumbering darkness and theological somnambulism.

I. An Overview of the History of the Medieval Church

To begin this study of the abiding significance of Anselm's understanding of the atonement of Christ,[5] let us place Anselm in his broader historical context by a brief summary of the contours of the Medieval Era. Following the lead of others, we can divide the Medieval Period into three eras, each reflecting a dominant theological motif that expresses its essence. *First*, The Benedictine Era, 600–1000 (The Era of the Explosive Growth of Monastic Life Under the Rule of Benedict); *Second*, The Scholastic Era, 1000–1300 (The Era of the Theological Synthesis of the Rediscovered Philosophy of Aristotle with Christian thought); *Third*, The Nominalist Era, 1300–1500 (The Era of the Dissolution of the Medieval Synthesis, Characterized by a Skepticism with Respect to the Value of Philosophy for Theological Development).

The Benedictine Era (600–1000), then, was a time of continuing mission growth for the Church. Gains were made in England, Ireland, Germany, the Low Countries, and in Italy. Significant losses to the Church, however, occurred in northern Africa, in the Near East and in Spain to the newly born Islamic faith of Mohammed. The spiritual life of the Church was marked by a profound concern for personal salvation that prompted a great influx into the monastic communities, which were often governed by The Rule of Benedict. During this time the rise of the Papacy occurred. Gregory the Great, for example, proclaimed that he possessed a universal bishopric emanating from Rome. The power of the occupant of the Papal see was greatly strengthened by the use of various documents attributed to Emperor Constantine, which granted to the Pope vast powers and lands. Although centuries later medieval scholars would demonstrate them to be spurious, their authenticity was immediately accepted, thereby justifying the territorial possessions and immense powers of the Bishop of Rome. The emerging dominance of the Popes in feudal society eventually caused them to clash with kings, particularly those who had converted from their pagan religions to Christianity, such as the dynasty of Charlemagne. Thus the issue of investiture resulted, with the Pope and King each claiming the right and vying to fill the vacant seats of power in the government of Church and state.

Nor was the Benedictine era bereft of theological discussions that are important for the history of doctrine. Issues debated and developed during this time include: the Monothelite controversy (Did Christ have only one will, that is, only a divine will, or two wills, a full human and a full divine will?), iconoclasm (May or must icons be used in Christian worship?), Spanish adoptionism (How did Jesus become the Son of God?), penance and indulgences (Must a man do anything to make amends for his sin and to prove his repentance to gain forgiveness for his sin? Can a financial payment be substituted for these acts of repentance for the convenience of the penitent, or the benefit of the Church?), the First Medieval Eucharistic debate (It anticipated some of the main theories of the Lord's Supper that would emerge in the Reformation. Paschasius Radbert held a sort of transubstantiation view, Rabanus Maurus taught a sort of symbolic presence, Ratramnus argued for a spiritual presence.), the Predestination Controversy (Was Augustine's double predestinarianism a required or even a legitimate theological view for the church? Gottschalk went to jail for defending Augustine's doctrine.), Filioque (Did the Holy Spirit proceed from the Father and the Son, or only from the Father? This debate resulted ultimately in the East/West Schism between the Roman Catholic and Greek Orthodox Churches). Thus even the earliest portion of the Medieval Era was rich in theological reflection.

The Scholastic Era (1000–1300) saw mission advances that impacted Scandinavia, Russia, Bohemia, Poland and Hungary. The spiritual life of the Church had been negatively impacted by the great growth, financial success and opulence of the monasteries. This was ironic since the monasteries were made up of those who had taken a vow of poverty. Thus monastic life was greatly reformed by the influence of the French Cluny monastic movement, as well as by the development of other new orders including the Dominicans and Franciscans. But with the Church's growth came the difficult setback of the Great Schism, which finally severed the Eastern Orthodox and the western Roman Catholic Churches due to their differing Trinitarian understanding of the *filioque*, whether the Holy Spirit precedes only from the Father (Orthodox) or from the Son as well (Catholic). When Innocent III arrived on the political/ecclesiastical scene, he brought the papacy to the acme of its power by using the church's sacramental power (particularly through the interdict, a claim to have the power to stay the efficacy of the sacramental grace by mere Papal declaration) and political claims (the possession of two swords, the power over church as well as state) to control and topple Kings. The crusades, various attempts to wrest the Holy Land from Muslim control, were launched during this era, sometimes offering plenary indulgences to recruit the necessary soldiers to assault the Muslim strongholds.

Several important theological debates also occurred which are significant for the history of doctrine. These include: the Second Eucharistic debate (again anticipating the Reformation debates on the Lord's Table), the theology and philosophy of Anselm (especially his ontological argument for the existence of God, and his substitutionary theory of the atonement), Abelard's theology (particularly his moral example theory of the atonement), the question of the Reordination of priests, and the necessity of the veneration of the Virgin Mary. Theological Education was formally born at this time by the creation of universities throughout Europe. Topics of the university scholars included canon law (the law of the Church), the four-fold exegesis of Scripture (typological and allegorical meanings that went beyond the literal and grammatical meanings of Scripture), Scholasticism – the integration of philosophy (especially the newly rediscovered Aristotelian philosophy) with theology. Leaders in this synthesis of theology and philosophy were Bonaventure, Albert Magnus and Thomas Aquinas. The inquisition developed to deal with heresy. Two of the more significant varieties of heresy were the Cathari and the Waldensians (A group that in the Protestant Reformation Era would merge with the Reformed Churches holding to the theology of John Calvin.) During this time, the Eastern Church also saw the rise of a new emphasis upon mystical theology. In view of these multiple and important developments, one can understand why Anselm's era has also been referred to as the High Middle Ages.

The Nominalist Era (1300–1500) saw success and failure with respect to the growth of Islam. While regaining Spain from Islam, the Eastern Byzantine Empire fell in 1453 to the invading Islamic Ottoman Turks, with Constantinople (the Second Rome) becoming Istanbul and Moscow (the Third Rome) becoming the new seat of government for the Eastern Orthodox Church. The spiritual life of the Catholic Church was marked by the emerging Italian Renaissance spirit. Material opulence, vast papal revenues and spectacularly ornate cathedrals were marks of the Church's worldly success. In the midst of this, the papacy moved to Avignon, France for almost 70 years. In the aftermath of the return of the papacy to Rome, a severe conflict occurred over the legitimate successor to the Papal throne, which resulted in what some have termed the

Western Schism which yielded three different Popes all in office at the same moment, and each excommunicating the others. The necessity of calling an ecclesiastical council to address this confusion and other problems resulted in the development of the Conciliar Movement (Two fundamental issues raised by the Conciliar Movement that would be important for the Protestant Reformation were first, which was more powerful – the Pope, or the gathering of the whole leadership of the Church in a Council?; the second, Who could call such a council into existence?). A further significant intellectual force impacting the Church that emerged in this era of the Renaissance spirit was Humanism. This movement can be described by the words, '*ad fontes*', an attempt to go back 'to the fountain' or the original sources, whether in classical, biblical or legal literature. This movement ultimately weakened papal temporal power by exposing some of the spurious documents that had been used to claim the extensive papal prerogatives, and also to expose the inadequate nature of the Latin Bible as compared with the original Greek and Hebrew texts.

There were also many important developments during this time for the history of doctrine. Nominalism was both a philosophical and a theological movement. Philosophically speaking, nominalism rejected the popularly held Platonic idea called Realism that asserted the existence of universals, or that the ideas of one's mind had a real and independent existence of their own. Nominalism rejected this theory of knowledge, and said that words and ideas do not exist in any other sense than thoughts in a person's mind ('nomina' is the Latin word for name). By its skeptical approach to the value of human reason, it undercut the trustworthiness of philosophy. Ultimately, nominalism helped to shatter the Medieval synthesis of Aristotelian and Christian thought worked out by Thomas Aquinas and others. By lessening the authority of Aristotle's philosophy, it also helped to prepare the way for the Protestant Reformation's strong emphasis upon the authority of Scripture. The philosophical leaders of nominalism were Scotus, Occam and Brabant (Significantly, Luther said, 'I am of Occam's school.'). Theologically, nominalism was committed to a view of salvation that was built upon the individual's meriting his own salvation from God by doing the best he could. The nominalists claimed that God's covenant could be defined by the phrase, 'to the ones who do their best, God would not withhold grace.' ('*Facientibus quod in se est, Deus non denegat gratiam.*') Biel and Holcot were two of the important leaders of theological nominalism.[6] This aspect of nominalism would be attacked with great force by the theology of the Protestant Reformers.[7] Other significant theological movements included mysticism (Led by Rhineland Neo-platonists Tauler and Eckhart, mysticism claimed that one could find God within one's own soul, without the necessity of the constant pursuit of the Church's sacramental administrations.), and Neo-Augustinianism (This was a return to Augustine's views of predestination and sovereign grace, led by such thinkers as Bradwardine, Rimini and Staupitz, marked by a rejection of the nominalist '*facientibus*' theology of merit.) The late Middle Ages also saw the rise of radical reformers such as Peter Bruys and Arnold of Brescia, as well as forerunners of the Protestant Reformation such as Savonarola, Hus and Wycliffe. This era finally gave birth to the Protestant Reformation with the advent of Luther's ministry. Mediated through these theological developments, Anselm's penetrating thought was brought to the Reformers.

II. Survey of Anselm's Life

Anselm was born in Aosta, Italy in AD 1033. A child of a pious mother who instructed him in spiritual matters and a father who evidently disapproved of his youthful monastic interests, Anselm wandered into youthful pleasures and away from his precocious theological pursuits. After leaving home at the age of 23 following a quarrel with his father, Anselm traversed Burgundy and France. It was in 1060 that Anselm, living in Normandy and 'torn between a desire for intellectual eminence and religious dedication,'[8] upon explicit invitation, entered the Abbey of Bec, where he began his apprenticeship under the famed Lanfranc, and lived under The Rule of Benedict. Only three years later, Lanfranc departed to become an abbot at another monastery, and Anselm was chosen to succeed him as prior. This rapid placement into a monastic office set the stage for the remainder of Anselm's life, as in the ensuing years, he became an abbot of Bec in 1078, a position in which he served for fifteen years. Succeeding Lanfranc again, he became the Archbishop of Canterbury in 1093, where he died during Holy Week in 1109. Anselm was as a man of gentle character, intractable conscience, and a keen mind, all of which propelled him into positions of ecclesiastical influence. Anselm's theology surged from the heart of a man sickened by his sin, and captivated by a burning desire to know God. Burdened with acute introspection, yet confident in his hope in Christ, he pleads,

> Almighty God, merciful Father, most kind Lord,
> have mercy upon me a sinner ....
> Grant me to believe and to hope for,
> to love and to live
> only what Thou willest,
> and in that degree ...
> Deliver me from every evil,
> and lead me to the life eternal,
> through the Lord.[9]

But how could the Almighty God have mercy and give eternal life to Anselm the sinner, and still maintain his perfect justice? Anselm's belief, as we shall now see, was however God chose to save sinners, he did so because that was the way it had to be done.

III. Anselm's Theological Principle of Economic Necessity as seen in his Argument for God's Existence

Before Anselm's classic explanation of the atonement is considered, however, we must understand one of his foundational ideas. A key idea for Anselm is the concept of economy or necessity. In Anselm's reasoning, there is an inviolable connection between ultimate being and what is necessary. Whatever is true of the created universe is so because of the nature of the eternal, Triune God. Even the existence of the 'smallest little worm'[10] is ultimately essential in order to maintain the integrity of the creation as a harmonious reflection of God's infinite and eternal being. We might call this the principle of economy, or, whatever is, is essential. Anselm argues that in an ultimate or metaphysical sense, nothing is superfluous, excessive or wasteful.

Anselm's argument for God's existence employs this principle of economy or necessity. Since his argument is based on the idea of a necessary being, it is called the 'ontological' argument (the word 'ontological' means 'being'). In the ontological argument, or the argument from necessary being, Anselm declares that all men can conceive of a being beyond which nothing greater can be thought. But if this being does not exist, then it is not really the conception of the greatest possible being. For a greater being can be imagined, namely, one that in fact exists, and even necessarily exists. So either God, the greatest possible being necessarily exists, or man is left with an inherent contradiction in his thought – the idea of the greatest possible being that is at the same time not the greatest possible being. Since man cannot logically think a contradiction, man's logical thought demands God's necessary existence. If one considers his argument in the historical setting of Medieval realism (the Platonic theory of knowledge discussed above), his argument gains added strength.

All this leads us to Anselm's understanding of the necessity of the atonement, or, why did God become man? On Anselm's terms, the incarnation and the cross could not be superfluous, any more than God could be superfluous. They too were necessary. As God's saving acts in human history, they had to be logically harmonious or congruous with God's very nature.

IV. The Necessity of the Cross flows Logically from the Goodness and Wisdom of God

Written as a dialogue between himself and his prized student at Bec named Boso, *Cur Deus Homo* rigorously probes the logical necessity for the atonement. Anselm's conception of atonement is framed from the start by a question asked by Boso, 'I desire that you should discover to me, what, as you know, many besides myself ask, for what necessity and cause God, who is omnipotent, should have assumed the littleness and weakness of human nature for the sake of its renewal?'[11] Anselm's carefully reasoned answer, as to why God became man to accomplish the renewal of man, is thus developed with the principle of economic necessity firmly in mind. This Anselm/Boso dialogue[12] actually reflects a historical discourse between these two men of like mind, through which Anselm sought to preserve the tight precision of his historically unprecedented argument.[13] According to Anselm, then, because 'all God's actions should preserve the order of the universe and dignity of God,'[14] the choice and means of God's accomplishing the atonement were neither random nor optional. The work of Christ on the cross, and the satisfaction of God's offended honor accomplished by the cross, were, in Anselm's mind, necessary acts. Prior to Anselm's explanation of how and why the atonement of Christ worked for sinners, there had been other popular and very different theories advanced by teachers in the church.[15] One of the most wide spread was the Ransom to Satan theory. Anselm's atonement theory is consciously developed as a polemic against the idea of God's indebtedness to Satan. Anselm avers, 'God owed the devil nothing but punishment.'[16] He insists, 'Whatever was required from man was due to God, not to the devil.'[17] Shifting his focus away from Satan as the object upon whom the atonement ends, Anselm crafts his argument with more biblical and theological reflection, logically demonstrating how the atonement begins and ends with God himself.

To begin, Anselm posits the critical question: 'For what reason or necessity did God become man and, as we believe and confess, by his death restore life to the world, when he could have done this through another person (angelic or human), or even by a sheer act of will?'[18] Three points in this question's formulation weigh heavily for the ensuing argument. *First*, Anselm assumes the existence of God, presupposing orthodox Trinitarian doctrine[19] as the buttress for his argumentation.[20] While reason and rational thought are integral, they are subordinate to faith in the Triune God of Scripture. *Second*, he assumes the historical reality of the incarnation and the personal union of Christ's human and divine natures. Operating with the assumption of evangelical faith, Anselm's intention is not to prove the *fact* of the atonement, but rather to prove the *reason* for it.[21] *Third*, the form of the question shapes the argument for a reasoned answer on the basis of his understanding of the absolute necessity of all that is.

With these assumptions in place, Anselm posits two alternatives. Either God could have redeemed man another way than by the cross but did not do so, or no other way existed for the forgiveness of man's sin. The former of these alternatives is not viable because of its inescapable and unacceptable implications. Either God could have redeemed man otherwise, and still chose to let Christ suffer, or, he must be evil, unwise, or impotent. For Anselm, neither of these conclusions is possible. God's *goodness* is necessarily manifest in his commitment to bring man to heaven: 'let us say that it [the atonement] is necessary, on account of his own changelessness, for God's goodness to complete what he undertook for man, even though the whole good that he does is of grace.'[22] God's goodness is even seen in his commitment to save men as a replacement for the fallen angels.[23] Since God is good, he demands the goodness of those who will dwell in his presence. Therefore, the atonement is necessary because only those redeemed by Christ can rectify the disorder created by the sin of the angels, and make fallen men 'good' so they can dwell with him. Furthermore, consistent with his nature, God's 'incomprehensible *wisdom*'[24] is expressly revealed, in his dealings with men, as he is impassible,[25] perfectly rational,[26] and absolutely sovereign.[27] God is both wise and good, so the atonement is necessarily both wise and good.

V. The Necessity of the Atonement is Logically Consistent with God's Omnipotence and His Love and Justice

But, Boso asks a penetrating question that goes to the very heart of God's nature: 'If he could not save sinners except by condemning the just, where is his omnipotence?'[28] Anselm replies, 'The fact is that the Son, with the Father and the Holy Spirit, had determined to show the loftiness of his *omnipotence* by no other means than death.'[29] God's infinite power is not compromised by the atonement, but gloriously displayed by it. The possibility that God would by divine fiat simply forgive the man who cannot pay the debt of sin he owes is an unacceptable position. Anselm insists that a mere royal pardon of what man ought freely to repay minimizes God's justice.[30] 'This kind of divine mercy is too directly opposed to God's justice, which allows nothing but punishment to be repaid for sin.'[31] An arbitrary cancellation of man's debt of sin causes mercy to emasculate justice, and puts God 'in opposition to himself,'[32] making God less than God.

Therefore, as Anselm sees it, God truly loves mankind. But God's love in isolation would have prevented the penal suffering for Christ, and in fact would never have demanded such penal suffering for the sinner. But God is both loving and just. God's justice demands legal satisfaction for sin. God is 'free' and 'subject to no law and to no one's judgment, and so kind that nothing kinder can be conceived, and nothing is right or fitting save what he wills.'[33] Accordingly, for God to ignore the dishonor caused by sin would not make him more loving, it would compromise his deity: 'the highest justice, which is none other than God himself, maintains nothing more justly than his honor, in the ordering of things.'[34] Therefore, any means of redeeming sinners must necessarily be done so as not to compromise any of God's attributes – whether his justice, goodness, wisdom, or omnipotence.

VI. The Atonement by a God-Man is Necessary because of God's Offended Honor and Man's Infinite Debt

Because of God's inherent worth, the creature owes him absolute obedience and unfailing honor. Accordingly, Anselm defines obedience and sin in terms of honor and debt. So obedience is giving God his due honor, and man's sin is 'the same thing as not to render his due to God.'[35] Anselm reiterates, 'One who does not render this honor to God takes away from God what belongs to him, and dishonors God, and to do this is to sin.'[36] It is precisely this failure to honor God[37] which Adam sustained in his disobedience,[38] staining all generations of men with his transgression.[39] This sin created an impossible dilemma. Man's sin not only violates the honor God deserves, but also incurs to the sinner an infinite debt to God by denying him his right to be honored. So the guilt of sin cannot simply be eradicated by a return to obedience. Satisfaction and sin must correspond. In view of the infinite debt in man's sin and his inherent sinful constitution, he is incapable of making satisfactory amends: 'you do not make satisfaction unless you repay something greater than that for the sake of which you were obliged not to commit the sin.'[40] Because present and future obedience cannot make restitution for past dishonor, man can never repay 'to God the whole of what he took from him.'[41] On this basis, man is entirely incapable of solving his problem of guilt. In fact, 'the very inability is a fault.'[42] Even though it is impossible for corrupted man to render to God the honor due him by fulfilling the law perfectly and suffering the law's penalty for past sins, he is *still responsible* for the debt.

Furthermore, if man is punished eternally for his sin, even then he will never attain the blessedness of the celestial city for which he was created.[43] But this is not merely bad news for man, since man's failure to arrive in heaven would seem to make God's creation of man itself a failure. Such a conclusion of things would be thoroughly inconsistent with God's honor. As Boso acknowledges, at stake is the very honor of God: 'I understand now how it is necessary for God to carry out what he began; otherwise he would appear to fail in his undertaking, and this is not fitting.'[44] Therefore, since man could do nothing to rectify his situation, and since it is impossible for a sinner to justify a sinner,[45] the only possible resolution resides exclusively within the power of God. Though man *ought* to make the needed satisfaction as the debtor,[46] only God *could* make the needed satisfaction; accordingly, it was necessary 'for a God-Man to make it.'[47] Manifesting the intrinsic character of the triune God, and rectifying the incongruity of sin produced by fallen angels and fallen man, *of necessity* the God-Man, born of a virgin,[48] united himself in solidarity with those of Adam's race,[49] and obediently died on the cross. This death produced infinite satisfaction before God, a satisfaction outweighing the 'number and greatness of all sins.'[50]

VII. The Necessity of the Atonement is Consistent with the Trinity and the Divine Freedom of the God-Man

Anselm ensures us that Christ's death was not necessary by any compulsion outside of God nor or by some coercion within the Trinity itself. 'God's will is not constrained by any necessity, but ... maintains itself by its own free changelessness.'[51] In no way did the Father 'force him [Jesus] to die or allow him to be slain against his will; on the contrary, he himself readily endured death in order to save men.'[52] The Son of God preferred 'to suffer death rather than leave the human race unsaved.'[53]

Moreover, this act of self-sacrifice was perfectly consistent with the Son's own divine honor: 'he offered himself for his own honor to himself, as he did to the Father and the Holy Spirit.'[54] The atonement, therefore, was absolutely necessary because of God's commitment to himself, to his own honor and to his character. Jesus desired to die because as incarnate Son, he 'owed this obedience to God the Father, and his manhood owed it to his divinity, and the Father required this of him.'[55] As *God*-Man, his desire could only be consistent with his own divine will.

VIII. The God-Man's Worthy Atonement Necessitated a Reward Freely Applied to Unworthy Sinners

But how did the satisfaction accomplished by Christ find its way to fallen men? It is one thing to recognize the satisfaction accomplished by Christ's death; it is quite another thing to demonstrate the reality of its application to those in need. With meticulous scrutiny, Anselm clinches his argument by describing the application of Christ's redemption in terms of the all-sufficiency and supremacy of God. Christ's death, accomplishing a full satisfaction of the offended divine honor, necessitated a reward: 'You will not suppose that he who freely gives God so great a gift ought to be left unrewarded.'[56]

Yet Christ, being God, has need of nothing. No reward could add to his state of blessedness as very God. Once again, Anselm presents a quandary: God the Father owes God the Son a reward, but God the Son 'is in need of nothing and there is nothing that can be given or forgiven him.'[57] The dilemma is resolved in view of the freedom of Christ to transfer the reward upon others. Christ was free to extend and apply this reward as he wished, and he desired to pay the reward to men, he sought to usher into the blessedness of heaven. 'To whom would it be more fitting for him to assign the fruit and recompense of his death than to those for whose salvation (as truthful reasoning has taught us) he made himself man?'[58] Thus the atoning work of Christ perfectly reflects the immutable character of God, and it 'establishes the New Testament and proves the truth of the Old.'[59]

IX. The Impact of the Anselmic View of the Atonement on the Reformers

Anselm's argument is Copernican in nature. His approach to the atonement was a profound departure from both his predecessors and his contemporaries. Anselm 'took a step beyond anything he had written in the past: consciously and deliberately he went against the tradition.'[60] While there is evidence that some earlier theologians to varying degrees recognized that the atonement had God's justice as its goal, this notion was undeveloped. Most held to the idea that the cross was a ransom paid to Satan to secure the release of humanity, which he had taken hostage by the Adamic Fall.[61]

The theological impact of his new atonement paradigm has been vast in scope. Though Medieval theologians such as Abelard and Lombard did not follow Anselm's lead, it is clear that the sixteenth century reformers followed the Archbishop's scheme. In fact, the warp and woof of Anselm's argument produced the theological fabric from which the reformers tailored their own further clarified expressions of the atoning work of Christ. Anselm's notion of sin as *dishonor* fell short of the reformers' perspective. Following Augustine, he had an inadequate understanding of sin as a positive evil.[62] With a fuller biblical view, the reformers characterized sin as a violent transgression of the law of God. Calvin, for example, substituted the Anselmic concept of *honor* with the more biblical concept of *holiness*, thereby clarifying the necessity of satisfying not merely the honor of God, but also his wrath against sin and sinner. Yet Calvin consciously developed his view of the atonement in dialog with Patristic and Medieval theologians. He writes,

> ... it is said that God declared his love toward us in giving his only-begotten Son to die [John 3:16]; and, conversely, that God was our enemy before he was again made favorable to us by Christ's death [Rom. 5:10]. But to render these things more certain among those who require the testimony of the ancient church, I shall quote a passage of Augustine where the very thing is taught: 'God's love,' says he, 'is incomprehensible and unchangeable. For it was not

after we were reconciled to him through the blood of his Son that he began to love us. Rather, he has loved us before the world was created, that we also might be his sons along with his only-begotten Son – before we became anything at all. The fact that we were reconciled through Christ's death must not be understood as if his Son reconciled us to him that he might now begin to love those whom he had hated. Rather, we have already been reconciled to him who loves us, with whom we were enemies on account of sin. The apostle will testify whether I am speaking the truth: 'God shows his love for us in that while we were yet sinners Christ died for us' [Rom. 5:8]. Therefore, he loved us even when we practiced enmity toward him and committed wickedness. Thus in a marvelous and divine way he loved us even when he hated us. For he hated us for what we were that he had not made; yet because our wickedness had not entirely consumed his handiwork, he knew how, at the same time, to hate in each one of us what we had made, and to love what he had made.' These are Augustine's words.[63]

For on the beginning of justification there is no quarrel between us and the sounder Schoolmen: that a sinner freely liberated from condemnation may obtain righteousness, and that through the forgiveness of sins; except that they include under the term 'justification' a renewal, by which through the Spirit of God we are remade to obedience to the law.... For Christ ever remains the Mediator to reconcile the Father to us; and his death has everlasting efficacy: namely, cleansing, satisfaction, atonement, and finally perfect obedience, with which all our iniquities are covered. And Paul does not say to the Ephesians that we have the beginning of salvation from grace but that we have been saved through grace, 'not by works, lest any man should boast' [Eph. 2:8-9].[64]

Calvin rejected the idea that satisfaction and punishment are mutually exclusive choices for sin's atonement. Instead, he saw them as inseparable in the work of Christ so that his punishment *was* the satisfaction, the propitiation of the wrath of God.[65] In this way the reformers improved upon Anselm. Yet there was not an absolute dearth of gospel truth during the Middle Ages. In spite of the merit theology of medieval scholastic theology, the truth of the gospel was not entirely devoid during these days. While it is important to emphasize the polemical character of Calvin's theology against medieval scholasticism, it is also true that Calvin was at times appreciative of and reliant upon the insights of the Schoolmen.[66]

As Anselm's theory of substitutionary atonement illustrates, medieval scholarship could uphold central tenets of the gospel, *including* justification by faith. Consider the following quotation from Anselm's pastoral study, entitled, 'Direction for Visitation of the Sick':

> Dost thou believe that thou canst not be saved but by the death of Christ? The sick man answereth, yes. Then let it be said to him: Go to, then, and whilst thy soul abideth in thee, put all thy confidence in this death alone, place thy trust in no other thing, commit thyself wholly to this death, cover thyself wholly with this alone, cast thyself wholly on this death, wrap thyself wholly in this death. And if God would judge thee, say, Lord, I place the death of our Lord Jesus Christ between me and thy judgment; and otherwise I will not contend, or enter into judgment with thee. And if he shall say unto thee, that thou art a sinner, say, I place the death of our Lord Jesus Christ between thee and my sins. If he shall say unto thee, that thou hast deserved damnation, say, Lord, I put the death of our Lord Jesus Christ between thee and all my sins; and offer his merits instead of my own, which I ought to have, but have not. If he shall say that he is angry with thee, say, Lord, I place the death of our Lord Jesus Christ between me and thy anger.[67]

As he ministers to the sinner on his deathbed, Anselm here presents a *sola fide* salvation. Faith alone is the instrument of receiving Christ's death. While human merit is the individual's responsibility, it is not claimed before God for salvation, because Christ's merit alone grounds personal redemption. Further, Anselm recognizes that man stands in judgment before God, under his wrath, and beneath the verdict of damnation – all ideas linked to propitiation which the reformers integrated into their doctrine of the substitutionary atonement of Christ. Anselm makes clear that it is only the mediation of Christ's death that prevents the unleashing of God's judgment upon this soul. Finally, though Anselm does not use the phrase 'justification by faith', the concept is implicit, demonstrating the precursory nature of Anselm's thought for the subsequent Protestant Reformation.

In his summary of Anselm, Eugene R. Fairweather contends, 'Anselm avoids the slightest suggestion that the atonement is the placating of an angry God, the satisfaction of an offended Father by the punishment of a loving Son.'[68] To this contention we must reply in two ways. It is true in *Cur Deus Homo* that Anselm does not develop the propitiatory character of the atonement as its central focus. Anselm's understanding of sin as a privation of good and a debt of dishonor understates the magnitude of sin, and consequently dilutes the wrath of God associated with its judgment. However, as the pastorally sensitive text above reveals, God's wrath at the sinner for his sin is very real to Anselm, making the mediation of Christ's merit very necessary. In view of God's anger, believing in Christ's death alone is the dying sinner's only hope of salvation. It is intriguing to note the distinction this presents between the theoretical and practical aspects of Anselm's thought. The *practical* and *pastoral* Anselm directed the ailing believer's attention to both the wrath of God and to the merit of Christ's death, rather than to matters of economy and necessity, or to honor and dishonor, the emphases of his theoretical treatise, '*Why the God Man?*'. Thus contrary to Fairweather's assessment, in *Cur Deus Homo*, propitiation does appear in Anselm's thought. For example, consider Boso's comments to Anselm about defending the atonement before the skeptic: 'He redeemed us from sins and from his own *wrath* and from *hell* and from the power of the devil, whom he came himself to conquer for us, since we could not do it ourselves.'[69] To Anselm (and Boso), God is angry at sin, an anger that reflects his holiness. The outpouring of final judgment attests to God's holy character. In the economy of God's perfect justice, eternal torment and punishment are both necessary and consistent with God's indignation regarding sin.[70] Placating God's wrath toward sin is not only present in Anselm's thought, he declares it to be indispensable in the work of Christ.

X. Conclusion: Satisfaction of a Historical Debt to the Honor of Anselm

Although the language of *honor* and *satisfaction*, rather than the reformers' terms of *holiness* and *propitiation*, dominate in Anselm's *Cur Deus Homo*,[71] to find contradiction between Anselm and the reformers at this point is unwarranted.[72] In general, Anselm's theory of the atonement proposed in *Cur Deus Homo* and pastorally summarized in his 'Direction for Visitation of the Sick' prepares the way for the reformational biblical theology of the sixteenth century. Though some have sought to alienate the reformers from Anselm,[73] it appears that his thinking not only prepares for, but also anticipates the later Protestant view of the atonement.

Trusting that there is an atonement that will propitiate not only the wrath of God but also the wrath of theological-historians for sins committed in life and in theology, let us seek to satisfy a debt we owe to Anselm, giving him his due honor. In the economy of theological development, there is ultimately a necessity to recognize a significant congruity between Anselm's explanation of why God became man, and the view of the atonement that is offered by his theological successors in the Reformation era. If Anselm is not to be conceived of as the greatest possible theologian, is it not at least appropriate to posit that his remarkable theology was historically and logically necessary for the emergence of the penal substitutionary atonement taught by the greatest theologians of the Reformation? Can we not also agree – at least in the case of Anselm – that the theological sun shone in the 'Dark Ages' after all?

NOTES

1. It is my privilege along with editing this volume, to offer this study in honor of my professor, dissertation adviser, colleague, fellow-presbyter and friend, Dr. D. Clair Davis. The first course I ever taught on a Seminary level was Dr. Davis' M. Div. Medieval Church History classes at Westminster Seminary, during his study leave in 1981. I also wish to express my thanks to David Garner, a Ph.D. candidate at Westminster Seminary, for his assistance in preparing this paper for publication.

2. Selected Bibliography on Anselm's Life and Theory of the Atonement includes: Church, R. W. *Saint Anselm.* London: Macmillan & Co., 1870; Eadmer, *The Life of St Anselm: Archbishop of Canterbury.* Edited and translated by R. W. Southern. Oxford: Clarendon Press, 1962; Evans, Gillian R. *Anselm and Talking About God.* Oxford: Clarendon Press, 1978; Foley, George Cadwalader. *Anselm's Theory of the Atonement.* London: Longmans, Green, and Co., 1909; Hannah, John D. 'Anselm on the Doctrine of Atonement.' *Bibliotheca Sacra* 135 (1978): 333-44; Hopkins, Jasper. *A Companion to the Study of St. Anselm.* Minneapolis: University of Minnesota Press, 1972; McIntyre, John. *St. Anselm and His Critics: A Re-Interpretation of the* Cur Deus Homo. Edinburgh: Oliver and Boyd, 1954; Southern, R. W. *Saint Anselm: A Portrait in a Landscape.* Cambridge: Cambridge University Press, 1990; Strimple, Robert B. 'Anselm and the Theology of Atonement.' Th.M. thesis, Westminster Theological Seminary, Philadelphia, 1964.

3. Anselm wrote many works, including *De Grammatico* in which he probes a section of Aristotle's *Categories, De Veritate* where he defines truth as rectitude of thought, *De Libertate Arbitrii* in which he seeks to discern the nature of freedom and bondage, and *De Conceptu Virginali et de Peccato Orginiali* which serves as an explanatory appendix to his classic *Cur Deus Homo* or 'Why the God-Man?' which is the subject of this study. In addition, he wrote *Proslogion*, wherein he states his famous ontological argument for the existence of God, which is still

significant for scholars from both theological and philosophical perspectives. See Southern, *Saint Anselm*, 411; Gillian R. Evans, *Anselm and Talking About God* (Oxford: Clarendon Press, 1978), 127, 132-33, 172-93.

4. A. N. S. Lane writes, '*Proslogion* was of particular significance for one modern theologian: Karl Barth. In his *Fides Quaerens Intellectum* (*Faith Seeking Understanding*; 1931), Barth analysed Anselm's method of 'faith seeking understanding' and found in it a precedent for his own approach to theology in the 20th century.' In *New Dictionary of Theology*, (Downers Grove: Inter-Varsity Press, 1988), p. 27. See also, Alvin Plantinga, *The Ontological Argument; from St. Anselm to Contemporary Philosophers*, (New York: Anchor Books, 1965). Lane again writes, 'The debate about the validity of the ontological argument continues to rage and shows no signs of abating.' Ibid.

5. The word 'atonement' is the theological word that is typically used to describe how Christ accomplished the salvation of sinners through his Gospel ministry in his incarnation. The word itself comes from an old English word meaning reconciliation. Hence, 'at-one-ment' implies the restoration of enemies into the oneness of reconciliation. The classic theological views of the atonement of Christ have been well summarized by Louis Berkhof, *Systematic Theology* (Grand Rapids: Eerdmans, 1996), pp. 373-391. He discusses eight different views: The Penal Substitutionary Theory; The Ransom-To-Satan theory; The Satisfaction Theory of Anselm (Commercial Theory); The Moral Influence Theory; The Example Theory; The Governmental Theory; The Mystical Theory; The Theory of Vicarious Repentance.

6. The classic study of theological nominalism is Heiko A. Oberman, *The Harvest of Medieval Theology*, (Durham: The Labyrinth Press, 1983).

7. See, Peter A. Lillback, *The Binding of God: Calvin's Role in the Development of Covenant Theology*, Texts and Studies in Reformation and Post-Reformation Thought, ed. Richard A. Muller (Grand Rapids: Baker Book House Company, 2001), pp. 74-76.

8. R. W. Southern, *Saint Anselm: A Portrait in a Landscape* (Cambridge: Cambridge University Press, 1990), 12-13.

9. Anselm, *Prayers and Meditations* (trans. A Religious of C. S. M. V.; London: A. R. Mowbray & Co., 1952), 13-14.

10. Anselm, *Cur Deus Homo,* in *A Scholastic Miscellany: Anselm to Ockham* (*The Library of Christian Classics* 10; ed. and trans. Eugene R. Fairweather; Philadelphia: The Westminster Press, 1956), 128. All references to *Cur Deus Homo* will from this work, unless otherwise noted.

11. St. Anselm, *Proslogium; Monologium; An Appendix in Behalf of the Fool by Gaunilon; and Cur Deus Homo,* Trans. Sidney Norton Deane, (Chicago: The Open Court Publishing Company, 1926), p. 178.

12. See Evans, *Anselm,* 161-67.

13. The importance of Anselm's work on the atonement for the history of doctrine is underscored in that the students of the history of theology do not fail to include a discussion of his contributions. For representative examples, consider the following: Louis Berkhof, *The History of Christian Doctrines*, (Grand Rapids: Baker, 1976), pp. 171ff.; David Knowles, 'The Middle Ages 604-1350' in *A History of Christian Doctrine*, ed. Hubert Cunliffe-Jones, (Philadelphia: Fortress Press, 1978), p. 247-249; K. R. Hagenbach, *Compendium of the History of Doctrines*, trans. Carl W. Buch (Edinburgh: T. & T. Clark, 1847), vol. II:32-38; E. H. Klotsche, *The History of Christian Doctrine*, (Grand Rapids: Baker, 1979), p. 140-142; Reinhold Seeburg, *The History of Doctrines*, (Grand Rapids: Baker, 1977), vol.

The Practical Calvinist

II:66-70; William G. T. Shedd, *A History of Christian Doctrine*, (Minneapolis: Klock & Klock Christian Publishers, 1978), Vol. II:273-286. Berkhof sums up the common view of these authors, 'Anselm of Canterbury made the first attempt at a harmonious and consistent representation of the doctrine of atonement. His *Cur Deus Homo* is an epoch-making book, a masterpiece of theological learning, in which the author combines metaphysical depth with clearness of presentation.' Berkhof, op. cit., p. 171.

14. Southern, *Saint Anselm*, 201.

15. B. B. Warfield presents an impressive summary of the logical categories of the atonement, which he calls 'the five chief theories of the atonement.' The first two were present in Anselm's historical context, the third immediately followed him, the fifth was his own conception. Thus only the fourth logical category of atonement theory was not present in the Medieval Era. Warfield explains them as follows: 1. Theories which conceive the work of Christ as *terminating upon Satan*, so affecting him as to secure the release of the souls held in bondage by him. These theories, which have been described as emphasizing the 'triumphantorial' aspect of Christ's work ... had very considerable vogue in the patristic age (e.g. Irenaeus, Hippolytus, Clement of Alexandria, Origen, Basil, the two Gregories, Cyril of Alexandria, down to and including John of Damascus and Nicholas of Methone; Hilary, Rufinus, Jerome, Augustine, Leo the Great, and even so late as Bernard). They passed out of view only gradually as the doctrine of 'satisfaction' became more widely known. Not only does the thought of a Bernard still run in this channel, but even Luther utilized the conception. The idea runs through many forms – speaking in some of them of buying off, in some of overcoming, in some even of outwitting (so e.g. Origen) the devil. But it would be unfair to suppose that such theories represent in any of their forms the whole thought as to the work of Christ of those who made use of them, or were considered by them a scientific statement of the work of Christ.... 2. Theories which conceive the work of Christ as *terminating physically on man*, so affecting him as to bring him by an interior and hidden working upon him into participation with the one life of Christ; the so-called 'mystical theories.' The fundamental characteristic of these theories is their discovery of the saving fact not in anything which Christ taught or did, but in what He was. It is upon the Incarnation, rather than upon Christ's teaching or His work that they throw stress attributing the saving power of Christ not to what He does for us but to what He does in us. Tendencies to this type of theory are already traceable in the Platonizing Fathers; and with the entrance of the more developed Neoplatonism into the stream of Christian thinking, through the writings of Pseudo-Dionysius naturalized in the West by Johannes Scotus Erigena, a constant tradition of mystical teaching began which never died out.... 3. Theories which conceive the work of Christ as *terminating on man, in the way of bringing to bear on him inducements to action*; so affecting man as to lead him to a better knowledge of God, or to a more lively sense of his real relation to God, or to a revolutionary change of heart and life with reference to God; the so-called 'moral influence theories.' The essence of all these theories is that they transfer the atoning fact from the work of Christ to the response of the human soul to the influences or appeals proceeding from the work of Christ. The work of Christ takes immediate effect not on God but on man, leading him to a state of mind and heart which will be acceptable to God, through the medium of which alone can the work of Chirst be said to affect God.... [Warfield here does not specifically mention Medieval theologian Abelard at this point, but Abelard's moral example theory of the atonement would fit here.] ... 4. Theories which conceive the work of Christ as *terminating on both man and God, but on man primarily and on God only secondarily*. The outstanding instance of this class of theories

is supplied by the so-called 'rectoral or governmental theories.' These suppose that the work of Christ so affects man by the spectacle of the sufferings borne by Him as to deter men from sin; and by thus deterring men from sin enables God to forgive sin with safety to His moral government of the world. In these theories the sufferings and death of Christ become, for the first time in this conspectus of theories, of cardinal importance, constituting indeed the very essence of the work of Christ. But the atoning fact here too, no less than in the 'moral influence' theories, is man's own reformation, though this reformation is supposed in the rectoral view to be wrought not primarily by breaking down man's opposition to God by a moving manifestation of the love of God in Christ, but by inducing in man a horror of sin, through the spectacle of God's hatred of sin afforded by the sufferings of Christ – through which, no doubt, the contemplation of man is led on to God's love to sinners as exhibited in His willingness to inflict all these sufferings on His own Son that He might be enabled with justice to His moral government, to forgive sins. This theory was worked out by the great Dutch jurist Hugo Grotius.... 5. Theories which conceive the work of Christ as *terminating primarily on God and secondarily on man*.... [one] theory supposes that our Lord, by sympathetically entering into our condition (an idea independently suggested by Schleiermacher...) so keenly felt our sins as His own, that He could confess and adequately repent of them before God; and this is all the expiation justice asks. Here 'sympathetic identification' replaces the conception of substitution ... the theory rises immeasurably above the mass of those already enumerated, in looking upon Christ as really a Saviour, who performs a really saving work, terminating immediately on God ... such theories, while preserving the sacrificial form of the Biblical doctrine, and, with it, its inseparable implication that the work of Christ has as its primary end to affect God and secure from Him favorable regard for man ... yet fall so far short of the Biblical doctrine of the nature and effect of Christ's sacrifice as to seem little less than travesties of it. The Biblical doctrine of the sacrifice of Christ finds full recognition in no other construction than that of the established church-doctrine of satisfaction. According to it, our Lord's redeeming work is at its core a true and perfect sacrifice offered to God, of intrinsic value ample for the expiation of our guilt; and at the same time is a true and perfect righteousness offered to God in fulfillment of the demands of His law; ... This doctrine, which has been incorporated in more or less fullness of statement in the creedal declarations of all the great branches of the Church, Greek, Latin, Lutheran, and Reformed, and which has been expounded with more or less insight and power by the leading doctors of the churches for the last eight hundred years, was first given scientific statement by Anselm in his '*Cur Deus Homo*' (1098); but reached its complete development only at the hands of the so-called Protestant Scholastics of the seventeenth century (Turretin, John Owen).' Benjamin B. Warfield, 'The Chief Theories of the Atonement' in *The Person and Work of Christ* (Presbyterian and Reformed, 1980), pp. 356-368.

16. Ibid., 181.

17. Ibid.

18. Anselm, *Cur Deus Homo*, 101. Boso (p. 176) restates this question: Why did God become man, to save man by his death, when it seems he could have done this thing another way?'

19. Ibid., 152. Cf. John D. Hannah, 'Anselm on the Doctrine of Atonement,' *Bibliotheca Sacra* 135 (1978): 337.

20. 'Those who [request this book] do not expect to come to faith through reason, but they hope to be gladdened by the understanding and contemplation of the things they believe, and as far as possible to be 'ready always to satisfy every one that asketh' them 'a reason of that hope which is in' them,' Anselm, *Cur Deus Homo*, 101.

21. Some have argued that while Anselm claims a presuppositional approach, he actually gravitates to a bald rationalism. While there are points at which Anselm's logical syllogisms appear coldly rational, the substantial tenor of the argument reflects a man whose heart has been stirred by faith in God. All of Anselm's reflections, in varying degrees of transparency, presuppose God in his intrinsic being and in his economic activity. Accordingly, Evans (*Anselm,* 138) is undoubtedly correct in his conclusion, 'When [Anselm] says that he intends to prove by reason alone, he means that proof to be slotted into the scheme of faith as soon as it is devised.' Cf. John McIntyre, *St. Anselm and His Critics: A Re-Interpretation of the* Cur Deus Homo (Edinburgh: Oliver and Boyd, 1954), 1-55; Robert B. Strimple, 'Anselm and the Theology of the Atonement' (Th.M. thesis, Westminster Theological Seminary, Philadelphia), 78-86.

22. Anselm, *Cur Deus Homo,* 150. Cf. p. 116.

23. See Ibid., 125-34, 168.

24. Ibid., 108, emphasis added. Cf. p. 124.

25. Ibid., 110.

26. Ibid.

27. Ibid., 108.

28. Ibid., 111.

29. Ibid., 113, emphasis added.

30. Ibid., 143.

31. Ibid.

32. Ibid.

33. Ibid., 120.

34. Ibid., 122.

35. Ibid., 119.

36. Ibid.

37. Though sin violates God's honor, Anselm is quick to assert that because of God's immutability ('He himself is honor incorruptible and absolutely unchangeable,' ibid., 123.), the robbery of honor is not one which compromises God's essence: 'No one can honor or dishonor God, *as he is in himself*; at the same time, anyone who submits his will to God's will, or withdraws it, *seems* to do one or the other, as far as lies in him' (p. 124, emphasis added). This disobedience/dishonor of man brings dishonor to God in the sense of disturbing the 'order and beauty of the universe,' but 'it cannot injure or stain the power and dignity of God' (p. 124).

38. Ibid., 140.

39. Ibid., 141. 'Strong and immortal in power, man freely accepted the devil's temptation to sin, and thus justly incurred the penalty of mortality; now, weak and mortal as he made himself he ought through the distress of death to conquer the devil, so as not to sin at all. But this is what he cannot do as long as, through the wound of the first sin, he is conceived and born in sin' (p. 140).

40. Ibid., 139. This 'greater' implies a 'greater than the simple maintenance of obedience to God's will' (p. 139, n25).

41. Ibid., 141.

42. Ibid., 142. He continues, 'The inability to repay to God what a man owes, which is the cause of his not repaying it, does not excuse him when he fails to make repayment, since the effect of sin does not excuse the sin that causes it.' Anselm illustrates the fault inherent in inability: 'Suppose that a man enjoins some task on his servant, and charges him not to throw himself into a pit which he points out to him, out of which he cannot possibly escape. But that servant despises the command and the

warning of his master and, of his own free will, throws himself into the pit that has been shown him, so that he is unable to carry out his assigned task. Do you think that this inability is worth anything as an excuse for not performing the assigned task?'

43. Ibid., 146-48.

44. Ibid., 148.

45. Ibid., 142.

46. Ibid., 151.

47. Ibid.

48. Ibid., 153-54.

49. Ibid., 152-53.

50. Ibid., 163.

51. Ibid., 170.

52. Ibid., 111.

53. Ibid., 115.

54. Ibid., 179.

55. Ibid., 112.

56. Ibid., 180.

57. Ibid.

58. Ibid.

59. Ibid., 183.

60. Southern, *Saint Anselm*, 205.

61. See, e.g., George Cadwalader Foley, *Anselm's Theory of the Atonement* (London: Longmans, Green, and Co., 1909), 15-99.

62. In his explanatory volume to *Cur Deus Homo*, Anselm writes, 'Therefore, by original sin I do not understand anything different from what is in the infant as soon as it has a rational soul, whatever may have happened in its body before it was animated – for instance, some corruption of the members – or whatever is to befall it afterward, either in soul or in body. For the reasons given above, I think that this is equal in all infants naturally begotten, and that all who die in it alone are condemned equally. Whatever sin is added in man beyond this is personal, and just as the person is born sinful because of the nature, so the nature is made more sinful by the person, because when any person sins, man sins.'
He continues, 'In these infants, I cannot interpret this sin which I call original, as anything but that deprivation of due justice, which, as I said above, is the outcome of Adam's disobedience.' Concluding that both original sin and acts of sin are deprivation of due honor, he writes, 'These two deprivations leave them unprotected in this life's exile, and open to the sins and miseries which ceaselessly befall them everywhere and attack them on every side, except in so far as they are protected by the divine government,' Anselm, *The Virgin Conception and Original Sin*, in *A Scholastic Miscellany: Anselm to Ockham* (*The Library of Christian Classics* 10; ed. and trans. Eugene R. Fairweather; Philadelphia: The Westminster Press, 1956), 199-200.

63. John Calvin, *The Institutes of the Christian Religion*, trans. Ford Lewis Battles, (Philadelphia: Westminster Press, 1975), II. XVI. 4, pp. 506-507.

64. Calvin, *Institutes*, III. XIV.11, pp. 778-779.

65. Calvin says, 'Surely he is addressing believers, to whom, while he sets forth Christ as the propitiation of sins, he shows that there is no other satisfaction whereby offended God can be propitiated or appeased ... he makes him a perpetual advocate in order that by his intercession he may always restore us to the Father's favor; an everlasting propitiation by which sins may be expiated. For what the other John said is ever true: 'Behold the Lamb of God, who takes away the sins of the world!' [John 1:29]. He, I say,

not another, takes them away; that is since he alone is the Lamb of God, he also is the sole offering for sin, the sole expiation, the sole satisfaction. For while the right and power of forgiving sins properly belong to the Father, in which respect he is distinguished from the Son, as we have already seen, Christ is here placed on another level because, taking upon himself the penalty that we owe, he has wiped out our guilt before God's judgment. From this it follows that we shall share in the expiation made by Christ only if that honor rests with him which those who try to appease God by their own recompense seize for themselves.' *Institutes*, III. IV.26, pp. 652-653.

66. Cf. Lillback, *The Binding of God*, pp. 194-206.

67. This translation of Anselm's 'Direction for Visitation of the Sick' can be found in Shedd's *History of Christian Doctrine*, II. 281-282, and the original is in *Opera* I. 686, ed. Migne. Shedd adds a significant insight about the theology here expressed and its relationship to the Mariolatry of the Medieval tradition. He writes, 'In Migne's edition, after the self-commendation of the soul into the hands of God, there follows an invocation of the Virgin which is manifestly an interpolation of some zealous and unscrupulous Papist. It is as follows: 'Postea dicat, Maria mater gratiae, mater misericordiae, tu nos ab hoste protege, et hora mortis suscipe: per tuum ergo, Virgo, Filium, per Patrem, et Spiritu Sanctum, praesens adsis ad obitum meum, quia imminet exitus. Amen.' The difference between the Mariolatry of this passage, and the Paulinism of the 'direction' for visiting the sick is too great to have proceeded from the same intuition. The us of 'nos' indicates that is part of an ecclesiastical liturgy. In the first extract, the first person singular is intense all the way through.' Shedd, op. cit. II.282.

68. Eugene R. Fairweather, 'Introduction to Anselm,' in *A Scholastic Miscellany: Anselm to Ockham* (*The Library of Christian Classics* 10; ed. and trans. Eugene R. Fairweather; Philadelphia: The Westminster Press, 1956), 57.

69. Anselm, *Cur Deus Homo,* 106, emphasis added.

70. Cf. Ibid., 181.

71. Lane writes, 'Anselm's case is impressive, but not without its weaknesses. He has been criticized on a number of grounds, some of which amount to blaming him for addressing his own particular context, where, for instance, talk of honour and satisfaction was familiar because of the penitential system in the church and because of feudal concepts in society. He has with some justice been criticized for locating the salvific work of Christ exclusively in the *cross*, neglecting the life of Christ and his resurrection and ascension. But it must be remembered that his aim was precisely to give reasons why the cross, the great scandal to unbelievers, was necessary. Anselm also went beyond the usual Christian claim that the cross was necessary (*i.e.* God had to do something) to claim that it was *absolutely* necessary (*i.e.* God could not have done anything else.). Here again he reflects the 11th century confidence in the power of reason. But the attractiveness of Anselm's case is that it is very flexible. His basic case, suitably modified, makes a powerful argument today that the incarnation and cross are indeed fitting and reasonable.' A. N. S. Lane, 'Anselm' in *New Dictionary of Theology*, p. 28.

72. Shedd's enthusiastic assessment emphasizes this point, 'In closing this brief sketch of Anselm's theory of the Atonement, it is evident that if his views and experience, as exhibited in the *Cur Deus Homo?*, could have become those of the church of which he was a member and an ornament, the revival of the doctrine of justification by faith in the Lutheran Reformation would not have been needed. Such a profound and spiritual conception of sin, such a clear and penetrating consciousness of guilt, such adoring and humbling views of the divine majesty, such calm and searching apprehensions of the divine justice, such annihilation of

human merit in the eye of law, and such an evangelic estimate of the atonement of the God-Man, if they could have been made elements and influences in the general religious experience of the Western Church, that eleventh century would have exhibited a spirit of judgment and of burning, of profound humility and self-denial, of purity and self-consecration, that would have been a dazzling contrast to the actual religious character which it presents. But the soteriology of Anselm, though exerting no little influence through his immediate pupils, did not pass over into the church at large.' Shedd, op. cit., pp. 285-286.

73. While Berkhof, the historical theologian has high praise for Anselm (see note 13 above), when he writes as a systematic theologian, he is more critical. His discussion in his *Systematic Theology* argues for a significant difference between Anselm and the Reformers. He writes, 'The theory of Anselm is sometimes identified with that of the Reformers, which is also known as the satisfaction theory, but the two are not identical. Some seek to prejudice others against it by calling it 'the commercial theory'.... However, it is open to several points of criticism. 1. It is not consistent in its representation of the necessity of the atonement. It ostensibly does not ground this necessity in the justice of God which cannot brook sin, but in the honor of God which calls for amends or reparation.... 2. This theory really has no place for the idea that Christ by suffering endured the penalty of sin, and that His suffering was strictly vicarious.... 3. The scheme is also one-sided and therefore insufficient in that it bases redemption exclusively on the death of Christ ... and excludes the active obedience of Christ as a contributing factor to His atoning work. The whole emphasis is on the death of Christ, and no justice is done to the redemptive significance of His life. 4. In Anselm's representation there is merely an external transfer of the merits of Christ to man.... There is no hint of the mystical union of Christ and believers, nor of faith as accepting the righteousness of Christ. Since the whole transaction appears to be rather commercial, the theory is often called the commercial theory.' Berkhof, *Systematic Theology*, pp. 385-86. In light of this discussion, it appears he has overstated the differences. Warfield's approach of placing the Reformers' and Anselm's theories of the atonement in the same logical category of 'theories which conceive the work of Christ as *terminating primarily on God and secondarily on man*' seems more accurate. Warfield contends, 'This doctrine, which has been incorporated in more or less fullness of statement in the creedal declarations of all the great branches of the Church, Greek, Latin, Lutheran, and Reformed, and which has been expounded with more or less insight and power by the leading doctors of the churches for the last eight hundred years, was first given scientific statement by Anselm in his '*Cur Deus Homo*' (1098); but reached its complete development only at the hands of the so-called Protestant Scholastics....' See Warfield, 'The Chief Theories of the Atonement,' p. 368.

INTRODUCTION
TO JOHN CALVIN'S
CHRIST THE END OF THE LAW

Editor's Note

The original French title of this work is '*A Tous Amateurs De Jesus Christ et De Son Evangile, Salut*'. When first translated into English by Thomas Weeden in 1848, it was entitled, '*Christ the End of the Law, Being the Preface to the Geneva Bible of 1550*' by John Calvin.[1] This little writing, however, was printed anonymously in the original 1535 French Bible of Pierre Robert Olevitan.

In defense of Calvin's authorship of *Christ the End of the Law*, we do know that Calvin was intimately involved in the early French Bible, since Calvin wrote and signed another Latin preface to Olevitan's 1535 French Bible.[2] Moreover, by 1545, *Christ The End of the Law* was linked with Calvin.[3] It is also evident that Theodore Beza attributed it to Calvin, as can be seen in Beza's collection of Calvin's letters.[4] Beza entitled it, *Praefatio in N.T. Cuius Haec Summa Est: Christum Esse Legis Finem*. Moreover, the editors of Calvin's works included it as an authentic writing of Calvin.[5] Recent scholars have also identified Calvin as its author.[6]

One of the reasons for the importance of *Christ the End of the Law* is that it reveals the remarkable covenantal harmony between Calvin and Bullinger.[7] As an extended summary of the unity of the Bible in both the Old and New Testaments, its argument clearly reflects the ideas of Bullinger's *De Testamento seu Foedere*, written only a year earlier in 1534.

Some may question, however, the propriety of the inclusion of a historical writing in a festschrift to honor a contemporary scholar. While, this may seem unusual, the reasons for doing so are threefold. First, I had planned to present it in my *Binding of God*. [8] But due to editorial and publishing considerations, it was not included. Hence, it seemed appropriate to incorporate it here, thereby completing an unfulfilled promise. Second, since my writing on Calvin began under Dr. Davis' oversight, its presentation is a further testimony of my appreciation for his impact upon my studies. Third, it seems wise to include it here, since this little work by Calvin is almost unknown to students of the Reformation. Given its emphasis on covenant continuity, the essence of the Reformed biblical hermeneutic, this opportunity for its rediscovery is irresistible. This is particularly so in a study intended to introduce students to the Presbyterian and Reformed heritage.

Finally, I wish to express a special thanks to Flavien Partigon, a Ph.D. student at Westminster Seminary, and to Dr. David B. Garner for their excellent labors in comparing, and correcting Thomas Weeden's English translation of the French version of Calvin's *Christ the End of the Law*, and in the process giving us what is in reality an entirely new and vastly improved translation. I am truly indebted to them for their excellent scholarly labors.

CHRIST THE END OF THE LAW[9]

John Calvin

God the Creator, very perfect and excellent Maker of all things, made man – in whom one can contemplate a special excellence – as a masterpiece, even more than his other creatures, in which he had already shown Himself more than admirable. For He formed him in His own likeness and image, so much so that the light of His glory shone brightly in him. Now, that which would have enabled man to remain in that condition in which he had been established was that he would always lower himself in humility before the majesty of God, magnifying it with thanksgiving, and that he should not seek his glory in himself; but, seeing that all things come from above, he would also always look above, to thank for them the one and only God, to whom belongs the praise for them.

But the wretched being, wishing to be something in himself, soon began to forget and fail to recognize the source[10] of his good, and by outrageous ingratitude undertook to elevate himself, and to puff himself up against his Maker and Author of all his graces. For this cause he stumbled into ruin; he lost all the dignity and excellence of his first creation; he was despoiled and stripped of all his glory; he was alienated of the gifts which had been placed in him – in order to confound him in his pride, and make him learn by force[11] that which he did not want to understand of his good will; namely, that he was only vanity, and that he never was anything else, except as much as the Lord of power assisted him.[12]

Hence God also began to hate him,[13] and, as he well merited, to disavow him as His work; seeing that His image and likeness was effaced from him, and that the gifts of His goodness were no longer in it. And, as He had set and ordained him in order to please and delight Himself in him, like a father in his well-beloved child; so, on the contrary, He held him in disdain and abomination, so much that all which had pleased Him before, now displeased Him; that which used to delight Him, angered Him; that which He used to contemplate with benign and parental regards, He now took to detest and to behold with regret. In short, the whole man with all his belongings, his deeds, his thoughts, his words, and his life, totally displeased God, as if he was His special and adversarial enemy, even to the point of saying that He repented that He had made him. After having been cast down into such confusion, he has been fruitful in his cursed seed to beget a race similar to him, that is to say vicious, perverse, corrupt, void and deprived of any good, rich and abounding in evil.

Nevertheless, the Lord of mercy (who not only loves, but Himself is love and charity), wishing still, of His infinite goodness, to love that which is no longer worthy of His love, did not at all waste, doom and sink men into the abyss as their iniquity required; but[14] has sustained and supported them in tenderness and in patience, giving them time and leisure to return to Him, and to come back to the obedience from which they had diverted. And though He hid and kept silent (as if He wanted to hide Himself from them), letting them follow the desires and wishes of their concupiscence, without law, without government, without any correction of His Word, nevertheless, He sent them enough warnings which were meant to incite them to seek, to grope for, and to find Him in order to know Him and to honor Him as is fitting.

For He has raised everywhere, in every place, and in every thing, His ensigns and armorial standards, even under blazons of such clear intelligence, that there is none who can claim ignorance of not knowing such a sovereign Lord, who has so widely exalted His magnificence, when He has written and almost engraved in all parts of the world, in the heavens and in the earth, the glory of His power, goodness, wisdom, and eternity. Therefore, St. Paul has truly said that the Lord did not leave Himself without witnesses, even towards those to whom He has not sent any knowledge of His Word. Seeing that all creatures from the firmament down to the center of the earth, could be witnesses and messengers of His glory to all men, in order to draw them to seek Him and, after finding Him, to do Him service and homage, according to the dignity of a Lord so good, so powerful, so wise and eternal, and they even help, each in its place, in that pursuit. For the singing young birds sing for God, the beasts clamor for Him, the elements of nature dread His might; the mountains echo Him; the rivers and fountains make eyes at Him; the herbs and flowers laugh before Him. However, it is truly not necessary to seek Him afar, seeing that everyone can find Him in himself, inasmuch as we are all upheld and preserved by His sustaining power dwelling in us.

Nevertheless, to manifest even more largely His goodness and infinite clemency among men, He did not rest satisfied with instructing them all by such teachings as those we have already set forth, but He made His voice heard in a special manner to a certain people, which, of His good will and free grace, He had elected and chosen from among all the nations of the earth. It was the children of Israel, to whom He clearly showed by His Word who He is, and by His marvelous works declared what He can do. For He brought them out from subjection to Pharaoh King of Egypt (under which they were detained and oppressed) to emancipate them and set them at liberty. He accompanied them night and day in their flight, being, as it were, a fugitive in the midst of them. He fed them in the desert; He made them possessors of the promised territory; He gave victories and triumphs into their hands. And, as if He were nothing to the other nations, He expressly wanted to be called 'God of Israel,' and this one nation to be called His people, under the agreement that they would never recognize any other lord nor receive any other god. And this covenant was confirmed and ratified by the testament and witness which He gave them as a surety.

Nevertheless, men, exhibiting all their cursed origin, and showing themselves true heirs of the iniquity of their father Adam, were not at all aroused by such remonstrances, and would not listen to the doctrine by which God warned them. The creatures on which is written the glory and magnificence of God were of no avail to the Gentiles to have them glorify Him of whom they testified. The law and the prophecies had no authority over the Jews to conduct them into the right way. All were blind to the light, deaf to the admonitions, and hardened against the commandments.

It is very true that the Gentiles, astonished and convinced by so many benefits which they beheld around them, were constrained to know the secret Benefactor, from whom so much goodness proceeded. But, instead of giving to the true God the glory which is due Him, they forged for themselves a god after their own desire, and according to that which their mad fancy, in its vanity and lie, imagined. And not one god only, but as many as their rash presumptuousness could pretend and found, so that there was neither people nor region which did not make to itself new gods, as seemed good to it. From there did idolatry – the treacherous madam – take its dominion, who has caused men to turn away from God, and to distract themselves with a host of travesties, to which they themselves gave form, name and being.

Touching the Jews, although they had received and accepted the messages and summons which the Lord was sending them by His servants, yet, they immediately broke faith with Him, lightly turned away from Him, violated and despised His law, which they hated. They walked in the law with regret; they alienated themselves from His house, and dissolutely ran after the other gods, committing idolatry after the manner of the Gentiles against His will.

Wherefore, in order to bring men to God, as well Jews as Gentiles, it was necessary that a new covenant would be made: certain, assured, and inviolable. And to establish and confirm it, there was need of a mediator, who would interpose and intercede with the two parties in order to reconcile them, without whom, man remains always under the wrath and indignation of God, and has no means of relieving himself from the curse, misery, and confusion into which he has stumbled. It was our Lord and Savior Jesus Christ, true and only eternal Son of God, who was to be sent and given to men on the part of the Father, to be the Restorer of the world, otherwise dispersed, destroyed, and laid waste, in whom from the beginning of the world was always the hope of recovering the loss made in Adam. For even to Adam, immediately after his ruin, to console and comfort him, was given the promise that by the seed of the woman the head of the serpent would be crushed, which meant that by Jesus Christ born of a virgin, the power of Satan would be beaten down and destroyed.

Since then, this same promise was more amply renewed to Abraham, when God told him that by his seed, all the nations of the earth will be blessed, as from his seed would come forth, according to the flesh, Jesus Christ, by whose blessing all men (of whatever region they might be), will be sanctified. And again, it was continued to Isaac, in the same form and in the same words. And afterwards, many times proclaimed, repeated, and confirmed by the testimony of divers prophets, even to showing fully, for greater confidence, of whom He would be born, at what time, in what place, what afflictions and death He should suffer, the glory in which He should resurrect, what would His reign be, and to what salvation He would conduct His people.

It was first predicted to us in Isaiah how He would be born of a virgin, saying, 'The virgin will be with child and will give birth to a son, and will call him Immanuel' (Isa. 7:14 NIV). In Moses the time is set forth to us when the good Jacob said, 'The scepter shall not depart from Judah, Nor the ruler's staff from between his feet, Until Shiloh comes, and to him *shall be* the obedience of the peoples' (Gen. 49:10 NASB), which was verified at the time when Jesus Christ came into the world. For the Romans, after having divested the Jews of all government and control, had about thirty-seven years before appointed Herod as king over them, a king who was a stranger, his father Antipater being an Idumaean and his mother from Arabia. It had at times happened that the Jews had been without kings, but they had never been seen like then – without counselors, governors, or magistrates. And another description of it is given in Daniel, by the computation of the seventy weeks. The place of His birth was clearly pointed out to us by Micah, saying, 'But you, Bethlehem Ephrathah, though you are small among the clans of Judah, out of you will come for me one who will be ruler over Israel, whose origins are from of old, from ancient times' (Mic. 5:2 NIV). As to the afflictions which He had to bear for our deliverance, and the death which He had to suffer for our redemption, Isaiah and Zechariah have spoken of them amply and with certainty. The glory of His resurrection, the quality of His reign, and the grace of salvation which He should bring to His people have been richly treated by Isaiah, Jeremiah, and Zechariah.

In such promises, announced and testified by these holy persons filled with the Spirit of God, the children and elect of God have rested in peace and comforted themselves, and in them have nourished, sustained, and strengthened their hope, waiting for the Lord to will to exhibit what He had promised them, among whom many kings and prophets strongly desired to see their accomplishment. Yet, nevertheless, they did not fail to apprehend in their hearts and minds by faith that which they could not see with their eyes. And in order to strengthen them even more in all ways in the long wait for this great Messiah, God gave them as a pledge His written law, in which were comprised many ceremonies, purifications and sacrifices, which things were only figures and shadows of the great good things to come by Christ, who alone is the body and truth of them. For the Law could not bring anyone to perfection; in that way it only pointed out and, like a schoolmaster, directed and conducted to Christ, who was (as St. Paul says) its end and fulfillment.

In like manner, at many times and in different seasons He has sent them some kings, princes and captains to deliver them from the power of their enemies, to govern them in good peace, to recover them their losses, to make their kingdom flourish, and by great feats[15] to make them renowned among all the other people, in order to give them some taste of the great marvels which they will receive from that great Messiah, to whom will be deployed all the might and power of the kingdom of God.

But when the fullness of time had come and the period preordained by God had expired, this much promised and much awaited great Messiah came, perfecting and accomplishing all that was necessary for our redemption and salvation. He was given not only to the Israelites, but also to all men, from all peoples, and regions, in order that by Him human nature would be reconciled to God.[16] *This reconciliation is fully contained and plainly demonstrated in the following book, which we have translated as faithfully as possible according to the truth and properties of the Greek language. The production of this translation is intended to enable all French-speaking Christians to hear and acknowledge the law they must keep and the faith they must follow.*[17] And this book is called the New Testament in regard to the Old, which, inasmuch as it was to be reduced and reported to the other, being in itself weak and imperfect, and thereupon has been abolished and abrogated. But this Testament is the new and eternal one which will never grow old or fail, because Jesus Christ has been its Mediator, who ratified and confirmed it by His death, in which He accomplished full and complete remission of all transgressions which remained under the first Testament.[18]

The Scripture also calls it Gospel, that is to say, good news and joyful, inasmuch as in it is declared that Christ, the only natural and eternal Son of the living God, was made man to make us children of God His Father by adoption. And thus he is our only

Savior, in whom lays entirely our redemption, peace, justice, sanctification, salvation, and life; who died for our sins, resurrected for our justification, who ascended into heaven to make for us an entry there, to take possession for us and in our name, and to remain forever before His Father as our perpetual Advocate and Priest; who sits at His right hand as King, constituted Lord and Master over all, in order to restore all things in heaven and in the earth; that which all the angels, patriarchs, prophets, apostles would never have been able nor have known how to do, for unto that they were not ordained by God.

And, as the Messiah had been so often promised in the Old Testament by many witnesses of the Prophets, so Jesus Christ has by certain and indubitable witnesses been declared to be Him without equal, who was to come and who was awaited. For the Lord God by His voice and His Spirit, by His angels, prophets, and apostles, even by all His creatures, has rendered us so sufficiently certain of it, that no one can contradict it without resisting and rebelling against His power. First, God Eternal by His voice itself (which is without any doubt irrevocable truth), has testified of it to us saying, 'This is my Son, whom I love; with him I am well pleased. Listen to him!' (Matt. 17:5 NIV). The Holy Spirit is a great witness of it to us in our hearts, as St. John says. The Angel Gabriel sent to the virgin Mary told her, 'You will be with child and give birth to a son, and you are to give him the name Jesus. He will be great and will be called the Son of the Most High. The Lord God will give him the throne of his father David, and he will reign over the house of Jacob forever; his kingdom will never end' (Luke 1:31-33 NIV). The same message in substance was delivered to Joseph, and also afterwards to the shepherds, to whom it was said that the Savior was born, who is Christ the Lord. And this message was not only brought by an angel, but it was approved by a great multitude of angels, who all together rendered glory to the Lord, and announced peace on earth. Simeon the Just, in prophetic spirit, confessed Him aloud, and taking the little child between his arms, he said: 'Sovereign Lord, as you have promised, you now dismiss your servant in peace. For my eyes have seen your salvation, which you have prepared in the sight of all people' (Luke 2:29-31 NIV). John the Baptist also spoke of Him as was suitable, when, seeing Him coming at the river Jordan, he said, 'Look, the Lamb of God, who takes away the sin of the world!' (John 1:29 NIV). Peter and all the apostles confessed, bore witness, and preached, all things that concerned salvation and were predicted by the prophets, to be done in Christ the true Son of God. And those, whom the Lord had ordained to be witnesses up to our age, have amply demonstrated it by their writings, as the readers can sufficiently perceive.

All these testimonies unite so well in one, and agree together in such a manner, that by such an agreement it is easy to understand that it is very certain truth. For there could not be in lies such an agreement. Nevertheless, not only the Father, the Son, the Holy Spirit, the angels, the prophets and the apostles bear witness of Jesus Christ, but even His marvelous works demonstrate His very excellent power. The sick, lame, blind, deaf, mute, paralytic, leprous, lunatics, demoniacs, nay, even the dead by Him resurrected, bore the ensigns of it. In His power He resurrected Himself, and in His name He remitted sins. And therefore, it was not without cause that He said that the works which His Father had given Him to do were sufficiently good witnesses to Him. Moreover, even the wicked and the enemies of His glory were constrained by the force of truth, to confess and to acknowledge something of it, like Caiaphas, Pilate and his wife. I do not want to bring forward the testimonies of the devils and foul spirits, seeing that Jesus Christ rejected them.

In sum, all the elements and all the created things have given glory to Jesus Christ. At His command the winds ceased, the troubled sea became calm, the fish brought the didrachma in his belly, the rocks (to bear witness to Him) were crushed, the veil of the temple rent itself down the middle, the sun darkened, the tombs opened themselves, and many bodies resurrected. There was nothing, either in heaven or in earth, which did not testify that Jesus Christ is its God, Lord, and Master, and the great Ambassador of the Father sent here below to effect the salvation of humankind. All these things are announced, demonstrated, written and signed to us in that Testament, by which Jesus Christ makes us His heirs to the kingdom of God His Father, and declares to us His will (as a testator does to his heirs) for it to be executed.

Now we are all called to this heritage without exception of persons: male or female, small or great, servant or lord, master or disciple, clergy or laity, Hebrew or Greek, French or Latin. No one is rejected from it, whoever by sure faith will receive that which is sent to him, will embrace that which is presented to him, in short, who will acknowledge Jesus Christ as He is given of the Father.

And yet shall we, who bear the name of Christians, let that

Testament be robbed from us, hidden and corrupted? That which so justly belongs to us, without which we cannot pretend any right to the kingdom of God, without which we are ignorant of the great goods and promises which Jesus Christ has given us, the glory and beatitude which He has prepared for us? We know not what God has commanded or forbidden, we cannot discern good from evil, light from darkness, the commandments of God from the constitutions of men. Without the Gospel we are useless and vain; without the Gospel we are not Christians; without the Gospel, all wealth is poverty, wisdom is folly before God, strength is weakness, all human justice is damned of God. But by the knowledge of the Gospel we are made children of God, brothers of Jesus Christ, fellows with the saints, citizens of the kingdom of heaven, heirs of God with Jesus Christ, by whom the poor are made rich, the feeble powerful, the fools wise, the sinners justified, the afflicted consoled, the doubters certain, the slaves free.

The Gospel is word of life and of truth. It is the power of God unto the salvation of all believers, and the key of the knowledge of God which opens the door of the kingdom of heaven to the faithful, unbinding them from their sins, and shuts it against the unbelieving, binding them in their sins. Blessed are all those who hear it and keep it, for thereby they show that they are children of God. Wretched are those who will not hear nor follow it, for they are children of the devil.

O Christians, hear and learn this, for indeed the ignorant will perish with his ignorance, and the blind following the other blind will fall with him into the pit. The one and only way unto life and salvation is the faith and certainty in the promises of God, which cannot be had without the Gospel, by the hearing and understanding of which living faith is given, with certain hope and perfect charity in God, and ardent love toward one's neighbor. Where then is your hope if you despise and disdain to hear, to see, to read, and to hold fast this holy Gospel? Those who have their affections stuck in this world pursue by every means what they think belongs to their felicity, without sparing their labor, or body, or life, or renown. And all these things are done to serve this wretched body, of which life is so vain, miserable, and uncertain. When it is a question of the life immortal and incorruptible, of the beatitude eternal and inestimable, of all the treasures of paradise, shall we not constrain ourselves to pursue them? Those who apply themselves to the mechanical arts (however base and vile those may be) undergo much trouble and labor to learn and know them, and those who wish to be reputed the most virtuous torment their spirits night and day to understand something of the human sciences, which are but wind and smoke. How much more ought we to employ ourselves, and to strive in the study of that heavenly wisdom which passes the whole world and penetrates even to the mysteries of God, which He has been pleased to reveal by His holy Word.

What then will be able to estrange and alienate us from this holy Gospel? Will it be insults, curses, opprobriums, privations of worldly honor? But we know well that Jesus Christ passed through such a road, which we must follow if we want to be His disciples, and which is not in refusing to suffer contempt, be mocked, abased and rejected before men, in order to be honored, prized, glorified and exalted at the judgment of God. Will it be banishment, proscriptions, deprivations of goods and wealth? But we know well when we will be banished from one country, that the earth is the Lord's. And when we will be cast out from all the earth, that we will nevertheless not be out of His kingdom; that when we will be plundered and made poor, we have a Father sufficiently rich to nourish us, and even that Jesus Christ made Himself poor, so that we would follow Him in poverty. Will it be afflictions, prisons, tortures, torments? But we know by the example of Jesus Christ that it is the way to reach glory. Finally, shall it be death? But she does not take away from us the life to be desired.

In short, if we have Christ with us, we will find nothing so cursed that it will not be made blessed by Him; nothing so execrable that will not be sanctified; nothing so bad that will not turn into good for us. Let us not be discouraged when we will see all the worldly mights and powers against us. For the promise cannot fail us, that the Lord, from on high, will laugh at all the assemblings and efforts of men who would want to gather themselves together against Him. Let us not be disconsolate (as if all hope was lost) when we see the true servants of God dying and perishing before our eyes. For it was truly said by Tertullian, and has always been proven and will be until the consummation of the age, that the blood of the martyrs is the seed of the Church.[19]

And we even have a better and firmer consolation: it is to turn our eyes away from this world, and to forsake all that we can see before us, awaiting in patience the great judgment of God, by which, in a moment, all that men have ever plotted against Him will be beaten down, annihilated, and overturned. That will be when the reign of God, which we now see in hope, will be manifested, and when Jesus Christ will appear in His majesty with the angels. Then, both the good and the bad must be present before the judgment seat of that great King. Those who will have remained firm in that Testament, and will have followed and kept the will of that good Father, will be on the right hand, as true children, and will receive the blessing, which is the end of their faith, the eternal salvation. And inasmuch as they were not ashamed to avow and confess Jesus Christ, at the time when he was despised and suffered contempt before men, so they will be partakers of His glory, crowned with Him eternally. But the perverse, rebellious, and reprobate, who will have suffered contempt and rejected that holy Gospel, and likewise those who, to entertain their honors, riches and high estates, were unwilling to humble and lower themselves with Jesus Christ, and for fear of men will have forsaken the fear of God, as they were bastards and disobedient to this Father, will be on the left hand. They will be cast into cursing, and as wages for their faithlessness will receive eternal death.

Now, since you have heard that the Gospel presents to you Jesus Christ, in whom all the promises and graces of God are accomplished, and declares to you that He was sent from the Father, came down on earth, conversed with men, perfected all that was of our salvation, as it had been predicted in the law and the prophets, it ought to be very certain and manifest to you that the treasures of paradise are open, the riches of God deployed, and the eternal life revealed to you in it. For this is eternal life, to know the one and only true God, and Him whom He sent, Jesus Christ, whom He has constituted the beginning, the middle, and the end of our salvation. This One is Isaac the well-beloved Son of the Father, who was offered in sacrifice, and yet did not succumb to the power of death. This is the vigilant Shepherd Jacob, taking such great care of the sheep He has charge over. This is the good and pitiable Brother Joseph, who in His glory was not ashamed to recognize His brothers, however contemptible and abject as they were. This is the great Priest and Bishop Melchizedek, having made eternal sacrifice once for all. This is the sovereign Lawgiver Moses, writing His law on the tables of our hearts by His Spirit. This is the faithful Captain and Guide Joshua to conduct us to the promised land. This is the noble and victorious King David, subduing under His hand every rebellious power. This is the magnificent and triumphant

King Solomon, governing His kingdom in peace and prosperity. This is the strong and mighty Samson, who, by His death, overwhelmed all His enemies.

And even any good that could be thought or desired is found in this Jesus Christ alone. For He humbled Himself to exalt us; He made Himself a slave to set us free; He became poor to enrich us; He was sold to redeem us, captive to deliver us, condemned to absolve us; He was made malediction for our benediction, oblation of sins for our justice; He was disfigured to re-figure us; He died for our life, in such manner that by Him harshness is softened, wrath appeased, darkness enlightened, iniquity justified, weakness is made strength, affliction is consoled, sin is impeached, despite is despised, dread is emboldened, debt is acquitted, labor is lightened, sorrow turned into joy, misfortune into fortune, difficulty is made easy, disorder made ordered, division united, ignominy is ennobled, rebellion subjected, threat is threatened, ambushes are driven out, assaults assailed, striving is overpowered, combat is combated, war is warred, vengeance is avenged, torment tormented, damnation damned, abyss is thrown into the abyss, hell is helled, death is dead, mortality immortality. In short, mercy has swallowed up all misery, and goodness all wretchedness. For all those things which used to be the arms of the devil to combat us and the sting of death to pierce us, are turned for us into an exercise of which we can profit, so that we can boast with the apostle, saying, 'O death,[20] where is your victory? O death, where is your sting?' (1 Cor. 15:55 NASB). From there it comes, that by such a Spirit of Christ promised to His elect, we no longer live, but Christ in us, and we are in spirit seated among the heavenlies, as the world is no longer world to us, though we have our conversation in it, but being content in all, either in countries, places, conditions, clothes, meats, and other like things. And we are comforted in tribulation, joyful in sorrow, glorious in vituperation, abounding in poverty, warmed in nakedness, patient in evil, living in death.

This[21] is in sum what we should seek in the whole Scripture: it is to know well Jesus Christ and the infinite riches which are comprised in Him, and are, by Him, offered to us from God His Father. For when the law and the prophets are carefully searched, there is not to be found in them one word which does not reduce and lead us to Him. And in fact, since all the treasures of wisdom and intelligence are hid in Him, there is no question of having any other end or object, if we wish not, as of deliberate intention, to turn ourselves away from the light of truth, in order to lose our way into the darkness of lies. For this reason does St. Paul rightly say in another passage that he resolved to know nothing except Jesus Christ and Him crucified. For though the flesh has the opinion that that knowledge is something vulgar and contemptible, the acquiring of it is sufficient to occupy our whole life. And we will not have wasted our time, when we will have employed all our study and applied all our understanding, to profit of it. What more could we ask, for the spiritual doctrine of our souls, than to know God, in order to be transformed into Him, and to have His glorious image imprinted in us, in order to be partakers of His justice, heirs of His kingdom, and to possess it fully to the end? Now it is thus, that from the beginning He gave Himself, and now even more clearly gives Himself to be contemplated in the face of His Christ. It is therefore not lawful that we turn ourselves away and wander here and there, however little it may be. But our understanding must be altogether stopped at this point, to learn in the Scripture to know only Jesus Christ, in order to be conducted by Him straight to the Father, who contains in Himself all perfection.

Behold, *I say again, here*[22] *is contained* all the wisdom that men can understand, and must learn in this life, to which neither angel, nor man, nor dead, nor alive, can add or take anything. For this reason it is the goal where we must stop and limit our understanding, without mixing anything of our own, not receiving any doctrine which is added thereto. For whoever dares undertake to teach one syllable beyond, or above that which is there taught to us, must be cursed before God and His Church.[23]

And you Christian kings, princes and lords, who are ordained by God to punish the wicked, and entertain the good in peace according to the Word of God, it is your responsibility to have that holy doctrine so useful and necessary published, taught, and heard by all your countries, regions, and lordships, in order that God be magnified by you, and His Gospel will be exalted. Do so as legitimately it falls to all kings and kingdoms in all humility to obey and to serve His glory. *Remember*[24] *that the sovereign Empire, above all kingdoms, principalities and lordships, has been given by the Father to the Lord Jesus, in order that He be feared, dreaded, honored and obeyed everywhere by both great and small. Remember all that was predicted by the prophets – that all kings of the earth will pay Him homage as their Superior and will adore*

Him as their Savior and their God – must be verified in you. Do not think of it as an infringement to be subjects of such a great Lord, because it is the greatest honor for you to desire to be acknowledged and held as officers and lieutenants of God. By His lordship your majesty and highness is in no way lessened; your honor can exist only as Jesus Christ, in whom God wants to be exalted and glorified, dominates over you. And in fact, it is only reasonable for you to give Him such preeminence, since your power is founded on no one but Him alone. Otherwise, what kind of ungratefulness would it be to want to deny the rights to the one who constituted, maintains, and preserves you in the position of power you occupy? Furthermore, it is imperative for you to know that no better nor firmer foundation exists to maintain your lordships in prosperity, than to have Him for Head and Master, and to govern your peoples under His hand. And also that without Him, not only can your lordships not be permanent or of long duration, but they are cursed of God and will thereby fall into confusion and ruin. Whereas, God has put the sword in your hand to govern your subject in His Name and in His authority; whereas, He granted you the honor to give you His Name and His title;[25] and whereas, He has sanctified your estate above others, in order for His glory and majesty to shine in it, let each one with regard to Him employ himself to magnify and exalt the One who is His true glorious Image, in which He fully presents Himself. Now, to do so, it is not enough solely to confess Jesus Christ and to profess to be His. Rather to bear this title truly and actually, one must yield to His holy Gospel and receive it in perfect obedience and humility – which is indeed everyone's office. But it is especially your responsibility that the Gospel would have an audience, and for it to be published in your countries, so that it would be heard by all who are committed in your charge, that they would recognize you as servants and ministers of this great King, in order to serve and honor Him, obeying you under His hand and leadership.

That is what the Lord requires of you when, by His prophet, He calls you tutors of His Church. For this tutelage or protection does not lay in increasing riches, privileges and honors to the clergy – of which it thereby prides and elevates itself, lives pompously and a fully dissolute life, against the order of its estate. Even less does it lay in maintaining the clergy in its pride and its disorderly pomps. On the contrary, this tutelage lays in providing for the doctrine of truth and purity of the Gospel to remain complete, the holy Scriptures to be faithfully preached and read, God to be honored according to the rule of Scripture, the Church to be well ordered, and all that contravenes either to God's honor or to the orderliness of the Church, to be corrected and thrown down, so that the reign of Jesus Christ would flourish in the power of His Word.

O, all of you who are called bishops and pastors of the poor people, see that the sheep of Jesus Christ are not deprived of their proper pasture. Ensure that it not be prohibited nor forbidden that every Christian might read, consider, and hear this holy Gospel freely in his own language, since God wants it, Jesus Christ commands it, and to accomplish this has sent his apostles and servants in the whole world, giving them the grace to speak all tongues, so that they would preach in all languages to all creatures. He has made them debtors to the Greeks and the barbarians, to the wise and to the simple, so that none would be excluded from their teaching. Certainly, if you are truly vicars, successors, and imitators of them, your office is to emulate them, watching the flock, and seeking all possible means for everyone to be instructed in the faith of Jesus Christ by the pure Word of God. Otherwise, the sentence is already pronounced and registered: God will demand their souls from your hands.

May the Lord of lights will to teach the ignorant, strengthen the weak, illumine the blind with His holy and salutary Gospel by His Holy Spirit, and cause His truth to reign over all peoples and nations, so that the whole world would know only one God and only one Savior, Jesus Christ, one faith, and one Gospel. Amen.

NOTES

1. The English translation is *Christ the End of the Law, Being the Preface to the Geneva Bible of 1550* by John Calvin, trans. Thoman Weeden (London: Henry George Collins, 1848).
2. The original text of Calvin's signed Latin Preface to Olevitan's 1535 French Bible may be found in *Opera Calvini* 9.787-790. In all subsequent editions, it was printed in French. For an English translation, see John Calvin, *Institutes of the Christian Religion, 1536 edition, printed at Basel*, trans. Ford Lewis Battles (Eerdmans Publishing Company), pp. 373-377.
3. For internal evidence of this, see note 17 below.
4. See Beza'a 1576 *Epistolareum et Consilium Calvini.*

5. Both the French and the Latin versions of this work can be found in *CO*, IX, p. 791-822.

6. See *La Vraie Piete: Divers traites de Jean Calvin et Confession de foi de Guillame Forel*, ed. Irena Bachus and Claire Chimelli (Geneva, 1986) p. 17-23.

7. Ibid. See also Peter A. Lillback, *The Binding of God: Calvin's Role in the Development of Covenant Theology* (Baker, 2001), pp. 162-165.

8. See *The Binding of God*, p. 165.

9. The following new translation is based upon the first and only known English translation of Calvin's *Preface to the Geneva Bible of 1550* by Thomas Weedon, Esq., published in 1848 by Henry George Collins (London). This present translation corrects, emends, and supplements Weedon's work, and provides a literal reflection of Calvin's French, with periodic reference to the Latin for clarification of textual variants. Because of certain appreciable gaps in Weedon's translation, several sections of this preface are now provided in English for the very first time. The footnotes serve as a critical apparatus for referencing the original French and Latin in the *CO*, and for referencing Weedon's editorial comments and English phrases which derive from undisclosed sources. In *CO* IX: 791-822, the French title of this work is 'A Tous Amateurs De Iesus Christ et de son Evangile, Salut.,' translated, 'To Those Who Love Jesus Christ and His Gospel, Greetings.' The title as written here is an abbreviation of that written in the Bibles and New Testaments printed in Geneva and elsewhere, where the preface is reproduced. This title was 'Epistre aux fideles monstrant comment (que) Christ est la fin de la Loy,' translated, 'Letter to the Faithful Showing That Christ is the End of the Law'.

10. In *CO* IX: 791, the text reads in French, 'dont'. In 1562 and in following editions, this word reads, 'd'où,' meaning 'from where'. For English clarity, we have translated the French 'd'où' as 'source'.

11. In all editions prior to 1543, 'by force' is missing.

12. Thomas Weedon's translation includes the concluding phrase, 'and supported him in the state to which He had created him'. This phrase is not contained in any French editions known to the present translators.

13. Weedon adds in brackets, 'except those whom He from that time made partakers of his mercy'. This phrase is not contained in any French editions known to the present translators.

14. Weedon inserts, 'in order to preserve the Human Race, as much to draw out from it His elect as to render other men more inexcusable'. This phrase is not contained in any French editions known to the present translators.

15. According to *CO* IX: 801, in the Bible of Olivetan, the French word 'prouesses' (feats, prowesses) incorrectly reads 'promesses'. The editors of the *CO* note that all other editions that they have read correct this mistake.

16. The first two sentences of this paragraph are not included in Weedon's translation.

17. In lieu of the italicized passage in the text, we read in the Treatise of 1543 and in all the editions of the Bible that reproduce it, the following sentences: 'To declare which, the Lord Jesus, who was the foundation and the substance of it, [after that He had executed His function among the Jews,] ordained His Apostles, to whom He has given charge and commandment to publish His grace through all the world. Now, the Apostles, in order well and completely to fulfill their duty, not only took labor and diligence to execute their embassy by oral preaching, but, after the example of Moses and the Prophets, to leave the eternal memory of their teaching, reduced it to writing; in which they first recited the history of that which our Lord Jesus did and suffered for our salvation; then, afterwards, showed the

value of it all, and what benefit we receive from it, and in what way we must take it. All this collection is called the New Testament.' The bracketed phrase is included in Weedon's translation, but is not contained in any French editions known to the present translators. *Editor's Note:* This substitution may suggest that Calvin had written the 1535 edition, and allowed the translator of the New Testament, Olevitan, to add his words as translator. Later, when Calvin's name is directly linked to this work, the language of the translator is removed, suggesting all was now his direct words.

18. Weedon adds, 'inasmuch as He brought them back to that which ought to be exhibited and performed under the New.' This phrase is not contained in any French editions known to the present translators.

19. This expression of Tertullian's is actually not a direct quotation, but rather summarizes an idea from his *Apology.* However, the concept is frequently repeatedly by the church fathers.

20. Calvin in *CO* IX: 813 reads 'hell' (French, *enfer*) for the first occurrence of 'death'.

21. This paragraph is not found in the Bible of 1535, but is found for the first time in the Treatise of 1543, and has continued in the different Genevan editions of the New Testament.

22. I.e., in the Scriptures.

23. Several Genevan editions of the New Testament conclude the preface here. This is true also for the Latin text which is complete only in the edition of Lausanne and Hanau.

24. The following italicized text is missing in the 1535 edition. It is found in the Treatise of 1543, and the New Testament editions that reproduced it in its entirety. However, it is not retained in the Latin version.

25. I.e., Lord, King, Ruler, etc.

MANIFESTED IN THE FLESH

John Calvin on the Reality of the Incarnation

Sinclair B. Ferguson

The question of whether there is a central theme in John Calvin's theology has long been debated and will surely continue to be so. The options placed on the table of Calvin scholarship have varied from the now passé assumption that he was obsessed with predestination to more recent attempts to place Christology at the center and core. Insofar as Calvin was a remarkably sensitive biblical (and not a narrowly systematic) theologian, this diversity of perspective is not surprising. An analogous diversity of answers is found among contemporary biblical scholars when asked what the central motif of the Old Testament is. It was part of Calvin's wisdom that he did not commit himself to view biblical revelation through a single controlling principle.

This essay does not attempt to resolve these long standing issues, but simply pursues a motif which was certainly central to Calvin personally, as a Christian believer: Jesus Christ, God's incarnate Son, clothed in the garments of the gospel. With Paul he held that 'the knowledge of Christ so far surpasses everything else by its sublimity that, compared with it, there is nothing that is not contemptible.'[1]

Calvin did not view this in isolation from the rest of his theology: the knowledge of God and his sovereignty, the wonder of his providence, the reliability of his revelation, and the importance of belonging to the Christian community. But his knowledge of the Person of Christ, and particularly his humanity seems, increasingly, to have played an important role in shaping his sense of the sheer privilege of belonging to the Lord. This, in turn, created the distinctive atmosphere of the Christian life which he himself sought to live as a 'practical Calvinist'.[2]

Calvin's teaching on the work of Christ incarnate as Savior can be readily explored in three stages: the necessity of the incarnation; the precise nature of the incarnation; and the relationship between the incarnation and the atonement.

The Necessity of the Incarnation

In an arresting passage in the *Institutes,* Calvin distinguishes between the pre- and post-Fall mediation of Christ: 'Even if man had remained free from all stain, his condition would have been too lowly for him to reach God without a Mediator.'[3] Now, however, that man has sinned and lapsed from the divine glory, there is (to express it technically) a consequent contingent necessity for the incarnation. It is *consequent upon,* yet not logically determined by the Fall. It is *necessary* insofar as God has determined to save fallen man. The incarnation has no *a priori* necessity attached to it (e.g. in the nature of God); rather it is a free action of God, determined by his own will. In this sense

> Christ suffered by His appointment and not by necessity [i.e. of a logically *a priori* kind] because, being 'in the form of God' He could have escaped this necessity, but nevertheless He suffered 'through weakness' because He 'emptied himself'.[4]

A Mediator adequate for man's needs, must be both divine and human. The atonement required can come only from man. But fallen man is disqualified from making atonement. God the Son incarnate is alone free from sin and able to offer himself as an atoning sacrifice.

Stylistically, Calvin delights to express this in a mode which illustrates a deep-seated pattern in his theological thinking, what

Hermann Bauke called a *complexio oppositorum*.[5] This pattern of thought is so deeply embedded in Calvin's thinking about Christ that it frequently surfaces even in the basic structure of his sentences, as the following characteristic statement indicates:

[Christ's] task was so to restore us to God's grace as to make

- of the **children of men**,
  children of God;
- of the **heirs of Gehenna**,
  heirs of the heavenly kingdom.

Who could have done this had not

- the self-same **Son of God**
  become the *Son of Man*,

and had not

- so taken **what was ours**
  as to impart ... *what was his* to us,

and

- to make what was **his by nature**
  ours by grace?[6]

What is so significant here is the extent to which salvation, and consequently the confidence of faith, are derived from the fact that the antithesis/oppositeness between what we are and what Christ is has been turned through 180 degrees. Thus everything lacking in us is given to us by Christ, everything sinful in us is imputed to Christ, and all judgment merited by us is borne by Christ.

Faith unites us directly with Christ thus clothed in his gospel and relieves us instantaneously from condemnation. Faith properly exercised drinks deeply from these springs of grace and sees that Christ is not only perfectly equipped to become the Savior, but actually is *my* Savior.

Calvin seems instinctively to have recognized the proclivity (often unspoken) in the faithful to seek assurance apart from faith in Christ. There is a native tendency (and perversity) to ask: 'How can I enjoy assurance even if I am not exercising faith?' His answer is that it cannot be done. We cannot have the assurance that comes from Christ on a *remoto Christo* principle (Anselm) in which we place Christ in abeyance and rest on other grounds! Assurance is possible only through Christ; Christ is known and received only through faith. There is no alternative to this correlation. Assurance is, after all, the assurance of faith in Christ.

This helps to explain why Calvin devotes so much detailed attention to the way in which Christ has really taken our flesh and accomplished our redemption. He thereby portrays Christ as so perfectly suited to our need for salvation, that Christ so portrayed masters faith and brings the conviction that in Christ one cannot but be saved.

As we have noted, Calvin holds, with Anselm and others, that reparation in atonement must be made from among those who owe it (humanity); but humanity lacks the resources to do this. Since all have sinned and fallen short of the divine glory, what is due from below can now be effected only from outside of corrupt humanity. Thus an impasse is reached. But this insolvable dilemma is divinely resolved: the Son comes from above into our humanity to do for us what we cannot accomplish for ourselves.

In his exposition of the assumption of our humanity by the divine Logos, Calvin clearly stands on the shoulders of Athanasius in his conviction that the doctrine of the incarnation must be formulated soteriologically. Thus, in contrast to Osiander, he argues that unless Adam had fallen, the Son never would have become incarnate.

But the incarnation *per se* is not saving. While Calvin's theology reflects the most biblical elements of Eastern theology's stress on the healing of humanity through Christ, for him the redemption of man is not to be viewed as a transformation of our flesh by the mere fact of its assumption and resurrection by the Holy Son. The ultimate consummation of salvation (which will be seen in the healing of our flesh involved in the final resurrection glory) is grounded in Christ's obedience as incarnate. This obedience of the incarnate Christ is in the whole course of his life and in his atoning death – in what he experienced and accomplished in our flesh – not simply in the taking of and living in our flesh in and of itself.

The controlling principle of the work of Christ in Calvin's thought is the concept of exchange. In order to restore fallen man to sinless God, the Son must take what is ours (sin, guilt, bondage, condemnation, death) and deal with it in such a way that what was ours becomes his and what is his also becomes ours. But what does this involve?

Christ appeared in 'the name and the person of sinners' in order genuinely and righteously to accomplish what we could not do for ourselves:

That is why it is here narrated to us that not only our Lord Jesus Christ has been willing to suffer death and has offered Himself as a sacrifice to pacify the wrath of God His Father, but in order that He might be truly and wholly our pledge, He did not refuse to bear the agonies which are prepared for all those whose consciences rebuke them and who feel themselves guilty of eternal death and damnation before God. Let us note well, then, that the Son of God was not content merely to offer His flesh and blood and to subject them to death, but He willed in full measure to appear before the judgment seat of God His Father in the name and in the person of all sinners, being then ready to be condemned, inasmuch as he bore our burden.[7]

Because Christ bears our name and our nature even the weakest believer may look to Christ and find assurance of grace and salvation in him. Here Calvin's exposition of the Gospels' testimony is profound and telling: Jesus' ministry reveals to us the humanity of a Savior who can be trusted, who understands and who is able to bring reassurance of the adequacy and fittingness of his grace. Much of what he does and experiences is intended to show us how near to us he came. The revelation of his frailty and weakness is all intended to assure us that he is one with us and has taken our place.

Calvin places great stress on the fact that the atonement was offered by Christ in his humanity:

We know that the two natures of Christ were so conformed in one person that each retained what was proper to it; in particular the Divinity was silent (*quievit Divinitas*) and made no assertion of itself whenever it was the business of the human nature to act alone in its own terms in fulfillment of the office of Mediator.[8]

While this is stated explicitly in connection with Christ's confession of ignorance in Matthew 24:36, it is a principle which surfaces throughout Calvin's writings.[9] True, were he not God, Christ could not have accomplished all that was necessary for reconciliation. Nevertheless, 'it is certain that he carried out all these acts according to his human nature.'[10] Calvin regularly strikes an additional note in his comments on the Savior's life and work: Christ did not need to experience what he did. He did so to persuade us that he knows, understands and sympathizes with us in our weakness. He can be trusted to support us in our times of darkness:

It was not because the Son of God needed to experience it to become accustomed to the emotion of mercy, but because he could not persuade us that He is kind and ready to help us, unless he had been tested by our misfortunes.... Whenever, therefore, all kinds of evils press upon us, let this be our immediate consolation, that nothing befalls us which the Son of God has not experienced Himself, so that He can sympathize with us; and let us not doubt that He is with us in it as if He were distressed along with us.[11]

In other words, the key to salvation and assurance lies in the extent to which the Son of God has come near to us in his incarnation, actually entering into our situation, tasting our experience from the inside, and exchanging his strength and confidence for our fears and frailties. This sense – that Christ enters into our life and bears the cursed condition from underneath, as it were, so that we may make the faith-discovery that all that is lacking in us is to be found in Christ – is nowhere in all Christian literature given more exquisite expression than in these words:

We see that our salvation and all its parts are comprehended in Christ (Acts 4:12). We should therefore take care not to derive the least portion of it from anywhere else. If we seek salvation, we are taught by the very name of Jesus that it is 'of him' (1 Cor. 1:30).... If we seek strength it lies in his dominion; if purity, in his conception; if gentleness, it appears in his birth. For by his birth he was made like us in all respects (Heb. 2:17) that he might learn to feel our pain (cf. Heb. 5:2) ... in short, since rich store of every kind of good abounds in him, let us drink our fill from this fountain, and from no other.[12]

But what, exactly, was involved in the Logos assuming our human nature?

The Nature of the Incarnation
The Son of God's motivation in assuming humanity was to redeem us. Calvin has shown that the precise way in which he assumes humanity brings Christ within trusting distance, as it were.

What, then, was the nature of the humanity the Logos assumed?

It was, first and foremost, *our* flesh he took in the Virgin Mary's womb. Calvin had no time for a theology without a genuine incarnation.[13] Christ was genuinely conceived in the womb of Mary – she was not merely a conduit for a humanity forged in heaven (contra Menno Simons who taught that the Logos became man 'not of the womb, but in the womb' of Mary).[14] He came near to us, says Calvin, 'indeed touches us, since he is our flesh'.[15]

Such flesh was like ours. In it Christ grew in wisdom and knowledge because, as a man, he was 'subject to ignorance' (albeit voluntarily, not necessarily like ourselves). Calvin thus starkly accepts what some of the Fathers had found so difficult to come to terms with: if the Logos really took human nature, then in that nature he experienced an innocent ignorance akin to that of Adam before the Fall. 'He freely took that which cannot be separated from human nature.'[16] This included all the emotions and affections of our common humanity in its weakness and infirmity. Commenting on Jesus' response of inner groaning at the grave of Lazarus, Calvin notes:

> When the Son of God put on our flesh He also of His own accord put on human feelings, so that he differed in nothing from His brethren, sin only excepted.... Our feelings are sinful because they rush on unrestrainedly and immoderately; but in Christ they were composed and regulated in obedience to God and were completely free from sin.[17]

Christ is not 'an idle spectator'[18] of the human condition, but a participant in it. Indeed so much is this the case, Calvin argues, that if we did not recognize the significance of Christ's humanity we would, like the Jews, find it an immense stumbling block that he took on a 'lowly and earthly body subject to many infirmities'.[19] In a word, the Logos became real flesh. Thus Calvin comments on John 1:14 ('the Word became flesh ...'):

> This word [sarx] expresses his meaning more forcibly than if he had said that He was made man. He wanted to show to what a low and abject state the Son of God descended from the height of His heavenly glory for our sake. When Scripture speaks of man derogatorily it calls him 'flesh'. How great is the distance between the spiritual glory of the Word of God and the stinking filth of our flesh. Yet the Son of God stooped so low as to take to Himself that flesh addicted to so many wretchednesses.[20]

Elsewhere Calvin can speak of Christ joining the infinite glory of God 'to our polluted flesh so that the two become one',[21] and of the 'weakness' and 'abasement' of the flesh which the Son assumed.[22] It had 'the appearance of being sinful' and 'a certain resemblance to our sinful nature'.[23] He saves from within, underneath and surrounded by this humanity, flesh of our flesh, bone of our bone.

Undoubtedly the most striking exposition of this in Calvin appears in his understanding of the experience of our Lord in Gethsemane (which he thinks of as a village). Alongside, perhaps even beyond Christ's admission of ignorance, the nature of Christ's suffering in Gethsemane and the apparent ambivalence of his will had long been seen as an intractable difficulty for those who believed in his absolute divinity. Calvin summarizes the struggles of the church's theologians to come to terms with this. Since it 'seems to be below the dignity of Christ's divine glory that He was affected with panic and sorrow, many interpreters are vehemently concerned to find a way out.'[24]

Calvin's response to these interpreters is illuminating: 'Their efforts were thoughtless and fruitless; if we are ashamed of His fear and sorrow, our redemption will trickle away and be lost.... Those who pretend the Son of God was immune from human passions do not truly and seriously acknowledge Him as man.'[25]

In a sermon on Gethsemane, preached towards the end of his own life, Calvin justifies the theological coherence of his exegesis at this point on the grounds that men are creatures who experience affections that do not belong by rights to God.[26] And in his *Harmony of the Gospels* he writes with similar vigor:

> But within the capacity of a sane and unspoiled human nature, He was struck with fright and seized with anguish, and so compelled to shift (as it were) between the violent waves of trial from one prayer to another. This is the reason why He prays to be spared death, then holds Himself in check, submits Himself to the Father's command, and corrects and revokes the wish that had suddenly escaped Him.... This was no rehearsed prayer of Christ's, but the force and onset of grief wrung a cry from Him on the instant, which he at once went on to correct. The same vehemence took from Him any thoughts of the decree of heaven, so that for a moment He did not think how He was sent to be the Redeemer of the human race. Often heavy anxiety clouds the eyes from seeing everything at once....

Yet,

> As various musical sounds, different from each other, make no discord but compose a tuneful and sweet harmony, so in Christ there exists a remarkable example of balance between the wills of God and of man; they differ without conflict or contradiction.[27]

The point of such quotations is not necessarily to defend every part of Calvin's exegesis, or the self-consistency of the whole as a theological construct, but to underline the seriousness with which he took the incarnation. For Calvin, Christ really can act for us because he is one with us, sin apart. We should not be alarmed to discover Christ's weakness, since the Savior held it in such check. But we should learn to recognize that the extent to which he is able to save us is correlative to the extent to which he became fully like us, while 'pure and free from all vice and stain'[28] because of his sanctification by the Spirit in the womb of the virgin Mary at the moment of his generation.[29]

Incarnation and Atonement

The Son of God took our human nature in order to redeem us. It is axiomatic with Calvin that unless Christ is really one of us, united to us by a common nature, *and* that his human nature is identical to ours (sin apart), he cannot be our Savior. This explains his problem with the Lutheran doctrine of the ubiquity of the resurrected humanity of Christ (which lies behind the Lutheran view of the real presence of Christ in the Lord's Supper) – it no longer remains authentic humanity.[30] The one who possesses it could not save us because he is not really one of us.

But the Son goes beyond assuming our nature; he also assumes our name and place, so that we see 'the person of a sinner and evildoer represented in Christ.' Commenting on Galatians 3:13, Calvin notes:

> He took our place and thus became a sinner and subject to the curse, not in Himself indeed, but in us; yet in such a way that it was necessary for Him to act in our Name.[31]

What Calvin additionally emphasizes, however, is that while Christ's saving work climaxes in his death and resurrection, this bearing of our name and nature is to be traced back to the very beginning of his life: 'from the time he took on the form of a servant, he began to pay the price of liberation in order to redeem us.'[32] Again, 'How has Christ abolished sin, banished the separation between us and God, and acquired righteousness to render God favorable and kindly toward us? To this we can in general reply that he has achieved this for us by the whole course of his obedience.' His obedience is an obedience unto (even *into*) death, as well as in death.[33]

But, in addition to this ongoing (active) obedience, Christ accomplished our salvation 'more exactly'[34] on the cross when he bore the judgment curse of death as sin's wages. Here again we see him bearing the name and person of Adam. He brings this out in the remarkable way in which he treats the Gospel passion narrative as a theological as well as an historical drama. Christ is explicitly charged with the two great Adamic sin-crimes: blasphemy, in that he sought to be equal with God; and treason, in that he rebelled against his lawfully constituted authority. This is what it means for Christ to bear 'our person' as Calvin so often puts it. Taking the character of a sinner, he undergoes the just judgment of God against our sins. Repeatedly pronounced innocent before human tribunals – as he is before every tribunal in heaven and earth, yet he is executed as though he had the character of a sinner under the law of God. This is the ultimate explanation for his trembling in Gethsemane:

> It was not simple horror of death, the passing away from the world, but the sight of the dread tribunal of God that came to Him, the Judge Himself armed with vengeance beyond understanding.... No wonder if death's fearful abyss tormented him grievously.... There is nothing more dreadful than to feel God as Judge, whose wrath is worse than all deaths. When the trial came on Christ in this form, that He was now against God and doomed to ruin, he was overcome with dread ... as though under the wrath of God, He were cast into the labyrinth of evil.[35]

But when Calvin has said that the life and death of Christ involved obedience and bearing the penalty of sin, he has not spoken his final word. That word has been spoken only when he has added that all this was *pro nobis*, for us. It was substitutionary (for us) as well as penal (for sin). Grasp this and we grasp both the wonder of God's love and receive the assurance of salvation. For Calvin, one cannot read the passion narrative without being confronted by the substitutionary nature of what is happening and by the soteriological implications it carries. Here, on the stage of history an exchange is being played out. Thus, in commenting on Matthew's passion narrative he highlights the fact that a theological transaction is taking place.

The powerful combination of chiasmic rhythm and contrasting statements underline the wonder of the great exchange involved in the work of atonement. First he comments on Christ being spat upon:

(A) The *face* of Christ,
   (B) marred with *spittle* and *blows*
(A) has restored to us that *image*
   (B)which sin had *corrupted*, indeed *destroyed*.[36]

Calvin continues:

(A) Christ *said nothing*

   (B) when the priests *pressed* Him from every side,
(A) in order to *open* our *mouths* by His silence.
   (B) Hence the glorious *freedom* which Paul acclaims that
(A) we can call out with a *full voice* 'Abba, Father.'[37]

(A) Thus He was
   (B) reckoned worse than a *thief*,
(A) to
   (B) bring us into the company of the *angels*.[38]

(A) Whatever might be
   (B) Pilate's *purpose*,
   (B) God *wishes*
      (C) his Son's *innocence*
         (D) *attested* in this way,
         (D) that it might be more *clear*
      (C) that our *sins*
         (D) were *condemned* in Him.[39]

(A) So the
   (B) *ugliness*
      (C) He once endured on *earth*
      (C) now wins us grace in *heaven*,
   (B) and also restores the *image* of God,
      (C) which had not only been *polluted* with the filth of sin,
      (C) but almost *effaced*.
(A) So also
   (B) God's inestimable mercy *upon us* shines out,
      (C)in *lowering*
      (C) His only-begotten Son to these *depths*,
   (B) for *our sake*.[40]

(A) God willed
>(B) His Son to be *stripped*
>>(C) that we should *appear freely*, with the angels,
>(B) in the *garments* of His righteousness and fullness of all good things,
>>(C) whereas formerly *foul disgrace*,
>(B) in torn *clothes*,
>>(C) *kept us away* from the approach to the heavens.

(A) Christ Himself allows
>(B) His *raiment* to be torn apart like booty
>>(C) *to make us rich* with the riches of His victory.[41]

Here, for Calvin, is the solid ground on which salvation rests. In the *fact* that Christ has entered our life, shared our nature, taken our place, borne our sin, received our judgment lies the foundation of our justification and acceptance with God.

But in addition, the *manner* in which this is accomplished encourages assurance. For the manner in which he has made the exchange – so evidently taking our place, bearing our guilt, facing our judgment, dying our death, rising for our triumph *in our flesh* – assures us that what he has done is both for us and suited to our needs. For here, in the climactic display of Jesus' love (John 13:1ff) we are given the clearest demonstration of:

- *The love of God for us in his not-spared Son.* If he gives his Son for us, he will give to us everything necessary to effect the purposes for which he gave his Son. Calvin believes that this apostolic logic, and behind it the logic of God, is irrefutable.
- *The forgiveness of sins.* The fact that in the Gospels we see Christ bearing sins before our eyes – (as it were placarded before us, Galatians 3:1) – leaves us in no doubt that our guilt has been objectively removed, our judgment absorbed in Christ. The sense of guilt, and the uncertainty it fosters, must yield to this solvent.
- *The hope of glory.* The Innocent One who appears in silence before the earthly tribunal thereby accepts the condemnation of the heavenly one. His mouth is shut; he is held to be guilty before God (Rom. 3:19). Because of his silence before the divine tribunal, we will be able to say 'Abba, Father' there.

For Calvin, nothing is more relevant than this to being a practical Calvinist. For the most practical Calvinists will be those who know such trust in, love for, and assurance of, Jesus Christ. The assurance that he is their Savior sets them free to serve him in a life whose *leitmotif* is grace.

Against this background, it does not require vivid imagination to transport oneself to the congregation gathered in St Peter's Church, Geneva on Wednesday June 29, 1558. The asthmatic, disease-ridden Calvin, now some twenty minutes into his sermon, momentarily clears his throat, and makes his moving appeal:

Since then there is in us nothing but spiritual infection and leprosy
and that we are corrupt in our iniquities,
what shall we do?
What remedy is there?

Shall we go to seek help from the angels in Paradise?
Alas! They can do nothing for us.

No, we must come to our Lord Jesus Christ,
who was willing to be disfigured
from the top of His head even to the sole of His feet
and was a mass of wounds,
flogged with many stripes and crowned with thorns,
nailed and fastened to the cross and pierced through the side.

This is how we are healed;
here is our true medicine, with which we must be content,
and which we must embrace wholeheartedly,
knowing that otherwise we can never have inward peace
but must always be tormented and tortured to the extreme,
unless Jesus Christ comforts us and appeases God's wrath against us.
When we are certain of that,
we have cause to sing His praises,[42]
instead of being capable of nothing but trembling and confusion.[43]

Clair – greetings to you on your seventieth birthday! Thank you for twenty years of friendship in which I have learned much from you. I join my prayers with your many friends that the singing of Christ's praises (of which Calvin here speaks) may constantly mark your faith in Christ and your assurance of grace. May you have energy all your days to continue to live as a 'practical Calvinist' for the honour of Christ, in the power of the Spirit, to the glory of God and in the service of his church.

NOTES

1. John Calvin, *The Epistles of Paul to the Galatians, Ephesians, Philippians and Colossians*, tr. T. H. L. Parker, ed., D. W. and T. F. Torrance, Edinburgh, 1965, p. 272.

2. That Calvin viewed his theology as 'practical' is beautifully expressed in *De Vita Hominis Christiani* , first published in 1550, material drawn from the *Institutes*. See *The Golden Booklet of the True Christian Walk*, Grand Rapids, 1952.

3. *Institutes of the Christian Religion*, tr. F. L. Battles, ed., J. T. McNeill, Philadelphia 1960, II. 12. 1. Cf. his comments on Galatians 3:19 in *The Epistles of Paul to the Galatians*, p. 62.

4. *Commentary on The Second Epistle of Paul to the Corinthians and the Epistles to Timothy, Titus and Philemon*, tr. T. A. Smail, ed., D. W. and T. F. Torrance, Edinburgh 1964, p.172. Cf. *Institutes* II. 12. 1.

5. Hermann Bauke, *Die Probleme der Theologie Calvins*, Leipzig 1922.

6. *Institutes* II. 12. 2.

7. *Sermons on the Deity of Christ*, selected and translated by Leroy Nixon, Grand Rapids, 1950, p.52.

8. *Harmony of the Gospels, Matthew, Mark and Luke*, tr. A. W. Morrison, ed. D. W. and T. F. Torrance, Edinburgh 1972, vol. III, p. 99.

9. See, e.g. his commentaries on Luke 2:40; 19:41; Philippians 2:7; cf. also *Institutes* II. 14. 3.

10. *Institutes* III. 11. 9. Cf. his commentaries on Isaiah 42: 1 and Hebrews 5:1.

11. *Commentary on Hebrews*, tr., W. B. Johnston, ed., D. W. and T. F. Torrance, Edinburgh, 1963, p. 33 (on 2:17). Cf his comments on Heb. 4:14, ibid., p. 55.

12. *Institutes* II. 16.19.

13. *Institutes* II. 13. 1.

14. *Institutes* II. 13. 3.

15. *Institutes* II. 12. 1.

16. Ibid.

17. *Commentary on The Gospel according to St. John*, 11-21, tr., T. H. L. Parker; ed., D. W. and T. F. Torrance, Edinburgh 1961, p. 12 (on John 11:33).

18. Ibid., p. 13 (on John 11:36).

19. *Commentary on Galatians, Ephesians, Philippians and Colossians*, pp. 314-15 (on Colossians 1:22).

20. *Commentary on The Gospel according to St. John*, 1-10, pp. 10-20 (on John 1:14).

21. *Commentary on The Second Epistle of Paul to the Corinthians and the Epistles to Timothy, Titus and Philemon*, p. 233 (on 1 Timothy 3:16). Calvin's language here (cum hac nostra carnis putredine) is characteristically strong, conveying the notion of something that has gone rotten.

22. *Commentary on The Epistles of Paul to the Galatians, Ephesians, Philippians and Colossians*, p. 248 (on Philippians 2:7).

23. *Commentary on The Epistles of Paul the Apostle to the Romans and to the Thessalonians*, tr., R. Mackenzie, ed., D. W. and T. F. Torrance, p. 159 (on

Romans 8:3). Calvin is at pains however to point out that 'the flesh of Christ was unpolluted by any stain'.

24. *Harmony of the Gospels*, III, p. 147 (on Matthew 26:37).

25. Ibid.

26. *Sermons on the Deity of Christ*, p. 58.

27. *Harmony of the Gospels*, III pp. 149-151 (on Matthew 26:37-39).

28. *Institutes* II. 13. 4.

29. See *The Catechism of the Church of Geneva* (1541), questions 53 and 54 in which the sanctifying ministry of the Spirit in the conception of Christ is spelled out. Cf. his comments in *Institutes* II. 13.4 and also on Luke 1:35 in the *Harmony of the Gospels*.

30. *Institutes* IV. 17.17.

31. *Commentary on The Epistles of Paul to the Galatians, Ephesians, Philippians and Colossians*, p. 55.

32. *Institutes*, II. 16. 5. Cf. III. 8. 1 and also his commentaries on John 17:19, Romans 5:19 and Galatians 4:4-5.

33. *Institutes* II. 16.5.

34. Ibid.

35. *Harmony of the Gospels*, III p. 148, 207-208 (on Matthew 26:37 and 27:46).

36. Ibid. p. 168 (on Matthew 26:67).

37. Ibid. p 179 (on Matthew 27:11).

38. Ibid. p. 184 (on Matthew 27:15)

39. Ibid. p. 187 (on Matthew 27:24).

40. Ibid. p. 189 (on Matthew 27:27).

41. Ibid. p. 194 (on Matthew 27:35).

42. In the light of this exploration of Calvin's thinking, it is difficult to avoid the conclusion that the hymn *Je te salue, mon certain Redempteur* ('I greet thee, who my sure Redeemer art') was indeed written by Calvin himself (to whom it has been attributed) or by someone both intimately acquainted with his theology and sharing much of his personal experience.

43. John Calvin, *Sermons on Isaiah's Prophecy of the Death and Passion of Christ*, tr. and ed. T. H. L. Parker, London, 1956, p. 75.

WAS LUTHER AN EVANGELICAL?

Carl Trueman

Luther and the Reformation: The basic problem

The basic problem for any evangelical historian approaching Luther is, of course, the centuries of mythology, literary, visual, anecdotal, that have come to surround the man and the Reformation in the evangelical tradition. How many third rate Protestant artists have painted their pictures of an angry Luther nailing the theses to the castle wall and thus symbolically putting a nail in the coffin of medieval catholicism? And how often have the sentiments of such artworks been echoed and reinforced in evangelical sermons and tracts over the years? Yet Luther himself in 1545 tells us that 'when I began that cause.... I was so drunk, yes, submerged in the pope's dogmas, that I would have been ready to murder all, if I could have, or to co-operate willingly with the murderers of all who would take but a syllable from obedience to the pope.'[1] Clearly Luther's own professed understanding of himself at this point in time has largely fallen on deaf ears in the tradition. Far from nailing up the coffin of the medieval church, he saw himself as operating within its framework for the furtherance of its mission.[2]

There is a sense in which, of course, the scholar should not be influenced by the popular images and arguments of popular Protestant apologists. Few who have ever read Luther will fail to see the irony of a man who rejected Zwingli as a Christian brother because of his eucharistic beliefs being used as an icon by the most hardline Protestant conspiracy theorists in their crusades against the influence of the Papacy. Yet it is also very difficult for the evangelical scholar, with the theological commitments that implies, to approach the Reformation without trying to read the Reformation in terms of how it anticipates or legitimates movements of the eighteenth century and beyond. All I wish to do in this essay is raise a number of points which, I hope, will allow us to see once again, in the words of L. P. Hartley, that the past is a different country – and they did indeed do things differently there.

Luther's Reformation as a Precursor of Later Evangelicalism

At the start, it is worth noting a number of similarities between Luther and later revivalism and evangelicalism which have allowed the later tradition to see its embryonic form in the work of Luther.

First, there is Luther's conversion. The famous Tower Experience looms large in the evangelical awareness of Luther, as do the constant references to faith as leading to a movement for the believer from wrath to grace which permeate his mature theology.[3] While few of us have perhaps spent much time reflecting upon exactly what the relationship is between what Luther is saying and what we find in later evangelicalism and revivalism, we instinctively feel that there is some close connection between the two. This is in part the result of the fact that Luther's development of this Augustinian tradition on turning to God has indeed exerted a powerful influence within the evangelical tradition's own self-understanding. John Bunyan was famously moved and helped by Luther on Galatians, and his allegorical masterpiece, *Pilgrim's Progress,* along with the lesser known but still influential autobiography, *Grace Abounding to the Chief of Sinners* gave literary expression to the kind of conversion outlined by Luther and mediated it to countless others as something approaching normative Christian experience. Luther was also, of course, a significant influence on the conversion of John Wesley who, along with George Whitefield, exerted a profound influence on the early shape of Anglo-American revivalism. Indeed, Whitefield's modern biographer, Harry S. Stout, points on a number of occasions to the similarities between the conversion struggles of his subject and those of Martin Luther. Luther's experience of the transition from wrath to grace thus indirectly became part of the canon of evangelical experience and one important source for evangelicalism's understanding of conversion.[4]

Second (and this almost goes without saying), it is also true that preaching was central to the Reformation program. At a pragmatic level, it was the best way to communicate a message in a culture with high levels of illiteracy. Theologically, it was one of the distinguishing features of Protestantism: not that medieval Catholicism had no place for preaching; but that Reformation Protestantism ascribed to the act of preaching an overwhelming theological importance which the church had never really given it before.[5] This is most clearly seen in the Reformers' insistence that the sacraments could not be faithfully or truly administered unless the word was also attached to the sign; to do otherwise would make a nonsense of the centrality of promise and faith in Reformation theology. The extent, then, to which evangelicalism and revivalism in the eighteenth century and beyond continued to place the practice of preaching the word at the centre of its life represents a significant point of continuity with the tradition of the Reformers.[6]

When we get beyond these apparent similarities, however, the question of the relationship of the Reformation to later movement becomes more complex. For example, did Luther understand his Tower Experience in a manner which is substantially continuous with the way in which later evangelicals were to come to understand their own? Or was Luther more used by the later tradition than correctly understood? And did later revivalists and evangelicals see preaching as fulfilling the same function in the life of the church and its member Christians as Luther himself did? Such questions, if they can be answered at all given the evidence, are too complex to be resolved here; but what I want to start to do is to provide a context in which answers may be possible.

Luther's Reformation: The Centrality of Sacramental Theology

While there is at least one comment of Luther which might lead us to believe that the success of the Reformation depended on little more, humanly speaking, than his ability to drink beer (a point which, incidentally, certainly marks him off from much later revivalism), a more fruitful avenue for looking at Reformation priorities is almost certainly the literary output of the central year of 1520. It was at this point that Luther laid out in its fullest form his manifesto for Reformation in the three great treatises: *The Babylonian Captivity of the Church; The Freedom of the Christian;* and *An Address to the German Nobility.* These three works, produced at the point in Luther's career when it was becoming clear that the Church of Rome was not going to institute a theological reformation from within, laid out for all to see the implications of Luther's understanding of justification by faith for the realms of the sacraments, the Christian life, and the secular authorities.

It is primarily with the concerns of the first of these treatises, *The Babylonian Captivity*, with which I wish to deal in this essay. To place sacramental theology at the heart of Luther's Reformation should require no justification: the fact, as I mentioned earlier, that he was willing to anathematise Zwingli precisely on sacramental grounds should indicate to us that importance of this to Luther's program; and the fact that one of the three major treatises of 1520 is devoted to this topic is scarcely coincidental to Luther's overall vision of Reformation. Furthermore, this point should immediately alert us to the fact that Luther's understanding of what the Reformation is all about has a sacramental dimension which is not something which stands out in the later evangelical tradition.

The sacramental revisions which Luther proposes in *The Babylonian Captivity* present in pointed form ideas that had been developing in his mind throughout the previous five years and which had become increasingly focused in late 1518 and 1519. In brief, he reduces the number of sacraments from seven to three (penance still being considered a sacrament at this stage) and redefines them in terms of his understanding of the centrality of promise and faith. Thus, the sacraments come to function as outward symbols whose inner reality (and usefulness) is only available to the eyes of faith.

Most striking for the evangelical approaching Luther on the sacraments is his view of baptism, for it is at this point that Luther's theology sits most uncomfortably with any reading of his spiritual life in terms of later conversionism. At the start of the baptism section in *The Babylonian Captivity*, Luther makes the following point:

> But Satan, though unable to do away with the virtue of baptizing little children, has shown his power by putting an end to it among adults. Today there is scarcely anyone who calls to mind his own baptism, still less takes pride in it; because so many other ways have been found of getting sins forgiven and entering heaven.[7]

What Luther is alluding to here is the medieval stress upon baptism as a 'first plank' for salvation which, once the recipient has again fallen into sin, is more or less abandoned in favour of the 'second plank' of the church's penitential system. Such an approach effectively reduces the significance of baptism to a point in the past and focuses the mind far more upon the various means which the church provides in the present for dealing with sin. As a result, baptism becomes less important than the present penitential system with which believers have to do.

Several comments are in order here. First, it is worth noting that, as with so much of Luther's Reformation thought, his critique of the status quo is motivated by a deep pastoral concern. This is a point which can often be lost in discussions of Reformation theology but which was central to Luther's own understanding of what Reformation was all about. From the Romans commentary onwards, Luther's thought is being shaped by the issue of how individuals are to relate to the God of the Bible in a manner which does justice to the heinous nature of sin and the graciousness of a holy God. Second, and following from this, Luther's vision of the Reformation is not one where the sacraments become less important than they had been in the Middle Ages but actually more important. True, the medieval system is pruned from seven to three – but this is in part to enhance and sharpen the importance of those that remained. For Luther, the sacraments – baptism, the mass, and, at this point, penance – are outward signs attached to God's promise and are to be accepted and grasped as such by faith. Justification by faith, therefore, precisely because it relates to God's promise, also relates to the physical signs of the sacraments: the water in baptism, the bread and wine in the mass, and the declaration of absolution in penance.

Given this, it should be no surprise to discover that the development of Luther's sacramental theology, including that of baptism goes hand-in-hand, and is indeed an integral part, of the theological development which culminates in his breakthrough to the notion of justification by faith. While later popular evangelical piety may have found the sacraments something akin to optional extras within their theological framework, something which has resulted, for example, in the celebration of the Lord's Supper as an appendage at the end of the real church service – there is no doubt that Luther's breakthrough on justification was part of the same movement of thought which saw him transforming the way in which sacraments should be understood as absolutely central to the life of the church and the believer.

On the issue of baptism, this is in large measure because of his increasingly radical and anti-Pelagian understanding of sin. Unlike the medieval tradition in which he had been schooled and against which he was to react, Luther came to regard innate human sin after baptism as far more than a mere *fomes* or piece of kindling-wood which could be defeated by the efforts of the baptized. No: sin was something which dominated and controlled the whole human being and therefore baptism needed to be something total and comprehensive in order to match up to the seriousness of sin. In his *Lectures on Romans,* he makes the following comment, after noting the need for the believer to die in a manner analogous to Christ:

> But we must note that it is not necessary for all men to be found immediately in this state of perfection [of being dead to sin], as soon as they have been baptized into a death of this kind. For they are baptized 'into death', that is, toward death, which is to say, they have begun to live in such a way that they are pursuing this kind of death and reach out toward this their goal. For although they are baptized unto eternal life and the kingdom of heaven, yet they do not all at once possess this goal fully, but they have begun to act in such a way that they may attain to it-for Baptism was established to direct us toward death and through this death to life-therefore it is necessary that we come to it in the order which has been prescribed.[8]

To anyone familiar first-hand with the theology of Luther, this passage will appear striking for its use of the Pauline language of life and death which is so characteristic of Luther's theology of justification. What is of central importance to note is that this was written during the very period when Luther's theology was moving towards its mature Reformation position on justification and that the two issues are thus inextricably linked. In *The Babylonian Captivity,* the same emphasis upon death and resurrection in baptism is to be found, all of a piece with Luther's understanding of law and gospel, and the nature of justification by faith.[9] The believer does not need to be washed clean of sin; no, he or she needs to die, to be buried and to rise again to newness of life – and this is what baptism both symbolizes and, if Luther's language is to be taken at face value, in a sense effects. Later historiography and mythology may have isolated the doctrine of justification from Luther's broader theological biography but that is an error of later tradition not something for which we can blame Luther. To excise Luther's doctrine of justification from its wider situation in the doctrinal matrix that is his anti-Pelagian soteriology, which embodies his new understanding of the sacraments, is not a legitimate historical or, one might add, theological move.

Given the importance of baptism to Luther's theological vision for the Reformation, the question now arises as to how we can tie together those elements in his life which lend themselves to a conversionist reading with this high sacramentalism. The problem centres on the fact that Luther, in common with all the Magisterial Reformers, is a paedobaptist. If it were not for this element in his thinking, understanding Luther's theology of justification, and, indeed, his experience in the Tower, might well be relatively straightforward. Once one introduces the paedobaptist element, however, the situation is far more complex.

There are, broadly speaking, two dimensions to Luther's understanding of paedobaptism, one of which remains constant throughout his mature career, and one of which shifts in a subtle fashion. As to the first, the necessity of baptizing infants, Luther never wavers, rooting the immediate reason for so doing in the command of God. As he declares in the *Large Catechism*:

> We bring the child with the intent and hope that it may believe, and we pray God to grant it faith. But we do not baptize on this basis, but solely on the command of God. Why? Because we know that God does not lie.[10]

As to the second reason, what we might call the secondary rationale for paedobaptism, this does change somewhat, mainly as a result of the explosive controversies between Magisterial Reformers and Anabaptists in the early 1520s. Given his understanding of the relationship between the sign and the word of promise in sacraments, he could not argue for an *ex opere operato* view of baptism but had to root its efficacy in the faith response of the recipient. This is clearly problematic with regard to infants, and Luther appears to have wrestled with this issue over an extended period of time. Early in his reforming career, he had tended towards the view that children were baptized on the basis of the vicarious faith of their parents. This is the position he advocates in *The Babylonian Captivity*:

> As against what I have been saying, it may be objected that, when infants are baptized, they cannot receive the promises of God; are incapable of accepting the baptismal faith; and that, therefore, either faith is not a requisite, or else it is useless to baptize infants. On this matter I agree with everyone in saying that infants are helped by vicarious faith: the faith of those who present them for baptism.[11]

Then, sometime around 1522–23, he shifted to arguing on occasion that infants themselves possessed faith. Later still, he became more cautious, no doubt in the context of anabaptism concerned about making the sacrament dependent upon the precondition of the presence of faith, and saw the sacrament as anticipating future faith. What is certain is that baptism's validity was rooted in the word and not in the individual faith of the baptized.[12]

The question now arises: how is this to be squared with the strongly conversionist reading of Luther which enjoys popular currency in evangelical circles and, if accurate, would represent a direct point of continuity between Luther and later revivalism? The question is difficult, and that in large part because of the historical distance between historian and subject. It is a simple fact that Luther appears to have felt no tension between his emphasis on innate human sinfulness and the necessity of the sacraments. Thus, even to pose the question of how he reconciled the two is to pose a question to him which his own theology never raised.

That Luther felt no tension on this score, and that his theology is significantly different in this area from later evangelical revivalism and conversionism is demonstrated by the way in which baptism functions in his understanding of assurance. It is this function of baptism for Luther that really marks his thought off from that of later evangelical practice. The latter would frequently root personal assurance of the individual's status before God in the experience of salvation at the point of conversion, whether such a point was momentary or an extended period of time. This is reflected in the significant role that has often been ascribed to personal testimonies in the life and ministry of evangelical churches where both the one giving the testimony and those listening are expected to be encouraged, challenged, and generally helped by the process of sharing the common experience of conversion. For Luther, however, the conversion experience as such appears to play no role in assurance. Rather, the focus in on the word and the signs or sacraments which are attached to the word. Here are some examples which highlight this:

[N]oone should be terrified if he feels evil lust or love, nor should he despair even if he falls. Rather he should remember his baptism, and comfort himself joyfully with the fact that God has there pledged himself to slay his sin for him and not to count it a cause for condemnation, if only he does not say Yes to sin and remain in it.[13]

Heaven is given unto me freely, for nothing. I have assurance hereof confirmed unto me by sealed covenants, that is, I am baptized, and frequent the sacrament of the Lord's Supper. Therefore I keep the bond safe and sure, lest the devil tear it in pieces; that is, I live and remain in God's fear and pray daily unto him. God could not have given me better security of my salvation, and of the gospel, than by the death and passion of his only Son: when I believe that he overcame death, and died for me, and therewith behold the promise of the Father, then I have the bond complete. And when I have the seal of baptism and the Lord's Supper prefixed thereto, then I am well provided for.[14]

The role of the sacraments, and particularly baptism, in Luther's thinking on assurance is thus clear: they occupy a central place in the believer's experience of God's love and grace. In the culture of later evangelical revivalism, such a notion would no doubt appear bizarre: assurance rooted not in an experience of conversion of any other kind but in the fact of baptism, and that as an infant! Obviously, from our later perspective, loose wires hang out: what is the difference between Luther being baptized and Tetzel or the Pope being baptized? Can they enjoy the same assurance as Luther himself? Clearly not, as that would imply that baptism acted *ex opere operato*, a position which Luther emphatically rejects. He would no doubt have responded to such a challenge by arguing that the sign should never be confused with the reality; and the reality of baptism is the promise rooted in the death and resurrection of Christ, a reality which is grasped by faith, not by the sprinkling of a few drops of water. If that is the case, then, by implication, the moment of transition from unbelief to belief is crucial, and is that not akin to later conversionism? That is certainly true; and yet Luther's self-understanding is clearly still not that which will become so common in later evangelicalism. The emphasis on conversion, the language of subject conversionist experience, is simply absent. The sacramental language and categories which he is using in order to articulate his assurance of salvation set him off from later evangelical subjectivism or mysticism and indicate quite clearly that this is a man occupying a very different thought world. The emphasis here is not upon the subjectivity of personal faith but rather upon the objectivity of the sacraments and the objectivity of the promise and the christology which lie behind the sacraments. As far as my amateur knowledge of the eighteenth century revivals goes, this represents something largely alien, even if there are perhaps elements within it which, in retrospect, anticipate in a certain sense those things which will develop later.

This then is the first point: Luther saw the Reformation program's success as inextricably linked with pastoral issues; and these pastoral issues could only be successfully resolved by a careful revision and reformation of the sacramental system of the church. This, in turn, must have an impact upon how we understand the later evangelical and revivalist tradition's appropriation of things such as Luther's Tower Experience. To this we shall return in the conclusion.

Luther's Reformation: The Importance of the Church as an Institutional Body in Relationship to the Priesthood of All Believers

This sacramental discussion brings me to what will be my second point, and another issue which must be taken into account when relating Luther's Reformation to later evangelicalism and revivalism: the importance of the church as an institutional body. There are many ways of approaching this issue, but given my purpose of relating Luther to later revivalism, I have chosen perhaps the most obvious probable source of continuity: the priesthood of all believers. Luther formulated his understanding of the universal priesthood of all believers in 1520.[15] This is significant: on one level, the term captures in a nutshell Luther's understanding of grace, justification, and salvation. Union with Christ is the central idea here: as Christ is priest, so those united to Christ by faith are themselves priests. Hence, this priesthood is not mediated via the institutional church or the priestly hierarchy of that church but is the direct privilege of every believer who, through faith, can have dealings with God in Christ on a direct, personal basis.

This is effected via the Word of God – in scripture, in preaching, and in the sacraments. In each case, there is an immediate grasping of God in Christ via faith by the individual; and, in each case, the believer is assured of God's favour – not by his or her standing in the visible church, but by the personal possession of what God has done for them in Christ. Within this scheme, the role of the church, of the institutional priesthood, and of the sacrament of the mass is radically transformed: the church is rather the servant of Christ, proclaiming his word to the world; the institutional priesthood becomes the group who, as much for convenience sake as for anything else, is there to preach the word and point to God's promises; and the mass becomes not a sacrifice which makes grace available in and of itself, but an act which, like preaching, underlines and offers God's promise of salvation in Christ. The whole notion of an elite priesthood as in some way an intermediate spiritual group between the laity and God is thus abandoned.[16]

At another level, however, we must beware of placing too much stock in the actual terminology of universal priesthood itself and seeing it as a wholesale rejection of the importance of structure and authority in the church, as if spiritual egalitarianism should inevitably manifest itself in the outward structures of the church. This is not Luther's point: rather, universal priesthood has more immediate ethical, than institutional, implications, underlining the fact that believers are to conceive of their priesthood as Christ did his – an avenue of service to others rather than an opportunity for self-advancement. Thus, Luther uses the language of universal priesthood in 1520 in large part to make a specific polemical point against the overweening social, theological and soteriological pretensions of the Roman clergy, and it is not in itself as theologically significant as the ideas which underlie it. 1520 was in many ways the make-or-break year of the Lutheran Reformation. After the inconclusive meetings with church authorities in Augsburg and Leipzig, and while waiting the inevitable bull of excommunication, Luther published his three great treatises in which he both stated his emerging Reformation theology in a sharply polemical manner and made a last – perhaps somewhat unconvincing – attempt to appeal to the Pope. It was in this climate that the language of universal priesthood came to the fore, though this did not in and of itself represent an underlying change or radical development in theological perspective. It was rather an attempt to give full expression to the content and implications of salvation by grace through faith which had been developing in Luther's mind since around 1515, while at the same time making a sharp polemical criticism of the Roman church's priestly pretensions. In the early 1520s, therefore, the rhetorical power of the term was in many ways as significant as the theological point being made – a point which had in effect been made by Luther on earlier occasions without using this kind of language.[17]

Furthermore, it is also important to note that what Luther is emphatically not doing is using the concept of universal priesthood as a means for determining the institutional structure of the church. In the mind of the German Reformer at least, this priesthood is intended as pointing towards an anti-hierarchical understanding of salvation; it is not intended in the first instance as pointing towards or demanding a democratic or anti-hierarchical view of church government. It gives the laity a theological significance they did not have before by tearing down pretensions of the medieval priesthood; but for Luther, it gives no mandate for tearing down all the notions of hierarchy in the visible church, even though it requires a rethinking of the functions of that hierarchy.[18]

That Luther's language of universal priesthood did not point towards anti-hierarchical, individualist anarchy in the church is indicated by the research of David Bagchi on Luther's earliest Catholic opponents. In the context of a discussion of the priesthood of all believers, Bagchi makes the following observation:

> [T]he controversialists in general were much less antagonistic to Luther's doctrine of the priesthood of all believers than might have been supposed. Their objection, as with some of Luther's other teachings, was prompted largely by the possibility that the rabble might understand it out of ignorance or malice. Cochlaeus, Fisher, Bartholomeus, Usingen, Eck, Arnoldi Von Chiernsee, Johannes Gropper, and Jodocus Clichtoveus all accepted the universal priesthood, provided that it did not detract from the special priesthood.[19]

The last caveat, referring to the fact that Luther's Catholic opponents still held to an elite priesthood above and beyond that of all believers, should not obscure the fact that Luther's use of this terminology in itself does not appear to have overly concerned orthodox Catholics -indeed, Bagchi mentions only one Catholic who wrote against the idea, and that from a perspective eerily reminiscent of John Wyclif![20] What was of concern was the way in which the language of universal priesthood could be abused by more radical and less subtly learned elements for more anarchic and disruptive ends.

In fact, as regards the universal priesthood, what we have in Luther is, I believe, two related but formally separable phenomena. On the one hand, we have the theology of grace, justification, and conversion which places the individual in union with Christ firmly at the center, with no hierarchical mediation whatsoever. From this flow various consequences: the need for comprehensible preaching of the word; for the vernacular mass; for accurate and clear translations of the scriptures into the vulgar tongue; an emphasis upon the individual wrestling with God. All of these point towards lay participation in church life and represent an empowerment of the laity as they are, effectively, handed direct responsibility for their own salvation.

On the other hand, however, we have the rhetorical language of universal priesthood, of Christian freedom from the law, and of the spiritual equality of all earthly callings, the spiritual and the non-spiritual. In theological and historical context, this rhetoric is simply a particularly pointed way of expressing the theological underpinnings of Luther's Reformation programme; to the untrained ear, however, in the context of early sixteenth century Saxony and beyond, they have a socially revolutionary sound which makes them very attractive to various nascent nationalist and radical groupings. To the oppressed peasants, labouring under intolerable conditions, and to the German knights, resentful of German taxes paying for Italian excess, the rhetoric of Luther was a rallying call for revolution and rebellion.

This is an important point as it helps to explain both the dramatic success of the initial Lutheran reform programme in Germany and, more significantly for this study, the disappearance of the rhetorical emphasis on universal priesthood and freedom from the rhetoric of the Protestantism of the later Reformation and Post-Reformation periods. First, particularly talk of Christian, but also of universal priesthood, struck a clear chord with the crescendo of nationalism, anti-clericalism, and peasant unrest which the German territories were witnesses to in the early sixteenth century. Luther's rhetoric was seized on by various groups as providing them with a vocabulary for articulating and justifying their various protests and a means of making the social grievances, which had been the stock-in-trade of ale-house conversation for some 150 years, into a religious crusade.[21] As such, they divorced the language from the theology and turned Luther's Reformation into a social and political revolution. The disasters of the so called Peasants'

War and Muenster served to demonstrate to Luther, and to others, the dangerous way in which the rhetoric of freedom and priesthood could be used and thus, once the polemical heat from the Catholic side in 1520 had passed, and the anarchic aspirations of the anabaptists started to surface, we find that such language becomes less frequent in Luther.

That Luther's emphasis upon universal priesthood was not an attempt to articulate a general opposition to all forms of authority is indicated by Luther's attitude to the laity in their relation to the church and its leaders. The old despotic hierarchy of institutional grace may have gone; and Luther may have dealt a death blow to many of the institutional church's pretensions - both political and theological-but he did not, for example, put the Bible into the hands of the laity for each and every believer to do with it what they would. Emphasis upon the fundamental perspicuity of scripture did not mean that there was no place in the church for theological professionals, nor that everyone was as competent to discern the meaning of scripture as everyone else.[22] Thus, the need for proper theological education was maintained by Luther and his followers as essential, and the respect for church tradition, particularly patristic theology, remained within the Reformation programme despite the adherence to the notion of scripture alone.[23] Both factors reflected Luther's acknowledgment that scriptural authority could not exist in a vacuum but needed to be set in a critical relationship to the doctrinal and exegetical traditions of the church; and, once that basic factor is acknowledged, theology becomes in part at least the corporate activity of the educated church leadership and not something in which just anyone can indulge.

All of this, of course, points towards substantial areas of discontinuity with later revivalism and the evangelicalism to which it gave birth. The pragmatic and democratic 'can do' mentality of much of the movement, the suspicion of learning, and the lack of any real ecclesiology were characteristic of revival movements from the eighteenth century onwards. From Whitefield and Wesley to Billy Graham, the result of revivalist religion has almost always involved a weakening of both the doctrine of the church and of the doctrinal content of theology. This is not, of course, to say that these characteristics were always evident in the leaders of the movement. Jonathan Edwards, for example, was clearly a most learned individual with a profound knowledge of the tradition and well-thought out convictions on theological issues. Nevertheless, it has been argued that it was the Edwardsean moment in American Reformed theology that contributed to the ultimate downgrading of ecclesiology and confessional subscription that one finds within the so-called New School presbyterians in the nineteenth century. The influence of Edwards' revival literature on the theologians of the Old School presbyterianism, the Hodges, Warfield and Machen to name a few, is conspicuous by its absence. Indeed, in a famous essay on Edwards, Warfield explicitly criticized his followers for their revivalist zeal and implicitly connected this with the doctrinal flux and declension which marked the leaders of the so-called 'New Divinity'.[24] But, even if this were not so, Edwards is still something of an exception. To put it bluntly, the pragmatism of revivalist leaders, rooted in general, though not exclusively, in a semi-Pelagian theology which comported well with the attitude of 'if it works for individual conversions, then it must be good', led to a practical contempt for the church as a creedal institution and for the historical tradition of theology which demanded intellectual engagement. No less a revivalist than Charles Finney ultimately had to concede, with some regret that this was the case.[25] Luther's priesthood of all believers was never intended as a means of turning the church into an unstructured, amorphous collection of saved individuals or of generating the lowest-common-denominator practice and theology which has often been the hallmark of revivalism. Rather, it was a means of highlighting one important aspect of salvation – union with Christ – and thus a way of revising people's understanding of what priesthood was all about. If further evidence is needed of this strongly ecclesiological dimension of Luther's understanding of the status of believers, just reflect for a moment upon the significance of baptism in particular, and the sacraments in general, for his understanding of faith and salvation. A soteriology which puts such stress on the sacraments is inevitably a soteriology which places a high premium on ecclesiology. Sacraments as Luther understands them militate against the kind of individualism upon which revivalism thrived.

Conclusion

Let us now turn to the question which lies behind the title of this paper. If we could ask Luther why the Reformation succeeded, he would no doubt respond that it was a movement of God's Word, accompanied by the effective power of God's Spirit. Ask a nineteenth century revivalist why his revival succeeded, and one would no doubt receive the same answer. But ask them each how this movement of Word and Spirit manifested itself and I would argue that significant differences would immediately emerge. For the revivalist, the answer would certainly be that many souls were saved, that many individuals turned to Christ, that many were able to testify that they had been lost but had now been found. Were our revivalist in a point-scoring mood, he may well also add that the Spirit chose to work outside of the framework of the church, undermining its stuffy structures and adherence to tradition and theology by raising up preachers who had no learning or theology, just the one book, and that through these foolish things God chose to shame the wise ones of the conventional churches, denominations, and seminaries. Asked how these individuals knew that they had been saved, the revivalist would no doubt respond that, at a point in time, they had come under conviction of sin and had then come to know – or perhaps to feel – that Christ was their saviour.

Luther's answer, I suspect, would be somewhat different. He would say that many had come to see that Christ was their righteousness, to be grasped solely through faith; and that, through this, they had come to a deeper understanding of their baptism, of the importance of the mass, of the fact that they were part of the body of Christ and must therefore give themselves for the service of others. Asked how they knew this, he would respond by saying that they had come to see that, by undergoing baptism, they had been baptized into Christ's death and resurrection and, through baptism and trusting in the promise of that baptism, had been united with their saviour.

The differences are perhaps at points ones of emphasis. But, even so, the sacramental *emphasis* in Luther's answer points away from a straightforward equation of his understanding of salvation with that later conversionism of the revivals. Luther's Tower Experience plays a large part in the evangelical appropriation of Luther; but Luther himself does not seem to ascribe to it quite the functional importance which we might have expected. After all, we only hear about it in 1545, the year before Luther himself dies. Clearly, his understanding of the functional importance of this testimony in the public sphere of the church (whatever its private significance may have been – and about that we can only speculate) was radically different to the attitudes to personal testimony and conversion narratives in later evangelicalism where they came to validate the individual's standing within the church community. Furthermore, this sacramental dimension of Luther at this point also points towards the corporate, rather than the individual, concerns of much of his thinking. Bultmann may have turned Lutheranism into a radically individualist movement, but this finds little precedent in Luther himself. I suspect that this corporate, sacramental focus decisively distances Luther from revivalism as well as from Bultmann and, indeed, from contemporary evangelicalism. If evangelical bookshops and publishing houses are good gauges of what evangelicals read and think, then one has to say that neither the sacraments nor corporate actions (outside of the realm of political activism) seem to hold as much interest for evangelicals today as they would have done for Luther. Books on individual acts of piety abound; books on the corporate aspects of Christianity are somewhat less common. As for the sacraments, understanding of baptism and of the Lord's Supper are, in my experience, minimal in both baptist and paedobaptist circles. Far from being integral to the church's practice of piety, they are frequently considered as added extras, traditions we do for the sake of it, or simply as confusing. I know of one leading evangelical Anglican minister in England who has not baptized his children in order to show to his congregation that it is faith, not baptism, which really matters. I can see what he is getting at, but one can only wonder at what Luther would have said to such a person. There is a pathway from Luther to the revivalism and to the evangelicalism of the modern day, but it is far more complex certainly than I myself envisaged and, I suspect, than many evangelicals either suspect or will admit.

NOTES

1. This sentence occurs in the autobiographical reflections contained in the 1545 preface to Luther's Latin works, translated in John Dillenberger, *Martin Luther* (New York: Anchor Books, 1961), p. 4.

2. The best modern one-volume account of Luther's theology is Bernhard Lohse, *Martin Luther's Theology: Its Historical and Systematic Development* (Edinburgh: T. and T. Clark, 1999); the older study of E. G. Rupp, *The Righteousness of God: Luther Studies* (London: Hodder and Stoughton, 1953) is still worth consulting. More recent works, setting Luther against the background of medieval trajectories of life and thought include Heiko Oberman, *Luther: Man Between God and the Devil* (Yale:YUP, 1989); and David C. Steinmetz, *Luther in Context* (Grand Rapids: Baker, 1995). On Luther's changing reputation, and his function as an icon of theological rebellion, see Robert Kolb, *Martin Luther as Prophet, Teacher, and Hero* (Grand Rapids: Baker, 1999).

3. The account is found in the 1545 preface to Luther's Latin works: Dillenberger, pp. 11-12.

4. See Harry S. Stout, *The Divine Dramatist: George Whitefield and the Rise of Modern Evangelicalism* (Grand Rapids: Eerdmans, 1991), pp. 14, 26; for a highly controversial and, in my opinion, basically incorrect understanding of how Augustine lies in the background of much of the West's reading of Paul (of which Luther's conversion experience is now a part) see K. Stendahl, 'The Apostle Paul and the Introspective Conscience of theWest', *HarvardTheologicalReview* 56 (1963), 199-215.

5. On medieval preaching, see Hughes Oliphant Old, *The Reading and Preaching of the Scriptures in the Worship of the Christian Church :The Medieval Church* (Grand Rapids: Eerdmans, 1999); also the individual studies D. Catherine Brown, *Pastor and Laity in the Theology of Jean Gerson* (Cambridge: CUP, 1987); and Cecelia A. Hatt, *English Works of John Fisher: Sermons and Other Writings* (Oxford: OUP, 2002).

6. See, for example, Luther's *Babylonian Captivity of the Church*, translated in full in Dillenberger, pp. 249-359; also Calvin's comments in *Institutes* 4.17.39.

7. Dillenberger, p. 292.

8. J. Pelikan and H. T. Lehmann (eds), *Luther's Works* (Philadelphia: Concordia Publishing House, 1955-86), hereafter *LW*, vol. 25, p. 312.

9. Dillenberger, pp. 301-302.

10. Rober Kolb and Timothy J. Wengert (eds) *The Book of Concord* (Minneapolis: Fortress Press, 2000), p. 464.

11. Dillenberger, p. 307.

12. On Luther's developing baptismal theology with regard to infants, see Lohse, pp. 302-05.

13. 'The Holy and Blessed Sacrament of Baptism', *LW* 35, p. 35.

14. *Table Talk*, no. 341

15. The definitive account of Luther's development up to, and including, the crucial year of 1520 is Martin Brecht, *Martin Luther: His Road to Reformation. 1483-1521*, trans. James L.s Schaaf (Minneapolis: Fortress Press, 1985).

16. Luther's soteriology is expressed in two of the major treatise of 1520, *On the Freedom of the Christian* and *The Babylonian Captivity of the Church*. Translations of both can be found in Dillenberger.

17. See especially Dillenberger pp. 345, 349, 407-08.

18. Thus, preaching and administration of the sacraments are still tasks reserved for a particular group, but this is essentially for the sake of convenience, and on the basis of mutual consent: Dillenberger, p. 349.

19. David V. N. Bagchi, *Luther's Earliest Opponents: Catholic Controversialists, 1518–1525* (Minneapolis: Fortress, 1991), pp. 137-38.

20. The controversialist's name was WolfgangWulfter: Bagchi, p. 138.

21. On this, see Heiko A. Oberman, 'The Gospel of Social Unrest: 450 Years After the So-Called 'German Peasants' War' of 1525' in idem, *The Dawn of the Reformation* (Edinburgh: T and T Clark, 1992), pp. 155-78.

22. On university life and pedagogy in the Reformation, see Heiko A. Oberman, *Masters of the Reformation* (Cambridge: CUP, 1981).

23. On the importance of patristic studies to the Lutheran Reformation, see P. Fraenkel, *Testimonia Patrum: The Function of the Patristic Argument in the Theology of Philip Melanchthon* (Geneva: Droz, 1961). See also the collection of essays edited by Irena Backus, *The Reception of the Church Fathers in the West: From the Carolingians to the Maurists* (Leiden: Brill, 1997).

24. See his essay, 'Edwards and the New England Theology', *Studies in Theology* (Edinburgh: Banner of Truth, 1988), pp. 515-38, esp. pp. 532-33.

25. See Charles Hambrick-Stowe, *Charles G. Finney and the Spirit of American Evangelicalism* (Grand Rapids: Eerdmans, 1996), p. 218.

PETER MARTYR VERMIGLI

Probing his Puritan Influence

Frank A. James III

I. Introduction

It is high praise indeed when the Regius Professor of Divinity at Cambridge, Patrick Collinson, locates Peter Martyr Vermigli at the theological center of the early Anglican church: '[I]f we were to identify one author and one book which represented the center of theological gravity of the Elizabethan church it would not be Calvin's *Institutes*, but the *Common Places* of Peter Martyr...'[1] Rarely will a Cambridge man grant such an accolade to an Oxford man. If nothing else, Collinson's recognition of Vermigli's influence underscores his pivotal importance for early English Protestantism.

Although not a household name, Peter Martyr Vermigli (1499–1562) was indeed one of the leading lights from that constellation of theologians who gave formative shape to early Reformed theology. In the last century, the German historian, Charles Schmidt, said of Vermigli, 'few have done so much for the establishment and determination of the doctrine of the Reformed Church.'[2] The Italian underwent an unprecedented theological transformation in sixteenth century Europe – from being an eminent Roman Catholic theologian into one of the leading Protestant Reformers of his day.[3] Indeed, his importance was such that one Protestant contemporary, Joseph Scaliger, could say, 'the two most excellent theologians of our times are John Calvin and Peter Martyr.'[4] Given his prominence throughout England and the continent in the world of the sixteenth century and the relative dearth of contemporary research on this Catholic turned Protestant, it is worthwhile to consider Vermigli's role in the development of Puritanism.

II. Peter Martyr in England

Although he might have wished differently, Peter Martyr was a peripatetic Protestant. Never in any location more than seven years[5], he found himself in positions of influence in three key Protestant cities – Strasbourg, Oxford and Zurich. After his first five years as a Protestant under Martin Bucer in Strasbourg, Vermigli's reputation was substantial enough that Archbishop Thomas Cranmer invited him to England to help inculcate a generation of Anglican priests with Protestant theology.[6] To this end he was appointed Regius Professor of Divinity at Oxford University (1547–1553). Vermigli was the first major Protestant theologian to heed the Archbishop's call and he remained at Cranmer's side until expelled by the Catholic authorities in 1553.[7] His nearly six years in England were among the most fruitful of his entire career, and there can be little doubt that he exercised an 'incalculable impact'[8] on the English Church. He single-handedly upheld Protestant Eucharistic teaching at the famous Oxford Disputation of 1549, consulted with Bishop Hooper in the Vestiarian controversy in 1550, assisted Cranmer in the revision of the 1552 Prayer Book and in the formulation of the Forty-Two Articles of Religion in 1553, and played a pivotal role in writing the *Reformatio Legum Ecclesiasticarum* from 1551–1553. Some have concluded that this time in England was 'the most useful period of Martyr's life.'[9] Vermigli's name would no doubt have been better remembered today if his sojourn in England had not been cut short by Mary Tudor's ascension to the throne in 1553. [10]

The single most impressive measure of Vermigli's importance as a theologian was the repeated publication of his books throughout Europe and England. His works went through 110 separate printings in the century following his death in 1562.[11] He made his mark primarily as a biblical commentator, but also as an important theologian of the Reformed branch of Protestantism. He exerted enormous influence through commentaries published during his lifetime (I Corinthians, Romans and Judges) as well as his posthumously published commentaries (Genesis, Lamentations,

I and II Samuel, and I and II Kings).[12] He also wrote theological treatises, most notably on the Eucharist. His *Defensio* against the 'persecuting prelate'[13] Stephen Gardiner, Bishop of Winchester, on the Eucharist was a lengthy tome of impressive erudition. In the words of Philip McNair, it was 'incontestably the weightiest single treatise on the Eucharist of the entire Reformation.'[14] While Eucharistic concerns tended to predominate, Vermigli's theological interests were wide ranging. His theological attentions extended to such matters as clerical celibacy and the two natures of Christ, subjects he addressed in published treatises. Easily the most influential of Vermigli's writings was the *Loci Communes* a posthumous compilation of various *loci* from his biblical commentaries arranged according to key theological topics.[15]

Although expelled from England, he never lost his interest and concern for the English Church. His connection to England was forged in the church battles of the Edwardian reformation and the fires of Marian persecution. Many of the Edwardian church leaders fled to protection of Zurich and to the fatherly support of Vermigli. John Jewel for example actually lived with Vermigli and continued a life-long correspondence with his mentor. Indeed, it was due in part to Jewel, later bishop of Salisbury, that Vermigli was invited to return to England in the reign of Elizabeth.[16] To the end of his life, Vermigli remained a faithful friend to many of the English church leaders and in times of struggle they turned to him for advice.

Even after his death in 1562, Vermigli continued to be a theological referent for many in the English church. Edmund Grindal, archbishop of Canterbury, spoke of his important role at the famous Colloquy of Poissy (1561) to Sir William Cecil saying: 'I am of the judgment that no man alive is more fit than Peter Martyr for such a conference ... for he is better versed in old doctors, councils and ecclesiastical histories than any Romish doctor of Christendom.'[17] His influence was felt in England for well over a century.

III. Vermigli and Puritanism

It has become something of a truism that Puritanism is difficult to define.[18] There have always been those well-intentioned religious persons who sought to purge or purify the Christian church of what they deemed unseemly ideas or activities. The difficulties of definition are compounded by the many caricatures that began in the sixteenth century and are unfortunately carried over to the present time. Whatever difficulties attend the term 'puritan', we are nevertheless compelled to employ it. Whatever ambiguities remain, it cannot be denied that religious convictions played a pivotal role in defining who the Puritans were. It is a fundamental failure to view Puritanism simply as a sociological, economical, or a political movement. While there were sociological, economical, political implications, which in some cases led to opposing positions, they were motivated largely by religious convictions.

For our purposes Puritanism refers to an identifiable group of English Protestants from the period of Elizabeth I to the Interregnum, who embraced Reformed theology to a substantial degree and viewed themselves as belonging to the Reformed camp. It was this theological orientation that gave Puritanism both an historical referent and its most distinctive features. To be sure, some Puritans took their Reformed theology in directions that would have certainly been rejected by the original Protestant reformers such as Calvin and Luther, neither of whom would have sanctioned the regicide of Charles I. One must even grant some measure of theological fluidity in defining Puritanism. The Puritan Richard Baxter, famous for his pastoral writings, deviated in significant ways from historic Reformed theology.[19] Despite differences, Puritans quite deliberately sought to work out the implications of their Reformed theology in the English church. Elizabethan puritans desired a 'further reformation' of her majesty's ecclesiastical compromise, especially its liturgy.[20] Puritans also attempted to work out the implications of a Reformed theology politically in the public square. Frustration with the crown over the progress of religious reform prompted many to become involved in the political process, many taking a seat in Parliament. Puritans could differ in church polity, in theology, or even in their expressions of piety, but all wanted the English Church to resemble more closely the Reformed Churches on the continent.

A. Vermigli and the origins of English Puritanism
Vermigli's influence among these Puritans was substantive and long term. He had a particularly significant influence on the origins of the Puritan movement through his relationship with the Marian Exiles.[21] With the ascension of Mary to the throne in 1553, Vermigli's sojourn was cut short. He managed to leave England in

mid-September 1553 and returned to Strasbourg in October 1553 to take up his former duties as professor in that city for a second tour of duty.[22] Shortly thereafter, Englishmen began arriving seeking refuge from Marian persecution. In a letter to Bullinger, he wrote on February 1554 that 'English youths have come over to us in great numbers within the past few days, partly from Oxford, partly from Cambridge...'[23] With their old mentor Peter Martyr resident in Strasbourg it is not surprising that it was one of the main destination of English exiles.[24] John Foxe informs us that some 800 English men and women fled Marian persecution to the safety of the continent, and Dickens confirms this.[25] It was only natural that many of these English Protestants would gravitate to Cranmer's champion and former Regius Professor of Divinity at Oxford. As a consequence, deep and abiding relationships were established between Vermigli and many of the English exiles who would later assume leadership in the Elizabethan church.

Among those who found refuge in Strasbourg with Vermigli for some length of time was John Ponet, Cranmer's chaplain, Bishop of Winchester, and the 'highest ranking ecclesiastic in exile.'[26] He arrived in Strasbourg in July 1554 and enjoyed close fellowship with Vermigli before succumbing to the plague in August 1556.[27] Strasbourg also welcomed another English refugee, Richard Cox, former Dean of Christ Church, Oxford, who was not only a good friend, but had presided over the famous Oxford Disputation in 1549 declaring Peter Martyr victorious against three Catholic opponents. Cox was one of the 'foremost' English exiles[28] and, upon returning to England, he was made Bishop of Ely. Another close associate was Edmund Grindal, later Archbishop of Canterbury, who spent time in Strasbourg during Vermigli's tenure there. Leading English scholars such as Sir Anthony Coke and Sir John Cheke, both of whom were tutors to Edward VI, also came to Strasbourg. Something of the esteem for Vermigli among English exiles in Strasbourg is captured in the words of another English refugee, Thomas Becon, who described Vermigli as 'that precious pearl and marvelous marguerite.'[29]

Some of the Marian exiles were so devoted to him that they followed him from Strasbourg to Zurich. John Jewel, later Bishop of Salisbury and the final revisor of the Thirty-Nine articles under Elizabeth, fled to Strasbourg in 1554 and, when Vermigli accepted the Chair of Old Testament in Zurich (1556) upon the death of

Conrad Pelikan, followed him and lived as a son in his home. Martyr's importance for Jewel and the English church cannot be overestimated. Jewel explicitly identifies the theology of the Thirty-Nine articles with Vermigli, saying: 'as to matters of doctrine, we … do not differ from your doctrine by a nail's breadth.'[30] Jewel was not alone in his devotion to Martyr. Edwin Sandys[31] had been the Vice-Chancellor of Cambridge University when Mary Tudor came to the throne in 1553 and was later Archbishop of York. He too fled Marian persecution to Strasbourg and, when Peter Martyr moved to Zurich, Sandys followed. If it can be said that the first bloom of Puritanism arose from among these exiled Englishmen, then one must acknowledge that Vermigli was a formative influence on the origins of Puritanism.

Vermigli's influence continued among the early Puritans.[32] Having returned from exile, many of Vermigli's friends became leading members of the Elizabethan church. And as one might expect of English exiles from such cities as Geneva and Zurich, there were serious concerns about the value of Elizabeth's religious settlement. One of the most significant controversies to arise among these returning exiles concerned the wearing of vestments. This dispute surfaced several times during and after Martyr's death in 1562. The matter of vestments first erupted in 1551 when John Hooper was consecrated bishop of Gloucester. Hooper had qualms about wearing vestments and sought the advice of two theologians he respected – Vermigli and Bucer. Although Vermigli personally preferred vestments not be worn, he viewed them as *adiaphora* (things indifferent). His advice (and Bucer's) to Hooper was to wear the vestments and preach the gospel. Hooper accepted the counsel.[33]

There were two other eruptions over vestments in Elizabeth's reign and, in both cases, Martyr served as a theological referent. Upon returning from exile, Thomas Sampson was under consideration for the Bishopric of Norwich, but he, like Hooper before him, had doubts about the wearing of vestments that seemed to be 'relics of Popery'.[34] Again Vermigli advised conformity on vestments as a sacrifice necessary to the furtherance of the gospel in England. Sampson, however, could not overcome his reservations and removed his name from consideration.

B. Vermigli and early Puritanism

Sampson's convictions surfaced again in a second vestments controversy in 1566. This latest eruption over vestments was initially prompted by the Archbishop of Canterbury, Matthew Parker, who wrote against two of Martyr's disciples, Thomas Sampson, by then dean of Christ Church, Oxford and Laurence Humphrey, the President of Magdalen College, Oxford. The issue under debate moved beyond the mere wearing of popish vestments to whether the Christian was obligated to obey the Queen in such matters. Sampson sought the advice of Bullinger, whose reply landed like a 'bomb-shell.'[35] Instead of supporting nonconformity, Bullinger sided with Archbishop Parker and the Queen. What is more, Bullinger appealed directly to the authority of Vermigli, citing many of the same arguments his Italian cohort employed with Hooper sixteen years earlier.[36]

Other controversies erupted in the English Church after Vermigli's death and still appeal was made to his theological authority. In the Admonition controversy of the early 1570's, disputes erupted over submission to the Queen and Episcopal church polity. The chief adversaries were John Whitgift, dean of Lincoln Cathedral and the future Archbishop of Canterbury, who squared off against Thomas Cartwright, Lady Margaret Professor at Cambridge, the former advocating for episcopacy, the latter Presbyterianism.[37] One of the more intriguing aspects of this debate was the fact that both held the teaching of Vermigli in high regard. Indeed, at times their polemics seemed to be little more than quibbling over Vermigli's words.[38] Whitgift, advocating for conformity, appealed especially to Vermigli's earlier letters to Hooper, and Cartwright, cited Vermigli's personal preference to advance the cause of nonconformity. Apart from the question of where Martyr's real sympathies lay, the fact that both parties appealed to him reveals his enduring legacy among Anglicans and Puritans alike.[39]

C. Vermigli and Puritan millennial trends

In recent years, new research has unearthed a hitherto unknown trajectory of Vermiglian influence among Puritans. It seems to be the case that he exercised a determinative impact in the emergence of millennial trends in Puritanism, especially the eschatological belief in the future conversion of the Jews. Ian H. Murray has concluded that '[t]he first volume in English to expound at some length [the conviction of a future general conversion of the Jews] was the translation of Peter Martyr's Commentary on Romans, published in London in 1568'.[40] The historical evidence suggests the 'strong probability' that the acceptance of Vermigli's exegesis of Romans 11 inclined many English Puritans to adopt the belief in the future conversion of the Jewish nation. Murray traces Vermigli's eschatological influence to such distinguished Puritan divines as William Perkins, John Owen, Thomas Manton, John Flavel, Jeremiah Burroughs and Increase Mather.[41] Building on the work of Murray, John Hesselink has also identified a connection between the influence of Vermigli's commentary on Romans (chs. 9-11) with the rise of premillennialism in Puritan England.[42] Although Vermigli was no premillennialist, his belief in a future conversion of the Jews does seem to have been fodder for some Puritans. For example, Henry Jessey (1601-1663), one of the Fifth Monarchy Men, recognizes him as an authority for his interpretation. Another millennialist, Natham Homes cites Vermigli favorably in his *A Brief Chronicle Concerning the Jews*.[43] Although enthusiasm for premillennialism proved in time to be no more than a passing phenomenon among Puritans, Vermigli's exegetical prowess proved to have enduring significance.[44] Along this same line, Vermigli seems to have been a factor in the rise in the seventeenth century of 'philo-semitism', a heightened Christian appreciation of Jews and Judaism in English eschatological thought, especially the belief in the return of the Jews to the Land of Israel.[45] The evidence seems to suggest that Vermigli was instrumental in this development.[46]

D. Vermigli and the Westminster Assembly

Although the pressing issues of theological debate had changed in sixteenth century England, Peter Martyr's memory was still vivid enough among the divines at the Westminster Assembly. For instance, one of 'the most influential members of the Assembly'[47] was Anthony Tuckney (1599-1670), a Presbyterian Puritan who had a 'primary' role in developing the Confession and the Catechisms.[48] Indeed, some even have judged Tuckney to have 'the most influential writer of the Shorter Catechism.'[49] After his death, forty of his sermons were published and they contain a number of favorable citations from Vermigli among others.[50] Another of the Westminster Divines, Anthony Burgess, refered repeatedly to Vermigli in his writings.[51] In his *Vindiciae Legis: A Vindication of the Moral Law and the Covenants*, Burgess appealed to his commentary on Romans.[52] Again in his treatise on the Lord's Supper, he drew from Vermigli's insights from his commentary on First Corinthians.[53] Thomas Gataker (1574-1654) was another influential divine at the Assembly, especially in its deliberations on the doctrine of justification.[54] So taken was he with Vermigli that he wrote a short life of Martyr.[55]

Peter Martyr was actually cited on a number of occasions at the Assembly as an authority. William Bridge, one of the most active of the Independent divines at Westminster, attempted to invoke the authority of both Calvin and Vermigli in support of his view that I Corinthians 5 taught the power of excommunication was to be exercised by the whole congregation.[56] John Strickland, one of the lesser known divines at Westminster Assembly, preached a sermon to the Westminster divines on 5 November 1544 in which he gave Vermigli honorable mention.[57] That Martyr remained one of the most popular Continental divines among English Puritans through the late sixteenth and seventeenth centuries is evident from the fact that the venerable John Milton considered him 'a divine of foremost rank'[58] and probably used Martyr's Genesis commentary in preparation for his *Paradise Lost.*[59]

If Patrick Collinson recognized the vital importance of Vermigli on the Elizabethan Church and the origins of the Puritan movement, then Diarmaid MacCulloch has highlighted his transatlantic influence in New England. '[T]he works of Peter Martyr,' he writes, 'were turned into a sort of themed theological textbook. If you looked in the library ... at Harvard in 1636, I suspect that it would be the most thumbed book you would find.'[60] Samuel Morison noted that more copies of Vermigli were possessed by seventeenth century Harvard divinity students than of Calvin's works.[61] There can be little doubt that Martyr's influence found a favored place among the American Puritans. The Puritan John Cotton considered him one of the leading Protestant theologians along with Luther, Calvin and Melanchthon.[62] Cotton Mather recommended Vermigli's writings in his *Maducation ad Ministrium* and personally possessed seven volumes of Martyr's biblical commentaries.[63] Vermigli found his way to the American colonies and thus retained a significant hold on the theological imagination of both English and American Puritans.

IV. Conclusion

One of the more helpful fruits of recent reformation research has been the increasing recognition that the origins of Reformed theology do not derive exclusively or even primarily from John Calvin, but rather from a collaboration of like minded theologians, including (besides Calvin) Heinrich Bullinger, Peter Martyr Vermigli and Martin Bucer.[64] Vermigli's role in the development of English Protestantism reminds us that the vitality of Reformed thought was like a pebble dropped in an English pond: the ripples changed the theological landscape for well over a century.

NOTES

1. Patrick Collinson, 'England and International Calvinism: 1558-1640,' in Menna Prestwich, ed., *International Calvinism: 1541–1715* (Oxford: Oxford University Press, 1985), 214.

2. Charles Schmidt, *Peter Martyr Vermigli, Leben und ausgewahlte Schriften nach handschristlichen und gleichzeitigen Quellen* (Elberfeld: Verlag von R. L. Friderich, 1858), v: 'Wenige haben so viel getan wie er für die Begründung und Festelling der reformierten Kirchenlehre.'

3. Vermigli's only other contender would be Pier Paolo Vergerio, Bishop of Capodistria. Although he had risen to the rank of Bishop, Vergerio never reached the status of Vermigli as a major Protestant theologian. See Anne Jacobson Schutte, *Pier Paolo Vergerio: The Making of an Italian Reformer* (Geneva: Librairie Droz, 1977).

4. Gordon Huelin, 'Peter Martyr and the English Reformation' (Ph.D. diss., University of London, 1954), 178.

5. Vermigli served two terms in Strasbourg from December 1542 to October 1547 and again from November 1553 to July 1556. He was also in Oxford from November 1547 to October 1553 and finished his days at Zurich from July 1556 to November 1562.

6. It was almost certainly Bucer who recommended Vermigli to Cranmer. See Diarmaid MacCulloch, *Thomas Cranmer: A Life* (New Haven: Yale University Press, 1996), 174 .

7. Ibid., 380-383, 435-436, 551-552.

8. R.T. Kendall, 'The Puritan Modification of Calvin's Theology,' in *John Calvin: His Influence in the Western World*, ed. W. Stanford Reid (Grand Rapids: Zondervan, 1982), 199.

9. M[ary] Young, *The Life and Times of Aonio Paleario: The History of the Italian Reformers in the Sixteenth Century*, 2 vols. (London, 1860), II: 435.

10. Kendall, judges correctly that when Mary Tudor came to the throne in 1553, 'the name of Calvin, though known in England, was not revered nearly as much as those of Martyr, Bucer or Bullinger.' See his 'The Puritan Modification,' 199.

11. John Patrick Donnelly, *Calvinism and Scholasticism in Vermigli's Doctrine of Man and Grace*, (Leiden: E.J. Brill, 1976), 171.

12. See John Patrick Donnelly in collaboration with Robert M. Kingdon and Marvin

W. Anderson, *A Bibliography of the Works of Peter Martyr Vermigil,* Sixteenth Century Essays & Studies 13 (Kirksville, MO, Sixteenth Century Journal Publishers, 1990).

13. Leonard J. Trinterud, ed., *Elizabethan Puritanism,* (Oxford: Oxford University Press, 1971), 78.

14. Philip McNair, 'Biographical Introduction', in *Early Writings: Creed, Scripture and Church,* The Peter Martyr Library 1, ed. Joseph C. McLelland (Kirksville, MO: Sixteenth Century Journal Publishers, 1994), 12. He also wrote two smaller Eucharistic treatises on the famous Oxford debate of 1549, in which he represented the Protestant cause.

15. It was Theodore Beza who suggested that Vermigli's *Loci* be gathered into a book. See his letter to Bullinger, 1 July 1563, in *Correspondance de Theodore de Bèze,* ed. F. Aubert, H. Meylan and A. Tripet (Geneva: Librairie Droz, 1960-), IV: 162. The *Loci Communes* was not actually the work of Vermigli himself, but of Robert Masson (French Pastor in London) and was deliberately calibrated to coincide with the organizational structure of Calvin's *Institutes.* Reciprocally, the first Latin edition of the *Institutes* to appear in England, the Vautrollier edition of 1576, was keyed to the *Loci Communes* of Vermigli. This pattern of coordination between Calvin and Vermigli reflected the prevailing conviction that two of the most important Reformed theologians of this period were in significant theological agreement. This arrangement is splendidly maintained in the modern edition of the *Institutes,* edited by John T. McNeill and translated by Ford Lewis Battles.

16. J. C. McLelland, *The Visible Words of God: An Exposition of the Sacramental Theology of Peter Martyr Vermigli, 1500-1562,* (Edinburgh: Oliver and Boyd, 1957), 56-58.

17. William Nicholson, ed. *The Remains of Edmund Grindal, D.D.,* (Cambridge: Parker Society, 1843), 244-245. I have modernized slightly the English to make it clearer. Also cited in Marvin Anderson, 'Peter Martyr on Romans,' *Scottish Journal of Theology* 26 (1973): 401.

18. See Basil Hall, 'Puritanism: the Problem of Definition,' *Studies in Church History* (Oxford: Basil Blackwell, 1965), 283-296 and Peter Lake, 'Defining Puritanism – again?' in *Puritanism: Transatlantic Perspectives on a Seventeenth-Century Anglo-American Faith,* ed. Francis J. Bremer (Boston: Northeastern University Press for Massachusetts Historical Society, 1993), 3-54.

19. See J. I. Packer's introduction to Baxter's *The Reformed Pastor* (Edinburgh: Banner of Truth Trust, 1974), 9-19.

20. Patrick Collinson, *The Elizabethan Puritan Movement* (Oxford: Clarendon Press, 1967), 12-13.

21. Although there is debate among contemporary scholars about the extent to which the Puritan movement arose from the Marian exiles, the historical fact is that significant numbers of the exiles returned to positions of leadership in the Elizabethan church with a greater appreciation for continental reformed theology.

22. George C. Gorham, *Gleanings of a Few Scattered Ears, During the Period of the Reformation in England and of the Times Succeeding, AD 1533 to AD 1589,* (London, 1857), 306, (Vermigli letter to Calvin 3 November 1553), cited in C. H. Garrett, *The Marian Exiles: A Study in the Origins of Elizabethan Puritanism* (Cambridge: University Press, 1938), 48.

23. *Original Letters Relative to the English Reformation, 1531–1558,* ed. Hastings Robinson, 2 vols. (Cambridge: Parker Society, 1846-47), II: 514.

24. Garrett, *Marian Exiles,* 47. During the Marian disapora English exiles fled to various Protestant cites on the continent: among the more important were Emden, Zurich, Strasbourg, Frankfurt, Geneva, and Basel.

25. A. G. Dickens, *The English Reformation* (University Park, PA.: Pennsylvania State University Press, second edition, 1989), 339.

26. Garrett, *Marian Exiles*, 254.

27. Ibid., 258.

28. Ibid., 136.

29. Chilton L. Powell, *English Domestic Relations, 1487-1653* (New York, 1917), 75, cited by Donnelly, *Calvinism and Scholasticism*, 179.

30. McLelland, *The Visible Words*, 42.

31. Donnelly, *Calvinism and Scholasticism*, 181, notes that Sandys was living in Vermigli's home in Zurich when word reached them of Mary Tudor's death in 1558.

32. Gary Jenkins, 'Peter Martyr and the Church of England After 1558,' in Frank A. James III. Ed. *Peter Martyr Vermigli and the European Reformations*, Studies in the History of Christian Thought (Leiden: E.J. Brill, forthcoming , 2002).

33. Letter of 15 February 1551 from Hooper to Cranmer, cited by C. Hopf, *Martin Bucer and the English Reformation* (Oxford: Oxford University Press, 1946), 132.

34. *The Zurich Letters*, ed. Hastings Robinson, 4 vols. (Cambridge: Parker Society, 1842–45), IV: 66, (letter of Vermigli to Sampson on 4 November 1559).

35. Torrance Kirby, ' 'Relics of the Amorites' or 'Things Indifferent'? Peter Martyr Vermigli's Authority and the Threat of Schism in the Elizabethan Vestarian Controversy,' unpublished paper presented at the Sixteenth Century Studies Conference, (Denver, Colorado, October, 2001), 6.

36. Letter of Bullinger to Sampson and Humphrey, 1 May, 1566, *Zurich Letters*, 214-224.

37. See Peter Lake, *Anglicans and Puritans? Presbyterian and English Conformist Thought from Whitgift to Hooker* (London, 1988)

38. See for example, Whitgift, *Works*, Cambridge: Parker Society, 1845) , I: 484-85.

39. J. F. H. New, *Anglican and Puritan: The Basis of their Opposition 1558–1640* (Stanford: Stanford University Press, 1964), 59-60: that 'Peter Martyr ... was an acknowledged authority on sacramental theology ... respected by Anglican and Puritan alike.' . cf. Donnelly, *Calvinism and Scholasticism*, 179.

40. Iain Murray, *The Puritan Hope* (Edinburgh: Banner of Truth, 1971), 42.

41. Ibid., 44-45.

42. I. John Hesselink, 'The Millennium in the Reformed Tradition,' *Reformed Review* 52/2 (Winter, 1998–1999), 101-102.

43. Dan Shute, 'And All Israel Shall be Saved: Peter Martyr and John Calvin on the Jews According to Romans 9-11,' in Frank A. James III. Ed. *Peter Martyr Vermigli and the European Reformations*, Studies in the History of Christian Thought (Leiden: E.J. Brill, forthcoming , 2002).

44. Hesselink, 'Millennium,' 102

45. David S. Katz, *Philio-Semitism and the Readmission of the Jews to England 1603-1655* (Oxford, 1982), 94, 98, 123-124.

46. Shute, 'And All Israel Shall be Saved.'

47. John H. Leith, *Assembly at Westminster: Reformed Theology in the Making*, (Atlanta: John Knox Press, 1973), 32.

48. David W. Hall *Windows on Westminster: A Look at the Men, the Work and the Enduring Results of the Westminster Assembly (1643-1648)*, (Norcross, Georgia: Great Commission Publications, 1993), 150-151. Cf. Leith, *Assembly*, 46-47.

49. Leith, *Assembly*, 46.

50. Ibid.

51. I am indebted to Steven Casselli for the references to Burgess.

52. Anthony Burgess, *Vindiciae Legis Or A Vindication of the Morall Law and the Covenants, From the Errors of the Papists, Armininans, Socinians and more especially Antinomians* (London: James Young for Thomas Underhill, 1647), 3, 4, 20, 109,148,207, 208, 266.

53. Anthony Burgess, *A Treatise of Self-Judging, in order to the worthy receiving of the Lords Supper. Together with a Sermon of the generall Day of Judgement* (London: J. H. for T. Underhill & M. Keinton, 1658), 148. He cites Vermigli with reference to I Cor 11:31.

54. David Hall, *Windows on Westminster*, 16.

55. Thomas Gataker, 'The Life and Death of Peter Martyr' in *Abel redevivus: or, The dead yet speaking. The lives and deaths of moderne divines. Written by severall able and learned men (whose names ye shall finde in the Epistle to the Reader.) And now digested into one volumne, for the benefit and satisfaction of all those that desire to be acquainted with the Paths of piete and virtue*, Edited by Thomas Fuller (London: Tho. Brudenell for John Stafford, 1651), 205-216. I am indebted to Chad Van Dixhoorn for this citation.

5.6 Robert S. Paul, *The Assembly of the Lord: Politics and Religion in the Westminster Assembly and the 'G

rand Debate'* (Edinburgh: T. & T. Clark, 1985), 256.

57. John Strickland, *Immanuel, or The Church Triumphing in God with us. A sermon preached before the Right Honorable House of Lords, in the Abbey of Westminster; at their publique thanksgiving, November 5th 1644* (London: Matthew Simmons for Henry Overton, 1644) from Ps 46:7.

58. John Milton, *Tenure of Kings and Magistrates*, in *Works*, V: 25-26.

59. Arnold Williams, 'Milton and Renaissance Commentaries on Genesis,' *Modern Philology 37 (1939)*, 270.

60. Diarmaid MacCulloch, 'Can the English Think for Themselves? The Roots of English Protestantism,' *Harvard Divinity Bulletin* (Spring, 2001), 19.

61. Samuel Morrison, *Harvard College in the Seventeenth Century* (Cambridge: Harvard University Press, 1936), I: 273.

62. Cf. Perry Miller, *The New England Mind: The Seventeenth Century* (Cambridge: Harvard University Press, 1963), 104.

63. Giorgio Spini, 'Riforma Italiana e mediazione ginevrine nella nuova Inghilterra puritana' in *Ginevra*, edited by Delio Cantimori, (Florence: Sansoni, 1964), 477.

64. Richard A. Muller, *Christ and the Decree: Christology and Predestination in Reformed Theology from Calvin to Perkins*, (Durham, N.C., Duke University Press, 1988), 39. Cf. Donnelly, *Calvinism and Scholasticism*, 2, states that Reformed theology derived from a 'group of like-minded thinkers and scholars whose theologies developed along parallel lines during roughly the same period.' He includes such persons as: Beza, Viret, Farel and Myconius.

Puritan Preaching[1]

Joseph A. Pipa Jr.

The crowd waited expectantly as John Cotton mounted the great pulpit of St. Mary's church in Cambridge. His fame had drawn many to hear him preach the University sermon, for, even though a young man, he had already exhibited great learning and ability. In a previous University sermon he regaled the auditory with the eloquence of his witty and metaphysical style, which was the mark of high Anglican preaching. But as he began to preach, a wave of disappointment swept across the audience. This master orator was preaching in the form and plain style of the Puritans. What had happened? In the time-lapse between the two University sermons, John Cotton had been converted through the preaching of Richard Sibbes. His conversion affected the way he approached preaching. His biographer relates what happened:

> Hereupon Mr. Cotton resolved that he would preach a plain sermon, even such a sermon as in his own conscience he thought would be most pleasing unto the Lord Jesus Christ; and he discoursed practically and powerfully, but very solidly, upon the plain doctrine of repentance.[2]

Mr. Cotton did not easily reach this decision. When he had been invited to preach the University sermon at St. Mary's, he agonized on the horns of a dilemma:

On the one side, he considered that if he should preach with scriptural and Christian plainness, he should not only wound his own fame exceedingly, but also tempt carnal men to revive an old cavil, 'that religion made scholars turn dunces,' whereby the name of God might suffer not a little. On the other side, he considered that it was his duty to preach with such a plainness, as became the *oracles* of God, which are intended for the conduct of men and not for *theatrical* ostentations and entertainments, and the Lord needed not any *sin* of ours to maintain his own glory.[3]

His conflict with its resolution gives great insight into the philosophy of Puritan preaching. By the time Cotton preached this sermon (between 1610 and 1612), Puritan preaching was marked by a set form and style. This approach to preaching was not simply a party badge, but had developed out of theological convictions concerning the task of preaching. Therefore, in order to understand Cotton's new commitment, we need to survey briefly what was going on in Elizabethan pulpits.

The Puritans found themselves in a difficult situation. Not only was high Anglicanism besotted with corrupt practices of worship, but it also was infatuated with an approach to preaching that was soul stultifying. Prior to the second half of the 16th century there had principally been two main forms of sermon construction: the 'ancient' form and the 'modern' form. The 'ancient' form , which is the homily, originated with the Church Fathers. Blench writes,

The 'ancient' which was descended from the homilies of the Fathers, is without any elaborate scheme of arrangement peculiar to sermons, and consists either of the explication and application of a passage of Scripture (often the Gospel or Epistle of the Day), secundum ordinem textus; or of the topical treatment of any subject, according to reason and Scripture.[4]

The 'modern' form was more structured. Blench describes it as follows:

The 'modern,' which was the product of the university schools, shows the influence of Aristotelian logic rather than that of the form of the ancient classical oration.... In place of the usual six parts of the classical oration, Exordium, Narration, Division, Confirmation, Confutation and Conclusion, the 'modern' style consists of the following parts: the Theme; the Exordium or

Protheme or Antetheme; the Prayer; the Introduction of the Theme; the Division (with or without Subdivision); and lastly the Discussion.[5]

Since the Reformers were concerned to communicate the message of the Scripture to the people, they sought to simplify the sermon structure. They discarded the elaborate 'modern' form and used more simple methods of construction.[6] Some, like Calvin and many of the early English reformers, used the 'ancient' form. Others sought to simplify the 'modern' form and bring it more in line with the classical form of oratory.

Although the Reformers freed the 'modern' form from many of the scholastical accretions, the High Anglican preachers, trained in Aristotelian dialectic, soon began to abuse it. The order of the day was minute and fanciful divisions and subdivisions of the text, with a forced parallelism. If the sermon had four sub-points under the first section, it had to have four under the second. By this method, they forced the text into a straight jacket and often failed to teach the true meaning of the text. Consider as an example a sermon preached by Thomas Playfere on Luke 23:28. After introducing his text, he fancifully divides it into eight parts: 'In which sentence we may observe, as many words so many parts. Eight words, eight parts. the first, Weep Not: the second, but weep: the third, Weep not, but weep: the fourth, For me: the fifth, for yourselves: the sixth, for me, for yourselves: the seventh, weep not for me: the eight, but weep for yourselves.'

In addition to the abuses of form, the High Anglican preachers adopted a style that was overly elaborate and rhetorical. Under the influence of the court and the literary style of the day, some of the Elizabethan preachers adopted an ornate style of preaching. According to Blench, the ornate style had two forms – the florid and the witty.[7] Both of these forms make an abundant use of rhetorical devices such as repetition, heaping of examples, gradations or word-chains, and schemata. Moreover, both used innumerable quotations from the Church Fathers and various secular sources (frequently given in the original).

For the Puritans, such sermons were ceremonial swords, not the sharp two-edged sword of biblical preaching. It was in this context that the Puritans developed their philosophy of the practice of preaching – a practice that grew out of their theology of preaching.

Puritan Theology of Preaching

In order to understand Puritan preaching, we must begin with the Puritan theology of preaching. The Puritan theology of preaching was that of John Calvin.[8] Like him they exalted preaching as the supreme work of a pastor. For the Puritans preaching was their chief work because it was the chief work of Christ and his apostles.[9] William Gouge wrote in his learned commentary on Hebrews:

> If Christ the Lord vouchsafed to be a minister of the gospel, who shall scorn this function? The pope, cardinals, sundry bishops, and others that pretend to be Christ's vicars, are far from performing that which Christ did in this kind; and many that lay claim to Peter's keys, are far from observing the advice which he, for the right use of them, thus gave: 'Feed the flock of God which is among you, taking the oversight thereof, not by constraint, but willingly; not for lucre, but of a ready mind; neither as being lords over God's heritage, but being ensamples to the flock,' 1 Peter 5 v. 2, 3.[10]

The Puritans believed with Calvin that when the lawfully ordained man preached God's word, God Himself spoke, Gouge said:

> He who is sent of God, that is, set apart, according to the rule of God's word, to be a minister of the gospel, doth himself understand the mysteries thereof, and is enabled to make them known to others; he also standeth in God's room, and in God's name makes offer of salvation, 2 Corinthians 5:20. This moves men to believe and to be saved.[11]

To stand in God's room means not only to speak for God, but also that God spoke through the preacher. *The Larger Catechism* states this in response to question 160, *What is required of those that hear the word preached?* '...examine what they hear by the scriptures; receive the truth with faith, love, meekness, and readiness of mind, as the word of God.' Notice the last phrase, 'as the word of God.' The Reformers and the Puritans believed that when the lawfully ordained man preached the word it became the living word of God. They were not saying that the Bible becomes the Word of God in preaching; it never ceases to be the written Word of God. But it takes on a unique nature as the spoken Word of God in the act of preaching. Calvin says in the Institutes, '(H)e (God) deigns to consecrate to himself the mouths and tongues of men in order that his voice may resound in them.'[12] Paul teaches this clearly in Romans 10:14. How shall they believe in him whom they have not heard. Note it is not 'of whom they have not heard,' but 'whom they have not heard.' In other words Paul asks, 'How shall they hear Christ without a preacher?' When the lawfully ordained preacher proclaims the word Christ speaks through him. Thus the preached word becomes the living word.[13]

Thus for the Puritans the preaching of God's word was the primary means of grace. In a sermon on 1 Peter 2:2, Henry Smith applied the importance of the Bible to preaching: 'If ye did consider, my beloved, that ye cannot be nourished unto eternal life but by the milk of the word, ye would rather desire your bodies might be without souls, than your churches without preachers.'[14]

In another sermon on 1 Thessalonians 5:19-22, he stressed the importance of the preacher:

Have you need to be taught why Paul would have you make much of such? Because they are like lamps, which consume themselves to give light to others, so they consume themselves to give light to you; because they are like a hen, which clucketh her chickens together from the kite, so they cluck you together from the serpent; because they are like the shout, which did beat down the walls of Jericho, Joshua 6:20, so they beat down the walls of sin; because they are like the fiery pillar which went before the Israelites to the land of promise, so they go before you to the land of promise; because they are like good Andrew, which called his brother to see the Messias, John 1:41, so they call upon you to see the Messias; and therefore make much of such.[15]

The *Larger Catechism* points out the importance of preaching in question 155: *How is the word made effectual to salvation?*

The Spirit of God maketh the reading, but especially the preaching of the word, an effectual means of enlightening, convincing, and humbling sinners; of driving them out of themselves, and drawing them unto Christ; of conforming them to his image, and subduing them to his will; strengthening them against temptations and corruptions; of building them up in grace, and establishing their hearts in holiness and comfort through faith unto salvation.

The Puritans, therefore, devoted themselves to preaching and to a particular type of preaching.

The Distinguishing Characteristics of Puritan Preaching

How then did their theology effect their preaching? I would like to answer this question by discussing seven distinguishing marks of Puritan preaching.[16] It was scriptural, Christ-centered, logical, memorable, transforming, experimental, and clear. Though we ought not slavishly copy the puritan preaching, their approach, summarized by these seven marks, ought to shape our preaching.

First, the Puritans were committed to preaching that was Scriptural. We read of this commitment in the Westminster Directory of Public Worship: 'Ordinarily, the subject of his sermon is to be some text of scripture, holding forth some principle or head of religion, or suitable to some special occasion emergent; or he may go on in some chapter, psalm, or book of holy scripture, as he shall see fit.'[17]

According to them every sermon was to focus on the Word of God. They eschewed all cultural preaching, philosophical preaching, and social moralizing. This commitment was reflected in their emphasis on doctrine. The Puritans saw no conflict between doctrinal sermons and practical sermons. Doctrine is simply the unfolding of the meaning of Scripture. The Puritans believed that their people must know doctrine in order to live well. Their sermons were full of rich biblical truth.

They preferred the expository method, as we saw from the Westminster Directory, 'he may go on in some chapter, psalm, or book of holy scripture, as he shall see fit.' Oftentimes their method was more textual-topical than purely expository and they would at times miss the main point of the text, yet what they were attempting to do was to bring order to Calvin's expository method.

Their sermons were also scriptural in their method of illustration. Though they used illustrations from life and nature, they primarily used biblical allusions and references to open up the truth.

To summarize this first characteristic: their preaching was scriptural in content, method, and illustration. All faithful preaching must have this distinguishing characteristic.

The second mark of Puritan preaching was its Christ-centered nature. The Puritans had a much greater sense of the Christ-centered nature of the Bible than some moderns credit them. Packer says,

> Puritan preaching revolved around 'Christ, and him crucified' – for this is the hub of the Bible. The preachers' commission is to declare the whole counsel of God; but the cross is the center of that counsel,

and the Puritans knew that the traveller (sic) through the Bible landscape misses his way as soon as he loses sight of the hill called Calvary.[18]

Perkins concluded *The Art of Prophesying*: 'The heart of the matter is this: Preach one Christ, by Christ, to the praise of Christ.'[19] The Christ centered nature of their preaching and theology is illustrated in John Bunyan's *Pilgrim's Progress* and *Holy War*. Matthew Henry's *Commentary* is full of illustrations of the Puritan's emphasis on Christ. For example, commenting on David's defeat of Goliath, he wrote: 'David's victory over Goliath was typical of the triumphs of the son of David over Satan and all the powers of darkness, who he *spoiled, and made a show of them openly* (Col. 1:15), and we through him are *more than conquerors*.'[20] Again we can learn much from them in this essential element of preaching.

The third mark of the Puritan preaching was its logicality. They believed that God is logical and his revelation, though at times beyond our comprehension, is reasonable. Moreover, they believed that the proper way to approach the will and affections was through the mind. For them, the order was inviolable. First, one deals with the mind, convincing the person of the truth. Once convinced of the truth, he is ready to respond to that truth. To accomplish this chain of communication, they developed a particular structure of preaching called 'the new reformed method' or 'the triple schema,' which consists of doctrine, proofs, and uses. Perkins, who popularized the method in *The Art of Prophesying*, summarized it:

1. Reading the text clearly from the canonical Scriptures.
2. Explaining the meaning of it, once it has been read, in the light of the Scriptures themselves.
3. Gather a few profitable points of doctrine from the natural sense of the passage.
4. If the preacher is suitably gifted, applying the doctrines thus explained to the life and practice of the congregation in straightforward, plain speech.[21]

They began their sermons with a contextual introduction and a fairly brief exegetical discussion of the verse or verses with which they are dealing, explaining the terms and any particular grammatical construct that were important to the understanding of the text. Next they derived a doctrine from the text. That doctrine is not dissimilar from what we call a sermon proposition: a one-sentence summary of the truth taught in that text. Then they would offer a few proofs, primarily drawn from Scripture to support the truth derived from the text. Once the doctrine was confirmed they would then apply it in what they called 'uses.' Sometimes they would derive only one doctrine from a text, but other times they would derive two or three. In each instance, they would develop the doctrine with its proofs and uses before proceeding to the next doctrine.

In reality the triple schema was but a logical structure placed on the homiletical method used by John Calvin. Calvin preached by the 'Ancient Method.' He would explain a portion of his text, prove the truth, and apply it (In fact, though not consistently Calvin would use the terms 'doctrine' and 'use' in the development of a text.) The Puritans simply imposed method on Calvin's 'running commentary.'

Though we may not agree with their particular method, we should learn from them the importance of being logical and orderly in our preaching. Too often listening to some sermons is like sitting in a traffic jam in Atlanta or New York, moving only in fits and spurts, and really going nowhere. Our sermons need a logical order that gives coherence and momentum.

The fourth mark is closely connected to the third. The Puritans believed a sermon should be memorable. The triple schema, with its numbered heads, gave people handles by which to carry the sermon home. We might be overwhelmed by all the numbered headings, but in their day the sermons were very effective.[22] Horton Davies wrote:

> The Puritan sermon structure was simple because it drew its lessons as the narrative proceeded. It was amply illustrated by godly examples drawn from other parts of the Bible to supplement the text. It was easily remembered, because to reread the texts at home was to recall the preacher's commentary and application of the passage.[23]

The hearers were expected to review the sermon at home. On Monday mornings, Puritan schools masters required their students to recite the previous day's sermons. The Westminster Divines incorporated this responsibility into *The Larger Catechism* question 160, 'What is required of those that hear the word preached? ... meditate and confer (discuss) of it.' Thus, the Puritan preacher's responsibility was to structure the sermon in such a way that his hearers could remember it. We need to structure our sermons so that our hearers may remember and review our main points and application.

Fifth, the sermon was to be transforming. The holy practicality of truth was one of the trademarks of Puritan piety. In a sermon on James 1:22, Thomas Manton said:

> That doers of the word are the best hearers. That is good when we hear things that are to be done, and do things that are to be heard. That knowledge is best which is most practical, and that hearing is best which ended in practice.... That is wisdom, to come to the word so as we may go away the better.[24]

The Westminster Directory for Worship summarizes the Puritan commitment to application:

> He (the preacher) is not to rest in general doctrine, although never so much cleared and confirmed, but to bring it home to special use, by application to his hearers: which albeit it prove a work of great difficulty to himself, requiring much prudence, zeal, and meditation, and to the natural and corrupt man will be very unpleasant; yet he is to endeavour to perform it in such a manner, that his auditors may feel the word of God to be quick and powerful, and a discerner of the thoughts and intents of the heart; and that, if any unbeliever or ignorant person be present, he may have the secrets of his heart made manifest, and give glory to God.[25]

Modern reformed preaching, tends to concentrate mostly on content and gives little application. In fact, there are those that argue against making any exhortative application. The Puritans, though, like Calvin, believed that one had not preached until he had applied the word. William Haller wrote of their approach to the sermon:

> Their function was to probe the conscience of the down-hearted sinner, to name and cure the malady of his soul, and then to send him out strengthened and emboldened for the continuance of his lifelong battle with the world and the devil.[26]

As careful physicians of the soul, they carefully thought through what they were doing in application. They studied the various types of application that one should make. Building on the framework of 2 Timothy 3:16-17, *The Directory of Worship* identifies six types of application.[27] The first type is instruction or information, pointing out truths that were to be believed on the basis of the doctrine stated. The second is the confutation of false doctrines, drawing attention to theological errors that the doctrine of the text condemns. The third is exhortation to perform the duties required by the text. The fourth, is dehortation (reprehension and admonition), calling people to repent and turn from sinful thoughts, words, and acts. The fifth is comfort, bringing the hope and resources of the gospel to those who are troubled. And the sixth are notes of trial. '[S]igns clearly grounded on the holy scripture, whereby the hearers may be able to examine themselves whether they have attained those graces, and performed those duties to which he exhorteth, or be guilty of the sin reprehended, and in danger of the judgments threatened, or are such to whom the consolations propounded do belong.'

To these six types I add a seventh, doxological. Puritan sermons are full of the beauty and glory of God. You can scarcely read a Puritan sermon without being moved to adore our God.

In addition to types of hearers, the Puritans also gave a great deal of thought to the categories of hearers and what truths and emphases each type needed. William Perkins gives the most thorough catalogue.[28] He catalogued seven types of hearers. The first four categories are unconverted: the ignorant and unteachable, the ignorant but teachable, those who have knowledge but are not humbled, and those who are humbled. Perkins gave much practical advice on how to deal with each type as the preacher seeks to bring men and women to repentance and faith. The ignorant and unteachable need to be prepared to receive the gospel. This preparation consist of reasoning with them about their 'attitude and disposition' and reproving them of their sin, 'so that their consciences may be aroused and touched with fear and they may become teachable.' If it appears they have become teachable, declare to them in general terms the message of the Word. If they do not respond positively, but remain unteachable, they should be left.[29] The ignorant but teachable need to be instructed in the basic doctrines of the Christian religion by means of a catechism.[30] The unhumbled that have knowledge, need to be brought to a true view of their sin. Perkins said the preacher should be specific:

In order to arouse this legal sorrow it is appropriate to use some choice section of the law, which may reprove any obvious sin in those who have not yet been humbled. Sorrow for and repentance from even one sin is in substance sorrow for and repentance of all sin.[31]

With respect to the humbled, he says they should be probed as to the nature of their humility. The partially humbled need to hear the law, tempered with the gospel, and the fully humbled, faith and repentance, with the hope of the gospel pressed on them.[32] The Puritans did not withhold the Gospel, but they wisely used the law and gospel to deal with the unconverted.

Perkins next listed 3 types of Christians to be addressed in our preaching: those who believe, those who are fallen, and the mixed. Believers need to be taught the key doctrines of justification, sanctification and perseverance, along with the law as the rule of conduct. They also need to hear of the heinousness of sin that they might not fall into carnal security.[33] The fallen are those who have fallen in faith or lifestyle. There are two types of falling in faith: knowledge of the doctrine of the gospel and apprehension of Christ. If they have fallen into error they need to be instructed in the particular doctrine from which they have erred. Falling with respect to faith is to lose assurance of salvation. The preacher is to use trial and remedy. Trial is a search of the cause of temptation or of their estate. If they have lost assurance, because they have fallen into sin, they are to be brought to repentance and confession. Trial of their estate is to determine if they have truly come to Christ. He recommends two sets of questions: 'Do they hate sin *as sin*? That is the foundation of the repentance, which brings salvation. Then, secondly we must ask whether they have or feel in their heart a desire to be reconciled with God. This is the groundwork for a living faith.'[34] Remedy consisted of the application of some specific promises of the gospel.

To fall in lifestyle is to fall into the practice of some sinful behavior. Those who fall in practice are to be brought to repentance by the preaching of the law and the gospel.[35]

The last category, 'the mixed' refers to the nature of the congregation. I think that he has in mind something like 1 John 2:12-14, the fathers, the young men, and the children. Every congregation has a mixed auditory, and the preacher must be able to speak to them according to the needs of each.[36] If we just aim at baby Christians, we are doing a great disservice to a great portion of the flock of the Lord Jesus Christ. And if we just aim at the mature, we are not communicating the Gospel to the unconverted nor teaching the young Christian.

In their application, the Puritans also sought to teach the people how to work out the duties and how to die to sin. With respect to exhortation *The Directory* says, 'In exhorting to duties, he is, as he seeth cause, to teach also the means that help to the performance of them.'[37] The Puritans teach us that application is a science. You will not learn to make effective application overnight; you must begin to study and practice this great work.

The sixth mark was experiential or experimental. The Puritan preacher believed that he should preach known and felt truth. The heart of the theology of John Calvin is experiential theology. Truth is not sought as an end in itself, but rather as a means by which we know, love, and worship God. Charles Bridges writes, there must be 'an application of the didactic system to the sympathies of the heart.'[38] Each Christian should know the truth through his experience of it and let every experience be shaped by the truth. Preaching then must come from the heart and experience of the pastor to the heart and experience of God's people. John Owen said that preachers must experience in their own souls the power of what they preached:

> Without this they will themselves be lifeless and heartless in their own work, and their labour for the most part will be unprofitable towards others. It is, to such men, attended unto as a task for their advantage, or as that which carries some satisfaction in it from ostentation and supposed reputation wherewith it is accompanied. But a man preacheth that sermon only well unto others which preacheth itself in his own soul. And he that doth not feed on and thrive in the digestion of the food which he provides for others will scarce make it savoury unto them; yea, he knows not but the food he hath provided may be poison, unless he have really tasted of it himself. If the word do not dwell with power *in* us, it will not pass with power *from* us. And no man lives in a more woeful condition than those who really believe not themselves what they persuade others to believe continually. The want of this experience of the power of the gospel truth on their own souls is that which gives us so many lifeless, sapless orations, quaint in words and dead as to power, instead of preaching the gospel in the demonstration of the Spirit.[39]

If one preaches known belief and felt truth, one will preach with passion. On principle the Puritan preachers would never enter the pulpit without first having preached the sermon to themselves and warmed their hearts with its truth. When they applied it to themselves, they were on fire with what they had to preach. They teach us to preach from an experimental grasp of the truth. The experimental element is probably the most conspicuously absent element in modern reformed preaching. We need to learn to think and preach this way.

The last mark of Puritan preaching is clarity. In addition to the triple schema, the other hallmark of Puritan preaching was the plain style. The plain style was not a dull, drab, unadorned style, but rather a style of communication that was direct and in the language of the hearers. Rhetoric, therefore, took second seat to truth. To the Puritan it would have violated his hearers and the word of God to bypass the minds of the hearers with the tricks of rhetoric. They did not want to encrust the clear teaching of the word of God with metaphysical wit. John Owen, after describing a number of the rhetorical flourishes of the metaphysical styles wrote:

> Such things become not the authority, majesty, greatness, and holiness, of Him who speaks therein. An earthly monarch that should make use of them in his edicts, laws, or proclamations, would but prostitute his authority to contempt, and invite his subjects to disobedience by so doing. How much more would they unbecome the declaration of His mind and will, given unto *poor worms*, who is the great possessor of heaven and earth![40]

Positively, the Puritans adopted this style because it was designed for effective communication. If people were to be changed by the sermon, they had to understand and remember it. Plain style was part of a theory of communication that desired to make the word clear to the common people. The intent was not to dazzle, but to teach.

The plain style did not lack imagination and feeling. It was not devoid of metaphors, similes, and other figures. But rhetorical devices were not to be ends in themselves. Once his hearers understood the meaning of the text with its doctrines, the Puritan preacher wanted him to feel the truth. Rhetoric was the means to cement the truth into the heart. Richard Sibbes wrote in a preface to a treatise by John Smith:

This good man's aim was to convey himself by all manner of ways into the heart, which made him willingly heard of all sorts; for witty things only, as they are spoken to the brain, so they rest in the brain and sink no deeper; but the heart (which vain and obnoxious men love not to be touched), that is the mark a faithful teacher aims to hit. But because the way to come to the heart is often through the fancy, therefore this godly man studied lively representations to help men's faith by the fancy.[41]

Perkins develops the principles of plain style in chapter 10 of *The Art of Prophesying*. He emphasizes two things: the hiding of human wisdom, and the demonstration of the Spirit. Human wisdom is to be hidden both in the content of the sermon and in its delivery: 'The preaching of the word is the testimony of God, and the profession of the knowledge of Christ, and not of human skill. Furthermore, the hearers ought not to ascribe their faith to the gifts of men, but to the power of God's word.'[42] The preacher thus used a vocabulary readily grasped by his hearers. Most newspapers and magazines today are written at a Middle School level of vocabulary. We need to preach at that level. This commitment does not mean that we fail to use the great theological terms of the Bible; election, justification, sanctification, etc. We must not cheat our people by failing to expose them to the great words of Scripture. In using these terms, however, we should remember periodically to define them.

But there is more to plain style than just a philosophy of communication. It also stressed the spiritual nature of preaching. Perkins said that the demonstration of the Spirit is manifest when the audience judges that the Spirit is speaking through the words and gestures of the minister.[43] The work of the Spirit is evident when the minister's speech is spiritual and gracious. Spiritual speech is marked by words that are simple and clear, expressing the majesty of the Spirit. The minister's language must be plain so that the people will understand him.[44] Gracious speech is manifest when the grace of the heart is evident in the sermon. Gracious speech includes both the grace of a holy life and the grace of the ministry. A minister must be a holy man. After pressing the importance of ministerial holiness, Perkins listed six things that comprise the grace of life: 1) a good conscience, 2) an inward feeling of the doctrine to be delivered, 3) the fear of God, 4) the love of the people, 5) sobriety and constancy of life, and 6) temperance.[45]

The grace of ministry includes three things: 1) aptness to teach, 2) authority in teaching, and 3) zeal in teaching. A minister must demonstrate the appropriate gifts for preaching. And his preaching should bear the marks, the authority and zeal of the Holy Spirit that is best described by the term unction. Perkins combines plainness and unction:

> To preach in the demonstration of God's Spirit is to preach with such plainness, and yet with such power, that even the least intellectually gifted recognize that it is not man but God himself who is teaching them. Yet at the same time, the conscience of the mightiest may feel not man but God reproving them through the power of the Spirit.[46]

Pierre Marcel gives an excellent definition of unction:

> When, in preaching, a man abandons himself to the freedom of the Spirit, he discovers that his faculties are developed above normal: freedom is given not only to the soul but also to the tongue, his mental penetration is deeper; his ability to picture things in his mind is greater; truth works a greater power in his soul; his faith is more intense; he feels himself involved in a living and compact reality. His feelings are much more sensitive and spontaneously permeate his heart. He comes to think the thoughts of Christ, to experience the feelings and emotions of Christ.... The spirit endows his word, his expression, with a natural freshness and vitality which gives the word a new and original appearance *and which belong only to the spoken style.*[47]

The minister must prayerfully seek the ministry of the Spirit both during his preparation and for his proclamation. Baxter exhorted in *The Reformed Pastor*:

> Our whole work must be carried on under a deep sense of our own insufficiency, and of our entire dependence on Christ. We must go for light, and life, and strength to him, who sends us on the work.... Must I daily plead with sinners about everlasting life and everlasting death, and have no more belief or feeling of these things myself.... Prayer must carry on our work as well as preaching; he preacheth not heartily to his people, that prayeth not earnestly for them. If we prevail not with God to give them faith and repentance we shall never prevail with them to believe and repent?[48]

When the Spirit is upon a man there will be an obvious zeal in his preaching. This zeal will manifest itself in each man differently, according to his gifts and personality, but each man must preach with a passion. Richard Baxter insists on the need to have one's heart stirred up:

> I confess I must speak it by lamentable experience, that I publish to my flock the distempers of my own soul. When I let my heart go cold, my preaching is cold; ... and so I can oft observe also in the best of my hearers that when I have grown cold in preaching, they have grown cold too; and the next prayers which I have heard from them have been too like my preaching[49]

Later he gives this counsel:

> O sirs, how plainly, how closely, how earnestly, should we deliver a message of such moment as ours, when the everlasting life or everlasting death of our fellow-men is involved in it! Methinks we are in nothing so wanting as in this seriousness; yet is there nothing more unsuitable to such a business, than to be slight and dull. What! Speak coldly for God, and for men's salvation? Can we believe that our people must be converted or condemned, and yet speak in a drowsy tone? In the name of God, brethren, labour to awaken your own hearts, before you go to the pulpit, that you may be fit to awaken the hearts of sinners. Remember they must be awakened or damned, and that a sleepy preacher will hardly awaken drowsy sinners. Though you give the holy things of God the highest praise in words, yet, if you do it coldly, you will seem by your manner to unsay what you said in the matter.... The manner, as well as the words, must set them forth....
>
> Though I move you not to constant loudness in your delivery (for that will make your fervency contemptible), yet see that you have a constant seriousness; and when the matter requireth it (as it should do, in the application at least), then lift up your voice, and spare not your spirits, Speak to your people as to men that must be awakened, wither here or in hell.[50]

The Directory of Worship summarizes the basic elements of plain style:

> Plainly, that the meanest may understand; delivering the truth not in the enticing words of man's wisdom, but in demonstration of

the Spirit and of power, lest the cross of Christ should be made of none effect; abstaining also form an unprofitable use of unknown tongues, strange phrases, and cadences of sounds and words; sparingly citing sentences of ecclesiastical or other human writers, ancient or modern, be they never so elegant.[51]

These seven distinguishing characteristics marked John Cotton's sermon preached at St. Mary's. He preached in a way that was Scriptural, Christ centered, logical, memorable, transforming, experimental, and plain. These marks are summarized in *The Larger Catechism* 159, '*How is the word of God to be preached by those that are called thereunto?*'

They that are called to labour in the ministry of the word, are to preach sound doctrine, diligently, in season and out of season; plainly, not in the enticing words of man's wisdom, but in demonstration of the Spirit, and of power; making known the whole counsel of God; wisely, applying themselves to the necessities and capacities of the hearers; zealously, with fervent love to God and the souls of his people; sincerely, aiming at his glory, and their conversion, edification, and salvation.

Today Puritan preaching receives a good deal of bad press. I agree, however, with J. I. Packer when he says, 'the well-being of the church today depends in large measure on a revival of preaching in the Puritan vein.'[52] Though we ought not to mimic their sermon structure and must not fall into Elizabethan language patterns (they of all people would caution us against this), the seven characteristics of their preaching are timeless. Let us learn from them.

NOTES

1. I thank the editor for the privilege of contributing to this Festschrift in honor of Dr. Clair Davis. I have adapted some of the material in this chapter from my dissertation 'William Perkins and the Development of Puritan Preaching.' I did the work at Westminster Theological Seminary in Philadelphia and Dr. Davis served as my Advisor. I fondly remember our afternoon discussions in the faculty lounge as he asked the probing questions and helped me to stay on track. Then as now, he combined the attitude of a scholar with the heart of a pastor.
2. Cotton Mather. *Magnalia Christi Americana; or The Ecclesiastical history of New England.* 2 vols. (Edinburgh: The Banner of Truth Trust, 1979), 1:256.
3. Ibid., 1:256.

4. J.W. Blench. *Preaching in England in the Late Fifteenth and Sixteenth Centuries. A Study of English sermons 1450–1600.* (Oxford: Basil Blackwell, 1964), 71-2.

5. Ibid., 72.

6. Ibid., 87.

7. A. F. Herr. *The Elizabethan Sermon.* (New York: Octagon Books, 1969), 89-103. See also Blench, 188.

8. For an excellent study of Calvin's Theology of preaching see Pierre Marcel. *The Relevance of Preaching.*

9. Horton Davies. *The Worship of the English Puritans.* (London: Dacre Press, 1948), 183.

10. William Gouge. *Commentary on Hebrews.* (Grand Rapids: Kregel Publications, 1980), 101

11. Ibid., 101.

12. John Calvin. *Institutes of the Christian Religion.* 2 vols. (Philadelphia: The Westminster Press, 1967), 2. 1018.

13. Pierre Marcel. *The Relevance of Preaching.* (Seoul/New York: Westminster Publishing House, 2000), 21,22. See the *Second Helvetic Confession* says in chapter 1, entitled *The Preaching of the Word of God is the Word of God.*

14. Henry Smith. *Works.* 2 vols. (Edinburgh: James Nichol, 1866), 1:495.

15. Ibid., 1:135.

16. J. I. Packer. *A Quest for Godliness.* (Wheaton: Crossways Books, 1990), pp.

17. 'The Directory for the Publick Worship of God.' *The Westminster Confession of Faith.* (Inverness: The Publications Committee of the Free Presbyterian Church of Scotland, 1985), 379.

18. Packer, 286.

19. Perkins, 79.

20. Matthew Henry. *Matthew Henry's Commentary on the Whole Bible* (6 vols.). (McLean, VA: Macdonald Publishing Company) vol. II, 378.

21. Perkins, 79.

22. Some of the printed sermons with innumerable headings probably were not preached that way. In some cases they were printed from the more exhaustive preparation of the minister, and he did not preach all the points. On other occasions they were printed from notes of the hearers, without being edited.

23. Horton Davies. *Worship and Theology in England form Cranmer to Hooker 1534–1603.* (Princeton: Princeton University Press, 1970), 307.

24. Thomas Manton. *The Complete Works of Thomas Manton.* 22 vols. (Worthington, PA: Maranatha Publications), 4: 153.

25. *The Directory*, p. 380.

26. Haller, 27

27. *Directory*, 380.

28. Perkins, 56-73.

29. Ibid., 56.

30. Ibid., 56.

31. Ibid., 58.

32. Ibid., 59.

33. Ibid., 59, 60.

34. Ibid., 61.

35. Ibid., 62.

36. Ibid., 62.

37. *Directory*, 380.

38. Charles Bridges. *The Christian Ministry.* (London: The Banner of Truth Trust,

1967), 259.

39. John Owen. *The Works of John Owen*. 16 vols. (London: The Banner of Truth Trust, 1967), 16:76.

40. John Owen. *An Exposition of Hebrews*. 4 vols. (Marshalltown, DE: The National Foundation for Christian Education, 1960), 1:52.

41. Richard Sibbes. *Works of Richard Sibbes*. 7 vols. (Edinburgh: The Banner of Truth Trust, 19e73–82), ci.

42. Perkins, 71.

43. Ibid., 72,73.

44. Ibid., 72.

45. Ibid., 74.

46. Ibid., 86.

47. Pierre Marcel. *The Relevance of Preaching*. (Grand Rapids: Baker Book House, 1977), 100, 101.

48. Richard Baxter. *The Reformed Pastor*. (Edinburgh: The Banner of Truth Trust, 1974.), 122, 123.

49. Ibid., 61.

50. Ibid., 147f.

51. Directory, 381.

52. Packer, 281.

WILLIAM PERKINS
ON
PREDESTINATION, PREACHING, AND
CONVERSION

Joel R. Beeke

'I am fully aware that liberty places me on a tightrope – a greased, slippery one – but I have no intention of falling.' So said union chief Lech Welesa when released by Soviet-backed militia in Poland.

Similarly, when Elizabethan England's premier Puritan preacher William Perkins (1558–1602)[1] proceeded (eighteen years prior to his untimely death at age 44) to write, teach, and preach predestinarian theology, he stepped forward on a taut theological cable, stretched between his conviction that God must be glorified in all things and his concern for the salvation of sinful men. Perkins believed that the proper balance between divine sovereignty and human responsibility depended on preaching that was practical, experimental,[2] and predestinarian. Interweaving supralapsarian predestination with experimental soul-examination, Perkins attempted the daring feat of setting forth a lively order of salvation (*ordo salutis*) that challenged all people, whether converted or not, to search for the fruits of predestination within their own souls on the basis of Christ's work.

Perkins, often called the 'father of Puritanism,'[3] has been evaluated by many scholars.[4] They have offered positive as well as negative commentary about his political, ethical, revivalistic, and ecclesiastical interests, but many have also offered contradictory assertions about his theological stand.[5] In the areas of predestination and preaching, this commentary has been particularly divisive.[6]

While Perkins cannot escape all charges of promoting confusion with his tightrope theology, his synthesis of decretal and experimental predestination is Christologically stable and a natural outgrowth of Calvinism. It is particularly faithful to the theology of Theodore Beza, which promotes a healthy combination of Reformed theology and Puritan piety.[7] I reject William H. Chalker's assertion that Perkins kills Calvin's theology as well as Robert T. Kendall's thesis that Beza – and thus Perkins – differ substantially from the Genevan Reformer. Rather, I concur with Richard Muller, who says, 'Perkins's thought is not a distortion of earlier Reformed Theology, but a positive outgrowth of the systematic beginnings of Protestant thought.'[8]

The Influence of William Perkins [9]

Perkins had exceptional gifts for preaching and an uncanny ability to reach common people with plain preaching and theology. He pioneered Puritan casuistry – the art of dealing with 'cases of conscience' by self-examination and scriptural diagnosis.[10] Many were convicted of sin and delivered from bondage under his preaching. The prisoners of the Cambridge jail were among the first to benefit from his powerful preaching. Thomas Fuller said that Perkins 'would pronounce the word *damne* with such an emphasis as left a dolefull Echo in his auditours ears a good while after.... Many an Onesimus in bonds was converted to Christ.'[11]

In time Perkins – a rhetorician, expositor, theologian, and pastor – became the principle architect of the young Puritan movement. His vision of reform for the church, combined with his intellect, piety, book writing, spiritual counseling, and communication skills enabled him to set the tone for seventeenth-century Puritans – in their accent on Reformed, experiential truth and self-examination, and in their polemic against Roman Catholicism and Arminianism. By the time of his death, Perkins's writings in England were outselling those of Calvin, Beza, and Bullinger combined.[12] He 'moulded the piety of a whole nation,' H. C. Porter said.[13] Eleven posthumous editions of Perkins's writings, containing nearly fifty treatises, were printed by 1635.[14] Perkins's influence continued through such theologians as William Ames (1576–1633), Richard Sibbes (1577–1635), John Cotton (1585–1652), and John Preston

(1587–1628). Perkins's ministry is what Cotton considered the 'one good reason why there came so many excellent preachers out of Cambridge in England, more than out of Oxford.'[15]

The translation of Perkins's writings prompted greater theological discussion between England and the Continent.[16] J. van der Haar records 185 seventeenth-century printings in Dutch of Perkins's individual or collected works,[17] twice as many as any other Puritan.[18] He and Ames, his most influential student on the continent, influenced Gisbertus Voetius (1589–1676) and numerous Dutch *Nadere Reformatie* (Dutch Second Reformation) theologians.[19] At least fifty editions of Perkins's works were printed in Switzerland and in various parts of Germany.[20] His writings were also translated into Spanish, French, Italian, Irish, Welsh, Hungarian, and Czech.[21]

In New England, nearly one hundred Cambridge men who led early migrations, including William Brewster of Plymouth, Thomas Hooker of Connecticut, John Winthrop of Massachusetts Bay, and Roger Williams of Rhode Island, grew up in Perkins's shadow. Samuel Morison remarks that 'your typical Plymouth Colony library comprised a large and a small bible, Ainsworth's translation of the Psalms, and the works of William Perkins, a favorite theologian.'[22] 'Anyone who reads the writings of early New England learns that Perkins was indeed a towering figure in their eyes,' writes Perry Miller. Perkins and his followers were 'the most quoted, most respected, and most influential of contemporary authors in the writings and sermons of early Massachusetts.'[23]

The Immovable Will of God: Preaching Predestination
A Christocentric Supralapsarian Position

Though William Perkins rejoiced with other Englishmen at the defeat of Spain – and Rome – in the Armada, the battle with anti-Calvinists was far from over.[24] Deploring the way in which students were avoiding Protestant writers, Perkins determined to tell everyone that he stood for the truth – the Calvinist doctrine.[25]

Primarily concerned with the conversion of souls and subsequent growth in godliness, Perkins believed that a biblical realization of God's sovereign grace in predestination was vital for spiritual comfort and assurance. He believed that predestination worked out experimentally in the souls of believers was inseparable from sovereign predestination in Christ. Far from being harsh and cold, sovereign predestination was the foundation upon which experimental faith could be built. It was the hope, expectation, and guarantee of salvation for the true believer.

In the introduction to his *Armilla Aurea* (1590), translated as *A Golden Chaine* (1591),[26] in which he first articulates his doctrine of predestination, Perkins identifies four viewpoints:

- The old and new Pelagians, who place the cause of predestination in man, in that God ordained men to life or death according to his foreknowledge of their free will rejection or receiving of offered grace.
- The Lutherans, who teach that God decided to choose some to salvation by His mere mercy but to reject the rest because He foresaw they would reject His grace.
- The semi-Pelagian Roman Catholics, who ascribe God's predestination partly to mercy and partly to foreseen human preparations and meritorious works.
- Finally, those who teach that the cause of the execution of God's predestination is God's mercy in those who are saved and man's fall and corruption in those who perish, but that the divine decree concerning both has no other cause than His will and pleasure.

Perkins concludes, 'Of these four opinions, the three former I labour to oppugn as erroneous, and to maintain the last, as being truth which will bear weight in the balance of the sanctuary.'[27]

The most notable feature of Perkins's *Golden Chaine* is his supralapsarian doctrine of double predestination. It is outlined in his famous chart titled: 'A Survey or Table declaring the order of the causes of salvation and damnation according to Gods word.'[28] Like Theodore Beza's chart, though more detailed, Perkins's chart begins with God and His decree of predestination, is divided into two chains of causes for the execution of election and reprobation, then traces the orderly progression of those executions from the eternal decrees of God to the final consummation of all things, where the elect and reprobate mutually end in glorifying God.

Predestination is the means by which God manifests the glory of the Godhead outside of Himself to the human race. He returns glory to Himself via mercy to the elect and justice to the reprobate. Both proceed from His sovereignty. Election is God's decree 'whereby on his owne free will, he hath ordained certaine men to salvation, to the praise of the glorie of his grace.' Reprobation is 'that part of predestination, whereby God, according to the most free and just purpose of his will, hath determined to reject certaine men unto eternal destruction, and miserie, and that to the praise of his justice.'[29]

Pure glory and absolute sovereignty in double predestination: these are the heartbeats of Perkins's theology. Like Beza, Perkins upheld a supralapsarian position by denying that God, in reprobating, considered man as fallen. He also used Beza's argument for support, that the end is first in the intention of an agent. Thus God first decided the end – the manifestation of His glory in saving and damning – before He considered the means, such as creation and the fall. [30] Ultimately, predestination must not be understood in terms of what it does for man, but in terms of its highest goal – the glory of God.

As a theological tightrope walker, Perkins knew that his supralapsarian view prompted two objections: (1) it makes God the author of sin; (2) it subordinates Christ.[31] In addressing the first objection, Perkins adamantly rejected the idea that God is the author of sin. Yes, God permitted the fall of man, but that doesn't mean that he caused the fall, Perkins said. He explained how God was not the cause of the fall by using the illustration of an unpropped house in a windstorm. As an unsupported house would fall with the blowing of the wind, so man without the help of God falls. Thus, the cause of the fall may not be imputed to the owner but to the wind.

Likewise, when God left Adam to himself, He did not will Adam's fall or cause his sin. Rather, Adam's fall was due to his own wilful disobedience of God in eating the forbidden fruit. Without constraint, men willingly fall from integrity. And God leaves them to their own desires, freely suffering them to fall. As Perkins says, we must not think that man's fall was by chance, or by God's failure to know it, or by barely winking at it, or by permitting it, or by allowing it against his will. Rather, miraculously, it happened, 'not without the will of God, yet without all approbation of it.'[32]

God did not make Adam sin. He did not infuse corruption in any form or withdraw any gift that had been Adam's from creation. He merely ceased for a time to give Adam the grace necessary to stand. He did not confer the confirming grace that He had every right to withhold.

The devil and Adam – not God – are responsible for sin. The devil is guilty because he tempted Adam to sin as representative head of the entire human race, and Adam is guilty for voluntarily falling away from God and His help. The proper cause of the fall, according to Perkins, was ' the diuell [devil] attempting our ouerthrow, and Adams will, which when it began to bee prooued by tentations [temptations], did not desire Gods assistance, but voluntarily bent it selfe to fal away.'[33]

Perkins denied that God creates anyone to damnation; rather, He creates the reprobate to manifest His justice and glory in their deserved damnation. God decreed damnation not as damnation but as an execution of His justice. Sin, therefore, is not an effect but a consequence of the decree of reprobation. Sin, however, is the meriting cause of actual damnation.[34]

This distinction is critical for Perkins's theological balancing act between supralapsarianism and God's freedom from sin. God decides to forsake some men not only 'in order that Adam and his posterity might know that they could fall by themselves, but also that they could not stand, much less rise again,' Perkins says.[35] God did not forsake men because He found them in sin. Rather, as every man is like a lump of clay in the potter's hand, so God, according to His sovereign will, makes vessels of wrath. Reprobation must not be grounded in God foreseeing that sinners would reject Him, for this would make reprobation depend upon men. Rather, for His own wise, sovereign reasons, God fitted vessels for wrath by the first act of reprobation (sovereign will of decree) as well as by the second act of reprobation (an ordination to just punishment on account of voluntary sin).

Though Adam's fall allows no one to make any claim on God, the holy God wills to take His elect out of the mass of mankind for His own everlasting love and glory.[36] The elect become vessels of God's mercy solely out of God's will and without regard to their good or evil. They are ordained to salvation and heavenly glory.

Along with Calvin, Dort, and Westminster, Perkins would wholeheartedly concur that reprobation is both sovereign and just.[37] No one is the victim of injustice, for God is under no obligation to grant mercy to sinners. The decree of creation and the fall is the means God used to allow Adam and his posterity to fall away from Him, but also to carry predestination to its glorious, happy end in Christ-centered salvation. Only in the sense that Adam's fall opened the way for the sacrifice of Christ upon the cross can Perkins call it a 'happy fault,' for no matter how tragic sin may be, it cannot compare to the righteousness of Christ.

In sum, God stands above and beyond human sin – though He chooses to save some men out of it. He is not the author of sin, for

He is never unjust. 'It stands more with equitie a thousand fold, that all the creatures in heaven and earth should jointly serve to set forth the glory and maijestie of God the creator in their eternall destruction, then the striking of a flie or the killing of a flea should serve for the dignities of all men in the world,' Perkin concludes.[38] Indeed, without sovereign predestination God's glory would be lost and all mankind would be lost. Thus God must be glorified as divine Goldsmith for the salvation of the elect in Christ and as divine Potter for the damnation of the reprobate outside of Christ.

As for the charge that supralapsarianism subordinates Christ, Perkins firmly maintains that not election *per se,* but election *in Christ* draws the line of separation between the elect and reprobate. Contrary to accusations, Perkins emphasizes Christ-centered predestination. For Perkins, salvation is never focused on a bare decree, but always upon the decreed Christ. The election and work of Christ is not commanded by God's decree; rather, it is voluntarily chosen by the Son.

Perkins goes on to say that this act – i.e., the purpose of saving or conferring glory, as he explains in more detail in *A Treatise of Predestination* – has 'no inward impulsive cause over and beside the good pleasure of God: and it is with regard to Christ the Mediator, in whom all are elected to grace and saluation; and to dreame of any election out of him, is against all sense: because he is the foundation of election to be executed, in regard of the beginning, the meanes, and the end.'[39]

Perkins states that there are five degrees in the act of election: 'the ordaining of a Mediatour, the promising of him beeing ordained, the exhibiting of him beeing promised, the applying of him beeing exhibited or to bee exhibited, and the accomplishment of the application.' He then adds: 'The ordaining of a Mediatour is that, whereby the second person beeing the Sonne of God, is appointed from all eternitie to bee a Mediatour betweene God himself and men. And hence it is that Peter saith, that Christ was foreknowne before the foundation of the world. And well saith Augustine, that Christ was predestinated to bee our head. For howsoeuer as hee is the substantiall word (*logos*) of the Father, or the Sonne, hee doth predestinate with the Father, and the Holy Ghost; yet as hee is the Mediator, hee is.'[40]

With approval, Perkins quotes Cyril, who wrote, 'Christ knoweth his sheepe, electing and foreseeing them unto euerlasting life.' He also cites Augustine, who wrote, 'Christ by his secret dispensation hath out of an unfaithful people predestinated some to euerlasting liberty, quickening them of his free mercy: and damned others in euerlasting death, in leauing them by his hidden iudgement in their wickednesse.'[41]

Perkins was more Christ-centered in his predestinarianism than most scholars realize. Breward, who is usually sympathetic to Perkins, attributes the 'withering Christ' view to Perkins. Breward is correct in saying that Perkins's 'definition of theology was a combination of Peter Ramus and John Calvin, and the arrangement of the whole work [*A Golden Chaine*], prefaced as it was by a formidable looking diagram, owed a good deal to Ramist categories of arrangement and aristotelian logic.'[42] But he errs in failing to add Perkins's 'in Christ' note in this summary: 'Calvin insisted that Christ was the mirror in which we contemplated election; Perkins taught that predestination was a glass in which we beheld God's majesty.'[43]

Though Perkins centered predestination in a Trinitarian framework more than Calvin did, by no means did his views denigrate Christ. It is true that Perkins was influenced by the Italian, Girolamo Zanchi, who was less Christocentric in predestination and was more grounded in scholastic theology and aristotelianism. For this reason, some scholars, including Breward, have assumed a lack of Christocentrism in Perkins, which is unfortunate as well as unjustified.[44]

Muller offers a more accurate picture of Perkins's Christocentric predestination.[45] He takes Perkins seriously when Perkins says that to dream of an election outside of Christ is 'against all sense!'[46] From the framework of High Calvinism, specifically, a Christocentric, supralapsarian position, Perkins believed that preaching predestination meant proclaiming the whole counsel of God from eternal, decretal sovereign pleasure to eternal, sovereign glory via a divine soteriological chain of election and reprobation. To this chain, viewed from God's side as the means of decretal execution, we must now turn.

Sovereign Pleasure to Sovereign Glory: A Golden Chain of Election and Reprobation

In his most famous work, *Armilla Aurea* (*A Golden Chaine*, 1591), Perkins stresses that the will of God in Christ is immovable, not only in sovereign decree, but also in the execution of sovereign decree. The title page expresses this conviction by describing *A*

Golden Chaine as *THE DESCRIPTION OF THEOLOGIE, Containing the order of the causes of Saluation and Damnation, according to Gods word. A view whereof is to be seene in the Table annexed. Hereunto is adioyned the order which M. Theodore Beza vsed in comforting afflicted consciences.*[47]

The next page, which contains 'The Table', shows that Perkins bases his soteriological system on election and reprobation as the primary structuring principle of his theology. 'The redde [gray] line sheweth the order of the causes of saluation from the first to the last [and] the blacke line, sheweth the order of the causes of damnation,' Perkins says. This order of causes leads to the image of a chain in which all the links are inseparably united.[48] Thus, every individual is tied to his predetermined destiny, which is inescapably linked to divine covenant grace in Christ or inevitable divine wrath outside of Christ. Neither the elect nor the reprobate is able to break out of this chain of eternal destiny; any attempts to do so will be futile, for all are tied to the eternal decree of predestined election or reprobation.

The foundation of Perkins's theology is that God not only decreed man's destiny but also the means through which the elect might attain eternal life, and without which the reprobate could not be saved. The means are grounded in the execution of predestination, which involves its foundation in Jesus Christ; its being carried out in the covenants of works and grace; and its becoming made evident through calling, justification, sanctification, and glorification.

The Foundation of Decretal Execution: Jesus Christ
Predestination does not affect anyone apart from the work of Jesus Christ. Thus Perkins states that, from God's viewpoint, the reprobate has no possibility of salvation because he has absolutely no link with Christ in the golden chain. Without Christ, man is totally hopeless.

Christ is the foundation of election, as the center column of Perkins's chart shows. He is predestined to be Mediator. He is promised to the elect. He is offered by grace to the elect. And, finally, He is personally applied to their souls in all His benefits, natures, offices, and states.[49]

This Christ-centeredness is what sets Perkins's theological chart apart from Beza's *Tabula*. Perkins's chart is similar to Beza's in showing the following contrasts:

- God's love for His elect versus His hatred for the reprobate
- The effectual calling of the elect versus the ineffectual calling of the reprobate
- The softening of the heart of the elect versus the hardening of the heart of the reprobate
- Faith versus ignorance
- Justification and sanctification versus unrighteousness and pollution
- The glorification of the elect versus the damnation of the reprobate.

In his diagram, Perkins shows that the 'imputation of righteousness' to believers is achieved only through faith in Christ. Faith is grounded in 'the holiness of [Christ's] manhood,' and His 'fulfilling of the law.' Sanctification follows the imputation of righteousness. The mortification of sinful flesh, results from faithful apprehension of Christ's accursed death, His burial, and His 'bondage under the grave.' The believer's new life grows out of Christ's resurrection. Perkins's diagram, therefore, emphasizes how Christ's work applies to every part of the order of salvation. In sum, Perkins's chart asserts that the God-centeredness of election is paralleled by the Christ-centeredness of salvation.[50]

The Means of Decretal Execution: The Covenant of Works and the Covenant of Grace

After introducing Christ as the foundation of election, Perkins explains how election is carried out through the two covenants. Although his chart does not show this connection, a major part of his discussion falls under covenantal headings.[51]

Incorporating parts of Calvin's covenant concept as well as Beza's system, Perkins explains that God's covenant is 'his contract with man concerning the obtaining of life eternall, upon a certen condition. This covenant consisteth of two parts: God's promise to man, Man's promise to God. God's promise to man, is that, whereby hee bindeth himselfe to man to bee his God, if hee performe the condition. Man's promise to God, is that, whereby he voweth his allegiance unto his Lord, and to performe the condition betweene them.'[52]

In a dipleuric (two-sided) view of covenant, the pact between God and man implies voluntary action: God makes demands, and man obeys. This view is consistent with Perkins's emphasis on apprehending Christ's benefits to unbolt the door that prevents the application of such benefits. To this Perkins adds a monopleuric (one-sided) view of covenant as a testament in which sinners are made heirs through God's gracious and unmerited gift of salvation in Christ.

Perkins combines these views of covenant as if no tension exists between them. He validates both, first by making a sharp distinction between the antelapsarian covenant of works and the postlapsarian covenant of grace. The former is God's covenant 'made with condition of perfect obedience and is expressed in the moral law.'[53] After the fall, the covenant of works still finds expression in the Ten Commandments. This law contains two parts: the edict, which commands obedience; and the condition, eternal life to those who fulfill the law. No fallen man can obey the law, of course, which only serves to bind man to God and His grace all the more. After a lengthy discussion of the Ten Commandments, Perkins states that the use of the law is:

- 'To lay open sinne, and make it knowne'
- 'To effect and augmente sinne'
- 'To denounce eternall damnation for the least disobedience, without offering any hope of pardon' which shows man his need for God and leads him to repentance that 'frees' him in Christ
- To guide the regenerate 'to new obedience'.

Because the law condemns man, God has established the covenant of grace, 'whereby God freely promising Christ and his benefits, exacts againe of man, that hee would by faith receive Christ, and repent of his sinnes.' Just as the law is linked with the covenant of works, so the gospel is tied to the covenant of grace. [54]

By teaching how this covenant of grace operates, Perkins offers another way to relieve the tension between God's sovereignty and man's responsibility. Without the covenant of grace, man cannot fulfill God's demands, whereas with it, man finds his will renewed through the Holy Spirit to the point that he is capable of choosing repentance. In Perkins's diagram, man becomes active in 'mortification and vivification' which lead to 'repentance and new obedience.' For Perkins, conversion is the point of reconciliation around which the monopleuric and dipleuric aspects of covenant theology can unite. This allowed the Christian life, considered as a covenantal warfare of conscience, to be systematized and stated as a vast series of 'cases of conscience.' It also allowed the covenant to be presented in the form of a voluntary act by the regenerate in their search for personal assurance. The greatest case of conscience would naturally be 'whether a man be a childe of God or no,' that is, whether a man is savingly brought into the covenant of grace and converted.[55]

Consequently, Perkins could say that though faith and repentance are the conditions of the covenant of grace, man is totally incapable of initiating or meriting the covenant relation through any goodness or obedience in himself. Ultimately, the decree of election and the covenant of grace is based upon the good pleasure of God. God chooses to be in covenant with man; God initiates the covenant relation; God freely, out of His sovereign will alone, invites man into the covenant of grace by granting him conditional faith and repentance. The decreeing, establishing, and maintaining of the covenant are all dependent on the free grace and sovereign will of God. Man does not tie up God, as Perry Miller claims; rather, God ties Himself to man in covenant.

In sum, for Perkins, the covenant brings to our understanding in time what God has already done past understanding from eternity. The covenant is God's condescending love, which, far from dragging God down to man's level – as Perry Miller implies[56] – constrains the elect to exalt their sovereign God all the more. For Perkins, God retains sovereign control of the covenant: predestination is the primary structuring principle of theology, and covenant the way in which God works it out via preaching.

The Degrees of Decretal Execution: Effectual Calling, Justification, Sanctification, Glorification

According to Perkins, God shows 'degrees of loue [love]' in carrying out election in Jesus Christ by means of covenant. Effectual calling, the first part of the process, represents the saving grace 'whereby a sinner beeing severed from the world, is entertained into God's family.'[57]

The first part of effectual calling is a right hearing of the Word by those who were dead in sin; their minds are illuminated by the Spirit with irresistible truth. The preaching of the Word accomplishes two things: 'the Law shewing a man his sin and the punishment thereof, which is eternall death' and 'the Gospel, shewing saluation by Christ Jesus, to such as beleeue [believe].'

Both become so real that 'the eyes of the mind are enlightened, the heart and eares opened, that he [the elect sinner] may see, heare, and vnderstand the preaching of the word of God.'[58]

The second part of this process is the breaking of the sinner's heart. It is 'bruised in peeces [under the preaching of the Word], that it may be fit to receiue Gods sauing grace offered vnto it.' To accomplish this, God uses four 'principall hammers':

- The knowledge of the law of God
- The knowledge of sinne, both original and actual, and what punishment is due vnto them
- Compounction, or pricking of the heart, namely a sense and feeling of the wrath of God for the same sinnes
- An holy desperation of a man's own power, in the obtaining of eternall life.[59]

The product of effectual calling is saving faith, which Perkins defines as 'a miraculous and supernatural facultie of the heart, apprehending Christ Iesus being applyed by the operation of the holy Ghost, and receiuing him to it selfe.'[60] The act of receiving Christ is not something that man does in his own strength; rather, by Spirit-wrought faith the elect receives the grace that Christ brings, thereby bringing the believer into union with every aspect of Christ's saving work through faith. According to Perkins, God 'accepts the very seeds and rudiments of faith and repentance at the first, though they be but in measure, as a grain of musterd seede.'[61]

Once a sinner has been effectually called, he is justified. According to Perkins, justification, as the 'declaration of God's loue,' is the process 'whereby such as beleeue, are accounted iust before God, through the obedience of Christ Iesus.' The foundation of justification is the obedience of Christ, expressed in 'his Passion in life and death, and his fulfilling of the Law ioyned [joined] therewith.' Christ frees the elect from the debt of fulfilling the law 'every moment, from our first beginning, both in regard of purity of nature and purity of action,' and of making 'satisfaction for the breach of the law.' Christ is become our surety for this debt, and God accepts His obedience for us, 'it beeing full satisfaction.' Justification thus consists of 'remission of sins, and imputation of Christ's righteousnesse.'[62] It takes place when a sinner is brought before God's judgment seat, pleads guilty, and flees to Christ as his only refuge for acquittal.[63] Justification is clearly a judicial, sovereign act of God's eternal good pleasure.

Justification includes other benefits as well. Outwardly it offers reconciliation, afflictions that serve as chastisements rather than punishments, and eternal life. Inwardly, it offers peace, quietness of conscience, entrance into God's favor, boldness at the throne of grace, an abiding sense of spiritual joy, and intimate awareness of the love of God.[64]

Sanctification, the third part of this process, receives more attention from Perkins than any other part. He defines sanctification as that work 'By which a Christian in his mind, in his will and in his affections is freed from the bondage and tyranny of sin and Satan and is little by little enabled through the Spirit of Christ to desire and approve that which is good and walk in it.'

Sanctification has two parts. 'The first is mortification when the power of sin is continually weakened, consumed and diminished. The second is vivification by which inherent righteousness is really put into them and afterward is continually increased.'[65] Sanctification includes a changed life, repentance, and new obedience – in short, the entire field of 'Christian warfare.' All the benefits of salvation that begin with regeneration are tied to a living relationship with Jesus Christ, to whom the believer is bound by the Holy Spirit. Perkins was optimistic about sanctification, not because of anything in man, but entirely because of Christ Jesus (1 Cor. 1:30).

Perkins taught that just as a fire without fuel will soon go out; so, unless God of His goodness, by new and daily supplies continues His grace in His children, they will grow cold and fall away.[66]

After sanctification comes the final step: glorification. This part of God's love is 'the perfect transforming of the Saints into the image of the Sonne of God,' Perkins says. Glorification awaits the fulfillment of the Last Judgment, when the elect shall enjoy 'blessednesse ... whereby God himselfe is all in all his elect.' By sovereign grace the elect will be ushered into perfect glory, a 'wonderfull excelencie' that includes beholding the glory and majesty of God, fully conforming to Christ, and inheriting 'the new heauens and the new earth.'[67]

God's Hatred of the Reprobate

Perkins's chart reveals that he developed reprobation as carefully as he did election. Indeed, the dark chain of reprobation from man's perspective is really a golden chain from God's perspective, for it, too, issues in the glory of God at the last.

According to Perkins, there are two types of reprobates: those who are not called, and those who are called, but not effectually. Those with no calling proceed from 'ignorance and vanitie of minde' to 'heart hardening' to 'a reprobate sense' to 'greedines in sinne' to 'fulnes of sinne.' Those who are called may go as far as 'yielding to God's calling' – which may include 'a generall illumination, penitence, temporarie faith, a tast [taste], [and] zeale' – before they 'relapse' into sin by means of 'the deceit of sinne, the hardening of the heart, an euill heart, an vnbeleeuing heart, [and] apostasie.' Ultimately, also the ineffectually called are led to 'fullnes of sinne,' so that the two streams of reprobates become one prior to death. For the reprobate, all calls remain ineffectual because all fail to bring them to Christ. Taken captive by their own sins, of which the greatest sin is 'an vnbeleeuing heart,' the reprobate make themselves ripe for divine judgment and damnation.[68]

Understanding the covenantal grace in Christ and inescapable wrath outside of this grace inevitably prompts questions, such as 'Am I one of God's favored elect? How can I avail myself of the salvation wrought in Christ? How can I be sure that I have true faith? If reprobates can also behave in ways that seem motivated by grace, how can I know whether I am a child of God?'[69]

The preacher must address such critical questions, for preaching predestination decretally necessitates preaching predestination experimentally and practically. Sinners must be shown how God, from His immovable will, moves the will of man. They must be biblically instructed how to look for marks of predestination and covenant inclusion in their own hearts, and be closely questioned if they are working out their election by a life consonant with God's choice.

Perkins's concluding argument questions readers concerning 'the right applying of Predestination to the persons of men.' The elect are known only to themselves and to God. They do not know that from 'the first causes of election, but rather from the last effects thereof – the testimonie of Gods Spirit and the works of Sanctification.'[70]

Someone who lacks this testimony should not conclude that he is reprobate, however. Rather, he should seek the aid of God's Word – particularly in preaching – and in the sacraments so that he might feel the power of Christ in him.

The Moved Will of Man: Predestinarian Preaching

The Need for Predestinarian Preaching: Bringing in the Elect

No Puritan was more concerned about preaching than William Perkins. Detesting the substitution of eloquence for the 'lost art' of preaching, Perkins led the Puritan movement to reform preaching. He did this in his instructions to theological students at Cambridge; in his manual on preaching, *The Arte of Prophecying*, which quickly became a classic among Puritans; in advocating a method and plain style of preaching in his own pulpit exercises; and, above all, in stressing the experimental application of predestinarian doctrines.

Ultimately, it was the lack of this notion of predestinating grace as personally experienced (rightly called 'experimental predestinarianism')[71] that Perkins missed in the preaching of his day. Fighting against Elizabethan opposition to experimental predestinarianism, Perkins told listeners that good preachers were hard to find. He urged rulers and magistrates to support universities and theological schools that produced experimental preachers. Without such support, good pastors would decline from 'one of 1,000' to 'not one in 2,000.'[72]

Perkins viewed preaching as the 'mighty arme of God' to draw in the elect, or the chariot on which salvation comes riding into the hearts of men. He defined preaching as 'prophecying in the name and roome of Christ, whereby men are called to the state of grace and conserued in it.'[73] In essence, Perkins's goal was to help preachers realize their responsibility as God's instruments to explain election and the covenant. Biblically balanced preaching was paramount, for the Word preached is the power of God unto salvation, without which there would be no salvation.[74] With such a high view of preaching, Perkins did not hesitate to assert that the sermon was the climax of public worship.

For Perkins, preaching was the gateway to heaven. There were four ways to listen to it, however.

- People could hear the Word without zeal.
- They could listen, know, and even approve the Word.
- They could hear and taste the Word.
- They could hear the Word and yield in obedience to it.

Of these four ways of listening, only the last is 'effectual hearing,' Perkins says, for those who are ordained to salvation are also ordained to the means. The elect respond favorably to the Word as willing servants, whereas the reprobate, who hear the Word and may even be led by the Spirit to understand God's will in it, do not respond in obedience to it.[75]

Since the elect are only known to God, Perkins assumed that everyone who listened to a sermon could potentially be gathered into gospel grace. He thus pressed every sinner to accept God's offer of salvation in Christ. The gospel promise must be offered freely to every hearer as a 'precious jewel,' Perkins said.[76] At the same time, he explained that there were two ways of regarding election: 'One especially whereby God knows who are his. The other is more generall, whereby we repute all men to bee Elect that professe faith in Christ, leaving secret iudgments to God. Thus Paul writes to the Ephesians, Philippians, & [etc.] as Elect. And the ministers of the word are to speake to their congregations, as to the Elect people of God.'[77]

This effectively eliminates any need for a preacher to determine who might be elect and who might be reprobate. Rather, a preacher must so clearly preach the marks of saving grace that, with the help of the Holy Spirit, the sinner's heart may confirm God's judgment concerning his eternal welfare.

Preaching sound theology is totally consistent with the serious intent to save souls, says Perkins, for the purpose of preaching is to deliver souls from hell and to make sinful men into new creatures like Christ. Perkins calls preaching the way to 'lay hold of Christ,' to 'repair the image of God,' and to 'form Christ in the hearts of all believers.'[78] The elect are not just called by preaching, then neglected; rather, preaching serves as a continual 'converter' in repairing the image of God in a believer.

The Essence of Predestinarian Preaching: Proclaiming the Moving Work of God

According to Perkins, the golden chain of salvation (effectual calling, justification, sanctification, and glorification) is applied to the elect via the preaching of God's covenant. Consequently, Perkins was not only interested in preaching God's sovereign grace to His elect from eternity but also God's covenant acts of salvation by which election is realized. He was deeply concerned about how this personal, redemptive process breaks into man's experience – how the elect respond to God's overtures and acts as well as how the will of God is carried out in the hearts of the elect.[79]

The Divine Goldsmith: Preaching Election
The stages of human transformation in true conversion, according to Perkins, can be listed under the following four headings: humilation, faith, repentance, and new obedience.

The First Step in Conversion: Humiliation. Perkins includes four 'actions of grace' that flow out of this first step of conversion:

- Attentive hearing of the Word. With this grace, 'The ministrie of the word [and with it] some outward or inward crosse, breake and subdue the stubborness of our nature, that it may be plyable to the will of God.'
- Awareness of God's law. With this grace, 'God brings the minde of man to a consideration of the Law, and therein generally to see what is good and what is euill.'
- Conviction of sin. With this grace, 'God makes a man particularly to see and know his owne peculiar and proper sinnes, whereby he offends God.'
- Despair of salvation. With this grace, 'God smites the heart with a legall feare, whereby when man seeth his sinnes, he makes him to feare punishment and hell, and to despaire of saluation, in regard to any thing in himselfe.'

These four actions are 'workes of preparation' that precede the work of grace. Perkins does not consider these to be fruits of grace, since the reprobate may actually go this far in the process of temporary faith. This prompts some critics to label Perkins as a preparationist. But that is not accurate for two reasons: First, these works are not attributed to the hearers (as is the case in preparationism) but are wrought in the hearers by the Spirit's grace. Second, a careful reading of Perkins shows that he sees these actions as preparatory, not because they do not show saving grace in the elect, but rather because it would be impossible to know if these steps were saving until a person went beyond these actions to further actions of grace. As Shaw says, 'All these works could be wrought in the lives of the non-elect by a common operation of the Spirit but when in retrospect a true believer analyzed these steps they were in fact works of regeneration and therefore fruits of faith.'[80]

It does not appear that Perkins ever addressed the question of whether a sinner who died before progressing beyond these four steps was truly saved. He probably would have begged the question by stating that God will lead all His elect to further stages of faith in Christ, for Perkins did not attribute to fallen man any ability in his natural will to move Godward.

The Second Step in Conversion: Faith in Christ. In this second step of conversion, the divine Goldsmith smelts out the impurities of false faith and grants His elect true, saving faith. With these actions, the reprobate and elect are definitively separated. This step also includes four actions (actions #5-8), which do the following, according to Perkins:

- Stirre vp the minde to a serious consideration of the promise of saluation, propounded and published in the Gospell.
- Kindle in the heart some seedes or sparkes of faith, that is, a will and desire to beleeue, and grace to striue against doubting and despaire.
- Fight with doubting, despaire, and distrust, [evidenced by] feruent, constant and earnest inuocation for pardon: and ... a prevailing of this desire.
- [Experience that] God in mercy quiets and settles the Conscience, as touching the saluation of the soule, and the promise of life, whereupon it resteth and staieth it selfe.[81]

For Perkins, faith is a supernatural gift given by God to the sinner to take hold of Christ with all the promises of salvation.[82] The object of faith is not the sinner or his experiences or faith itself; it is Jesus Christ alone. Faith sees Christ, first, as the sacrifice on the cross for the remission of sins, then learns to experience Him as the strength to battle temptation, the comfort in a storm of affliction, and ultimately as everything needed in this life and in the life to come.[83] In sum, faith shows itself when 'euery seuerall person doth particularly applie vnto himselfe, Christ with his merits, by an inward persuasion of the heart which commeth none other way, but by the effectuall certificate of the Holy Ghost concerning the mercie of God in Christ Iesus.'[84]

Faith has no meaning outside of Jesus Christ. 'Faith is ... a principall grace of God, whereby man is ingrafted into Christ and thereby becomes one with Christ, and Christ one with him,' Perkins says.[85] All of Perkins's references to faith as an 'instrument' or 'hand' must be understood in this context. Faith is a gift of God's sovereign pleasure that moves man to respond to Christ through the preaching of the Word. Yet precisely at the moment when Christ is received, faith responds to the gift of grace. Thus the response is most active when it has completely yielded to and is centered in the Person it has received.

This concept of faith, within the context of covenant, is the genius of Perkins's theology. His intense concern for the godly life rises alongside his equally intense concern to maintain the Reformation principle of salvation by grace alone. For man is never granted salvation because of faith but by means of faith. There are five steps in saving faith:

- Knowing the gospel by the illumination of God's Spirit.
- Hoping for pardon, 'whereby a sinner, albeit hee yet feeleth not that his sinnes are certenly pardoned, yet hee beleeueth that they are pardonable'.
- Hungering and thirsting after the grace offered in Christ Jesus, 'as a man hungreth and thirsteth after meate and drinke.'
- Approaching the throne of grace, 'that there flying from the terrour of the Law, hee may take holde of Christ, and finde fauour with God.' The first part of this is 'an humble confession of our sinnes before God particularly, if they be knowne sins, and generally, if vnknowne.' The second part is 'crauing pardon of some sinnes, with vnspeakeable sighes, and in perseuerance.'
- Applying, by the Spirit's persuasion, 'vnto himselfe those promises which are made in the Gospel.'[86]

These steps of faith are dependent upon the preaching of the Word of God as well as the inner witness of the Spirit, which leads to a personal assurance of having been 'grasped' by God's grace to embrace Christ. In this context, Perkins develops his major contribution to the discussion of assurance by making a distinction between *weak faith* and *strong faith*. Weak faith is like a grain of mustard seed or smoking flax, 'which can neither giue out heat nor flame, but only smoke.' Weak faith has low levels of illuminating knowledge and of applying to the promises (the first and last steps of saving faith mentioned above), but shows itself by 'a serious desire to beleeue, & an endeauour to obtaine Gods fauour.' God does not despise even the least spark of faith, Perkins says, providing the weak believer diligently uses the means of grace to increase it. He must 'stirre vp his faith by meditation of Gods word, serious prayers, and other exercises belonging vnto faith.'[87]

For Perkins, even weak faith is a 'certaine and true' persuasion, since there can be no doubt in faith, but strong faith is a 'full perswasion of the heart, whereby a Christian much more firmly taking hold on Christ Iesus, maketh full and resolute account that God loueth him, and that he will giue to him by name, Christ and all his graces pertaining to eternall life.'[88] Strong faith, or 'full assurance,' claims God's promises as a personal possession. Then, Perkins says, 'to beleeue in Christ, is not confusedly to beleeue that he is a Redeemer of mankind, but withal to beleeue that he is my Sauiour, and I am elected, iustified, sanctified, and shall be glorified.'[89]

Perkins thus moves with his golden chain from God's assurance of salvation from eternity to the elect's assurance in time. The chain of divine sovereignty, covenant-establishment, mediatorial satisfaction, faith in Christ and the Spirit's corroborating witness, results in assurance within the soul through what was called the 'practical syllogism' *(syllogismus practicus)*. A practical syllogism is, simply put, a conclusion drawn from an action. It involves three components: a major premise, a minor premise, and a conclusion. The basic form of the syllogism Perkins uses when it pertains to salvation is as follows:

> *Major premise:* Those only who repent and believe in Christ alone for salvation, are children of God.
> *Minor premise:* By the gracious work of the Spirit, I repent and believe in Christ alone for salvation.
> *Conclusion:* Therefore I am a child of God.[90]

Though assurance by syllogism provides only secondary grounds of assurance that depend on the primary grounds (the sovereign work of the Father, the redeeming work of the Son, and the applying work of the Spirit), such assurance is nonetheless real and vital. Packer agrees: 'In my opinion, Perkins was right, first to analyse conscience as operating by practical syllogisms, and second to affirm that scriptural self-examination will ordinarily yield the Christian solid grounds for confidence as to his or her regeneration and standing with God.'[91]

Perkins stresses that the human spirit's syllogistic response to the inward, saving work of the Triune God does not degrade Christ in any way. Rather, it magnifies the unbreakable strength of God's golden chain of salvation merited by the Son and applied by His Spirit. Though one might argue that Perkins linked these secondary grounds of assurance to a personal profession of faith, these grounds were only valid as evidence of the primary grounds. With Calvin, Perkins maintained that works do not save the elect, but often succeed in assuring them. Works are the evidence of election, not the cause of it.[92]

The Third Step of Conversion: Repentance. In saying that repentance follows faith, Perkins does not mean legal repentance but evangelical repentance that refines the soul and persuades the elect to live wholly unto God, hating sin and loving obedience for His sake. Such repentance, which corresponds with his ninth action of grace, flows from the conviction that 'we have offended so merciful a God and loving Father' and produces a wholehearted changed toward God in 'the mind and whole man in affection, life and conversation.'[93]

Like Luther and Calvin, Perkins sees repentance as a lifelong process. It is not merely the start of the Christian life; it *is* the Christian life. It involves growth in holiness that is marked by continual confession of sin. Perkins went so far as to say, 'The chiefest feeling that we must have in this life, must be the feeling of our sinnes.'[94]

For Perkins, repentance is a necessity; without it a person must question whether he has true faith. Repentance is a necessary condition of the covenant, but happily, God enables the believer to fulfil that condition. Perkins was no voluntarist. 'He that turnes to God must first of all be turned of God, and after that we are turned, then we repent,' he wrote.[95] The Spirit uses the gospel to reveal the way of repentance, though He also uses the law to serve as a guide in the believer's repentant life.[96]

The Fourth Step of Conversion: New Obedience. This step of conversion, in which grace reaches its climax, corresponds with Perkins's tenth action of grace, which he defines as 'new obedience when the believer obeys the commands of God and begins to walk in newness of life'.[97]

Three things are necessary in this step:

- It must be a fruit of the spirit of Christ in us, 'for when we doe any good thing, it is Christ that doth it in us'.
- It requires keeping every commandment of God.
- It involves striving to keep the whole law in every part of a sinner's 'minde, will, affections, and all the faculties of soule and body.'

According to Perkins, this means the sinner 'must not live in the practise of any outward sinne.' It also means 'there must be in him an inward resisting and restraining of the corruption of nature, and of the heart, that he may truly obey God, by the grace of the spirit of God.' And it means that he exercises the inward man 'by all spirituall motions of Faith, Joy, Love, Hope and the praise of God.'[98]

New obedience augments the believer's assurance, strengthening the conscience by the means of grace, such as prayer and the sacraments. True prayer and a right use of the sacraments strengthen the believer's faith that he is elect.

Believers must press on in obedience, even if Spirit-given assurance diminishes in the midst of strong temptations. As long as they are 'in this world according to their own feeling, there is an access and recess of the Spirit,' Perkins said.[99] Lack of feeling could be due to a weak conscience, strong doubts, failure to grasp any part of the golden chain of salvation, or simply the Spirit's sovereignty. The testimony of the Spirit, which can be temporarily lost at any moment, emphasizes the need for continual self-examination, repentance, and obedience.

Perkins makes a serious attempt to link divine election with Reformed piety. The elect walk in godly piety as the fruit of divine decree, he says. They perform good works, but only in the strength of Christ who must cleanse these works from remnants of corruption. The Triune God of sovereign grace proves His elect in His fiery furnace to bring them forth as gold, shaped and formed according to His sovereign will. Indeed, on the Day of Judgment, all remaining imperfections will be removed. The golden chain will be finished to the glory of an electing God.

The Divine Potter: Preaching Reprobation

The reprobation of the divine Potter must be preached to warn the ungodly to flee from sin and seek grace to obey the revealed will of God as well as for the benefit of the elect, Perkins says. Preaching reprobation helps the elect in three ways:

- It shows how far a reprobate can go in the appearance of 'actions of grace'. Reprobation preaching lovingly urges the elect to seek further exercises of grace and to make their calling and election sure in Christ (2 Pet. 1:10).

- It moves the godly to examine themselves for marks of election.
- It provides an antidote to pride and a foundation for grateful humility before the Lord, who chose His own purely out of sovereign grace.[100]

This teaching of Perkins is evident in Dort's 1618-1619 doctrine of reprobation, in 'illustrating and recommending' (I, 15) the elect to humble thanksgiving and complete self-negation before God. Three decades after Dort, this teaching also became part of the Westminster Confession, which states that double predestination grants the elect 'matter of praise, reverence, and admiration of God; and of humility, diligence, and abundant consolation.'[101]

Conclusion

Perkins earned the titles of both 'scholastic, high Calvinist' and 'father of pietism'.[102] His theology affirms divine sovereignty in the predestination decree of the Father, the satisfaction made by Christ for the elect, and the saving work of the Spirit. Yet, Perkins never allows sovereignty to prevent a practical, evangelical emphasis on the individual believer working out his own salvation as hearer of the Word, follower of Christ, and warrior of the conscience. Divine sovereignty, individual piety, and the gospel offer of salvation are always in view.

Perkins's emphasis on sound doctrine and the reform of souls influenced Puritanism for years to come.[103] J. I. Packer writes, 'Puritanism, with its complex of biblical, devotional, ecclesiastical, reformational, polemical and cultural concerns, came of age, we might say, with Perkins, and began to display characteristically a wholeness of spiritual vision and a maturity of Christian patience that had not been seen in it before.'[104]

Contemporary scholars have called Perkins 'the principal architect of Elizabethan Puritanism', 'the Puritan theologian of Tudor times,' 'the most important Puritan writer,' 'the prince of Puritan theologians,' 'the ideal Puritan clergyman of the quietist years,' 'the most famous of all Puritan divines,' and have classed him with Calvin and Beza as third in 'the trinity of the orthodox.'[105] He was the first theologian to be more widely published in England than Calvin and the first English Protestant theologian to have a major impact in the British isles, on the continent, and in North America. Little wonder that Puritan scholars marvel that Perkins's rare works remained largely unavailable until now.[106]

NOTES

1. I am indebted to D. Clair Davis, my dissertation advisor and longtime friend, for arousing my interest in Perkins in the early 1980s.

2. Experimental or experiential preaching addresses how a Christian experiences the truth of Christian doctrine in his life. The term *experimental* comes from *experimentum,* meaning trial, and is derived from the verb, *experior,* to know by experience, which in turn leads to 'experiential,' meaning knowledge gained by experiment. Calvin used experimental and experiential interchangeably, since both words indicate the need for measuring experienced knowledge against the touchstone of Scripture. Experimental preaching seeks to explain in terms of biblical truth how matters ought to go, how they do go, and what is the goal of the Christian life. It aims to apply divine truth to the whole range of the believer's personal experience as well as in his relationships with family, the church, and the world around him. Cf. Robert T. Kendall, *Calvin and English Calvinism to 1649* (New York: Oxford University Press, 1979), pp. 8-9; Joel R. Beeke, 'The Lasting Power of Reformed Experiential Preaching' (Morgan, Penn.: Soli Deo Gloria, forthcoming 2002).

3. Puritanism has been variously defined. I use the term 'Puritans' here of those who desired to reform and purify the Church of England and were concerned about living a godly life consonant with the Reformed doctrines of grace. As J. I. Packer writes, 'Puritanism was an evangelical holiness movement seeking to implement its vision of spiritual renewal, national and personal, in the church, the state, and the home; in education, evangelism, and economics; in individual discipleship and devotion, and in pastoral care and competence.... It was Perkins, quite specifically, who established Puritanism in this mould' *(An Anglican to Remember – William Perkins: Puritan Popularizer,* St. Antholin's Lectureship Charity Lecture [1996], pp. 1-2).

4. Dissertations and theses that contribute to an understanding of Perkins's theology include Ian Breward, 'The Life and Theology of William Perkins' (Ph.D., University of Manchester, 1963); William H. Chalker, 'Calvin and Some Seventeenth Century English Calvinists' (Ph.D., Duke University, 1961); Lionel Greve, 'Freedom and Discipline in the Theology of John Calvin, William Perkins, and John Wesley: An Examination of the Origin and Nature of Pietism' (Ph.D., Hartford Seminary Foundation, 1976); Robert W. A. Letham, 'Saving Faith and Assurance in Reformed Theology: Zwingli to the Synod of Dort,' 2 vols. (Ph.D., University of Aberdeen, 1979); R. David Lightfoot, 'William Perkins' View of Sanctification' (Th.M., Dallas Theological Seminary, 1984); Donald Keith McKim, *Ramism in William Perkins's Theology* (New York: Peter Lang, 1987); C.C. Markham, 'William Perkins' Understanding of the Function of Conscience' (Ph.D., Vanderbilt University, 1967); Richard Alfred Muller, 'Predestination and Christology in Sixteenth-Century Reformed Theology' (Ph.D. Duke University, 1976); Charles Robert Munson, 'William Perkins: Theologian of Transition' (Ph.D. dissertation, Case Western Reserve, 1971); Willem Jan op't Hof, *Engelse piëtistische geschriften in het Nederlands, 1598–1622* (Rotterdam: Lindenberg, 1987); Joseph A. Pipa, Jr., 'William Perkins and the Development of Puritan Preaching' (Ph.D., Westminster Theological Seminary, 1985); Victor L. Priebe, 'The Covenant Theology of William Perkins' (Ph.D., Drew University, 1967); Mark R. Shaw, 'The Marrow of Practical

Divinity: A Study in the Theology of William Perkins' (Ph.D., Westminister Theological Seminary, 1981); Paul R. Schaefer, Jr., 'The Spiritual Brotherhood on the Habits of the Heart: Cambridge Protestants and the Doctrine of Sanctification from William Perkins to Thomas Shepard' (Ph.D., Keble College, Oxford University, 1994); Rosemary Sisson, 'William Perkins' (M.A., University of Cambridge, 1952); C. J. Sommerville, 'Conversion, Sacrament and Assurance in the Puritan Covenant of Grace to 1650' (M.A., University of Kansas, 1963); Young Jae Timothy Song, *Theology and Piety in the Reformed Federal Thought of William Perkins and John Preston* (Lewiston, New York: Edwin Mellin, 1998); Lynn Baird Tipson, Jr., 'The Development of a Puritan Understanding of Conversion' (Ph.D., Yale University, 1972); J. R. Tufft, 'William Perkins, 1558–1602' (Ph.D., Edinburgh, 1952); Jan Jacobus van Baarsel, *William Perkins: eene bijdrage tot de Kennis der religieuse ontwikkeling in Engeland ten tijde, van Koningin Elisabeth* ('s-Gravenhage: H.P. De Swart & Zoon, 1912); William G. Wilcox, 'New England Covenant Theology: Its Precursors and Early American Exponents' (Ph.D. Duke University, 1959); James Eugene Williams, Jr., 'An Evaluation of William Perkins' Doctrine of Predestination in the Light of John Calvin's Writings' (Th.M., Dallas Theological Seminary, 1986); Andrew Alexander Woolsey, 'Unity and Continuity in Covenantal Thought: A Study in the Reformed Tradition to the Westminster Assembly' (Ph.D., University of Glasgow, 1988).

5. Perkins's critics – both positive and negative – agree that he provided a major link in Reformed thought between Beza and the Westminster Confession. Those who view that linkage as largely negative include Perry Miller (*Errand into the Wilderness* [Cambridge: Belknap Press, 1956]); Karl Barth (*Church Dogmatics*, III/4 [Edinburgh: T. & T. Clark, 1961], p. 8); Basil Hall ('Calvin Against the Calvinists,' in *John Calvin*, ed. G. E. Duffield [Appleford, England: Sutton Courtney Press, 1966], pp. 19-37); Robert T. Kendall (*Calvin and English Calvinism* 'Living the Christian Life in the Teaching of William Perkins and His Followers,' in *Living the Christian Life* [London: Westminster Conference, 1974]; 'John Cotton – First English Calvinist?,' *The Puritan Experiment in the New World* [London: Westminster Conferencee, 1976]; 'The Puritan Modification of Calvin's Theology,' in *John Calvin: His Influence in the Western World*, ed. W. Stanford Reid [Grand Rapids: Zondervan, 1982], pp. 199-214); Chalker and Knappen as noted above. Scholars who have reacted positively to Perkins include F. Ernest Stoeffler (*The Rise of Evangelical Pietism* [Leiden: Brill, 1965]); Ian Breward ('William Perkins and the Origins of Puritan Casuistry,' *Faith and a Good Conscience* [London: Puritan and Reformed Studies Conference, 1962]; 'The Significance of William Perkins,' *Journal of Religious History* 4 [1966]:113-28; 'William Perkins and the Origins of Puritan Casuistry,' *The Evangelist Quarterly* 40 [1968]:16-22); Richard Muller ('Perkins' *A Golden Chaine:* Predestinarian System or Schematized *Ordo Salutis?,' Sixteenth Century Journal* 9, 1 [1978]:69-81; 'Covenant and Conscience in English Reformed Theology,' *Westminster Theological Journal* 42 [1980]:308-34; *Christ and the Decrees: Christology and Predestination in Reformed Theology from Calvin to Perkins* [Grand Rapids: Baker, 1988]); Mark R. Shaw ('Drama in the Meeting House: the concept of Conversion in the Theology of William Perkins' *Westminster Theological Journal* 45 (1983):41-72; 'William Perkins and the New Pelagians: Another Look at the Cambridge Predestination Controversy of the 1590s,' *Westminster Theological Journal* 58 [1996]:267-302); Joel R. Beeke (*The Quest for Full Assurance: The Legacy of Calvin and His Successors* [Edinburgh: Banner of Truth Trust, 1999]); Greve, Markham, Munson, op't Hof, Pipa, Priebe, Schaefer, Sommerville, Song, van Baarsel, and Woolsey, as noted above). See Shaw, 'The Marrow of Practical Divinity,' pp. 4-29 for a summary of interpretations of

Perkins's thought.

6. M.M. Knappen, *Tudor Puritanism: A Chapter in the History of Idealism* (Chicago: University of Chicago Press, 1939), pp. 374-76; Ian Breward, intro. and ed., *The Work of William Perkins*, vol. 3 of The Courtenay Library of Reformation Classics (Abingdon, England: Sutton Courtenay Press, 1970), p. 86. Hereafter, *Work of Perkins*. For Perkins's writings, I used Breward's volume as well as *The Workes of That Famovs and VVorthy Minister of Christ in the Vniuersitie of Cambridge, Mr. William Perkins*, 3 vols. (London: John Legatt, 1612-13) – hereafter *Works*, and Thomas F. Merrill, ed., *William Perkins, 1558-1602, English Puritanist – His Pioneer Works on Casuistry: 'A Discourse of Conscience' and 'the Whole Treatise of Cases of Conscience'* (Nieuwkoop: B. DeGraaf, 1966) – hereafter *Works on Casuistry*. Additional printings of Perkins's writings include *A Commentary on Galatians*, ed. Gerald T. Sheppard (New York: Pilgrim Press, 1989), *A Commentary on Hebrews 11*, ed. John H. Augustine (New York: Pilgrim Press, 1991), and *The Art of Prophesying*, ed. Sinclair Ferguson (Edinburgh: Banner of Truth Trust, 1996).

7. *Work of Perkins*, p. xi.

8. 'Perkins' *A Golden Chaine*,' pp. 69-71, 79-81.

9. Thomas Fuller provided the basics of what is known about Perkins's life (*Abel Redevivus; or, The Dead Yet Speaking* [London: William Tegg, 1867], 2:145-54, and *The Holy and Profane State* [London: William Tegg, 1841]). See Breward, 'The Life and Theology of William Perkins,' and idem, introduction in *Work of Perkins*; Munson, 'William Perkins: Theologian of Transition'; Tufft, 'William Perkins, 1558–1602,' for the best accounts to date.

10. *Works on Casuistry*, pp. x-xv, xviii-xx; Breward, 'William Perkins and the Origins of Puritan Casuistry,' *The Evangelist Quarterly* 40 (1968):16-22; George L. Mosse, *The Holy Pretence: A Study in Christianity and Reason of State from William Perkins to John Winthrop* (Oxford: Blackwell, 1957), pp. 48-67.

11. *Abel Redevivus*, 2:145-46.

12. Louis B. Wright, *Middle-Class Culture in Elizabethan England* (Chapel Hill: University of North Carolina Press, 1935), pp. 281-84; Breward, 'The Significance of William Perkins,' *Journal of Religious History* 4 (1966):116.

13. *Reformation and Reaction in Tudor Cambridge* (London: Cambridge University Press, 1958), p. 260. Porter claims that more than fifty of the 210 books printed in Cambridge between 1585 and 1618 were written by Perkins (ibid., p. 264).

14. For a summary of Perkins's writings, see Packer, *An Anglican to Remember*, pp. 8-11.

15. Louis B. Wright, 'William Perkins: Elizabethan Apostle of 'Practical Divinity,'' *Huntington Library Quarterly* 3, 2 (1940):194.

16. Breward, 'The Significance of William Perkins,' p. 116.

17. *From Abbadie to Young: A Bibliography of English, mostly Puritan Works, Translated i/o Dutch Language* (Veenendaal: Kool, 1980), 1:96-108.

18. Cornelis W. Schoneveld, *Intertraffic of the Mind: Studies in Seventeenth-Century Anglo-Dutch Translation with a Checklist of Books Translated from English into Dutch, 1600–1700* (Leiden: Brill, 1983), pp. 220-26.

19. The *Nadere Reformatie* was a primarily seventeenth and early eighteenth century movement that paralleled English Puritanism in both time and substance. Voetius was to the *Nadere Reformatie* what John Owen, often called the prince of the Puritans, was to English Puritanism. Voetius called Perkins 'the Homer [that is, the magisterial classic], of practical Englishmen ' (Packer, *An Anglican to Remember*,

p. 3). Cf. Joel R. Beeke, *Gisbertus Voetius: Toward a Reformed Marriage of Knowledge and Piety* (Grand Rapids: Reformation Heritage Books, 1999), pp. 9, 11; Breward, 'The Significance of Perkins,' p. 128.

20. Breward, 'Life and Theology of Perkins,' Appendix 2.

21. Munson, 'William Perkins: Theologian of Transition,' pp. 56-59.

22. *The Intellectual Life of Colonial New England*, 2nd ed. (New York: New York University Press, 1956), p. 134.

23. *Errand into the Wilderness*, p. 57-59.

24. Irvonwy Morgan, *Puritan Spirituality* (London: Epworth Press, 1973), p.24.

25. Breward, 'Life and Theology of Perkins,' p. 16.

26. For a list of Perkins's writings, see Munson, 'William Perkins: Theologian of Transition,' pp. 231-34; McKim, 'Ramism in William Perkins,' pp. 335-37.

27. *Work of Perkins*, pp. 175-76. Cf. Michael T. Malone, 'The Doctrine of Predestination in the Thought of William Perkins and Richard Hooker,' *Anglican Theological Review* 52 (1970):103-117.

28. See Perkins's chart in the appendix, taken from Edward Hindson, ed., *Introduction to Puritan Theology* (Grand Rapids: Baker, 1976), p. 136. For an exposition of Perkins's chart, see Cornelis Graafland, *Van Calvijn tot Barth: Oorsprong en ontwikkeling van de leer der verkiezing in het Gereformeerd Protestantisme* ('s-Gravenhage: Boekencentrum, 1987), pp. 72-84.

29. *Works,* I:24, 106.

30. The terms supralapsarian and infralapsarian concern the moral order of God's decree related to man's eternal state. Supralapsarian literally means 'above the fall' and infralapsarian, 'below the fall' (supra=above; infra=below; lapsus=the fall). Supralapsarians believe that the decree of divine predestination must morally precede the decree concerning mankind's creation and fall in order to preserve an accent on the absolute sovereignty of God. Infralpsarians maintain that the decree of predestination must morally follow the decree of creation and the fall, believing it to be inconsistent with the nature of God for Him to reprobate any man without first contemplating him as created, fallen, and sinful. See Joel R. Beeke, 'Did Beza's Supralapsarianism Spoil Calvin's Theology?,' *Reformed Theological Journal* 13 (Nov 1997):58-60; William Hastie, *The Theology of the Reformed Church* (Edinburgh: T. & T. Clark, 1904); Klaas Dijk, *De Strijd over Infra- en Supralapsarisme in de Gereformeerde Kerken van Nederland* (Kampen: Kok, 1912).

31. The subordinate role of Christ in supralapsarian predestination has been revived in the twentieth century by those who say that Christ only becomes a 'carrier of salvation' – that He plays no active role since the decree of predestination is made prior to grace (J.K.S. Reid, 'The Office of Christ in Predestination,' *Scottish Journal of Theology* 1 [1948]:5-19, 166-83; James Daane, *The Freedom of God* [Grand Rapids: Eerdmans, 1973], chap. 7).

32. *Work of Perkins*, pp. 197-98.

33. *Works,* II:607.

34. *Works,* I:294.

35. *Works,* II:611.

36. *Works,* I:24. Here Perkins seems to be approaching some kind of synthesis between infra and supralapsarianism.

37. *Works,* II:606. Perkins would agree with Calvin that election and reprobation are equally ultimate but not parallel – election being sovereign and gratuitous, reprobation being sovereign and just (Fred Klooster, *Calvin's Doctrine of Predestination* [Grand Rapids: Baker, 1977], chap. 3.

38. *Works*, I:294.
39. *Work of Perkins*, pp. 197-98.
40. *Works*, II:608.
41. *Works*, II:607.
42. See McKim, 'Ramism in William Perkins.'
43. *Work of Perkins*, pp. 85-86.
44. Ibid., p. 83; Song, *Theology and Piety in Reformed Federal Thought*, pp. 44-49.
45. Muller, 'Perkins' *A Golden Chaine*,' pp. 71, 76.
46. Even G.C. Berkouwer, who devoted a lengthy chapter to how election takes place *in Christ*, appears unaware of Perkins's attempted solution (*Divine Election*, trans. Hugo Bekker [Grand Rapids: Eerdmans, 1960], pp. 132-71).
47. *Works*, I:9.
48. *Works*, II:177.
49. Cf. *Works*, II:608.
50. Muller, 'Perkins' *A Golden Chaine*,' pp. 76-77.
51. Shaw, 'The Marrow of Practical Divinity,' p. 124. Shaw concludes that 'the background of Perkins' covenant of grace was election in Christ as its formal cause and the work of Christ as its material cause.'
52. *Works*, I:32.
53. *Works*, I:32.
54. *Works*, I:70.
55. Muller, 'Covenant and Conscience,' pp. 310-11.
56. *Errand in the Wilderness*, pp. 48-98.
57. *Works*, I:77.
58. *Works*, I:78.
59. *Works*, I:79.
60. Ibid.
61. *Works*, I:79-80.
62. *Works*, I:81-82.
63. *Works*, II:204.
64. *Works*, I:368.
65. *Works*, I:541.
66. *Works on Casuistry*, p. 103.
67. *Works*, I:92, 94.
68. See first chart in the Appendix, taken from Heinrich Heppe, *Reformed Dogmatics*, ed. Ernst Bizer, trans. G.T.Thomson (London: George Allen & Unwiwin, 1950), pp. 147-48).
69. Chalker, 'Calvin and Some Seventeenth Century Calvinists,' p. 91.
70. Muller, '*A Golden Chaine*,' pp. 79-80.
71. Kendall, *Calvin and English Calvinism*, pp. 8-9.
72. *Works*, III:433.
73. *Work of Perkins*, p. 330.
74. *Works*, I:83.
75. *Works*, III:64.
76. *Work of Perkins*, p. 300.
77. *Works*, II:646ff.
78. *Works*, I:434; II:289, 294.
79. See Donald K. McKim, 'William Perkins and the Theology of the Covenant,' in *Studies of the Church in History*, ed. Horton Davies (Allison Park, Penn.: Pickwith, 1983), pp. 85-87; Priebe, 'Covenant Theology of Perkins.'
80. 'Norman Pettit has suggested that there were at least three continental attiudes on

the position of preparation. Peter Martyr represented one extreme with the idea that the heart is taken by storm, 'that grace comes only as an effectual call, with no preparatory dispositon of the heart.' Bullinger represented the opposite extreme, 'that grace follows the heart's response to God's offer of the covenant promises in preparatory repentance.' Coming down in the middle between these two positions is Calvin, that grace, while entirely a matter of seizure, may nevertheless involve preparation through divine constraint of the heart.' The English theologians opted broadly for the Calvin-Bullinger part of the spectrum but vacillated between the two Swiss reformers' (Shaw, 'The Marrow of Practical Divinity,' p. 128-29; Pettit, *The Heart Prepared: Grace and Conversion in Puritan Spiritual Life* [New Haven: Yale University Press, 1966], pp. 44-47).

81. *Works,* II:13.

82. *Works,* I:124.

83. *Works,* I:124.

84. *Works,* I:79.

85. *Works,* II:18.

86. *Works,* I:79-80.

87. *Works,* I:80.

88. Ibid.

89. *Works,* I:523.

90. Cf. Kendall, *Calvin and English Calvinism,* p. 71; Beeke, *Quest for Full Assurance,* pp. 65-72, 131-41.

91. *An Anglican to Remember,* p. 19.

92. Gordon J. Keddie, "Unfallible Certenty of the Pardon of Sinne and Life Everlasting": The Doctrine of Assurance in the Theology of William Perkins,' *The Evangelical Quarterly* 48 (1976):30-44; Joel R. Beeke, *Assurance of Faith: Calvin, English Puritanism, and the Dutch Second Reformation* (New York: Peter Lang, 1991), pp. 105-118.

93. *Works on Casuistry,* p. 106.

94. *Works,* I:599. Cf. Michael McGiggert, 'Weak Christians, Backsliders, and Carnal Gospelers: Assurance of Salvation and the Pastoral Origins of Puritan Practical Divinity in the 1580s,' *Church History* 70, 3 (2001):473-74.

95. *Works,* I:453.

96. *Works,* I:454. Cf. Woolsey, 'Unity and Continuity in Covenantal Thought,' p. 217.

97. Ibid., p. 107.

98. Ibid.

99. *Works,* I:413.

100. *Works,* II:620ff; William Haller, *The Rise of Puritanism* (New York: Columbia University Press, 1938), pp. 130-31; Kendall, *Calvin and English Calvinism,* pp. 67-74.

101. WCF 3.8; *Reformed Confessions Harmonized,* p. 31; cf. John Murray, 'Calvin, Dort, and Westminster on Predestination – A Comparative Study,' in *Crises in the Reformed Churches: Essays in Commemoration of the Great Synod of Dort, 1618-1619,* ed. Peter Y. De Jong (Grand Rapids: Reformed Fellowship, 1968), p. 157.

102. Heinrich Heppe, *Geschichte des Pietismus und der Mystik in der reformierten Kirche namentlich in der Niederlande* (Leiden: Brill, 1879), p. 24-26.

103. Richard Muller, 'William Perkins and the Protestant Exegetical Tradition: Interpretation, Style, and Method,' in Perkins, *Commentary on Hebrews 11,* p. 72.

104. *An Anglican to Remember,* p. 4.

105. John Eusden, *Puritans, Lawyers, and Politics* (New Haven: Yale University Press,

1958), p. 11; Knappen, *Tudor Puritanism*, p. 375; Haller, *Rise of Puritanism*, p. 91; Collinson, *Elizabethan Puritan Movement*, p. 125; Paul Seaver, *The Puritan Lectureships: The Politics of Religious Dessent, 1560-1662* (Palo Alto, Calif.: Stanford University Press, 1970), p. 114; Christopher Hill, *God's Englishman: Oliver Cromwell and the English Revolution* (New York: Harper & Row, 1970), p. 38; Packer, *An Anglican to Remember*, p. 1.

106. Louis Wright, 'William Perkins: Elizabethan Apostle of 'Practical Divinitie," *Huntington Library Quarterly* 3 (1940):171; Mosse, *The Holy Pretense*, p. 48. Volume 1 of Perkins's retypeset *Works* is scheduled to be printed by Tanski Publications in 2002, D.V., to be followed by an additional eight volumes. An extended version of this chapter will introduce the set in volume 1. Perkins's *Works* will no doubt revive Puritan studies as the father of Puritanism becomes accessible to all. They will show that Perkins's theology did not make him cold and heartless when dealing with sinners and saints in need of a Savior. Rather, his warm, practical theology set the tone for Puritan literature that would pour forth from the presses in the seventeenth century, and from which we benefit today. *The Works of William Perkins* is a fitting capstone to the past half-century of reprinted Puritan literature. For a comprehensive listing and annotated bibliography of Puritan literature reprinted since the 1950s, see Joel R. Beeke and Randall Pederson, *A Reader's Guide to Puritan Literature* (Edinburgh: Banner of Truth Trust, forthcoming).

THE CLASH OF KING AND KIRK

The 1690 Revolution Settlement in Presbyterian Scotland

Richard Gamble

The Presbyterian tradition in Scotland began in the early years of the Protestant Reformation, and in a very real sense, came to adulthood with the 1690 'Revolution Settlement' between the English King and the Scottish Kirk. The purpose of this study is first to survey the historical development that led to the culmination of this long conflict between Crown and Kirk, and then to seek to resolve the question: Was the Revolution Settlement in Scotland too strong, too weak, or the best that could be expected?

I. England and Scotland until 1649

The Protestant reformation was ushered into Scotland under the leadership of great men like John Knox. It advanced in the hearts and minds of God's people to the point that in 1580 they were ready to make a 'national covenant' with God. It was re-affirmed by the Scottish nation again in 1590 and 1596. Scottish Protestantism was always slightly different from that of England.[1]

Nevertheless, these forward steps did not go unchallenged! King Charles I of England (1633–1649) reintroduced bishops into the churches of Scotland as well as a new code of church law. His 'book of Canons', making him head of the church, was mandated. Eventually, any non-Episcopal worship was outlawed, and non-Episcopalians were barred from public office in Scotland.[2]

However, in response to these religious and political oppressions by King Charles, the old 'national covenant' (1580) of Scotland was brought out and was renewed with another signing in 1638.[3] This time, King Charles at least appeared to back down.[4] In the same year, there gathered the first free General Assembly of the Church of Scotland, since 1605, which met in Glasgow.[5]

A few years later, in 1640, after a Scottish/English battle when the English were bested, Charles I granted limited rule to Scotland to a national assembly seated in Glasgow. This political change ended episcopacy in the Church of Scotland, but those Episcopalian clerics who desired to remain in Scotland were invited to stay if they became Presbyterian.[6]

The Solemn League and Covenant

Charles I's politics also oppressed believers in England. Civil war broke out there in 1642. The English naturally turned to Scotland for aid. However, to obtain Scottish aid, since Scotland was 'a covenanted nation', a new document would have to be subscribed by the English.[7]

That new document was termed 'The Solemn League and Covenant'. Alexander Henderson, the Moderator of the Scottish General Assembly, wrote it. The stated goals of the Solemn League and Covenant were: 'The preservation of the reformed religion in the Church of Scotland', 'The reformation of religion in the kingdoms of England and Ireland' and 'to bring the Churches of God in the three kingdoms to the nearest conjunction and uniformity of religion, confession of faith, form of Church government, directory of worship and catechizing.' The people throughout England, Scotland and Ireland subscribed to the document in 1643.[8] It was also subscribed by the English parliament (both houses), and later by the divines meeting at Westminster to draft a new confession of faith, and the Scottish commissioners. It was then further ratified by the Scottish Parliament and also sent over to Ireland and sworn there too.[9]

The Westminster Assembly

An assembly was already meeting in England in 1643 to reorganize the government of the Church of England. At first, doctrine was relatively unimportant- the pressing need was for change in government and worship.[10] The parliament was determined to retain its power over the church. Thus, the Assembly was, according to Warfield, 'merely the creature of Parliament.'[11] Despite the original plan, the Solemn League and Covenant in some senses changed the task of the theologians at Westminster. It was now responsible to propose a new Form of Church Government, a new Directory for Worship (the Book of Common Prayer was now to be abolished), and a new Confession and Catechism.[12]

As the civil war progressed, King Charles I was captured on Scottish soil. The Scots returned him to the English upon the condition that they would preserve the Monarch's life. Unfortunately, with the King in their power and no further need for Scottish forces, the English then renounced their adherence to the Solemn League and Covenant. Charles I was subsequently executed in 1649. For these two acts, formally renouncing the Solemn League and Covenant and breaking their promise to preserve the king's life, the Scots felt as if the English had twice broken their word.

Meanwhile, one week before Charles' execution, the 'Act of Classes' was passed by the Scottish Parliament. That Act excluded non-covenanters from civil and military office. Certain Episcopal ministers were also deposed.[13]

II. From the Restoration of the King to the 'Act against Conventicles' (1660–1670)

Political Events

The English civil war and execution of King Charles I, plus Oliver Cromwell's invasion and defeat of Scotland, resulted in the establishment of what is termed the 'Commonwealth'. To unite England and Scotland, Cromwell was open to various Protestant churches, including the Presbyterian.[14]

However, the monarchy came back into power and the new King, Charles II, was restored in 1660. Scotland, which had earlier been under the political thumb of Cromwell, was now legally given her independence.

With the turn of the year there was a new Scottish parliament seated in Edinburgh. A commissioner from the King directed the Scottish Parliament. It lasted only 6.5 months and is known by historians as the 'drunken Parliament'. There are very few neutral attitudes toward this Parliament. 'Their aim was to re-establish despotism and to destroy Presbytery', says one, for 'there were no boundaries to the powers with which they invested the King.'[15] During this time, Presbyterianism was outlawed and bishops returned.[16]

Presbyterian problems: the 'Act Recissory'[17]
The most important action of this Parliament was passing the Act Recissory. The Act annulled the convention of Estates that had earlier sworn the Solemn League and Covenant. The Solemn League and Covenant was now without public and permanent obligation. They revoked all Acts of Parliament from the years 1640–1648. This revocation swept away the legal basis for Presbyterianism. This meant that any Presbyterian could now be called disloyal or traitorous.[18]

The 'Act against Conventicles'
While Presbyterianism may have been obliterated *de jure*, *de facto* it was still vibrant. The people of God continued to meet for worship. If a minister or licentiate were available, they would have a preaching service called a 'conventicle'. As time went on a fewer ministers were available, and the people of God had 'informal' worship and fellowship: without their former pastor but led by an elder. These smaller gatherings were outside the confines of the organized church. These meetings were oftentimes termed 'Society meetings' or 'the society'.

To bring law and reality together, in 1670 an 'Act against Conventicles', was passed. This Act severely fined those who might attend worship at homes or in the fields. Preachers, or those responsible for calling the meetings, were to be killed and their goods confiscated.[19] At the society meetings after 1670, usually with fewer than twelve members, the *Psalms* would be sung; there was a time of open prayer and sharing of Scripture. Members held each other accountable for their Christian walk. This was the people's only real opportunity for public worship, yet being without ministry and sacraments, for Presbyterians, it could not be considered formal public worship. They were not really a 'church' outside of the church, but more a general fellowship of praying societies.

III. From the 'United Societies' to King Charles II's Death (1681–1685)

The 'United Societies'

The various praying Societies throughout Scotland now banded together for what they called a General Correspondence of Society, with their first convention meeting at the end of 1681. The group was to assemble quarterly thereafter.[20] They were defined as neither civil nor ecclesiastical judicatories but rather Christian gatherings. They officially rejected the sin of schism.[21]

The United Societies could claim at this time 'the then dangerous and even treasonable honor of being a remnant of the true Presbyterian churches of Scotland, waiting, only until the defections be healed and the church will be re-established, to unite in full fellowship.'[22] They commissioned men to visit the reformed churches on the continent for help and commissioned others for the study of the gospel ministry.[23]

The 'Test Act' of 1681

This act required all that held positions of public trust to acknowledge the King as the head of the church. Yet, Jesus Christ is the only head of the church! Rather than taking 'the test', many godly men choose to give up their property and positions. In addition, to continue the campaign against Presbyterianism, while the Society meetings were already illegal, it also became illegal to stop attending the state supported church services. Failure to attend the curate's sermons resulted in persecution.[24]

From the time of the 'Act against Conventicles' 1670 to the 'Test Act' of 1681, the Scottish people as individuals and as families had to make difficult choices that bore grave consequences. Would they stop attending the Society meetings, where they could find food for the soul? Would they now attend what they considered to be ungodly worship thrust upon them by a foreign power? Each father had to decide for his own family. The stress was great on all who feared God.[25]

The 'Abjuration Oath'

The final loop of the noose to strangle Presbyterianism was tied in November 1684. The 'Abjuration Oath' required the people to renounce the Society meetings. God in His good providence now afforded no place for believers to hide, there was no room for 'lukewarm' Christianity. Yet, how could the common people consider their societies to be 'wrong'? The United Societies therefore wrote the *Apologetical Declaration* defending their existence. Their efforts proved fruitless. The government went on to establish a bounty for Society members and required all Scots to obtain written certificates vouching for their loyalty to the crown. Basically, Society members lost all rights of citizenship.[26] The stage of opposition was now properly set for one last act. That act unfortunately must include the shedding of innocent blood.

In conclusion, the Societies in general were people who had sided with the covenanters in their renunciation of the Stuart Kings and their various armed rebellions. They argued that the Kings had grievously failed to keep their oaths to support the Solemn League and Covenant, had unlawfully established an erastian church and had persecuted God's people for failing to obey the unrighteous laws. Failure to denounce those rebellions became a capital offense.[27] The Societies also rejected those preachers who had yielded to government demands and been 'indulged'. It is conservatively estimated that by the year 1683 there were about 80 organized Societies with a total membership of about 7,000.[28]

IV. From King James II to the Revolution Settlement (1685–1688)

The Persecution of the Covenanters

This era of Scottish history is also known as 'the killing times'. Many covenanters were condemned to transportation to the colonies and enforced servitude. In 1685, after a rebellion, some captives were sent as slaves to America, landing in New Jersey. Other covenanter slaves were sent to the Carolinas, Barbados and Jamaica.[29]

While there are various accounts of the persecution, we can verify that at least 362 people were judicially executed.[30] Another 498 were what is gently termed 'dispatched in the fields'.[31] A further 680 were killed fighting. 750 were banished from the kingdom. At least 1,700 believers were shipped away to the colonies. A further 2,800 suffered imprisonment.[32] Moreover, many others perished in wanderings.[33]

The hanging of the 26 year old Rev. James Renwick in 1688 was one of the very last martyrdoms.[34] After his death, the government declared all Covenanter literature to be illegal.[35] The persecution of God's people was severe and comprehensive. Their bodies were tortured, their goods confiscated and their literature destroyed. The Lord would soon answer their cries for help. Prince William of Holland would arrive in England about six months later.

V. The 'Revolution Settlement' of 1689–1690
Political developments 1688–1689
King James II had a son in 1688. That son's ascension to the British throne would have ensured a Roman Catholic succession, and England would have been lost to Protestantism. In that same year, William of Orange landed in England with 14,000 troops – and at Christmastime King James quietly fled the island. William Henry, the third Prince of Orange, was himself the son of a British princess and thus King James II's nephew. William's wife Mary was a legitimate heir to the English throne – she was James II's daughter.[36] William called a convention of English legislators in January 1689. Both the Commons and the Lords resolved that the throne of King James II was vacant and both offered the Crown to William and Mary.[37] The Scots Estates, in March of the same year, summoned by William by letter, passed the resolution that James had forfeited the throne.[38] After legally sweeping away King James II, the throne was prepared for William and Mary. The Scots sent delegates to London and the coronation oath was taken there.

As William and Mary came to power in England, an important change was made to their coronation oath.[39] The oath made no mention of the *Westminster Confession of Faith*, let alone a vow to support it, nor was there mention of any of the related Acts of Parliament.[40] In addition, William would also not agree to 'root out heresy'.[41]

The Convention of legislators was adjourned and re-called in June as an English Parliament – who ratified the new Sovereignty. The constituted English Parliament declared that King James II had, indeed, forfeited the throne. Their ground was 'that King James II, having endeavored to subvert the Constitution by breaking the original contract between the King and the people, did abdicate the throne.' The Scottish convention concurred, 'that King James, by his abuse of power, had forfeited all title to the crown, and that it be conferred upon the Prince of Orange.'[42]

Thus, the stated grounds for the deposition of King James II by both Parliament and Scottish convention were the same argument used earlier by the Covenanters to oppose him! The two principles enunciated by Parliament and the covenanters were that the abuse of power destroys the right to exercise it, and that a people may depose their rulers. Scholars agree that 'nothing vindicates the position of the covenanters through the persecuting years so much as the fact that their consistent arguments for renouncing their Stuart kings, which had led to the sacrifice of several thousand Presbyterian lives, became now the reasons offered to the world for the righteousness of the invasion of Britain by a foreign liberator.'[43]

The United Societies and the Cameronians

In January 1689, two groups addressed William. The Scots nobles asked for a free Parliament with no bishops as judges. The Presbyterian ministers asked for the elimination of Episcopacy. The United Societies at this time were not anxious to join with their Presbyterian brethren. They believed that the indulged ministers had to face up to their defections, and would only agree to attend meetings with them to convince them of error.[44] The United Societies also publicly acknowledged their sin and once again subscribed the covenants.[45] Why were the society people so dissatisfied with the indulged clergy?

The first 'indulgence' came in 1669. Presbyterian ministers could return to their churches if they were vacant, they promised to be orderly, and asked for permission. With the first indulgence act also came further suppression of the Conventicles and society meetings.[46] The second indulgence of 1672 provided for simultaneous communion in each diocese. Indulged ministers were certified by the magistrates and needed to obtain a license from the bishops to move. At this point, there were sufficient indulged ministers for Presbyteries to function. The third indulgence came in 1679 and involved obtaining a license from the crown. Now 'moderate' Presbyterians were allowed to hear indulged ministers in their homes.[47]

Meanwhile, even though King James was declared forfeit, he himself never renounced the crown. Although he had fled the country, there was still danger from Loyalists raising an army to restore the king by force. In fact, a few Scots nobles were still in the employ of King James.[48]

At this time of military crisis, there was a proposal to form a new regiment to protect the Sovereigns and Protestantism. The United Societies were asked to raise a regiment of soldiers, and they were to be their authoritative/commanding body.[49]

The soldiers, known as the Cameronians, were to be a separate congregation of armed Presbyterian, Covenanting worshippers. They were to have one minister and one elder for each company. They were to have regular worship and catechizing. They were all volunteers and refused any payment from the government.[50]

The fear of armed rebellion on behalf of King James became a reality. Led by a few Scottish nobles, wild and literally half-naked highlanders defeated King William's much larger forces at Killiecrankie, where 1800 of William and Mary's men were killed and 500 taken prisoners. Very few of James II men died.[51]

Unfortunately, the Cameronians could not arrive in time. When they arrived for battle, they were outnumbered six to one. 'This small force of Covenanters, consisting of a few hundred men, was now the only creditable fighting force that could deprive King James of victory.'[52] Their victory, over superior numbers, saved the throne for William and Mary in 1689.

The Revolution Settlement in 1690

At their first meeting, the newly created Scottish Parliament passed an 'Act abolishing prelacy'.[53] At their second session, in April 1690, they rescinded the 'Supremacy Act', which had legally made King Charles supreme in all causes.[54] At the same time, the evicted Presbyterian pastors were to receive back their homes and churches (there were only about 60 who had survived) and their Episcopalian successors had to leave those churches.[55]

Later, the Scottish Parliament approved what is sometimes termed the 'Charter of Presbyterianism'. In that Charter, they accepted the *Westminster Confession of Faith*, ratified previous acts against the Roman Catholic Church, which had asserted that Prelacy was a 'great and insupportable grievance and trouble to this nation', appointed the first meeting of the General Assembly of the Church of Scotland, and authorized the church to purge any scandalous ministers.[56]

It is also important to note what was either not considered in the Scottish Charter of Presbyterianism or was lost for inclusion. The form of Presbyterian Church government for Scotland was not included so as not to offend Anglican sensitivities. The catechisms and directory for worship were also ignored. Parliament did not repeal the 'Act Recissory', 'and the omission was a sore point with the Cameronians.'[57] Most importantly, the acts of Parliament that had dealt a deathblow to Presbyterianism, for example, the prohibition of the Solemn League and Covenant, were ignored. Thus, an oath to uphold the covenant was still illegal throughout the land.[58] Furthermore, an attempt was made to approve the 1647 Scots edition of the *Westminster Confession of Faith* (instead of the English version) that has a clause that the church can call her own assemblies. That motion was lost.[59]

At the first General Assembly of the Church of Scotland, the members were faced with a number of problems. The text of the *Confession of Faith*, in an inferior English version, had already been ratified by the Parliament. The General Assembly was left powerless to make any changes to the *Confession*. Thus, the church was denied its fundamental liberty. To make the matter more difficult, King William made it clear that Episcopalians who were willing to conform should also be tolerated in Scotland.[60]

Contemporary Result and Responses to the 'Revolution Settlement'
The settlement was hailed throughout Scotland. Eventually, all the ministers joined the new Presbyterian Church. However, there was some protestation against the union.[61] The Society people wrote a 'humble petition' against the revolution settlement. They requested a free Church assembly, as well as approval of the reproached national covenants, and protested the continued presence of Prelates, even though Parliament called Prelacy 'a grievance'.[62]

This 'humble petition' was rejected by the committee for church affairs and was not considered by the Scots Parliament. Now the Society people's hope turned to the General Assembly. At the first General Assembly, the petition was also not accepted; thus, the question of a free General Assembly and the place of the National Covenants were never addressed. [63]

The situation was politically hopeless for the Society people. Their legal petitions were denied everywhere. What could they do? They did make a decision – and to help understand their decision we should examine contemporary analysis of the settlement.

VI. Contemporary Analysis of the Revolution Settlement
There are four main positions concerning the settlement, under the general headings of positive and negative. Under positive analysis, the settlement was either 'perfect', or the best solution under the circumstances. Critical analysis finds the revolution settlement either too strong or too weak.

Positive analysis: the settlement was perfect
The settlement was 'in the main adopting what was universal, and rejecting what was exclusive or over-grasping in their views – was the consummation and triumph, civilly, and politically, and to a large extent ecclesiastically, of *the 50 year struggle of the Scottish covenanters*.'[64]

Positive analysis: the settlement was the best that could be expected
While acknowledging that 'the Act' had not been repealed, and that the Covenants had not been re-imposed, nevertheless the Covenanters 'had gained the substance of what they had contended for, but had at the same time forgotten that the Covenants were but a means to an end, called forth not only by the spirit of the time, but by the special circumstances of the day.'[65] Nevertheless, if it had shortcoming, 'it was the parent of abundant good.'[66] 'Despite its warts, the Revolution Settlement church was the church.'[67]

Negative evaluation: the Revolution Settlement was too strong!
Because Scotland only recognized the Presbyterian Church, some have held that such a position was unjust. Viewed from contemporary political/religious presuppositions, such a conclusion is understandable. However, the notion of true religious 'pluralism' would be conceived and born later and the past should not be judged by the standards of later developments.[68]

Negative evaluation: the Revolution Settlement was too weak!
While the covenanters had gained much in the settlement, they certainly did not obtain all that they thought was necessary. Most important, the revolution settlement did not revoke the Act Recissory. 'It left', said one scholar, 'the wicked decree untouched.'[69]

Also, all who had signed the Solemn League and Covenant had sworn to oppose Popery, Prelacy and Erastianism. Yet, King William was the head of the Episcopal Church of England as the 'true religion' which he was bound to defend. Meanwhile, Presbyterianism was established in Scotland only as most agreeable to the mind of the people.

Furthermore, Erastianism was interwoven into the very constitution under King William. While He was the head of the Church of England, he also exercised a limited supremacy over the Church of Scotland. He could call and dissolve the courts of the church. The General Assembly could not convene except by royal authority. Thus, the King exercised an authority over the Church of Scotland in a manner rightfully seen by many as contrary to the Word of God and the previous position of the Church of Scotland.[70]

VII. Conclusion

What was gained and what was lost by the revolution settlement? Certainly, peace was gained. There was no more bloody persecution of the people of God. In addition, Presbyterian Church government and the faith of the *Westminster Confession* were established in Scotland. For both of those blessings the Scots could rejoice.

However, what was lost? Lost were the advances made between the years 1638 to 1648. A new type of Presbyterian Church was born – one where the elders had to submit to a King to be permitted to assemble in ecclesiastical court. A new type of Presbyterian Church was born – where the people had to submit to a King who had the audacity to function as the head of this church. A new type of Presbyterian Church was born – one where her 'king' acknowledged that government by prelacy was according to the word of God; and not Presbyterianism alone.

What was lost by the revolution settlement? The men and women of Scotland, who had freely given their blood and material possessions for the crown rights of King Jesus, had to relinquish the victory that was sealed by the Solemn League and Covenant.[71]

For some, members of the United Societies, the loss was simply too great to be willing to participate in the newly established church. Sometimes, the price of peace is simply too dear. That group of believers developed into the Reformed Presbyterian Church of Scotland.[72]

NOTES

1. James Kerr, *The Covenants and the Covenanters*, Edinburgh, R. Hunter, 1895, pp. 12-13. B. B. Warfield, *The Westminster Assembly and its work*, New York, Oxford Press, 1931 p. 20. Warfield asserts that in Scotland, 'from the beginning of the Reformation, the ideal of a free Church in a free State had been sedulously cherished and repeatedly given effect; and the government of the Church was in representative courts which asserted and exercised their own independent spiritual jurisdiction.'
2. James Kerr, *The Covenants and the Covenanters*, pp. 16-18. J. D. Douglas, *Light in the North*, Devon, England, The Paternoster Press, 1964. pp. 22-24. The Book of

Canons was imposed in 1636. It acknowledged royal supremacy and transferred power to bishops. Excommunication was threatened to those who objected to the liturgy or to the bishops.

3. George Gillespie also wrote in response to this imposition from England, *Reasons for which the Service Book ... should be refused*. The text of the 1638 Covenant can be found in J. D. Douglas, *Light in the North*, pp. 200ff.

4. The King pretended to yield while writing at the same time to his commissioner in Scotland: 'I give you leave to flatter them with what hopes you please; your chief end being now to win time, until I be ready to suppress them ... I will rather die than yield to those impertinent and damnable demands' J. D. Douglas, *Light in the North*, p. 25

5. This assembly excommunicated eight bishops and deposed the rest, the Liturgy was condemned. J. D. Douglas, *Light in the North*, p. 27.

6. J. D. Douglas, *Light in the North*, p. 31.

7. B. B. Warfield, *The Westminster Assembly* pp. 19-22, 31.

8. David Scott, *Annals and Statistics of the original Secession Church*. Edinburgh, Andrew Elliott, 1886. Pp. 5-6. It had first been submitted to a joint committee of the English Parliament, the Scots convention of Estates and the Scottish General Assembly. They adopted it in August 1643.

9. James Kerr, *The Covenants and the Covenanters*, pp. 19-20. J. D. Douglas, *Light in the North*, p. 36. B. B. Warfield, *The Westminster Assembly* p. 24. 'By the terms of the engagement made in it, the difference in the actual ecclesiastical situations of the contracting parties was clearly recognized, and that in such terms as to make the actual situation in Scotland the model of the establishment agreed upon for both countries.'

10. B. B. Warfield, *The Westminster Assembly and its work*, New York, Oxford Press, 1931 pp. 12-13.

11. B. B. Warfield, *The Westminster Assembly* p. 15.

12. B. B. Warfield, *The Westminster Assembly* p. 26. 'The significance of the Solemn League and Covenant was, therefore, that it pledged the two nations to uniformity in their religious establishments and pledged them to a uniformity on the model of the establishment already existing in the Church of Scotland.' 'By the Solemn League and Covenant, therefore, the work of the Assembly of Divines was revolutionized, and not only directed to a new end but put upon a wholly new basis.' p. 34. Concerning the new form of worship, see pp. 45ff. 'The duty of preparing an entirely new Creed was imposed on them solely by the Solemn League and Covenant.' p. 53.

13. J. D. Douglas, *Light in the North*, p. 37.

14. Presbyterianism was established in England in June 1646 and the last General Assembly met in England in 1659. J. King Hewison, *The Covenanters*. Vol. II. pp. 50-51.

15. Smelie, *Men of the Covenant* p. 56-57. 'By which the drunken parliament in 1661 erased much that was where the esteemed the church's record of achievement.' J. D. Douglas, *Light in the North* p. 177.

16. James Barr, *The Scottish Covenanters*, Glasgow, John Smith and Son, 1946, pp. 43-48. J. D. Douglas, *Light in the North*, Devon, England, The Paternoster Press, 1964. pp. 98-110. James Dodds, *The fifty years' struggle of the Scottish covenanters*. London, Houlston and Sons, 1868. pp. 84-112-143. Roger Lockyer, *Tudor and Stuart Britain 1471-1714*, New York, St. Martin's Press, p. 419.

17. For a text of the act, see James Kerr, *The Covenants and the Covenanters*, Edinburgh, R. Hunter, 1895, pp. 398-407.

18. Smelie, *Men of the Covenant*, pp. 58-59.

19. James Kerr, *The Covenants and the Covenanters* pp. 412-414. 'Diverse disaffected persons, under the specious but false pretense of religion and religious exercises, presumed to make, and be present at conventicles and warrantable meetings and conventions of the subjects ... tending to the prejudice of the public worship of God in the churches, to the scandal of the reformed religion, to the reproach of his Majesty's authority and government, and to the alienation of the hearts and affections of the subjects from that duty and obedience they owe to his Majesty, and to the public laws of the kingdom.' 'No ousted ministers who are not licensed by the council, and no other person as not authorized, or tolerate by the bishop of the diocese, presumed to preach, expound Scripture, or pray in a meeting, except in their own houses, and to those of their own families; and that none be present at a meeting, without the family to which they belong, who are not licensed, authorized, nor tolerated as is said, shall preach, expound Scripture, or pray.' 'Any who should also preach, expound, or pray, shall be seized upon and imprisonment, till they find caution, under the pain of 5000 Merck's, not to do the light thereafter. And any person who shall be found to have been present at any such meetings shall be fined according to their qualities and imprisoned until they pay their fines.' 'Every man or woman having land and heritage life-around is to be fined the fourth part of his or her valued yearly rent.'

20. Edwin Nisbet Moore, *Our Covenant Heritage*, p. 93.

21. See W. H. Goold, *Commemoration of the Bicentenary of the Westminster Assembly of Divines and the Centenary of the Reformed Presbytery*, p. 172.

22. Roy Blackwood, *William Symington, Churchman and Theologian*. Ph.D. dissertation, University of Edinburgh, reprinted 1999. p. 5.

23. Edwin Nisbet Moore, *Our Covenant Heritage*, p. 95.

24. Every parish minister would submit a last of people who did not attend worship to the bishop, who then turned the list to the magistrate for prosecution. J. King Hewison, *The Covenanters* Vol. II. pp. 351-353. See Edwin Nisbet Moore, *Our Covenant Heritage*, pp. 96-97.

25. J. D. Douglas, *Light in the North*, has the text of the Test Act, pp. 209-211.

26. James Dodds, *The fifty years' struggle of the Scottish covenanters*, p. 288. Edwin Nisbet Moore, *Our Covenant Heritage*, p. 111.

27. Edwin Nisbet Moore, *Our Covenant Heritage*, 109.

28. James Dodds, *The fifty years' struggle of the Scottish covenanters* p. 286 thinks that the numbers grew significantly after that time. Edwin Nisbet Moore, *Our Covenant Heritage*, pp. 94-95.

29. J. D. Douglas, *Light in the North* p. 181-182. 'Oliver Cromwell dispatched Scottish prisoners in shiploads to the plantations of North America to be sold as slaves.' During the 38 years thereafter until the revolution, thousands of Scottish covenanters either were transported to America or went there to flee the persecution. The group of slaves sent to New Jersey included one Grisel Gamble. They arrived in mid-December, after 29 had already died, including two ministers as well as their leader, from rotten food and ill treatment. Two ministers from that sorry lot survived, Archibald Riddle and James Frazer. It is the same James Frazer who wrote: *A Treatise on Sanctification*. New Jersey, Old Paths publications, 1992.

30. The nature of the executions included beheading, with the head oftentimes placed on a stake. Sometimes cutting off hands. Women were also hanged and drowned. S. Bates, pp. 14-16. Edwin Nisbet Moore, *Our Covenant Heritage*, p. 96 gives accounts of the hanging of Robert Gray for writing to a prisoner advising him not to take the Black Oath.

31. This is the phrase used for those murdered without pretense of trial. Oftentimes

there were found worshipping in the fields and killed there. Bates, p. 17.

32. Edwin Nisbet Moore, *Our Covenant Heritage*, p. 110 recounts that more than one thousand were in the Dunnottar Castle prison for refusing the oath.

33. J. King Hewison, *The Covenanters A History of the Church in Scotland from the Reformation to the Revolution*. Glasgow, John Smith and Son, 1913. Vol. II p. 512.

34. Renwick asserted that he was about to be hanged for three reasons: disowning James, preaching that it was unlawful to pay the cess, and that it was lawful to bear arms to defend themselves during their meetings. J. King Hewison, *The Covenanters* Vol. II pp. 509-510. Dodds, *The fifty years struggle*, pp. 355-369. Feb. 1688. Smelie, *Men of the Covenant*, pp. 481-493.

35. Edwin Nisbet Moore, *Our Covenant Heritage*, p. 150.

36. J. King Hewison, *The Covenanters*. Vol. II. pp. 513-514.

37. J. King Hewison, *The Covenanters*. Vol. II. pp. 520-521.

38. J. King Hewison, *The Covenanters*. Vol. II. pp. 522-523.

39. James Barr, *The Scottish Covenanters*, p. 60.

40. J. King Hewison, *The Covenanters*. Vol. II. p. 523. Edwin Nisbet Moore, *Our Covenant Heritage*, p. 153.

41. Edwin Nisbet Moore, *Our Covenant Heritage*, p. 153.

42. W. Melanchthon Glasgow, *History of the Reformed Presbyterian Church in America*, Baltimore, Hill and Harvey 1888, p. 44. J. D. Douglas, *Light in the North*, pp. 175-176.

43. J. D. Douglas, *Light in the North*, p. 176. J. King Hewison, *The Covenanters*. Vol. II. p. 513 agrees: 'The identical arguments used by the Cameronians for justifying their renunciation of the Stuarts became the reasons offered to Europe for the righteousness of the invasion of Britain by a foreign liberator.' James Dodds, *The fifty years' struggle of the Scottish covenanters* pp. 292-293.

44. J. King Hewison, *The Covenanters*. Vol. II. p. 516. 'The General Society decried the defections of the Presbyterian brethren and refused to meet with previously Indulged ministers unless they repented.' Edwin Nisbet Moore, *Our Covenant Heritage*, p. 152.

45. J. King Hewison, *The Covenanters*. Vol. II. pp. 519-520.

46. J. King Hewison, *The Covenanters*. Vol. II. p. 226. 'An Erastian breech of the Covenant'.

47. J. King Hewison, *The Covenanters* Vol. II. pp. 225, 235, 321, 503.

48. J. King Hewison, *The Covenanters*, p. 534. Montgomery was the leader.

49. Edwin Nisbet Moore, *Our Covenant Heritage*, p. 153. They were the 'only body that both possessed the power and the inclination to protect their country's liberties, and might be trusted in this hour of peril'.

50. Dodds, *The fifty years struggle*, pp. 374-376. The regiment was 800 men but a total of 1200 served. They were engaged to 'resist Popery and Prelacy, and arbitrary power; and to recover and establish the work of Reformation in Scotland, in opposition to Popery, Prelacy, and arbitrary power in all the branches and steps thereof, till the government in Church and State be brought to that luster and integrity which it had in the best times.' J. King Hewison, *The Covenanters*. Vol. II. Pp. 524-532.

51. J. King Hewison, *The Covenanters*. Vol. II. p. 530.

52. Edwin Nisbet Moore, *Our Covenant Heritage*, P. 155.

53. J. King Hewison, *The Covenanters*. Vol. II. p. 525. See *John Calvin, his influence in the Western World*.

54. That act asserted the 'royal supremacy over all persons and in all causes ecclesiastical'.

James Barr, *The Scottish Covenanters*, Glasgow, John Smith and Son, 1946, p. 60. Also rescinded: The appointment of church officers superior to elders and the decrees against Conventicles. Smelie, *Men of the Covenant*, p. 504.

55. James King Hewison, *The Covenanters* Vol. II. p. 537.

56. James King Hewison, *The Covenanters* Vol. II. p. 536-538. At the same time, there was also the abolition of patronage. Smelie, *Men of the Covenant*, p. 505.

57. Michael Shields, 'Is there any positive act to be found amongst the archives of the nation, by which that heaven-daring Act is repealed? If there is not, the whole legal establishment of the true Protestant Presbyterian form of church government must stand yet publicly condemned.' As cited by J. D. Douglas, *Light in the North*, p. 177.

58. Edwin Nisbet Moore, *Our Covenant Heritage*, p. 154. 'Unfortunately, they left the acts that had undone the work of the Second Reformation on the books; consequently, the Solemn League and Covenant remained an illegal oath. The net result was an abandonment of the pledge contained in the Solemn League and Covenant for the preservation and reformation of religion.'

59. Edwin Nisbet Moore, *Our Covenant Heritage*, p. 154.

60. J. King Hewison, *The Covenanters* Vol. II. p. 540. 'This disregard for the spiritual independence of the church, and intrusion upon its special province, was one which both Knox and Andrew Melville would have resented.'

61. James Kerr, *The Covenants and the Covenanters* pp. 419-434.

62. Thus, an episcopal presence remained in Scotland. There was a bishop in Glasgow into the 1700's. There were 890 parishes in Scotland. Between 300-400 Episcopalian ministers were allowed to continue in their living, and by 1707 of the 900 parishes there were still 165 serving. Edwin Nisbet Moore, *Our Covenant Heritage*, p. 156. J. King Hewison, *The Covenanters*. Vol. II. pp. 539-540. James Barr, *The Scottish Covenanters*, Glasgow, John Smith and Son, 1946, p. 61.

63. James King Hewison, *The Covenanters* p. 539. 'Thus the most faithful adherents of the covenanted church were turned away from the national Zion, veritable scapegoats consciously burdened with the sins of the people, and again driven into the wilderness. The society-men were quite logical and accurate in their conclusion that the Covenanters had paid too dearly for all that their Protestant patrons and protectors were offering in return for their sacrifices. Conscience alone rewarded them.' W. M. Glasgow, *History of the Reformed Presbyterian Church in America* p. 46.

64. James Dodds, *The fifty years' struggle*, p. 376.

65. J. D. Douglas, *Light in the North*, p. 177.

66. Smelie, *Men of the Covenant*, p. 506.

67. Edwin Nisbet Moore, *Our Covenant Heritage*, p. 157.

68. James Barr, *The Scottish Covenanters*, Glasgow, John Smith and Son, 1946, p. 61. 'But the settlement itself was narrow, unjust and opposed to every principle of civic and religious equality. The state recognized only one church. They establish, ratify and confirm the Presbyterian Church Government and discipline as being the only government of Christ's church within the kingdom. They established and confirmed the Protestant religion and the worship, discipline and government of the church to continue without any alteration to the people of this land in all succeeding generations.'

69. Smelie, *Men of the Covenant*, p. 506.

70. Here Kerr is partially correct, 'For nearly a hundred years this conflict was destined to continue till, at the Revolution Settlement, the divine right of kings was banished [from] the realm.' However, more caution should be taken between a nation's

ability to depose a king and a king's sovereignty over the church. Kerr, 15.

71. 'The net result was an abandonment of the pledge contained in the Solemn League and Covenant for the preservation and reformation of religion.' Edwin Nisbet Moore, *Our Covenant Heritage*, p. 154. 'The Presbyterianism that had forged an ideal blend of doctrinal purity, evangelical spirit, and cultural involvement during the Second Reformation ceased to exist.' p. 156.

72. Under the leadership of the layman Sir Robert Hamilton, some groups continued to meet in societies. John McMillan, a minister in the established church, agitated until 1703 that the Covenants should not be violated. He was then deposed and worked with the societies. In 1707, Reverend McMillan was joined by licentiate John McNeile who together wrote a 'Protestation and Testimony of the United Societies'. The following year they composed a 'Protestation, Declinature and Appeal'. In 1707, Scotland and England were united and in 1711, patronage was restored. These events led to a further covenant renewal by the societies in 1712. In 1743, Thomas Nairn, a minister in the associate presbytery, joined with John MacMillan and their respective elders, and formed a presbytery called The Reformed Presbytery. This presbytery 'professed to adhere and bear testimony to our covenanted reformation, as it was carried on in the nations betwixt the years 1638 and 1649.' In 1761, the Reformed Presbytery wrote an act declaring that it was the legitimate successor to the second Reformation churches, termed the 'Ploughlandhead Testimony'. See W. M. Glasgow, *History of the Reformed Presbyterian Church in America*, pp. 46-49.

JONATHAN EDWARDS AND THE 1734-35 NORTHAMPTON REVIVAL

Samuel T. Logan, Jr.

I. Methodology

It's always difficult to assess the work of a preacher. Should we tabulate statistics or is that too crassly materialistic? How do we evaluate the role of the human agent vis-à-vis the sovereign power of the Holy Spirit – especially when the human agent in question professed absolute and total dependence on the Spirit in everything he did, but most especially in his preaching? When the preacher under consideration is 200 years dead, having lived long before Sony made homiletical instant replays possible, the task becomes more difficult – and when his fame (or notoriety, depending upon one's perspective) has raised him to semi-mythical status thereby provoking all manner of distortions of his work, the task of assessment nearly provokes the would-be interpreter to despair. Nearly, but not quite.

Jonathan Edwards has variously been regarded as an anachronistic throw-back to the narrow bigotries of provincialized Puritanism and as the enlightened proponent of modern theological constructs built upon Newtonian science and Lockean epistemology.[1] His preaching has likewise occasioned something less than fully complementary analyses. His name evokes horrifying images of spiders, the blazing pits of hell, as well as admiration for brilliantly sophisticated theological constructs combined with a unique mastery of the English language. And he was involved in two revivals, the second of which shook the young British colonies in America like nothing before or since. But in spite of the incredible diversity of interpretations of Edwards and in spite of the difficulties cited earlier, we can, if we are careful, learn something of his work as a preacher and possibly even come to the kind of evaluation of his work that will allow us to learn from his experiences so that our own labors on behalf of the kingdom of Jesus Christ might be more effective.

Fortunately, our subject is the first and smaller (and therefore more manageable) of the revivals with which Edwards was involved – that which began in his church in Northampton in November of 1734. But before tackling even that limited objective, it would be well to specify the primary sources to be used in our analysis. We will not depend on anonymous so-called 'eye-witness' accounts of his preaching style ('He stared at the bell-rope as though he would stare through') and we will disregard what some historians believe 'must have happened' because of the subsequent events. Rather, we will utilize just a couple of specific sources, and those largely from Edwards' own hand. First, we will make a brief comment about the type of notes Edwards took with him into the pulpit in 1734 (which notes are available for inspection in the Beinecke Rare Book and Manuscript Library at Yale University). Then we will consider Edwards' own account of the events of 1734–35 as that account is provided in *A Faithful Narrative of the Surprising Work of God in the Conversion of Many Hundred Souls, in Northampton, and the Neighbouring Towns and Villages of New Hampshire, in New England; in a Letter to the Rev. Dr. Colman, of Boston* (hereafter, for obvious reasons, cited simply as *Narrative*).[2] Finally, we will look directly at one of the sermons actually preached by Edwards during the 1734–35 revival, *The Justice of God in the Damnation of Sinners* (hereafter cited simply as *Justice*).[3] All of this I do with the clear and profound conviction that Edwards's concern for revival 'to the glory of God' parallels the teaching and ministry of D. Clair Davis, in recognition for whose service to Christ this volume is being prepared.

II. Edwards' Use of Sermon Notes

Norman Fiering, in his recent profound and provocative work entitled *Jonathan Edwards' Moral Thought and Its British Context*, comments in his bibliographical section that, 'For the serious researcher on Edwards, there is no substitute for spending a summer at the Beinecke.'[4] Surely he is correct except that there is far more there than can be digested in a year of summers. However, even a brief visit (with proper advance permission by the authorities) will provide insights into Edwards unavailable in any other way. Among the treats in store for the scholar who would visit the Beinecke is the opportunity to hold in one's own hands Edwards' actual sermon notes, including those for *Sinners in the Hands of an Angry God*. Actually, 'notes' seems both an appropriate and an inappropriate description of that material. The pages are certainly small – 3 7/8 by 4 1/8 inches – and there are only a couple of them. But upon those pages, crawling from margin to margin, is the most microscopic and nearly undecipherable handwriting one would ever hope to see. But each of those sets of sheets contains an Edwards sermon written out word-for-word.

Writing out his sermons in full and reading them verbatim from the pulpit was Edwards' common practice, at least until George Whitefield visited Northampton in October of 1740.[5] Whitefield's own extemporaneous preaching style had its impact on Edwards and he (Edwards) began to utilize few notes (sometimes only outlines) in the pulpit. But in 1734, at the time of the first Northampton revival, Edwards was reading his sermons and obviously, as we shall see, was doing so quite effectively. Surely we must be careful of drawing conclusions prematurely and our overall assessment of Edwards' role in the 1734–35 revival must await a fuller description of his actions during that time, but it does seem appropriate at this point to suggest that his method of sermon delivery (which has been highly criticized in recent days) does not seem to have been a barrier to revival in Northampton.

III. Backgrounds of Revival

Located some two hundred miles west of Boston, Northampton, Massachusetts, in 1734, 'still belonged to that vague territory known to the Boston newspapers as "our western Frontiers"'.[6] Ola Winslow's further description of the physical aspects of the town is helpful.

Beyond the houses and completely encircling what had been the settlement, were the old fortifications: the trenches, earth-works, and spike fences (overgrown now in many places, but their outline still plainly visible). Farther out, and extending up the rough slopes of Mt. Tom and Rocky Hill, were the sheep pastures, cleared of underbrush and marked off in irregular plots with hurdle fences. An occasional shepherd moved about among the flocks. Along the river were the fertile fields, explaining why a settlement had been made in this lonely spot, which was really no more than a clearing between the woods and the river. Roads were merely paths, made for horseback travel only, and lost to view at the edge of the clearing. On all sides deep forests blotted out the horizon. Only the river led out. A town built here must be sufficient unto itself, and what concerned one would concern all.[7]

As important as what Northampton was distant from (Harvard and Boston) was what it was close to. Less than thirty miles north, also lying alongside the Connecticut River, was the town of Deerfield – or, one should say, the rebuilt town of Deerfield, for it was here, in 1704 – the year after Edwards' birth – that a nighttime raid by fifty French soldiers and two hundred Indians killed fifty of the inhabitants (one sixth of the total), carried off more than a hundred others, and destroyed most of the town.[8] To be sure, that raid had occurred thirty years earlier and it would not be until the 1750's that the full-scale French and Indian War (known across the Atlantic as the Seven Years War) would bring to a head the old lurking antagonisms. But again Ola Winslow does a masterful job of setting the scene.

> The burning of Deerfield by the Indians in 1704 had been the last horror of that sort, but the portholes in the meetinghouse and in the fortified houses around it still reminded residents who had reason to be reminded that such dangers had once been very real. Even yet, it was wise to take precautions. Occasionally a child wandered too far and was carried off. A man went into the woods to look for his cow, and was found scalped or never heard of again. Wolves were a continual menace to the flocks; sometimes to the children.[9]

It was not, however, the geographical setting with which Edwards was most concerned in his *Narrative*. Indeed, he barely mentions these factors at all. But it is crucial for us to remember where Edwards preached and where the Lord chose to begin the revival in New England. This was not the urbane, sophisticated, 'hub of the universe' Boston. And Edwards' people were not, for the most part, highly educated intellectuals. They were small merchants, farmers, young people, all still living more or less in one of the outposts of 18th century American civilization. We must remember this as we reflect upon the rigorous content of Edwards' preaching, upon the type of rhetoric he used, upon the events of 1734 and 1735, and upon the even greater events, which followed five years later.

Edwards certainly knew the geographical setting of Northampton, but his concern, when he described the events of that first revival, was more with the chronological and spiritual setting. He began the *Narrative* with an evocation of the memory of his predecessor in the Northampton pulpit, his grandfather, the Rev. Solomon Stoddard. Perry Miller may very well have been correct when he described Stoddard as the 'Pope' of the Connecticut Valley.[10] Given Northampton's distance from Boston, Stoddard made the most of his congregational autonomy and introduced ecclesiastical innovations in the criteria for church membership that made the eastern theological establishment (personified in the Mathers) gasp. The content of those innovations has been evaluated by various scholars as theological liberalism, nascent democracy, and pure Calvinism but fortunately, it is not necessary to resolve these differences here.[11] Suffice it to say that Stoddard's innovations brought new people into the meetinghouse, that Stoddard preached repentance to them, and that a series of mini-revivals resulted.

It was with these 'spiritual harvests' that Edwards was concerned in describing the context for the 1734–35 events. In the fourth paragraph of the *Narrative*, he described Stoddard's work like this:

> He continued in the work of the ministry here, from his first coming to town, near 60 years. And as he was eminent and *renowned* for his gifts and grace; so he was blessed, from the beginning, with *extraordinary success* in his ministry, in the conversion of many souls. He had *five harvests*, as he called them. The *first* was about 57 years ago; the *second* about 53; the *third* about 40; the *fourth* about 24; the *fifth* and last about 18 years ago. *Some* of these times were much more remarkable than others, and the ingathering of souls more plentiful. Those about 53, and 40, and 24 years ago, were much greater than either the *first* or the *last*: but in *each* of them, I have heard my grandfather say, the greater part of the *young* people in town, seemed to be mainly concerned with their eternal salvation.[12]

Why would Edwards have mentioned these revivals under Stoddard? Of what importance were they in understanding the Lord's work in 1734–35? First, we must remember that in 1734, Edwards was only thirty-one years of age and that he had been alone as Pastor at Northampton for just five years (Stoddard had died in 1729). He was a young man and he was laboring in the shadow of one of the most eminent of the New England divines. It was his concern (legitimate, I believe) to show that he was not, in his involvement with the 'Surprising Conversions' he was about to describe, departing from the mainstream of Puritanism. It seems appropriate to regard this reminder of Stoddard's spiritual harvests as of the same character as the Apostle Paul's comments at the end of Galatians, Chapter 1. Edwards and Paul both were seeking to validate the authority with which they spoke and to assure their readers thereby that the account and admonitions to follow were legitimate.

But there was at least one other reason for Edwards to remind his readers of what had happened earlier in Northampton. Edwards always tried to consider what we would call 'the big picture'.[13] He sought to discover the patterns in God's dealings with the people of Northampton, which unified both the Stoddard harvests and the 1734–35 revival just as, later in his life, he would write of the pattern being expressed in the entire Great Awakening.[14] All of this, of course, emerged from Edwards' belief in the sovereignty of God and from his thoroughly Biblical sense of the 'fitness', the beauty, which characterized both the movement of redemptive history and the very structure of creation itself. Edwards, even more than he wanted to legitimatize his own work, deeply desired his readers to catch a glimpse of the patterned movings of the Almighty, so that they would know their part in the cosmic drama which will one day climax in the New Heavens and the New Earth. What happened in Northampton, Edwards was saying, was not just an isolated blip on the screen of human history. It was a partial fulfillment of the work that the Lord did here earlier and, as a part of this kind of larger pattern, it especially deserved the reader's attention.

But unfortunately, this was not the only element in the Northampton context. Past blessing had given way to an

> ... extraordinary dullness in religion. *Licentiousness* for some years greatly prevailed among the *youth* of the town; they were many of

them very much addicted to *night-walking*, and frequenting the *tavern*, and *lewd* practices, wherein some, by their example, exceedingly corrupted others. It was their manner very frequently to get together, in conventions of both *sexes* for mirth and jollity, which they called *frolics;* and they would often spend the greater part of the *night* in them, without regard to any *order* in the families they belonged to: and indeed *family government* did too much fail in the town.[15]

Where grace had abounded, there sin now much more abounded. So Edwards was preaching in 1734 in a context of moral decline, but not only that. He further pointed out that 'About this time began the great noise, in this part of the country, about Arminianism, which seemed to appear with a very threatening aspect upon the interest of religion here.'[16] Winslow even sees this as the most significant of all the contexts for Edwards' 1734 sermons.

> The battle was already at hand. By 1734 heresy had filtered into his own parish. Men were beginning to take sides. He set himself to resist the oncoming tide. The result was a series of sermons designed to combat point by point what he believed to be the false doctrines of his theological opponents. His refutation was in Calvinistic idiom: the sovereignty of God, his inexorable justice, particularly justification by faith alone.[17]

Whether Edwards believed that the heresy produced the immorality (as is likely) or that the immorality led to the heresy, one thing is certain: he faced a difficult situation in the very place where, years earlier, there seemed such bright promise of the blessings of God.[18] Confronting the twin problems of Arminianism and immorality, and conscious of what the Lord had done (and might yet do again) in Northampton, Edwards chose his homiletical response carefully. Edwards determined, in the late fall of 1734, to preach a series of sermons on the Biblical doctrine of justification by faith alone. To modern minds, such a decision might seem the least likely to produce any kind of revival. After all, mustn't we, if we expect any significant response from our congregations, leave the heavy theology in our studies and excite that response by giving them material easy to assimilate and easier to respond to? Granted there may be a significant difference between Edwards' congregation and ours in terms of the homiletical diet to which they would be accustomed, nevertheless Edwards' decision was a daring one.

But it does make solid Biblical sense. Edwards was conscious first of all that what ultimately mattered was not the welfare of an isolated community called Northampton. His vision was cosmic and he knew that what really counted was the forward movement of the kingdom of Jesus Christ – Northampton counted only as it 'fit' into that movement. This sense of perspective kept Edwards from responding just to the immediacy of the moment. The cause is the Lord's, the kingdom is his, and therefore, any response to a specific situation would have to be made so as to promote the eschatological cause of the kingdom. Edwards would not, therefore, allow the pressures of the moment to lead him to narrow his focus. He would preach on the big issue, the truth which would forward the work of the kingdom begun earlier in Northampton, the truth at the heart of the Reformation – justification by faith alone.

But his commitment to this broader vision did not leave him blind to the specific needs in his community; indeed that vision heightened his pastoral sensitivities. To forward the kingdom of Jesus Christ in Northampton in 1734 was the motive behind Edwards' choice of sermon topics for that November and December. He analyzed his congregation's specific needs in terms of the broader advance of the kingdom and determined to preach on justification. For Edwards, Arminianism threatened the kingdom at precisely this point – how are sinners justified by God? And the licentious behavior of some in the community likewise threatened the kingdom by denying the difference God's sovereign, justifying grace *must* make in the life of the sinner. So Edwards preached to meet specific needs and genuine threats. But he did so by dealing directly and thoroughly with complex Biblical truths because he wanted to see the kingdom advanced even more than he wanted to see Northampton blessed. But as a matter of fact, he saw both.

This is not the place to analyze in detail the sophisticated content of Edwards' sermons on justification by faith alone. That has been done elsewhere.[19] Suffice it to say here that what Edwards said was both thoroughly orthodox and brilliantly creative – as most of his best work tended to be. Perhaps what would be of most help now would be simply to sketch the basic events of the revival and then to return to an assessment both of Edwards' preaching and of his overall handling of the situation.

IV. The Sequence of the Revival

The specific events which Edwards himself included in his description of the revival began in late 1733 when there was noted 'a very unusual flexibleness, and yielding to advice, in our young people'.[20] Apparently socializing after the second Sunday service had gotten a bit out of hand and was threatening the sanctity of the Lord's day, for Edwards specifically mentioned this problem and preached on it at a Sunday morning service. He urged 'heads of families that it should be a thing agreed upon, among them, to govern these families, and keep their children at home, at these times.'[21] The parents seemed to have agreed with Edwards and were prepared to take the appropriate disciplinary action when they discovered that action was unnecessary.

> But *parents* found little or no occasion for the exercise of government in the case. The *young people* declared themselves *convinced* by what they had heard from the *pulpit,* and were willing of themselves to comply with the counsel that had been given: and it was *immediately,* and, I suppose, almost *universally,* complied with; and there was a thorough *reformation* of these disorders thenceforward, which has continued ever since.[22]

Following this 'thorough reformation' by no more than five months was the 'very sudden and awful death of a young man in the bloom of his youth; who being violently seized with a pleurisy, and taken immediately very delirious, died in about two days; which (together with what was preached publicly on that occasion) much affected many young people.'[23] This death occurred in April of 1734 and

> ... was followed with another death of a young married woman, who had been considerably *exercised* in mind, about the salvation of her *soul,* before she was ill, and was in great *distress* in the beginning of her illness; but seemed to have *satisfying evidences* of God's saving *mercy* to her, before her death; so that she died very full of *comfort,* in a most earnest and moving manner warning, and counseling others. This seemed to *contribute* to render solemn spirits of many young persons; and there began evidently to appear more of a *religious concern* on people's minds.[24]

Early autumn found Edwards organizing small group meetings for his young people in order to build upon what the Lord had already done in Northampton.[25] But note that this was now a year since the discussions about the proper use of Sunday evenings. Edwards was a patient but persistent pastor and he was acutely sensitive to the ways in which seemingly diverse problems may become an opportunity for the Spirit's reviving work. That sensitivity was about to bear fruit for it was later that autumn (1734) that he began his series on justification by faith alone.

Those sermons were actually preached in November and December. 'And then it was,' Edwards commented, 'in the latter part of December, that the Spirit of God began extraordinarily to set in, and wonderfully to work amongst us; and there were, very suddenly, one after another, five or six persons, who were to all appearance savingly converted, and some of them wrought upon in a very remarkable manner.'[26] As often happens, the Spirit built upon his own work through the testimony of one of those converted. A young woman, a notorious 'company keeper' surprised even Edwards with her narrative of grace. But the effect upon the town was positively electric. In Edwards' words,

> God made it, I suppose, the *greatest occasion of awakening* to others, of any thing that ever came to pass in the town. I have had abundant opportunity to know the effect it had, by my private conversation with many. The news of it seemed to be almost like a *flash of lightning,* upon the hearts of young people, all over the town, and upon many others. Those persons amongst us, who used to be *farthest* from seriousness, and that I most feared would make an ill improvement of it, seemed greatly to be *awakened* with it. Many went to talk with her, concerning what she had met with: and what appeared in her seemed to be to the satisfaction of all that did so.[27]

Edwards did not date this woman's public testimony precisely, but presumably her conversion became public knowledge by late January or early February with the result that 'a great and earnest concern about the great things of religion, and the eternal world, became universal in all parts of the town, and among persons of all degrees, and all ages'.[28] Edwards himself was struck by the Biblical overtones of what was happening, commenting in terms reminiscent of the Lord's words to Ezekiel that 'The noise amongst the dry bones waxed louder and louder'.[29]

This dramatic sense of the Lord's special presence in Northampton continued for several months.

This work of God, as it was carried on, and the number of true saints multiplied, soon made a glorious alteration in the town: so that in the spring and summer following, *anno* 1735, the town seemed to be full of the presence of God: it never was so full of *love*, nor of *joy*, and yet so full of distress, as it was then. There were remarkable tokens of God's presence in almost every house. It was a time of joy in *families* on account of salvation being brought unto them; *parents* rejoicing over their children as new born, and *husbands* over their wives, and wives over their husbands. *The goings of God* were then *seen in his sanctuary*, God's *day* was a *delight*, and his *tabernacles* were *amiable*. Our public assemblies were then beautiful: the congregation was *alive* in God's service, every one earnestly intent on the public worship, every *hearer* eager to drink in the words of the *minister* as they came from his mouth; the assembly in general were, from time to time, *in tears* while the word was preached; *some* weeping with sorrow and distress, *others* with joy and love, *others* with pity and concern for the souls of their neighbours.[30]

By March of 1735, the revival had spread beyond Northampton to the neighboring towns of Suffield, Sunderland, Deerfield, Hatfield, West Springfield, Long Meadow, Enfield, Westfield, Hadley, Northfield, Windsor, Coventry, New Haven, Mansfield, and many others. And in a fascinating intimation of things to come, Edwards commented that the revival was spreading beyond the regional boundaries of New England.

But this shower of divine blessing has been yet more *extensive:* there was no small degree of it in some part of the *Jerseys;* as I was informed when I was at New York, (in a long journey I took at that time of the year for my health,) by some people of the Jerseys, whom I saw. Especially the Rev. William Tennent, a minister who seemed to have such things much at heart, told me of a very great awakening of many in a place called the *Mountains*, under the ministry of one Mr. Cross; and of a very considerable revival of religion in another place under the ministry of his brother the Rev. Gilbert Tennent; and also at another place, under the ministry of a very pious young gentleman, a Dutch minister, whose name as I remember was Freelinghousa.[31]

Jonathan Edwards, the Tennents, and Frelinghuysen (even if Edwards did misspell his name) – were all involved in the revival work of the Spirit of God in the mid-1730's and Edwards especially, because of his penchant for seeing the big picture, sensed the unity behind the apparent diversity.[32] Just as clearly but in this case somewhat regrettably, Edwards became all too aware of the quantitative aspects of the revival, but his comments remain valuable to us who would understand the exact scope of what was happening.

> This dispensation has also appeared very extraordinary in the *numbers* of those on whom we have reason to hope it has had a saving effect. We have about *six hundred and twenty communicants*, which include almost all our adult persons. The church was very *large* before; but persons never *thronged* into it, as they did in the late extraordinary time. – Our *sacraments* are eight weeks asunder, and I received into our communion about a *hundred* before one sacrament, *fourscore* of them at one time, whose appearance, when they presented themselves together to make an open explicit *profession* of Christianity, was very affecting to the congregation. I took in near *sixty* before the next sacrament day: and I had very sufficient evidence of the conversion of their souls, through divine grace, though it is not the custom here, as it is in many other churches in this country, to make credible relation of their inward experiences the ground of admission to the Lord's supper.
>
> . . .
>
> This work seemed to be at its greatest height in this town, in the former part of the spring, in March and April. At that time, God's work in the conversion of souls was carried on amongst us in so wonderful a manner, that, so far as I can judge, it appears to have been at the rate, at least, of four personas a day; or nearly thirty in a week, take one with another, for five or six weeks together. When God in so remarkable a manner took the work into his own hands, there was as much done in a *day or two* as at ordinary times, with all endeavours that men can use, and with such a blessing as we commonly have, is done in a *year*.[33]

But by May of 1735, some disturbing signs had begun to appear as well. First, Thomas Stebbins, a 'poor weak man' with a family history of emotional disturbances, being, as Edwards said, 'in great spiritual trouble', attempted to cut his own throat.[34] Fortunately, Stebbins was unsuccessful and recovered. But unfortunately, his action was repeated, this time with deadly success by Joseph Hawley, one of the town leaders and Edwards' own uncle. Winslow's description of the effect of these events is striking.

A fast was appointed, and the congregation prostrated itself before God. But the turning point had come: the spell was broken, the emotional climate changed at once, and the long delayed reaction set in. For the first time sobered men and women began to question the wholesomeness of the excitement under which they had been living. As a matter of fact, the limit of endurable ecstasies had been reached; but before equilibrium could be established and life could proceed normally once more there were to be many blots on the record. Hawley's death proved to be only the beginning, even in suicides. 'Multitudes', to quote the pastor's own word, were impelled to do likewise, feeling it 'urged upon them as if somebody had spoke to them "Cut your own throat. Now is a good opportunity."' Fortunately not all succeeded. Others suffered from equally strange delusions, until at length it was clear to all that God had withdrawn his spirit. The heavenly shower was over.[35]

As the summer of 1735 drew to a close, Edwards noted two other disturbing facts. First, there were 'remarkable instances of persons led away with strange enthusiastic delusions'.[36] In at least one case the delusion consisted of an individual's claim to be receiving direct revelation from God, a not-uncommon phenomenon in the midst of revivalist fervor. Second, conversions were becoming more rare and the attention of the people was being refocused on more earthly concerns – such as Indian treaties and the details of building a new meetinghouse with enough room for all the recent converts.[37] Clearly, to Edwards' practiced pastoral eye, 'there was a gradual decline of that general, engaged, lively spirit in religion, which had been.'[38] But this decline, while disappointing to one who desired nothing less than the full and immediate triumph of the kingdom of Christ, did not negate the value of what had happened. Edwards summarized the results of the revival in this way:

But as to those who have been thought converted at this time, they generally seem to have had an abiding change wrought on them. I have had particular acquaintance with many of them since; and they generally appear to be persons who have a new sense of things, new apprehensions and views of God, of the divine attributes of *Jesus Christ,* and the great things of the gospel. They have a new sense of their truth, and they affect them in a new manner; though it is very far from being always alike with them, neither can they revive a sense of things when they please. Their hearts are often touched, and sometimes filled, with new sweetnesses and delights; there seems to express an inward ardour and burning of heart, like to which they never experienced before; sometimes, perhaps, occasioned only by the mention of *Christ's* name, or some one of the divine perfections. There are new appetites, and a new kind of breathings and pantings of heart, *and groanings that cannot be uttered.* There is a new kind of inward labour and struggle of soul towards heaven and holiness.[39]

Edwards' use, in this description, of phrases like 'new sense', 'new apprehensions', 'new sweetnesses and delights', and 'inward ardour and burning of heart' shows that he was already thinking in the categories which appear so explicitly in his masterpiece, the *Treatise Concerning Religious Affections.* And the fact that he used these terms here, in 1737, to describe those who have been converted tells us something about the terms in which he saw conversion and therefore about the perspective from which he saw his own preaching. As we shall note shortly, Edwards' preaching was designed specifically to stir the affections, to elicit new apprehensions, and by God's grace, it did.

All to which I have thus far referred in Edwards' *Narrative* has focused on the chronological sequence of events in the revival as a whole. I would like now to turn briefly to Edwards' description of the chronological sequence of events in the lives of those who were savingly touched by the Spirit during those days. In other words, I would like to turn to the morphology of conversion developed implicitly by Edwards in his description of the revival. I use the word 'implicitly' on purpose. We must remember that Edwards, in the *Narrative* is seeking to be primarily an historian. That is, his intention was to narrate the events of the 1734–35 revival. To be sure, he is an apologetic historian in that he wished to defend the Biblical character of what happened but he is still much more the historian here than he is, for example, in his treatises on *Religious Affections, The Freedom of the Will, Original Sin, True Virtue,* etc.

This is an important point here because the tendency otherwise might be to read the morphology which emerges from the *Narrative* as a kind of rigid preparationism, which, in the normal connotation of that phrase, it definitely was not.[40] Edwards simply saw a pattern emerging from the Spirit's dealings with the people of Northampton and, as he did on a much larger scale in his *History of the Work of Redemption,* he sought to describe that pattern to his readers.

But if it is possible to read too much into Edwards' morphology, it is also possible to read too little out of it. Edwards included it in the *Narrative* and he did so with a purpose. Both pastor and parishioner (in the new millennium as well as in the 1730's) should be aware of how the Spirit seems normally to work in bringing someone into justification by faith. They should be aware of this in order better to know how to act, what to say or do, when confronting the Spirit's work in progress – in themselves or in others.

This is again not to say that each so-called step had to be experienced by each individual in precisely the same order and on precisely the same timetable. The Spirit could very well leap over some steps or add others. As Edwards put it with resounding clarity, 'God has appeared far from limiting himself to any certain method in his proceedings with sinners under legal conviction. In some instances, it seems easy for our reasoning powers to discern the methods of divine wisdom, in his dealings with the soul under awakenings; in others, his footsteps cannot be traced, and his ways are past finding out.'[41] But even with this caveat, knowing the Spirit's normal operations may help us to avoid misinterpreting a brother's spiritual situation which misinterpretation could lead us to give him exactly the wrong counsel. Edwards saw the morphology he provided in the *Narrative* as guidance for those who are experiencing the Spirit's work and for those who deal with those who are – nothing less than that and certainly nothing more.

Edwards did not present his material in the form of morphology, and other readers of the *Narrative* may quarrel with the way in which I have grouped and divided that material. I have, however, tried to be sensitive to Edwards' language here and in his other writings in order to present accurately his perceptions of what happened in 1734–35. This first step in the conversion process, observed Edwards, frequently seemed to be the awakening of the individual to a sense of the miserable danger of their natural condition.[42] This initial awakening had a broader rather than a narrower focus and led the individuals in question to begin seeking ways of avoiding a spiritual danger which, though not precisely specific, was deeply felt. Two types of response seemed frequently to have categorized persons under this sort of awakening – first, they sought to avoid behavior which might be considered sinful (the result being, as Edwards reported, that 'the tavern was soon left empty'), and second, they began positively seeking after answers in, for example, 'prayer, meditation, the ordinances of God's house, and private conferences' with their pastor.[43]

Edwards described in great detail the degrees of distress experienced by such individuals, but the next discrete 'step' in the process was the development of a sense of 'conviction of their absolute dependence on his (God's) sovereign power and grace, and by a universal necessity of a mediator.'[44] The progress or development here seems clear. The vague sense of danger and need now began to lead toward the recognition of where help must come from if it is to come at all. These factors are implicit in the responses described above but they are made explicit here by the increasing sense that the source of danger was also the only possible source of deliverance from danger. Here already we see emerging what was for Edwards an absolutely crucial factor – wrong doctrine and wrong behavior are tied inextricably together. One cannot be dealt with without the other, and there is no possibility of revival without dealing with both. If debauchery and Arminianism went hand in hand in Northampton's spiritual mess, so orthodox doctrine and reformation of lifestyle went hand in hand in the Spirit's revival of Northampton.

The third stage outlined by Edwards reinforced the second. Being awakened to a sense of their sin and becoming aware that God himself must provide some kind of protection for them, these persons then '... set themselves upon a new course of fruitless endeavours, in their own strength, to make themselves better; and still met with new disappointments.'[45] Having realized conceptually that the work of salvation was God's alone, they now realized it experientially with the result that they now may enter the fourth stage, '... a conviction of the justice of God in their condemnation, appearing in a sense of their own exceeding sinfulness, and the vileness of their own performances.'[46] Again the progress is clear. From the first step in which they became aware that they were in danger, those with whom the Spirit worked now came to understand and to accept that they *deserved* to be in danger. The convergence of what might be called 'head knowledge and heart knowledge' is remarkable – the orthodox doctrines were 'sensed' (that's Edwards' word) to be true and as they were, the process continued toward fruition. But a word of assessment might be appropriate here before we move on to consider the rest of this process. Among his most helpful insights has been Edwards' realization (fully expressed in his *Treatise Concerning*

Religious Affections, to which we shall briefly turn later) that the preacher's primary aim must be to make sensible, lively, affecting, the grand truths of Scripture. The degree to which he did this well is seen in the morphology, which arose out of his preaching, and in the blessings God sent upon Northampton.

Thus far, the one being awakened, the one under conviction had been both negatively and selfishly affected. He had become aware of the fact that he was a sinner and deserved judgment at the hand of a sovereign God. But now, the focus seemed to shift and while continuing to be deeply aware of his own spiritual malaise and the justice of it, the individual for the first time, in what might be regarded as step number five, began 'to see feelingly' the beauty, the glory of God.[47] This turn-around of perspective, while still in Edwards' mind prior to the manifestation of God's saving grace, was nevertheless crucial, for Edwards emphasized long and hard, as we shall see more fully later, that genuinely gracious affections are concentrated on God and on the excellencies of his being, not on the benefits to be gleaned from faith in him. As sinners begin to see God, not as a reflection of their own need but as he is in himself, they are truly getting close to Heaven.

The first five steps constituted what Edwards called 'legal humiliation' and were, in his phrase, 'preparatory to grace'.[48] Great care must be used to understand Edwards' meaning here. Edwards was emphatically not saying that Northampton sinners completed these first five steps on their own and then grace intervened. In fact, in the very sentence where he used the phrase 'preparatory to grace', he described the individuals going through these steps as 'wrought upon' by the Spirit.[49] When Edwards suggested that the first five were steps preparatory to grace, he was maintaining that the Spirit accomplished *all* of the steps, that a person might be brought through these five and still never be saved, and that special, saving grace entered the individual's life later (logically if not chronologically). Again, the implications for Edwards as pastor were monumental (and they are no less so for us who would learn from his experience). An individual having experienced all five of the steps described this far was *not* to be counseled toward assurance. He was to be urged to rest in Jesus for he had not yet done this. The wrong advice at such a crucial point could be spiritually devastating – and that is one reason Edwards tried to be so careful in describing what had happened in Northampton.

'The way that grace seems sometimes first to appear', wrote Edwards in introducing the crucial sixth step, 'is in earnest longings of soul after God and Christ.'[50] It was one thing to recognize the glory of God but an entirely different one to desire to be with him. This understanding of human psychology, anticipatory of Edwards' work in both *Religious Affections* and *Freedom of the Will*, places a heavy emphasis on the individual's fundamental disposition of heart. One possibly oversimplified but nonetheless helpful way to summarize Edwards' argument in *Freedom of the Will* is to say that one can do what he wants, but one cannot want what he wants. That is, freedom consists in the absence of external restraints, not in a kind of ethical indifference out of which one chooses his direction randomly.[51] One's most fundamental 'wants' are given to him – either by his natural sinful disposition (in the case of the unregenerate person) or by Spirit-originated redeemed disposition (in the case of the regenerate). Thus, an unregenerate man cannot 'relish' (again Edwards' word) the glory of God even though he might recognize it. But the regenerate man can and, though imperfectly, does.

It was, therefore, in the desires, the genuine longings of individuals, that the specifically redemptive special grace of God was first seen. These longings, as Edwards described them, were divinely focused:

> ... to know God, to love him, to be humble before him, to have communion with Christ in his benefits; which longings, as they express them, seem evidently to be of such a nature as can arise from nothing but a sense of the superlative excellency of divine things, with a spiritual taste and relish of them, and an esteem of them as their highest happiness and best portion. Such longings as I speak of, are commonly attended with firm resolutions to pursue this good for ever, together with a hoping, waiting disposition. When persons have begun in such frames, commonly other experiences and discoveries have soon followed, which have yet more clearly manifested a change of heart.[52]

Gradually, Edwards noticed in those who had come to relish the Savior, a sort of holy repose of soul developed, a sweet complacency in which they were simply aware of being delighted in Christ. This constituted the seventh and penultimate step of the redemptive process. Individuals in this situation, Edwards noted, might not yet have been propositionally aware of their redeemed status and might even have talked about seeking their conversion, but Edwards himself had no doubt – those whose delight was truly in Jesus were just as truly his. And Edwards did not hesitate to say so, for he believed that the movement to the final step, assurance, was also a crucial one. Without that eighth step, individuals tended toward the kind of intensive self-questioning which hindered their growth into genuine Christian maturity.

So Edwards sought to bring his people into Biblical assurance, into a clear intellectual apprehension of what it meant that they truly relished God and his son Jesus Christ. And once having apprehended that, the fruit of the entire process, evangelical obedience coupled with verbal testimony regarding the Spirit's work, could be realized. These are not by Edwards counted another, ninth, step. Rather assurance, testimony, action blend together and, indeed, may be used by the Spirit to begin the process all over again in someone else's life. As he put it succinctly but accurately, 'There is no one thing that I know of which God has made such a means of promoting his work among us, as the news of other's conversion.'[53] Therein is seen another reason why Edwards was so concerned that his people keep moving from relish to repose to assurance – so that they could then, with assurance, testify of God's redemptive grace thereby, possibly, if the Spirit moved, influencing others.

This was the morphology Edwards noted in 1734–35. But it would be unwise to leave this aspect of the revival without once again hearing Edwards' own implicit warning as to how we must *not* take this material. It is a lengthy statement but one packed with wise pastoral advice.

Conversion is a great and glorious work of God's power, at once changing the heart, and infusing life into the dead soul; though the grace then implanted more gradually displays itself in some than in others. But as to fixing on the *precise time* when they put forth the very first act of grace, there is a great deal of difference in different persons; in some it seems to be very discernible when the very time was; but others are more at a loss. In *this respect, there are very many who do not know, even when they have it, that it is* the grace of conversion, and sometimes do not think it to be so till a long time after.

In *some*, converting light is like a glorious brightness suddenly shining *upon* a person, and all *around* him: they are in a remarkable manner brought *out of darkness into marvellous light.* In many *others* it has been like the dawning of the day, when at first but a *little* light appears again, and it may be is presently hid with a cloud; and then it appears again, and shines a little *brighter,* and gradually increases, with intervening darkness, till at length it breaks forth more clearly from behind the clouds. And many are, doubtless, ready to *date* their conversion wrong, throwing by those lesser degrees of light that appeared at *first* dawning, and calling some more remarkable experience they had *afterwards,* their conversion. This often, in a great measure, arises from a wrong understanding of what they have always been taught, that conversion is a *great* change, wherein *old things are done away, and all things become new,* or at least from a false inference from that doctrine.[54]

Edwards' description and interpretation of the data of the revival suggests scores of implications, only a few of which have been touched on even briefly. Certainly among the most important to the pastor who would properly preach to and counsel his people are the uses and the dangers of tracing the Spirit's usual steps, the role of doctrine in revival preaching, and the degree to which a person's desires are the key to his spiritual state. The next matter before us is a brief consideration of one of the sermons Edwards actually preached in late 1734 in the context of which God blessed Northampton with revival.

V. A Sermon of the Revival

The *Justice of God in the Damnation of Sinners* is a fairly typical Edwardsean sermon and is therefore useful for understanding both his preaching in 1734 and his general homiletical style. Here, however, any paraphrase would be clearly inferior to direct quotation in providing an understanding of what Edwards' preaching was like, and therefore I will provide several large chunks of the sermon and then make a few evaluatory comments. The text was Romans 3:19, 'Now we know that whatever the Law says, it speaks to those who are under the Law, that every mouth may be closed, and all the world may become accountable to God' (NASB). 'The main subject of the doctrinal part of this epistle', Edwards began,

is the free grace of God in the salvation of men by Jesus Christ; especially as it appears in the doctrine of justification by faith alone. And the more clearly to evince this doctrine, and show the reason of it, the apostle, in the first place, establishes that point, that no flesh living can be justified by the deeds of the law. And to prove it, he is very large and particular in showing, that all mankind, not only the Gentiles, but Jews, are under sin, and so under the condemnation of the law; which is what he insists upon from the beginning of the epistle to this place.[55]

After a detailed discussion of the general sinfulness of both Jews and Gentiles and an explanation of why the law is 'sufficient to stop the mouths of all mankind', Edwards then moved to draw his doctrine from his exegesis.

DOCTRINE

'It is just with God eternally to cast off and destroy sinners.' – For this is the punishment which the law condemns to – The truth of this doctrine may appear by the joint consideration of two things, *viz.* Man's *sinfulness,* and God's *sovereignty.*

I. It appears from the consideration of man's sinfulness. And that whether we consider the infinitely evil nature of all sin, or how much sin men are guilty of.

1. If we consider the infinite evil and heinousness of sin in general, it is not unjust in God to inflict what punishment is deserved; because the very notion of deserving any punishment is, that it may be justly inflicted. A deserved punishment and a just punishment are the same thing. To say that one *deserves* such a punishment, and yet to say that he does not *justly* deserve it, is a contradiction; and if he justly deserves it, then it may be justly *inflicted.*

Every crime or fault deserves a greater or less punishment, in proportion as the crime itself is greater or less. If any fault deserves punishment, then so much the greater the fault, so much greater is the punishment deserved.

. . .

Our obligation to love, honour, and obey any being, is in proportion to his loveliness, honourableness, and authority; for that is the very meaning of the words. When we say any one is very lovely, it is the same as to say, that he is one very much to be loved. Or if we say such a one is more honourable than another, the meaning of the words is, that he is one that we are more obliged to honour. If we say any one has great authority over us, it is the same as to say, that he has great right to our subjection and obedience. But God is a being infinitely lovely, because he hath infinite excellency and beauty. To have infinite excellency and beauty, is the same thing as to have

infinite loveliness. He is a being of infinite greatness, majesty, and glory; and therefore he is infinitely honourable. He is infinitely exalted above the greatest potentates of the earth, and highest angels in heaven; and therefore he is infinitely more honourable than they. His authority over us is infinite; and the ground of his right to our obedience is infinitely strong; for his is infinitely worthy to be obeyed himself, and we have an absolute, universal, and infinite dependence upon him.
So that sin against God, being a violation of infinite obligations, must be a crime infinitely heinous, and so deserving infinite punishment.[56]

This is, of course, much the same type of argument with which, in his treatise on *Original Sin,* Edwards responded to later and more sophisticated Arminian onslaughts.[57] Here, in his 1734 sermon, he used it as one of the reasons why God is just to destroy sinners. The second reason, Edwards believed, was even more fundamental.

II. If with man's sinfulness, we consider God's *sovereignty,* it may serve further to clear God's justice in the eternal rejection and condemnation of sinners, from men's cavils and objections. I shall not now pretend to determine precisely, what things are, and what things are not, proper acts and exercises of God's holy sovereignty; but only, that God's sovereignty extends to the following things.
1. That such is God's sovereign power and right, that he is originally under no *obligation* to keep men from sinning; but may in his providence permit and *leave* them to sin. He was not obliged to keep either angels or men from falling.[58]

After a lengthy discussion of God's role in the permission of sin, Edwards continued.

3. When men are fallen, and become sinful, God by his sovereignty has a right to determine about their redemption as he pleases. He has a right to determine whether he will redeem any or not. He might, if he had pleased, have left all to perish, or might have redeemed all. Or he may redeem some, and leave others; and if he doth so, he may take whom he pleases. To suppose that all have forfeited his favour, and deserved to perish, and to suppose that he may not leave any one individual of them to perish, implies a contradiction; because it supposes that such a one has a claim to

God's favour, and is not justly liable to perish; which is contrary to the supposition. It is meet that God should order all these things according to his own pleasure. By reason of his greatness and glory, by which he is infinitely above all, he is worthy to be sovereign, and that his pleasure should in all things take place. He is worthy that he should make himself his end, and that he should make nothing but his own wisdom his rule in perusing that end, without asking leave or counsel of any, and without giving account of any of his matters. It is fit that he who is absolutely perfect, and infinitely wise, and the Fountain of all wisdom, should determine every thing that he effects by his own will, even things of the greatest importance. It is meet that he should be thus sovereign, because he is the first being, the eternal being, whence all other beings are. He is the Creator of all things; and all are absolutely and universally dependent on him; and therefore it is meet that he should act as the sovereign possessor of heaven and earth.[59]

Immediately Edwards moved into his application, only small portions of which I will quote here.

APPLICATION

In the improvement of this doctrine, I would chiefly direct myself to sinners who are afraid of damnation, in a use of conviction. This may be matter of conviction to you, that it would be just and righteous with God eternally to reject and destroy you. This is what you are in danger of. You who are a Christless sinner, are a poor condemned creature: God's wrath still abides upon you; and the sentence of condemnation lies upon you. You are in God's hands, and it is uncertain what he will do with you. You are afraid what will become of you. You are afraid that it will be your portion to suffer eternal burnings; and your fears are not without grounds; you have reason to tremble every moment. But be you never so much afraid of it, let eternal damnation be never so dreadful, yet it is just. God may nevertheless do it, and be righteous, and holy, and glorious. Though eternal damnation be what you cannot bear, and how much soever your heart shrinks at the thoughts of it, yet God's justice may be glorious in it. The dreadfulness of the thing on your part, and the greatness of your dread of it, do not render it the less righteous on God's part. If you think otherwise, it is a sign that you do not see yourself, that you are not sensible what sin is, nor how much of it you have been guilty of. Therefore for your conviction, be directed. *First,* To look over your past life: inquire at the mouth of conscience, and hear what that has to testify concerning it.

Consider what you are, what light you have had, and what means you have lived under: and yet how you have behaved yourself! What have those many days and nights you have lived been filled up with? How have those years that have rolled over your heads, one after another, been spent? What has the sun shone upon you for, from day to day, while you have improved his light to serve Satan by it? What has God kept your breath in your nostrils for, and given you meat and drink, that you have spent your life and strength, supported by them, in opposing God, and rebellion against him?

How *many sorts* of wickedness have you not been guilty of! How manifold have been the abominations of your life! What profaneness and contempt of God has been exercised by you! How little regard have you had to the Scriptures, to the word preached, to sabbaths, and sacraments! How profanely have you talked, many of you, about those things that are holy! After what manner have many of you kept God's holy day, not regarding the holiness of the time, nor caring what you thought of in it! Yea, you have not only spent the time in worldly, vain, and unprofitable thoughts, but immoral thoughts; pleasing yourself with the reflection on past acts of wickedness, and in contriving new acts. Have not you spent much holy time in gratifying your lusts in your imaginations; yea, not only holy time, but the very time of God's public worship, when you have appeared in God's more immediate presence?

. . .

How much of a spirit of *pride* has appeared in you, which is in a peculiar manner the spirit and condemnation of the devil! How have some of you vaunted yourselves in your apparel! others in their riches! others in their knowledge and abilities! How has it galled you to see others above you! How much has it gone against the grain for you to give others their due honour! And how have you shown your pride by setting up your wills in opposing others, and stirring up and promoting division, and a party spirit in public affairs.[60]

. . .

I will finish what I have to say to natural men in the application of this doctrine, with a *caution* not to improve the doctrine to *discouragement*. For though it would be *righteous* in God for ever to cast you off, and destroy you, yet it would also be just in God to save you, in and through Christ, who has made complete satisfaction for all sin. Romans 3:25, 26, 'Whom God hath set forth to be a propitiation, through faith in his blood, to declare his righteousness for the remission of sins that are past, through the forbearance of God; to declare, I say, at this time his righteousness, that he might be just, and the justifier of him which believeth in Jesus.' Yea, God may, through this Mediator, not only justly, but honourably, show you mercy. The blood of Christ is so precious, that it is fully sufficient to pay the debt you have contracted, and perfectly to vindicate the Divine Majesty from all the dishonour cast upon it, by those many great sins of yours that have been mentioned. It was as great, and indeed a much greater thing, for Christ to die, than it would have been for you and all mankind to have burnt in hell to all eternity. Of such dignity and excellency is Christ in the eyes of God, that, seeing he has suffered so much for poor sinners, God is willing to be at peace with them, however vile and unworthy they have been, and on how many accounts soever the punishment would be *just*. So that you need not be at all discouraged from seeking mercy, for there is enough in Christ.

Indeed it would not become the glory of God's majesty to show mercy to you, so sinful and vile a creature, for anything that you have done; for such worthless and despicable things as your prayers, and other religious performances. It would be very dishonourable and unworthy of God so to do, and it is in vain to expect it. He will show mercy only on Christ's account, and that, according to his sovereign pleasure, on whom he pleases, when he pleases, and in what manner he pleases. You cannot bring him under *obligation* by your works; do what you will, he will not look on himself obliged. But if it be his pleasure, he can honourably show mercy through Christ to any sinner of you all, not one in this congregation excepted. – Therefore here is encouragement for you still to seek and wait, notwithstanding all your wickedness; agreeable to Samuel's speech to the children of Israel, when they were terrified with the thunder and rain that God sent, and when guilt stared them in the face, 1 Samuel 12:20, 'Fear not; ye have done all this wickedness; yet turn not aside from following the Lord, but serve the Lord will all your heart.'

I would conclude this discourse by putting the godly in mind of the freeness and wonderfulness of the grace of God towards them. For such were the same of you. – The case was just so with you as you have heard; you had such a wicked heart, you lived such a wicked life, and it would have been most just with God for ever to have cast you off: but he has had mercy upon you; he hath made his glorious grace appear in your everlasting salvation. You had no love to God; but yet he has exercised unspeakable love to you. You have condemned God, and set light by him; but so great a value has God's grace set on you and your happiness, that you have been redeemed at the price of the blood of his own Son. You chose to be with Satan in his service; but yet God hath made you a joint heir with Christ of his glory. You were ungrateful for past mercies; yet God not only continued those mercies, but bestowed unspeakable greater mercies upon you. You refused to hear when God called; yet God heard you when you called. You abused the infiniteness of God's mercy to encourage yourself in sin against him; yet God has manifested the infiniteness of that mercy, in the exercises of it towards you. You have rejected Christ, and set him at nought; and yet he is become your Saviour. You have neglected your own salvation; but God has not neglected it.

You have destroyed yourself; but yet in God has been your help. God has magnified his free grace towards you, and not to others; because he has chosen you, and it hath pleased him to set his love upon you. O! what cause is here for praise! What obligations you are under to bless the Lord who hath dealt bountifully with you, and magnify his holy name! What cause for you to praise God in humility, to walk humbly before him. Ezekiel 16:63, 'That thou mayest remember and be confounded, and never open thy mouth any more, because of thy shame, when I am pacified toward thee for all that thou hast done, saith the Lord God!' You shall never open your mouth in boasting, or self-justification; but lie the lower before God for his mercy to you. You have reason, the more abundantly, to open your mouth in God's praises, that they may be continually in your mouth, both here and to all eternity, for his rich, unspeakable, and sovereign mercy to you, whereby he, and he alone, hath made you to differ from others.[61]

So much could be said about even the small amount of his sermon which I have presented here, but let me make four points briefly and then a fifth a bit more fully. First of all, Edwards' use of the second person pronoun is overwhelming. Edwards was talking to his people face-to-face, and they knew it. And they responded. Second, Edwards did not, you will notice, spend much time urging a decision upon his people. He presented the Biblical facts, sketched their implications, made a few specific and concrete suggestions, and then left it to the Spirit to bring action in the context of the truth. Third, Edwards' focus throughout the sermon, but especially in the lengthy doctrinal section, was on the being and nature of God. His glory, his sovereignty, his prerogatives were consistently revealed to the congregation. Clearly, it was the creator and not the creature who was being worshipped. Fourth, in the sermon Edwards seems to have preached with the morphology he later outlined clearly in his mind. If one reads the sermon carefully, all eight steps or stages are addressed in one way or another. All in all, it is, it was, a remarkable sermon. And typically Edwardsean.

This brings me to the fifth and final point about this sermon and, indeed, about all of Edwards' preaching before, during, and after the revival of 1734–35. As has been suggested earlier, Edwards' greatest single published work was probably his *Treatise Concerning Religious Affections* and in that treatise, he said much of direct relevance to a proper understanding of his preaching style. We have already seen how and why Edwards believed that the individual's heart disposition is the foundation of all that he is and does. This disposition, Edwards went on to argue, is expressed in the individual's affections. But by 'affections', Edwards had in view more than mere passions – he defined the affections in terms that incorporated much of what often are considered passions, but his focus was more particularly on the basic orientation of one's being, one's essential loves and hatreds, those movements of the soul toward some things and away from others. As he put it,

> The *affections* and *passions* are frequently spoken of as the same; and yet, in the more common use of speech, there is in some respects a difference. *Affection* is a word, that, in its ordinary signification, seems to be something more extensive than *passion*, being used for all vigorous lively actings of the will or inclination; but *passion* is used for those that are more sudden, and whose effects on the animal spirits are more violent, the mind being more over-powered, and less in its own command. As all the exercises of inclination and will, are concerned either in approving and liking, or disapproving and rejecting; so the affections are of two sorts; they are those by which the soul is carried out to what is in view, cleaving *to* it, or *seeking* it; or those by which it is averse *from* it, and *opposes* it. Of the former sort are *love, desire, hope, joy, gratitude, complacence.* Of the latter kind are *hatred, fear, anger, grief,* and such like; which it is needless now to stand particularly to define.[62]

Another distinction between passions and affections makes it clear why the preaching of sound doctrine is crucial when the preacher would stir his people's affections.

> Holy affections are not heat without light; but evermore arise from some information of the understanding, some spiritual instruction

that the mind receives, some light or actual knowledge. The child of God is graciously affected, because he sees and understands something more of divine things than he did before, more of God or Christ, and of the glorious things exhibited in the gospel. He has a clearer and better view than he had before, when he was not affected; either he receives some new understanding of divine things, or has his former knowledge renewed after the view was decayed; 1 John 4:7, 'Every one that loveth, knoweth God.' Philippians 1:9, 'I pray that your love may abound more and more in knowledge, and in all judgment.' Romans 10:2, 'They have a zeal of God, but not according to knowledge.' Colossians 3:10, 'The new man, which is renewed in knowledge.' Psalm 43:3, 4, 'O send out thy light and thy truth; let them lead me, let them bring me unto thy holy hill.' John 6:45, 'It is written in the prophets, and they shall be all taught of God. Every man therefore that hath heard, and learned of the Father, cometh unto me.' Knowledge is the key that first opens the hard heart, enlarges the affections, and opens the way for men into the kingdom of heaven; Luke 11:52, 'Ye have taken away the key of knowledge.' Now there are many affections which do not arise from any light in the understanding; which is a sure evidence that these affections are not spiritual, let them be ever so high.[63]

Affections, in distinction from passions, are grounded in knowledge, and Edwards argued throughout his *Treatise*, genuinely gracious affections are grounded in knowledge of the truths of Christ's Gospel. Working with this basic psychological model (and developing it far more fully than I can here), Edwards then asserted the basic thesis of his *Treatise*, 'True Religion, in great part, consists in holy affections.'[64] The implications for the preacher are enormous and obvious, but Edwards did not want to leave any doubt.

And the impressing of divine things on the hearts and affections of men, is evidently one great end for which God has ordained, that his word delivered in the Holy Scriptures, should be opened, applied, and set home upon men, in *preaching*. And therefore it does not answer the aim which God had in this institution, merely for men to have good commentaries and expositions on the Scripture, and other good books of divinity; because, although these may tend, as well as preaching, to give a good doctrinal or speculative understanding of the word of God, yet they have not an equal tendency to impress them on men's hearts and affections. God hath appointed a particular and lively application to his word, in the preaching of it, as a fit means to affect sinners with the importance of religion, their own misery, the necessity of a remedy, and the glory and sufficiency of a remedy provided; to stir up the pure minds of the saints, quicken their affections by often bringing the great things of religion to their remembrance, and setting them in their proper colours, though they know them, and have been fully instructed in them already, 2 Peter 1:12, 13. And particularly, to promote those two affections in them, which are spoken of in the text, *love* and *joy*: 'Christ gave some, apostles; and some, prophets; and some evangelists; and some, pastors and teachers; that the body of Christ might be edified in love', Ephesians 4:11, 12, 16.[65]

And Edwards practiced what he preached. *The Justice of God in the Damnation of Sinners,* by the use of the second person pronoun, by the sound doctrine it embodied, by its concrete specificities, stirred the affections – not the passions, the affections – of Edwards' people and revival was the result.

VI. Assessment of Edwards' Role in the Revival

The revival in Northampton in 1734–35 was clearly the work of the Holy Spirit of God. So Edwards believed and so I believe. But since we also believe that human responsibility is not negated by Divine sovereignty, our belief in the agency of the Spirit in that revival should not obviate an assessment of the art Edwards played in the revival. First of all, it is clear that Edwards made some mistakes, both in the way he handled events at the time and in the way he reported them in the *Narrative.* He was young and relatively inexperienced in such matters and it showed. This Edwards himself admitted in a letter written in 1751 to the Rev. Thomas Gillespie of Carnock, Scotland. In seeking to explain the cause of his dismissal from his Northampton pastorate on 22nd June 1750, he said this:

One thing, that has contributed to bring things to such a pass at Northampton, was my youth, and want of more judgment and experience, in the time of that extraordinary awakening, about sixteen years ago. Instead of a youth, there was want of a giant, in judgment and discretion, among a people in such an extraordinary state of things. In some respects, doubtless, my confidence in myself was a great injury to me; but in other respects my diffidence of myself injured me. It was such, that I durst not act my own judgment, and had no strength to oppose received notions, and established customs, and to testify boldly against some glaring false appearances, and counterfeits of religion, till it was too late. And by this means, as well as others, many things got footing, which have proved a dreadful source of spiritual pride, and other things that are exceedingly contrary to true Christianity. If I had had more experience, and ripeness of judgment and courage, I should have guided my people in a better manner, and should have guarded them better from Satan's devices, and prevented the spiritual calamity of many souls, and perhaps the eternal ruin of some of them; and have done what would have tended to lengthen out the tranquility of the town.[66]

Of course, this is hindsight but in this case it is perceptive and helpful hindsight. It focuses attention on a problem which was to plague Edwards and other revival preachers through the 1730's and especially during the Great Awakening. The key is the word 'counterfeit' – how does one distinguish genuine from spurious religious experiences? This became such a sticking point in the early 1740's that Edwards explains his entire reason for writing his *Treatise on Religious Affections* (published 1746) in these terms:

It is by the mixture of counterfeit religion with true, not discerned and distinguished, that the devil has had his greatest advantage against the cause and kingdom of Christ. It is plainly by this means, principally, that he has prevailed against all revivals of religion, since the first Founding of the Christian church ... And so it is likely ever to be in the church, whenever religion revives remarkably, till we have learned well to distinguish between true and false religion, between saving affections and experiences, and those manifold fair shows, and glistering appearances, by which they are counterfeited; the consequences of which, when they are not distinguished, are often inexpressibly dreadful.[67]

Edwards apparently had realized his own failure to distinguish the genuine from the counterfeit in 1734–35, and this partially explains his writing the *Treatise on Religious Affections* a decade later. And Edwards' insight about the devil's work during revivals, because it is correct, explains why his *Treatise* may very well be the most important book outside the Scriptures themselves for the preacher/pastor to read. But what kinds of mistakes did Edwards make along this line in 1734–35? Ola Winslow once again provides a helpful analysis here:

Inexperienced as he was in such matters, he had been caught, like his people, by the more unusual manifestations; so much so that when he set himself to prove the signal presence and power of God in conversion he chose out of the several hundred conversions to which he might have borne witness, two of the most spectacular: the experience of a young woman in a morbid state of mind immediately preceding her own death, and the precocities of Phoebe Bartlett, aged four, who feared herself in danger of hell and shut herself up in the closet until she received assurances to the contrary. When the readers assumed that such behaviours did greater honour to God than less spectacular deliverances their conclusion was fair enough, and when in the next decade extravagance went out of bounds, and revival marvels were induced by a score of bizarre methods, Jonathan Edwards was himself in part to blame.[68]

Winslow is right. Edwards' *Narrative* does focus upon the more spectacular operations of the Spirit in the specific examples he gives of conversion and, by so doing, leaves the impression that such external manifestations are themselves marks of genuineness. Edwards further feeds this impression in his description of the large numbers of people who joined the church during and immediately after the revival. Neither in 1734–35 when he was involved in the revival nor in 1736 when he wrote the *Narrative* to describe it did he fully comprehend how easily Satan may indeed counterfeit dramatic events on a large scale and how profoundly subtle the marks of genuine affections may actually be. He learned these things during the early 1740's and embodied them in his *Treatise on Religious Affections* but by then some amount of damage had been done and some of the problems of the Great Awakening may thus be considered partially his fault.

But he did far more good than harm, even though he was just thirty-one years of age at the time of the revival. The two examples mentioned by Winslow and the references to large numbers of new church members constitute just a small part of the *Narrative* and such matters surely played an even smaller role in Edwards' actions during the revival. He was a pastor deeply sensitive to the spiritual needs of his people, he was convinced that the way to respond to those needs was by preaching the great truths of the faith, and he worked exceedingly hard to do that preaching well. Among the many valuable, Biblical lessons that we can learn from Edwards and the 1734–45 Northampton revival, this one stands out. Preaching that honors Christ, preaching that the Spirit honors, is affectionate, doctrinal preaching, preaching which turns the face of the congregation to the glory of God in his Son, Jesus. And so, both in his actions and in his writings, Edwards has bequeathed to the Church a superb theology of preaching. Our task is to appropriate it.

NOTES

1. For the former, see Vernon Parrington, *Main Currents in American Thought: Vol. I, The Colonial Mind, 1620–1800* (New York: Harcourt, Brace, and Co. 1927), and for the latter, see Perry Miller, *Jonathan Edwards* (New York: Dell Publishing Company, 1949).

2 .Jonathan Edwards, *A Faithful Narrative of the Surprising Work of God in the Conversion of Many Hundred Souls, in Northampton and the Neighbouring Towns and Villages of New Hampshire, in New England; in a letter to the Rev. Dr. Colman, of Boston* in *The Works of Jonathan Edwards, Vol. I* (Edinburgh: The Banner of Truth Trust, 1974), pp. 344-364..

3. Jonathan Edwards, *The Justice of God in the Damnation of Sinners* in *Works, Vol. I,* pp. 668-679. Hereafter, page numbers will be cited in the text.

4. Norman Fiering, *Jonathan Edwards' Moral Thought and Its British Context* (Chapel Hill: The University of North Carolina Press, 1981), p. 373.

5. See Ola Winslow's full description of Edwards' use of notes in *Jonathan Edwards, 1703–1758: A Biography* (New York: Farrar, Straus, and Giroux, 1979), pp. 135-37.

6. Ibid., p. 111.

7. Ibid.

8. Kenneth Silverman, *The Life and Times of Cotton Mather* (New York: Harper and Row, 1984), p. 211

9. Winslow, op.cit., pp. 111-12.

10. Miller, op.cit., p. 9. See also Perry Miller, *The New England Mind: From Colony to Province* (Boston: Beacon Press, 1961), pp. 227-29.

11. See, respectively, J. William T. Youngs, Jr. *God's Messengers,* pp. 82-83; Winslow, op.cit., pp. 105-107; and Miller, *Colony,* p. 235

12. Edwards, *Narrative,* p. 347.

13. See, for the best example of this, his *History of the Work of Redemption* in *Works, Vol. I,* pp. 533-619, especially his summary, pp. 615-19.

14. Ibid., pp. 600-1.

15. Edwards, *Narrative,* p. 347.

16. Ibid.

17. Winslow, op.cit., p. 160.

18. Patricia Tracy points out additional tensions in the Northampton of 1734, although her antisupernaturalistic bias and her tendency to psychoanalyze Edwards on the basis of exceedingly skimpy evidence leads to as much distortion as enlightenment. See her *Jonathan Edwards, Pastor: Religion and Society in Eighteenth-Century Northampton* (New York: Hill and Wang, 1979), pp. 71-145.

19. Samuel T. Logan, Jr., 'The Doctrine of Justification in the Theology of Jonathan Edwards', *The Westminster Theological Journal,* XLVI (Spring, 1984), pp. 26-52.

20. Edwards, *Narrative,* op.cit., p. 347.

21. Ibid.

22. Ibid.
23. Ibid.
24. Ibid.
25. Ibid.
26. Ibid., p. 348.
27. Ibid.
28. Ibid. The last part of this statement and other evidence from the *Narrative* contradicts the impression Tracy gives in *Jonathan Edwards, Pastor* that the 1734 revival was largely confined to the young and economically disadvantaged. See pp. 99-108
29. Edwards, *Narrative*, op.cit., p. 348.
30. Ibid.
31. Ibid., p. 349.
32. Alan Heimert has argued that the Great Awakening was the first truly intercolonial event and laid the foundation for political and economic cooperation among the colonies in 1776. See *Religion and the American Mind* (Cambridge: Harvard University Press, 1966) pp. 144-47, 398. But this passage from Edwards' *Narrative*, p. 349, makes it clear that the Great Awakening itself had been 'prepared for' by the earlier revival. And we must not think that Edwards was simply taking advantage of hindsight, for the *Narrative* was published in 1737, some three years before the Spirit brought the Great Awakening to the colonies.
33. Edwards, *Narrative*, op.cit., p. 350.
34. Ibid., p. 363.
35. Winslow, op.cit., p. 165.
36. Edwards, *Narrative*, op.cit., p. 363.
37. Ibid.
38. Ibid.
39. Ibid., p. 364.
40. It makes a world of difference whether we define a preparationist as an individual who believes there are certain prescribed steps through which one must, in one's own strength, go to be prepared for grace or as an individual who believes the Spirit normally (but not necessarily and not always) brings an elected person along a series of steps to faith. Edwards probably was a preparationist in the latter sense but certainly not in the former sense.
41. Edwards, *Narrative*, op.cit., p. 352
42. Ibid., p. 350.
43. Ibid., p. 351.
44. Ibid.
45. Ibid., p. 352.
46. Ibid., p. 353.
47. Ibid. The phrase 'to see feelingly' is, of course, a Shakespearean one, used originally by the blind Gloucester speaking to Lear upon the heath. But an excellent exposition of the concept, which meshes in so many ways with Edwards' notion of the affections, may be found in Maynard Mack, 'To See It Feelingly', *PMLA*, May, 1971. See also in this connection a fuller correlation of Edwards and Mack in Samuel T. Logan, Jr., 'Poetry in the Parsonage?' *The Bulletin of Westminster Theological Seminary*, Spring, 1981.
48. Edwards, *Narrative*, op.cit., p. 352.
49. Ibid.
50. Ibid., p. 354.
51. See Norman Fiering's excellent discussion of this in *Jonathan Edwards' Moral*

Thought, op.cit., pp. 261-321. See also Fiering's discussion of the backgrounds of this kind of approach in his *Moral Philosophy at Seventeenth Century Harvard: A Discipline in Transition* (Chapel Hill: University of North Carolina Press, 1981), pp. 118-20.

52. Edwards, *Narrative,* op.cit., p. 354.

53. Ibid., p. 355.

54. Ibid.

55. Jonathan Edwards, 'The Justice of God in the Damnation of Sinners', *Works, Vol. I,* op.cit., p. 668.

56. Ibid., p. 669.

57. Ibid., p. 669.

58. Jonathan Edwards, *The Great Christian Doctrine of Original Sin Defended, Works, Vol. I,* op.cit., p. 152-53.

59. Edwards, *Justice,* op.cit., p. 670.

60. Ibid., pp. 669-70.

61. Ibid., p. 671.

62. Jonathan Edwards, *A Treatise Concerning Religious Affections, Works, Vol. I,* op.cit., p. 237.

63. Ibid., pp. 281-82.

64. Ibid., p. 336.

65. Ibid., p. 242.

66. Jonathan Edwards, 'Letter to the Rev. Thomas Gillespie', *Works, Vol. I,* op.cit., p.cxxxii.

67. Edwards, *Religious Affections,* op.cit., p. 235.

68. Winslow, op.cit., p. 167.

LOVE AS THE FOUNDATION OF THEOLOGY

The Practical Implications of Jonathan Edwards' Doctrine of the Indwelling of the Spirit

John Hannah

There is an old adage that goes like this, 'A picture is worth a thousand words'. By this, it is implied that mental images are vehicles for the communication of ideas. Images are formed by the reception of words. It takes of lot of words to convey a mental image just as it does a lot of bricks to construct a huge wall. In the multiplication of words, images are formed in the minds of those who receive them.

Communication is not only made difficult because of the deficiencies of linguistics; it is complicated by the fact that subject matter is often not clearly perceived by the communicator. You cannot convey to a receiver with clarity what is not clearly understood by the sender. At the root of this latter difficulty in communication is that distortion or cloudiness of understanding comes because we frequently do not know what questions to ask of the material in the first place. Jonathan Edwards privately mused on this very point as he reflected on the doctrine of justification, 'Tis a hundred pities that men don't think what the question is, about which they dispute.'[1] A clear understanding of the issue at hand greatly facilitates its communication.

If the clarity of the question is a key to understanding, and understanding is important to communication, then what is the question before us? It is a question that has troubled me at a practical level since the completion of my formal academic training. What precisely is the nature of the indwelling of the Holy Spirit in the believer? Though the Bible states the fact of the Spirit's presence (Rom. 8:9-11, Eph. 1:13-14), what is the Spirit's indwelling presence? Further, what are the implications of this for the believer?

To access this question, I have chosen the writings of Jonathan Edwards (1703–58), the Northampton puritan-pastor-scholar. With Edwards as a lens, I will explore the doctrine of the indwelling presence of Holy Spirit in the believer.

The Holy Spirit as Divine Love

Like so many theological discussions, the place to begin is with the doctrine of the Trinity of God, the interrelationship of the Father, Son, and Holy Spirit in the revelation of Himself to mankind. Edwards believed that God is infinite beauty and holiness. These qualities consist in His infinite love for Himself.[2] Though he was quick to confess that the subject of God's nature was 'utterly inexplicable and inconceivable,'[3] he argued that the interpersonal love of God (God, therefore, of necessity being plural) is revealed by the incarnation of Christ and the work of the Spirit. The essence of His self-communication or emanation is love, the love of the Holy Spirit who is love. Love is harmony, beauty, and loveliness. It is this love that is infused into the soul in regeneration, the very being of God, the Holy Spirit, according to Edwards.[4]

In the grand self-glorifying revelation of Himself in condescending grace, Edwards claimed that we have a disclosure of God through each member of the Trinity. The Father is the one revealed through the Son and the Spirit. The incarnate Son is the revelation of the character of God and the Spirit the disclosure of the love of God. He expressed it this way, '… the Son is God's idea of himself, and the Spirit is God's love to and delight in himself.'[5] Employing an idealistic framework derived through Augustine, Edwards, according to Schafer, made 'the Holy Spirit the love whereby God loves himself, the love between the Father and the Son'.[6] The Holy Spirit is the revelation of God's infinite love.[7] The love which exists between the Father and the Son is revealed by the Spirit. The Son revealed God to us through His active and passive obedience obtaining the ground of divine forgiveness and imputed righteousness. The Spirit, through the workings of a definitive regeneration and progressive sanctification, reveals to the believer God's immense love. Indeed, He does more than that. He forms love in the saint by His divine presence in His sanctifying grace, which is love. He found evidence for this in the phrase, 'the Spirit of God,' suggesting that it implies that the Spirit is the activity or energy of God. 'It appears by the Holy Scriptures that the Holy Spirit is the perfect act of God ... the activity, vivacity and energy of God.'[8] The Godhead exists in three persons: God, the idea of God revealed in the incarnation by Christ, and the delight or love of God disclosed by the Spirit.

Edwards found in the image of the sun an analogy of the functional interrelationships within the Godhead. In Miscellany 362 he noted, 'The Father is as the substance of the sun; the Son is as the brightness and glory of the disk of the sun; the Holy Ghost is as the heat and continually emitted influence, the emanation by which the world is enlightened, warmed, enlivened and comforted.'[9] In another place he attempted to distinguish the persons within the Trinity functionally. 'It may be thus expressed: the Son is the Deity generated by God's understanding, or having an idea of himself; the Holy Ghost is the divine essence flowing out, or breathed forth, in infinite love and delight'.[10]

The exegetical basis for this conclusion, at least in part, is drawn from his understanding of 1 John 4: 8, 12-13, 16. From this passage he reasons that if God is love, if God dwells in the believer, and if God dwells in the believer in the form of the Holy Spirit, then the Holy Spirit and divine love are one and the same thing. The manner of the Spirit's indwelling is that of love. 'I think that in the 4th chapter of 1 John, in which we are twice told that God is love, it is intimated to us that this love is the Holy Spirit, in the 12th and 13th verses.... So here also we are told in what sense God dwells in us, in the first of these verses, viz. in that love dwells in us; which is explained in the next verse (which is evidently exegetical of the foregoing), that God dwells in us because the Holy Spirit dwells in us.'[11]

It can be argued that in the repetition by Edwards that the Spirit of God is God's love revealed that he was answering his enthusiastic opponents in the Great Awakening. Zealous advocates of renewal in the Great Awakening relegated the Spirit's presence to a mere feeling or religious experience, a portent of the reductionistic and personalized view of the 19th century revivalistic tradition which is the root of modern Evangelicalism. In so doing, his understanding of the work of the Spirit became one of the most cherished dimensions of his pneumatology. Wilson-Kastner writes, 'Love, the center of the Christian faith, was not, for Edwards, a pious abstraction, or a warm feeling of heart. Love was nothing other than the Holy Spirit, who came to dwell in the elect in order to make them children of God, united to God and acting as his children in the world.'[12]

The Holy Spirit as the Believer's Inheritance

Edwards' most sustained treatment of the Holy Spirit is perhaps found in the *Treatise on Grace*. As one reads the work, as well as scattered comments in the *Miscellanies*, several sermons, and portions of his larger works, it is evident that he views the work of the Spirit somewhat differently than those in his immediate Puritan heritage, such as writers Richard Sibbes and John Owen, or many contemporary authors. The Spirit not only applies the benefits procured by Christ and granted by the Father; He is the 'thing purchased' by Christ and given to the believer. Edwards states that to describe the work of the Spirit as only applying Christ's purchased benefits is to make the work of the Spirit less than that of the Son. He noted: 'Merely to apply to us or immediately to give or hand to us blessing purchased, after it is purchased, is subordinate to the other two persons.... But according to what is now proposed there is an equality. The price and the thing purchased with that price are of the same value ... the glory that belongs to Him that bestows the gospel, arises from the excellency and value of the gift, and therefore the glory is equal to that excellency of the benefit.'[13]

The biblical phrases that he cites to support the view are: 'that we might receive the promise of the Spirit through faith' (Gal. 3:13-14); 'who was given as a pledge of our inheritance' (Eph. 1:13-14); '[God] who also sealed us and gave us the Spirit in our hearts as a pledge' (2 Cor: 1:21); and Luke 24:49 where the Spirit is called the promise of the Father. Extracting insights from these verses, he writes: 'The Holy Spirit is the purchased possession and inheritance of the saints, as appears, because that little of it which the saints have in this world is said to be the earnest of that purchased inheritance.... This an earnest of that which we are to have of fullness hereafter.'[14] The most succinct summary of his view is, perhaps, found in this triune statement of God's redemptive work. 'All our good is *of* God the Father, and *through* the Son, and all is *in* the Holy Ghost, as He is Himself all our good' [italics mine].[15]

This insight is scattered throughout Edwards' writings. The Spirit is the giver of life and the gift of life itself. He was granted through regeneration and the application of Christ's redemptive work initially though incompletely. After some time, for every one of His elect, He is to be most fully given in glorification. 'That the Spirit of God is spiritual joy and delight, is confirmed by those places where we are told that the Holy Spirit is the 'earnest' of our future inheritance and the 'first fruits'. The earnest is a part of the inheritance; which shows that our inheritance, that happiness spoken of that God will give his saints, is nothing but a fullness of his Spirit.'[16] In his polemic against the Antinomian enthusiasts of the Great Awakening, Edwards made the point that the presence of the Spirit is not signified by ability to perform miracles as an evidence of spiritual power or in the exercise of any of the various spiritual gifts, but in holiness. The Spirit's presence in the soul is verified by the presence of His own character, not by external phenomena however impressive. 'The inheritance that Christ has purchased for the elect, *is* the Spirit of God; not in any extraordinary gifts, but in his vital indwelling in the heart, exerting and communicating himself there, in his own proper, holy and divine nature; and this is the total sum of the inheritance that Christ has purchased for the elect' (italics mine).[17]

Recent scholars of Edwards's pneumatology have recognized his insight into the role of the Holy Spirit in salvation. The Spirit is more than the provider of the benefits procured by Christ. He is the gift that is purchased. Anri Morimoto stated the point bluntly, 'The Holy Spirit according to Edwards' improvement, is not just "an applier" of what is achieved by the Son, but is himself what is achieved and given in the work of redemption'.[18] It is not incorrect to say with Edwards that the Holy Spirit is the grace of God that is given in redemption. He is the 'sum of the blessings that Christ died to procure, and that are the subject of gospel promises'; 'the fullness of good'; and 'the sum of the saint's inheritance'.[19]

The Holy Spirit as the Believer's Indweller

Sinclair Ferguson has argued that the indwelling of the Spirit in the believer is 'more than that of mere divine influence'. However, he adds that the exact relationship of the Spirit to us in His indwelling ministry is 'nowhere explained or explored' in Scripture.[20] Edwards would not have agreed with his conclusion in the matter.

The Holy Spirit is the love of God extended to His children. He defined the presence of the Spirit as 'an indwelling vital principle', 'a union of the mind of the believer with Himself', or 'an abiding principle'. These expressions are meant to distinguish the Spirit's work in the life of the believer from his work in the unbeliever. Whereas the Spirit's work in the unbeliever is external or from without, His influence upon the saint is internal or from within, the union of the Spirit with the believer's nature makes the Spirit's visible manifestations through the believer appear to be natural to him. 'Natural men may be influenced by the Spirit as a power from without; the Christian receives the Spirit who acts as an inward power. This inward influence is called indwelling, an indwelling principle, or union.'[21]

Edwards found in the Scripture many phrases from which he derived his understanding. In John 3:6 the indwelling presence of God is called 'spirit' as it is contrasted to its opposite, the flesh. He noted the same comparison in Galatians 5:17 and in Romans 7.[22] He felt that the phrase in Romans 8:2, 'Spirit of life', and the Spirit's 'quickening' work in John 4:63 were the same thing. Other texts included 2 Peter 1:4, 'partakers of the divine nature', and 1 Corinthians 3:16, 17, 'we are temples of the Holy Ghost'. Commenting on the meaning of the Peter passage, he noted, 'That holy and Divine love dwells in their hearts, and is so united to human faculties that tis itself become a principle of new nature.'[23] He made a similar notation in a private notebook. 'And whenever the Scriptures speak of the Spirit of God indwelling in us, of our being filled with the Spirit, it will signify much the same thing if it said, a divine temper and disposition or affection of God is no other than infinite love. This Holy Spirit of God, the divine temper, is that divine nature spoken of, 2 Peter 1:4.'[4]

Not only is the indweller the love of God, He is also denominated as the grace of God. Edwards wrote, '...when the Holy Spirit by his ordinary influences, bestows saving grace, he therein imparts himself to the soul in his own nature ... grace is as it were the holy nature of the Spirit imparted to the soul.'[25] While other passages can be multiplied in Edwards indicating that the Spirit is love and grace, it seems justifiable to say that the indwelling, vital principle in the saint called the Holy Spirit are the nine fruit(s) of the Spirit listed in Galatians 5:22-23. While together they are God's graces, these graces are infused by the Spirit at regeneration and are the essence of God's indwelling presence. The most profound of these evidences of the Spirit are love and joy.

The indwelling of the Spirit is, then, the infusion or communication of the life of God into the believer. It is the Spirit of God as expressed by the fruit(s) or moral character of God. The infusion of this grace, these fruits, or the Spirit is directly into the soul. He commented, 'I, for my part, am convinced of an immediate communication between the Spirit of God and the soul.'[26] The practical experience of the impartation of the moral character of God into the soul is that we not only become 'partakers of the divine,' but we become instantaneously attracted to the things of Christ. 'Indwelling is the communication of the character of the Spirit into the soul. It causes the 'partaker' to relish in God's beauty and Christ's joy which is true fellowship.'[27] The indwelling presence of the Spirit immediately gives the believer a sense of the loveliness of God's character. Indwelling may be defined as a fusion or uniting of the Spirit with the human soul renewing its faculties, turning the soul from the downward drag of sin and death toward the things of God and life. In a sermon he defined this experience of regeneration as an intuitive, immediate communication to the soul instantaneously altering the inclination, will, and heart.[28]

It seems that the reason he went at lengths to describe the experience of regeneration was that the question of divine assurance of God's mercy was one that was challenged throughout his ministry. He was concerned with the doctrine of regeneration because the gospel was being redefined by rationalists, moralists, and enthusiasts in England, Scotland, and his own neighborhood. From his first published sermon, 'God Glorified in Man's Dependence' (1731) to 'A Divine and Supernatural Light' ten years later, as well as his major treatises, he argued that salvation was an inward, immediate divine work of God in the soul. Contrary to the New Light Enthusiasts of his day, the sphere where God effects redemption is not in the feelings, the revelation of new truth, or mental intuitions or impressions. 'Many have been the mischiefs that have arisen from that false and delusive notion of the witness of the Spirit, that it is a kind of inward voice, suggestion, or declaration from God to a man, that he is beloved of him, and pardoned, elected, or the like, sometimes with, and sometimes without a text of Scripture,'[29] Edwards was not willing to say with the moralists of his day that regeneration is the infusion of the faculties of the soul with renewed propensities, such as a heightened conscience. These do not have the effect of contributing to one's salvation. If so, it would reduce salvation to mere moral resolve and sincerity. Instead, he described it as a supernatural intrusion into the soul wherein 'those principles are restored that were utterly destroyed by the fall'.[30] Wilson-Kastner summarizes the point well saying, 'True virtue, in Edwards' scheme, is not simply a conscience telling me to do good, for that would have no sustained or lasting effect. Rather, true virtue is love moving me to action. Love is no other than the Holy Spirit, and we are brought again to the core of all of Edwards' theology.'[31] To the rationalists, such as Charles Chauncy of Boston, Edwards argued that redemption is more than mental cognition and religious habits. Knowledge can tell a person that something is real, not that it is true. 'There is not only a rational belief that God is holy, and that holiness is a good thing, but there is a sense of the loveliness of God's holiness.'[32] Redemptive knowledge is not merely apprehension; it is knowledge experienced. To ask the unredeemed to describe the experience of salvation, to use one of Edwards's most used illustrations, is like asking a blind man to describe honey when a jar is placed into his hands. However, if he tastes the contents of the jar, though blind, he can describe it. The ability of the blind to taste is the effect of regeneration.

The Holy Spirit as Indweller and Practical Implications

If the Holy Spirit is the emanation of the love of God the Father and God the Son mutually expressed, if the Holy Spirit is the purchase of Christ in His redemptive action for all Christians, if the Holy Spirit is the union of heart with Christ in love, and if love and the Spirit, being one and the same, is what is infused into the believer as a new, vital principle of action into the inner most being as Edwards has argued, several important practical implications can be drawn. First, salvation is a work of God. It is not a work of man aided by God nor is it the strengthening of existing habits and abilities. It is God's work because the new life is the life of God infused into the soul; it is not the best of improved human efforts. It is the infinite life of God infused by miracle into the soul. It is the love of God, the love that He alone possesses toward Himself. Finitude simply cannot produce the infinite. Eternal life is the divine life infused into the soul and, thus, cannot be the result of even the most commendable finite activity. Neither moral resolve nor wise decision-making is the criteria for the entrance of the life of God in the soul. Paul Ramsey has stated Edwards' view of this point quite well. 'No creature has a natural capacity to actualize in itself knowledge of or love to God; that is the common teaching of classical Christian theology. In evangelical Christianity in America this was, of course, and still should be, the meaning of being 'born again".[33]

Second, Edwards' view of the Spirit as the manifestation of divine love is quite instructive of the meaning of being a Christian. The Liberal Tradition of American Christianity was not incorrect in identifying love as the essence of Christian faith. That love is at the heart of Christian faith is true because God, the author of faith, is love. However, Liberalism has greatly erred in defining love as the finite affection and kindness expressed between creatures or of a person to God. To be a Christian is not merely to possess creaturely love, that is a fruit of common grace. True love, which is true virtue to Edwards, is not to have a human love for God or a love for mankind; it is not a native quality in fallen creatures. It is to have God's love for God and mankind infused into the heart. This kind of love is not natively within the creature. The moralist errs at this point; this kind of love requires infusion. Its source, nature, and object are of God, not of man. It has God as its primary object, not the creature. It is impossible to have a love of this kind that is not rooted in renewed human faculties by infusion. That is, by something that is outside the creature. 'True virtue does primarily and most essentially consist in a supreme love to God; and that where this is wanting, there can be no true virtue.'[34]

Third, Edwards' understanding of the nature and sphere of regeneration, namely, that it is caused by a renovation of the natural faculties producing a new Godward focus, addresses the issue of lordship and 'free grace', an issue that has been a focus in evangelical circles recently. If the essence of the experience of rebirth is the infusion of the love of God into the soul of the creature and if that love is the Spirit of God indwelling us, then it is senseless to argue that redemption does not result in a heart and life change. While no one, except for the liberal traditions of the church, would argue that lordship is the cause of salvation, lordship is most certainly the essence of the new life infused into the soul at regeneration. Love to God and lordship are the same thing. Since regeneration is the infusion of love and love is a heart-rooted desire to please God, lordship must be inherent in what it means to have become a Christian. How can one be transformed by the love of God into the character of that love by the Spirit and not possess love? This seems so utterly senseless. Edwards argued, 'The holy Ghost influences the minds of the godly by living in the godly.'[35] It is simply not an optional lifestyle for the insightful. John Gerstner stated it plainly, 'The [regenerate] human soul voluntarily determines to do good, but this is what the influence of God's Spirit determines.'[36] Those who have argued so strongly for 'free grace' have perceived correctly that divine grace is absolutely unmerited, but they seem not to have understood its essence. Edwards' comment is pertinent, '... he who receives Christ by saving faith closes with him as Lord and King, and not only as a Priest to make atonement for him. But to close as King is the same thing as to close with subjection to his laws, and obedience to his commands.'[37] Wilson-Kastner has insightfully written, 'Divine love in the soul of the saints is the Holy Spirit himself, who becomes the well-spring of activity and the divine life itself for us.' [38]

Fourth, evidence of the divine life in the soul is rooted in works. The evidence of a life without God is described in Galatians 5 as the fruit of the flesh, contrarily, the evidence of the life of God in the soul are the nine fruit(s) of the Spirit. As Edwards attempted to ameliorate the unbiblical emphases of many of the enthusiasts during the Great Awakening, he argued that the *virtues* of the Spirit, not the *gifts* of the Spirit were the ground of assurance of the divine life in the soul.

According to Edwards, the grace of God is the love of God. The love of God is infused into our souls by the indwelling of the Holy Spirit. This principle of love or grace produces an outward practice of that love and grace in the Christian. His axiom is bold, 'All true Christian grace tends to practice.'[39] He argues that this must be the case because the indwelling presence of love and grace are rooted in the faculty of the will, the decision-making faculty of the soul as well as the understanding, the rational faculty. Since it is rooted in the will, it of necessity must be transformed by the infusion of love. Said Edwards, '... if the principle of true grace be rooted in this faculty, it must necessarily tend to practice, as much as the flow of water in the fountain tends to its flowing in the stream.'[40]

The Christian practice of love, the foremost of the virtues, is inherent within the conversion experience because in the renewing of the mind the Spirit comes to reside in His moral dimensions as a transforming and abiding principle to direct us. In giving the believer what Edwards called 'a natural relish of the sweetness of that which is holy. And of everything that is holy,' the manifestation of that love is guaranteed. Commenting on Luke 6:44 in answer to the enthusiasts of his day, he wrote, 'Christ nowhere says, ye shall know the tree by its leaves or flowers, or ye shall know men by their talk, or ye shall know them by the manner and air of their speaking, and emphasis and pathos of expression, or by their speaking feelingly, or by making a very great show of abundance of talk, or by many tears and affectionate expressions, or by the affections ye feel in your hearts towards them; but by their fruits shall ye know them'.[41] Without the virtues of the Spirit, though one may simultaneously have the giftedness of the Spirit, there can be no spiritual life according to Edwards. A recent writer has stated the point succinctly, 'Without exception, all who have been given the *Holy* Spirit will pursue *holiness*. His holy presence and holy ministry within us cause us to love holiness, to long for it, and at times to grieve over our lack of it.'[42]

Conclusion

Wilson-Kastner was correct when she argued that Edwards made pneumatology, the doctrine of the Holy Spirit, central in his thought. The Spirit, who is the love between the Father and the Son, is at the center of his understanding of the Christian faith. To possess divine love is to be a partaker of the Spirit who is eternal life. Divine love is the gift of God; it is the Spirit's presence in our heart, mind, and will. Without the Spirit, there can be no divine love within us acting out from us. God, God the Holy Spirit, is love. Without this kind of love, there is no divine life within. However, to possess the Spirit is to express that Spirit. Paul said it rather succinctly, 'If I speak with the tongues of men and of angels, but do not have love. I have become a noisy gong or a clanging cymbal, And if I have the gift of prophesy, and know all mysteries and all knowledge; and if I have all faith, so as to remove mountains, but do not have love, I am nothing.'[43] I conclude with a quotation that is both greatly assuring for the believer and disconcerting for the mere professor of Christian faith. 'When the Holy Spirit comes into our lives at our salvation, He comes to make us holy in practice. If there is not then, at least a yearning in our hearts to live a holy life pleasing to God, we need to seriously question whether our faith in Christ is genuine.'[44]

NOTES

1. Thomas A. Schafer, ed., *The 'Miscellanies,' a-500*, vol.13 in *The Works of Jonathan Edwards*, (New Haven, CT: Yale University Press, 1994): 219 [36]. Edwards numbered the entries in this notebook. These appear within the brackets hereafter.

2. Wallace E. Anderson, ed., *The Mind* in *Scientific and Philosophical Writings*, vol. 6, *The Works of Jonathan Edwards* (New Haven, CT: Yale University Press, 1980), 363 [45].

3. Alexander B. Grosart (ed.), *Treatise on Grace*, in *Selections from the Unpublished Writings of Jonathan Edwards* (1865. Reprint. Ligonier, PA: Sola Deo Gloria Publications, 1992), 37.

4. This seems to be what Edwards was describing in the initial entry into his *Miscellanies*, the essence of the conversion experience. That entry is perhaps his clearest description of the experience of regeneration. Edwards (*The 'Miscellancies,' a-500*, 163 [a]).

5. Edwards, *The 'Miscellanies,' a-500*, 468 [405].

6. Thomas A. Schafer, 'Introduction' to *The 'Miscellanies,' a-500*, 57.

7. Edwards was quick to indicate that what he was discussing was beyond explanation (Grosart, ed., *Treatise on Grace*, 36).

8. Edwards, *The 'Miscellanies,' a-500*, 261 [94].

9. Edwards, *The 'Miscellanies,' a-500*, 434 [362]. Edwards uses the same analogy in Miscellany 370.

10. Edwards, *The 'Miscellanies,' a-500*, 468 [405].

11. Edwards, *The 'Miscellanies,' a-500*, 300 [146].

12. Patricia Wilson-Kastner, *Coherence in a Fragmented World: Jonathan Edwards' Theology of the Holy Spirit* (Washington, DC: University Press of America, 1978), 11.

13. Edwards, *Treatise on Grace*, 51.

14. Edwards, *Treatise on Grace*, 50.

15. Edwards, *Treatise on Grace*, 51.

16. Edwards, '*The Miscellanies,' a-500*, 436 [364].

17. John E. Smith, ed., *Treatise on Religious Affections*, vol. 2, *The Works of Jonathan Edwards* (New Haven, CT: Yale University Press, 1959), 236. I came to the same conclusion in a study of his relationship to the Toronto Blessing Movement. 'Of utmost importance is the insight that Edwards's emphasis is not on the power of the Spirit, but the presence of the Spirit; the presence of the Spirit is synonymous with having his power' ('Jonathan Edwards, The Toronto Blessing, and the Spiritual Gifts: Are the Extraordinary Ones Actually the Ordinary Ones,' *Trinity Journal* 17 [1996]: 181).

18. Anri Morimoto, *The Reality of Salvation in the Soteriology of Jonathan Edwards* (Ann Arbor, MI: University Microfilms, 1991), 61.

19. Mark Valeri, ed., 'God Glorified in Man's Dependence,' in *Sermons and Discourses, 1730–1733* , vol. 17, *The Works of Jonathan Edwards.* (New Haven, CT: Yale University Press, 1999), 209.

20. Sinclair B. Ferguson, *The Holy Spirit* (Downer's Grove, IL: InterVarsity Press, 1996), 176.

21. Edwards, '*The Miscellanies,' a-500*, 471 [512].

22. For Edwards gathering of several similar texts see, *Treatise on Grace*, 52-53.

23. Edwards, *Treatise on Grace*, 54.

24. Edwards, '*The Miscellanies,' a-500*, 396 [462].

25. Paul Ramsey, ed., *Charity and Its Fruits* in *Ethical Writings,* vol. 8. *The Works of Jonathan Edwards.* (New Haven, CT: Yale University Press, 1989), 158.

26. Edwards, 'The Miscellanies,' a-500, 296 [138].

27. Edwards, *Religious Affections,* 201.

28. Edwards, 'A Divine and Supernatural Light,' 414-15.

29. Edwards, *Religious Affections,* 239.

30. Edwards, 'A Divine and Supernatural Light,' 411.

31. Wilson-Kastner, *Coherence in a Fragmented World,* 57.

32. Edwards, 'A Divine and Supernatural Light,' 412.

33. Paul Ramsey, 'Introduction' to *Ethical Writings,* 21.

34. Paul Ramsey, ed., *The Nature of True Virtue* in *Ethical Writings,* vol. 8, *The Works of Jonathan Edwards* (New Haven, CT: Yale University Press, 1989), 554.

35. Edwards, 'The Miscellanies,' a-500, 513 [471].

36. John H. Gerstner *Jonathan Edwards: A Mini-Theology* (Wheaton, IL: Tyndale House, 1987), 63.

37. Edwards, *Charity and Its Fruits,* 301.

38. Wilson-Kastner, *Coherence in a Fragmented World,* 27.

39. Edwards, *Charity and Its Fruits,* 197.

40. Edwards, *Charity and Its Fruits,* 298.

41. Edwards, *Religious Affections,* 407

42. Donald S. Whitney, *Ten Questions To Diagnose Your Spiritual Health* (Colorado Springs, CO: NavPress, 2001), 94.

43. 1 Corinthians 13:1-2.

44. Jerry Bridges, The *Pursuit of Holiness* (Colorado Springs, CO: NavPress, 1978), 38.

THE LIGHT OF SCHLEIERMACHER IN RESTORATION FRANCE

The Test Cases of Samuel Vincent and Merle d'Aubigné

William Edgar

It is widely acknowledged that Friedrich Schleiermacher's theology represents one of the great turning points in the history of Christian thought. One index to the depth of the mark he left on Protestant theology in the nineteenth century and beyond is Karl Barth's nearly compulsive commentaries on him throughout his own career. In his *Foreword* to the famous 1923–24 Göttingen lectures on Schleiermacher, he states: 'The almost incomparable influence that he has had in the history of the Reformation is not surprising. We have in him a classical figure.'[1] And this from the man, himself a classical figure, whose own project began with a fundamental rejection of Schleiermacher.[2] Even in his last year, Barth was ambivalent. He recounts his discovery, along with his friend Thurneysen, that in order to effect a '"wholly other" theological foundation' he could no longer proceed any further on the basis of Schleiermacher. But then he goes on to describe his debt to him, and to add disqualifiers to his opposition to him, admitting how much he has learned from him, and even calling him a 'common denominator' in practically all the worthwhile theology of the twentieth century.[3]

What issues are at stake in trying to assess Schleiermacher's influence on the theologians of his era? One is surely the fascinating question of how one man could have held such sway. Was it his charisma, was it the timing of his presence, or was it the compelling content of his thought? Another, which is the main preoccupation of this article, is the extent and nature of his influence. Was he equally important for evangelical theology as well as the more liberal types? Did any reject him altogether? Did they receive his views but with particular filters? To listen to Karl Barth one might have the impression that Schleiermacher's influence went across the board, regardless of the position of those who came under his spell. To put it bluntly, could orthodox people recognize the flaws in Schleiermacher's theology, or did they only strain at the gnat of his doctrinal errors while swallowing the camel of his deep structure? To test this, we shall examine the basic contours of Schleiermacher's thought, and then attempt to measure his influence, using the test case of two French Protestants, one a pre-liberal, and the other an orthodox product of the awakening. The case of French theology is especially interesting in that it has been ignored, or nearly so, by historians of theology, including Barth. This essay is lovingly dedicated to D. Clair Davis, who has always had a keen interest in the nineteenth century in general, and in Schleiermacher in particular.

The Well is Dry

What is the background for Schleiermacher's task? At the end of the eighteenth century a certain exhaustion of options characterized theology. Biblical criticism had become rationalist. In fact, many of the greatest thinkers of the Enlightenment had drifted into a deep revulsion against orthodoxy, especially certain offensive doctrines such as predestination, the bloody sacrifice of Christ, original sin, and so forth. For example, Jean-Jacques Rousseau's (1712–1778) religion is reasonable, tolerant, humble, rather than dogmatic. In his extraordinary *Emile*, the Fourth Book bespeaks his own creed. Entitled *Confession of Faith of a Savoyard Vicar*, it is the narrative of a pastor giving advice to a young man on matters religious. The Vicar insists with his charge that nature is sufficient to instruct us in most essential truths, because the Creator has endowed mankind with the capacity to receive these truths with unaided reason. In a paradoxical manner, he tells his pupil that he had 'closed all the books,' because the one book that counts, opened for all to see, is the book of nature. But then he admits that the Gospel 'speaks to my heart.' What does it say to him? 'What sweetness, what purity in its manners, what touching grace in its instruction....'[4] So, on the one hand, Rousseau could plead for the exercise of reason alone, standing within the theater of nature, in order to discover the truth. On the other hand, he admits having a respect, even a reverence for biblical revelation. But what he saw in those pages turns out to be strangely selective. Strangely, not because it contradicts his most basic assumptions, which it certainly does not, but because Rousseau knew his Bible so well, and read it every day. But he derived from it what his unaided reason was seeking in the first place. The end result of his dual path to knowledge was a combination of tolerance, moralism, and the elevation of reason to a place it had never held in Christian tradition.

Immanuel Kant's (1724–1804) philosophy is the end point of the Enlightenment spirit. His attacks on supranaturalist systems placed theologians on the defensive. Over against traditional theological constructs, which derived a great deal from dogmatic *a priori*, Kant criticized the false security of human knowledge based on dogma. The only sure thing is moral consciousness. Religious faith belongs to pure reason, and is thus immune from any rational demonstration.[5] While intending to save religion from wrong-headed apologetics, the effect of this extraordinary move was to gag theologians from asserting anything verifiable about God and the supernatural. This is the more so in that to be absolutely authentic, the moral consciousness cannot allow us to conjecture that God is working in us by divine legislation. That would have the effect of denying the autonomy of the will, an impossibility for Kant. In keeping with the prevailing mood of the eighteenth century, then, Kant judges Scripture and doctrinal claims by their moral content alone. But theologians and philosophers alike would soon discover the emptiness of that outlook.

In addition to this legacy from the empty well of an eighteenth-century moralism, the nineteenth century in Europe was characterized by powerful trends whose underlying motives though not Christian, needed to be encountered by theology, if it was to stay alive. Chief among them was romanticism. This amorphous current could be said to begin in Germany in the 1790s, nurtured by Schiller and Herder, and come into its own in

Novalis, Schelling and Friedrich Schlegel. No doubt a reaction against the tight rationality of the Enlightenment, along with the moralism we've seen, and its official, neo-classical art, romanticism elevated the imagination, heroism, and spontaneity. For Friedrich Schelling (1775–1854) there is an unfolding spirit that inheres in all things. Going way beyond Rousseau, he saw nature as a creative spirit which tends ever more toward self-realization. Mankind should strive after unattainable ideals, and will find the best catalyst for this to be the arts, where nature and history are reconciled, and a bridge is extended between nature and intelligence.[6] Often the romantic vision includes a fall from paradise, where child-like innocence is lost because of an intellectual separation from nature. But the ultimate unity of all things can be regained by a journey through history, one that involves the often costly overcoming of obstacles. Thus, movement and process replace abstract truth. In the arts, color and sound, quests and pilgrimages replace monuments and strict form. How should Christians interact with romanticism?

Like a Sacred Music

With these challenges, something fresh was needed if the theological enterprise was to be renewed, or even survive. Who would speak out? Orthodoxy was in a sort of rear guard position, and seemed incapable of answering the skepticism of David Hume, let alone the firewall of Kant. The decisive turn was made by Friedrich Schleiermacher (1768–1834). He needed somehow to show that theology was both still possible and also necessary. Yet the traditional theology of Protestant orthodoxy he judged outdated: 'It is obvious that the textbooks of the seventeenth century can no longer serve the same purpose as they did then, but now in large measure belong merely to the realm of historical presentation.'[7] Nevertheless, neither could Schleiermacher accept Kant's grounding religious truth in the moral consciousness. He insisted on centering theology in historical Christianity. The Gospel had to be true and credible to outsiders, judged, as it were, by the canons of ordinary verification. He thus called for a *cultural* theology, one that had apologetical value for Christianity's would-be despisers. Hence the title of his extraordinary manifesto, *Speeches on Religion, to the Cultured among its Despisers.*[8]

Schleiermacher himself formulated his life's goal, 'to create an eternal covenant between the living Christian faith and an independent and freely working science, a covenant by the terms of which science is not hindered and faith not excluded.'[9] Somehow, faith must have its freedom of formulation, but also it has to have a relation to science. Not only to science, but to all of life. Schleiermacher believed that Christians should participate in political, artistic and social life. Unlike Hegel, he did not believe in a higher synthesis which went beyond theology and science into a grand resolution of all things. Unlike traditional Christian thought, religion is distinct from metaphysics as well as from simple ethics or morality. Religion for Schleiermacher is neither a kind of belief nor a set of moral actions. As he famously put it in the *Speeches*, religion 'resigns, at once, all claims on anything that belongs either to science or morality.'[10]

So where does it reside? He answers, 'but, while man does nothing from religion, he should do everything with religion. Uninterruptedly, like a sacred music, the religious feelings should accompany his active life.'[11] In other words, religion occupies its own sphere, and yet it must interact with every other sphere of life. This being the case, what is the fundamental character of religion? As everyone knows, it is not a formulation of beliefs, nor an ethical posture. Rather, it is the 'sense and taste for the infinite'. Religion is a feeling (*Gefühl*), the feeling of utter dependence.[12] All proper feelings are pious. Ideas and principles are foreign to religion, because they are in a different department of life from religion.[13] Yet at the same time religion informs them, and so it should be impossible for the truly religious man to be immoral or even artistically cold. This is because the feeling of dependence is a self-consciousness that links the person's deepest self to ultimate things. By ultimate, Schleiermacher means several things, including the universe as a whole, and God himself.

True piety is not merely subjective for Schleiermacher. There is an objective world which determines the shape of the subject. Religion must be particular, rather than abstract. It is historically grounded. Yet at the same time, the truly pious person cannot simply argue his way into faith. Nor may he receive it on authority. He must *decide* to embrace revelation. The only legitimate beginning point for all theological reflection is the firsthand, genuine relationship to the object of faith which precedes doctrinal formulations. The authority of Scripture does not depend on prior arguments about its inspiration or its factual authenticity. Nor does trust in Christ depend on the authority of Scripture. Indeed,

Schleiermacher, along with numerous other nineteenth-century theologians, is eager to move away from the empty well of the Enlightenment, which, in his judgment, was too limited by arguments and proofs to issue in anything genuine and lasting. Rather, it is the other way around: the authority of Scripture is arrived at only when the primary relationship to Christ is present.

But then the question is raised, how to construct a proper bridge between the experience of the ultimate and the formulations religious people in general, and Christian people in particular, must live by? In fact, what is to guarantee that Christian faith be somehow exclusive or even superior to other religions? The very method Schleiermacher sets forth resists a strictly logical linkage from this pristine, intuitive feeling to the doctrines of the church. However, he comes to the conclusion that in the evolution of different religions, none is equal to Christianity, with its redemptive theme, and its great holy man, Jesus Christ. Within the Christian faith, the traditional loci of theology have their place, but only as they are redefined in the light of our primary relation of dependence with the ultimate.

How does this work, specifically? Take, for example, the doctrine of redemption. It is given a new character. Our conscience feels the need for fulfillment, but our limitations and flaws prevent us from having the freedom we need. This freedom can only be achieved when our religious sentiment, now hidden, becomes the driving force of our life, we can then enter into full communion with God. How can this occur? By looking at the supreme example of a human being in full communion with his God, to wit, Jesus Christ. Jesus, in Schleiermacher's view, was the most complete human being. He never had to be redirected because he was never so distracted by his limitations that he needed to return to God. In Christ, then, there is a holiness which must be the gift of God. His redemptive work consists of communicating this holiness to believers.[14]

Although there are obvious parallels here to the traditional Protestant doctrine of redemption in Jesus Christ, we are a long way from the substitutionary atonement of orthodoxy. It is even questionable whether Jesus Christ was fully divine in Schleiermacher's theology. He certainly struggled with the credibility of the Holy Trinity. He redefined every major doctrine in order to accord with the beginning point, the immunity, yet constituent nature, of the feeling of dependence. Sin, for example, becomes the feeling of a battle between spirit and flesh. This battle is felt because our sensuality develops earlier than the feeling of dependence. In fact, the fall is not a historical moment defined by Adam's disobedience, but the typification of a generalized condition, that of human beings not yet in touch with the holiness of Jesus Christ.

One of the major consequences of this theological reconstruction was to 'liberate' the exegesis of the Scripture from doctrinal presuppositions. Henceforth, because the essence of religious experience was not determined by the Scriptures, they were completely open to historical and critical investigation. Of course, many precursors to Schleiermacher were heading in this direction. Herder had said before him that exegesis was crucial in order to verify the connection between the historical data surrounding Jesus' coming to earth and the dogmas of the church.[15] But Schleiermacher was bold to assert the necessity of theology as a science. And since science has no particular responsibility to establish faith, only to give it shape, nothing is particularly lost by giving it free reign.

A second consequence of this approach is that new limits are placed upon language, especially theological language. A careful study of the massive *The Christian Faith* will reveal that the doctrine of God, or theology proper, is not particularly concentrated in any one place, neither at the beginning, where one might expect it, not even in his ambiguous thoughts about the Trinity, almost an appendix at the end. Rather, they are spread throughout the *ordo salutis*, but culminate with the integrative affirmation that 'God is love.'[16] But what specifically can we say about God's attributes? how far may we talk of the way God acts in our world? Once again, we can do it only when we honor the starting point of our need for redemption and of our being utterly dependent upon God. From there, we can make statements about God's eternity, his omniscience, his justice, his love and wisdom. His bold assertion is that 'all attributes that we ascribe to God are not to be taken as denoting something special in God, but only something special in the way in which the feeling of utter dependence is related to him.'[17] Along with Kant, then, Schleiermacher asserted that God could not be defined or objectified. This would place God outside of any relation with human consciousness, which is inappropriate. These new limits on theological language were meant to free the enterprise from reifying God. Theology, a rather anthropological endeavor, safeguards the divine from human pollution.

A third major consequence of Schleiermacher's position is that the work of the church is now to foster the progress of the human spirit. The advancement of the kingdom of God is now the advancement of human culture. Theology, though limited because of its role to protect God, is nonetheless a positive discipline, moving out from the experience of the heart to the more conventional studies in the human sciences. It is closely tied to ethics and the philosophy of religion, though not contained in them.[18] And, as mentioned above, theology had implications for all of life, hence the motto about the eternal covenant between the living Christian faith and every sphere of life. The originality of this entire scheme would not go unnoticed in the nineteenth century.

The French Connection

Accurately measuring the influence of Schleiermacher on the theology of the generations following him is a formidable task, one that is not in view in the present study. Indeed, detecting the force of the figure known as the 'father of liberalism' on theologians and philosophers in the nineteenth century involves far more than looking for acknowledgments and quotes by the different players. It is well known that a person may leave his imprint even on those who disagree with his basic views, simply because there are certain 'classical figures' who impose themselves and define the terms in ways that few can recognize, let alone resist.

The assessment of Schleiermacher's influence upon French theology is even more difficult to make than for German, British, or even American theology.[19] This is for at least two reasons. The first is that the French at the beginning of the nineteenth century were, with significant exceptions, not as familiar with German culture, even the German language, as other countries could be. The second is that French Protestants to a large extent had been decimated by the eighteenth-century persecutions. The French Revolution, and the Napoleonic wars, had reshaped Europe in the image of the French Enlightenment. Protestants on the whole had welcomed and supported the Revolution. But Napoleon's defeat and France's humiliation resulted in the Congress of Vienna (ending 1815) and a Europe restored. France returned to a modified monarchy, and climbed into modernity at a slightly different rate than did other countries, though it was certainly to become a major player by mid century. The task of Protestants in the Restoration period, as a minority of around 2% of the population, was to rebuild when the foundations had been severely shaken. Besides a smaller bourgeoisie, the great number of Protestants lived in the countryside. Their relation to the monarchy were cordial, and by the July Monarchy (1830–48) Protestants no longer felt themselves to be a tolerated minority, but began to hold significant positions of leadership and respect both in political realms and cultural fields.

What were the characteristics of the theology of this era of *le retour des huguenots*, as Jean Baubérot would call it?[20] Specifically, what was Schleiermacher's influence, if any, on the restored Protestants? In the very short space allotted here, the best way to proceed is to take a couple of representative examples from among the many possible choices of theologians who are candidates for this question. In passing, we should note that Madame Germaine de Staël published her controversial *De l'Allemagne* in 1813, meant to introduce the French public to the glories of German culture.[21] Among other things, she praises the spirit of free examination which has made German religion far more erudite than French. Instead of spreading rationalism, it was able to combine a scientific spirit with the things of the soul, thanks in large part to the work of Friedrich Schleiermacher. His merit is to have fought against indifference, and to have promoted, with great warmth and great clarity, the feeling for the infinite.

The first major French theologian consciously to have testified to the greatness of Schleiermacher is Samuel Vincent (1787–1837), the pastor-theologian from Nîmes, in the Gard. Not an easy thinker to classify, some have called him liberal, and even '*le Schleiermacher français*.'[22] There are indeed strong parallels to Schleiermacher in Vincent, as we will see. Yet I hesitate to place him so squarely in the liberal camp. Perhaps 'pre-liberal' suits him better.[23] In point of fact, there are only three mentions of Schleiermacher by name in the works of Samuel Vincent.[24] Does this mean he did not identify himself with Schleiermacher to the extent it is sometimes held? The answer depends, first, on the content of those references, and, second, on the overall structure of Vincent's theology.

Vincent constantly mentions the way that England and Germany have been in the lead, but now that there is peace in France, it is the homeland's turn to make major contributions to the study of religion.[25] He saw with unusual perspicacity the need for a renewal in Protestant thinking at the dawn of a new century. In a famous text, *Vues sur le Protestantisme en France*, he writes:

> Everything is stirring in the intellectual and moral worlds, new ideas are fermenting in people's spirits, a more living, more elevated philosophy is replacing the moribund materialism, and the need for spirit, for life and future, inextinguishable in the human spirit, long hidden, awakens with new energy; the people is beginning to feel the need for religion.[26]

The pages of his writings are replete with this sort of eloquent call for renewal. Certainly the spirit of Schleiermacher is not far from this kind of statement. The question is how close they are, and whether there was any direct influence.

One of the first tasks to which he dedicated himself was the translation of works which in his judgment would help fill the void. He did this from 1810 to 1819. Vincent followed this early period of translations with a longer one, 1820–1831, where he gathered articles together in a regular periodical, called *Mélanges de religion, de morale et de critique sacrée*. Published in Nîmes, there were ten volumes over a five year period, from 1820 to 1825.[27] He wrote numerous shorter articles, often bound into anthologies during his lifetime. His one major book is a sort of treatise on ecclesiology, called *Vues sur le protestantisme en France*, published in 1829.

Among his earlier publications was the translation of the two volumes of William Paley's *Principles of Moral and Political Philosophy* in 1817. Then two years later he published Thomas Chalmers' *The Evidence and Authority of the Christian Revelation*. One could wonder at the reasons for his choice of books to translate. At first glance, Paley's volumes have little in common with the methods of a French pre-liberal. They contain a general view of ethics rather than a biblically derived approach to political science. But though the particular approach undertaken by Paley did not closely resemble Vincent's own methods, the work represented something French Protestants could use in their new position as 'returning Huguenots.' Vincent made the volume available in order to furnish French Protestants with a third way between rationalism and authoritarian religion. It was thus a method he deemed salutary for their present plight. Similarly, one could wonder at his choice of Chalmers, an evidentialist in the Scottish tradition of Common Sense philosophy. As a matter of fact, he was a great admirer of Chalmers and kept the readers of his periodical abreast of the Scotsman's labors. No doubt in this case Vincent's mission was to give French Protestants a sure refutation of Deism, using its own claims against itself. He was also committed to the results of experimental science, especially those that were used to verify the authenticity of the Scriptures. Unlike Deism, which found the God of the Bible too specific and personal, historic Christianity demonstrates the need for beginning from the texts, and not from rational preference. At the same time he was not unaware of the increasing romantic spirit of his day. In one place where Chalmers had written, 'We have the experience of men, but we do not have the experience of God,' Vincent feels compelled to respond, in a footnote, 'If there is not something certain in our experience of God ... we would not even know whether there were a God.'[28]

This understanding of Vincent's motives is corroborated by the articles and the book published subsequently. One of his principal concerns was with the relation of religion to the other disciplines. The natural sciences are a crucial enterprise for Christians. So are the human sciences, including fine arts. But they derive from something deeper. Not theology, which although a science, perhaps a bit more exalted than the others, is 'something entirely different' from religion, which is the 'intercourse of the human soul with its creator.'[29] This is clearly a statement in line with Schleiermacher. He put it similarly in 1830, in *Religion et Christianisme*, 'Religion in the first rank, theology and all that goes with it in the second rank; that's where we are called to go ... everything is in our domain, for everything ends in religion.'[30] His approach is again like Schleiermacher's in that it is apologetic. He is eager to show how in the modern era, Christianity can subsist, full of strength and vitality, right alongside the most critical scientific studies.[31]

Thus, for Vincent religion is the heart of all things, but never in isolation from the other disciplines. Philosophy assists religion by verifying that its claims to receive revelation are worthy of the name. In turn, philosophy benefits from theology, which is its 'sublime guide'. The natural sciences are not only no threat, but a boon to Christians. First, they reveal the grandeur of the Creator. In a Baconian fashion, Vincent praises the ability of science to investigate the book of nature. But they also provide a method for critical reflection which can inform the investigation of the world, and of literature, including the Bible. If certain preconceived notions based on traditional hermeneutics must be questioned, that is all to the good. Perhaps the earth was not created in six regular days, but over long stretches of time. Perhaps the formulations of the great sixteenth century reformers was on certain issues bound to their times. Yet he is careful not to go as far as some of his colleagues in questioning outright the doctrines of predestination, original sin, the substitutionary atonement, and so forth.

Vincent is thus somewhere between two worlds. As a descendent of the eighteenth century, he believes in free examination as the key to religious freedom. In his extensive debate with the Roman Catholic Félicité de Lamennais, he constantly pleads for allowing people to read the Bible in the light of their own conscience, and not to dictate to them ahead of time what they must believe.[32] Indeed, owing to the writings of Pierre Bayle and Jean-Jacques Rousseau, and many others, free examination had become something of a Protestant slogan, attaining mythic proportions, by the time of Samuel Vincent. His best known statement about it is 'The content of Protestantism is the Gospel, its form is free examination.'[33] His other world, though, is the nineteenth century, particularly the current of romanticism, spreading rapidly around the French landscape at his time. True religion is individual, internal, a matter of the soul's communion with God. From this root the tree and branches of theology, and all of the sciences grow forth.

I believe we do have here a man under the sway of Schleiermacher. Although direct references to him in his writings are rare, his presence abounds in the framework of his theology. Naturally, it is impossible to measure how much his thought was shaped specifically by reading and studying Schleiermacher's work, as opposed to simply breathing the same air as the classical German personage. In fact, it is impossible with any degree of certainty to decide how much his influence is direct or indirect for any of the French theologians of the nineteenth century. Bernard Reymond, in an article devoted to the rediscovery of

Samuel Vincent, states in a pregnant footnote, that because Schleiermacher only appeared in translation into French in the twentieth century, his influence on French Protestant theology had to be indirect.[34] André Encrevé, preeminent historian of the nineteenth century, takes issue with the suggestion. He points out that Schleiermacher's influence was often direct, for in point of fact most French theologians could read German, and so had access to his writings.[35] Encrevé has developed his view of Schleiermacher's influence in a thorough discussion in volume 11 of the series *Histoire du christianisme*, where he reviews the works of Edmond Scherer, Charles Secrétan and Alexandre Vinet.[36] His thesis is that often Schleiermacher had a direct influence on French theology, but that even when it was not direct, he was impossible to ignore. Even the more orthodox theologians, he maintains, were still under his shadow. I basically agree. While in my first study of this question, *La carte protestante*, I took issue with what I took to be Encrevé's lack of nuance on this matter, I now recognize that I had caricatured him somewhat.[37] I was pleading to see Schleiermacher's presence in French theology, but not always in the same manner, depending on the players, a point with which Encrevé surely agrees.

An Awakened Historian

As proof of this, consider briefly another Protestant thinker of the same epoch, J. H. Merle d'Aubigné (1794–1872). Merle belonged to the school born of the Réveil (the Awakening) in Switzerland and France. Linked to pietism and the renewal movements in other parts of Europe, the Réveil in the French world developed in part through the frustrations of students and others in Geneva to the cold rationalism of the Venerable Company, the official registry of pastors. A remarkable religious awakening occurred beginning around 1813. It led to a certain fragmentation of the churches, along theological lines. Merle stayed in the established church, but was definitely affected by the Réveil. One of the triggers of his own pilgrimage toward a living orthodoxy was in a series of Bible studies on the Book of Romans led by the Scottish missionary Robert Haldane, held for the students at the Theological Seminary in Geneva, during his visit, from 1816 to 1817.[38] As one of Haldane's interpreters would remark, 'Never since Francis Turrettini and Benedict Pictet, of holy and venerable memory, had a teacher exposited the council of God with such purity, such force, such fulness.' The flame of this new zeal for Scripture spread far and wide. Eventually an informal party, known variously as the 'orthodox,' or the 'awakened,' was brought about, one that had episodic conflicts with various more liberal (or pre-liberal) opponents.

Merle had been concerned to see Geneva overcome some of the contradictions he saw in its intellectual heritage. How could both its great Protestant tradition and the newer requirements for toleration and enlightened science be preserved? He became convinced that the basic thrust of the Réveil, would make this possible. He came to profess the Calvinistic doctrines set forth by Haldane because he believed they were biblical. Not that he sided politically with all the early members of the Réveil. In fact, he was ordained in the established church in July of 1817.[39] That same year saw the young Merle travel from his native Geneva to Germany, where he applied for the position of pastor in the French Reformed church at Hamburg.

While waiting for the paperwork to clear he studied in Berlin with none other than Schleiermacher. Merle was particularly drawn to what he perceived as the balance between the internal and the external aspects of Christian faith. He had longed to reconcile science and inner religion. Schleiermacher seemed to hold the key. He taught that the human soul had two aspects, one that establishes the independent individual, and the other that puts the individual in a relation of dependence with the external world. Later, the study of the individual in history became one of the basic historiographical methods in Merle's work. He believed, along with a number of others, that, 'The study of individuals in history becomes central to the study of religion because, if individuals have discovered an equilibrium between these two poles of the human soul, then this will establish the true Christian consciousness.[40]

One could go on showing places where Schleiermacher left his mark on Merle. Yet caution must be exercised here. First, Merle would later become fairly critical of Schleiermacher on specific issues. For example, he wrote in 1851 that, the theology of Schleiermacher has the interior character of Christianity, but it has neglected the positive, historical, and objective character.'[41] He would be troubled by Schleiermacher's permissive approach to Protestant doctrines. Second, as Roney points out, although he attended many lectures by Schleiermacher, his real mentor became the church historian August Neander. This fascinating figure converted from Judaism to Christian faith, and changed his name from David Mendel to Neander, meaning 'new man (in Christ)'. He was far more orthodox than Schleiermacher, believing in sin as guilt, and redemption through Christ's atonement. He spent much of his life combating rationalism in the Prussian church, and pleading for authentic personal faith. He was one of the greatest historians of his era, and as such looked to find the dynamic of the religious factor in human affairs. Finally, far better than Schleiermacher, in Merle's judgment, Neander was able to combine faith and science, and keep the proper balance between academics and personal piety.

Merle was thus influenced by Schleiermacher, because he represented so many of the ideals which would later nurture his own intellectual approach. But he was far from a disciple of the classical German. His real heros were Neander, as mentioned, but also Hengstenberg, Stier, and the Mediation School theologians such as Tholück. Merle was simply more conservative, or orthodox, than Schleiermacher. Though he believed in the power of reason, for example, Merle thought that if scientific integrity were to be maintained, the forces of human reason needed to be marshaled, 'under the influence of the Holy Spirit and of the Word, blessed from on high.'[42] Like Schleiermacher, he believed there was a difference between the essential principles of Christianity and the time-bound expression of doctrines and confessions in a particular age, say, the Reformation. But Merle was much closer to the actual formulations of the sixteenth century. More than Schleiermacher, for the sake of the health of the contemporary church, he thought one should adhere to those views, although, of course, they should be developed and applied by the church. Like Karl Ullmann, then, Merle believed, 'What the church requires, is not so much a radical and universal remodeling, as a development of the principles of the Reformation.' He stressed a closer continuity with Reformation doctrines.[43] Merle was simply orthodox. Not a thoughtless, mimicking orthodoxy, but one to which one could subscribe as is. The trouble with Schleiermacher's theology, taken at face value, was that it represented a serious departure from orthodoxy on numerous points.

Merle indeed developed a historiography which might be called 'romantic'. At the beginning of his treatise on the study of history, he cites Neander as his principal guide. Schleiermacher is not far in the background, perhaps. Merle intends to present a history which is as attentive to the internal elements as to the external. He looked for individual persons in whom the ideals of an age tend to be personified, for good or for ill.[44] In response to the eighteenth century's view, which questioned any Christian understanding, we should now acknowledge it. With the right view of the human soul, we could look for the 'soul of history', that is, the moral and emotional factors that drive great men in history. Yet only if scientific methods validate these findings can they be protected from being speculative. Here, he is going into territory not charted by Schleiermacher.

Merle's apologetics was a departure from Schleiermacher altogether. Whereas for the latter, revelation is very close to the awareness of God, for Merle, revelation was the Scripture. Here he even parted company with his true mentor, Neander. As Roney puts it, 'Merle disagreed with Schleiermacher and Neader because, in the final analysis, he could not accept their belief that conscience and personal experience confirmed Scripture.'[45] He even differed with Neander on the role of human agency in receiving written revelation: 'We do not entrust the Christian conscience to govern the Word, but we entrust the Word to govern the Christian conscience.'[46] According to Roney, his doctrine of divine sovereignty and the interpretation of Scripture was close to that of the Princeton school.[47] In short, Merle was far more orthodox than even his mentor Neander, and *a fortiori* Schleiermacher. He was able to filter various aspects of Schleiermacher's views and still use some of his themes, especially those that related to seeing God at work in the process of history.

A Partial Light

The end of the matter is this. Schleiermacher's conviction that theology needed to be overhauled at the beginning of the nineteenth century was shared by the bulk of Protestants, including the French, returning as they did from their fragile background to a more solid foothold. With his stress on the relation of the soul to the absolute, and the relationship of that primary feeling of utter dependence to the more positive work of science, Schleiermacher cast a strong ray of light over many of the French theologians, but in different degrees. The glare was not as intense for some as it was for others. One of the key differences in the way he was received was the theological conviction of those who stood in Schleiermacher's beam.

While André Encrevé is right that even the awakened (or orthodox) group was influenced by Schleiermacher, there are crucial differences between their understanding of the classical German and that of the pre-liberals.[48] What is at stake here? First, the question of whether theologians can be objective enough that while living under someone's sway they can, if need be, distance themselves from key elements of that person's authority. Our answer to this is affirmative, judging from the two cases in point, especially that of Merle. Second, the issue is whether the nineteenth century was an entirely liberal century, no matter what the particular differences might have been in the schools of theology it harbored. To that the answer would have to be yes and no. Yes, because almost everyone, from pre-liberal to rationalist to orthodox, and similarly in Roman Catholic circles, had to conjugate theology into the new, expanding Europe, the exhaustion of Enlightenment rationalism, and the crisis of a church increasingly separated from direct bonds with the central sectors of society. In this awareness it would have been impossible to avoid being in Schleiermacher's shadow. But, no, because at least the more orthodox theologians were profoundly conscious of the great distance that separated Schleiermacher from his sixteenth-century forebears. Many, especially the awakened, were willing to denounce his doctrinal errors, on questions that were central to the Christian faith.

NOTES

1. Karl Barth: *The Theology of Schleiermacher: lectures at Göttingen, Winter Semester of 1923/24*, Dietrich Ritschl, ed., Geoffrey W. Bromiley, transl., Grand Rapids: Eerdmans, 1982, p. xvi.
2. Karl Barth: *Der Römerbrief*, Munich, 1922, pp. 209, 242. Barth's gradual revolt against liberalism came to a head during his pastorate in Safenwil. The first edition of the *Römerbrief*, 1919, then its reworked second version, 1922, are the first manifestos critiquing liberalism that echoed around the world. They were not the first to be voiced, however. As Fred H. Klooster points out, both Abraham Kuyper and Herman Bavinck had done so, in 1834 and 1890 respectively. It is the inaccessibility of the Dutch language that kept them from being heard, Klooster avers. *The Significance of Barth's Theology*, Grand Rapids: Baker, 1961, p. 17.
3. Karl Barth: *Schleiermacher-Auswahl*, Siebenstern Taschenbuch 113/14, Munich & Hamburg, 1968, pp. 261-279.
4. Jean-Jacques Rousseau: *Emile*, in *Œuvres complètes*, vol. 4, Paris: Gallimard - La

Pléiade, 1969, pp. 614, 625.

5. Immanuel Kant: *Religion Within the Limits of Reason Alone*, T. M. Greene & H. H. Hudson, transl., New York: Harper & Row, 1960, *ad loc.*

6. *Vorlesung über die Methode des akademischen Studiums*, 1803.

7. *Der christliche Glaube*, 19.2. See *the Christian Faith*, H. R. Mackintosh & J. S. Stewart, editors and transl., Edinburgh, 1928.

8. First published in 1799. We will use the English edition, *On Religion: Speeches to Its Cultured Despisers*, John Oman, transl., Louisville: Westminster/John Knox Press, 1994, henceforth, *Speeches*.

9. *Sendschreiben an Dr. Lücke*, quoted in Claude Welch: *Protestant Thought in the Nineteenth Century*, New Haven: Yale University Press, 1972, p. 63.

10. *Speeches*, p. 35.

11. *Ibid.*, p. 59.

12. The translation of *das schlechthinige Abhängigkeitsgefühl* is debatable. On the whole, Schleiermacher specialists tend to avoid the more popular, 'feeling of absolute dependence,' and prefer 'utter,' or perhaps 'simple' (in the sense of unreserved) dependence.

13. *Ibid.*, p. 46.

14. *Der christliche Glaube*, *Op. Cit.*, ch. 15.

15. Numerous histories of biblical criticism exist. One of the most engaging is by Henning Graf Reventlow: *The Authority of the Bible and the Rise of the Modern World*, Philadelphia: Fortress Press, 1985. He traces the immediate background for nineteenth century hermeneutics not to Germany but to Great Britain, particularly the Deists.

16. *Der christliche Glaube*, *Op. Cit.*, ch. 167.

17. *Ibid.*, ch. 50.

18. Friedrich Schleiermacher: *Brief Outline on the Study of Theology*, Richmond, 1966, *ad loc.*

19. Tracing Schleiermacher's influence on American theology is a task in itself, one that would have been especially appropriate in an essay dedicated to D. Clair Davis. One of the most obvious candidates would be Horace Bushnell (1802–1876), whose influential writings had the effect of recasting traditional theology into new molds. Though Samuel Taylor Coleridge was the first influence on Bushnell, Schleiermacher was the strong second, seminal for much of his thinking. It would be interesting to compare him with a more orthodox American theologian to measure Schleiermacher's influence in the same way we are doing here with two French Protestants.

20. Jean Baubérot: *Le retour des huguenots, la vitalité protestante XIXe-XXe siècle*, Paris: Cerf & Labor et Fides, 1985.

21. London, 1813. The book was only published in Paris in 1814 because Mme de Staël was under surveillance by the imperial police. She was the daughter of Genevan financier Necker, who served under Louis XVI but dismissed because of his pre-revolutionary platform to tax even the rich.

22. Ferdinand Fontanès: *Introduction*, *Méditations religieuses* de Samuel Vincent, Valence, 1839.

23. The suggestion is from Daniel Robert: *Les Eglises réformées en France, 1800-1830*, Paris: P.U.F., 1961, p. 377.

24. See Roger Grossi: *Samuel Vincent, témoin de l'Evangile, 1787-1737*, Nîmes: S.H.P.N.G., 1997, p. 142.

25. Samuel Vincent: *Mélanges de religion, de morale et de critique sacrée*, vol. 1, Nîmes, 1820, p.3.

26. _____: *Vues sur le Protestantisme en France*, Nîmes-Paris-Genève, 1929.

27. It ceased publication no doubt because he hesitated to compete with Charles

Coquerel's Parisian periodical with similar goals, *La Revue protestante*. Vincent came back in 1830 with another revue, *Religion et Christianisme*, to coincide with the new July Monarchy. Its mission was to 'promote spirituality in the fullest sense, over against materialism.' Vol 1, p. 19.

28. From Vincent's French translation, p. 190.

29. *Vues sur le Protestantisme en France*, vol 2, p. 83.

30. Vol 1, p. 5.

31. *Ibid.*, p. 6.

32. Lamennais had written the massive *Essai sur l'indifférence en matière de religion*, published from 1817 to 1823. They contain strong criticism of Protestantism because of its supposed deficient view of the church. Vincent picket up the gauntlet in his lengthy *Observations sur l'unité religieuse*, Paris, 1820.

33. *Vues sur le Protestantisme en France*, vol 1, p. 19.

34. Bernard Reymond: 'Redécouvrir Samuel Vincent,' *Études théologiques et religieuses*, 1979, p. 423, n. 41.

35. André Encrevé: *Protestants français au milieux du XIXe siècle, Les réformés de 1848 à 1870*, Genève: Labor et Fides, 1986, p. 101, n.158.

36. ____: 'La pensée protestante,' *Histoire du christianisme des origines à nos jours*, vol 11, (1830–1914), Paris: Desclée, 1995, pp. 49-60.

37. William Edgar: *La carte protestante, Les réformés francophones et l'essor de la modernité (1815–1848)*, Genève: Labor et Fides, 1997, p. 308. I appreciate the gracious way in which Professor Encrevé has set me straight, in private correspondence.

38. Numerous accounts of the Réveil's first phase exist. One of the most engaging is Gabriel Mützenberg: *À l'écoute du Réveil, De Calvin à l'Alliance évangélique*, St-Légier: Eds Emmaüs, 1989, esp. pp. 68-84.

39. By far the best account of Merle's intellectual itinerary is John B. Roney: *The Inside of History: Jean Henri Merle d'Aubigné and Romantic Historiography*, Westport: Greenwood Press, 1996. Much of what follows draws on that work.

40. *Ibid.*, p. 51.

41. Merle d'Aubigné: *Sommaire de l'histoire des dogmes*, Genève: Société évangélique, 1851, p. 223.

42. ____: *Foi et science*, Paris, 1835, p. 16.

43. Quoted in John B. Roney: *Op. Cit.*, p. 176.

44. Merle d'Aubigné: *Discours sur l'étude de l'histoire du christianisme, et son utilité pour l'époque actuelle*, Paris-Genève, 1832, p. 6.

45. John B. Roney: *Op. Cit.*, p. 121.

46. Merle d'Aubigné: *Quelle est la théologie propre à guérir les maux du temps actuel?*, Genève, 1852, p. 22.

47. John B. Roney: *Op. Cit.*, p. 122.

48. André Encrevé: *Les protestants en France de 1800 à nos jours, Historie d'une réintégration*, Paris: Stock, 1985, p. 82.

THE STRUGGLE FOR ORTHODOXY IN THE CHRISTIAN REFORMED CHURCH

W. Robert Godfrey

In 1857 four congregations and one minister left the Reformed Church of America to form what is today the Christian Reformed Church. Many more joined them in the early 1880s. The causes for these secessions seem small: concern about hymns supplanting psalms in the church's worship, decline of catechetical preaching and instruction, lack of endorsement for the Secession of 1834 in the Netherlands, and toleration of freemasons as members of the church.[1] But for Dutch Reformed immigrants all these issues illustrated their concern to avoid the kind of Americanization that would make them conform to what they believed was the dominant American religion. Writing of these attitudes in the early twentieth century Calvin Seminary Professor Henry Stob observed: 'American religion, they believed, was Methodistic, and the Americanization of the church could only mean the dilution if not the dissolution of the Calvinistic faith.'[2] James Bratt, a keen historian, detailed some of the differences between American evangelicals and the Dutch Reformed immigrants: 'Evangelicals replaced catechism with Sunday School, Bible study with prayer meetings, doctrinal sermons with topical discourses. Having sacrificed the intellectual in Christianity, they had to resort to the emotions of the ignorant – revivals – or to the tastes of the respectable – "sound organization" pleasing the businessman and "social service" pleasing his wife. In each case they imitated "the world", whether of mass entertainment, of big business with its mergers and boards, or of charities with their assorted benevolences.'³ From its earliest days the CRC found itself struggling in America to maintain its Reformed orthodoxy.

This struggle was not unique to the small Dutch enclave in which the CRC functioned. Protected by ethnic, linguistic, geographical and institutional isolation as well as theological distinctiveness these Dutch Reformed pioneers were part of a larger struggle for Calvinism in America. Over a longer period of time American Presbyterians faced very parallel challenges. But for the Dutch Reformed community in their new homeland the duty to Calvinism was clear. As Henry Beets, an influential leader, wrote in 1907: 'Our great and peculiar duty and calling here was and is ... to become more and more what God in his providence in the past had designed us to be as a Calvinistic people.... To reach this purpose ... we had no right to be benevolently assimilated.... Christian isolation was a duty, isolation to develop ourselves quietly and without undue haste ... until we are prepared enough ... to cast us ... into the arena of American religious and political and social life.'⁴

The enemies of Calvinism in America were many. One enemy was theological liberalism undermining confidence in the Bible as God's revelation and in orthodox Christian teaching on God, Christ, salvation and the church. This enemy increasingly controlled various institutions of higher learning in America and over time would come to dominate institutions in the Netherlands to which those in the CRC had traditionally looked for solid Reformed education. Another enemy for Reformed Christianity in America was the unconfessional or anti-confessional evangelicalism. This enemy, identified as Methodism by the Dutch Reformed, was reductionistic in theology, concerned more for its own brand of piety than for comprehensive truth, and profoundly activist in spirit. Its focus on piety and activism strangely enough, were the basis on which, as the Dutch Reformed confessionalists would learn to their regret, evangelicals and liberals could sometimes agree and cooperate. A third enemy, less obvious and more invidious, was the gradual growth of the economic and social standing of the Dutch in America. Beginning as farmers and lower middle class workers they moved up over the decades through education and hard work to the upper middle class. Perhaps it is harder to believe that one is totally depraved with a college degree and white collar job. Cottages by the lake became at least as great a problem for orthodoxy as theological liberalism.

While the common enemy was relatively clear, Bratt's study has shown that in the early part of the twentieth century the Dutch Reformed community had several different emphases and therefore tensions as to the precise direction that it should pursue. In the CRC three such emphases came to expression: the confessionalist, the antithetical and the positive Calvinist.[5] The confessionalist stressed traditional Reformed doctrine and piety, looking with varying degrees of concern at some of the innovations of the followers of Kuyper. The antitheticals and the positive Calvinists both followed Kuyper more enthusiastically, the antitheticals embracing particularly his stress on the absolute antitheses between all regenerate and unregenerate thought, while the positive Calvinists followed his stress on common grace as a link between Christians and non-Christians. Yet within those tensions a fundamental unity was to be found and within that unity there was a clear hegemony of the confessionalists.[6]

Those tensions at times did become divisive and led to disciplinary actions: in 1922 Ralph Janssen was deposed from the ministry accused of embracing aspects of higher biblical criticism and in 1924 Herman Hoeksema was deposed because of his rejection of common grace. Still the center of the CRC seemed to be holding. Under the leadership of the faculty of Calvin Theological Seminary and stalwarts of orthodoxy like Louis Berkhof, H. J. Kuiper and R. B. Kiuper the CRC seemed secure in its orthodoxy.

Nevertheless the struggle continued. The life and career of Henry Stob illustrates the emergence and concerns of a powerful progressive movement in the CRC. Henry Stob (1908–1996) taught at Calvin College and Calvin Theological Seminary and was a mentor to many who became leaders of the more progressive wing of the CRC. In his autobiography *Summoning Up Remembrance* (1995), Stob has given us a remarkable window into the church and the factors of change in it. The autobiography focuses most of its attention on the external events of his life, giving interesting snapshots of his experience in the Dutch-American subculture. For a man who was a philosopher and led a life of the mind, he was remarkably reticent about his thought and the development of his ideas. Still we get revealing glimpses through his eyes of what he believed was happening in the CRC.

He was raised in a pious Reformed Dutch immigrant home. His parents had very little formal education. After grammar school he worked several years before he attended a Christian high school in Chicago and then attended Calvin College (1928–1932) and Calvin Seminary (1932–1935). He studied as a graduate student at Hartford Seminary in Connecticut and the University of Goettingen, Germany (1935–1938). From 1939-1952 (except for his military service from 1943–1946) he taught philosophy at Calvin College and then in 1952, was appointed by the Synod of the CRC to teach at Calvin Seminary where he served until his retirement in 1975. He was ordained to the ministry in the CRC in 1953.

In many ways he was a loyal son of the Reformed Christianity in which he was raised. He seemed to have no crisis of faith and appreciated his heritage. He remembered the quiet, restful Sabbaths of his youth fondly and observed, 'and in retrospect I know of no better way to spend the day on which the Lord rose.'[7] He praised J. Gresham Machen's *Christianity and Liberalism* (1923)[8] and spent a 'delightful' evening with Machen and others at Westminster Seminary in Philadelphia in 1931.[9] He served as the national president of the League of Evangelical Students in 1933.[10] He commented on his experience of the theological liberalism at Hartford Seminary, 'I had grown skeptical of some features of the Reformed faith while at Calvin, but the shallowness of the 'modernist' alternative as expounded here turned me around and deepened my appreciation of my orthodox heritage.'[11] He believed that he represented sound and sensible Reformed theology. 'We [the faculty of Calvin College] were one in holding that reason should function within the boundaries of religion and that science should be pursued in alliance with the truth revealed in Scripture and received in faith.'[12]

Stob showed at several points in his story his concern about what he regarded as ultra-conservative elements in the Dutch Reformed tradition. He saw the beginning of the publication of the *Torch and Trumpet* (later *The Outlook*) in 1951 as the expression of those 'out to cultivate a mind that valued safety above advancement and militancy above engagement.'[13] He regretted 'a state of mind that, inclined toward safety on the one hand and toward militancy on the other, impeded the progress of thought and growth and encouraged the development of a narrow and stultifying conservatism.'[14] He seemed to see Cornelius Van Til of Westminster Seminary as an example of that excessive militancy.[15]

He was also concerned that the Neo-Calvinist philosophy of Dooyeweerd and Vollenhoven, too much involved 'a futile attempt to fit a philosopher into a preconceived slot'.[16] At the time of his appointment to teach at Calvin College he had doubts about the decision of the Synod of 1928 in regard to worldly amusements: 'though I expressed reservations about the "moral" restrictions imposed upon the faculty and students, I promised to observe the rules prohibiting movie attendance, card playing, and dancing.'[17] He continued to urge a less legalistic approach to avoiding worldliness.[18]

Some of his complaints about the narrowness of conservatism in the CRC may well have been justified. He was eager to be orthodox and advance the cause of sound Reformed thought. Yet in his own way he was remarkably parochial. His experience outside of Dutch communities in Chicago and western Michigan did not seem to stretch him beyond the rather insular quality of his life there. He was remarkably naïve about the character of Hartford Seminary when he went there. He wrote of one course that he took there: 'In it the professor gave expression to the vapid theological liberalism that, I soon realized, reflected the dominant spirit of the school.'[19] The only surprise about this is his surprise.

He also seemed rather naively positive about the theology of Karl Barth. At Hartford 'I fell upon Karl Barth.... I sensed that here was a man who, affirming a transcendent God and a veritable supernatural revelation expressed my own deepest sentiments.... I can fairly say that it was Karl Barth who, even in his Kiekegaardian existentialist phase, helped to established me more firmly in the Reformed faith.'[20] He certainly rejected Van Til's criticism of Barth. He heard Van Til speak on Barth in 1950: 'His five addresses on Barthianism were well attended, but his characterization of Barth as a malevolent 'neo-Modernist', while pleasing to some, struck a number of us as a representation suffering from misunderstanding and distortion.'[21] Like many of his contemporaries in the CRC he reacted more to the narrowness immediately around him than to the great threat of neo-orthodoxy for the churches.

In a variety of ways his autobiography showed his own deviations from confessional Reformed theology. He no doubt believed that his dissent was within the bounds of the confessions or was only over minor matters. He believed that he was refining and improving Reformed thought, and that he was relating the old theology to the church for a new era.

Yet the areas in which he dissented were important and pointed to problems that would grow and grow in the CRC. He seemed to have little regard for the inerrancy of the Bible. He wrote of the 'Bible's presumed inerrancy'[22] and commented on Professor Wyngaarden of Calvin Seminary that he sought 'refuge in a staid orthodoxy and the advocacy of a completely inerrant Bible.'[23] Of his state of mind in 1932 he wrote, '... I did not see in any supposed evolutionary development a threat to the biblical doctrine of creation, since creation and evolution are answers to quite different questions and need not come into conflict. The Bible remained for me an authoritative book, but I no longer read it without discrimination and I did not take all its pronouncements literally. I became, I suppose, more tolerant of divergent opinions, less prone to judge prematurely, and more disposed than formerly to take the middle road when disputes raged.'[24] He recorded that while he was at Calvin Seminary 'I had problems with an eternal decree of reprobation and with the doctrine of limited atonement.'[25]

His account of the controversy at Calvin Seminary in the early 1950s showed his sympathy for Harry Boer and his cousin George Stob against Professors Volbeda, Hendricksen, Rutgers and Wyngaarden. While Volbeda and the three who stood with him saw the issues as fundamentally theological,[26] Stob did not agree, and saw the problems as differences over 'policies, procedures and management.'[27] Yet he offered as an illustration of the tensions of that time the reactions in the seminary faculty to a sermon preached in October 1951 by a seminarian named Raymond Opperwall. In preaching on God's healing of Hezekiah, the seminarian said, as summarized by Stob, 'this seemed to indicate quite clearly that God could change his mind and revoke a plan of action he had previously adopted.'[28] The consistory of the church complained to the seminary faculty that the sermon had not upheld the doctrine of God's immutability. Stob observed, 'The faculty had now to adjudicate the case and determine whether Opperwall was guilty of doctrinal defection or had done no more than replace the staticism of Greek ontology with a slice of biblical historicism.'[29] The faculty was divided on how to proceed with this student, but clearly the majority believed the doctrinal issue was serious.[30] The investigating committee of the board early in 1952 concluded that the ideas on God in the sermon were 'in conflict with the Reformed faith' and that 'the position of Mr. Opperwall violates the express revelation of God which declares that God is immutable'.[31] Stob argued that George Stob and Harry Boer were vindicated when Opperwall, after a special examination, was declared a candidate for the ministry in the CRC by Synod 1952. Stob did not indicate, however, whether any change in Opperwall's sentiments or expressions had taken place by then. In any case on Stob's own evidence that matter seems fundamentally doctrinal however much procedural differences may have muddied the waters.

Stob perhaps gave the clearest indication of his own approach to the Reformed confessional theology that he had sworn before God and the church to uphold in his comments on a candidate for the ministry named Clarence Boersma. 'The board [of trustees] also dealt lightly with Clarence Boersma, who refused to sign the Form of Subscription because, as he said, he did not "detest the Anabaptists" and did not regard the Catholic mass as "an accursed idolatry". Some of us who had signed the Form shared Boersma's sentiments but considered that we were not bound by expressions formulated in the heat of sixteenth-century battles, and we judged that the accepted creeds are best left unaltered and for historical reasons preserved in their integrity.'[32] This attitude seems seriously at odds with the Form of Subscription that CRC ministers and professors sign. The confessions are not honorable museum pieces, nor are ministers free to decide which doctrinal elements they accept or reject. But the attitude expressed candidly by Stob – twenty years after his retirement – came to be held less openly by many.

In the case of Henry Stob and those like him we see the tendency for 'positive Calvinism' to become more progressive. These progressives moved beyond differing emphases under an orthodox umbrella to views in various ways accommodated to the unconfessional thinking of America and the Netherlands. The struggle for orthodoxy had entered a whole new stage.

After the disruption at Calvin Seminary in 1952 Bratt described the new faculty in these terms: 'More striking was the new state of ideological pluralism, signaled by the persistence rather than the purging of parties and their periodicals, and by the dedication of the new Calvin Seminary faculty above all to moderation, coexistence, and peace. This spelled the end of Confessionalist hegemony.'[33] While Bratt may have overstated the Confessionalist loss at this point, it is certainly true that Calvin Seminary no longer exercised the strong, public leadership in the church that it had in the past. Its faculty became very cautious. The challenges to the CRC's confessional character became more serious and intense.

In the years after the reorganization of Calvin Seminary a whole serious of developments showed the movement in the CRC in a less orthodox direction. One way of seeing the marginalization of the confessionalists in the CRC is to look at the editorial leadership of the *Torch and Trumpet* (later the *Outlook*), the leading conservative periodical in the CRC. While edited by young ministers after its founding in 1951, many leading figures in the church were frequent contributors to the magazine. Most notably perhaps was R. B. Kuiper (1886–1966). While most of his teaching ministry was at Westminster Theological Seminary in Philadelphia, he served as president of Calvin College 1930–1933 and as president of Calvin Seminary 1952–1956. In 1957 H. J. Kuiper became editor. Kuiper was one of the leading figures in the church and former editor of the *Banner*, the CRC's official denominational periodical. When Kuiper died in 1963, he was succeeded as editor by P. Y. DeJong, son of a famous CRC minister and professor of practical theology at Calvin Seminary (1964–1970). In 1970 John Vander Ploeg became editor, after he had retired from serving as H. J. Kuiper's successor as editor of the *Banner*. Vander Ploeg retired in 1978. His replacement by Peter DeJong marked the point at which leadership of the *Outlook* passed to those not centrally influential in the agencies of the CRC. This change exemplified the reality that the confessionalists had lost a presence in the center of the institutional life of the CRC. While the *Outlook* would continue to seek to shape the direction of the CRC under DeJong and after 1990 under Thomas and Laurie Vanden Heuvel, the CRC continued to move away from its orthodox past. After 1996 the *Outlook* turned its focus away from the CRC to other Reformed churches in North America.

Another way to see the declining influence of the confessionalists in the CRC is to look at the various theological issues which emerged in the church. Progressives advanced one challenge after another to the historic Reformed consensus in the church. One of the first was the question: should the CRC support a distinctively Reformed seminary for its mission work in Nigeria or support a union seminary. The Nigerians preferred a Reformed seminary but the progressives led by Harry Boer preferred a union seminary. The CRC ultimately supported the Reformed seminary.

Then came the debate over the love of God, stemming from the teaching of seminary professor Harold Dekker. Dekker wanted a more universal statement on God's love for mankind than had been historic among the Reformed. (Dr. Roger Nicole saw his views as simply classic Amyraldianism.) After much time Synod 1967 mildly chastised him for his views. Bratt saw the tepid character of the synod's reprimand as evidence that the 'Confessionalists' dominance was now broken on the official level.' Bratt related the declining influence of the confessionalists in part to generational change marked by the deaths of three leaders – Henry Van Til in 1961, H. J. Kuiper in 1962, and R. B. Kuiper in 1966.[34]

One area of considerable unity was the rejection of the charismatic movement in the 1970s. Synod 1973 accepted the conclusions of a report that recognized the unreformed character of the Pentecostal movement. Bratt recognized this decision as very much in keeping with early fears of Americanization: 'The argumentation of the '70s repeated exactly the charges brought three generations before against "Methodism": individualism and privatization (read "subjectivism'''); feeling at the expense of intellect; frenetic "practicality" that follows first the "soul saving", then the bureaucratic imperative (now in the form of evangelists' personal empires); and through it all an Arminian "bootstrap theology" ('human potential') that displaces divine grace for human faith (read "anthropocentrism").'[35]

Then there were recurring discussions about the authority and interpretation of the Bible. Synod 1959, with Confessionalists still strong, declared the commitment of the CRC to the inerrancy of the Bible. But the pressures from theological movements in the United States and the Netherlands continued to bring up questions about the Bible. In 1969 a study committee was appointed to examine the nature and extent of biblical authority. Its preliminary report to Synod 1971 (Report 36) raised a storm of protest from conservatives. The revision of the report presented to Synod 1972 (Report 44) was much more acceptable to conservatives was still too ambiguous at a number of points. Nevertheless its basic points were accepted, but enough concern about the report continued so that Synod 1979 sought to clarify the position of the CRC by reiterating the declaration of 1959 on the inerrancy of the Bible.

In 1977 Harry Boer submitted a gravamen to the synod calling on the CRC to reject the teaching of the Canons of Dort on reprobation. Here was an attack on confessionalism at its very heart. Synod 1980 rejected the gravamen, but Boer continued to teach his opposition to the doctrine in violation of his oath of subscription.

Another telling synodical action occurred in 1982. The synod adopted a number of pastoral guidelines that had the effect of permitting dancing in the church. This action, of course, actually only recognized what was already happening in many parts of the church. In reality it was a reversal of the warning of Synod 1928 against worldly amusements, but it wrapped itself in the neo-Kuyperian language of 'redeeming the dance'. While most in the church supported the decision or were indifferent to it, some sat and wept.

Questions on the relationship between science and Bible also produced a number of debates in the church. The decisions of Synod 1991 in response to a study committee report still reflected a rather conservative approach to issues of origins, evolution, and the early chapters of Genesis. But in these decisions as in so much, the decision of synod was more on the confessional than progressive side, but was less assertive and clear than confessionalists would have liked. Even more serious than the mild character of the decisions was the unwillingness of the church to enforce the decisions with discipline. Time and again relatively good decisions were ignored or flaunted by the progressives and the church had no will to discipline such behavior.

In some ways the culmination in the Americanization of the CRC was demonstrated in the report on worship, 'Authentic Worship and a Changing Culture,' submitted to Synod 1997. The report denied that Reformed worship was a distinctive form of worship and even endorsed the use of images in worship in direct contradiction of the Heidelberg Catechism. The report embraced the use of Christmas manger scenes, for example, without even a reflection on the possible idolatry of such use.

However important these and other theological debates were in the CRC, the climactic issue in the struggle for orthodoxy became the debate on the question as to whether women could hold the offices of deacon, elder and minister in the church. The discussion was brought into the church because of changes in the Netherlands. As early as 1973 the synod received a report that stated that 'the practice of excluding women from ecclesiastical office cannot be conclusively defended on biblical grounds'. To try to use such a statement to open the offices of the church to women was inherently unreformed and contrary to the Belgic Confession. Both the Confession and the Reformed heritage teach that the structure of the church and its offices must be established by the positive teaching of the Bible. But from 1973 to 1995 progressives pushed the issue often oblivious of the consequences for the theology and unity of the church. Study, discussion, debate and controversy would take up much time and energy in the CRC.

At Synod 1978 the decision was made to permit the ordination of women as deacons 'provided their work is distinguished from that of elders'. Synod 1979 delayed implementation of that decision. Synod 1981 appointed a committee to study the biblical teaching on headship. Synod 1984 in response to that study report declared that the Bible taught male headship in the church and home, but opened the office of deacon to women on the grounds that the office was one of service, not headship. Synod 1985 stated that the headship principle implies that only men may serve as ministers and elders. One conservative leader in the CRC heralded this decision insisting that the debate over women in ecclesiastical office was over and that the decision of 1985 was set in concrete.

The issue, however, did not go away. In an unexpected move Synod 1990 voted to change the rules of the church to permit the ordination of women as ministers and elders. Since the rules' change could only be implemented by a second concurring synod, Synod 1990 decided that the issue should be debated at Synod 1992. After intense debate in the churches Synod 1992 refused to change the rules, but sought a compromise by saying that women could 'expound the Word of God'. The compromise satisfied neither the progressives nor the confessionalists. The issue came to Synod 1994 and there a detailed biblical defense of the church's prohibition against women in office was adopted. That action should have ended the debate since the rules of the church stated that a decision of synod was settled and binding and could be changed only on the basis of the clear teaching of the Word of God. In spite of this rule, Synod 1995 permitted the ordination of women, not by presenting new arguments from Scripture or by changing the rules in the established manner long followed in the church, but by adopting a supplementary note to the rules that permitted the ordination of women in effect as an exception.

The definitive defeat of the confessionalists at the Synod of 1995 should not have come as a surprise. The confessionalists had long since lost influence in critical agencies of the church, particularly the Synodical Interim Committee (later the Board of Trustees), Calvin College, the Home Missions Board and the Christian Reformed World Relief Committee. (Ironically Calvin Seminary under the leadership of James DeJong who became president in 1984 had moved in a more conservative direction.)

In spite of steady successes at the synodical level for conservatives from the late 1950s to 1994, the battle for Reformed orthodoxy as a whole was lost. The CRC had often said the right thing, but was increasingly unwilling to insist on agreement with those decisions. I had a very telling conversation that illustrated that phenomenon. In Synod 1994 a minister I know voted to maintain the biblical prohibition to ordaining women as ministers and elders. The next year at synod the same minister voted to open the offices of the church to women. When I asked him why he had changed his opinion, he replied that he had come to realize that if he voted to maintain the decision of 1994, he had to be willing to discipline those who were violating the church order and ordaining women. He had decided that although he was still personally opposed to women in office, he was not willing to discipline those with whom he disagreed.

All of these changes in the theology, discipline and agencies of the church were not the result of conspiracy by some elite in the church. They reflected in fact what most in the church wanted or at least were willing to tolerate. The CRC experience paralleled what three religious sociologists documented about the Presbyterian Church USA in *First Things*. There in an article entitled 'Mainline Churches: The Real Reason for Decline' the sociologists observed: 'The erosion proceeded steadily and without instances of reversal, and no new standards requiring equal discipline and sacrifice were adopted in their place. Rules against worldly amusements and immodest dress went by the boards after World War I, standards for Sabbath observance were widely ignored by 1940, and in many congregations old norms concerning alcoholic beverages had become obsolete by the early 1950s.' What caused these changes? The conclusion is remarkable: 'The intriguing discovery, however, is the role the laity seems to have played in this process. A careful examination of General Assembly records suggests that the laity *chose* the course the church has taken. In other words, over the long term the erosion of old standards has been genuinely popular at the Presbyterian grass roots. The clergy and denominational elites did little or nothing to stop the process, but neither did they foist it upon the laity.'[36] In the democratized culture of America the people in the pew ultimately get what they want. Confessionalists in the CRC had lost the most important struggle of all, the struggle for the understanding and commitment of the ordinary members of the church.

Some confessionalists after 1995 left the CRC to help form the United Reformed Churches or to enter other Reformed churches. Other conservatives left for other denominations that seemed to them to be more biblical than the CRC. Still other confessionalists remained in the CRC reconciled to minority status. They decided to face the pressures of Americanization there rather than carry on the struggle in a more Reformed context. There continue to be solid Reformed folk in the CRC, but the CRC is no longer a solid Reformed denomination. The CRC has become another American methodist church.

NOTES

1. James Bratt, *Dutch Calvinism in Modern America*, Grand Rapids, Michigan (Eerdmans), 1984, p. 39.
2. Henry Stob, *Summoning Up Remembrance*, Grand Rapids, Michigan (Eerdmans), 1995, p. 29. In the Netherlands Abraham Kuyper had used this characterization of American church life as Methodist. Kuyper explained his opposition to Methodism, not as an opposition to a denomination, but to a religious outlook. He defined what he meant by Methodism in these terms: 'From vindicating the subjective rights of the individual it soon passed into antagonism against the objective rights of the community. This resulted dogmatically in the controversy about the objective work of God, viz., in His decree and His election, and ecclesiastically in antagonism against the objective work of the office through the confession. It gave supremacy to the subjective element in man's free will and to the individual element in deciding of unchurchly conflicts in the Church. And so it retained no other aim than the conversion of individual sinners; and for this work it abandoned the organic, and retained only the mechanical method.' *The Work of the Holy Spirit*, Grand Rapids, Michigan (Eerdmans), 1900, p. xiii. Interestingly David Martin, an English sociologist of religion, made a similar point about American religion in *Tongues of Fire*, Cambridge, MA (Blackwells), 1990, p. 21.
3. Bratt, p. 59.
4. Cited in Bratt, p. 41.
5. See Bratt, pp. 43-50.
6. Bratt, pp. 50, 54.
7. Stob, p. 31.
8. Stob, p. 56.
9. Stob, p. 104.
10. Stob, p. 127.
11. Stob, pp. 137f.
12. Stob, p. 207.
13. Stob, p. 299.
14. Stob, p. 335.
15. Stob, pp. 318, 335.

16. Stob, p. 191.
17. Stob, p. 197.
18. Stob, p. 281.
19. Stob, p. 137.
20. Stob, pp. 138f.
21. Stob, p. 295.
22. Stob, p. 54.
23. Stob, p. 132.
24. Stob, p. 117.
25. Stob, p. 130.
26. Stob, p. 329. See Bratt's account, p. 190, which sees personality differences as very important, but also sees theological issues in the background.
27. Stob, pp. 320f.
28. Stob, p. 321.
29. Stob, p. 321.
30. Stob, pp. 322f.
31. Stob, p. 323.
32. Stob, p. 297.
33. Bratt, p. 203.
34. Bratt, p. 207.
35. Bratt, p. 217.
36. Benton Johnson, Dean R. Hoge and Donald A. Luidens, 'Mainline Churches: The Real Reason for Decline,' *First Things*, March 1993, p. 17. For a more detailed analysis on the issue of the Sabbath in the Presbyterian Church USA, see Benton Johnson, 'On Dropping the Subject: Presbyterians and Sabbath Observance in the Twenieth Century,' in *The Presbyterian Predicament*, ed. by M. Coalter, J. Mulder and L. Weeks, Louisville (Westminster/Knox), c1990.

B. Distinctives of American Presbyterianism

An Historical Perspective on 'Joining and Receiving' and Its Impact on the OPC, PCA, and RPCES

William S. Barker

I. Background

Delegates to the General Synod of the Reformed Presbyterian Church, Evangelical Synod (RPCES) and to the General Assembly of the Orthodox Presbyterian Church (OPC) gathered on the campus of Geneva College in Beaver Falls, Pennsylvania on June 4, 1975 in order to take a decisive vote on union of the two denominations. For the Plan of Union to be adopted, both bodies needed a two-thirds vote. The OPC achieved this by three votes, 95-42 or 69%. The RPCES failed by twenty-one votes, 122-92 or 57%.[1] By this small measure an effort to reunite those who had separated from the Presbyterian Church USA, or Northern Presbyterian Church (PCUSA), in 1936, but who had divided in 1937-38, failed. Those who had stood for the doctrinal purity of the visible church in the 1930s were now concerned as well for the unity of the visible church. Some felt that the RPCES failure to achieve the necessary 67% came from its concern for the peace of the church, Francis Schaeffer having warned against spending the next ten years disputing over secondary issues if the union were to go through.

The union would indeed have been a reunion. Both groups stemmed in large part from the movement led by J. Gresham Machen in the 1920s and '30s to restore Reformed orthodoxy to the PCUSA. In 1929 Machen and others had left Princeton Seminary to form Westminster Seminary in Philadelphia for the sake of training sound ministers. In 1933 the Independent Board for Presbyterian Foreign Missions (IBPFM) had been formed to assure that the gospel would be conveyed to overseas mission fields. It was this strike at the PCUSA's board for foreign missions that led to the ecclesiastical trial and expulsion from the denomination of Machen and several others. They and their followers in 1936 formed the Presbyterian Church of America, which would later change its name to the Orthodox Presbyterian Church.

Tragically, the desire for a doctrinally pure church led to aspiration by many for a perfect church, with people on both sides of the 1937 split that produced the Bible Presbyterian Church (BPC), alongside the OPC, emphasizing secondary issues, such as total abstinence from alcoholic beverages vs. Christian liberty, a premillennial eschatology vs. amillennial, independent mission agencies (like the IBPFM) vs. boards subject to the General Assembly of the church. The 'Preamble' to the 1975 Plan of Union declared: 'Soon after the Presbyterian Church of America was established in 1936 to continue faithful witness to the Christ of the Scriptures, a grievous division brought reproach upon this testimony.... We do not claim to have achieved unanimity of opinion on all the issues that led to that division, but ... we do confess that the unity of Christ's church should not have been broken as it was in 1937 and that neither the newly formed Bible Presbyterian Church nor the church from which it was formed pursued reconciliation.'[2]

Both small groups had grown gradually. The OPC increased from a little over 4,000 members in 1938 to over 15,000 in 1975. The BPC grew from around 2,000 in 1938 to almost 9,000 in 1955, when a division occurred with Carl McIntire withdrawing his Collingswood, New Jersey congregation of 1,600 members along with 2,000 from thirty-five churches. When McIntire's Synod retained the name Bible Presbyterian, the majority body in 1961 renamed itself the Evangelical Presbyterian Church (EPC). In 1965, reversing the trend of three divisions, the EPC (with about 8,000 members) united with the smaller Reformed Presbyterian Church, General Synod (about 3,000 members) to form the RPCES. This happy union led to the prospect for uniting with the OPC in 1975, when the RPCES had over 23,000 members and the OPC over 15,000.[3]

Although the 1975 reunion attempt failed to achieve the necessary 67% vote in the RPCES, further efforts toward union of doctrinally conservative Presbyterians now focused on the newly formed Presbyterian Church in America (PCA), which had brought a larger group (over 41,000 members) out of the Presbyterian Church in the U.S. or Southern Presbyterian Church (PCUS), in 1973.

II. The Formation of the PCA in 1973

Many of the same issues that had called for the stand of Machen and his associates in the Northern Presbyterian Church (PCUSA) had become evident in the Southern Presbyterian Church (PCUS) by the 1960s and '70s. A critical approach to Scripture, denial of or indifference to cardinal doctrines of the Reformed faith, replacement of evangelistic zeal and missions by social concerns, the ordination of women, and ecumenical pursuits were causing conservatives in the PCUS to band together for doctrinal purity. Lacking a single articulate theological leader like Machen, the Southerners found several entities to be instrumental in bringing them together in the cause of reform. The *Southern Presbyterian Journal*, founded by L. Nelson Bell and others in 1942, edited by Henry B. Dendy and later by G. Aiken Taylor, was the voice of the conservatives. In 1965 the *Journal* led in the formation of Concerned Presbyterians, Inc., an organization of laymen, led by Kenneth S. Keyes. In 1968 an organization of clergymen, led by Donald B. Patterson, Morton H. Smith, and others, began meeting for prayer and discussion, and in 1969 as Presbyterian Churchmen United, they issued a 'Declaration of Commitment' to be signed by ministers and sessions. In the meantime, in 1966, Reformed Theological Seminary was established in Jackson, Mississippi for the training of sound ministers. The Presbyterian Evangelistic Fellowship, founded by William E. Hill in 1964, became the vehicle for overseas missionary efforts as the Executive Commission on Overseas Evangelism (ECOE) in 1970.[4]

Apparent in these developments are many parallels to the events in the Northern Presbyterian Church some thirty-seven years earlier. Conservatives in both cases believed that crucial issues were at stake: the authority of the Scriptures as the written word of God and the very nature of the gospel of salvation based on the person and work of Jesus Christ. Concern for the preparation of ministers who would preach the word was manifested in the establishment of Reformed Seminary in 1966 as well as that of Westminster Seminary in 1929. Concern for spread of the gospel was manifested in the founding of ECOE in 1970 as well as that of IBPFM in 1933.

Not only were there parallels between the developments in the North and in the South, but also there were direct influences and lessons out of the earlier Northern experience that would help to shape the cause in the South.

The National Presbyterian and Reformed Fellowship (NPRF) was formed in 1970 to provide informal fellowship among individual ministers from as many as ten different denominations who shared concerns about the liberal trends of the times. This brought together many leaders of the OPC (such as Edmund P. Clowney) and the RPCES (such as Robert G. Rayburn and Donald J. MacNair) with those who would help to bring the PCA into existence. In February of 1973 Francis Schaeffer of the RPCES addressed a rally in Atlanta that was attended by members of the Steering committee for a Continuing Presbyterian Church, the group that would provide the groundwork for the First General Assembly of the newly formed PCA in December of 1973 in Birmingham, Alabama. In contrast to the separation in the North in the 1930s, the movement in the South was largely led by laymen, Attorney W. Jack Williamson being elected Moderator of the First General Assembly. The theological counsel offered by such Northern leaders as Schaeffer, Clowney, Rayburn, and MacNair helped to infuse the Southerners' stand for truth with a spirit of love. The Northern separation in 1936 had included a harshness that left many moderate conservatives remaining in the PCUSA and then led to further division between the OPC and the BPC in 1937–38. The Southern separation in 1973 was done generally in a more charitable spirit, with the result that a larger number joined the PCA in the following years, and by 2001 the PCA has not experienced a significant split.

The First General Assembly, on December 7, 1973, adopted 'A Message to All Churches of Jesus Christ Throughout the World', on the model of the Southern Presbyterian Church's statement in 1861, similarly seeking to justify its existence and to declare its principles. Toward the conclusion of that document it states:

> We declare also that we believe the system of doctrine found in God's Word to be the system known as the Reformed faith. We are committed without reservation to the Reformed faith as set forth

in the Westminster Confession and Catechism. It is our conviction that the Reformed faith is not sectarian, but an authentic and valid expression of Biblical Christianity. We believe it is our duty to seek fellowship and unity with all who profess this faith. We particularly wish to labor with other Christians committed to this theology.[5]

Out of that commitment to fellowship and unity there came the formation in 1976 of the North American Presbyterian and Reformed Council (NAPARC), an organization that included from its beginning the Christian Reformed Church (CRC), the OPC, the PCA, the RPCES, and the Reformed Presbyterian Church of North America (RPCNA or 'Covenanters'). The purposes were discussion and joint action, including the possibility of eventual ecclesiastical union. For the PCA, whose origin was in part a reaction to liberal ecumenical zeal, there was caution with regard to union, especially while the newly formed church was still young and determining its identity. On the other hand, there was obvious strength and wisdom to be gained from those who had stood for the same convictions and had learned hard lessons from that stand. For the OPC and RPCES, the attempt at union in 1975 having failed, the newly formed PCA looked like a catalyst for bringing together the strengths of North and South with mutual reinforcement for a testimony to North America and the world.

III. The Development of 'Joining and Receiving'

For a variety of reasons the method for approaching church unity with the PCA was not the normal process of an official plan of union, but rather by a unique procedure termed 'Joining and Receiving,' (J&R). For a while the RPCNA was included in discussions of 'J&R', but because of its distinctives, such as exclusive psalm-singing and close communion, discussions with the RPCNA did not proceed to a serious level. The OPC and RPCES did proceed to mutual votes on 'J&R' with the PCA with the result that the RPCES joined, and was received by, the PCA in 1982, but the OPC was not received by the PCA in 1982, and in 1986 the OPC did not achieve the necessary two-thirds majority vote to join the PCA. Before considering the impact of 'J&R' on the RPCES, PCA, and OPC, it is necessary to understand the concept of 'Joining and Receiving' and why this procedure was adopted.

In 1976 the General Synod of the RPCES communicated to the General Assembly of the PCA a desire to seek 'a more united testimony.' The PCA Assembly was informed that the OPC was also considering a similar communication. By 1978 the PCA approved a study on 'the Biblical Basis for Church Union' and authorized its Interchurch Relations Committee to pursue discussions with the OPC and the RPCES toward a possible merger. In 1979 the PCA shied away from the idea of merger, but established a committee to 'determine possible areas of agreement, difference and difficulty that might exist' between the denominations. In 1980 the PCA adopted a ten-step procedure to bring the other denominations into a continuing Presbyterian Church in America, to become effective at the meetings of the judicatories in Grand Rapids, Michigan in June of 1982. This process, which would require approval by three-fourths of the PCA presbyteries after General Assembly approval in 1981, became known as 'Joining and Receiving' since it did not involve a normal merger by way of an official Plan of Union, but rather a joining of the PCA by the other denominations with their adoption of the PCA Book of Church Order (as well as the Westminster Confession and Catechisms, which they already shared).

This procedure was understandable since the PCA was less than ten years old and still developing its identity; moreover, it was significantly larger, with over 104,000 members, compared to the OPC's 17,000 members and the RPCES's almost 34,000 members in 1981.[6]

At the PCA's General Assembly in 1981 the issuing of an invitation to the RPCES to join the PCA was approved without much debate; however, the invitation to the OPC was clouded by discussion, focused in part on the views of Norman Shepherd, a professor of systematic theology at Westminster Seminary, on justification by faith. The invitation to the OPC was, nevertheless, approved by the General Assembly by more than a two-thirds majority. Then the issue went to the presbyteries. All twenty-five of the PCA presbyteries voted in favor of receiving the RPCES, whose presbyteries voted 13-4 in favor of joining the PCA. The vote of the PCA presbyteries to receive the OPC was 17-8, two votes short of the three-fourths majority needed. When this result was made known, the OPC presbyteries, having received from their General Assembly the action to join the PCA, did not proceed to vote.

At its General Synod in 1982, on June 12 at Calvin College in Grand Rapids, the RPCES voted 322-90, well over the two-thirds majority needed, to effect the joining of the PCA, and on June 14 the PCA received the RPCES.

In 1983 the enlarged PCA General Assembly voted to re-issue an invitation to the OPC for 'Joining and Receiving'. Twenty-nine of the thirty-seven PCA presbyteries approved this action, thus achieving the requisite three-fourths majority, by 1984. In 1985 the OPC General Assembly notified the PCA that it would put the matter to a vote at their Assembly in 1986, at which they would be celebrating the fiftieth anniversary of the denomination. On that occasion the OPC Assembly voted 76-68 in favor of joining the PCA, twenty votes short of the two-thirds needed to pass. Thus the OPC, jilted by the PCA in 1982, rebuffed the PCA proposal in 1986. Like the courtship of star-crossed lovers, when one seemed ready for a marriage, the other backed away, and vice versa.

In 1991 the OPC expressed interest in union by another method than 'Joining and Receiving,' but the 1992 PCA Assembly responded by sticking to the 'J&R' process. In 1994 the OPC again expressed concern over the 'J&R' method since the 'simple applying for membership in the PCA eliminates the possibility of addressing the issues that divide us'. The PCA responded, however, that the best procedure was for 'the OPC to take their necessary constitutional steps requesting to be received into the PCA,' with the corresponding denominational committees prepared to discuss issues relating to the 'J&R' process. A similar conclusion was reached in the 1996 PCA General Assembly, and the prospect for union with the OPC rested there.[7]

IV. The Impact of 'Joining and Receiving'
The vision when 'Joining and Receiving' was first broached, and the hope for the future, was a united Presbyterian testimony that could testify effectively to the truth of Scripture and could convey the gospel of Jesus Christ to North America and the world. What J. Gresham Machen had desired in the Northern context of the 1920s and '30s might be fulfilled with the addition of a more numerous Southern contingent in the 1970s and '80s, to produce a strong, doctrinally sound Presbyterian Church nationwide with global outreach. Obviously, without Machen's own denomination, the OPC, this dream is not yet realized. Yet, in the providence of God, the joining of the RPCES with the PCA has proved to be a happy union with prospects for an even more fruitful future.

The impact of 'J&R' on the RPCES has been immensely positive. In almost its final action of its concluding 160th General Synod in 1982, it communicated to the OPC a reiteration of part of the

'Preamble' to the failed Plan of Union of 1975 that acknowledged the 'grievous division' of 1937 and expressed 'our obligation and determination to achieve and maintain, by God's grace, the unity of the church in mutual faith, love, and confidence which we profess.'[8] After this look to the past the members and churches of the former RPCES have zealously hurled themselves into the ministries and pursuits of the PCA. Those who were already in the PCA have received well the agencies and leaders from the RPCES. In the first thirteen General Assemblies after 'J&R' four of the elected Moderators have been former RPCES men. In 1988, former Stated Clerk of the RPCES, Paul R. Gilchrist, succeeded Morton H. Smith in that position in the PCA. G. Aiken Taylor was succeeded as Editor of the *Presbyterian Journal* by the present writer in 1984. A smooth transition was made of missionaries and other personnel from World Presbyterian Missions and National Presbyterian Missions of the RPCES to Mission to the World and Mission to North America of the PCA, and likewise in the field of Christian Education. The higher educational institutions of the RPCES, Covenant College on Lookout Mountain near Chattanooga, Tennessee, and Covenant Seminary in St. Louis, have blossomed in enrollment, influence, and recognition since becoming schools of the PCA. Churches call pastors with little sense of whether their background was in the former RPCES or the previous PCA. Although losing some of the intimacy and sense of family that characterized the RPCES, those who may recall the former denomination nostalgically now relish the increased opportunities for service that the PCA affords.

The impact of 'J&R' on the PCA has been increased growth and the realization of becoming a national (and Canadian) church, not just a denomination concentrated mainly in the region of the South. Before 1982 the PCA had one presbytery north of the Mason-Dixon line and one on the west coast. With the addition of the RPCES, presbyteries covered most of the continental United States and parts of both eastern and western Canada. Membership in 1982 jumped to over 151,000. Rather steady growth has continued over the past two decades to over 299,000 by 1999. Foreign missions work has flourished, with outreach in every continent of the world and an equal number of missionary personnel to the much larger mainline denomination which she left in 1973.[9] As already mentioned, leadership from the RPCES has been welcomed within the PCA. Covenant Seminary and Covenant

College have contributed to the preparation of ministers and lay leadership for the denomination. In general, the marriage of the PCA and the RPCES has proven to be one of great compatibility. One historian of the PCA struggles to assess the theological effect of the PCA's receiving of the RPCES, concluding:

> Perhaps one could consider the RPCES a Northern Old School church - somewhere between a 'New School' position and a strict, Southern 'Old School' position. In practical terms, this would mean that the former RPCESers would tend to react against the more strict view, thereby increasing the tendency to 'loosen' the Standards.[10]

On the other hand, a Moderator of the PCA General Assembly and one of the founding fathers of the PCA, has commented concerning the reception of the RPCES:

> A word needs to be said here about the way the RPCES buried their very significant past history, and came to the PCA with all of their institutions and agencies, their leadership and resources, their missionaries and church planters and in a very very real sense, just gave it all to us. In my mind it is certainly one of the most unselfish and significant things that has ever happened in the history of the Church.[11]

Opinions may vary, but the spirit in which the majority of the enlarged PCA functions is reminiscent of the Presbyterian Church after the reunion of Old Side and New Side in 1758, when orthodoxy in doctrine and polity was combined with evangelistic zeal.

The impact of 'Joining and Receiving' on the OPC is more difficult to analyze. There obviously was frustration over the failure of the necessary three-fourths of PCA presbyteries to vote in favor of receiving the OPC in 1982 and then over the failure of the OPC General Assembly to achieve the requisite two-thirds vote to join the PCA in 1986. The latter vote was no doubt affected by the celebration of the OPC's fiftieth anniversary, emphasizing the blessings the Lord had brought to them and through their testimony. After that vote there was a protest signed by thirty-eight commissioners 'which claimed that the decision was 'a serious setback to our hopes for a united, vital, biblical and nationwide Presbyterian church' and that the vote communicated an 'attitude of superiority' on the part of the OPC.'[12] In the ensuing years some ministers and churches followed a policy of 'voluntary realignment,' moving from the OPC to the PCA. This includes the various churches of the 'New Life' network, founded by C. John Miller, and such leaders as Edmund P. Clowney, former President of Westminster Seminary, and D. Clair Davis, Professor of Church History at Westminster. As a result, membership in the OPC dipped from over 19,000 in 1989 to approximately 18,000 in 1991. Fairly steady growth followed, however, as the denomination seemed to firm up its identity, and membership exceeded 25,000 in 1999.[13] The OPC tends to see itself as 'a pilgrim people,' a church with a unique commitment to the Reformed faith, a church that, by God's grace, 'has recognized that the troubles of this life are swallowed up in the sweet communion God has with his people and that the church's task, no matter how irrelevant it may seem, is to make known the good news that God offers rest to the weary soul in the saving work of Christ Jesus.'[14]

V. The Future Prospect

The historians of the OPC who wrote the words above concluded with reference to J. Gresham Machen's vision of the task of the church in modern times. Machen saw the church as radically doctrinal, radically intolerant, and radically ethical. 'The responsibility of the church in the new age,' he said in 1933, 'is the same as its responsibility in every age.' That is to testify to the salvation from sin that is to be found in Christ alone and that is communicated through the Scriptures.[15]

No doubt it is because the OPC knows what it stands for that it has experienced growth in recent years. The same can be said for the PCA. While it has grown more than sevenfold since its beginning in 1973, the PCUSA and most mainline, liberal denominations have been in decline. Machen took a stand for the purity of the visible church in the 1930s. By the 1970s, as we have seen, the OPC and the RPCES had come to cherish the unity and peace of the church as well. The ordination vows for elders in the PCA promise to strive for the purity, peace, unity, and edification of the church. While there may sometimes be tension between purity on the one hand and peace and unity on the other, the edification of the church - on the basis of Scriptural Mandate – requires the maintenance of all of these traits. The doctrinal commitment that the OPC possesses could strengthen the PCA. The growth and outreach of the PCA could afford greater opportunity for the OPC. Because of the OPC's history and integrity, the PCA should be willing to consider union on a basis other than 'Joining and Receiving'. Because of the PCA's desire not to be hampered in its carrying out the Great Commission, the OPC should be willing to accommodate to the 'Joining and Receiving' process. Either way, the Scriptural mandate for the purity, peace, unity, and edification of the church must be obeyed. And thus will Machen's vision for a sound, faithful, and fruitful Presbyterian church be fulfilled.

Commitment to the gospel of salvation through Jesus Christ alone may be perceived by some to be irrelevant to the times, but it is actually the unchanging truth that is most relevant to the ever-changing world. The PCA has brought some of the strengths of the Southern Presbyterian tradition into a nationwide context. The OPC represents some of the best of the Northern Presbyterian tradition. It is time that distinctions of the past, whether Northern or Southern, be appreciated and put behind us to see what God may yet do with a fully united American Presbyterian Church that is committed to the Scriptures and to the Reformed faith and to carrying out the Great Commission of our Lord Jesus Christ.

NOTES

1. See D. G. Hart and John Muether, *Fighting the Good Fight: A Brief History of the Orthodox Presbyterian Church* (Philadelphia: Committee on Christian Education and Committee for the Historian of the OPC, 1995) pp.135-136 for one view of this vote.

2 .For the 'Preamble' to the Plan of Union, see *Minutes of the 153rd General Synod of the RPCES* (1975), pp. 111-112.

3. OPC statistics are derived from Hart and Muether, *Fighting the Good Fight*, p. 69 and *The Orthodox Presbyterian Church 1936-1986*, ed. Charles G. Dennison (Philadelphia: Committee for the Historian of the OPC, 1986), p. 317. BPC, EPC, and RPCES statistics are from George P. Hutchinson, *The History Behind the Reformed Presbyterian Church, Evangelical Synod* (Cherry Hill, N.J.: Mack Publishing Co., 1974), pp. 252, 306, 345, 403 and from the *Minutes of the 158th General Synod of the RPCES* (1980), p. 218. The RPC, General Synod figure is derived from *Minutes of General Synod, Reformed Presbyterian Church in North America, Session CXXXIX* (1962), insert between pp. 38 and 39.

4. The background and origins of the PCA are thoroughly described in Frank J. Smith, *The History of the Presbyterian Church in America*, 2nd ed.; (Lawrenceville, Ga. : Presbyterian Scholars Press, 1995), pp. 15-85.

5. The entire document is to be found as Appendix A in Smith, *History of the*

PCA, 2nd ed., pp. 559-562.

6. The statistics of the PCA are from Smith, *History of the PCA*, 2nd ed., p. 570; of the OPC from *Yearbook of Churches in America and Canada 1983*; of the RPCES from *Minutes of the 160th General Synod of the RPCES* (1982), p. 180.

7. Discussion of 'Joining and Receiving' from a PCA viewpoint is to be found in Smith, *History of the PCA*, 2nd ed., pp. 369-385; from an OPC viewpoint in John P. Galbraith, 'The Ecumenical Vision of the OPC' in *Pressing Toward the Mark: Essays Commemorating Fifty Years of the Orthodox Presbyterian Church*, ed. Charles G. Dennison and Richard C. Gamble (Philadelphia: Committee for the Historian of the OPC, 1986), pp. 417-418, and in Hart and Muether, *Fighting the Good Fight*, pp. 136-138. The tally of RPCES presbyteries in 1982 is from *Minutes of the 160th General Assembly of the RPCES* (1982), p. 65.

8. *Minutes of the 160th General Synod of the RPCES* (1982), pp. 13-14, 75-76.

9. In 1973 the Southern Presbyterian Church (PCUS) had over 900,000 members. By 1982, membership had declined to around 815,000. In 1983 the PCUS united with the Northern United Presbyterian Church with approximately 2,343,000 members, to form the PCUSA with a total of over 3,122,000 members. According to John H. Leith, *Crisis in the Church: The Plight of Theological Education* (Louisville, Ky.: Westminster John Knox Press, 1997), p. 1, the combined membership of the UPCUSA and the PCUS has declined from 4,250,000 in 1966 to 2,665,375 in 1996.

10. Frank J. Smith, *History of the PCA*, 2nd ed., p. 552, n. 38.

11. Kennedy Smartt, *I Am Reminded: An Autobiographical, Anecdotal History of the Presbyterian Church in America* (Chestnut Mountain, Ga., 1994), p. 156.

12. Hart and Muether, *Fighting the Good Fight*, p. 137.

13. The latest statistics are from *Yearbook of American and Canadian Churches 20001*, ed. Eileen W. Lindner (Nashville: Abingdon Press, 2001), pp. 345-357. Hart and Muether, *Fighting the Good Fight*, pp. 63-65, describes the 'New Life Story' from an OPC perspective.

14. See Hart and Muether, *Fighting the Good Fight*, pp. 190-195.

15. J. Gresham Machen, 'The Responsibility of the Church in Our New Age,' in Hart and Muether, *Fighting the Good Fight*, p. 209. The entire essay is on pp. 197-209.

THE JUSTIFICATION OF CONFESSIONS AND THE LOGIC OF CONFESSIONAL SUBSCRIPTION

David F. Coffin, Jr.

Introduction

The 29th General Assembly of The Presbyterian Church in America held a pre-Assembly convocation entitled 'How Shall We Then Live Together – Subscription and the Future of the PCA.' From these terms it is not unfair to presume that the sponsors had concluded that questions relating to the use of the doctrinal standards had in some way become an occasion for disunity, a lack of peace, difficulty in living together, perhaps even a threat to the future of The Presbyterian Church in America.[1]

No doubt there are grounds for such a conclusion, but here I would notice how ironic this state of affairs is in light of the traditional Presbyterian rationale for the use of confessions. Consider the testimony of the PCUSA General Assembly in 1824:

> *Resolved*, 1. That in the opinion of this Assembly confessions of faith, containing formulas of doctrine and rules for conducting the discipline and worship proper to be maintained in the house of God, are not only recognized as necessary and expedient, but as the character of human nature is continually aiming at innovation, absolutely requisite to the settled peace of the Church, and to the happy and orderly existence of Christian communion. Within the

limits of Christendom few are to be found in the attitude of avowed hostility to Christianity. The name of Christian is claimed by all, and all are ready to profess their belief in the holy Scriptures; to many reserving to themselves the right of putting upon them what construction they please. In such a state of things, without the aid of confessions, Christian fellowship can exist only in a very limited degree....

2. [T]he Confession of Faith and standards of our Church ... form a bond of fellowship in the faith of the gospel....

4. Finally, the General Assembly recommend to all who are under their care, steadfastly to resist every temptation, however presented, which may have for its object the relaxation of those bonds of Christian fellowship which have hitherto been so eminently blessed of God, for the order, edification, and extension of the Presbyterian Church....[2]

Such an emphasis is commonplace in conservative American discussions of the subject. One of the 'founding fathers' of American Presbyterianism, Samuel Miller, reflected this perspective when in his *The Utility and Importance of Creeds and Confessions: Addressed Particularly to Candidates for the Ministry*[3] he urged that candidates for the ministry must understand 'the importance of Creeds and Confessions for maintaining the *unity* and purity of the visible Church'.[4] Later in that century A. A. Hodge argued from the same perspective when he urged that doctrinal standards 'secure the real co-operation of those who profess to work together in the same cause, so that public teachers in the same communion may not contradict one another, and the one pull down what the other is striving to build up'.[5] That one of the means for maintaining unity among the members and teachers of a church, should itself be a cause for division among that same people, is a most lamentable circumstance.

I have no doubt that in large part the reason for this unhappy state of affairs lies in the fact that Presbyterians generally have had no constitutional standard as to what confessional subscription amounts to, and what powers belong to courts of original jurisdiction to allow for officers to subscribe to the *Confession*[6] while denying the biblical fidelity of some portion of the teaching.[7] When a confessional church has no agreement as to how the articles of agreement should function to maintain agreement, but rather each one 'does what is right in his own eyes', it is profoundly incapacitated in functioning as a confessional church, and is thus prevented from reaping the promised benefits.

In this paper I will offer some arguments as to how one *ought* to think about subscription to the *Confession,* with the hope that this discussion might contribute to a greater unity with respect to what the courts of the church are called to actually do in the course of fulfilling their Christ-appointed responsibilities. The heart of what I hope to show is this: that the justification for having a confession ought logically to determine the manner of subscription to that confession.

The Justification of Confessions

Though Presbyterians have historically affirmed that the Bible is the only rule of faith and practice, they have been known as well for their vigorous commitment to the Westminster Standards, which are understood and prized as a true and faithful summary statement of the teachings of the Word of God. This commitment to a confessional standard is made concrete in the requirement that all *officers* of the church *subscribe* to the standards. The grounds of this distinction are ably set forth by A.A. Hodge:

> In all churches a distinction is made between the terms upon which private members are admitted to membership, and the terms upon which office-bearers are admitted to their sacred trusts of teaching and ruling. A Church has no right to make anything a condition of membership which Christ has not made a condition of salvation. The Church is Christ's fold. The Sacraments are the seals of his covenant. All have a right to claim admittance who make a credible profession of the true religion – that is, who are presumptively the people of Christ. This credible profession of course involves a competent knowledge of the fundamental doctrine of Christianity – a declaration of personal faith in Christ and consecration to his service, and a temper of mind and habit consistent therewith. On the other hand, no man can be inducted into any office in any Church who does not profess to believe in the truth and wisdom of the constitution and laws which it will be his duty to conserve and administer. Otherwise all harmony of sentiment and all efficient co-operation in action would be impossible.[8]

American Presbyterians have long debated the meaning of confessional subscription. When a ministerial candidate responds affirmatively to the question: 'Do you sincerely receive and adopt the Confession of Faith and the Catechism of this Church, as containing the system of doctrine taught in the Holy Scriptures....'[9]

what precisely is he affirming? The answers to this question have been varied, and the parties formed around the various answers have continued to find advocates to the present day. Most often the discussions have centered on the meaning of the Adopting Act in 1729 and the actions of various church courts soon thereafter. Years of debate about this history, however, has not done much to settle the matter. Further, it is not entirely clear what relevance such historical proofs might have for Presbyterians today, operating without any constitutional standard that would establish the historical position as the rule of the church. There is clearly a need for some other means of helping presbyters understand how to fulfill their practical duty in the examination and approval of candidates in relation to the *Confession*. Rather than seeking the meaning of the first subscription, perhaps we would do better to return to first principles.

In contemporary discussions, one matter is notable in its absence, i.e., how does the use of a 'man-made' confession by the Church find any justification at all? This problem is particularly acute for Presbyterians. The very confession they defend and affirm appears at first glance to contradict creed making as well as creed subscribing. The *Confession of Faith* teaches that:

> The whole counsel of God concerning all things necessary for His own glory, man's salvation, faith and life, is either expressly set down in Scripture, or by good and necessary consequence may be deduced from Scripture; unto which nothing at any time is to be added, whether by new revelations of the Spirit or traditions of men. (1.6) The Old Testament ... and the New Testament ... being immediately inspired by God ... in all controversies of religion, the Church is finally to appeal unto them. (1.8) The supreme judge by which all controversies of religion are to be determined, ... and in whose sentence we are to rest, can be no other but the Holy Spirit speaking in the Scripture. (1.10) God alone is Lord of the conscience, and hath left it free from the doctrines and commandments of men, which are, in any thing, contrary to His Word; or beside it, if matters of faith and worship. (20.2)

How can the propositions that God alone is Lord of the conscience, and that the Holy Spirit speaking in Scripture is the supreme judge of all controversies, be consistent with subscription to the *Westminster Confession* as a standard for ministerial admission and a rule for doctrinal controversy? In light of these bold statements of Scriptural sufficiency and authority the burden of proof on those who would defend confessional authority in this context appears significant.

Our Presbyterian forefathers, however, were not unaware of this burden, nor unwilling to bear it. Earlier discussions of the issue of confessional *subscription*, almost without exception, began with a statement of the *warrant* for doctrinal confessions, and only then moved on to consider their appropriate use.[10] This, of course, raises the issue I wish to discuss: Is there a logical relation between the justification for the use of confessions in the Church, and the nature of the subscription that is, or ought to be required to them? A corollary question also arises: if one's view of subscription contradicts or undermines the rationale for the Church's confession, does not that, in itself, count as presumptive evidence against the view?

In considering this question, I first offer a standard description of a doctrinal confession from Samuel Miller:

> By a Creed, or Confession of Faith, I mean, an exhibition, in human language, of those great doctrines which are believed by the framers of it to be taught in the Holy Scriptures; and which are drawn out in regular order, *for the purpose of ascertaining how far those who wish to unite in church fellowship are really agreed in the fundamental principles of Christianity.*[11]

Notice that in Miller's understanding the purpose of the confession *itself* is to state what its adopters agree to as the fundamental principles of Christianity. It is not framed to *contain* such principles among others, for what would be the point of including articles not agreed upon in articles of agreement?

In discussing his view Miller takes pains to emphasize that a confession adopted is not a law enacted by the Church, for he denies that the Church has any properly legislative power.

> Creeds and Confessions do not claim to be in themselves laws of Christ's house, or legislative enactments, by which any set of opinions are constituted truths, and which require, on that account, to be received as truths among the members of his family. They only profess to be *summaries*, extracted from the Scriptures, of a few of those great Gospel doctrines, which are taught by Christ himself; and which those who make the summary in particular case, concur in deeming important, and agree to make the test of their religious union.[12]

Here Miller reflects the consensus set forth in the General Assembly's earlier deliverance on the matter: 'though the Confession of Faith and standards of our Church are of no original authority, independent of the Scriptures, yet we regard them as a summary of those divine truths which are diffused throughout the sacred volume....'[13]

Now it is the formal *summarizing* that historically Presbyterians have unambiguously affirmed as, 'not only lawful and expedient,' 'but also indispensably necessary to the harmony and purity of the visible Church.'[14] Miller offers nine arguments in favor of the necessity of creeds: they are necessary for the sake of unity, truth, candor, for study, from the experience of the Church past, from the character of their opponents of creeds, from the fact that even those opposed to them use them, from the need for accredited manuals of doctrine, and for the transmission of doctrine from one generation to another. A. A. Hodge stated the necessity in question in these words:

> Creeds and Confessions, therefore, have been found necessary in all ages and branches of the Church, and, when not abused, have been useful for the following purposes: (1.) To mark, disseminate and preserve the attainments made in the knowledge of Christian truth by any branch of the Church in any crisis of its development. (2.) To discriminate the truth from the glosses of false teachers, and to present it in its integrity and due proportions. (3.) To act as the basis of ecclesiastical fellowship among those so nearly agreed as to be able to labor together in harmony. (4.) To be used as instruments in the great work of popular instruction.[15]

Both Miller and Hodge reflect a tradition of longstanding. Consider the representative statement recorded in the Assembly's *Digest* from 1805:

> Under the specious pretence of honoring the sacred scriptures, they [the opponents of creeds] would persuade you to reject all written or printed creeds and forms of discipline, alleging that those who adopt such, substitute them for divine inspiration.
>
> But, dear brethren, we presume you need scarcely be informed of the absurdity of such insinuations – You know that *we;* you know that *you yourselves* consider them differently. Confessions or creeds are only the doctrines which we believe to be revealed to us from heaven, collected from different parts of sacred scripture, and

brought into one view. – Must not all who read their bibles and believe them, form some opinion of what is taught therein? And where can be the criminality, when they have thus searched and collected, to publish what they believe to be the truth of God? – In so doing, we act in open day, as children of light, and do not leave the world to conjecture, whether we be Pelagians, Semi-Pelagians, Catholics, Arminians, or Calvinists; or whether we differ essentially from them all. We do not leave those with whom we would unite in the most tender and endearing bonds, at a loss to know whether we believe, or disbelieve, what they esteem the essential doctrines of Christianity....[16]

The rationale for the necessity of creeds may be epitomized as follows. Each teacher in the church is bound to teach the message that Christ has set forth in his Word. Some parts of that message are absolutely essential to salvation; other parts, though not essential to salvation, are essential to the well-being of the Church, because her master instructed her to teach his disciples to obey all that he had commanded. All Protestants acknowledge the right of private judgment – that the meaning of the Word as the recipient understands it in good conscience is the word of Christ to him. Yet because of their imperfections, professed believers sincerely differ as to the correct understanding of the Scriptures. Each is duty-bound to teach as he understands the Word of Christ. There is no infallible arbiter available to the Church in this age to sort out the differences between teachers. It follows that it is impossible for professed believers to live in complete unity with such differences as exist, without the fellowship either tending to indifference with respect to the disputed doctrines, or suffering a constant theological warfare. In such a state either truth or peace will be sacrificed. Thus, professed believers who are agreed as to the heart of the gospel, but who differ from one another in matters of real significance, must exist as separate denominations of Christians, charitably respecting each other's right and duty to maintain their differences, while affirming that together they make up the visible Church.[17] To that end, each denomination must set forth its understanding of the teaching of Scripture in a confession, for the purpose of uniting those who are of like mind in fellowship and mission in a voluntary society.[18]

The basic principles of the rationale stated above are clearly discernable in the views of the PCUSA Assembly in 1811, addressed in a letter to Rev. J. W. Stephenson:

Adhere sacredly to our adopted standards, whilst you extend the hand of fellowship to others who, you have reason to hope, love our Lord Jesus Christ. In this way alone, do we conceive, peace can be cultivated, and union, in the end, established between differing Christians. To relinquish principles for the sake of peace, is too dear a sacrifice. And every overture made to us from any quarter, to produce a union at such an expense, we unhesitatingly reject.... Take your stand, therefore, on the ground of the confession of faith, and the book of discipline. Keep that ground. If these men wish to join our church, they know the terms. Their wish to alter these terms is not very modest; for it is requesting the majority to yield to the minority. As we force no one to adopt our standards, there is no oppression exercised over any by our adherence to our own principles.... Whilst we thus exhort you to receive none upon *any modification* of our standards, we recommend to you a conciliatory, mild, and forbearing conduct to those who are out of our communion.[19]

Miller reasoned soundly within this tradition when he concluded:

The inference then plainly is, that no church can hope to maintain a homogeneous character; – no church can be secure either of purity or peace ... without some test of truth, explicitly agreed upon, and adopted by her; ... something recorded; something publicly known; something capable of being referred to when most needed; which not merely this or that private member supposes to have been received; but to which the church as such has agreed to adhere, as a bond of union.[20]

The Logic of Subscription

Is there a logical relation between this justification for the use of confessions in the Church, and the nature of the subscription that is, or ought to be, required to such confessions? It appears to me quite clear that any view of subscription which allows the church court to receive candidates, and qualify them to preach and teach in their communion, while those candidates avowedly deny the doctrines of the standards, is contradictory to the justification of confessions set forth above. Subscription understood in this sense actually undermines the functioning of a doctrinal standard, as can be seen by briefly comparing such a subscription to the main ends which a confession is designed to achieve.[21]

In the first place, such subscription does little to maintain the unity of the church. Rather than a clear, stable and certain statement of what is agreed upon as the teaching of the Scripture, this view leaves this portion of the body of Christ adrift, always searching for that essential core which must be affirmed, while ready to allow defection from those doctrines not so essential. And of course this judgment may vary from year to year, from Presbytery to Presbytery, from one Presbytery meeting to another, or, most damnably, from one candidate to another (based on some unstated extra-biblical criterion).

Second, such a view cannot aid the Church in its duty as a depository, a guardian, and a witness to the truth. At best this 'loose' subscription makes the confession a collection of propositions which may or may not be asserted by most or some of its teachers as true. Rather than an honest and straightforward statement of its Biblical convictions, published abroad for all to consider, the Church is left to equivocate, easily bending with the prevailing cultural winds.

But the reality is, that those who oppose the 'strict' view in favor of at least a theoretical commitment to a 'looser' approach, actually find themselves in practice adopting a rigorous position quite at odds with their profession. With respect to certain doctrines, all subscriptionists are strict subscriptionists. That is to say for each subscriber, there are some parts of his confession which are non-negotiable. Some want the extent of their confession to coincide with the non-negotiable parts; others are content to have the non-negotiable parts lie somewhere within their confession. This latter class typically will not or cannot not say beforehand what the non-negotiable, strictly-subscribed-to-core amounts to, but rather define it *ad hoc*, depending upon the mood of the court, the candidate in question, and the will of the current majority. But this practice clearly undermines the very rationale of having a confession in the first place. In this light it can be seen that the debate about subscription is really a conflict about which articles ought to be subscribed to, not the strictness, or looseness, of the subscription. Some maintain that one ought to strictly subscribe to all the doctrines of the *Confession*; others maintain that one ought to strictly subscribe to a more limited number within the *Confession*. Contrary to this latter view, here I want to briefly argue that the following practical principles of confessional subscription are those logically consistent with a sound justification of the use of confessions in the Church.

Practical Principles of Subscription

1. The Confession is a subordinate standard; but it is nonetheless a real standard. The *Confession's* subordination is not in its *functioning* in the church, as if in every case of its use one might appeal to Scripture in opposition to the *Confession*. On such a view the Confession is not a standard at all. Its true subordination is in its *derivation* from Scripture, as framed and adopted. But once adopted the *Confession* functions as the standard setting forth the understanding of Scripture that the officers of the Church have agreed to uphold. Francis Turretin, whose *Elenctica* was of enormous influence among American Presbyterians, argued for this authority with typical precision:

> The authority of these [public confessions of the Church] should be great in the Churches among the godly, yet it falls below the authority of Scripture. The latter is the rule, the former is the thing regulated. The latter alone is autoupisto' and both in words and in matter is divine and infallible. The former, as in matter they are divine, yet in language and in mode of treatment are human documents. To the latter faith is due directly and absolutely, the former must be judged, and by such mediation be believed, if they agree with the word. The latter is the fixed and unchangeable rule of faith, but the former are liable to fresh revision and examination, in which it is right not only to explain and expand them, but also to correct any flaw noticed in them and to reform them by the norm of the word. Whence it is clear that they err in excess here, who make such confessions replace the norm of actual truth and equate them with the word of God, since at most they are but secondary norms, not of truth but of the doctrine received in a particular Church, since by them may be perceived and discerned, what agrees with the Church's doctrine or what disagrees with it.
>
> Thus their true authority is to be found in the fact that they are binding on those who are liable to them in the forum of the outward fellowship, because written by the Churches or in the name of the Churches, by which the individual members in the outward communion are bound, 1 Corinthians 14:32.... Thus they cannot bind in the inward court of conscience, except so far as they are found to agree with the word of God, which alone has the power to bind conscience.[22]

James H. Thornwell explained the relation between Scripture and confession in similar language:

> The Constitution is, with Presbyterians, the accredited interpretation of the Word of God. It is not an inference from it, nor an addition to it, but the very system of the Bible.... That Word has to be interpreted. If the Constitution is what we profess to believe, we have the interpretation to our hand – we have already wrought out for us the only result we could reach, if we made the interpretation anew in every instance....[23]

2. The church in her Confession sets forth what she has determined to be some of the important points of Scripture's teaching, but by no means does the *Confession* seek to set forth all the truth of the Scripture. Thus Presbyterians have no confessional determination of the proper interpretation of various texts of Scripture, nor have they an approved Bible commentary.[24] In fact, generally the texts that are listed in support of the doctrines of the Standards are not subscribed to, but are only suggestive, what proofs there may be being finally left to the judgement of each subscriber.[25]

3. The proper number of articles in a confession is a question to be determined by prudence, but that number should certainly include some doctrines that are broader than the fundamentals of the Gospel. So Samuel Miller ably argued:

> The extent to which we ought to go in multiplying articles [of a creed], is a secondary question, the answer to which must depend on the exigencies of the church framing the Creed....
>
> I have no hesitation in saying, that in my opinion, church Creeds not only lawfully *may*, but always *ought*, to contain a number of articles besides those which are fundamental.... [T]here are many points confessedly not fundamental, concerning which, nevertheless, it is of the utmost importance to Christian peace and edification, that the members, and especially the ministers of every church should be harmonious in their views and practice....
>
> To exemplify my meaning [instances of churches opposed to an ordained ministry, anti-pedobaptists and Prelatists described].... In all these cases, it is evident there is nothing fundamental to the existence of vital piety. Yet it is equally evident, that those who differ entirely and zealously concerning the points supposed, cannot be comfortable in the same ecclesiastical communion. But how is their coming together, and the consequent discord and strife, which would be inevitable, to be prevented? I know of no method but so constructing their Confessions of Faith as to form different families

or denominations, and to shut out from each those who are hostile to its distinguishing principles of order.

It is plain, then, that unless Confessions of Faith contain articles, not, strictly speaking, fundamental, they cannot possible answer one principal purpose for which they are formed, viz. guarding churches which receive the pure order and discipline, as well as truth, of Scripture, from the intrusion of teachers, who, though they may be pious, yet could not fail to disturb the peace, and mar the edification of the more correct and sound part of the body.[26]

4. Matters not addressed by the *Confession* are not properly a part of the articles of agreement, and thus differences of opinion in such matters should be dealt with in charity, as a part of the respectful, brotherly wrestling with Scripture that is the ongoing calling of the Church. Thus, for example, one must affirm the 'decrees' (chap. 3), but neither infra- nor supra-lapsarianism is specified; a universal 'providence' (chap. 5), but no method specified, e.g., concursus; a sin 'imputed' (chap. 6.3), but neither mediate nor immediate required; Adam as the 'root of all mankind' (6.3), but no theory of the propagation of the soul specified (neither agnostic, nor creationist nor traducianist); Christ's work 'fully satisfied' (8.5), but no determination between a quantitative/commercial view and a moral/legal equivalence view; a 'free will' insisted upon (9.1), but not the doctrine of philosophical necessity nor a power of contrary choice; Adam created upright, but 'mutably' (9.2), yet no theory of how the change was wrought specified; 'elect infants' (10.3), but no further discrimination between the agnostic, those supposing some infants dying in infancy are saved, those supposing all infants of believers dying in infancy are saved, or those supposing all infants dying in infancy are saved. Dabney argued that the *Confession's* underspecificity in such cases is an example of its great moderation.[27]

5. An exception to the *Confession*, from the point of view of the Church confessing, is an exception to the teaching of Scripture (although obviously not from the point of view of the sincere exceptor). This plain inference, apparently repugnant to many in contemporary debates, has typically been stated without embarrassment by our forefathers. The PCUSA Assembly of 1824 freely acknowledged that their doctrinal standards, 'as a system of doctrines, cannot be abandoned, in

our opinion, without an abandonment of the word of God....'[28] John Murray exemplified this ancient tradition in the 20th Century when he argued that

> The persons subscribing to that creed are bound to adhere to its teachings as long as they enjoy the privileges accruing from that subscription and from the fellowship it entails. They must relinquish these privileges whenever they are no longer able to avow the tenets expressed in the creed. In this sense a creed may be said to be normative within the communion adopting it. For the Church concerned officially declares in the creed what it believes the teaching of Scripture to be. And so the person who has come to renounce the tenets of the creed to which he once subscribed has no right to continue to exercise the privileges contingent upon subscription. He may not in such a case protest his right to these privileges by appeal to Scripture as the supreme authority. It is entirely conceivable that the creed may be in error and his renunciation of it warranted and required by Scripture. But his resort in such a case must be to renounce subscription and with such renunciation the privileges incident to it. Then he may proceed to expose the falsity of the creedal position in the light of Scripture.[29]

6. In subscribing to the *Confession* the candidate for office enters into a solemn compact with the assembly of elders that authorizes him to teach in their branch of the church, and thus the candidate must make plain all that is in his heart and mind with respect to the *Confession*, and the assembly of elders must carefully and sympathetically examine all those who profess to subscribe. For example, in Potomac Presbytery a candidate must prepare a written statement, based upon a conscientious examination of the Constitution of the PCA, responding to the following: 'Are you doubtful about, or in disagreement with, the biblical fidelity of any of the doctrines, concepts, phrases or wording of the doctrinal standards of the PCA? In each case, state in detail your views.' It then belongs to the court to determine whether or not these doubts or disagreements provide any impediment to a credible subscription to the system of doctrine. Samuel Miller early described the true nature and proper procedure of this transaction with clarity and insight:

> We may see from what has been said, that subscribing to a Church Creed, is not a mere formality; but a very solemn transaction, which means much, and infers the most serious obligations.... For myself,

I know of no transaction, in which insincerity is more justly chargeable with the dreadful sin of 'lying to the Holy Ghost,' than this....

Set it down, then, as a first principle of common honesty, as well as of Christian truth, that subscription to Articles of Faith, is a weighty transaction, which really means what it professes to mean; that no man is ever at liberty to subscribe articles which he does not truly and fully believe; and that, in subscribing, he brings himself under a solemn, covenant engagement to the church which he enters, to walk with it 'in the unity of faith,' and 'in the bond of peace and love.' If he cannot do this honestly, let him not profess to do it at all....

You will, perhaps, ask me, what shall be done by a man who loves the Presbyterian Church; who considers it as approaching nearer to the scriptural model than any other with which he is acquainted; who regards its Confession of Faith as by far the best, in its great outlines, and in all its fundamental articles, that he knows; and who yet, in some of its minor details cannot entirely concur? Can such an one honestly subscribe, without any previous explanation of his views? I answer by no means. Ought he, then, you will ask, to abandon all thoughts of uniting himself with our Church, when he is in cordial harmony with it in all fundamental principles, and nearer to it, in all respects, than to any other Church on earth? I again answer by no means. I know of no other mode of proceeding in such a case as this which Christian candor, and a pure conscience will justify, than the following: Let the candidate for admission unfold to the Presbytery before which he presents himself, all his doubts and scruples, with perfect frankness; opening his whole heart, as if on oath; and neither softening nor concealing any thing. Let him cause them distinctly to understand, that if he subscribe the Confession of Faith, he must be understood to do it in consistency with the exceptions and explanations which he specifies. If the Presbytery, after this fair understanding, should be of the opinion, that the excepted points were of little or no importance, and interfered with no article of faith, and should be willing to receive his subscription in the usual way, he may proceed. Such a method of proceeding will best accord with every principle of truth and honor; and will remove all ground of either self-reproach, or of reproach on the part of others, afterwards.[30]

7. Subscription to the very words of the *Confession* is not properly a part of what is required, but rather subscription to the propositions expressed in those words. Here a little care for the basic principles of logic will be of aid to the presbyter. Logicians distinguish between sentences and the propositions they may be used to assert. A proposition is an assertion or denial that may be true or

false, and is capable of being expressed in a variety of words and sentences. For example, the sentence 'Bill has faith in Jesus' and the sentence 'Jesus is trusted by Bill' assert the same proposition. So too, 'de gustibus non est disputandum' and 'there is no disputing about tastes' express the same proposition. Now the *Confession of Faith* contains a number sentences, most expressing a proposition, some expressing more than one. Those sentences together make up certain doctrines, which doctrines, related one with another in the Confession, make up the system of doctrine. What does a candidate do when he subscribes to the *Confession* 'as containing the system of doctrine taught in Holy Scripture'? Clearly it is possible for him to affirm the requisite propositions, without committing himself to the particular words and sentences of the *Confession*. Who should decide? In the first instance, the candidate. He must decide for himself, but then he must declare his judgement to the presbytery, so that the body receiving his pledge can confirm or disconfirm his judgement.

Thus an officer candidate might well take exception to the *form* of the *Confession* in some particular. Here the candidate professes to affirm the Standards' doctrine, but in words other than those of the Standards. For example, a candidate might object to the word '*passions*' (chap. 2.1), supposing the term to suggest a lack of care for his creatures on God's behalf, while agreeing that God has no 'passive powers' and affirming the active affections of His will. So too a candidate might object to the phrase 'the regenerate *part*' (13.3), as giving the impression that the soul is partitioned, without denying the nature of the conflict in view. With respect to baptism, a candidate might object to the phrase 'the grace promised is not only offered, but really ... *conferred*' (28.6), as suggesting 'received in present experience,' without denying the idea of title granted. In all such case the court must judge whether the candidate's words are an essentially faithful expression of the standard's teaching, or in fact an exception of substance. Surely it would follow that exceptions of form, if approved, may be freely taught, for they present no obvious threat to the peace or the purity of the church.[31]

8. Subscription to the *all* that might be, or has been, construed as the sense of the words of the Confession is not properly a part of what is required, but only *essential* agreement. Thus an officer candidate might well profess to affirm the words of the Confession

while taking exception to a particular construction of those words. For example, a candidate might affirm that 'God ... neither is nor can be the author ... of sin' (chs. 3.1, 5.4), in the sense of God is never the agent of sin, while insisting that there is a sense in which God is the one who authors the story of creation and redemption, and is, as such, the author of sin.[32] A candidate might agree that 'recreations' (ch. 21.8) are forbidden on the Sabbath, in the sense that organized sports are forbidden, but a walk in the park for some exercise on that day is not. In these cases the candidate professes to affirm the words of the Standards, but in a sense that the candidate supposes may differ in some way with the manner in which the Standards may have been traditionally understood. The court must judge whether that professed sense is in essential agreement with the Standards, or in fact an exception of substance. And again, surely it would follow that exceptions of sense, if approved, may be freely taught, for they present no obvious threat to the peace or the purity of the church.

9. The historical sense of the terms as first propounded provides the framework for a proper understanding of the *Confession*, but that sense does not necessarily preclude the possibility of a permissible development in understanding which nonetheless maintains an essential agreement with that historical sense. Thus, for example, one might affirm the *Confession's* teaching concerning the 'light of nature' (1.1. et al) in the non-Puritan Van Tilian sense; one might affirm the *Confession's* teaching concerning the 'covenant' (7), but as a unilateral treaty, not in the typically Puritan sense of 'contract'; one might affirm the *Confession's* 'necessity' with respect to the permissible works of the Sabbath (21.8), but in the sense of the post-industrial revolution necessities of modern society; one might agree with the *Confession's* understanding of the resurrection as including 'the selfsame bodies, and none other' (32.2), but with a formal, or some other non-material, sense of identity; one might affirm the *Confession's* 'space of six days' (4.1), but without having in view the 24 hour days that were probably in the minds of the Divines.[33]

10. It is inconsistent with the very purpose of, and justification for, confessions to allow those to subscribe who, without any qualification, simply deny the biblical fidelity of its doctrines, i.e., take exceptions of substance. Such a view appears to inform the

position of the Old School General Assembly in answer to a query in 1848:

> When Ministers and other officers are ordained in the Presbyterian Church, and give an affirmative answer to the question: 'Do you sincerely receive and adopt the Confession of this Church as containing the system of doctrines taught in the holy Scripture?' are such Ministers and officers to be understood as embracing and assenting to the doctrines, principles, precepts, and statements contained in the Larger and Shorter Catechisms, in the same unqualified sense in which they are understood to embrace and assent to the doctrines, principles, precepts, and statements contained in other parts of the Confession of Faith?.... The committee recommended that the question be answered in the affirmative, and the recommendation was adopted.[34]

It is important to note, at this juncture, that there is no spiritual tyranny in requiring such a subscription – no violation of liberty of conscience – for the subscription is voluntary, the *Confession* having been set forth for the very purpose of uniting in fellowship those who from biblical conviction can agree. So A. A. Hodge ably argued:

> It must be remembered, however, that the matter of these Creeds and Confessions binds the consciences of men only so far as it is purely scriptural, and because it is so; and as to the form in which the matter is stated, they bind those only who have voluntarily subscribed the Confession, and because of that subscription.[35]

11. An officer cannot, submitting to the authority of the church, give the impression that he believes what he does not. Therefore all officers must have the right to testify to their conscience in a matter wherein they differ with the Church's *Confession*. So too one cannot, submitting to the authority of the church, absolutely refrain from declaring what Christ has called one to teach. John Murray expressed this point powerfully when he urged:

> The person who adopts a creed and subscribes to it is never justified in doing so merely on the authority of the Church or simply because it is the creed of the Church to which be belongs. Creedal adoption or subscription must always proceed from the conviction that the creed is in accord with Scripture and declares its truth. The person adopting can never pass on the responsibility for such personal and

individual conviction to the Church and its official action. The moment acceptance is conceded on the basis that it is the interpretation and formulation of the Church rather than on the basis of consonance with Scripture, in that moment the Church is accorded the place of God and the authority of the Church is substituted for the authority of God's Word. The gravity of such a spiritual catastrophe cannot be measured. For in principle the idolatry perpetrated by Rome has been conceded and the basis has been laid for the gross impieties and tyrannies that have followed the career of the Romish Church.[36]

Nevertheless an officer can properly and prudentially regulate the manner, and limit the forums, in which he expresses his views.[37] Further, an officer can, and should, fairly commend the teaching of the Church, concerning the meaning of the Scripture, as worthy of more solemn consideration than his own private judgment. So the PCUSA Assembly wisely declared in 1824:

> [T]he General Assembly cannot but believe the precious immortals under their care to be more safe, in receiving the truth of God's holy word as exhibited in the standards of our Church, than in being subject to the guidance of any instructor, whoever he may be, who may have confidence enough to set up his own opinions in opposition to the system of doctrines....[38]

12. The courts of original jurisdiction should consider carefully any professed exceptions to the substance of the *Confession's* teaching, and may, under certain circumstances, allow such exceptions. In an exception of substance the candidate supposes that he disagrees with the *Confession*, credibly believing the Bible to teach other than what the Standards teach. What is to be done? The court must judge whether the excepted doctrine so undermines the integrity of the system of doctrine, government, discipline and worship of the Standards as to 1) make doubtful the candidate's profession of that system, or, 2) make impossible the candidate's practice under that system; in either of which cases, the exception should not be permitted. The emphasis on 'system of doctrine' is a key element in understanding the court's responsibility. Consider the testimony of J. Gresham Machen, instructing what would become the Orthodox Presbyterian Church, in the days of her infancy:

> Subscription to the Westminster Standards ... is not to every word in those Standards, but only to the *system* of doctrine which those

standards contain.... It is no new thing to take this position regarding creed subscription. It is the position which has long been taken by orthodox Calvinistic theologians.[39]

Yet even with this wholesome emphasis, further clarification is needed. In subscribing to the *Confession* as containing the system of doctrine contained in Scripture, one is not subscribing to the system of doctrine of the Holy Scripture, and to the *Confession* only so far as it contains that scriptural system. Rather, one is subscribing to the *Confession of Faith*, agreeing that the system of doctrine set forth in the *Confession of Faith*, is the Scriptural system.

How does one judge what is essential to the scriptural system as set forth in the *Confession*? Machen thought that pre-millenialism was not inconsistent with the *Confession's* system of doctrine.[40] But surely it is fair to ask, is this obvious? Suppose someone disagrees? Who decides? The presbytery, in the case of ministers, at first. What is the standard for the presbytery's judgment? Is it the standard if the view violates mere Christianity, as some would urge? Or perhaps it is the core elements of soteriological Calvinism that must be maintained?[41] There have been a variety of answers to this question, but as we urged above, the only answer that is logically consistent with the purpose of the *Confession* is to insist that the standard is found in what is essential to the system of doctrine of the *Confession* itself.

In other words, the test for the presbytery is this: is the excepted matter so integral to the system of doctrine of the *Confession*, that the allowance of an exception in this case would vitiate the justification of having a confession. Can one contemplate a body persevering in unity and peace, with common cause preserving and propagating the truth, with such a disagreement permitted among its authorized teachers and rulers? The contemplation requisite should be informed by a careful consideration of the practical force of the logic of the matter ('ideas have consequences'), as well as by the practical lessons evident in the church's past and present experience.

What then of the status of the candidate with respect to his permissible exception of substance? If the exception is found permissible, the candidate should be approved only under the following conditions: a) that he is able and willing to teach the doctrine of the Standards with sympathy and deference, and bring his practice into conformity with the Standards' teaching; b) that he shall be permitted to express his own conscience on the matter in the course of his teaching on the subject; and c) that he shall be permitted peacefully and respectfully to advocate his views before the courts of the church in order to persuade the church to modify its Standards.

13. Once ordained, if an officer finds his study of Scripture leading to conclusions contrary to the *Confession*, he should first raise his concerns, not in public, nor with people he serves, but with his brother officers. The matter should be raised for discussion, so that the church may help resolve the doubts, or become persuaded that a change in her *Confession* is necessary. Turretin spoke well for the course of wisdom when he argued:

> Accordingly if they think they see in them anything worth correcting, they should undertake nothing rashly or *ataktos* and unseasonable, so as vitally to disturb their mother's innards, as schismatics do, but should commend the difficulties they have to their Church; or either put her public opinion before their own private judgment, or break away from her communion, if conscience cannot acquiesce in her judgment.[42]

14. The Presbytery, of course, as important as it is, cannot be the final word on the permissibility of exceptions. As this matter has to do with teachers and rulers who are authorized on behalf of the whole church,[43] and as it is the peace or purity of the whole church (members, officers, and the graded system of courts as well) that is in view as the good to be obtained by confessional subscription, there must finally be recourse to the judgment of the highest, or most inclusive, assembly of elders. Thus by the wholesome procedures of appeal and complaint, used with restraint and modesty, the Church defines and refines the boundaries of the language of her Confession through judgment in particular cases. Princeton's Frances L. Patton clearly expressed Presbyterian first-principles when he observed:

> There is no doubt that there is an area of tolerated divergence from the Confession of Faith. How large that area is will depend upon the degree of readiness there may be in the Church to move the ecclesiastical courts, and upon the decisions reached in the court of last resort. Historical students may tell us what the Church has thought upon the subject, and dogmatic theologians may tell us what the

Church ought to think; but it is only as the General Assembly decides concrete cases in appellate jurisdiction, and the principle of *stare decisis* may be supposed to govern subsequent deliverances, that the area of tolerated divergence can be defined.[44]

Such principles as these, it appears to me, inform a view of subscription that alone is consistent with a sound justification of confessions. The burden of proof lies, in my judgment, with those who would advocate other views to come up with a defense for their use of confessions that does not amount to a re-articulation of the faulty arguments employed by those who oppose them outright, and is able to make some sense out of their continued employment for the unity, purity, and peace of the Church.

How Shall We Then Live Together?

First, a few preliminary observations. I think it would be fair to say that the PCA, in its brief history, has not been uniformly operating according to the principles set forth above.[45] What do I make of that fact? I suppose the denomination is the weaker for it, but that imperfection certainly does not undo the church. This is a matter of the well-being of the Church, not its very existence. We must all learn to live with imperfection while we labor with our eyes on the prize. But though the view I have articulated has not been generally embraced, I see no reason why it should trouble the church for me to charitably and peaceably argue in its favor. Yet some seem to find in this advocacy a threat, and as such, find the very thought of such debates something to lament. I would like to understand more of why this is the case, but I am well persuaded that without such discussion neither the purity nor the peace of the PCA as she is now constituted will be sustained.

The fact is, however, that since the PCA has not uniformly operated on such principles as above, the denomination may have considerably less confessional unity than it might otherwise have had. What should be done, from the point of view that I am urging, to remedy this circumstance?

First, I would have the PCA devote serious efforts toward establishing a constitutional standard for subscription.[46] Some public standard, reflecting real agreement, even if not all that I would seek, is far better than no standard at all. In my judgment until the PCA establishes such a standard it will continually be troubled with controversy concerning subscription and have no ready means of resolution. Of course the work in seeking to establish such a standard will require great self-discipline, for the temptation will lurk near at hand to affirm a theory of subscription sustaining one's own peculiarities, rather than that which is consistent with the rule of Christ and is adapted to the good of the Church. Further, it is important to remember that such an achievement will provide no panacea. As Dr. Davis has so wisely insisted, 'in the final analysis there simply is no constitutional device that will guarantee continued orthodoxy,' or, I might add, continued peace.[47]

Second, in my judgment a faulty theory and practice of subscription is far more dangerous to the health of the Church than an imprudent (either to few or to many) specification of doctrines in the *Confession*. Thus if the PCA could agree on what I take to be a sound view of subscription, I, for one, would be amenable to discussing what elements in the *Confession* must be removed in order for the PCA to find in that *Confession* a genuine statement of her articles of unity. Thus I would favor a consideration of amendments to the *Confession* where it simply does not constitute the articles of agreement in the Presbyterian Church in America today.[48]

Third, I would have the courts of the church insist that the seminaries serving the PCA devotedly teach the *Confession* itself as providing the foundational outline of their theological study, and not just as a minor survey course offered in the final year to prepare the candidate for ordination exams. In the many years I have served on the credentials committee of Potomac Presbytery, I have seen evidence of a continuing lack of depth in understanding of our *Confession* on the part of our candidates, candidates who have been uniformly able and diligent, but who have clearly not been taught to embrace the *Confession* as a precious gift of God's providence for our good, and a 'form of sound words' marvelously adapted to the public expression of their biblical faith. I would have the seminaries teach the *Confession* as derived from the Scriptures, set forth in its original historical context, compared carefully to the views it rejects, pursued in its use among American Presbyterians, and displayed in its contemporary significance for the glory of Christ and the good of His Church. The need expressed long ago by George A. Baxter, professor of theology at Union Theological Seminary (Virginia) and principle leader of the Old School Presbyterians, South, should demand the church's attention afresh:

I think it desirable that preachers trained in this Seminary, would be imbued with a cordial attachment to our Confession of Faith. The Scriptures are an infallible guide; the creed is only the best exposition which a fallible church could give of the Scriptures. As such, however, they must take [make?] it the bond of union in all their operations. It is therefore not only desirable but necessary that the ministers of a church should be imbued with a cordial attachment to its creed as the bond of its union. The creed of a church cannot be broken up, or trampled under foot, without such a complete destruction of its harmony as would ruin its usefulness....[49]

Finally, I can do no better in closing, than add my 'amen' to the counsel recently offered by Dr. Davis, whose principled yet ever-practical labors on behalf of Christ in His Church we honor in this volume: the Presbytery must require candidates to read the *Confession*! Said he:

There are 31,000 words in the Confession and Catechisms. I tell my students, if you don't find something in there that puzzles you or that sounds right but you're not sure the Bible says it – then I doubt you've been paying attention. Get some stronger coffee and read the Standards again, slower this time.[50]

NOTES

1. Throughout this discussion I shall refer to the circumstances of The Presbyterian Church in America as a case on point, but I suppose that with suitable adjustments the arguments of this paper would apply to any seriously confessional body. For an insightful discussion of this question in the Orthodox Presbyterian Church see John R. Muether, 'Confidence in Our Brethren: Creedal Subscription in the Orthodox Presbyterian Church,' in *The Practice of Confessional Subscription*, 2nd ed., edited by David W. Hall (Oak Ridge, TN: The Covenant Foundation, 2001), pp. 301-310. See also the thoughtful questions raised by Dr. Davis in his comparison of the OPC and the RPCES on subscription in 'Creedal Changes and Subscription to the *System of Doctrine*,' *The Presbyterian Guardian* 36 (March 1967): 45-47.
2. Samuel J. Baird, *A Collection of the Acts, Deliverances, and Testimonies of the Supreme Judicatory of the Presbyterian Church. . . ,* 2nd ed. (Philadelphia: Presbyterian Board of Publication, 1858), pp. 41-42. Hereafter 'Baird, *Digest,* p. #.'
3. (Philadelphia: Presbyterian Board of Publication, 1839); reprinted under the title *Miller On Creeds* (Greenville, SC: A. Press, 1987). It is from this reprint that I will be citing.
4. Ibid., p. 6. Emphasis added.
5. *A Commentary on The Confession of Faith. With Questions for Theological Students and Bible Classes* (Philadelphia: Presbyterian Board of Publication, 1869); reprint,

with an essay of the life of Hodge, retitled *The Confession of Faith. A Handbook of Christian Doctrine Expounding the Westminster Confession* (Edinburgh: Banner of Truth, 1983), p. 2.

6. Though the doctrinal standards of the PCA include the *Confession of Faith*, and the *Larger* and *Shorter Catechisms*, for the sake of brevity and clarity I will use the term '*Confession*' throughout this paper as referring to all.

7. This is popularly known as permitting 'exceptions.'

8. *The Confession of Faith*, p. 3. Cf. Robert Lewis Dabney: 'It is only of the pastors and the doctors of the church, and of such other officers as exercise spiritual rule therein, that we rightfully require the adoption of our whole creed.' From 'The Doctrinal Contents of the Confession of Faith – Its Fundamental and Regulative Ideas, and the Necessity and Value of Creeds,' in *Memorial Volume of the Westminster Assembly, 1647–1897*, Francis Beattie, et al., editors (Richmond, VA: PCP, 1897), pp. 87-114; reprint, *DRLD*, V:119-142. The quoted text appears on p. 133 of the reprint.

9. PCA *BCO* 21-5.(2). The language quoted was originally adopted in 1788.

10. See for example Francis R. Beattie, 'The Nature and Uses of Religious Creeds,' in *The Presbyterian Standards* (Richmond, VA: The Presbyterian Committee on Publication, 1896), pp. 29-39; Robert L. Dabney, 'The Doctrinal Contents of the Confession: Its Fundamental and Regulative Ideas, and the Necessity and Value of Creeds,' in *Memorial Volume of the Westminster Assembly*, ed. by F. R. Beattie, et al. (Richmond, VA: Presbyterian Board of Publications, 1897), pp. 87-114; A.A. Hodge, *A Commentary on The Confession of Faith. With Questions for Theological Students and Bible Classes* (Philadelphia, PA: Presbyterian Board of Publication, 1869), pp. 19-21; Ashbel Green, 'Lecture I. – Introductory,' in *Lectures on the Shorter Catechism of the Presbyterian Church in the United States of America Addressed to Youth*, 2 vols. (Philadelphia: Presbyterian Board of Publication and Sabbath School Work, 1841), 1:13-32; Samuel Miller, *The Utility and Importance of Creeds and Confessions: Addressed Particularly to Candidates for the Ministry* (Philadelphia: Presbyterian Board of Publication, 1839).

11. *Miller on Creeds*, p. 7. Emphasis added.

12. Ibid.

13. Baird, *Digest*, p. 41.

14. *Miller on Creeds*, p. 8.

1.5 *The Confession of Faith*, p. 2-3.

16. *A Digest, Complied From the Records of the General Assembly of the Presbyterian Church in the United States of America, and From the Records of the Late Synod of New York and Philadelphia, of Their Acts and Proceedings, That Appear to be of Permanent Authority and Interest; Together With a Short Account of the Missions Conducted by the Presbyterian Church*, by order of the General Assembly (Philadelphia, PA: Printed for the Trustees of the Assembly by R. P. M'Culloh, 1820), pp. 133-34.

17. Cf. *BCO* 2.2.

18. Summarizing Robert L. Dabney, 'The Form of Sound Words,' *The Central Presbyterian* 6:43 (May 18, 1871): 1; reprinted as 'Broad Churchism,' in *Discussions by Robert L. Dabney, D.D., L.L.D.,,* ed. by C.R. Vaughan. (Richmond: Presbyterian Committee of Publication, 1890), II:447-463.

19. *A Digest, Complied From the Records of the General Assembly of the Presbyterian Church in the United States of America*, pp. 140-142.

20. *Miller on Creeds*, p. 15-16.

21. This view has been called the 'substance of doctrine' view of subscription. Cf.

Minutes of the Tenth General Assembly of the Presbyterian Church in America (1982), 221 ff.

22. *Institutio Theologiæ Elencticæ,* vol. 3 (Edinburgh: John D. Lowe, 1847-48), XVIII, xxx, 9-10, cited in Heinrich Heppe, *Reformed Dogmatics set out and illustrated from the sources,* rev. and ed. by Ernst Bizer; trans. by G. T. Thomson (Grand Rapids: Baker Book House, 1978), pp. 687-688.

23. *The Collected Writings of James Henley Thornwell, D.D., LL.D.* 4 vols. (Richmond, VA: Presbyterian Committee of Publication, 1871-75); reprint (Edinburgh: Banner of Truth, 1974), IV:367. It is worth noting here that a commonly-used argument against 'strict' subscription is clearly fallacious. The argument runs roughly as follows. One should not require subscription to everything in the Confession, because that would imply that there are no errors in the Confession (or that it is unchangeable), and such an errorless (or unchangeable) Confession would be a threat to the unique infallibility, finality, and authority of Scripture. But the Confession is subordinate to Scripture, not because it may err whereas Scripture may not, or because it may be changed whereas the Scriptures may not, but because Scripture is the Divinely approved source of our Confession. Strictly speaking, it would not be much trouble to pen an infallible confession, if it had few enough propositions and was stated with reasonable simplicity and care; but such an infallible confession would still be subordinate to Scripture, because both its infallibility and its authority are derivative.

24. Cf. Charles Hodge, 'Church Commentary on the Bible,' in *The Church and Its Polity* (London: Thomas Nelson and Sons, 1879), pp. 380-384. 'If the mere suggestion of such an idea does not strike a man dumb with awe, he must be impervious to all argument.'

25. Cf. the insight and admission of William Cunningham: 'The duty of a church in settling her symbols, or arranging her terms of communion, is to be regulated by different principles from those which determine the duty of individuals, who are simply bound to acquire and to profess as much a of accurate and distinct knowledge of truth as they can attain to, on all matters, whether important or not. When a church is arranging her terms of communion, other considerations in addition to that of the mere truth of the statements, must be brought to bear upon the question, of what it is right, necessary, and expedient to do, or of what amount of unity in matters of opinion ought to be required. The principles applicable to this branch of the church's duty have never been subjected to a thorough discussion by competent parties, though they are very important in their bearings; and the right application of them is attended with great difficulty....' *The Reformers and the Theology of the Reformation* (Edinburgh, 1862); reprint (Edinburgh: Banner of Truth, 1979), 412.

26. *Miller On Creeds,* pp. 44, 88-94.

27. 'The Doctrinal Contents of the Confession of Faith,' pp. 87-114.

28. Baird, *Digest,* pp. 41-42.

29. 'Tradition: Romish and Protestant,' in *Collected Writings of John Murray,* vol. 4, *Studies in Theology* (Edinburgh: Banner of Truth, 1982), p. 272.

30. *Miller on Creeds,* pp. 98, 100-102.

31. Here it is worth noting, however, the warning offered by George A. Baxter, early 19th century professor of theology at Union Theological Seminary, Virginia: 'A minister may disturb the peace of his church, by appearing to deviate from its creed, when he does not do so in reality. He may do this by the substitution of new terms, to give the air of novelty to his speculations.... Much of the new divinity would become old divinity, if the terms of our Confession, or similar terms, were used to

express, what, on fair explanation, appear to be the real sentiments of its authors.' Cited in William Henry Foote, *Sketches of Virginia, Historical and Biographical,* second series (Philadelphia, PA: J.B. Lippincott and Company, 1856), p. 458.

32. Cf. Jonathan Edwards, *Freedom of the Will,* IV.IX.

33. On this last see Francis R. Beattie, *The Presbyterian Standards* (Richmond, VA: The Presbyterian Committee on Publication, 1896), pp. 80-81, or A.A. Hodge, *The Confession of Faith,* pp. 82-83.

34. Baird, *Digest,* p. 43.

35. *Confession of Faith,* p. 3. Cf. *BCO,* Preface, II. Preliminary Principles. 1-2.

36. 'Tradition: Romish and Protestant,' in *Collected Writings of John Murray,* vol. 4, *Studies in Theology* (Edinburgh: Banner of Truth, 1982), pp. 272-273.

37. Cf. the example of Jesus: John 16:12, 'I have many more things to say to you, but you cannot bear *them* now.'

38. Baird, *Digest,* p. 42.

39. J. Gresham Machen, *The Presbyterian Guardian* 3:2, p. 21, cited in Clair Davis, 'Creedal Changes and Subscription to the *System of Doctrine,*' *The Presbyterian Guardian* 36 (March 1967), p. 45.

40. '[W]e think that a man who holds that the return of Christ and the final judgment take place not in one act, as the Westminster Standards contemplate them as doing ... yet may honestly say that he holds the system of doctrine that the Standards contain.' Machen cited in Davis, 'Creedal Changes,' p. 45.

41. This appears to have been Machen's view.

42. *Institutio Theologiæ Elencticæ,* vol. 3 (Edinburgh: John D. Lowe, 1847-48), XVIII, xxx, 9-10, cited in Heinrich Heppe, *Reformed Dogmatics set out and illustrated from the sources,* rev. and ed. by Ernst Bizer; trans. by G.T. Thomson (Grand Rapids: Baker Book House, 1978), pp. 687-688.

43. Cf. *BCO* 11-4.

44. *The Revision of the Confession of Faith.* Read before the Presbyterian Social Union, New York, December 2, 1889, p. 6.

45. Though I should say that Potomac Presbytery, without formally endorsing such a view, has never in fact (to my memory) acted contrary to these principles in dealing with candidates.

46. Cf. the counsel of the 22nd General Assembly: '... with respect to the question concerning subscription, the Assembly suggests that interested Ruling and Teaching Elders (particularly from ostensibly differing points of view) could serve the church well by producing and circulating among themselves draft language for a new section IV of the Preface of *The Book of Church Order* (to be titled: 'Of the Church's Confession and Subscription') where in brief paragraphs would be stated the nature and authority of the Confession and Catechisms, their justification and purposes, and the meaning of subscription to the doctrinal standards in the PCA. Such drafts as perfected through prayerful study and charitable discussion, without the pressures and politics of an impending vote, could then be proposed to the Presbyteries for study, perfection, and circulation among themselves, in hope that some measure of consensus could be achieved in the church before the formal amending process of sending an overture to the General Assembly even begins. Perhaps this course, with the Lord's blessing, would provide a way for securing both the bonds of our unity, and the purity of our faith, while maintaining peace in the church under the reign of our Lord Jesus Christ.' *M22GA* (1994), pp. 233-34.

47. Clair Davis, 'Creedal Changes and Subscription to the System of Doctrine,' *Presbyterian Guardian* 36 (March 1967): 46.

48. Something like this, for example, appears to have been Thornwell's counsel.

See James Henley Thornwell, 'The General Assembly of 1847,' in *The Collected Writings of James Henley Thornwell, D.D., LL.D.,* 4 vols. (Richmond, VA: Presbyterian Committee of Publication, 1871-75); reprint (Edinburgh: Banner of Truth, 1974), IV:493.

49. Cited in William Henry Foote, *Sketches of Virginia, Historical and Biographical,* second series (Philadelphia, PA: J.B. Lippincott and Company, 1856), p. 458.

50. 'Another Word on Subscription.' PCANews (April 30, 2002).

J. Gresham Machen

Confessionalism and the History of American Presbyterianism

Darryl. G. Hart

J. Gresham Machen was a biblical scholar by training and so may be forgiven if his evaluation of American Presbyterianism in his day was not as informed by the study of church history as it could have been. For instance, in the midst of debates about the reorganization of Princeton Seminary in 1929, in which conservatives lost control of the school, Machen asserted that the proposed changes would 'mark the end of an epoch in the history of the modern Church.'[1] His reason for making this claim, of course, stemmed from his estimate of liberal Protestant theology and the inroads it was making into the Presbyterian Church in the U.S.A. As he had argued in *Christianity and Liberalism* (1923), liberal Protestantism and evangelical Christianity were diametrically at odds, so much so that liberalism constituted another religion. So the loss of Princeton to the evangelical faith was indeed a grave matter, nothing less than the elimination of orthodoxy's last line of defense in the onslaught of modernism. Machen was not alone in this outlook. Samuel G. Craig, a member of Princeton's board of directors and one of Westminster Seminary's original board members quoted Princeton Seminary's first president, Francis Landey Patton when justifying the creation of a new seminary to carry on the Princeton tradition. According to Patton, the new theology that, in Craig's estimation, had captured Princeton Seminary 'was not an amendment' to historic Christianity, nor a 'restatement'; 'it [was] a revolution' that 'we must be ready to fight, and, if need be, to die, in defense of the blood-bought truths of the common salvation'.[2]

As courageous and insightful as these interpretations were, Machen, Craig, and their supporters ignored the longer trajectory of a more deep-seated tension in the history of American Presbyterianism of which the so-called fundamentalist controversy was yet another manifestation. What appeared to leading conservatives as a new development in American Protestantism actually stemmed from an older tension that had afflicted Presbyterians in the New World since the eighteenth century. This older antagonism was not simply the result of orthodoxy's opposition to theological naturalism of the Enlightenment but also stemmed from the influences of pietist Protestantism. In fact, one way of interpreting American Presbyterian history is to look for a perennial conflict between pietists and confessionalists. Pietism, as many scholars have observed, is a form of Protestant devotion that arose in the seventeenth century in reaction to the apparent formalism of Protestant orthodoxy and insisted upon the simpler truths of Bible study, personal experience, and holy living. It surfaced in North American Presbyterian circles during the revivals of the eighteenth century and periodically did battle against the formalities of creed, polity and liturgy when such structures seemed to become barriers to more genuine and vital expressions of faith.[3] Confessionalism, in contrast, conserved the historic forms of the Reformed faith as the ordained means by which believers should be nurtured and as the signs of a healthy church.[4] To put this difference in simple terms, pietists stressed the subjective side of Christianity while confessionalists emphasized the objective aspects of the gospel and its ministry. For the former, the individual's experience or decision was the decisive element of genuine faith, while for the latter inheriting and conforming to the corporate expressions of faith, both in the family and church, were determinative of Presbyterian faith and practice.

A significant element in this opposition between Presbyterian pietists and confessionalists was a debate over practical Calvinism. Two different answers, accordingly, emerged in response to the question of what made the Reformed faith relevant. For pietists, practical Calvinism resulted in godly lives and transformed societies. For confessionalists, in turn, the relevance of the Reformed faith was more otherworldly than visible, manifesting itself in the marks of the church – reformed preaching, sacraments and discipline – that then became the means of calling the elect and sustaining them through their earthly pilgrimage until their final arrival in the new heavens and new earth.

The history of American Presbyterianism unfolded with this tension between pietism and confessionalism as the central dynamic. In particular it was responsible for the major divisions in the Presbyterian Church, from the eighteenth-century Old-Side/New-Side controversy, the nineteenth-century conflict between Old School and New School Presbyterians, down to the so-called modernist-fundamentalist controversy of the early twentieth century. What follows is a brief survey of American Presbyterian history that highlights this fundamental rivalry between pietism and confessionalism. Had Machen and other conservatives of the 1920s been aware of this dynamic, the conflicts of the 1920s would not necessarily have turned out any differently than they did. Still, an awareness of this tension on the part of those Presbyterians who identify with Machen may yield a better understanding of the factors that led to the departure of conservative Presbyterians from the mainline church (both the Orthodox Presbyterian Church and the Presbyterian Church in America), and greater insight into the ways in which an otherworldly faith such as Calvinism is truly practical.

The Perennial Conflict

At the time of the First Great Awakening, the Presbyterian Church was a very young and untested communion. The first Presbyterian congregations in the New World developed more on the basis of migration patterns of the Scots and Scotch-Irish than the missions strategy of Presbyterian churches in Great Britain. By 1706, when the Presbytery of Philadelphia was founded and was the first official Presbyterian body, only seven churches existed. American Presbyterianism would continue to grow independently of Old World Presbyterianism, so that by 1716, seventeen churches existed, organized into four presbyteries and one synod. But despite the fragility of the young churches and efforts to build them into a stronger unity, it did not take long for the tension between pietism and confessionalism to surface. And when it did, it altered significantly the course of Presbyterianism in America.

One of the first crises the new denomination faced was the basis for ministerial fellowship. Although the *Westminster Confession of Faith* and *Larger* and *Shorter Catechisms* were only eight decades old, colonial Presbyterians followed the example of the Scottish Kirk and in 1729 adopted these creeds as their doctrinal standard. Much has been written about the nature of subscription in American Presbyterianism and part of the reason for this ongoing discussion is whether or not the Adopting Act of 1729 was strict or allowed for some flexibility by those who subscribed to the Westminster Standards.[5] The Scotch-Irish ministers tended to insist that ministers not be allowed to take exceptions, except for the chapter on the civil magistrate. Those Presbyterians from Puritan backgrounds, in contrast, were not as strict. For this reason, plausible arguments exist on both sides about the character of subscription among American Presbyterians. But often overlooked is an important difference between the two sides over the meaning of subscription. For the Scotch-Irish, subscription was sufficient for a minister to be received into the fellowship thanks in part to his baptism and profession of faith. But for the Presbyterians with Puritan backgrounds, prospective ministers not only were required to subscribe to the Standards but also to show signs of authentic religious experience.[6]

These differences led in turn to the first significant division in American Presbyterianism, that between the Old Side and New Side denominations, which lasted from 1741 until 1758. Part of what brought this conflict to a head, even though it had been simmering since 1729, was the form of revivalism that George Whitefield made so popular during his campaign of 1739. The English evangelist popularized a style of preaching and ministry that until then had been practiced by a handful of pastors. Whitefield preached with great emotional fervor and did so in a way designed to elicit a deeply felt experience from hearers. Some who heard Whitefield wept, some fainted, some shrieked, partly because they were convicted but also because the evangelist's preaching was so different from standard sermons. Whatever the reason, the conversion experience, not creed, liturgy, or church polity, became the defining feature of entrance into the Christian life. What is more, even though the Protestant creeds had spoken of conversion as a life long process, the pattern encouraged by Whitefield's revivals tended to reduce conversion to an instantaneous and immediate work of God in response to preaching also enlivened by the Spirit.[7]

Despite Whitefield's success and warm reception by many Presbyterians, some in the young church raised questions about his methods, which in turn prompted a controversy over qualifications for the ministry. In the midst of this conflict, Gilbert Tennent in 1740 preached his famous sermon, 'The Danger of An Unconverted Ministry,' in which he compared Whitefield's critics to the Pharisees and insisted that anyone opposed to the revival was likely unconverted. A year later Presbyterians split forming two separate denominations. The Old Side, those skeptical of revivals, continued to require traditional theological training and subscription to the Westminster Standards as sufficient guides to a candidate's fitness. The New Side, those who supported revivals, also stressed the importance of theological training and creedal subscription but added that ministerial candidates needed to give evidence of a conversion experience. Other factors also contributed to the split. But pivotal to it was the question of conversion and whether or not prospective ministers who could subscribe to the Westminster Standards also needed to demonstrate evidence of vital Christianity.

Church historians have had little difficulty caricaturing both sides in this controversy, though the Old Side most often has been the object of ridicule. Sometimes described as rationalists, immoderate in their consumption of alcohol, and forerunners of theological liberalism, Old Side ministers have not received sympathetic treatment in large measure because the revivals about which they raised concerns were, by seemingly universal consent, beneficent. The New Side, in contrast, has sometimes attracted criticism for self-righteousness and a tendency toward enthusiasm. However inaccurate these depictions may be, the Old Side-New Side split does reveal the fundamental discord between confessionalism and pietism. For the Old Side, Christian devotion was to be judged by outward forms, such as subscription to a corporate confession of faith, not because individual experience did not matter but because looking into the heart of a professing believer was impossible. Confessionalism, accordingly, holds that the forms of the faith, creeds, liturgy, and polity, although fallible are the proper criteria for evaluating the health of a church or individual believer. For the New Side, however, these religious externals went only skin deep – conceivably anyone could subscribe to the Westminster Standards. Instead, genuine faith needed a surer measure, one that demonstrated the presence of the Spirit. From the pietist perspective, then, new life in Christ might take shape in certain religious externals, but these were not as reliable as the life-changing experience of revivals and the holy form of living they encouraged.

Almost a century after the Old Side-New Side controversy, American Presbyterianism experienced another division, again in the context of revival. This was the split in 1837–1838 between Old School and New School Presbyterian denominations (it is important to observe that by the time of the Civil War both the North and the South had Old and New School churches). As significant as the differences were between the eighteenth and nineteenth-century controversies – theology being an important one with prominent New School ministers denying the imputation of Adam's sin – the Old School-New School division was another form of a deeper tension between confessionalism and pietism. The acuteness of this strain was particularly evident in the doctrine of the church that leading Old School and New School Presbyterians formulated during the controversy.[8]

As most students of American Presbyterianism readily admit, one of the important factors contributing to division in the church during the first quarter of the nineteenth century was church polity. Since 1801 Presbyterians and Congregationalists had agreed to a form of cooperation that made the expansion of the churches into the new territories of the United States a joint enterprise. New congregations could call either a Congregationalist or Presbyterian as pastor, while the two denominations cooperated through the courts of the Presbyterian Church. But the disagreement between Old School and New School Presbyterians went deeper than differences between Presbyterian and Congregationalist polity. Each side maintained an understanding of the nature and mission of the church that proved difficult to harmonize in one communion. The Old School view, sometimes called 'the Spirituality of the Church', asserted the uniqueness of the church and her responsibilities when compared to other institutions, whether the state or the family. In contrast, the New School conception, which undergirded many of the social reforms of the Protestant-led 'Benevolent Empire', insisted that the church had a pivotal role to play in the improvement of society.

For New School Presbyterians, the church needed to take an active role in American public life. According to Albert Barnes, a prominent Philadelphia pastor, the Christian church:

> owes an important duty to society and to God...; and its mission will not be accomplished by securing merely the sanctification of its own members, or even by the drawing within its fold multitudes of those who shall be saved ... the burden which is laid upon it may not be primarily the conversion of the heathen or the diffusion of Bibles and tracts abroad; the work which God requires it to do, and for which specifically it has been planted there, may be to diffuse a definite moral influence in respect to an existing evil institution. On all that is wrong in social life, in the modes of intercourse, in the habits of training the young, and in the prevailing sentiments in the community that have grown out of existing institutions, God may have planted the church there to exert a definite moral influence – a work for himself.[9]

This conception of the church would appear to be nothing more than the idea commonly understood in Reformed circles that all of life has religious significance and so efforts to separate the realm of the church from other spheres is a rejection of a Reformed world-and-life-view.[10]

But from the Old School perspective, the New Schoolers had too readily merged the notions of the church and religion so that everything with religious significance was also properly a sphere of the church. The Old School, accordingly, represented an older strain of Reformed thought, clearly stated in chapter thirty-one of the Westminster Confession, that put significant limits on church power. According to the Southern Presbyterian theologian, James Henley Thornwell:

> The church is not, as we fear too many are disposed to regard it, a moral institute of universal good, whose business it is to wage war upon every form of human ill, whether social, civil, political, moral, and to patronize every expedient which a romantic benevolence may suggest as likely to contribute to human comfort. We freely grant, and sincerely rejoice in the truth, that the healthful operations of the Church, in its own appropriate sphere, react upon all the interests of man, and contribute to the progress and prosperity of society; but we are far from admitting either that it is the purpose of God, that, under the present dispensation of religion, all ill shall

be banished from this sublunary state, and earth be converted into a paradise; or, that the proper end of the Church is the direct promotion of universal good. It has no commission to construct society afresh, to adjust its elements in different proportions, to rearrange the distribution of its classes, or to change the forms of its political institutions.... The power of the Church, accordingly, is only ministerial and declarative. The Bible, and the Bible alone, is her rule of faith and practice. She can announce what it teaches, enjoin what it commands, prohibit what it condemns, and enforce her testimonies by spiritual sanctions. Beyond the Bible she can never go, and apart from the Bible she can never speak.[11]

One important matter of social policy before nineteenth-century Americans was slavery and the New School and Old School views of the church developed very much in the context of that political and moral conflict. The Old School argued that the Bible did not condemn slavery and neither could the church, whereas the New School insisted that the Bible did condemn the motivation for slavery and so should the church. Although the American nation would go to the lengths of a civil war to resolve the dispute about slavery, the Old School-New School division did not bring an end to disagreements over the nature of the church and its ministry. After the Civil War the divided Presbyterian churches on both sides of the Mason-Dixon Line reunited, first the southerners in 1867 (PCUS) and then the northerners two years later (PCUSA). These reunions in turn spawned a series of cooperative endeavors among American Protestants more generally, from the Evangelical Alliance (1873) to the Federal Council of Churches (1908), in which Presbyterians would assume positions of leadership. The doctrine of the church that informed Protestant ecumenism was decidedly New School. Many Protestant leaders were alarmed by the spread of secularism and the rising prominence of Roman Catholicism in American society and believed that Protestant cooperation was crucial to winning the culture wars. Some Presbyterians opposed these endeavors, most of them from Old School backgrounds. But theirs was a decidedly minority point of view. [12]

In addition to endorsing implicitly the New School conception of the church, the ecumenical spirit that dominated early twentieth-century Presbyterianism was also decidedly pietist. It insisted upon the primacy of the individual's experience in coming to faith in Christ. Likewise, it defended the right of the laity to study and interpret the Bible for themselves, irrespective of church teaching. Furthermore, the pietist strain in American ecumenism also looked for signs of genuine faith in deeds of moral earnestness. In sum, ecumenical Protestants – Presbyterians included – were looking for a piety with direct application to individuals and society's needs; it was a this-worldly faith that stood in marked contrast to the churchly forms of devotion advocated by confessional Presbyterians.

Of course, pietism's common denominator was a logical development if Protestants as diverse as Presbyterians, Baptists, and Episcopalians, for instance, were to cooperate. Experience, the Bible and holy living had a much better chance of supplying unity than did polity, creed, or worship. Nevertheless, the ecumenical movement, building upon the foundation of interdenominational cooperation supplied by American revivalism, further weakened the confessional identity of American Presbyterianism. As Presbyterians entered into greater levels of collaboration with Protestants in other denominations, those confessionalists who defended the particular beliefs and practices of the Reformed heritage were sure to look sectarian if not perverse.

The Presbyterian Conflict of the 1920s

The differences between pietist and confessional Presbyterians is crucial for understanding the realignment of American Presbyterianism during the 1920s. The most common way of interpreting that controversy involves the identification of three different parties, conservatives (or fundamentalists) moderates (or evangelicals), and liberals. Representatives of each group include J. Gresham Machen, a conservative, his colleague at Princeton Seminary, Charles Erdman, an evangelical, and Henry Sloan Coffin, president of Union Seminary in New York and well known liberal theologian. According to this perspective, conservatives and evangelicals split over the issue of whether or not the church should tolerate liberals, with the former opposing, and the latter affirming a degree of ecclesiastical breadth. The division between evangelicals and conservatives, the reasoning goes, allowed liberals to take control of the church, a power shift that became apparent once conservatives in the 1930s set up a rogue missions agency, the Independent Board for Presbyterian Foreign Missions, and were forced to leave the denomination. Because of this interpretation, conservatives such as Machen have been faulted for playing the game of ecclesiastical politics poorly, insisting on the purity of the church when in fact compromise may have been necessary for conservatives to maintain control of the Presbyterian Church.[13]

A recent address by Barbara Wheeler, the current president of Auburn Seminary, calls into question this now standard assessment of the Presbyterian controversy and implicitly lends credibility to the idea that only two parties existed in American Presbyterianism, namely, pietists and confessionalists. Wheeler argues that evangelicals such as Erdman and liberals like Coffin, rather than representing two separate streams of Presbyterianism, actually shared a number of significant traits that made the alliance between evangelical and liberal Presbyterians likely if not inevitable. She writes:

> Erdman and Coffin shared a piety, and I think that fact explains how they could so readily join forces to hold the church together.... [T]he bond between them was not similar life experiences, or friends in common or shared theological ideas. The bond was not Presbyterian patriotism either. Though both loved the Presbyterian Church as the home in which they had met Jesus Christ, neither made denominational loyalty a basic value. Coffin crusaded for Protestant unity, and Erdman, like Moody, cared much more about Christianity than any of its branches. They joined and worked together ... because they wanted to lead the same kind of Christian lives.[14]

What united the evangelical and liberal contingents into one party was a commitment to a strand of piety, one unencumbered by denominational particulars or theological labels but driven by the pursuit of a holy life, church and society.

If Wheeler is correct, then the conservatives' defeat in the struggles of the 1920s is much easier to understand. For Machen stood for a version of piety very different from the generic faith of Erdman and Coffin. In fact, the fundamental point of Machen's critique of liberalism was modernism's wrongheaded effort to separate the kernel of Christianity (its general ideals) from its husk (the outward forms). But this task was impossible, he argued, because the 'essence' of Christianity could never be isolated from its particulars such as the person of Christ, and redemption through his death and resurrection. And even though Machen believed Protestants and Catholics could be co-belligerents against modernism, he refused to join other evangelicals in an effort to find a lowest common denominator upon which all Bible-believing Christians could unite. As he explained in his rejection of the invitation from the trustees of Bryan Memorial University to be the new school's president:

> I am somewhat loathe, for the present at least, to relinquish my connection with distinctively Presbyterian work.... [T]horoughly consistent Christianity, to my mind, is found only in the Reformed or Calvinistic Faith; ... Hence I never call myself a 'Fundamentalist' ... what I prefer to call myself is ... a 'Calvinist' – that is, an adherent of the Reformed Faith. ... which flows down from the Word of God through Augustine and Calvin and which has found noteworthy expression in America in the great tradition represented by Charles Hodge and Benjamin Breckinridge Warfield.[15]

This was a piety that regarded Christianity not from the perspective of the individual believers's own experience but rather from that of the corporate body of Presbyterianism as articulated in the church's creed and polity.

At the same time, Machen's confessional piety looked for the benefits of Christianity in places other than simply righteous individuals, denominations, or nations. At the close of his classic book, *Christianity and Liberalism*, Machen identified the bottom line in the battle with liberalism; it was corporate worship. Whatever the solution to the controversy, one thing was clear, he wrote:

> There must be somewhere groups of redeemed men and women who can gather together humbly in the name of Christ, to give thanks to Him for His unspeakable gift and to worship the Father through him. Such groups alone can satisfy the needs of the soul.

Machen conceded that this was an otherworldly devotion, one that transcended the things 'that divide nation from nation and race from race', 'the passions of war', and the 'puzzling problems of industrial strife'.[16] But confessionalism's deficiency in the realm of short term relevance could also turn out to be a blessing, such as when it prevented the church from identifying the most important matters with things earthly and thereby used the gospel for purposes that were ultimately peripheral to the life of faith.

One instance where the differences between Presbyterian pietists and confessionalists was clearly displayed was the matter of alcohol and the Presbyterian Church's support for Prohibition and the

Volstead Act. Evangelicals like Erdman and liberals like Coffin believed that the consumption of alcohol was a grave evil that was at odds with the gospel and was destroying the possibility for Christian civilization in the United States. For that reason, throughout the 1920s the church passed resolutions in support of the federal government's legislation. Machen, however, believed the Bible forbade immoderate consumption of alcohol but did not require total abstinence. In addition, he held that the church abused its power when it endorsed the state's legislation since this was a political matter on which the church should be silent. Ironically, Machen's opposition to Prohibition was a major reason for the 1926 General Assembly's refusal to promote him to the chair of apologetics and ethics at Princeton Seminary. But over time not simply the repeal of the Eighteenth Amendment but also the demise of total abstinence among Presbyterians vindicated the confessional piety of Machen. Pietism's concern for holy living did carry the day during the 1920s and literally transformed the culture by making the consumption of alcohol illegal. Yet, this crusade turned out to have a short shelf life and proved to be a distraction for the church from its much weightier tasks of word, sacrament and discipline. The lesson taught by this episode of Presbyterian history in the 1920s is that confessionalism's apparent irrelevance turns out to offer and to yield a longer lasting utility, one that reminds the corporate church of its chief calling and permits believers a measure of freedom in determining how to relate the gospel to daily life.

What is more, the differences between confessionalists like Machen and pietists like the evangelical Erdman and the liberal Coffin are helpful not only for understanding the way the Presbyterian controversy of the 1920s unfolded but also for clarifying the relationship between the Old School-New School division and twentieth-century Presbyterianism. In a thoughtful article on the heritage of New School Presbyterianism, George M. Marsden rightly observed that the trend among the New School's twentieth-century heirs ran as much toward fundamentalism as it did toward liberalism. Marsden's point is especially useful because it addresses a fact often overlooked by historians who generally trace modernist Protestantism's doctrinal laxity to the New School's departure from Calvinist orthodoxy.[17] As he observes, such doctrinal indifference also surfaced among fundamentalists along with the New School's moral activism and experimental piety.

But what Marsden does not recognize is that one of the reasons why New Schoolers could wind up in either the fundamentalist or liberal camps is because deep down both were pietists. Liberals *and* fundamentalists resisted the corporate and churchly piety of confessionalism. To be sure, as Machen would learn during the 1920s the number of Presbyterian confessionalists was small. Many who considered themselves conservative, such as Erdman, had a very different agenda from the confessionalists. Unfortunately, historians of American Presbyterianism have ignored the differences between pietism and confessionalism, preferring instead to interpret the twentieth-century church through the lens of evangelicalism's antagonism to liberalism.[18] But as the Presbyterian controversy of the 1920s reveals, the real divide in American Presbyterianism may be that between those like Machen who stressed the objectivity of the Christian faith and the uniqueness of the Presbyterian expression, and those like Erdman and Coffin who emphasized religious experience and holy living, thus blurring the differences between Presbyterians and other Christians.

J. Gresham Machen himself did not understand the dynamics at work between pietism and confessionalism in his own day. And this failure is responsible for the considerable surprise and anguish he experienced as many conservatives stood by and watched the unraveling of the Presbyterian Church's confessional identity. Nevertheless, the controversies in which he played such a large role did expose the fault lines in the American Presbyterian terrain. And even though Machen was confused by the actions of many evangelicals, the contrast that he drew between Presbyterians who stressed Reformed doctrine and those who emphasized religious experience was precisely the fault line in the church. If twenty-first-century Presbyterians are to offer a meaningful alternative to both evangelicalism and mainline Protestantism, they will have to devote more study to the differences between pietism and confessionalism, and what those differences involve for the development and witness of American Presbyterianism. More importantly, they will need to recognize that pietism's promise of practical and vital religion is in the long run unable to provide the solid and lasting food that confessionalism has endeavored to conserve.

NOTES

1. J. Gresham Machen, *The Attack upon Princeton Seminary: A Plea for Fair Play* (privately published, 1927), 33.

2. Samuel G. Craig, *Westminster Seminary and the Reformed Faith* (privately published, 1934), 14.

3. See F. Ernest Stoeffler, *German Pietism during the Eighteenth Century* (Leiden: Brill, 1973); and Donald G. Bloesch, *The Evangelical Renaissance* (Grand Rapids: Eerdmans, 1973).

4. See D. G. Hart, *The Lost Soul of American Protestantism* (Lanham, Md.: Rowman & Littlefield, forthcoming), ch. 2.

5. For the most recent contribution, See David W. Hall, ed., *The Practice of Confessional Subscription* (Lanham, Md.: University Press of America, 1997).

6. On colonial Presbyterian developments, See Leonard J. Trinterud, *The Forming of an American Tradition: A Re-examination of Colonial Presbyterianism* (Philadelphia: Westminster Press, 1949); Milton J. Coalter, Jr., *Gilbert Tennent, Son of Thunder: A Case Study of Continental Pietism's Impact on the First Great Awakening in the Middle Colonies* (Westport, Conn.: Greenwood Press, 1986); and Elizabeth I. Nybakken, 'New Light on the Old Side: Irish Influences on Colonial Presbyterianism,' *Journal of American History* 66 (1981–1982) 813-32.

7. See Harry S. Stout, *The Divine Dramatist: George Whitefield and the Rise of Modern Evangelicalism* (Grand Rapids: Eerdmans, 1991); and Frank Lambert, *'Pedlar in Divinity': George Whitefield and the Transatlantic Revivals* (Princeton: Princeton University Press, 1994).

8. On the Old School-New School split, See George M. Marsden, *The Evangelical Mind and the New School Presbyterian Experience: A Case Study of Thought and Theology in Nineteenth-Century America* (New Haven: Yale University Press, 1970); and Ernest Trice Thompson, *Presbyterians in the South*, vol. 1 (Richmond: John Knox Press, 1961).

9. Albert Barnes, *The Church and Slavery* (1857; New York: Negro Universities Press, 1969), 21.

10. Here it may be worth noting that James Bratt, perhaps the leading scholar on Abraham Kuyper, concludes that the great Dutch theologian and politician was, in American categories, New School in outlook. See James D. Bratt, 'Abraham Kuyper, J. Gresham Machen, and the Dynamics of Reformed Anti-Modernism,' *Journal of Presbyterian History* 75 (1997), 247-58.

11. James Henley Thornwell, 'The Relation of the Church to Slavery,' in *The Collected Writings of James Henley Thornwell*, vol. 4, ed., B. M. Palmer, (1875; Edinburgh: Banner of Truth Trust, 1974), 383-84.

12. See D. G. Hart, 'The Tie that Divides: Presbyterian Ecumenism, Fundamentalism, and the History of Twentieth-Century American Protestantism,' *Westminster Theological Journal* 60 (1998), 85-107.

13. On the 1920s, See Bradley J. Longfield, *The Presbyterian Controversy: Fundamentalists, Modernists, and Moderates* (New York: Oxford University Press, 1991); D. G. Hart, *Defending the Faith: J. Gresham Machen and the Crisis of Conservative Protestantism in Modern America* (Baltimore: Johns Hopkins University Press, 1994); and William J. Weston, *The Presbyterian Pluralism: Competition in a Protestant House* (Knoxville, Tenn.: University of Tennessee Press, 1997).

14. Barbara G. Wheeler, 'Henry Sloane Coffin and Charles R. Erdman and Our Search

for a Livable Piety,' *Princeton Seminary Bulletin* 21 new series (2000) 34.

15. Quoted in Ned Bernhard Stonehouse, *J. Gresham Machen: A Biographical Memoir* (Grand Rapids, Mich.: Eerdmans, 1954).

16. J. Gresham Machen, *Christianity and Liberalism* (New York: Macmillan, 1923), 179, 180.

17. George M. Marsden, 'The New School Heritage and Presbyterian Fundamentalism,' *Westminster Theological Journal* 32 (1970) 129-47.

18. On the harmful effects of this perspective for American Protestant history, See Douglas Jacobsen and William Vance Trollinger, Jr., 'Historiography of American Protestantism: The Two-Party Paradigm,' *Fides et Historia* 25.3 (1993) 4-15.

NON SOLA RATIONE

Three Presbyterians and the Postmodern Mind[1]

K. Scott Oliphint

My task is to attempt to show the abiding relevance and underlying unity of three influential and penetrating thinkers in the contemporary Reformed theological tradition. This may seem, at least initially, like a difficult task. One of the things that the Reformed tradition is particularly adept at (and this should be seen as one of its strengths) is delineating differences in emphases and nuances that can help clarify the truth and application of Scripture. Because of the caliber of these three men, clarifications and nuances in ideas and applications are abundant, and there should be no question that there are disagreements between them. There is enough written on their differences, however, that anyone interested could see those differences delineated for them.[2] The differences are important. They are so important that understanding them will profoundly impact one's approach to apologetics, as well as one's approach to, and delineation of, theology generally. In that sense, understanding the differences will help one to know how best to 'glorify God and enjoy Him forever' with respect to these disciplines.

As important as those differences are, however, there are significant areas of concern and critique that serve to bring these three together. These areas of agreement could easily be seen as grounded in the Reformed and Presbyterian tradition which each of them shared.[3] Their commitment to the theology that became prominent again after the Reformation, together with their commitment to the church as the vehicle through which God would bring people to Himself and thereby influence the culture, generated some penetrating and fascinating themes in each of these men, themes that run through their own respective works and careers. Given these themes, it might be helpful to emphasize the contribution that these three can make to the current cultural and intellectual climate. We will attempt to argue, therefore, that (at least part of) the emphases of these three can provide for the church today a helpful and needful path through the morass of confusion that most secular thinkers, as well as many biblical scholars and theologians of the day seem to savor.

In this study, I would like to highlight one central and crucial aspect of the contributions that conspired together to make Gordon Clark (1902–1985), Francis Schaeffer (1912–1984) and Cornelius Van Til (1895–1987) men of significant influence in the church of Jesus Christ, both during their lifetimes and during ours. This particular aspect, I will suggest, is the very one that alone is able adequately, and radically, to challenge the principles and perils of unbelieving thought, no matter what its forms. In that way, the contributions of these theologians are as relevant (if not more so) for the church now as they ever were.

The best way, it seems to me, to begin to emphasize the underlying and unified critique of these three presbyterians is to see that critique against the backdrop of current discussions. In that light, perhaps the most penetrating and relevant critique given by these three can be seen in the application of their analyses to what has come to be called postmodernism.[4] That may sound strange, given the fact that postmodernism was less influential during the heyday of their respective careers. As I will try to show, however, postmodernism is just modernism in costume, so that any critique of the latter will entail a critique of the former. The trenchant critique given by each man, therefore, penetrates as deeply into postmodern as into modern thought and life. Fundamentally, and radically, each man saw all unbelieving thought, which would include postmodernism, as a crisis of ultimate authority.

Postmodernism is likely the most explicit expression of that crisis to date and is therefore most susceptible to the radical critique that each of these men brought. Before presenting their critique, however, we should look at postmodernism itself.

Postmodern thought is notoriously difficult to categorize. That, of course, is part of its charm. A position not clearly categorized is even less clearly refuted. Its very allure, therefore, is the ability it seems to have to hide behind its own obfuscation, virtually impervious to criticism, since any one point can quickly and with apparent ease turn into its opposite. One who holds to postmodern thought pretends to hold to no ultimate commitments. Thus, any critique is thought to be of minimal interest to a postmodern mind. A critique of one postmodern hypothesis will provoke a postmodern's about face so that another, opposing, hypothesis can be immediately defended. Since the appearance of no real commitments is given, a true postmodern can easily defend one position, or its opposite, depending on context. And 'round and round' it goes. To the extent, then, that people love the dark and tenebrous rather than the light and luminous, postmodernism is one of the more lovable options currently available. But just what is this dark and lovable thing called postmodernism?

Fundamentally, it seems, it is the consistent outworking (or, at least, historical progression) of Kantian thought.[5] It is the natural implication, perhaps even the culmination, of a certain reading of Kant's monumental and influential work, *Critique of Pure Reason*. In that sense, postmodernism is what we might expect of post-Kantian thought. It is, to put it another way, Kantian creative anti-realism writ large.[6]

Creative anti-realism, in its most radical, ontological (i.e., with respect to being) form, is the view that whatever exists, exists by virtue of the powers and categories of our own minds. In its most radical, epistemological (i.e., with respect to knowledge) form, creative anti-realism holds that truth is a product, solely and completely, of one's own mental processes and activity. In either case, the source of being and truth is seen to be the human mind, reason itself.[7] We create (creative) the world through our own mental categories, and our creations cannot 'connect' (anti-realism) with the 'outside' world itself.

In thinking of truth and existence in this way, postmodernism has sought to emphasize the contribution of the individual (or a small group of individuals) to the process of philosophical (or theological, or linguistic, or social, or ...) debate. The postmodern would want to demolish any notion of 'the way things are' and substitute for it the more up-to-date idea of 'the way things are *to me*', or '*to us*'. To speak of *a* way things are is to speak in modernist language; it is to assume that the world 'out there' is in some way accessible to us, able to be understood and interpreted by us all.

But this cannot be the case for a postmodern. The world is beyond our grasp. The sheer disagreement over what the world is like is evidence aplenty that it cannot be rightly understood. This was the trap that ensnared modernism. Modernists assumed that our reason was able to grasp and understand the world with some kind of universal objectivity. For postmoderns, however, our reason provides little help for us when it is the outside world that we want to know. In this way, postmodernism has been seen (wrongly, it seems to me) as rejecting the autonomy of reason.

Along with the rejection of reason's autonomy, a further, perhaps central, tenet of postmodernism is a rejection of (what some have called) classical foundationalism. Classical foundationalism is a theory of the *structure* of knowledge. On a foundationalist model, it was thought that beliefs could be categorized in one of two ways, and that such categorizations would allow us to understand the world, and all of its parts, as fundamentally and universally reason*able*. Not only so, but this kind of reasonable world is governed and maintained by the laws and dictates of reason itself. Thus, classical foundationalism was a way of seeing, and thus of knowing, the world. In a foundationalist structure, our connection with the world was expressed either by the way in which the world 'presented' itself to us, which would create in us basic beliefs about the things presented, or by the way in which we formed beliefs by gathering, analyzing and synthesizing other facts, *based on those basic beliefs*.

But this, so we're told by postmoderns, gave to reason the ability to understand and know the world from the outside in. In other words, in a foundationalist scheme of the world, we simply responded to what the world had to offer, surrendering to its imposition, forming beliefs and justifying them on the basis, and in the context of, the way things are 'out there'. This scenario gave to reason a kind of universal, and universalizing, quality (at least in theory). All that was needed for us to know the world, and to see in it universal laws, criteria and regulations, was the proper and persistent use of our reasoning faculty.

In a post-Kantian world, however, reason is thought to be much more limited in its use. For post-Kantians, the world is neither understood nor coherent until and unless we bring our own mental categories to bear on it, which, of course, we must do. This means that, while there may be a world 'out there,' it is both unknown and unknowable. The fact that it *is* 'out there' makes its existence necessary as a pre-condition of what we know, but also, by definition (since it is 'out there'), inaccessible to the mind. Reason cannot take us from its own inner categories to the outside world of (initial) chaos.

Thus, whatever we claim to know, we know only because of the creatively constructive activity of our minds. This is not to say that the creative activity of the mind is all that there is. There is, and must be, according to Kant, more. But the 'more' that is there is a noumenal 'more' and thus, while necessary (at least for 'practical reason'), is nevertheless separated from the activity of the mind; it is, in every important way, beyond us.

Kant saw his philosophy as an epistemological Copernican revolution in which knowledge was no longer a response to an external world. Instead the world that we know revolved around the categories and capacities of our minds. Whereas the external world occupied a central place in discussions of knowledge prior to Kant, after Kant, the mind, though thought to be far more limited than before, became, nevertheless, the center of the epistemological universe. The Kantian revolution had begun.

This Kantian revolution has been able after him, like a child at Halloween, to don divers costumes as it moves from historical house to historical house and to trick away the tastiest treats of various disciplines, rendering them empty in the end. In its more current, postmodern, costume, it has given rise to all kinds of stimulating and shocking statements (which is another part of postmodernism's current appeal) statements like, 'there is nothing outside the text', (Derrida) or, 'truth is whatever our peers will let us get away with saying' (Rorty). Part of the problem with these statements, as we noted above, is that they are inherently (intentionally?) unclear and opaque. They seem either to be saying nothing of any real interest, or something so shocking that it is difficult to take them seriously.[8]

Perhaps we can take Rorty's statement as a case in point. Does Rorty really mean to say that truth is determined by our peer group? On one read, probably not. On one read, what Rorty is really saying with respect to epistemology is close to what Thomas Kuhn said with respect to science.[9] He is simply attempting to say that our theories of knowledge (or of anything else) are in fact justified, or not, within our respective groups. So, no matter how loudly I want to proclaim my theory, if my group doesn't, in the end, find the argument convincing, then it remains my own theory and not something acceptable.

If that is all that Rorty is saying, then his contribution to postmodernism is, for all intents and purposes, jejune and vapid. One would be hard-pressed to find any theory or argument – one, that is, that has been, at some point in time, accepted – that has not been argued in the context of its peers. As a matter of fact, if one found an accepted argument that had not been argued in the context of its peers, it simply would not be, by definition, an *accepted* argument. If that is all Rorty, and by extension postmodernism, wishes to say, then the real conundrum might be found in an attempt to justify the ink spilt over such a view.

There is likely more to it than that, however. It is more plausible to suppose that what postmoderns wish to say is something more radical than the obvious. It is likely that what they, or at least Rorty and those like him, wish to say is something a bit more Kantian, more Copernican, something more cosmically neoteric than the above. Perhaps Rorty wants us to think that the belief or position justified (or not) by our peers is, as far as we can tell, all that there is of the matter at hand. There is not, or at least we cannot access, anything other than the justified (or not) belief-cum-peers. The truth of the matter, in this case, would reside, not in anything external to us – a real world, for example – but in the group itself.

Now this *is* a radical claim and if it is true it might pose real problems for Christianity.[10] If the truth of the matter depends on us and if that is all there is to the truth of the matter, then my belief that Christianity is objectively true can itself only be true if my peers agree, or let me get away with saying it. But then my belief of the objective truth of Christianity is only true because of my peers. Thus, the objective truth of the matter is never really known, knowable or accessible. No wonder then that it is common in these postmodern days to hear that postmodernism has called 'such and such' Christian belief into question.

We should see postmodernism's critique, however, in its proper context. Just what is it, we could ask, that makes us think that there really *is* a critique, given the postmodern position? Alvin Plantinga's response to such a question bears repeating here:

But you don't automatically produce a defeater for Christian belief just by standing on your roof and proclaiming (even loudly and slowly), 'God is dead!' (Not even if you add: 'And everybody I know says so too.') Nor can you call Christian belief (or anything else) into question just by declaring, 'I hereby call *that* into question!' You can't destroy a way of thinking just by announcing, 'I hereby destroy that way of thinking!' This will not do the job, not even if it is embodied in writing of coruscating wit and style, and not even if you adopt a superior air and elegant gestures while intoning it. Something further is required.[11]

At least part of the 'further' that is required is some kind of argument that truth is what the postmoderns want to say it is, or that no correspondence with the outside world is needed for the justification of a given belief. But postmoderns are reluctant to give such an argument, or at least to *say* that they are. To give such an argument is to fall again into the terrible trap of Enlightenment thought wherein reason is the arbiter of truth. To give such an argument, they will tell us, is to violate the very principle that they are seeking to establish. So, the obfuscation continues. How, then, does one address the postmodern situation?

Perhaps the best way to address the problem is the way that Clark, Schaeffer and Van Til taught us to address every other form of unbelief. Perhaps it is best to try to get at the underlying presuppositions of such a position, to see if the position itself is standing on solid ground, or if (as is the case with all unbelieving thought) it is sinking in its own quicksand.

As we look more closely at postmodernism, we should see that *the* problem surrounding it, and the problem that has thus filtered down to the thinking of our western culture, is, as we said above, the problem of authority. If there is a consensus in postmodern thought (and that is still a live question), it would likely center around postmodernism's rejection of traditional notions of anything, but preeminently traditional notions of authority.

One who considers himself to be centrally postmodern in his thinking will no doubt deride any and every appeal to an authoritative system or source of thinking and living.[12] Postmoderns reject all attempts at systematizing, whether in philosophy, theology or any other discipline (except, of course, their systematized principles that are designed to reject systematizing). To systematize is to artificially impose something on a text or a context that is, in fact, not there. Postmoderns would like to convince us that any appeal to a unifying, systematizing 'whole' has been shown to be an abysmal failure in the past, that our best approach as we face the future is to have the courage to reject this approach now.[13]

But just what *is* postmodernism's ground for its claims? Why should we seriously entertain notions that call into question so much of what we need to take for granted for life and thought?[14] To what can the postmodernist point that should give us pause to consider this position?

One thing to which every postmodern will point is, as was said, the failure of the modern. Because modernism sought to bring all truth and life under the big umbrella of autonomous reason, and because it has failed in its task, we should be willing, if not eager, to consider an alternate, opposing viewpoint. This analysis has some real appeal. It is certainly true that modernism, with its insistence on the near godlike capabilities of reason to deliver us from evil, has done little to help us intellectually and, practically speaking, seems to have left almost unspeakable evil in its wake. The quest for universalizing and systematizing rationality has ended, they tell us, in oppression and destruction. Surely, that fact alone would cause us to cry out for something else.

The (initial) appeal of this kind of analysis is likely the best, and perhaps the *only*, explanation for any influence that postmodernism has had in our time. As we're weary of things well-worn we're only too willing to discard them, like an old pair of shoes, and to put our money on what is currently, in culture and in intellectual life, fashionable. To do so may (and historically speaking *will*) itself end in failure, but it will at least keep us, for the moment, well, fashionable. We'll remain on the 'cutting edge' and we'll maintain an air of relevance that modernism cannot give. In remaining fashionable (and this is particularly true in academic circles) we can keep up with the (postmodern) Joneses, speaking to and with them, putting our names in all the right circles. Our intellectual and academic careers will follow the avant-garde.

It should be noted, however, that, in spite of this appeal, such an analysis is not new in the history of the west, or of western thought (and if it's not new, one wonders why it would appeal to a postmodern). Thales' water gave way to Anaximander's *apeiron*, which gave way to Anaximenes' (hot?) air. Heraclitus' becoming gave way to Parmenides' being. Descartes' clear and distinct ideas gave way to Hume's clear and distinct skepticism. Kant's abstract universal gave way to Hegel's concrete universal. And on the story goes.

The history of western thought would hardly be intelligible without the pattern of the failure of one philosophy, then that philosophy being discarded and replaced by another, which then itself fails only to be replaced by yet another. So, the appeal of postmodernism is, in one important sense, just more of the same. But it is not just the pattern and response that is the same. Unfortunately, for postmodernism and those who love it, its foundation and ground are the same as modernism's. For postmodernism is, in the final analysis, the same as modernism.

Gary Gutting, who is himself somewhat sympathetic with Rorty's postmodern project, detects, in spite of that sympathy, the underlying problem with it. He notes:

> Rorty's pragmatism is certainly critical of classical formulations of the Enlightenment project. But, as I will show, properly clarified and modified, it renews rather than rejects the fundamental Enlightenment idea of human autonomy through reason.[15]

In the end, postmodernism is yet another attempt (doomed to failure like the rest of unbelieving thought) to make the mind and practice of human beings the final arbiter and judge of truth and life. The problem – as it was in the beginning, is now and ever shall be (until the end of history, at least) – is that the Kantian Copernican revolution was no radical revolution at all; it was only window dressing.

The attempt to reject reason's hegemony and to substitute for it another, more enlightened mode of inquiry and truth, is fundamentally just another attempt, maybe with different terminology or methodology, to assert reason's hegemony after all. That, we should notice, is the problem. And the problem is not simply a problem of authority in the abstract, it is a deeper problem. It is the problem of attempting to base our thought and lives on our own minds, an attempt that leads to futility. Furthermore, it is not simply that we have encountered this problem after Kant; this problem can be detected, without much effort, in virtually *all* of western thought and culture. The crux or essence of a crisis or problem of authority, put simply, is the attempt to apply the principle of *homo mensura* – 'man as the measure' of all things.

Now one Latin phrase certainly deserves another in response. The only proper response to *homo mensura* is the emphasis and methodology that Clark, Schaeffer and Van Til sought to appropriate throughout their respective ministries – *non sola ratione* – not reason alone. This may seem to be an obvious and not so significant insight for a Christian. What is obvious, however, is the way in which this tenet has been virtually ignored in the history of the church.

It seems to me that the Presbyterian triad – Clark, Schaeffer and Van Til – stand together on this most crucial point. Unless and until we have a Word from God, *the* Word *of* God, we simply cannot make sense of the world around us or the 'world' within us, not to mention the more important truth of how we can please God. We have no means by which to explain why we trust that the world in which we live, move and exist is, in fact, something that is known by us.

It is not, of course, that (at least in the typical case) we don't believe the world to be a certain way. People do, in fact, trust that the house that they leave each day will, under normal circumstances, be there when they return, and will be in roughly the same shape as when they left. The living room will not have changed to the bathroom, or to a warehouse, or to a unicorn while they were away. That fact, and countless others that we need for living each day, is something on which we do and must rely. The problem, however, is that, apart from God's revelation to us, we have no *reason* why we *ought to* or *can* trust such facts. Schaeffer was insistent on this point:

> When people refuse God's answer, they are living against the revelation of the universe and against the revelation of themselves. They are denying the revelation of God in *who* they themselves are. I am not saying that non-Christians do not live in the light of real existence. I am saying that they do not have any answer for living in it. I am not saying that they do not have moral motions, but they have no basis for them. I am not saying that the person with a non-Christian system (even a radical system like Buddhism or Hinduism or the modern Western thinking of chance) does not know that the object exists – the problem is that they have no system to explain the subject-object correlation. As a matter of fact, this is their damnation, this is their tension, that they have to live in the light of their existence, the light of reality – the total reality in all these areas – and they do live there, and yet they

have no sufficient explanation for any of these areas. So, the wiser they are, the more honest they are, the more they feel that tension and that is their present damnation.[16]

Perhaps postmodernism is, in Schaeffer's sense, 'wiser' and 'more honest' with respect to the world. Perhaps its denial of any objectivity should be applauded for its honest look at the state of things. But, if so, it should also be exposed for what it, in fact, is. It is the natural conclusion to a long history of relying on the limited and errant faculty of reason alone as the ground on which we stand in order to make sense of the world. Reason, on this view, is given the right to ultimate authority.

Christians cannot, in this sense, give ground to the postmodern agenda. One of our more fundamental beliefs as Christians is that we, happily and boldly (because of God's grace), live as a people under authority. Not only so, but as Christians we confess that the authority under which we live is a *universal* authority. It is God's authority and as such it applies to everything that is.

God's authority is not something that has been kept secret. It has been revealed to us by God. Whereas, in past times and in different ways, God revealed Himself and His will through various means, in these last days He has spoken through His Son (Heb. 1:1f.). That revelation, which is preeminently the Scriptures but includes also the revelation through creation, because it is *God's* revelation, carries with it all the authority of God Himself. Thus, Christians are, as God's willing servants (by grace), preeminently 'people of the book.' That book is the Bible; it is God's authoritative Word to His people.[17]

The truth of Scripture, then, is at least a part, and a significant part, of the answer to the problems posed by postmodernism. That should not surprise us, since that truth is the answer to the problems posed in any generation. It is the Reformed and Presbyterian view of Scripture, of God's revelation, as that view is explained, for example, in the *Westminster Confession of Faith*, Chapter I, that forms the basis for a sound, biblical apologetic.

When people challenge us to 'give a reason for the hope that is within us' (1 Peter 3:15), we should immediately realize that the 'reason' given comes, not ultimately from ourselves, but from God's own revelation. It is revelation *itself* that provides a response to the challenges brought against Christianity. Clark, Schaeffer and Van Til all understood this, and so were able to provide answers to the challenges of postmodernism, and to whatever else will soon take its place.

Because postmodernism is, at its roots, modernism in costume, it falls prey to the very rationalism that it seeks to negate. Note Schaeffer on rationalism:

> ...a rationalist is a person who thinks man and his reason can come to final answers without information from any other source. No one stresses more than I that people have no final answers in regard to truth, morals, or epistemology without God's revelation in the Bible. This is true in philosophy, science and theology. Rationalism can take a secular or theological form. In both, the rationalist thinks that on the basis of man's reason, plus what he can see about him, final answers are possible. My books stress that man cannot generate final answers from himself.[18]

Whether an individual or a group of individuals, we simply are not able to create the truth. The issue, then, is the authority of God's revelation and its application to the struggles and questions that come to human beings who live in God's world, all the while attempting to refuse His revelation. That refusal, however, is culpable. In any form, modern or postmodern, unbelief is rightly understood as a denial of God's revelation. It is not as though people who refuse God's answer are honestly seeking Him, or wandering about with no axe to grind.[19]

In this way Schaeffer, Clark and Van Til, were self-consciously applying their own Presbyterian and Reformed heritage to the cultural, philosophical and theological issues of the day, or of any day for that matter. They were, all three, also unified in their rejection of the liberalism, modernism and neo-orthodoxy that had stolen the Reformed gospel from so many of the churches. In that rejection, they together sought to demonstrate, in thought and in life, that no other answer could be found than that given by Reformed theology, as expressed in its creeds (particularly, for them, the Westminster Standards).

To use one illustration of this, Schaeffer's emphasis, in so many of his books, on the erroneous dichotomy of the so-called 'upper story' and 'lower story' came from his own discussion with Karl Barth, and his conviction, after that discussion, that Barth had nothing more to offer the modern world than a kind of spiritualized, existential secularism.[20] All that Barthianism could offer was a 'pre-postmodern' postmodernism. The world according to Barth, if it was even God's creation, simply did not matter. What did matter for Barth was the revelation-event. But that event, no matter how loudly Barth would protest to the contrary, could only be grounded in a person's own reason.

So also for Clark. In his analysis of Kenneth Hamilton's, *Words and the WORD*, Clark's description of Hamilton's notion of language could be pulled from virtually any postmodern text.

For example, Hamilton, expounding Cassirer, says;

> Intelligence ... is not man's decisive characteristic. What really distinguishes him from other animals is his ability to construct symbols ... He does not first understand the world, and then learn how to put his knowledge into words. Rather his invention of verbal symbols provides the possibility of his having knowledge...

Clark responds:

> This is patently backwards. It takes intelligence to construct symbols, and in particular before constructing the symbol the man must have something in mind to symbolize. A primitive man would never invent the sound or vocal symbol *cat*, unless he had first seen a little tail and heard its other end say meow. Does anyone believe that he said to himself, '*Cat* is such a nice sound, I shall use it to symbolize whatever I see tomorrow at noon'?[21]

Clark then goes on to argue that unless one presupposes the truth of God's revelation in Scripture, one is destined for this kind of (postmodern) absurdity. In fact, as Clark argues throughout his career, presupposing the truth of God's revelation in Scripture is the *only* position that escapes absurdity. To assume the sufficiency of reason alone in such matters, is intellectual suicide.[22]

Van Til as well dedicated his career to making this same point. For him, there were really only two principial options when it came to the issue of authority. Either one presupposes the Christian position as it is given to us infallibly in God's revelation, or one presupposes oneself as ultimate, which results in a crisis of the deepest magnitude. If one presupposes oneself, then one rejects the revelation of God and tries in vain to make sense of the world 'out there'. With respect to a theory of knowledge (epistemology), Van Til put it this way:

When therefore we examine the various epistemological views with regard to their 'objectivity,' we are interested most of all in knowing whether or not these views have sought the knowledge of an object by placing it into its right relation with the self-conscious God. The other questions are interesting enough in themselves but are comparatively speaking not of great importance. Even if one were not anxious about the truth of the matter, it ought still to be plain to him that there can be no more fundamental question in epistemology than the question whether or not facts can be known without reference to God. ... Suppose then the existence of God. Then it would be a fact that every fact would be known truly only with reference to him. If then one did not place a fact into relation with God, he would be in error about the fact under investigation. Or suppose that one would just begin his investigations as a scientist, without even asking whether or not it is necessary to make reference to such a God in his investigations, such a one would be in constant and in fundamental ignorance all the while. And this ignorance would be culpable ignorance, since it is God who gives him life and all good things. It ought to be obvious then that one should settle for himself this most fundamental of all epistemological questions, whether or not God exists. Christ says that as the Son of God, he will come to judge and condemn all those who have not come to the Father by him.[23]

The point that Van Til is making here is, again, the same that Clark and Schaeffer attempted to make – unless one presupposes the revelation of God as itself the infallible ground on which we stand, for knowing and living, then one stands not only in error with respect to the world and its facts, but one stands condemned before the God whose revelation is clearly seen and understood in that world (Rom. 1:20).

So, the so-called 'Reformation *solas*' – *Sola Scriptura, Sola Fide, Sola Gratia, Solo Christo, Soli Deo Gloria* – rightly leave one 'sola' out of the equation that was predominant in all of western philosophy, as well as much of church history. It was a 'sola' that had plagued the church for centuries, a 'sola' that was based on a fundamental misunderstanding of the fall and its consequences, a 'sola' that was grounded, not only in the history of western thought, but in much of Christian apologetics as well. It was *sola ratione*; a cry that thankfully fell on deaf ears during the Reformation.

Unfortunately, ears have not remained deaf to this cry. In spite of its theological fallacy and its philosophical failure, *sola ratione* has remained as strong in the present postmodern climate as it has ever been. Not only in philosophy, but in theology as well, some still want to set forth the postmodern agenda as in some way *more* enlightened than the modernist's 'Enlightenment' agenda. That, of course, is erroneous thinking. It is the kind of erroneous thinking to which our triad devoted themselves to responding. The answer to that kind of fallacy of thinking and failure of nerve – *non sola ratione* – can be found in the works of these three Presbyterian apologists, the reading of which reaps rich rewards – *tolle, lege, tolle, lege*.[24]

NOTES

1. I count it a privilege to contribute to this volume for my teacher, colleague and friend Clair Davis. Clair has repeatedly said that he'll wait to retire before he tells me what he *really* thinks of Van Til's thought. I'm not sure what he'll say about that, but, whatever he says, the emphasis of this chapter remains true to Clair's own emphasis in his life and teaching – *non sola ratione*.

2. See, for example, William Edgar, 'Two Christian Warriors: Cornelius Van Til and Francis A. Schaeffer Compared,' *Westminster Theological Seminary* 57, no. 1 (1995)., John M. Frame, *The Doctrine of the Knowledge of God* (New Jersey: Presbyterian and Reformed Publishing Co., 1987)., and Herman Hoeksema, *The Clark-Van Til Controversy* (The Trinity Foundation, 1995), for an analysis of differences between these three.

3. Gordon Clark was a minister in the Orthodox Presbyterian Church (1944–48), the United Presbyterian Church of North America (1948–1965) and the Reformed Presbyterian Church of North America, General Synod (1965) until his death. Frances Schaeffer was reputedly the first minister ordained in the Bible Presbyterian Church and later began a presbyterian denomination in Europe. Cornelius Van Til served as a minister in the Christian Reformed Church early in his life and was a minister in the Orthodox Presbyterian Church from 1936 until his death.

4. Given that the literature on postmodernism is so vast, and confusing, it is probably best to consult Victor E. Taylor and Charles E. Winquist, eds., *Encycolpedia of Postmodernism* (New York: Routledge, 2001), for further information and resources. Most would hold that postmodernism came to its own somewhere between the late 70s and the late 80s.

5. Whether or not it is the thought of Kant *himself* is a question we need not deal with here. It is, without question, an implication of certain aspects of Kantianism.

6. For a nice discussion of creative anti-realism, see Alvin Plantinga, 'On Christian Scholarship,' in *The Challenge and Promise of a Catholic University*, ed. Theodore Hesburgh (Notre Dame and London: University of Notre Dame Press, 1994).

7. By 'reason' I mean something like the sum of intellective processes and powers. So, it would include the process of reasoning as well as some notion of reason as a faculty or tool. It should *not*, however, be seen as something religiously neutral.

8. For many who have tried to read philosophy, this may be the perception of the entire discipline. Some might think that it continually vacillates between irrelevance and vacuity. Postmodernism can be entertaining, however, a trait not common to much of philosophy and one that is appealing to our current cultural climate. For example, I remember taking a class in which the assigned text was Stanley Fish's,

Is There A Text In This Class? You have to at least appreciate the humor of it.

9. See Thomas S. Kuhn, *The Structure of Scientific Revolutions* (Chicago: University of Chicago Press, 1970).

10. But if it is true, then it is true if and only if our peers will let us get away with saying it. But if our Christian peers would let us get away with saying it, then there would be no, or little, sense in which they were Christian at all. So, if it is true, then it still poses no threat to Christianity *per se*. It does, however, pose a threat to the claims of Christianity that truth includes, first of all, a Person Who *is* Truth itself, and then, on a created level, it includes some kind of correspondence between what is known or believed and the way the world is.

11. Alvin Plantinga, *Warranted Christian Belief* (New York, etc.: Oxford University Press, 2000), 425-26.

12. This very rejection depends on a postmodern consensus of authority, and in that way it is self-defeating.

13. Speaking of courage, it is interesting to note Plantinga's suggestion that postmodernism is, in the end, a failure of nerve. See Plantinga, *Warranted Christian Belief*, 436-37.

14. In this context, postmodernism's rejection of all foundationalism is, like much of philosophy, irrational. No matter how loudly they protest against it, they still must rely on basic beliefs even to make their arguments. If they simply want to reject the lack of *foundation* for foundationalism, that is another, and nobler, project.

15. Gary Gutting, *Pragmatic Liberalism and the Critique of Modernity* (Cambridge: Cambridge University Press, 1999), 8.

16. Francis A. Schaeffer, *A Christian View of Philosophy and Culture*, vol. 1, *The Complete Works of Francis A Schaeffer: A Christian Worldview* (Westchester, Illinois: Crossway Books, 1982), 180.

17. As Calvin reminds us, 'the book' is like a pair of spectacles through which we can see everything else, including natural revelation, aright.

18. Ibid., 184.

19. Ibid., 180.

20. In one interview with Barth, Schaeffer asked him the question, 'Did God create the world?' Barth's answer was, 'God created the world in the first century AD' Schaeffer then asked him, 'This world?,' to which Barth responded, 'This world does not matter.' See Edith Schaeffer, *The Tapestry* (Waco, Texas: Word Books, 1981), 314.

21. Gordon Haddon Clark, *God's Hammer: The Bible and Its Critics* (Jefferson, Maryland: The Trinity Foundation, 1982), 158.

22. See, for example, Gordon Haddon Clark, *Religion, Reason, and Revelation* (Philadelphia,: Presbyterian and Reformed Publishing Company, 1961). and Ronald H. Nash, ed., *The Philosophy of Gordon H. Clark* (Philadelphia, Pennsylvania: Presbyterian and Reformed Publishing Company, 1968).

23. Cornelius Van Til, *A Survey of Christian Epistemology*, vol. II, *In Defense of the Faith* (Phillipsburg, New Jersey: Presbyterian and Reformed Publishing Company, 1969), 4.

24. 'Take and read, take and read.' This was the instruction from a child that changed Augustine's entire outlook as he searched and searched for the truth. He found that truth, not in Platonism or Manicheaism, but in the Bible alone.

C. Reformed and Presbyterian Biblical Hermeneutics

THE MILLENNIAL STUDY BIBLE OF HEINRICH HORCH (1652-1729)

A Case Study in Early Modern Reformed Hermeneutics

Douglas H. Shantz

Introduction

Heinrich Horch (1652-1729), theologian and pastor in the German Reformed Church, has been described as 'without doubt one of the most interesting figures of the Pietist movement in Hessen.'[1] Called in 1690 to the Reformed Academy in Herborn as Professor of theology, Horch gained a reputation as a noteworthy champion of Reformed teaching. Horch authorized some sixty-three works in his lifetime. By far 'the most well known and influential' of these was his *Mystische und Profetische Bibel (The Mystical and Prophetical Bible)*, published in Marburg in 1712.[2] Horch's *Mystical and Prophetical Bible* represents one of the most ambitious hermeneutical achievements of Hessen Pietism. Known as the 'Marburg Bible',[3] it became the model and forerunner of the better known multi-volume 'Berleburg Bible', published between 1726 and 1742.[4] In its time, Horch's *Marburg Bible* won recognition among Reformed Pietist preachers such as Conrad Mel and Friedrich Adolf Lampe. Lampe praised Horch's work, noting that the *Marburg Bible* 'has given much encouragement in the discovery of the secret and prophetical meaning of the most difficult Biblical books.' Lampe qualified his praise, however, lamenting that 'so many expressions and observations had been introduced here and there which concede too much to present day separatist ideas, for which reason one hesitates to recommend this otherwise not unprofitable work to the unlearned.'[5]

Since his death, right up to the present time, Horch has suffered from relative scholarly neglect even in comparison with other radical Pietist figures such as Gottfried Arnold and Johann Heinrich Reitz. Horch's eighteenth century biographer, Carl Haas, expressed amazement that this extraordinary man, of such wide learning, prolific writing, and devotion to Christian unity, should be so ignored by church and literary historians.[6] Rudolf Mohr has identified two pressing tasks facing Horch researchers: the need to shed light on the sources and background to Horch's *Mystische und Profetische Bible*, and the need for an historical comparison of the hermeneutic of Reformed theologian Campegius Vitringa with that of Horch. Both Horch and Vitringa, for example, set the *Psalms* in close relation to the book of *Revelation*, and both described the latter as a 'completely mystical and prophetical book.'[7] The present study undertakes the first of Mohr's tasks by pursuing a twofold goal: to situate Horch's Pietist-Philadelphian hermeneutic within the context of medieval and early modern Biblical commentary, and, secondly, to locate Horch within the late 17th– early 18th century social context of German Hessen.

The study shows that Horch's *Marburg Bible* understood John's *Revelation* as a prophetic portrayal of the principle events in the history of the church and the world. Horch's apocalyptic reading strategy found the *Song of Solomon* to be in 'delightful harmony' with the book of *Revelation*. This hermeneutic was not original with Horch, but had debts to the medieval and Reformation heirs of Joachim of Fiore and Gregorian monastic commentators. This tradition of interpretation stood ready and available to Horch as a kind of hermeneutical tool, one aptly suited to his own apocalyptic temperament, worldview and times. Horch's comments in the *Marburg Bible* reflect a time of crisis, specifically the 'crisis of the body' that was widespread among Protestant radicals in late 17th century Germany. His was a hermeneutic of psychological and historical asceticism aimed at Protestant renewal. Primary source materials for the study are the *Mystische und Profetische Bibel*, and the near contemporary biography of Horch by Carl Haas.[8]

Johann Heinrich Horch: Reformed Theologian and Radical Pietist

Johann Heinrich Horch was born to Reformed parents on December 12, 1652, in the small community of Eschwege, Hessen, where his father served as a Court baker and Councillor to a Reformed Count. At age eighteen, thanks to a stipend from church Superintendent Johannes Hütterodt, Horch began studies in philosophy and mathematics at the Philipps-University in Marburg.[9] During this time he was attracted to Pietism as preached by Theodor Undereyck, father of Reformed Pietism.[10] 'The desire for a rebirth of the church was the ideal which had powerfully moved [Horch], and for which he felt himself called to work in word and deed.'[11] In 1671 when Undereyck was called to Martin's Church in Bremen, Horch and 'many other young men from Hessen' followed him to Bremen, Horch to pursue studies in theology.[12] The unexpected death of his father on April 18th, 1672 pained Horch deeply and brought on a kind of hypochondria that would continue to affect Horch in later life.[13] In that same year Horch returned to Marburg to study medicine and in 1674 defended a dissertation in this field. Horch served for a time as an instructor in Cartesian Philosophy at Marburg. From 1679-1681 Horch acted as tutor to the son of the Baron of Somnitz, accompanying the young noble to Danzig as *Informator* and then to the Universities of Frankfurt/Oder and Leiden. In 1681 Horch married Anna Katharina Eckhard of Wetter in Hessen.

Between 1683 and 1690 Horch served in Reformed pastorates in Heidelberg, Kreuznach and Frankfurt am Main. In November 1686 he was awarded the Doctor of Theology degree by the Reformed Heidelberg University, defending a dissertation investigating 'the dimensions of divine grace.'[14] In 1690 Horch was appointed professor of theology at the Reformed Seminary in Herborn. Here he won his reputation as a distinguished advocate of Reformed theology.

However, contacts with the separatist Pietists Balthasar Christoph Klopfer and Johann Heinrich Reitz sowed doubts in Horch's mind on the Reformed practices of infant baptism and the Lord's Supper. Klopfer, a Pietist from Kassel 'without extensive education but great conviction', persuaded Horch that Reformed Christians indeed had the truth, 'but only on paper, not in their hearts and lives'. Klopfer called on true Christians to stay away from the churches and their sacraments.[15] Horch became an advocate of baptism by total immersion of infants, and argued that celebration of the Lord's Table should also include the love feast.[16] Horch's conflicts with the seminary faculty and Reformed clergy resulted in a series of public debates. Horch was suspended in November 1697, and formally removed from office by a letter from Prince Heinrich of Nassau-Dillenburg dated February 15, 1698. Despite repeated efforts, he did not win reinstatement. Horch left the city of Herborn on March 28, 1698, accompanied by 'a great crowd of students and residents … who with many tears saw him to the city gate.'[17] Horch made his way to Offenbach, the residence city of the tolerant Reformed Count Johann Philipp of Ysenburg-Büdingen and his radical chiliastic court preacher, Conrad Bröske.[18]

In 1698 Horch began what Max Goebel called 'a restless and fanatical life, lasting ten years, in which he sought to escape the deep pain gnawing at his inner being over the willfully surrendered circle of influence' that he had left behind in Herborn.[19] Horch renounced his doctor title, and grew his beard long after the fashion of the Anabaptists.[20] In this new phase of Horch's career, his Reformed identity was syncretized with the outlook of German Philadelphianism. Influenced by the English author Jane Leade, the Philadelphian movement was inspired by a post-millennial eschatology that worked for the soon dawning of a new church age marked by ecumenical peace and unity among Christians.

In 1699 Horch returned to his home town of Eschwege where he fell in with other radical Pietists and Philadelphians. In July of 1699 Horch met Samuel König, the chiliastic preacher from Bern, Switzerland. Together they organized separatist Philadelphian communities in Herborn and Niederhessen, including the region around Eschwege.[21] Horch organized Bible studies in homes in the region. In 1699 Horch offered a description of these gatherings:

> We gather once or twice a day in a private house, numbering about two hundred people. The discussion has to do solely and exclusively with the holy Scriptures. Although, like the first Christians who in their assemblies read aloud as well from other spiritual writings and letters, we do not entirely reject [non-Scriptural writings] so long as the hearers can be edified by them … to the praise of God and the strengthening of their hope in the coming kingdom of Jesus Christ. Thus we hold that these [other writings] are in no way to be

confused with but rather carefully distinguished from the books of holy Scripture, the only perfect guide for our faith and life, and therefore can be read properly [only] before or after prayer and worship. But I do not wish to reject or condemn entirely catechetical instruction, since my concern is merely to show how the Word of God and that of men can properly be distinguished, as in the early church the catechism students were separated from believers and catechism instruction distinguished from the worship of God in public assemblies and the gathering of believers.... In the short period of about five months [I] was able in the Bible classes to discuss a part of the Old Testament and almost the whole New Testament, although the letters to the Romans, Galatians and the Revelation of John were explained in quite a bit of detail.[22]

Soon the sitting rooms were too small and the gatherings were moved to the city gate where Horch preached and taught daily.[23]

Repeated instances of unbridled prophetic enthusiasm and conflicts with authorities resulted in Horch's arrest and imprisonment for nine months in the Marburg castle in 1699-1700. In the course of his imprisonment, Horch's ideas concerning the approaching kingdom became ever more concrete and corporeal. 'He expected a change to come about in his body, from the inside out, as the beginning of the "new man".' A friend visiting Horch in prison spoke of their conversation:

Horch shared with [his friend] in confidence: he had the feeling in his back that he was completely changed and transformed. Little by little it came about. To help the change along, he tore out his hair and his teeth.[24]

Earlier, Klopfer had told Horch of his oneness with Christ and of his immortality:

Where there is no sin, there death cannot reign.... For I feel no more sin in me, meaning I have died to sin and been made alive in Christ. Now Christ no longer dies, and so I also, since I have become Christ, I no longer die....[25]

These notions were an interpretation of 1 Corinthians 6:15, 17, 'your bodies are members of Christ; the one who joins himself to the Lord is one spirit with Him.' The examples of Klopfer and Horch demonstrate that in radical Pietist circles around the year

1700 the experience of imprisonment in a body had become a serious problem, demanding some kind of solution. 'Horch sought the answer in a God-inspired change in the body, resulting in bringing forth the new human being.'[26]

After six months in prison, Horch began to suffer under mental derangement, and made several suicide attempts.[27] Under these conditions he was released and sent to his home town of Eschwege on July 12, 1700. Upon his return to Eschwege Horch again became involved in leading Philadelphian conventicle gatherings, resulting in his eventual banishment from that part of Hessen. His travels took him to Holland and England, and for a time he considered emigration to Pennsylvania before abandoning the idea due to the opposition of his family.[28]

Despite his Philadelphian involvements during this time, it is clear that Horch never intended to forsake his Reformed roots. 'He did not wish to deviate a hair's breadth from the doctrine of the Reformers as expressed in the Heidelberg Catechism.'[29] Horch's dissatisfaction with the church of his day focussed upon the way of life, not the dogmas. His ideal was to re-establish worship according to the principles of a 'purified Protestantism', to restore it to 'the condition of the time of the apostles'.[30]

When Horch's attempt to return to his birthplace, Eschwege, was frustrated by his reputation and involvement in Philadelphian conventicles, Horch decided to settle in Kirchhain, Hessen, just outside of Marburg. Horch and his family lived in Kirchhain for the last two decades of his life, from 1708 to 1729, longer than in any other previous place of residence.[31] Zeller suggested several reasons as to why the Horch family chose to reside in Kirchhain. One was its proximity to Marburg University where Horch had spent several years as a student and teacher. For a short time in 1709 Horch may have offered lectures in the Philosophy faculty at the University.[32] Also, Marburg offered easy access to a printing press for publication of Horch's many writings. Another reason for settling here was that in this otherwise largely Lutheran region there was a Reformed church in Kirchhain where the Horch family could worship.[33] Furthermore, there is evidence of Pietist influence within the Reformed church in Kirchhain. Pastors included a possible relative of chiliast Johanna Eleonora Petersen and also Johann Christoph Mel, son of the influential Hessian Pietist Konrad Mel.[34] Finally, and most significantly, it appears that Horch's wife Anna Katharina, born Eckhard, had some family relations in Kirchhain. A town mayor was named Eckhardt.[35]

By 1708 in Kirchhain, Horch was apparently ready to settle down to a quieter, more even-tempered and withdrawn life. Horch became a member of the Reformed church community there.[36] Church records mention the confirmation of Horch's daughter Anna Katharina Horch in 1710, and of his youngest daughter Anna Christina Horch in 1718, and in 1721 the consecration of his son Philipp Burckhard Horch. On the 4th of January, 1727 Anna Christina was married to Johann Georg Kießelbach. Church records note that at the baptism of their first two grandchildren the grandparents Horch served as godparents.[37] Clearly in later life Horch had given up his earlier scruples about the practice of baptism in Reformed churches.[38]

The church *Totenbuch* records that Horch died in Kirchhain on August 5, 1729. The church book notes his burial on August 8th: 'On the 8th of August of 1729 Doctor of Theology Heinrich Horch born in Eschwege. Text: 2 Timothy 4:7, 8.' The passage reads, 'I have fought a good fight, I have finished the course, I have kept the faith; henceforth is reserved for me the crown of righteousness.'[39]

Horch's *Mystische und Profetische Bibel* (1712): Radical Reformed Pietist Hermeneutics

Horch worked on *The Mystical and Prophetical Bible* in the later years of his life, while living in Kirchhain. Horch was prolific during this time, publishing seventeen different titles between 1708 and 1721, all printed and published legally in Marburg and most at his own expense.[40] These writings consisted of numerous commentaries on Biblical books, and apologetic treatises opposing Spinozism and Islam, as well as works pleading for Protestant unity – 'brotherly love among all true believers within the Lutheran and Reformed churches regardless of the disputed questions that they have between them.'[41] In 1712, the same year Horch's *Marburg Bible* appeared, Horch published a two volume work written in a Philadelphian spirit and entitled, *Filadelfia, das ist, Bruderliebe unter den rechtschaffenen Gläubigen in denen sogenannten Lutherischen und Reformirten Gemeinen ungeachtet der Streitfragen, welche dieselben unter einander haben.* The first volume dealt with the Lord's Supper, the second with election and related questions. 'In Horch's irenic discussion of confessional doctrinal differences, it is noteworthy how the Reformed school tradition of this former theology professor comes again into consideration.'[42]

The Bible commentaries that Horch worked on while in Kirchhain served as important 'preliminary works' for his massive theological work on the stages of salvation history in the *Mystical and Prophetical Bible*. His typological-allegorical interpretation of the *Song of Solomon*, the OT poetical books and the book of *Revelation* indicated the main steps in salvation history and pointed to their near realization in his own time.[43] This outlook shaped the *Mystical and Prophetical Bible* of 1712. Horch received help with the Bible from Ludwig Christoph Schefer, Pietist Court Preacher and Church Inspector in Berleburg.[44]

Horch's *Marburg Bible* consisted of an edition of the Luther Bible along with a general foreword, introductions to all the Biblical books, and explanations of individual chapters and verses. The full title of the *Marburg Bible* should be noted: 'Mystical and Prophetical Bible, that is, the entire Holy Scripture of the Old and New Testament, newly and thoroughly Improved, including an Explanation of the Main Symbols and Prophecies, especially of the Song of Solomon and the Revelation of Jesus Christ, as well as of the Chief Teachings which in advance are Adapted to these last Days.'[45] As the title indicates, Horch's treatment of the Biblical message and Biblical history made *Song of Solomon* and *John's Revelation* the interpretive key to the whole Bible. We shall now examine principles of Horch's radical Pietist hermeneutic, investigating the *Marburg Bible's* general foreword to the reader, then the introduction and comments that accompanied the *Song of Solomon* and the *Book of Revelation*.

General Foreword to the Reader

Horch's purpose in publishing the work was to awaken in his 'Beloved Readers' a new desire to consider the word of God so that in dark times and in the last days it might provide light for the way and a spiritual sword for confronting temptations in the hour of trial.[46] Christ himself stated long ago that 'the hour of temptation would come upon all who live on the earth, and even the elect would be in extreme danger of being led astray.'[47] Just as Christ overcame the tempter by the word of God, so it is by this same means that Christian people must be delivered from their temptations in the last days.

Horch explained the meaning of the term, 'mystical Bible'. He emphasized that the right use of the Bible demanded that its message be grasped not merely with mind and mouth but with the heart and faith. By the Spirit of Christ the interpreter must take the 'letter' of OT law and history and relate these outer symbols to the inner life of the Christian. The 'hidden kernel' and essence must be removed from the outer shell of the letter, and laid before the spiritually hungry for their enjoyment.[48] Horch gave a couple of examples. In reference to the description in Genesis of how, in the beginning, God made heaven and earth, Horch suggested that the Christian reader take this passage as an occasion to reflect upon how God has created believers anew by his almighty power. When Genesis says that the earth was a desolate waste and dark abyss until God called forth the light, one should recall the natural condition of humanity before God, how sin has made all the children of Adam a desolation and darkness, and how God's grace in Christ has brought light and new life.[49] With such an approach, the scripture becomes 'a pharmacy containing the most precious medicines'.[50]

As for the term, 'prophetical Bible', Horch indicated that his Bible would seek to explain the principal prophecies according to their proper time sequence, including the stages leading to Christ's future coming and the day of the Lord. The prophetical symbols and signs of the OT held great significance for Horch, as Horch's comments throughout the Bible indicate. Horch explained, for example, that in *Deuteronomy* 33 the whole church of Christ was set forth, from beginning to end, under the symbol of the ancient patriarchs.

Horch treated *Song of Solomon* 6:8 as a 'clever puzzle' ('geistreiche Rätzel') needing to be solved. The text reads:

Sixty queens there may be and eighty concubines, and virgins beyond number; but there is only one dove, my perfect one, the only daughter of her mother, the favourite of the one who bore her. When the maidens saw her, they called her blessed; the queens and concubines praised her.[51]

'Without doubt,' wrote Horch, this passage and its references to Solomon's harum portrayed the condition of the Christian church. The challenge, of course, was to explain the significance of the queens, concubines and virgins. Clearly Solomon's words in this passage indirectly address 'not only the breakdown of the true church but also the great depravity of the false one.' Horch suggested that once this was understood, 'we easily understand that the queens, over against the one true bride of Christ, represent those churches which rule over Christ's inheritance in the spirit of antichrist.' In *Revelation* 18:7, 8 Babylon the Great is compared to a boasting, adulterous queen who will be consumed by fire. The number sixty identifies these churches with the number of the beast, six hundred and sixty-six.[52] This church of antichrist refers to Catholic and Protestant churches where false worship of Christ takes place.

The *concubines*, wrote Horch, point to the religion of Islam, represented among Turks, Persians and Tartars. They are children of Ishmael, son of Hagar the concubine of Abraham. 'Because they do not believe that Christ was offered up for our sins and rose again for our justification, so long as they remain in their unbelief, they remain mere concubines, servants, not children of the kingdom, and so cannot inherit along with Isaac the son of the promise but are cast out along with Hagar and Ishmael.'[53] Finally, the *virgins* or maidens are the heathen who are in no way bound to Christ nor know God. Horch numbered the Jews here, as well, as those whom God called 'not my people.' (Hos. 2:25). Just as the false churches were numbered sixty, so the Muslims are numbered eighty and the heathen the numberless crowd found in China, India, Africa and America. The *beloved daughter* of her mother is one of a kind, and corresponds to a church that resembles the first apostolic church, a church of true Christian love, the church of Philadelphia in *Revelation* where brotherly love prevails. When such a church arises, all peoples under heaven will convert in response to the gospel.[54]

Horch's introduction highlights themes and methods of interpretation that Horch applied consistently throughout his Bible commentary. Horch approached Scripture as a 'puzzle', more specifically an eschatological puzzle whose solution would reveal the special eschatological significance of the early 18th century in the divine calendar. Also noteworthy is Horch's metaphorical reading of queens, concubines and virgins, and the spiritual references to the church that he found in the sexually-laden passages of *Song of Solomon*.

Commentary on the *Song of Solomon*

Horch's introduction to the *Song of Solomon* repeated some of the same material as found above but with added detail. Horch explained that readers would only derive 'the true significance of the divine wisdom contained in Solomon's writing' if they purified their hearts by faith in the blood of the lamb, and allowed Christ's Spirit to complete the work of sanctification.[55] Only then would they find nothing earthly or sexual in this 'spiritual and divine love drama'. According to Horch, the *Song of Solomon* portrayed 'the various forms of the Christian church from the beginning to the end of the world.'

Horch presented the fourfold condition of the church, noting the chronological limits of each. The church 'under the Jews and heathen' lasted until 312 AD; the church under the Christian emperors unfortunately did not enjoy even a hundred years of peace due to the invasions of the Goths and barbarian peoples, with the final fall of Roman empire in 475 AD; the church under the antichrist reached its peak in 1260 and beyond; finally, there was the church of freedom, which had two or three stages: the 'former Reformation' time in the sixteenth century, lasting almost two hundred years, but now with its original life and power greatly diminished; the second stage, with a more complete time of widespread purifying when the gospel would be preached to all peoples, which Horch expected to arrive any time; followed, finally, by the thousand year kingdom of peace when the dragon would be bound and cast into the abyss.[56] Horch divided the *Song of Solomon* into the same four historical divisions as noted above. *Song of Solomon* 1:5 to 3:6 represented 'the church under the Jews and Heathen.' *SS* 3:7 to 5:1 was 'the church under the Christian Emperors'. *SS* 5:2 to 5:16 was 'the church under Antichrist.' And finally, *SS* 6:1 to 8:14 was 'the church under Freedom'.

Horch then took this simple historical scheme, and amplified it by reference to the seven churches of Revelation 2 and 3, which Horch took to be 'symbols of the whole church age, from beginning to end.'[57] It will suffice to observe that Horch identified Sardis, the fifth church, with the Reformation age when Christians lived under Protestant authorities, but sadly misused their freedom. The sixth church was the church of Philadelphia, of brotherly love. This church belonged to the age of the second and more complete Reformation when an open door was offered to the nations for their conversion.

The peaceful condition of the church under Constantine and his Christian successors was portrayed by *Song of Solomon* in 3:6, 7: 'Who is this coming up from the desert like a column of smoke, perfumed with myrrh and incense made from all the spices of the merchant?' Horch commented:

Is this not the multitude of Christians who are burnt alive by the heathen and martyred in all manner of ways? And see they are a sweet aroma to the Lord, indeed for the heathen themselves who frequently come and accept the Christian faith.

The next verse reads: 'Look, it is the litter of Solomon! Around it are sixty mighty men of the mighty men of Israel. They all have swords, are experienced in battle, and each has his sword at his side prepared for the terrors of the night.' The peace and freedom of Christians under the Christian Roman emperors corresponded to the image of the soft bed of Solomon. Horch further noted:

> See here the peace of my church under Constantine, the first Christian emperor. But it is still insecure on account of the remaining heathen chiefs, so I provide them with a strong guard chosen from my believing people.[58]

Song of Solomon 4:1 reads, 'How beautiful you are my darling! Oh how beautiful! Your eyes behind your veil are doves. Your hair is like a flock of goats descending from Mount Gilead.' Horch interpreted:

> Here has grown a crowd of believers without number who have escaped the tyrannous power of the heathen gods, as the herds of Jacob [taken] from the persecuting hand of Laban.[59]

'... the flocks of goats which move down the slopes of Gilead,' represent the great crowd of believers escaping the power of the antichrist, represented by the Church of Christ from the time of the Christian emperors.[60] Interestingly, the same image of 'a flock of goats descending from Gilead,' appears in *Song of Solomon* 6:5 where Horch's explanation referred to 'the freedom of the church during the first Reformation.'[61]

Horch concluded his comments on *Song of Solomon* on an impassioned prophetic note, combining allegorical interpretation of the book with an apocalyptic sense of the dawning of a new age for the church. He warned that God's prophetic clock had already struck and the time of God's gracious visitation was near.

> Heed with me, people, this prophetic clock so that we may know how often this clock of God's providence has already struck ... and when it will strike again in the same fashion in future, although to be sure we cannot count the minutes, as if we could discern the time

of God's gracious visitation upon us and insinuate ourselves by God's grace into the future.[62]

The foundation for all Christian hope was that the bridegroom had come, in flesh and blood, and honored humankind with his kiss of love. To receive his loving gifts one need only kiss him with sincere and believing love. Then one could love him with a purified virgin heart, as he has loved us.

Christians in Horch's day had reached the first stage of freedom, when they no longer worshipped a false Christ made by the Catholic priest out of the host.[63] There was need for the church to come out of the lingering dark shadows into the morning light to attain a new level of spiritual freedom and purity. Christians should invite the bridegroom to come with the words of the bride, 'Come my beloved, let us go out into the field and abide in the villages, and I will give you my love.' (*Song* 7:11, 12) We see that Horch's hermeneutic involved playful allegory, drawing out the image of lover and beloved as it applied to the church in the last days. One of Horch's disciples, Eva Buttlar, would take this imagery in a more literal direction, suggesting that lovemaking with her brought spiritual benefits to believers in the last days.[64]

Commentary on the *Book of Revelation*

Horch began his comments on *Revelation* by affirming that, 'this book should be carefully considered above all other prophecies.' Horch justified such a claim from the book's early verses which identify the book as, 'the revelation of Jesus Christ,' and which promise a special blessing to the reader: 'blessed is the one who reads and hears the words of this prophecy and accepts what is written in it, for the time is near.'[65] Horch affirmed enthusiastically, 'Yes indeed, one could say then, and how much more can one say now, 'See, he is coming!''

For example, he is evidently pouring out his Spirit; he is converting the heathen; he has destroyed the temple and power of the Jews; he has overcome the heathen emperors; he has vanquished the antichrist by taking away his people from him. See, he is coming! He is once again giving courage to many to die as martyrs for the truth, in prisons and as slaves on the galleys, as has happened recently in France.... He incites the kings of the beast against each other; indeed, the kings of Sardis are provoked by each other, and he has awakened the Assyrians, the ferocious Turks!

Horch observed that in order rightly to understand the mysteries of this book, and to consider them for our improvement and comfort, 'it is necessary above all, that we be servants of God and not of the world and of the beast of antichrist, for it is given to John to speak to these [people],' verse 1. Those in Christ's true church 'must be bought along with the virgins of the lamb from the earth and its people, but, above all, not be stained with women, that is by the ungodly churches' (14:3).[66]

Horch's treatment of the seven letters to the churches in *Revelation* chapters two and three deserves special note. Horch affirmed that 'the *Revelation* introduces the principle events [in the history] both of the church and the world by means of the seven churches, seven seals and seven trumpets.'[67] Horch related the seven lamps to the seven candlesticks on which they were placed; the seven eyes to the seven seals whose secrets they sought to discover; the seven horns to the seven trumpets which announced the wars in which the horns crush their enemies. In this threefold ordering Horch found 'a threefold cord that cannot be broken' (Eccles. 4:12).

Horch offered a couple of principles for understanding the significance of the seven churches, in particular. First, it should be recognized that the seven angels were sent not only to churches in the seven cities in Asia Minor, but also 'to the whole earth, and to all periods of history.' Secondly, to investigate rightly the meaning of the seven churches it was necessary to consider the working of God as presented in history and in the prophets. At this point Horch referred the 'devoted reader' to his introduction to the *Song of Solomon*, 'which harmonizes in delightful fashion with the book of *Revelation*'.[68]

The church in 'Ephesus' signified, for Horch, the first Christian age of the church in which the apostles untiringly sought to spread the gospel of divine truth and to remove the ungodly from the church of the Lord. (1 Cor. 5:1). Unfortunately, this early zeal soon cooled off as the spirit of antichrist infiltrated and sought to rule over the Christian people (1 John 2:18).

Horch noted that 'Smyrna' means myrrh, appropriate because in the next age the churches were persecuted under heathen emperors and were set on fire, offering a sweet aroma to the Lord. (*Song* 3:6). Following Christian tradition, Horch noted that 'one can count as many such persecutions as there are fingers on a person's hands.'[69] The last persecution lasted ten years, until the beginning of Constantine's reign in 312 AD.

'Pergamus' was the church under the Christian emperors in Rome. This was also the first church which had to suffer under the rebellion of antichrist and the popes. Many true believers had to endure persecutions and death (11:7). The church in 'Thyatira' was the second age of antichrist when the 'Roman Jezebel' claimed to speak prophetically as a teacher of the faith, when in fact she taught the doctrine of Balaam and heathen abominations received from Satan. That her later works were better than the first signified the beginning of Reformation when people stood up to oppose the evils, although the kings of the day persecuted this opposition to Rome, as happened in sixteenth and seventeenth century France.[70]

The church of 'Sardis' pointed especially to the church of the Reformation, which although it had the name Evangelical and Reformed, was in fact an incomplete, somnolent, even dead, church. Yet in this church, signifying Horch's own time, there were some Christians who had unsoiled garments. Those who still worshipped in 'Babylon' prayed to a false Christ and god of bread in the mass, and bowed the knee to dumb idols. In the church of 'Philadelphia' the first love of the early Christians would be restored, as believers were of one heart and soul and put away the strife of brother against brother in the churches. The door of the gospel would be opened to all the peoples on earth.[71] Finally, the church in 'Laodicea' will be one in which Philadelphian love again cooled off. Christ will judge the world as in the days of Noah, and usher in for his people a time 'of such glory that we cannot even fathom much less describe it.'[72]

Summing up, we see that according to Horch's hermeneutic the seven angels of *Revelation* were sent not only to churches in the seven cities in Asia Minor, but also 'to the whole earth, and to all periods of history.' He was confident that John's *Revelation* introduced the principle events in the history of the church and the world. Especially noteworthy is the way Horch found in the *Song of Solomon* a 'delightful harmony' with the book of *Revelation*. His was a hermeneutic of psychological and historical asceticism that aimed at restoring the Protestant churches of his day to a level of spiritual freedom, purity and simplicity.

Horch's Hermeneutic in Context

In order to understand Horch as a Reformed thinker it is important to situate his interpretive comments in *The Marburg Bible* within the contexts of medieval and early modern hermeneutics, as well as in the social context of the times.

The *Apocalypse* and *Song of Solomon* in Medieval and Early Modern Exegesis

In his understanding of the *Apocalypse* Horch was very much in a tradition of interpretation going back to the Reformation and the middle ages. Comparison of Horch with sixteenth century Schwenckfelders, for example, reveals virtually identical understandings of the seven churches of *Revelation* 2 and 3 as seven periods of Christian history, revising, however, the time frame for the dawning of the millennium. Valentin Crautwald's reading of Joachim of Fiore shaped this Schwenkfeldian optimistic strain.[73] The mystical writer Jakob Böhme and his disciples represent a key link connecting the sixteenth century Reformation radicals with English Philadelphians and German Pietism.[74]

The medieval beginnings of this model can only be hinted at here. In contrast to Augustine, Joachim of Fiore (ca. 1135–1202) saw the *Apocalypse* as a 'detailed account of the course of history', a history that unfolded in three ages belonging to the Father, Son and Holy Spirit respectively. The third age was marked by the freedom of the Spirit when the millennium would arrive in fullness. Joachim thus 'opened the door for the reemergence of chiliasm... [shaping] the thought of visionaries and prophets for many centuries to come.'[75]

The immediate result of Joachim's work was the emergence of interpretations that treated the *Apocalypse* as a detailed map of the course of history. Commentators argued that the book prophesied events from the time of Jesus until their own day, whether that day was in the thirteenth, fourteenth or any other century.... The church-historical interpretation that came into fashion in the Middle Ages was still in vogue until the middle of the nineteenth century.[76]

In his commentary on the *Apocalypse* Peter Aureoli, contemporary of Pope John XXII (1316–1334), saw *Revelation* as a prophetic history of the Church. He reckoned seven periods between the first and the second advent of Christ: a period of the apostles, the Roman persecutions, establishment, divisions, pacification, antichristian persecution, the glory of paradise.[77] In the seventeenth century millennialism again became popular in Protestantism, as evidenced by the German Calvinist Johann Heinrich Alsted (1588–1638), Johann Amos Comenius (1592–1670), Joseph Mede (1586–1638), and French Protestant Pierre Jurieu (1637–1713). Many of them continued to understand the

Apocalypse as a 'synopsis of church history.'[78] Heinrich Horch should be understood as a lively member of this interpretive tradition. He found in this tradition one that reflected his own concern for restoring the church in his day to its former glory.

Horch likewise was indebted to a long tradition that interpreted the *Song of Songs* in a way that saw its close prophetic commonalities with the *Apocalypse*. Acknowledging debts to Beryl Smalley's work,[79] Ann Matter has recently shown that the *Song of Songs* was 'the most frequently interpreted book of medieval Christianity,' and that this interpretive tradition was one of 'great allegorical complexity.'[80] A key to most of these medieval interpretations of the book was the love between God and the Church. 'Each author who wrote in the allegorical mode reworked the assumptions of interpretation which he had inherited to explain to each Christian century how the *Song of Songs* is the portrait of love between God and the Church.'[81]

As the Catholic Church experienced increasing turmoil and schism, and concerns about the Church's purity became more widespread, the *Song of Songs* was read in a way that reflected these concerns in light of the *Apocalypse*. Given the reforming context, 'It is no historical accident that so many medieval exegetes commented on both the *Apocalypse* and the *Song of Songs*.'[82] The Benedictine monk Robert of Tombelaine (d. ca. 1090), for example, lived in the times of eleventh century Gregorian reform. He spent his career attacking various abuses and laxity in both the hierarchical church and the monasteries. Not surprisingly, Robert's commentary on the *Song of Songs* is full of 'apocalyptic expectations for the final wedding of the lamb with the Church of the elect'.[83] In the twelfth century one witnesses an 'increasingly common perception' of the close connection between the *Song of Songs* and the *Apocalypse*.'[84]

This tradition of interpretation took on new life in the seventeenth century.[85] Most noteworthy is Thomas Brightman's *Commentary on the Canticles*, first published in 1644. Brightman's works were available to Horch in Latin from German publishers.[86] In Brightman one finds 'a much developed apocalypticism with regard to *the Song of Solomon*'. Brightman's interpretation of the book treats it as a history of the church, in two parts: the first three and a half chapters of *Song of Solomon* provide the 'legal history of the church from David to Christ'; the rest of the book covers the period from Christ to the second coming. Of special note is his treatment of chapters six to eight, which portray events leading to a full restoration and renewal in the last days.[87] The queens, concubines and virgins of 6:8 Brightman understood to refer to the churches of the Reformation 'according to their degrees of purity'.[88] Queens included the churches in England, Ireland, Scotland and Geneva; the concubines were the less impressive Lutheran churches in Germany and Denmark; virgins without number included the least impressive churches of all – Anabaptists, Arians and Unitarians. Brightman taught that the year 1650 would see the conversion of the Jews and destruction of antichrist, and dawning of the millennium. John Cotton closely followed Brightman's understanding, and interpreted *Song of Solomon* 6:8 in similar fashion: the queens were the 'true Reformed churches', that is Congregationalists; concubines were churches 'with a ministry thrust upon them'; and the virgins were 'those groups with no satisfactory ministry.'[89]

One can see that this tradition of interpretation stood ready and available to Horch as a kind of hermeneutical tool, one aptly suited to his own apocalyptic temperament and worldview. Horch obviously brought his own distinctive outlook to bear, however, interpreting queens as the churches of antichrist, concubines as Muslims, and virgins as heathen, and the beloved daughter as the true church.

Horch and the Crisis of the Body in German Culture

The 17th century was an age of crisis, marked by accelerating cultural, social, religious and political transformations.[90] It was an age when heterodox publications and religious views tested restrictions on freedom of the press and religious association. In the period 1700–1750, German lands located in the Lahn and Werra valleys, from Kassel, Herborn and Marburg to Frankfurt and Erfurt, became the center of unusual spiritual manifestations, bearing comparison, noted Goebel, with the region of Phrygia in the second century! In early 18th century Germany these manifestations were of a Pietist, enthusiast and separatist nature. It was these lands, dominated by Reformed Counts, that welcomed the French Huguenots when Louis XIV allowed renewed persecutions against the Reformed in France. The welcome extended by these German princes extended to a group that fell outside the three tolerated confessions, with the result that from around 1700 this comparatively small German region became a safe haven ('eine feste Burg') for other persecuted German Christians who because of their faith could find toleration nowhere else – Anabaptists, Pietists, Separatists, Inspired and Herrnhuters.[91] Heinrich Horch's career belongs to the story of enthusiasm in these German lands. This situation of crisis and anxiety helps to account for Horch's inclination to use the *Song of Solomon* and the *Apocalypse* as apocalyptic keys to Scripture.

Willi Temme has recently shown that 'in Pietism around the year 1700 there was a crisis of corporality, of embodiment, a collective experience of having to deal with the body and its sensations.'[92] We have seen that Heinrich Horch taught a 'transformation of the human body in the thousand year kingdom.'[93] The utopia of a new, redeemed human body constituted the content of his chiliasm.[94]

Conclusion

For Heinrich Horch, Scripture was a 'puzzle,' more specifically an eschatological puzzle whose solution revealed the special eschatological significance of the early 18th century in the divine calendar. Especially noteworthy is the way Horch found in the *Song of Solomon* a 'delightful harmony' with the book of *Revelation*. Horch's metaphorical reading of sexually-laden passages in *Song of Solomon* served Horch's desire to see the Protestant churches of his day attain a new level of spiritual freedom and purity. His was a hermeneutic of psychological and historical asceticism aimed at Protestant renewal. We have seen that this hermeneutic was not original with Horch, but had debts to the medieval and Reformation heirs of Joachim of Fiore and Gregorian monastic commentators. This tradition of interpretation stood ready and available to Horch as a kind of hermeneutical tool, one aptly suited to his own apocalyptic temperament and worldview.

This paper has further argued that Horch's *Marburg Bible* reflected a time of crisis, specifically a 'crisis of the body' that was widespread among Protestant radicals in the late 17th century in Germany. Horch was clearly a man not at home in his own body; a true hypochondriac. He was also a man not at home in the Reformed churches of his day. Horch's hermeneutic at once accounted for these discomforts, and offered hope of new earthly forms, for both body and church, when integrity and peace would be restored to God's creation in a time of millennial peace.

Max Goebel's words in 1852 offer a fitting tribute to Horch's career and significance: 'Horch was a man of admirable gifts and abilities, passionate temperament, deep seriousness of mind and Christian zeal, a victim of his own pride and stubbornness and of his own times.' Compared to Gottfried Arnold, Goebel found Horch to be 'much more imprudent, more harsh, more impulsive, and more unbalanced, and therefore also more unsettled and more unfortunate.'[95]

NOTES

1. Winfried Zeller, 'Heinrich Horche in Kirchhain,' *Jahrbuch der Hessischen Kirchengeschichtlichen Vereinigung* 11 (1960), p. 129.
2. 'Horche,' in Carl Meusel, *Kirchliches Handlexikon, 3ter Band* (Leipzig: Verlag von Justus Naumann, 1891), p. 361.
3. Horch worked on *The Mystical and Prophetical Bible* in the last period of his life, while living in Kirchhain, near Marburg.
4. Zeller, p. 135.
5. Hans Schneider, 'Radikal Pietismus im 18. Jahrhundert,' in Martin Brecht, ed., *Der Pietismus im achtzehnten Jahrhundert* (Göttingen: Vandenhoeck & Ruprecht, 1995), p. 121. 'Friedrich Adolf Lampe lobte, daß die 'Marburger Bibel' 'viel Anleitung zur Entdeckung des geheimen und Prophetischen Sinns der schwersten Bücher gegeben' habe, doch hätte er sich gewünscht, 'daß nicht hin und wieder viele Redensarten und Anmerckungen wären eingeflossen, die dem heutigen Separatismo zuviel einräumen, dadurch man sehr verhindert wird, diese sonst nicht unnützliche Arbeit den Einfältigen anzupreisen.''
6. Carl Franz Lubert Haas, *Lebensbeschreibung des berühmten D. Henrich Horchens aus Hessen* (Cassell: Johann Jacob Cramer, 1769). 'Ich verwunderte mich nicht ohne Ursache darüber, daß ein in vielen Wissenschaften erfahrner Mann; ein Verfasser einer großen Anzahl von Schriften; ein Mann, der gar besondre Schicksale gehabt; dessen Streitigkeiten mit andern gar bekannten und wichtigen in einiger Verbindung stehen; der sich viele Mühe gegeben, die beyden Protestantischen Kirchen zu einer Art der Vereinigung zu bringen; der so sehr vor den Gebrauch der deutschen Sprache geeifert; mit einem Worte, ein Gelehrter der gar nicht unter die gemeinen Köpfe gehöret, so wenig sey beschrieben worden, daß fast nirgends auch nur eine kurze Anzeige von ihm gefunden wird.' (Vorrede).
7. Rudolf Mohr, Review of Norbert Fehringer, 'Philadelphia und Babel. Der hessische Pietist Heinrich Horche und das Ideal des wahren Christentums,' Dissertation theol. Marburg, 1971; review appearing in *Pietismus und Neuzeit* (1977), p. 153.
8. Carl Franz Lubert Haas, *Lebensbeschreibung des berühmten D. Henrich Horchens aus Hessen* (Cassell: Johann Jacob Cramer, 1769). This work was obtained in microfiche from the Herzog August Bibliothek in Wolfenbüttel, Germany.
9. C. W. H. Hochhuth, *Heinrich Horch und die philadelphischen Gemeinden in Hessen* (Gütersloh: Verlag von C. Bertelsmann, 1876), p. 1.
10. Willi Temme, *Krise der Leiblichkeit: Die Sozietät der Mutter Eva (Buttlarsche Rotte) und der Radikale Pietismus um 1700* (Göttingen: Vandenhoeck & Ruprecht,

1998), p. 84 n.22.

11. Hochhuth, p. 1.

12. Hochhuth, p. 2.

13. Hochhuth, p. 2.

14. Zeller, p. 129 and Hochhuth, p. 7.

15. Max Goebel, *Geschichte des christlichen Lebens in der rheinisch-westphalischen evangelischen Kirche, Zweiter Bd.* (Coblenz: Karl Bädeker, 1852), p. 744. Klopfer 'behauptete, die Reformirten hätten zwar die Wahrheit, aber nur auf dem Papier, nicht aber im Herzen und in der That; man dürfe wegen des verderbten Zustandes der Kirche weder zur Kirche gehen noch die Sacramente gebrauchen.'

16. Goebel, p. 746.

17. Goebel, p. 747.

18. My book length manuscript on Bröske, *Conrad Bröske (1660–1713): First Preacher of Offenbach, Herald of the Millennium; The Response of a German Pietist Court Preacher to 17th C. Crisis*, is presently under consideration at Brill press.

19. Max Goebel, pp 747f: 'Er begann hiermit ein zehn Jahre dauerndes unstetes und schwärmerisches Leben, in welchem er den tief in seinem Innern nagenden Schmerz über den muthwillig aufgegebenen segensreichen Wirkungskreis und zugleich der Sorge um Brod und Amt zu entgehen suchte.' Without any quotation marks or acknowledgement of Goebel, Hochhuth cited almost verbatim the above words of Goebel from twenty-four years earlier regarding Horch's activities from 1698 to 1708. Hochhuth wrote: 'Es begann für ihn ein zehn Jahre dauerndes, unstetes und schwärmerisches Leben, in welchem er den tief in seinem Innern nagenden Schmerz über den muthwillig aufgegebenen segensreichenden Wirkungskreis und zugleich die Sorge um Brot und Amt zu vergessen suchte.' See Hochhuth, pp. 101f.

20. Goebel, p. 746.

21. Hans Schneider, 'Radikal Pietismus im 17. Jahrhundert,' in Martin Brecht, ed., *Der Pietismus im siebzehnten Jahrhundert* (Göttingen: Vandenhoeck & Ruprecht, 1993), p. 409.

22. Hochhuth, pp. 97f.

23. Willi Temme, *Krise der Leiblichkeit: Die Sozietät der Mutter Eva (Buttlarsche Rotte) und der Radikale Pietismus um 1700* (Göttingen: Vandenhoeck & Ruprecht, 1998), p. 95.

24. Willi Temme, *Krise der Leiblichkeit*, p. 99.

25. Willi Temme, *Krise der Leiblichkeit*, p. 91.

26. Willi Temme, *Krise der Leiblichkeit*, p. 103.

27. See Goebel p. 748. Later that year, in December 1700, Horch's mental condition and delusions were such that he mistreated his son and wife. Fellow Pietists attributed the behaviour to the Holy Spirit. See Hochhuth, pp. 134f and Hans Schneider, 'Radikal Pietismus im 18. Jahrhundert,' in Martin Brecht, ed., *Der Pietismus im achtzehnten Jahrhundert* (Göttingen: Vandenhoeck & Ruprecht, 1995), p. 120.

28. Zeller, p. 130.

29. Hochhuth, p. 91.

30. Hochhuth, p. 92.

31. Zeller, 'Heinrich Horche in Kirchhain,' p. 130.

32. Zeller asserted this teaching activity. See Zeller, p. 130. Schneider denies that Horch taught at this time at Marburg University. See Hans Schneider, 'Der radikale

Pietismus im 18. Jahrhundert,' pp. 120 and n. 113.

33. Zeller, p. 130.

34. Zeller, p. 131. See Hans Schneider, 'Der radikale Pietismus im 18. Jahrhundert,' p. 120.

35. Zeller, p. 132.

36. Hans Schneider, 'Radikal Pietismus im 18. Jahrhundert,' in Martin Brecht, ed., *Der Pietismus im achtzehnten Jahrhundert* (Göttingen: Vandenhoeck & Ruprecht, 1995), pp. 119f. Hans Schneider has called into question Fehringer's argument that by 1700 Horch experienced a change of heart and decided to forsake his radical separatism and return to the Reformed Church. But by 1708 such a change was evident. 'Die Nachrichten, die ab 1708 wieder vorliegen, lassen ihn ruhiger und ausgeglichener erscheinen...Hier führte Horch, der einstige Babelstürmer, ein zurückgezogenes Leben als Mitglied der reformierten Kirchengemeinde, seine Familie hielt sich zum Gottesdienst und nahm kirchliche Amtshandlungen in Anspruch.'

37. Zeller, p. 132.

38. Zeller, p. 133.

39. Zeller, p. 133.

40. Schneider, p. 120.

41. Zeller, p. 134.

42. Hans Schneider, 'Radikal Pietismus im 18. Jahrhundert,' in Martin Brecht, ed., *Der Pietismus im achtzehnten Jahrhundert* (Göttingen: Vandenhoeck & Ruprecht, 1995), p. 121.

43. Schneider, 'Radikal Pietismus im 18. Jahrhundert,' p. 120.

44. Goebel, p. 750 n. 1.

45. *Mystische und Profetische Bibel, Das ist Die gantze Heil. Schrifft, Altes und Neues Testament, Auffs neue nach dem Grund verbessert, Sampt Erklärung der fürnemsten Sinnbilder und Weissagungen, Sonderlich Des H. Lieds Salomons Und der Offenbarung J. C. Wie auch Denen fürnemsten Lehren, bevoraus die sich in diese letzte Zeiten schicken* (Marburg: Joh. Kürßner, Universitäts Buchdrucker, 1712).

46. *Mystische und Profetische Bibel*, Vorwort, p. i.

47. *Mystische und Profetische Bibel*, Vorwort, p. i.

48. *Mystische und Profetische Bibel*, p. i.

49. *Mystische und Profetische Bibel*, p. ii.

50. *Mystische und Profetische Bibel*, p. ii.

51. Song of Songs 6:8, 9 in *The Holy Bible, New International Version* (Grand Rapids: Zondervan, 1978).

52. *Mystische und Profetische Bibel*, p. iii.

53. *Mystische und Profetische Bibel*, p. iv.

54. *Mystische und Profetische Bibel*, p. v.

55. *Mystische und Profetische Bibel*, 'Das Hohe Lied Salomons,' p. 1.

56. *Mystische und Profetische Bibel*, 'Das Hohe Lied Salomons,' p. 1.

57. *Mystische und Profetische Bibel*, 'Das Hohe Lied Salomons,' p. 1. '... voraus der Offenbarung, als des warhaften schlüssels aller weissagungen die in 7. gemeinen bestehet als sinnbildern der gantzen kirchen von anfang biß ans ende. Off. 2 u. 3.'

58. *Mystische und Profetische Bibel*, 'Das Hohe Lied Salomons,' p. 7.

59. *Mystische und Profetische Bibel*, 'Das Hohe Lied Salomons,' p. 7.

60. *Mystische und Profetische Bibel*, 'Das Hohe Lied Salomons,' p. 10.

61. *Mystische und Profetische Bibel*, 'Das Hohe Lied Salomons,' p. 1.

62. *Mystische und Profetische Bibel*, 'Das Hohe Lied Salomons,' p. 14. 'Beschalle dan nun o mensch alhier mit mir diesen Profetischen uhrzeiger daß wir wissen

mögen wie viel die glocke der fursehung Gottes, die über sein wort wachet, bereits schon geschlagen u. was sie nach demselben ins künftige noch schlagen werde, wiewol wir eben die minuten nit zehlen können, damit wir die zeit der gnädigen heimsuchung Gottes an uns erkennen u. uns aufs künftige durch seine gnade bey zeiten schicken mögen.' In 1697 Horch wrote: 'We take pleasure in the expectation of the Kingdom either in the course of this century or at the beginning of the following, but the actual year, of the time and hour, God has in his hand and kept hidden there.' ('Wir wollen uns vergnügen, dasselbe entweder im Ablauf dieses Jahrhunderts oder im Anfang folgenden zu erwarten, das eigentliche Jahr aber Gott, dem Herrn der Zeit und Stunde in seiner Hand hat, heimgestellt sein lassen.') (Temme, p. 92)

63. *Mystische und Profetische Bibel*, 'Das Hohe Lied Salomons,' p. 14.

64. See Temme, pp. 123-60, 382-427.

65. *Mystische und Profetische Bibel*, 'Die Offenbarung Jesu Christi,' p. 1.

66. *Mystische und Profetische Bibel*, 'Die Offenbarung Jesu Christi,' p. 2.

67. *Mystische und Profetische Bibel*, 'Die Offenbarung Jesu Christi,' p. 3.

68. *Mystische und Profetische Bibel*, 'Die Offenbarung Jesu Christi,' p. 3.

69. *Mystische und Profetische Bibel*, 'Die Offenbarung Jesu Christi,' p. 3. Das sind die 10 tage der trübsal weil man solcher grausamen verfolgungen so viel zehlen mag als finger an des menschen hände sind u. daurete dazu die letzte zehen jahr lang bis ins jahr Christi 312...'

70. *Mystische und Profetische Bibel*, 'Die Offenbarung Jesu Christi,' p. 4.

71. *Mystische und Profetische Bibel*, 'Die Offenbarung Jesu Christi,' p. 4.

72. *Mystische und Profetische Bibel*, 'Die Offenbarung Jesu Christi,' p. 4.

73. See Douglas H. Shantz, *Crautwald and Erasmus: A Study in Humanism and Radical Reform in Sixteenth Century Silesia* (Baden-Baden: Valentin Koerner, 1992), chapter three.

74. 'In the mystic spiritualism of the seventeenth century [in Germany], with Jakaob Böhme and some of his students, the conviction grew that future salvation would begin in Germany with the rediscovery of the gospel of the Reformation.' Gottfried Seebaß, 'The Importance of Apocalyptic for the History of Protestantism,' *Colloquium: The Australian and New Zealand Theological Review*, 13, #1 (October 1980), p. 27.

75. Arthur W. Wainwright, *Mysterious Apocalypse: Interpreting the Book of Revelation* (Nashville: Abingdon Press, 1993), pp. 50f.

76. Wainwright, pp. 53, 65.

77. See D. H. Kr60omminga, *The Millennium in the Church* (Grand Rapids: Eerdmans, 1945), pp. 161, 335.

78. Wainwright, pp. 56, 68-73. 'During the seventeenth century, millenarianism became a leading doctrine in many areas of Protestantism. Although condemned by official Lutheranism and some Calvinists, it had a large number of adherents in Britain, Holland and the Protestant parts of France. Even in Germany it was surmounting the obstacle of official opposition.' (p. 73).

79. See especially Beryl Smalley, *The Study of the Bible in the Middle Ages, 3rd. ed.* (Oxford: Blackwell, 1983).

80. E. Ann Matter, *The Voice of My Beloved: The Song of Songs in Western Medieval Christianity* (Philadelphia: University of Pennsylvania Press, 1990), pp. 6, 4.

81. Ann Matter, p. 86.

82. Matter, p. 111.

83. Matter, p. 108.

84. Matter, p. 106.

85. See Bryan W. Ball, *A Great Expectation: Eschatological Thought in English Protestantism to 1660* (Leiden: E.J. Brill, 1975), especially Appendix I, 'The Apocalyptic Significance of the Song of Solomon.'

86. See for example, Thomas Brightman. *Apocalypsis Apocalypseos. Id est, Apocalypsis D. Johannis. Refutatio Rob. Bellarmini de Antichristo libro tertio de Romano Pontifice* (Frankfurt: 1609 und Heidelberg: Commelinianus, 1618). [Wolfenbüttel 573 Theol.].

87. Ball, p. 241.

88. Ball, p. 241.

89. Ball, pp. 241f.

90. Hartmut Lehmann, 'Die Krisen des 17. Jahrhunderts als Problem der Forschung,' in M. Jakubowski-Tiessen (ed.), *Krisen des 17. Jahrhunderts* (Göttingen: Vandenhoeck & Ruprecht, 1999), p. 21. 'Beide Formen schärfen unseren Blick für das 17. Jahrhundert als einer Epoche akzelerierter kultureller, sozialer, religiöser und politischer Transformationen.'

91. Max Goebel, *Geschichte des christlichen Lebens in der rheinisch-westphalischen evangelischen Kirche, Zweiter Bd.* (Coblenz: Karl Bädeker, 1852), p. 740.

92. Willi Temme, *Krise der Leiblichkeit: Die Sozietät der Mutter Eva (Buttlarsche Rotte) und der Radikale Pietismus um 1700* (Göttingen: Vandenhoeck & Ruprecht, 1998), p. 452. This book is based upon Temme's doctoral dissertation at Marburg.

93. Temme, *Krise der Leiblichkeit*, p. 98.

94. Willi Temme, 'Gott im Fleisch,' paper read at the Doktoranden Kolloq in Giessen, December 1992. As Horch told a visitor in the year 1700 in the Marburg castle: 'He felt it, that he was completely changed and converted. Little by little he arrived ever further along in this transformation; to attain ever further he tore out his own hair and teeth.' Horch had the notion of utopia, and a violent adaptation to the picture of a new life.

95. Max Goebel, p. 751. 'So ward Horch, ein Mann von ausgezeichneter Gabe, heftiger Gemüthsart, tiefem Ernst und christlichem Eifer, ein Opfer seines Hochmuthes und Eigensinnes wie auch seiner Zeit; an Denkart und Schicksalen war er vielfach unserm Gottfried Arnold ähnlich, aber viel unvorsichtiger, schroffer, leidenschaftlicher und verkehrter, und darum auch unruhiger und unglücklicher.'

PRESBYTERIANISM AND DISPENSATIONALISM

Vern Sheridan Poythress

At first glance, presbyterianism and dispensationalism might seem to be opposites. How is it, then, that two of the most representative and influential American dispensationalists, Cyrus I. Scofield and Lewis Sperry Chafer, both sprang from presbyterian-related denominational roots? Lewis Sperry Chafer (1871–1952), a presbyterian, was founder of Dallas Theological Seminary, and served as its president and professor of systematic theology.[1] His eight-volume work *Systematic Theology* remains a classical presentation of dispensationalism within the structure of a complete systematic theology. The second figure, C. I. Scofield (1843–1921), had ties with congregationalism, a close relative to presbyterianism. He was ordained to the congregational ministry in 1882, and then in later years devoted much energy to two projects that helped form the very definition of American dispensationalism, namely the Scofield Correspondence Bible School and *The Scofield Reference Bible*.[2]

Differences in Roots

The juxtaposition of dispensationalism with presbyterian or congregationalist roots might seem all the more strange if we travel back to earlier stages in presbyterian and dispensationalist history. Presbyterianism received its definitive formulation in the seventeenth century in the *Westminster Confession of Faith* and the *Westminster Larger* and *Shorter Catechisms*. Dispensationalism arose in the nineteenth century primarily through John Nelson Darby (1800–1882) and the Plymouth Brethren.

The defining stages of the two positions displayed deep differences. The Westminster Standards emphasized the unity of Old and New Testament revelation under the overall structure of the covenant of grace. Darby, by contrast, distinguished sharply between the Old Testament and the New. According to his view, the Old Testament focuses on law and the earthly destiny for Israel, while the New Testament focuses on grace and the heavenly destiny of the church.

Darby's view of the church differed from Westminster presbyterianism not only in his strict separation of the New Testament church from Old Testament Israel, but in its stance toward 'Christendom'. Darby was a 'restorationist', who thought that the past history of the church represented such a mass of corruption and degeneration that the church had to be refounded by the Plymouth Brethren, who alone really met in Christ's name.[3] Presbyterian thinking, by contrast, recognized substantial continuity with the church throughout the ages, along with the need for reform. Darby believed in independency in church government, while the presbyterians saw a biblical basis for wider expressions of church unity in the form of presbyterian government.

In sum, Darby and his followers among the Plymouth Brethren differed sharply from presbyterians on a number of matters, but preeminently in their interpretation of the relation of law to grace and old covenant to new.

Eschatology in American Dispensationalism

But American dispensationalism soon went its own way, and did not reproduce every aspect of Darby's thinking. Daniel Fuller comments:

> It appears, then, that America was attracted more by Darby's idea of an any-moment Coming than they [*sic*] were by his foundational concept of the two peoples of God.... Postmillennialism made the event of the millennium the great object of hope; but Darby, by his insistence on the possibility of Christ's coming at any moment, made Christ Himself, totally

apart from any event, the great object of hope. Darby was accepted [in America] because, as is so often the case, those revolting from one extreme took the alternative presented by the other extreme.[4]

American dispensationalists did accept Darby's sharp distinction between Israel and the church, but the teaching on the last things (eschatology) rather than the teaching on the church (ecclesiology) was the main point of emphasis and interest.

Eschatology in Presbyterianism

The focus on the last things in American dispensationalism meant that possible conflicts with presbyterianism remained more in the background. Historic presbyterianism – and Reformed theology more broadly – has never committed itself creedally to details of the millennium or the idea of an any-moment coming. For the most part, the Reformed creeds confine themselves to general statements about the last judgment and the resurrection, such as Christians throughout the centuries have believed.

But some points of conflict nevertheless remain. The *Westminster Larger Catechism* in particular becomes more specific on some issues. Question 87 and its answer run as follows:

Q. 87. What are we to believe concerning the resurrection?
A. We are to believe, that at the last day there shall be a general resurrection of the dead, both of the just and unjust: when they that are then found alive shall in a moment be changed; and the self-same bodies of the dead which were laid in the grave, being then again united to their souls for ever, shall be raised up by the power of Christ. The bodies of the just, by the Spirit of Christ, and by virtue of his resurrection as their head, shall be raised in power, spiritual, incorruptible, and made like to his glorious body; and the bodies of the wicked shall be raised up in dishonour by him, as an offended judge.

Question 87 is framed as a question about 'the resurrection', not several distinct resurrections. In the *Catechism*'s answer, the language about 'the last day' and 'a general resurrection' seems to imply *one* day of judgment, not several. By contrast, dispensationalists postulate at least three judgments and three resurrections, one for church-age believers at the Rapture, one for the nations at the visible Second Coming of Christ, and still a third at the end of the millennium. The first of these judgments includes bodily resurrection for Christian believers, but no bodily resurrection for the wicked until the visible Second Coming.

The *Larger Catechism* seems to exclude not only dispensationalism, but any form of premillennialism, because all premillennialists believe in at least two distinct times of judgment and resurrection, one at the beginning of the millennium and the other at the end.[5]

But does the *Catechism* answer actually exclude premillennialism? If we allow a slight stretch in interpretation, the *Catechism* answer might be interpreted as describing the general resurrection at the end of the millennium. Dispensationalists and other premillennialists could agree with such a description of the very last resurrection. They would only introduce the further explanation that they still believe in an additional resurrection before the beginning of the millennium.

However, the troubles for dispensationalists are not quite over. In Question 88 the *Catechism* discusses 'the general and final judgment'. To accept this language, a dispensationalist would have to interpret it as the judgment at the end of the millennium. Question 89 discusses the destiny of the wicked. Question 90 then turns to describe the destiny of the righteous:

> Q. 90. What shall be done to the righteous at the day of judgment?
> A. At the day of judgment, the righteous, being caught up to Christ in the clouds, shall be set on his right hand, and there openly acknowledged and acquitted, shall join with him in the judging of reprobate angels and men, and shall be received into heaven, where they shall be fully and for ever freed from all sin and misery; filled with inconceivable joys, made perfectly holy and happy both in body and soul, in the company of innumerable saints and holy angels, but especially in the immediate vision and fruition of God the Father, of our Lord Jesus Christ, and of the Holy Spirit, to all eternity. And this is the perfect and full communion, which the members of the invisible church shall enjoy with Christ in glory, at the resurrection and day of judgment.

The expression 'being caught up to Christ in the clouds', together with the footnoted proof-text from 1 Thessalonians 4:17, indicates that church-age believers are in view, not subsequent believers during the millennium. 'The day of judgment,' in the light of the immediately preceding questions, must refer to 'the general and final judgment of angels and men' (Answer 88), not to a judgment at a time before the beginning of the millennium. Taken together, the answers to Questions 87-90 force us to dissolve the distinction between an earlier judgment for the church and a later one for millennial believers. The *Catechism* is clearly thinking in amillennial terms.

Yet technically there still remains a way to escape an amillennial conclusion. Generally speaking, the footnotes that supply Scripture proofs have not been considered to be part of the standards to which ministers subscribe, but only illustrative support to the standards. Thus, a dispensationalist might reject the prooftext from 1 Thessalonians 4:17 as inapplicable, and still say that Answer 90 accurately describes the judgment at the end of the millennium. Yet this leaves the *Catechism* in a position where it says nothing about the resurrection and judgment that will take place for Christians in the church age. The practical design of the *Catechism* demands that it say something practical about the hope that we have as Christians. Thus, an interpretation that shifts Questions 87-90 to another time period (the time 1000 years after the Second Coming) is not historically plausible.

Focus on Salvation in Reformed Theology

Thus, it is difficult to square the detailed language of the *Catechism* with either dispensationalism or historical premillennialism. Yet in practice presbyterians have usually considered the millennial issue to be debatable, and premillennialists have been numbered within the bounds of presbyterian belief. Why so? Millennial differences have seemed to many Reformed people to be minor differences, not touching on main points of doctrine.[6] Moreover, Reformed people with a sense of the historical roots of the church recognize that premillennialism is an ancient belief, dating back at least to Justin Martyr in the second century.

In fact, the issue of last things was not a central focus for presbyterianism. Presbyterianism stems from the Reformation and from English and Scottish Puritanism, both of which were fighting primarily for the doctrine of salvation, in opposition to Roman Catholic and other views that compromised the sovereignty of God's grace and the certainty of salvation based on Christ's work alone. Thus the Reformed creeds in general and the Westminster Standards in particular devote much space to discussion of issues of salvation.

Hence, when the *Larger Catechism* treats the doctrine of last things, as it does in Questions 87-90, it still discusses the issue largely from the perspective of the salvation or damnation of individuals. The main point of the *Catechism* is not to decide the millennial debates in the abstract, but to talk about the final destiny of believers and unbelievers. According to Question 90, the 'righteous ... shall be ... openly acknowledged and acquited', as the culmination and confirmation of the earlier act of justification. They shall be 'for ever freed from all sin and misery,' which constitutes a reversal of the 'estate of sin and misery' into which the fall of Adam brought mankind (Question 23). They shall be 'made perfectly holy,' which is the completion of their sanctification. The last things are enumerated primarily so that believers may see that God completes the work that he has begun in them. The last things mentioned in Question 90 correspond to earlier points that the *Catechism* has made about the fall and about redemption from sin.

In short, the *Larger Catechism* is thinking in practical, pastoral terms. It recites teachings about the last things in order to comfort believers and warn unbelievers. Salvation here and now means something not only because of its present effects, but because it issues in eternal bliss. Conversely, not to be saved results in eternal damnation. Thus, all human beings must in this life consider the issues of salvation and damnation with full awareness of the weight of the consequences. Almost all dispensationalists would agree heartily with these basically pastoral concerns of the *Catechism*, even though they would have to differ with respect to the details. We must not overlook the details, but neither must we exaggerate their importance in the scheme of the Westminster Standards. The differences over the last things do not by themselves touch on the heart of presbyterianism.

Unity of the Covenant of Grace

An important dispute nevertheless remains that does touch on the doctrine of salvation. The doctrine of the covenant of grace, as a covenant characterizing redemption from beginning to end, unifies the message of the Old and New Testaments. By contrast, dispensationalists emphasize the discontinuities. They speak of different 'dispensations' with characteristically different modes in which God relates to man.[7] In the eyes of many Reformed people, this differentiation threatens to break up the unity of the Bible and deprive Christians of the use of the Old Testament.[8]

And indeed there is a danger. At times some dispensationalists, in their zeal to distinguish grace from law, used language that suggested there might be different ways of salvation offered for different dispensations. For example, the *Scofield Reference Bible*, in its note on 1 John 3:7, says baldly, 'The righteous man under law became righteous by doing righteously; under grace he does righteously because he has been made righteous' (Rom. 3:22; Rom. 10:3, *note*). Commenting on the petition in the Lord's Prayer to 'forgive us our debts', the *Scofield Reference Bible* states, 'This is legal ground. Cf. Ephesians 4:32, which is grace. Under law forgiveness is conditioned upon a like spirit in us; under grace we are forgiven for Christ's sake, and exhorted to forgive because we have been forgiven. See Matthew 18:32; 26:28, *note*.' We hope that Scofield did not intend it, but it sounds as if the Israelites under Moses were saved by works, whereas now the church is saved by grace.

Representative dispensationalists today all repudiate the idea of two ways of salvation, and insist of the unity of one way. In this respect, they are affirming the heart of the theology of the covenant of grace, whose main function is to articulate precisely this unity. But more subtle differences still crop up. The sharp distinction between grace and law can tempt some dispensationalists into formulations that leave out or deny the fact that Christian believers should be careful to obey God's standards (the third use of the law). Dispensationalism's founder, J. N. Darby, shows the same tendency in a pronounced and even denunciatory form. Darby says:

> All this [the Westminster Confession's statement on the covenant and on the law of God] is a fable and a mischievous fable. And I notice it because it is the foundation of the whole religious system to which it belongs.... The basis of the entire system of moral relationship with God in Presbyterianism is false; and it has tainted the whole Evangelical system everywhere.[9]

In return, warnings were issued by Presbyterians. In the 1944 General Assembly of the Presbyterian Church in the U.S., a committee appointed to study dispensationalism reported that it was incompatible with presbyterian beliefs:

> It is the unanimous opinion of your Committee that Dispensationalism as defined and set forth above is out of accord with the system of the doctrine set forth in the Confession of Faith,

not primarily or simply in the field of eschatology, but because it attacks the very heart of the Theology of our Church, which is unquestionably a Theology of one Covenant of Grace. As Dr. Chafer clearly recognizes, there are two schools of interpretation here which he rightly designates as 'Covenantism' as over against 'Dispensationalism'.[10]

That is, the 'covenantism' of the Westminster Standards is diametrically opposed to 'dispensationalism'. This judgment is accurate, if what we mean by 'dispensationalism' includes the suggestion of different ways of salvation or a pronounced antinomianism that dispenses with any requirement of obedience for New Testament Christians.

But over time, biblical sanity wins out over the zeal for sharp distinctions or the attraction of one-sided formulations. The idea of more than one way of salvation retreats as people observe Christ's central role in salvation throughout the Bible. The warnings in the New Testament against Christian disobedience – from James 2, from 1 John, and even from Galatians 5–6 – are too obvious to allow Bible students to remain comfortable for long with virulent antinomianism in their own thinking. Christians must admit that requiring obedience belongs to New Testament Christianity, not exclusively to the Old Testament. Moreover, the pastoral dangers of antinomianism soon become evident in people's lives, and pastors begin instinctively to recognize that their words are being applied in an unhealthy way.

If, then, in the course of time these excesses of dispensationalism disappear, what is left? We still have a zeal from distinguishing grace from law. But if it is no longer coupled with antinomianism, how much does it differ in its overall function from the distinction between grace and works that the Reformation discovered in its fight for the sovereignty of God's grace in salvation? How much does it differ from the distinction as embodied in the Westminster Standards, between the covenant of works and the covenant of grace?

We still find among dispensationalists an interest in distinguishing different 'dispensations' within God's plan for history. But the Westminster Confession of Faith itself distinguishes between different 'administrations' of the covenant of grace:

> This covenant [of grace] was differently administered in the time of the law, and in the time of the gospel: under the law it was administered by promises, prophecies, sacrifices, circumcision, the

paschal lamb, and other types and ordinances delivered to the people of the Jews, all foresignifying Christ to come; which were, for that time, sufficient and efficacious, through the operation of the Spirit, to instruct and build up the elect in faith in the promised Messiah, by whom they had full remission of sins, and eternal salvation; and is called the old Testament.[11]

In this formulation the primary interest is still in the unity of the covenant of grace. The Confession wants to make sure that we see this unity under the two different 'administrations' or external forms of the two times. But why this focus on unity? Precisely because the Confession is interested in articulating the one way of salvation. Faith in Christ to come, and operation of the Spirit resting on his coming work, are 'sufficient and efficacious' for the elect, that is, sufficient to provide forgiveness and secure eternal salvation. If dispensationalists focus on this one issue of the way of salvation, they too must end up saying what the Confession says. There is only one way.

Leading dispensationalists today acknowledge this much. But then they choose to focus primarily on other issues, relating to the differences in concrete expression and form that piety takes in the different redemptive epochs. Within Reformed tradition, the developments in biblical theology stemming from Geerhardus Vos have resulted in an analogous interest in differences.[12] On the Reformed side people articulate more overtly differences among redemptive epochs. On the dispensationalist side, people recognize the importance of articulating the one way of salvation. Especially among 'progressive dispensationalists' we find willingness to affirm continuities between different dispensations and preliminary prophetic fulfillment in the church.[13] These affirmations bring us into a situation where differences remain, but the differences look more minor and less antagonistic than they did in the days of mutual denunciation.

NOTES

1. J. D. Douglas, ed., *New 20th-Century Encyclopedia of Religious Knowledge* (2nd. ed.; Grand Rapids: Baker, 1991), 160.
2. Ibid., 741.
3. John N. Darby, *Writings* 20:240-41; Clarence B. Bass, *Backgrounds to Dispensationalism: Its Historical Genesis and Ecclesiastical Implications* (Grand Rapids: Eerdmans, 1960), 106-9. See also Vern S. Poythress, *Understanding Dispensationalists* (2d ed.; Phillipsburg, NJ: Presbyterian and Reformed, 1994),

7-38.

4. Daniel P. Fuller, 'The Hermeneutics of Dispensationalism,' Th.D. dissertation, Northern Baptist Theological Seminary, Chicago, 1957, pp. 92-93, quoted in Poythress, *Understanding Dispensationalists*, 19.

5. For a discussion of the variant millennial views, see Loraine Boettner, *The Millennium* (Philadelphia: Presbyterian and Reformed, 1957); Robert G. Clouse, *The Meaning of the Millennium: Four Views* (Downers Grove, IL: InterVarsity, 1977); Millard J. Erickson, *Contemporary Options in Eschatology: A Study of the Millennium* (Grand Rapids: Baker, 1977); Stanley Grenz, *The Millennial Maze: Sorting Out Evangelical Options* (Downers Grove, IL: InterVarsity, 1992).

6. Thus J. Gresham Machen and Ned B. Stonehouse write:

It is true, the Westminster Confession of Faith and Catechisms teach not the Premillennial view but a view that is opposed to the Premillennial view. That is particularly plain in the Larger Catechism (Q. 87 and 88).

. . .

The real question, then, is whether a person who holds the Premillennial view can hold that system. Can a person who holds the Premillennial view be a true Calvinist; can he, in other words, hold truly to the Calvinistic or Reformed system of doctrine which is set forth in the Westminster Standards? We think that he can; and for that reasons we think that Premillennialists as well as those who hold the opposing view may become ministers or elders or deacons in The Presbyterian Church of America ('Premillennialism,' *The Presbyterian Guardian* 3/2 [October 24, 1936]: 21; this, the lead article, is unsigned; J. Gresham Machen and Ned B. Stonehouse were editors at the time, so the article comes from one or both of them. My thanks are due to Dr. William Barker for alerting me to this quotation in his unpublished paper, 'System Subscription,' 5-15-2000).

7. See especially the classic formulation by Lewis Sperry Chafer, 'Dispensationalism,' *Bibliotheca Sacra* 93 (1936): 390-449.

8. See Poythress, *Understanding Dispensationalists*, 30-33.

9. John N. Darby, 'Presbyterianism,' *Collected Writings* 14:528, quoted in O. T. Allis, *Prophecy and the Church* (Philadelphia: Presbyterian and Reformed, 1969), 47-48.

10. O. T. Allis, *Prophecy*, 296n59, quoted from *Minutes*, pp. 123-24.

11. Westminster Confession of Faith 7.5.

12. See, e.g., my discussion in *Understanding Dispensationalists*, 39-51.

13. For ongoing developments, especially in 'progressive dispensationalism,' see especially Craig A. Blaising and Darrell L. Bock, eds., *Dispensationalism, Israel, and the Church* (Grand Rapids: Zondervan, 1992); Craig A. Blaising and Darrell L. Bock, eds., *Progressive Dispensationalism: An Up-to-Date Handbook of Contemporary Dispensational Thought* (Wheaton, IL: Victor, 1993); W. R. Willis and J. R. Master, eds., *Issues in Dispensationalism* (Chicago: Moody, 1994); Herbert W. Bateman, IV, *Three Central Issues in Contemporary Dispensationalism: A Comparison of Traditional and Progressive Views* (Grand Rapids: Kregel, 1999); and the bibliography in the last of these.

BIBLICAL THEOLOGY
AND THE
WESTMINSTER STANDARDS

Richard B. Gaffin, Jr.

If it is fair to view Geerhardus Vos as the father of Reformed biblical theology, then we are now at a point several generations later where we can begin assessing something of the lasting impact of that theology, particularly within Reformed churches.[1] The following reflections, no more than partial, are an effort at such an assessment.

Among pastors, teachers and other interested persons more or less conversant with Vosian biblical theology, it's fair to say, a fairly sharp difference of opinion presently exists. On the one side are those enthusiastic about biblical theology (or redemptive-historical interpretation of Scripture) and who see themselves in their own work as building on the insights of Vos and others (like Meredith Kline and Herman Ridderbos). Others, however, question the value of biblical theology, if they have not already concluded that it has introduced novelties detrimental to the well-being of the church. Still others are at various points in between these clashing views, often wondering what to think.

While I would certainly include myself among the first group just mentioned, the 'enthusiasts', some of the reservations voiced by the second deserve to be taken seriously. One among these is the concern that biblical theology, despite its avowed intention to serve systematic theology, is in fact undermining doctrinal stability by diminishing interest and confidence in the formulations of classic Reformed theology. This is seen to have the further deleterious effect of weakening cordial commitment to the Reformed confessions and so, inevitably, of impairing their proper functioning, so necessary for the church's well-being.

This concern, if substantiated, would certainly be cause for alarm. In my view, however, it is largely misplaced. In fact, as I hope to help show here, a deep compatibility exists between the Westminster Standards and biblical theology. While my comments have these Standards primarily in view, they are largely applicable as well, I take it, to other Reformed confessions, like the Three Forms of Unity, although I make no effort to show that here.

I.

I begin with two observations of a more general sort pertaining to the often alleged or perceived novelty of biblical theology. Without for a moment wanting to slight the epoch-making value of Vos's work, for which my admiration continues undiminished, it has always been important to me to recognize his continuity with those who came before him. Contrary to the impression occasionally left by some, it is not as if the church were stumbling about in interpretive darkness until he burst onto the scene, lightening-like, toward the close of the 19th century. In fact, already in the second century in the first great struggle for its existence, the battle with Gnosticism, the church had impressed upon it indelibly the controlling insight, as much as any, of biblical theology, namely that salvation resides ultimately not in who God is or what he has said, but in what he has *done* in history, once for all, in Christ. Virtually from its beginning on and more or less consistently, the church has been incipiently biblical-theological.

Narrowing the scope to Reformed theology, Vos himself has observed that it

> has from the beginning shown itself possessed of a true historic sense in the apprehension of the progressive character of the deliverance of truth. Its doctrine of the covenants on its historical side represents the first attempt at constructing a history of revelation and may be justly considered the precursor of what is at present called biblical theology.[2]

This is a particularly clear indication, present frequently throughout his work, of the substantive continuity Vos saw between his own work and earlier Reformed theology and so how those who build on that work ought to view theirs, as well as what they (and others) should expect of it by way of continuity with the past. The Reformed confessions, and the theological framework they entail, particularly thinking on the covenant, far from being hostile, are quite hospitable toward – in fact they anticipate – giving greater, more methodologically self-conscious attention to the redemptive-historical substance of Scripture.

The preceding paragraph begs at least two questions. First, is Vos right? Did his work perhaps, despite his intention, set in motion factors of which he was unaware but which we at a distance are now able to see are in tension or even conflict with Reformed theology and its confessions? Second, if he is right, are there not, nonetheless, elements in that theology and its confessions at odds with its own underlying covenant-historical disposition? These are large and important questions. With them and the issues they raise on the horizon, I want to consider, as space allows, the role of the *ordo salutis* in the Westminster Standards.

II.

In his magisterial book on Paul's theology Herman Ridderbos observes repeatedly and on a variety of topics, sometimes explicitly, more often implicitly, that the apostle's interest is primarily the history of salvation (*historia salutis*), not the order of salvation (*ordo salutis*).[3] This distinction, its formulation apparently original with Ridderbos,[4] signals not only what Paul's controlling concern is, redemptive-historical, but also what it is not. Why the negative as well as the positive? In large part because of his perception, expressed already in the opening pages, that increasingly since the Reformation preponderant interest within Lutheran and Reformed theology and church life has shifted to the personal appropriation of salvation, to questions of *ordo salutis*, and so moved away from where it was for Luther and Calvin, like Paul and following him, on salvation as revealed once for all in Christ's death and resurrection (*historia salutis*) .[5]

This perception has validity, as long as what is *primarily* the case is in view, both for Paul and the Reformation tradition. As he proceeds, however, Ridderbos tends to leave the impression on a variety of topics that Paul has little or no interest in issues of *ordo salutis*. This has the effect, as I will try to show, of unnecessarily widening the difference between Paul and Calvin, on the one hand, and subsequent Reformed theology, on the other.

At this juncture it may be helpful to make a clarifying comment about the expression *ordo salutis*, at least as I am using it here. It can have two distinct senses, one broader, the other more specific. The latter, more technical sense is the more common and has in view the logical and/or causal, or even temporal 'order' or sequence of various discrete saving acts and benefits, as unfolded within the actual life of the individual sinner.[6] It may also be used, however, without having yet settled on a particular 'order' or even that there is one in the sense just indicated, to refer, more generally, to the ongoing application of salvation, in distinction from its once-for-all accomplishment. Understood in this sense, the *historia salutis/ordo salutis* distinction reformulates the classic Reformed distinction between redemption accomplished and applied, but in a way that accents the redemptive-historical nature of the accomplishment (impetration) and so the need to keep that in view in discussing issues of application (individual appropriation).

It is important not to confuse or otherwise equivocate on these two senses of *ordo salutis*. The narrower concept is subject to the criticism of tending in effect, in some instances more than others, to focus on *ordo* at the expense of *salutis*, of being so preoccupied with various acts of application in their logical/causal and even temporal sequence and interconnections that salvation itself, in its wholeness, becomes eclipsed, of so concentrating on the benefits of Christ's work in their variety and mutual relations, that he, in his person and work, recedes into the background. However, in making such criticisms, particularly from a redemptive-historical perspective, we must avoid the opposite extreme of depreciating all *ordo salutis* issues as unnecessary or even inappropriate. In fact, it is not putting it too strongly, the integrity of the gospel itself stands or falls with the *ordo salutis* in the broader sense, equivalent to the application of salvation (*applicatio salutis*) and distinct from its accomplishment.

That necessity can be highlighted by briefly noting Karl Barth's rejection of the notion of *ordo salutis*.[7] His dismissal, perhaps the most resolute and sweeping to date, turns on his idea of *Geschichte* ('historicity' or 'historicness'), involving the radically undivided contemporaneity or simultaneity, in all its aspects, of the single event of salvation (in this sense often termed 'the Christ-event'). Such a notion plainly has no place for the distinction between accomplishment and application, for a salvation in history, finished 2000 years ago, having its own integrity and historically distinct from its ongoing appropriation. Accordingly, Barth rejects any notion of *ordo salutis*, maintaining that it leads inevitably to psychologizing distortions of Christian existence.

But Barth's idea of *Geschichte*, leaving no room for the accomplishment-application distinction and so for any *ordo salutis* notion, excludes as well a temporal distinction or sequence between the two states of Christ; he denies their historical before and after, that in history Christ's exaltation followed his humiliation.[8] He sees, quite rightly, that the distinction between accomplishment and application is given with the sequence in time of humiliation followed by exaltation. To affirm or deny the latter is to affirm or deny the former; they stand or fall together.

Barth's view, it should be clear, involves a radical departure from biblical revelation, one that strikes at the very heart of the gospel. If Christ's state of exaltation is not separate from and subsequent to his state of humiliation, if his being 'highly exalted' and 'given the name above every name' did not follow, temporally, his 'obedience unto death' (Phil. 2:8-9), that is, if it is not the case that the incarnate Christ was for a time in the past, in history, actually exposed to God's just wrath on the sins of his people, but now, subsequently and permanently, for all eternity future, is no longer under God's wrath but restored to his favor under conditions of eschatological life, then, as Van Til tirelessly pointed out in critiquing Barth's theology, 'there is no transition from wrath to grace in history.'[9] But if there is no transition from wrath to grace in history, then there is no gospel and we are, as the apostle says, in the most pitiable condition of still being 'in our sins' (1 Cor. 15:18-19). The gospel, the salvation of sinners, stands or falls with the historical before and after of Christ's humiliation and exaltation.

Accordingly, with that before and after, with the historical distinction between them, is given the irreducible distinction between redemption accomplished and applied, between *historia salutis* and *ordo salutis*, where neither one may be allowed to diminish or eclipse the other. The unavoidable question of application, of the *ordo salutis* in the more general sense, is this: How does the then and there of Christ's transition from wrath to favor relate to the here and now of the sinner's transition from wrath to grace? How do Christ's death and resurrection, then and there, benefit sinners, here and now? What are those benefits and what is the pattern (ordo) in which they are communicated to sinners?

III.

From Barth I turn to Calvin and for two closely related reasons. In a most instructive and edifying way, unparalleled in the Reformed tradition as far as I have seen, he shows the absolute necessity of *ordo salutis* concerns and at the same time has led the way in pointing us to an *ordo salutis* faithful to the *historia salutis*, to an appropriation of salvation that honors the redemptive-historical structure and substance of Scripture.[10]

Book 3 of the *Institutes* is entitled, 'The Way in Which We Receive the Grace of Christ: What Benefits Come to Us from It, and What Effects Follow.' This title plainly shows that Calvin understands himself to be concerned throughout with the application of salvation ('the grace of Christ'), its 'benefits' and consequent 'effects' (in their irreducible plurality and diversity, as he will go on to show). All told, his concern is 'the way' (Latin: not *ordo*, but *modus*, 'mode', 'manner', 'method'), in which 'we' (believers) 'receive' this grace, in which this salvation is appropriated by 'us.' With this concern restated in the opening words of 3:1:1, the very next sentence reads:

> First, we must understand that as long as Christ remains outside of us, and we are separated from him, all that he has suffered and done for the salvation of the human race remains useless and of no value to us.[11]

In my opinion, on the matter before us no more important words have been written than these. Incisively and in a fundamental way, they address both the *necessity* and *nature* of application, the basic concerns of an *ordo salutis*. So far as necessity is concerned, to put it somewhat provocatively with an eye to some current debates, Calvin is saying something like, 'the redemptive-historical Christ, the Christ of redemptive history, as often conceived, is not enough'; in fact, he says, this Christ is 'useless and of no value to us'!

Certainly this Christ, his death and resurrection, including his ascension and Pentecost, as the culmination of redemptive history, are the heart-core of the gospel. They are 'of first importance,' as

Paul says (1 Cor. 15:3); he and other New Testament writers make that abundantly clear. That centrality is not at issue here. But to punctuate the gospel, particularly its proclamation, with a full stop after Christ's death, resurrection and ascension (allowing for his future return) does not do the gospel full justice, as 'the power of God unto salvation', and as it involves 'the revelation of the righteousness of God' (Rom 1:16-17). In fact, as Calvin intimates, such a parsing of the gospel misses an integral component, something absolutely essential.

Or as subsequent Reformed theology affirmed aphoristically: 'Dempta applicatione, redemptio non est redemptio' ('Without application, redemption is not redemption').[12] Herman Bavinck makes a sweeping and quite striking observation to put the importance of application in proper perspective. Taking the activity of God in its entirety, he says, there are just three great *initiating* works: the creation of the world, the incarnation of the Word, and the outpouring of the Holy Spirit.[13] In other words, seen in a most basic profile, the work of the triune God consists in creation, and, given the fall, redemption accomplished/*historia salutis* and redemption applied/*ordo salutis*.

In the course of his lengthy treatment of the *ordo salutis* as a topic, Bavinck makes another statement, one that over the years has continued to challenge my thinking, 'In his state of exaltation there still remains much for Christ to do.'[14] This statement is surely faithful to Scripture (e.g., Rom. 8:33-34; Heb. 7:25, 8:1-2) and the Reformed confessions (e.g., *Westminster Shorter Catechism*, 23-26; *Larger Catechism*, 42-45, 52-55; *Belgic Confession*, 26; *Heidelberg Catechism*, 46-47, 49-51). We may ask, however, whether, with its implications, it has been developed in those confessions as it might, or functioned in the life of the church as it should. All told, the 'it is finished' of the cross is true, preciously true; it points to the end of his humiliation and, together with his resurrection, to remission of sin and entitlement to eschatological life as definitively achieved and secured. But it is only *relatively* true, relative to the 'much,' as Bavinck says, that it remains for the exalted Christ to do.

It should be apparent, then, that Christ is not only active in redemption accomplished but also in redemption applied; the one just as much as the other is *his* work. In fact, from the perspective of his present exaltation the distinction between redemption accomplished and applied, between *historia salutis* and *ordo salutis* begins to blur. The way it is often put, that accomplishment is Christ's task, application the Holy Spirit's, is helpful but can also be misleading. The latter, no less than the former, is Christ-centered.

The question, then, is not only, as I put it earlier, how the once-for-all 'there and then' of Christ's work relates to the 'here and now' of my/the church's life, but also, how the 'there and *now*' of his (present) activity relates to the 'here and now' of my life, or, given that the ascended Christ indwells the church by his Spirit, that, in fact, he is also present with the church *as* 'the life-giving Spirit' (1 Cor. 15:45),[15] how does the '*here* and *now*' of his activity relate to the 'here and now' of my life?

The second sentence of Book 3 of the *Institutes*, quoted above, not only highlights the necessity of *ordo salutis* concerns but also their essence. The pivotal, absolutely crucial consideration, the heart of the matter, put negatively as Calvin does here, is that Christ not remain 'outside us' (extra nos), that we not be 'separated from him' (ab eo). Or, expressed positively, as he presently does, that 'we grow into one body [in unum] with him'. Here Calvin has in view the union that exists between Christ and the believer, referred to repeatedly and in a variety of ways throughout Book 3 and elsewhere in his writings. This union he sees to be central and most decisive in the application of redemption.

It is essential to be clear about this union, about its nature and scope, especially since it is easy to equivocate on or otherwise overlook irreducible distinctions in discussing union with Christ. Expressed categorically, the union of which Calvin speaks here is neither 'predestinarian,' in the sense of election in Christ 'before the foundation of the world' (Eph. 1:4-5), nor 'redemptive-historical,' being contemplated in him and represented by him in his work, as the last Adam, in 'the fullness of time' (Gal. 4:4). Rather, in view is union, he immediately specifies, as it is 'obtained by faith' (fide), union as it does not exist apart from or prior to faith but is given with, in fact is inseparable from faith; as it has been categorized, union that is 'spiritual' or 'mystical.'

This mention of faith, and the key role accorded to it, prompts Calvin, still within this opening section (3:1:1), to touch on what would become a central question in subsequent discussions about the *ordo salutis*, namely the origin of faith, giving rise eventually in Reformed theology to the doctrine of regeneration in a narrower sense. We observe, so Calvin, 'that not all indiscriminately embrace that communion with Christ which is offered through the gospel.'

Why? Not because of some differentiating factor on our side. The answer is not to be found by looking into ourselves or contemplating the mystery of human freedom and willing. Rather, consistent with his uniform teaching elsewhere about the total inability of the will due to sin, we must 'climb higher' and consider 'the secret energy of the Spirit' (arcana Spiritus efficacia). Faith is Spirit-worked, sovereignly and efficaciously.

The union Calvin has in view is forged by the Spirit's working faith in us, a faith that 'puts on' Christ (citing Gal. 3:27), that embraces Christ as he is offered to faith in the gospel. Faith is the bond of that union seen from our side. 'To sum up, the Holy Spirit is the bond by which Christ effectually unites us to himself.'

This, in a nutshell, is Calvin's *ordo salutis*: union with Christ by (Spirit-worked) faith; being and continuing to be united with Christ by faith, faith that, through the power of the Spirit, 'embraces Christ, freely offered to us in the gospel' (*Westminster Shorter Catechism*, 31). This 'ordo' is at once simple as well as profound and comprehensive, because on matters of application it keeps the focus squarely on *Christ* – specifically on the crucified and resurrected Christ, on Christ who is what he now is as he has suffered and is now glorified. It does not lose sight of the various 'benefits' and 'effects' of salvation (cf. the title of Book 3), in all of their multiplicity, but recognizes, as he goes on to show, that these have their place only within union with this presently exalted Christ, as they are its specific outworkings, its inseparable as well as mutually irreducible manifestations. It is an 'ordo,' I take it, that captures, better than other proposals, the essence of 'the great eschatological *ordo salutis*'[16] taught in the New Testament, especially by the apostle Paul.

IV.

Subsequent, post-Reformation theology, in this regard, represents something of an obscuring of Calvin. We must be on guard against overstating this criticism. Certainly, in the area of application important advances took place in developing specific doctrines of grace, for instance, the doctrine of regeneration in the aftermath of the emergence of Arminianism. But a prevailing tendency down to the present has been to be preoccupied with the various benefits of Christ's work, and their interrelations – logical, causal and sometimes even temporal,[17] *ordo* in this sense – so that while Christ himself is certainly there, the danger is that he fades, more or less, into the background, and where to put union with Christ – spiritual, mystical union – in the *ordo salutis* remains a conundrum. Ironically, the better the biblical doctrine is understood – union as an all-encompassing reality that resists being correlated as one benefit among others, like a link in a chain – the more keenly this conundrum is felt. This is the case particularly within the Reformed tradition.[18] Lutheran theology senses no problem here, since union is regularly put after justification, as just one among others of its attendant benefits.

Where, then, do the Westminster Standards fall within this assessment of post-Reformation developments? Three observations are in order. First, in distinction from positions no doubt held by a number of the framers, the Standards themselves do not spell out a particular *ordo salutis* (of causally concatenated acts or works of God). Within the bounds of what they do teach, an explicitly articulated *ordo salutis* is left an open question. The Standards do not foreclose that issue for those who subscribe to them.[19]

Second, such indications as the Standards do contain point to a position close to Calvin's. That can be seen most easily from two parallel sections of the *Larger* and *Shorter Catechisms*.[20] At question and answer 58 the *Larger Catechism* begins to take up 'the application' of 'the benefits which Christ hath procured'. Following questions dealing primarily with the visible church/invisible church (the elect) distinction and the 'special privileges' of the former (59-64), question 65 asks about the 'special benefits' of the latter, with the answer: 'The members of the invisible church by Christ enjoy union and communion with him in grace and glory.' This answer structures the basic flow all the way through question and answer 90: union with Christ (66-68); communion in grace with Christ (69-81); communion in glory with Christ (82-90). Within the scope of the application of redemption to the elect, then, union and communion with Christ are seen as most basic, encompassing all other benefits.

Answer 66 goes on to describe this union as being 'joined to Christ,' and specifies that the union in view is effected 'spiritually and mystically, yet really and inseparably.' The next two answers also refer to this union, as the goal of effectual calling, as being 'draw[n] ... to Jesus Christ' (67) and 'truly com[ing] to Jesus Christ' (68). Then answer 69, in addressing 'the communion in grace which the members of the invisible church have with Christ,' speaks of 'their justification, adoption, sanctification, and whatever else, in this life, *manifests their union with him* (emphasis added). So far as I can see, answer 69 is the most forthright assertion in the Westminster Standards on *ordo salutis* issues as usually discussed, and what is noteworthy is that union with Christ is clearly not put in series with the other benefits mentioned, like a link in a chain. Rather, those benefits 'manifest' being united with Christ; that is, the former are functions or aspects of the latter.

Shorter Catechism 29-32 are to the same effect, though less clearly. Answer 29 brings into view 'the effectual application' of redemption. Answer 30 is properly read as expressing the essence of that application: taking place in effectual calling, it is the Spirit's 'working faith in us, and thereby uniting us to Christ.' Answer 31 reinforces that the union in view ('to embrace Jesus Christ') is the goal of effectual calling.

Question and answer 32 enumerate the present benefits of redemption applied, but are silent about union with Christ. This omission is somewhat surprising and unlike the parallel in *Larger Catechism* 69. In light of the latter as well as their own immediate context, a better wording might have been: Question: 'What benefits do they that are *united to Christ* partake of in this life? Answer: 'They that are *united to Christ* do in this life partake of justification, adoption, and sanctification, and the several benefits which ...' (changed wording in italics).[21]

We may conclude, then, that in the Westminster Standards the heart of the application of salvation, underlying all further consideration of *ordo salutis* questions, is being united to Christ by Spirit-worked faith, a union providing for multiple other benefits, without any one benefit either being confused with or existing separately from the others. This is essentially Calvin's '*ordo salutis*,' though not as clearly elaborated as one might wish.

Third, in the light of these observations, I offer for further reflection and testing the following thesis on the overall relationship between biblical theology and the Westminster Standards. The concern of biblical theology, as it has developed, has been predominantly the once-for-all accomplishment of salvation; for the Standards, predominantly its ongoing application. Both, biblical theology and the Standards, share both concerns, accomplishment and application, but with different emphases. In terms of the *historia salutis*/*ordo salutis* distinction, the former is biblical theology's major focus, the latter, its minor focus; for the Standards these foci are reversed. Both, biblical theology and the Standards, have the same dual or elliptical concern but with differing accents. These respective accents need not be seen as mutually exclusive; they are not antagonistic but complementary. There is no good reason, at least for the large area of the salvation revealed in Christ, both its once-for-all accomplishment and its ongoing application, why biblical theology cannot work compatibly within the theological framework of the Standards, to enrich that framework and at points perhaps improve its formulations without fear of undermining it. The same may be said, as far as I can see, of the other areas covered in the Standards.

V.

Calvin's approach to *ordo salutis* issues, provided for as well in the Westminster Standards, has multiple strengths. In the space that remains to me here, I highlight just two that emerge as he deals with the application of redemption in Book 3 of the *Institutes*. Both have a bearing on the doctrine of justification and its biblically faithful maintenance today.

First, the basic flow of Book 3 is noteworthy. Chapter 1, as already noted, introduces union with Christ by Spirit-created faith; chapter 2 further treats faith (its 'definition' and 'properties'); chapters 3–10 take up 'regeneration by faith' (regeneration here used in a broader sense, equivalent to sanctification in subsequent theology) and the Christian life; chapters 11-18 then focus on justification by faith (followed by chapters on Christian freedom, prayer, election and the final resurrection). What is remarkable here is the 'ordo' (!): Calvin discusses the change that takes place within the sinner, our ongoing inner renewal and personal transformation, *before* the definitive change effected in the sinner's legal status, our forensic standing *coram Deo*. He addresses the removal of the corrupting slavery of sin before considering the abolition of the guilt it incurs. All told, he treats sanctification, at length, before justification. Such an approach contrasts conspicuously with subsequent Reformed and Lutheran theology, where justification always (without exception?) precedes sanctification.

Why does Calvin proceed as he does? More importantly, what enables him to take this approach without compromising or minimizing the Reformation doctrine of justification, but rather, in taking it, to provide one of the classic discussions of that doctrine?

One can only admire what Calvin has achieved in structuring the first 18 chapters of Book 3 as he did. Here is one of the great moments in church history, a truly impressive theological coup.

The constantly echoing charge from Rome at that time (and ever since) is that the Protestant doctrine of justification, of a graciously imputed righteousness received by faith alone, ministers spiritual slothfulness and indifference to holy living. Subsequent Reformed and Lutheran theology, intent on safeguarding the priority of justification to sanctification, especially against what was in effect Rome's reversal in suspending justification on an ongoing process of sanctification, responded to this charge by asserting forcefully, and more or less adequately, that faith as the alone instrument of justification is never alone in the person justified but a working, obedient faith, in the sense that it is 'ever accompanied with all other saving graces' (*Westminster Confession*, 11:2).

Calvin's approach is different. He counters Rome's charge, masterfully and, in my opinion, much more effectively, by dwelling at great length (133 pages!) on the nature of faith, particularly its inherent disposition and concern for holiness, distinct from the issue of justification and before beginning to discuss justification. He concerns himself extensively with sanctification and faith in its sanctified expressions, largely bypassing justification and without having yet said virtually anything about the role of faith in justification. He has taken this approach, he says in a transitional passage right at the beginning of chapter 11, the first on justification, because 'It was more to the point to understand first how little devoid of good works is the faith, through which alone we obtain free righteousness by the mercy of God.' Calvin destroys Rome's charge by showing that faith, in its Protestant understanding, entails a disposition to holiness without particular reference to justification, a concern for Godliness that is not to be understood only as a consequence of justification.

Calvin proceeds as he does, and is *free* to do so, because for him the relative 'ordo' or priority of justification and sanctification is indifferent theologically. Rather, what has controlling soteriological importance is the priority to both of (spiritual, 'existential,' faith-) union with Christ.[22] This bond is such that it provides both justification and sanctification ('a double grace'), as each is distinct and essential. Because of this union both, being reckoned righteous and being renewed in righteousness, are given without confusion, yet also without separation.

To illustrate Calvin uses a metaphor that seems hard to improve on (3:11:6): Christ, our righteousness, is the Sun, justification, its light, sanctification, its heat. The Sun is at once the source of both, so that light and heat are inseparable. But only light illumines and only heat warms, not the reverse; both are always present, without the one becoming the other. Or as he puts it elsewhere, Christ 'cannot be divided into pieces.'[23] There is no partial union with Christ, no sharing in only some of his benefits. If believers do not have the whole Christ, they have no Christ; unless they share in all of his benefits they share in none of them. Justification and sanctification are inseparable not because God has decided that subsequent to forgiving sinners and extrinsic to that forgiveness, he will also renew them. Rather, they are inseparable because of who Christ is and the nature of our union with him. Calvin calls justification 'the main hinge on which religion turns,'[24] but clearly it is that for him only as that hinge is firmly anchored, and religion pivots, within the believer's union with Christ.

Second, prominent in Protestant, especially Lutheran, development of the doctrine of justification is the notion of the imputation Christ's righteousness as an 'alien' righteousness; the righteousness that justifies is apart from us, it is not our own but Christ's. At issue here is the concern, not only understandable but necessary, not to confuse Christ's righteousness, as the sole ground for justification, with anything that takes place within the sinner, the concern not to obscure that justifying righteousness is perfect and complete, apart from anything the believer does, in what Christ has done, once for all, in his finished work. In that sense, to speak of 'alien righteousness' is surely defensible.

At the same time, we should recognize, a definite liability attaches to this expression. 'Alien' suggests what is remote, at a distance; it can easily leave the impression of an isolated imputative act, without a clear relationship to Christ and the other aspects of salvation. In this regard, I have the impression that some Reformed thinking on justification centers on a line, focused on the individual sinner, that moves from my eternal election to its realization and documentation in history by my faith, produced by regeneration, that receives justification. On this view Christ and his work are surely essential but recede into the background, along with other aspects of salvation.

A different tone is heard in Calvin. In expressing himself on justification, including imputation, he always, explicitly or implicitly, relates it to union with Christ. Perhaps his most pointed statement on imputation in this regard is the following:

> Therefore, that joining together of Head and members, that indwelling of Christ in our heart – in short, that *mystical union* – are accorded by us the highest degree of importance, so that Christ, having been made ours, makes us sharers with him in the gifts with which he has been endowed. *We do not, therefore, contemplate him outside ourselves from afar in order that his righteousness may be imputed to us but because we put on Christ and are engrafted into his body – in short, because he deigns to make us one with him.* For this reason, we glory that we have *fellowship of righteousness* with him.[25]

Here there is no mingling of Christ's righteousness with some presumed righteousness of our own. But, at the same time, that righteousness, as imputed, is, in an absolutely crucial sense, anything but 'alien.'

Such remarkable and compelling words, I dare say, could only be written by someone with the *ordo salutis* intimated in *Institutes*, 3:1:1, and who has also incisively anticipated subsequent insights into the redemptive-historical substance of Scripture and the gospel, particularly the soteriology of the apostle Paul. These words are no less timely today, when, perhaps as never before, the notion of imputed righteousness is either misunderstood or rejected.[26] Only as we maintain imputation as a facet of what Calvin calls our 'fellowship of righteousness' (*iustitiae societatem*) with Christ, as an integral aspect of our union with Christ crucified and exalted, will we do so in a fashion that is fully cogent biblically. As added value, doing that will provide a much more effective response to the persisting misunderstanding of Roman Catholics and others that the Reformation doctrine of justification renders sanctification unnecessary. It will also help the heirs of the Reformation to keep clear to themselves something they have not always or uniformly appreciated, how it is that sanctification, involving as it does the pursuit of that 'holiness without which no one will see the Lord' (Heb. 12:14), is as integral to the salvation accomplished and applied in Christ as is justification.

NOTES

1. Vos (1862–1949) was Professor of Biblical Theology at Princeton Seminary from 1893 until his retirement in 1932.

2. *Redemptive History and Biblical Interpretation. The Shorter Writings of Geerhardus Vos* (ed. R. B. Gaffin, Jr.; Phillipsburg, NJ: P & R, 1980), p. 232.

3. *Paul. An Outline of His Theology* (Grand Rapids: Eerdmans, 1975), e.g., pp. 14, 45, 63, 91, 177/n.53, 205-06,211, 214ff., 221-22, 268, 365, 378, 404.

4. I have not found it earlier than in his 1957 essay, 'The Redemptive-Historical Character of Paul's Preaching', in *When the Time Had Fully Come* (Grand Rapids: Eerdmans, 1957), pp. 48, 49. It is apparently not present in pertinent discussions in Herman Bavinck,Vos or G. C. Berkouwer, althoughVos, *The Pauline Eschatology* (Grand Rapids: Baker, 1979/1930), chapter 2 ('The Interaction Between Eschatology and Soteriology') clearly anticipates it.

5. *Paul,* p. 14.

6. The first occurrence of *ordo salutis,* apparently, is in this sense, in the 18th century within emerging pietism from where it is taken over and eventually becomes widely current in both Lutheran and Reformed orthodoxy. A precursor is present already at the time of the Reformation in Bullinger, who speaks of the *dispensatio salutis* ['dispensing' or 'administering of salvation']. While that expression does not take hold, the basic area that Bullinger (and later *ordo salutis* thinking) have in view, the application of salvation, is a major concern for other reformers, like Luther and Calvin, as well as subsequent Reformation orthodoxy, for Reformed theology increasingly in the period after the Synod of Dort on the 'ordo' aspect.The reference to Bullinger is cited by G. C. Berkouwer, *Geloof en rechtvaardiging* (Kampen: Kok, 1949), p. 24 [omitted from the ET, *Faith and Justification* (Grand Rapids: Eerdmans, 1949)], p. 26; cf. O. Weber, *Foundations of Dogmatics* (ET; Grand Rapids: Eerdmans, 1983), 2:336-38 andW. H. Velema, *Wet en evangelie* (Kampen: Kok, 1987), pp. 125-28.

7. *Church Dogmatics* (Edinburgh: T & T Clark, 1958, 1962), 4/2: 502-03; 4/3: 505-06.

8. Correlatively and most radically, he denies as well the historicity of the fall, in the sense of the historical sequence of creation (a time of original beatitude at the beginning of human history where sin was not yet present) and fall.

9. 'The present writer is of the opinion that, for all its verbal similarity to historic Protestantism, Barth's theology is, in effect, a denial of it. There is, he believes, in Barth's view no 'transition from wrath to grace' in history. This was the writer's opinion in 1946 when he published *The New Modernism.* A careful consideration of Barth's more recent writings has only established him more firmly in this conviction' (C. Van Til, *Christianity and Barthianism* [Philadelphia: Presbyterian and Reformed, 1962], Preface, vii). A search of the phrase 'transition from wrath to grace' in *The Works of Cornelius Van Til* (CD-ROM; New York: Labels Army Co., 1997) indicates 74 occurrences in 59 different books and articles; almost all refer to its denial, and of these the large majority have in view Barth's theology, either explicitly or implicitly.

10. C. Graafland, "Heeft Calvijn een bepaalde orde des heils geleerd?," in ed. J. van Oort, *Verbi Divini Minister* (Amsterdam: ton Bolland, 1983), pp. 109-127, concludes: "... so strongly did Calvin put Christ and faith as the work of the Holy Spirit at the center that a particular order or sequence in the application of salvation remains subordinate to that emphasis. In that sense Calvin's theology is not to be termed an

ordo salutis theology, and he would have never been able to summarize his theology, as W. Perkins did his, under the title, 'the golden chain of salvation' " (p. 127). ["... Calvijn zo sterk Christus en het geloof als werk van de Heilige Geest in het centrum heeft gesteld, dat en bepaalde orde of volgorde in de applicatie van het heil duidelijk daaraan ondergeschikt blijft. Calvijns theologie is in die zin geen heilsordelijke theologie te noemen en hij zou, zoals b.v. W. Perkins, zijn theologie nooit hebben kunnen samenvatten onder de titel: 'de gouden keten des heils.'"]

11. J. Calvin, *Institutes of the Christian Religion*, trans. F. L. Battles (ed. J. T. McNeill, The Library of Christian Classics, 20; Philadelphia: Westminster, 1960), 1:537.

12. Quoted in H. Bavinck, *Gereformeerde Dogmatiek* (Kampen: Kok, 1976), 3:520.

13. *Dogmatiek*, 3:494.

14. *Dogmatiek*, 3:571; cf. 573.

15. I take it that careful exegesis has settled that the reference here is to the Holy Spirit; see, building on Vos, Ridderbos and John Murray among others, my 'Life-Giving Spirit': Probing the Center of Paul's Pneumatology,' *Journal of the Evangelical Theological Society*, 41, 4 (December 1998): 573-89, esp. 575-82 and *Resurrection and Redemption. A Study in Paul's Soteriology* (2nd ed., = *The Centrality of the Resurrection* [Grand Rapids: Baker, 1978]; Phillipsburg, NJ: Presbyterian and Reformed, 1987), pp. 85-87; see also, e.g., 2 Cor. 3:17; Rom. 8:9-10; 1 Cor. 6:17.

16. Adapting the language of Ridderbos, *Paul*, p. 200.

17. A glaring instance, not unknown among some Reformed teachers and pastors, is to maintain that a person, as a grown child or adult, may be regenerate for some time, before becoming a believer. John Murray's trenchant classroom comment on this (as I recall it): biblically considered, the notion of a regenerate unbeliever is a 'monstrosity'!

18. Two instances where the problem is palpable though not really addressed or resolved are A. A. Hodge, 'The Ordo Salutis: or, Relation in the Order of Nature of Holy Character and Divine Favor,' *The Princeton Review*, 54 (1878): 304-21, and, more recently, J. Murray, *Redemption – Accomplished and Applied* (Grand Rapids: Eerdmans, 1955). Murray is clear that union with Christ 'is in itself a very broad and embracive subject (p. 201) and 'underlies every aspect of redemption both in its accomplishment and its application' (p. 205). But how, in application specifically, ('spiritual,' 'mystical') union is related to other aspects in the *ordo* he maintains is not made clear.

19. Some semblance of an *ordo* might seem to be implied by the sequence of pertinent chapters in the Confession and questions and answers in the Catechisms, but a comparison of the three documents also reveals differences in sequence; the Standards do not provide a uniform sequence.

20. I make no claim for a complete survey of the Standards here, although I hope not to have overlooked anything important or counterindicative.

21. LC 69 and SC 32 also differ in perspective: in the former justification, adoption, sanctification and whatever other blessings, all 'manifest' union with Christ, while in the latter these other 'several benefits' are said to 'either accompany or flow from' justification, adoption and sanctification (cf. SC, Q. 36). Both perspectives are true, but that of the LC is more basic.

22. 'Let us sum these ['benefits of God'] up. Christ was given to us by God's generosity, to be grasped and possessed by us in faith. By partaking of him, we principally receive a double grace: namely, [justification and sanctification]' (*Institutes*, 1:725 [3:11:1]).

23. *Institutes*, 1:798 (3:16:1).

24. *Institutes*, 1:726 (3:11:1).

25. *Institutes*, 1:737 (3:11:10), emphasis added. Note that this statement occurs just in a context where he is intent on refuting Osiander's serious error that justifying righteousness consists of the believer's 'essential righteousness'. In other words, the root of that error, a false understanding of union, does not lead Calvin to tone down on his own understanding of union in relation to justification bur rather to assert that union most emphatically.

26. See, e.g., the recent sweeping rejection of R. H. Gundry, *Books & Culture*, January/February 2001, pp. 6-9.

D. Ministry in the Life of the Church

PASTORAL MINISTRY IN UNION WITH CHRIST

Philip Graham Ryken

Rightly or wrongly, Calvinism has often been criticized for giving inadequate attention to practical theology. Fearing that Calvinist clergy are too weighed down with doctrine to attend to the more practical aspects of pastoral ministry, those who make this criticism seek to put the practicality back into theology.

There may be some truth to the conventional criticism. But there are also good reasons to have the opposite concern, namely, that the Reformed community has given insufficient attention to the theological basis for pastoral ministry. If practical theology ought to be practical, it must also be theological. That is to say, it must delineate from Scripture the doctrinal dimensions of gospel ministry. With this goal in mind, the present essay highlights an important and often neglected doctrine that can be used to construct a theology of pastoral ministry that is really and truly a *theology*. It takes as its starting point the apostolic aspiration of Philippians 3:10-11: 'I want to know Christ and the power of his resurrection and the fellowship of sharing in his sufferings, becoming like him in his death, and so, somehow, to attain to the resurrection from the dead.' Its thesis is that pastoral ministry is exercised in union with Christ, both in his humiliation and in his exaltation.[1]

The Doctrine of Union with Christ

There is little question as to the importance of the doctrine of union with Christ. Being connected to Christ is one of the central concerns of the New Testament. Over and over again, the apostle Paul emphasizes the necessity of being found 'in Christ' (Phil. 3:9). He emphasizes this because it is in Christ that all of salvation's blessings are located: 'Praise be to the God and Father of our Lord Jesus Christ, who has blessed us in the heavenly realms with every spiritual blessing *in Christ*' (Eph. 1:3). This vital unitive relationship virtually comprehends our salvation: we are saved in Christ. It also summarizes the Christian life: the life that we now live is a new life in Christ. 'Therefore, if anyone is *in Christ*, he is a new creation' (2 Cor. 5:17).

Given the consistent biblical emphasis on being in Christ, the doctrine of union with Christ properly occupies a central place in systematic theology. We were predestined and elected in Christ. On the basis of our union with him we are justified, and through his Spirit we are adopted and sanctified. It is in Christ that we persevere, and it is into his image that one day we will be glorified. Therefore, as John Murray has written, 'Union with Christ is really the central truth of the whole doctrine of salvation.... It embraces the wide span of salvation from its ultimate source in the eternal election of God to its final fruition in the glorification of the elect.'[2] Without beginning and without end, every aspect of salvation is wrapped up in union with Christ, the central dogmatic principle that unites the several doctrines of Reformed soteriology.

Union with Christ was a prominent theme in the theology of the Reformers. To give the most notable example, it served as one of the organizing principles for Calvin's *Institutes*. 'We must understand,' wrote Calvin, 'that as long as Christ remains outside of us, and we are separated from him, all that he has suffered and done for the salvation of the human race remains useless and of no value for us.... All that he possesses is nothing to us until we grow into one body with him.'[3] Calvin went on to teach that it is the Holy Spirit who unites us to Christ by faith.[4] By the faith the Spirit provides, we bind ourselves to Christ; by his Spirit, Christ binds us to himself, and thereby 'makes us participants not only in all his benefits but also in himself.'[5] This experiential union with Christ finds its ultimate basis in the incarnation and also in the 'wonderful exchange' whereby Christ was pleased to 'present our flesh as the price of satisfaction to God's righteous judgment, and in the same flesh, to pay the penalty that we had deserved'.[6]

Many later Reformed theologians adopted Calvin's emphasis on union and communion with Christ. The doctrine is present in the writings of post-Reformation theologians such as Beza and Zanchius.[7] It exercised a formative influence on the theology of the English Puritans and Scottish Presbyterians, some of whom considered union with Christ the conduit for all spiritual life and the fountainhead of every spiritual blessing.[8] In his book on Puritan spirituality, Gordon Wakefield went so far as to identify the doctrine as 'the normative dogma of Reformed Christianity.'[9] The Puritan John Brinsley wrote an entire book on the subject, entitled *Mystical Implantation; or, The Great Gospel Mystery of the Christian's Union and Communion with, and Conformity to Jesus Christ, both in his Death and Resurrection, Opened and Applied*. As Brinsley's subtitle indicates, the believer's union with Christ is tied to the redemptive history of Christ's saving work. To be united to Christ is to participate in his death and resurrection.

At the same time, union with Christ involves Christ's present and active work in the life of the believer. This is how the Puritan John Preston described the experiential aspect of the doctrine: 'That is, when, there is an union made between Christ and us, when he comes into the heart, when he dwells in us and we in him; when Christ is so brought into our hearts, that he lives there, and when we are so united to him, that we live in him; when he grows in us, as the Vine in the branches; and we grow in him, as the branches in the Vine: when faith hath done this, then it is an effectual faith, when it knits and unites us to Christ.'[10] Clearly, union with Christ is not a matter of sterile speculation. On the contrary, for the practical Calvinist it pulses with the heartbeat of genuine piety – a heart of faith joined to the Savior of love. In the words of the Puritan Paul Bayne, 'by faith we are united with Christ, so that we come to have Communion in all that is Christ's.'[11] Or as the Old Princetonian Archibald Alexander insisted, 'If Christ be in us there will be communion.... He will sometimes speak to us – He will speak comfortably to us – He will give tokens of his love. He will invite our confidence and will shed abroad his love in our hearts. And if Christ be formed within us we cannot remain altogether ignorant of his presence. Our hearts, while he communes with us, will sometimes burn within us.'[12]

I want to know Christ

When the Puritans considered the work of Christ, they often made a distinction between his humiliation and his exaltation. Humiliation was the work of Christ in suffering and dying for sin. According to the *Westminster Shorter Catechism*, it 'consisted in his being born, and that in a low condition, made under the law, undergoing the miseries of this life, the wrath of God, and the cursed death of the cross; in being buried, and continuing under the power of death for a time' (A. 27). Exaltation is the work of Christ in conquering sin and death through his resurrection and ascension. To quote again from the *Shorter Catechism*, this consisted 'in his rising again from the dead on the third day, in ascending up into heaven, in sitting at the right hand of God the Father, and in coming to judge the world at the last day' (A. 28).

These two aspects of Christ's work – humiliation and exaltation – are clearly in view in Philippians 3:10-11, which mentions both the sufferings and the glories of Christ.[13] The *kais* in verse 10 are *epexegetical*. In other words, what follows serves to explain what Paul meant by knowing Christ. He meant knowing him in his crucifixion and resurrection. He wanted the kind of 'fellowship with Christ, or union with him, in which all that Christ had done for him in his life, death, resurrection and ascension was brought into his life through the ministry of the Holy Spirit.'[14] Earlier in the Philippians letter the apostle traced the trajectory of Christ's work, the grand parabola of redemption that swept from equality with God down to the obedience of crucifixion, and then back up to the highest place (Phil. 2:5-11). In order to accomplish salvation, God the Son went from glory to glory by way of the cross. This was the Christ whom Paul wanted to know: the Christ who suffered, died, and rose again. To put this in the categories of systematic theology, he wanted to be united to Christ in both his humiliation and exaltation.

In order to attain this knowledge of Christ, it was necessary for Paul to declare spiritual bankruptcy. All the things he formerly had counted as assets – his ethnic heritage, his educational background, his ecclesiastical pedigree, his ethical standards – all these things had to be written off as liabilities (Phil. 3:4-7). Furthermore, compared to the superlative joy of knowing Christ, Paul calculated that his religious achievements added up to nothing more than a filthy pile of refuse (*skubala*; Phil. 3:8). The best thing, the most valuable thing, the surpassingly great thing was to know Christ and to be found in him. Paul gave up everything else to be united to Jesus Christ, receiving in him salvation by faith.

Now the apostle's burning and passionate desire was 'to know Christ and the power of his resurrection and the fellowship of sharing in his sufferings, becoming like him in his death' (Phil. 3:10). Paul knew Christ already, of course. He had known him for decades, ever since he met him on the Damascus Road (Acts 9). But knowing Christ only made Paul want to know him all the more. He wanted to become ever more closely identified with the crucified and glorified Christ.

Paul's aspiration to know Christ in his humiliation and exaltation usually is taken as a general comment on the Christian life. That is to say, as we live in Christ we are conformed to the realities of the cross and the empty tomb. But what the apostle says about being united to Christ in suffering and glory should also be considered from the vantage point of Christian ministry. Paul was writing these words not simply as a Christian, but also as a minister of the gospel. It was in his ministry – more than anywhere else – that God would satisfy his desire to be humiliated and exalted with Christ. Like everything else in the Christian life, the ministry of word and sacrament is exercised in union with Christ. In order to proclaim Christ, the minister must know Christ in both his crucifixion and resurrection. The doctrine of union with Christ thus provides the paradigm for a theology of pastoral ministry.[15]

Becoming Like Him in His Death

To follow the pattern of Christ's own ministry, in which the cross came before the crown, one must begin with the sufferings of the ministry. Pastoral ministry is not a matter of life and death, but a matter of death, then life: 'we share in his sufferings in order that we may also share in his glory' (Rom. 8:17; cf. 1 Pet. 4:13). And Philippians 3:10-11 leads us to expect pastoral ministry to contain suffering as well as glory. As Stu Webber has written, 'The pastor who is most Christlike is not the one who is most gloriously fulfilled in every moment of his ministry, but the one whose ministry has in it unbelievable elements of crucifixion.'[16]

The biblical history of gospel proclamation is primarily a story of suffering. Few of the biblical preachers were successful, at least by any worldly standard. And for every success there seem to be dozens of failures and flameouts. For every man who turned the nation back to God, many others were mocked and persecuted, some so severely that they were tempted to leave the ministry, or even to despair of life itself. God said, 'I will send them prophets and apostles, some of whom they will kill and others they will persecute' (Luke 11:49).

Consider the Old Testament prophets. Their call narratives make for inspiring reading; however, what most of them were called to do was to suffer. Samuel heard God's voice in the night, yet the message he received made his ears tingle with fear: judgment on Eli, his father in the faith (1 Sam. 3:11-14). Jeremiah was assured that God would always be with him, but at the same time he was informed that the entire nation – all the people, priests, and politicians – would fight against him (Jer. 1:17-19). Hosea was told to marry a whore (Hos. 1:2). The story of Isaiah's call is the most inspiring of all, with its thrilling response: 'Here am I. Send me!' (Isa. 6:8). But what was Isaiah sent to do? God said, 'Go and tell this people: 'Be ever hearing, but never understanding; be ever seeing, but never perceiving.' Make the heart of this people calloused; make their ears dull and close their eyes. Otherwise they might see with their eyes, hear with their ears, understand with their hearts, and turn and be healed' (Isa. 6:9-10). From the outset, Isaiah's preaching ministry was doomed to fail. Its purpose was not to help people come to faith, but to confirm them in their unbelief!

Many prophets faced rebellion from God's people. The supreme example is Moses, who had people grumbling about his leadership style from the very beginning of his ministry. They complained about their meal plan (Exod. 15:24; 16:3). They refused to follow instructions (Exod. 16:20, 27). They accused him of attempted homicide (Exod. 17:3). They even tried to stone him (Exod. 17:4). And when Moses was ready to lead them to the Promised Land, they refused to go.

Other prophets suffered persecution. One was Elijah, who in many ways was the most successful prophet in the Old Testament. Elijah saw fire come down from heaven. He watched the people fall down in the dust to worship Israel's God, and then he killed hundreds of false prophets (1 Kings 19:38-40). But the next day he was afraid of his enemies and ran for his life. Elijah's discouragement led to depression so deep that he begged God to take his life (1 Kings 19:3-4). Or consider Jeremiah, who had such a difficult ministry that the ancient rabbis called him 'the Weeping Prophet.' Jeremiah was tormented by false prophets (Jer. 14:14).

He was beaten, imprisoned, and left to die (Jer. 20:1-6; 38:13). He was mocked for being God's servant (Jer. 20:7-10). When he interceded for God's people, his prayers went unanswered (Jer. 15:1). Then at the end of his life he saw the city he loved surrounded and destroyed, while the people he loved suffered and died in the streets (Jer. 14:17-18; Lam. 1–5). It is little wonder that Jeremiah once cursed the day he was born (Jer. 10:14-18).

Even this brief survey shows how the Old Testament prophets anticipated the sufferings of Christ. It is said of Moses that he suffered 'disgrace for the sake of Christ' (Heb. 11:26). The same could be said of the other prophets. They too suffered in union with Christ, for Jesus proved the necessity of his humiliation from what they endured. 'Did not the Christ have to suffer these things and then enter his glory?' he asked his disciples on the road to Emmaus. 'And beginning with Moses and all the Prophets, he explained to them what was said in all the Scriptures concerning himself' (Luke 24:25-27; cf. 1 Pet. 1:11). Jesus suffered many indignities at the hands of the evil men who plotted to have him killed. He was unlawfully arrested, unfairly accused, unjustly convicted, and unmercifully beaten. But he endured his greatest sufferings on the cross, where he died a God-forsaken death. His crucifixion was the apotheosis of the humiliation suffered by his prophets (see Luke 11:47-51). As Stephen said in his challenge to the Sanhedrin, 'Was there ever a prophet your fathers did not persecute? They even killed those who predicted the coming of the Righteous One. And now you have betrayed and murdered him' (Acts 7:52-53).

Remarkably, at the time of his death Jesus had virtually nothing to show for his ministry. Nearly everyone had rejected him. He had relatively few followers to begin with, but at the end he had only eleven, and even they abandoned him. His ministry turned out to be no more successful than Isaiah's. People were forever hearing Jesus, but never understanding him; forever seeing his miracles, but not perceiving his message (Matt. 13:13-15; cf. Isa. 6:9-10). And Jesus suffered for this. 'O unbelieving generation,' he groaned, 'how long shall I stay with you? How long shall I put up with you?' (Mark 9:19). The lament of this Suffering Servant was previously recorded in the book of Isaiah: 'He [God] said to me, "You are my servant, Israel, in whom I will display my splendor." But I said, "I have labored to no purpose; I have spent my strength in vain and for nothing"' (Isa. 49:3-4a). At the time of his death, the preaching ministry of Jesus Christ could hardly be judged anything except a failure. The main thing it seemed to accomplish was getting him killed.

And what of his followers? What happened to them? Think of the original disciples. According to the best historical records, nearly every one of them died a violent death. Or think of Stephen, who as far as Scripture records, preached only one great sermon before being stoned. These men suffered all these things because they were united to Jesus Christ in his sufferings and death.

The one who endured the most excruciating torment was the apostle Paul. When Paul first came to Christ, God showed him how much he would suffer for the sake of the gospel (Acts 9:16). And suffer he did. Paul faced trouble, hardship, and distress. He was frequently imprisoned and often on the run – in danger by land and by sea. He was whipped, beaten, stoned, and left for dead (2 Cor. 6:4-10; 11:23-27). 'To this very hour,' he wrote, 'we go hungry and thirsty, we are in rags, we are brutally treated, we are homeless.... Up to this moment we have become the scum of the earth, the refuse of the world' (1 Cor. 4:11, 13b). Then there were all the sufferings he experienced in ministry: his anguish for lost souls (Rom. 9:1-5), his ceaseless spiritual concern for the church (2 Cor. 11:28-29), his tearful entreaties with Christians who were struggling to follow Christ (Acts 20:31). Thus Paul's prayers were answered: in the context of his gospel ministry, he became like Christ in his death.

The Fellowship of Sharing in His Sufferings

What does this litany of misery teach about pastoral ministry? Obviously it teaches that a call to pastoral ministry is not to be trifled with. One night at bedtime a minister read his four-year-old son the story of Stephen. He explained that God's servants often suffer for speaking God's Word, and that sometimes they are even killed. 'Are they going to kill you, Daddy?' the boy asked, his eyes open wide. 'I hope not!' his father answered, but given the biblical history, it was a fair question.

Any minister who knows his Bible can hardly expect to escape suffering – specifically suffering for the cause of Christ. Martin Luther wrote: 'Those who are in the teaching office should teach with the greatest faithfulness and expect no other remuneration than to be killed by the world, trampled under foot, and despised by their own.... [T]each purely and faithfully, and in all you do expect not glory but dishonor and contempt, not wealth but poverty, violence, prison, death, and every danger.'[17] Some, especially those who enjoy the comforts of Western civilization, may object that Luther's view of gospel ministry is unduly negative. No doubt it was colored by the unique difficulties of his time and place. However, an authentic pastoral theology must be adequate to the task of ministry under conditions of the most extreme hardship, such as many ministers suffer today in many parts of the world. The truth is that being united to Christ in the ministry of his gospel always involves conflict within the church and some measure of opposition from without. Inevitably there will be unfair criticisms, unfortunate misunderstandings, unfounded rumors, and unjust accusations. These hardships cannot be avoided; they are to be expected. It is simply a fact: 'the sufferings of Christ flow over into our lives' (2 Cor. 1:5). Pastoral ministry could not be in union with Christ unless it entailed difficulty, discouragement, and even death.

Nevertheless, many ministers are surprised by suffering. Perhaps this is one reason why some become discouraged and unproductive, or even leave the ministry altogether. Often there has been a failure to grasp the implications of pastoral ministry in union with Christ. The words of Thomas a Kempis are striking for their contemporary relevance: 'Jesus today has many who love his heavenly kingdom, but few who carry his cross; many who yearn for comfort, few who long for distress. Plenty of people he finds to share his banquet, few to share his fast. Everyone desires to take part in his rejoicing, but few are willing to suffer anything for his sake. There are many that follow Jesus as far as the breaking of bread, few as far as drinking the cup of suffering; many that revere his miracles, few that follow him in the indignity of the cross.'[18]

How rare it is – especially in America – to find a minister who desires fellowship with Christ if it includes sharing in his sufferings. Such a minister is able not simply to endure difficulty, but actually to embrace it. And the trials of pastoral ministry are to be embraced, for Paul said, 'I *want* to know Christ, and the fellowship of sharing in his sufferings.' Here the emphasis is on knowing Christ, but that knowledge is specifically placed in the context of sharing in Christ's humiliation. This perspective flies in the face of the career goals of the average pastor. Indeed, Paul's statement is one that all too few ministers would be able to make honestly and sincerely. A willingness to suffer with Christ cannot come from the human nature, but only from God's Spirit.

In his epistles, the apostle Paul often reflected on the role of suffering in gospel ministry. One of the striking things about these reflections is his manifest joy in suffering for the cause of Christ. 'Now I rejoice in what was suffered for you,' he wrote in Colossians 1:24. Or to the Corinthians: 'I delight in weaknesses, in insults, in hardships, in persecutions, in difficulties' (2 Cor. 12:10). Paul really *did* want to know Christ in the fellowship of his sufferings! He was like the apostles in Jerusalem, who left the Sanhedrin 'rejoicing because they had been counted worthy of suffering disgrace for the Name' (Acts 5:41).

There were two reasons for Paul's readiness to share in Christ's sufferings. One was his belief that they were necessary for the evangelization of the lost. The world could not understand the message of the cross unless those who preached it were themselves marked by its suffering and shame. This is the meaning – at least in part – of Paul's enigmatic claim, 'I fill up in my flesh what is still lacking in regard to Christ's afflictions' (Col. 1:24). This verse has nothing to do with the extent of the atonement, of course, but everything to do with missions and evangelism. What is still lacking is the communication of the gospel by a suffering church. The unsaved people of the world cannot see Jesus hanging on the cross. What they can see is a community that shares in his sufferings, and thus confirms the truth of his passion. The sufferings of the apostles – and by implication, the sufferings of the church and its ministers – were public demonstrations of Christ and his cross. Paul thus described himself as part of a procession constantly being led out 'to die in the arena' (1 Cor. 4:9) or to die for the honor of a conquering king (2 Cor. 2:14).[19] Sharing in suffering was the very heart of his strategy for making known the crucified Christ: 'We always carry around in our body the death of Jesus' (2 Cor. 4:10a).

The other reason for Paul's passion to know Christ in his sufferings is that such fellowship affords a deep, personal knowledge of Christ. This is one of the promised blessings of gospel ministry. As George Whitefield observed, 'Ministers never write or preach so well as when under the cross; the Spirit of Christ and of glory then rests upon them.'[20] Anyone who is in the pastorate inevitably faces one form of suffering or another, and in the fellowship of sharing Christ's sufferings will enjoy the fruit of union and communion with him. In his Latin translation, Jerome rendered 'the fellowship of his sufferings' as 'the society of his passion'. It is during times of hardship and difficulty that the minister becomes a member of that intimate society, experiencing the closest possible identification with Christ. At the same time Christ makes the closest possible identification with his suffering ministers. Paul learned of this identification at the time of his conversion, when the Lord said to him, 'I am Jesus of Nazareth, whom you are persecuting' (Acts 22:8; cf. 9:5). As these words indicate, because he is united to his people, Christ considers every incarceration and abuse they endure to be an assault on his own person.

All of this explains why Paul wanted so very badly for the humiliation of Christ to be worked out in his own life and ministry. What he desired was not the sufferings themselves, but the fellowship of sharing them with Christ. He reasoned that since he was a minister of the gospel, difficulties were bound to come. And when they came, it would be much better to experience them in union with Christ. Paul knew that hardship is woven into the fabric of any faithful pastoral ministry. It is not only to be expected, but also embraced as part of the minister's communion with Christ. Suffering is one of God's gifts; 'For it has been granted to you on behalf of Christ not only to believe on him, but also to suffer for him' (Phil. 1:29).

This does not mean that suffering needs to be sought out. It will come on its own, according to the will of God, in the manner and measure that he intends. It will come in all the sorrows a shepherd shares with his flock, and in all the burdens he bears on their behalf. In the meantime, there are other ways for a minister to nurture his communion with the crucified Christ. The kind of spiritual intimacy that Paul sought comes not only from outward suffering, but also inwardly from dying to self. This too is part of what it means to be united with Christ in his death, following the way of his cross. The minister must be able to say, with the apostles, 'We do not preach ourselves' (2 Cor. 4:5a); 'but we preach Christ crucified' (1 Cor. 1:23a). However, in order to preach this way, he must first be able to say, 'I have been crucified with Christ and I no longer live, but Christ lives in me' (Gal. 2:20).

As one aspect of his union with Christ, the pastor must die to self in all its hideous forms: self-indulgence, self-aggrandizement, self-love, and self-will. He must be dead to pride, dead to financial gain, dead to recognition and approval. All of this must be put to death – if a pastor is to know Christ and the fellowship of sharing in his sufferings. The notable Scottish minister William Still (1911–

1997) gave his spiritual autobiography the significant title *Dying to Live*. In it he wrote: 'The deaths one dies before ministry can be of long duration – it can be hours and days before we minister, before the resurrection experience of anointed preaching. And then there is another death afterwards, sometimes worse than the death before. From the moment that you stand there dead in Christ and dead to everything you are and have and ever shall be and have, every breath you breathe thereafter, every thought you think, every word you say and deed you do, must be done over the top of your own corpse or reaching over it in your preaching to others. Then it can only be Jesus that comes over and no one else. And I believe that every preacher must bear the mark of that death. Your life must be signed by the Cross, not just Christ's Cross (there is really no other) but your cross in his Cross, your particular and unique cross that no one ever died – the cross that no one ever could die but you and you alone: your death in Christ's death.'[21]

The Power of His Resurrection

Paul had much to say about knowing Christ in his sufferings and death. However, he understood that union with Christ entails exaltation as well as humiliation. His ministry was, after all a *gospel* ministry – one grounded in the crucifixion and resurrection of Jesus Christ.

In Philippians 3:10-11 – the summary statement for his theology of pastoral ministry – the apostle did not begin with suffering, but with glory: 'I want to know Christ and the power of his resurrection' (Phil. 3:10a). He also ended with glory, hoping 'somehow to attain to the resurrection from the dead' (Phil. 3:11). The word 'somehow' does not indicate doubt, as if Paul lacked the certainty of his salvation. Elsewhere he is emphatic in the assurance of his eternal hope (e.g. Rom. 8:38-39; 2 Tim. 1:12). What he expresses in Philippians 3, therefore, is not so much doubt as amazement – amazement that God would raise a sinful man like him from the dead. And this is precisely what Paul wanted to know: God's resurrection power.

What is the power of Christ's resurrection? It is the life-giving power of God the Holy Spirit. The Scripture teaches that 'through the Spirit of holiness' Christ 'was declared with power to be the Son of God by his resurrection from the dead' (Rom. 1:4). The Holy Spirit is the effective transforming agent of God's resurrection power. This was true for Christ, and it remains true for the Christian. As Paul later wrote, 'If the Spirit of him who raised Jesus from the dead is living in you, he who raised Christ from the dead will also give life to your mortal bodies through his Spirit, who lives in you' (Rom. 8:11). The same Spirit who brought Jesus back to life also vitalizes and revitalizes the believer. To know the power of the resurrection, therefore, is to know the power of the Holy Spirit. When Paul asserted his desire to know Christ's resurrection power, he was announcing his intention to live (and minister) by the power of God's Spirit.

The resurrection gives power for gospel ministry. This was true in the ministry of Jesus Christ. It was not until Jesus was raised from the dead that his preaching achieved lasting effect. Prior to the resurrection, his followers remained uncertain of his identity and thus lacked the courage to live for his cause. It was only when Jesus rose from the dead that they came to a full understanding of his saving work.

Once the apostles believed in the risen Christ, they were commissioned to proclaim his saving message. That message was the good news of salvation for sinners through both the cross and the empty tomb. Thus the resurrection was partially constitutive of apostolic preaching. When Peter preached in Jerusalem, and when Paul preached in places like Pisidian Antioch and Athens, it was not simply the crucifixion, but also the resurrection that animated their presentation of the gospel (see Acts 2:24-32; 13:30-37; 17:31-32). Whenever the apostles preached, they said, 'We are witnesses' (e.g. Acts 2:32; 3:15; 5:32; 13:31), meaning eyewitnesses of the resurrection. Hughes Oliphant Old explains, 'It was the risen and exalted Christ who sent those who experienced him as risen and exalted to proclaim his resurrection glory. Not only that, but the proclamation that Jesus is the risen and exalted Christ was constitutive of the Church. It planted it; it brought it into being. It was the essence of the apostolic ministry. The highest and holiest office of the apostle is to proclaim that Christ has risen. The proclamation of the resurrection is the heart and center of all Christian preaching.'[22]

The resurrection was significant to the apostles for another reason as well. It was not simply the basis for their message, but it was also the source of their power. The same Spirit who raised Jesus from the dead was now at work in their ministry of his gospel. Jesus had ascended to glory, and from his place of exaltation he had sent his Spirit. This is why he had promised his disciples that by faith they would do even greater things than he had done (John 14:12): He was sending them by his Holy Spirit, so that the very power of his resurrection would be at work in their ministry.

As we have seen, the ministry of the Old Testament prophets was marked primarily by humiliation. The same can be said of the ministry of Jesus Christ – up until the time of his death. It too was humiliating. But everything changed with the resurrection. Then the Spirit was unleashed in all his saving power. And now the ministry of the gospel reveals God's power to save sinners. This ministry is not exercised without suffering; the 'already/not yet' dynamic is evident in the pastorate as much as anywhere. But through the preaching of the risen Christ, the Spirit is inaugurating the glories of the coming age. Therefore, for the minister in union with Christ, there is exaltation as well as humiliation in the duties of his calling. His practical theology is not merely a theology of the cross, but also a theology of glory.

The resurrection power of the Holy Spirit is the source of all effective gospel ministry. First, the Holy Spirit has the power to regenerate (see John 3:5). Paul experienced this in his own conversion. When he met the risen Christ on the Damascus road, the light was so dazzling that he was blind for three days. But one of Christ's ministers came and said to him, 'Jesus .... has sent me so that you may see again and be filled with the Holy Spirit' (Acts 9:17). As the scales fell away from Paul's eyes, he was filled with the Spirit, and at once he began preaching that Jesus is the Son of God (Acts 9:20). Paul's ministry of the gospel, in turn, led to the conversion of others. The same resurrection power was at work in his preaching, as it is in all preaching, to bring spiritual life from spiritual death. It is through the preaching of God's Word that sinners receive eternal life by the Holy Spirit. Through the proclamation of a risen Savior, they are granted all the blessings of resurrection life.

The Holy Spirit also has the power to sanctify. Paul had experienced this as well. He was growing in godliness, and it was partly on the basis of his own spiritual experience that he was able to write: 'Those who live according to the sinful nature have their minds set on what that nature desires; but those who live in accordance with the Spirit have their minds set on what the Spirit desires. The mind of sinful man is death, but the mind controlled by the Spirit is life and peace' (Rom. 8:5-6). He went on in the same passage to make it clear that the Spirit who sanctifies is also 'the Spirit of him who raised Jesus from the dead' (Rom. 8:11). Therefore, just as Christ relied on the Spirit for his resurrection, so too the minister who is united to Christ relies on the Spirit to raise the dead to new spiritual life. The minister prays, as Paul prayed, for God's blessing on his ministry of God's Word, through the powerful work of God's Spirit: 'I pray also that the eyes of your heart may be enlightened in order that you may know the hope to which he has called you, the riches of his glorious inheritance in the saints, and his incomparably great power for us who believe. That power is like the working of his mighty strength, which he exerted in Christ when he raised him from the dead' (Eph. 1:18-20a). Another way to say this is that Paul wanted others to know what he knew: the resurrection power of Christ.

If it is to be effective, everything a minister does must be done in the resurrection power of the Spirit. When Paul announced that he wanted 'to know Christ and the power of his resurrection,' he was asking for the sovereign work of God's Spirit, who alone enables the various duties of pastoral ministry to fulfill their divinely-appointed purpose. It is the Spirit who answers pastoral prayer. It is the Spirit who transforms sinners through the private application of biblical teaching. It is the Spirit who makes baptism an effectual sign of God's saving grace. It is the Spirit who makes Christ present in the bread and the wine of the Lord's Supper. Most of all, it is the Spirit who blesses the public ministry of God's Word by doing his saving and sanctifying work. Charles Spurgeon is reported to have mounted each of the fifteen steps of the Metropolitan Tabernacle pulpit saying, 'I believe in the Holy Ghost.'[23] If this story is true, then Spurgeon was conducting his ministry in union with the Christ who is present in the church by his living Spirit.

The Spirit is at work not only in a minister's evident successes, but also in his apparent failures. Here again the example is Paul, who, especially when he faced difficulty in ministry, was compelled to depend on the Holy Spirit. Paul did this in his preaching. He often preached 'in weakness and fear, and with much trembling', yet his message came 'with a demonstration of the Spirit's power, so that (he explained to the Corinthians) your faith might not rest on men's wisdom, but on God's power' (1 Cor. 2:3-4). What was true of Paul's preaching was true of his ministry generally. He informed his friends of the hardships he had faced in Asia: 'We were under great pressure, far beyond our ability to endure, so that we despaired even of life. Indeed, in our hearts we felt the sentence of death' (2 Cor. 1:8b-9a). Nevertheless, God had a sovereign purpose in this experience of sharing in Christ's sufferings. As Paul went on to testify, 'This happened that we might not rely on ourselves but on God, who raises the dead' (2 Cor. 1:9b).

As he ministered in union with Christ, Paul experienced both humiliation and exaltation. And often it was humiliation that compelled him to rely more completely on the exalting power of God's Spirit. The weakness he suffered served to demonstrate the glory of God's grace. 'Therefore,' he said, 'I will boast all the more gladly about my weaknesses, so that Christ's power may rest on me. That is why, for Christ's sake, I delight in weaknesses, in insults, in hardships, in persecutions, in difficulties. For when I am weak, then I am strong' (2 Cor. 12:9b-10; cf. 4:7). Paul's sufferings in ministry strengthened his grasp on God's resurrection power, so that he was able to say, 'We always carry around in our body the death of Jesus, so that the life of Jesus may also be revealed in our body. For we who are alive are always being given over to death for Jesus' sake, so that his life may be revealed in our mortal body' (2 Cor. 4:10-11). Or again, 'He was crucified in weakness, yet he lives by God's power. Likewise, we are weak in him, yet by God's power we will live with him to serve you' (2 Cor. 13:4).

These verses show that it was partly through his suffering that Paul came to know Christ in the power of his resurrection. Christ has already suffered his humiliation and entered his exaltation. Now we are one step behind, still waiting to be exalted. It is of some encouragement to know, as we suffer, that Christ has passed this way before. But more than that, we now have the risen and exalted Christ to sustain and comfort us in our humiliation. Ultimately his resurrection will raise us beyond all suffering, but in the meantime we experience the power of his grace.

Finally, the Holy Spirit has the power to glorify. Here it must be emphasized that many of the greatest glories of preaching are deferred benefits. This was true in the ministry of Christ. Earlier we noted the humiliation of the Suffering Servant, who said, 'I have labored to no purpose; I have spent my strength in vain and for nothing.' Yet the Servant went on to declare his expectation of his coming exaltation: 'What is due me is in the Lord's hand, and my reward is with my God' (Isa. 49:4). The same movement from suffering to glory occurs again in chapter 53: 'It was the Lord's will to crush him and cause him to suffer.... After the suffering of his soul, he will see the light of life and be satisfied.... Therefore I will give him a portion among the great' (Isa. 53:10a, 11a, 12a).

The hope of deferred glory is of particular encouragement to men who are discouraged by their apparent fruitlessness in gospel ministry. As it was for Christ, so it is for his ministers: exaltation comes only after humiliation. The gospel minister labors in his field with the hope of a harvest that will not be reaped until eternity, when his ministry of suffering will become a ministry of glory. The Puritan Richard Sibbes thus advised ministers to wait for the rewards of their ministry: 'Let us commit the fame and credit, of what we are or do to God. *He will take care of that*, let us take care to be and to do as we should, and then *for noise and report*, let it be good or ill as God will send it.... Therefore let us labour to be good *in secret*.... We should be carried with the Spirit of God, and with a holy desire to serve God and our brethren, and to do all the good we can, and never care for the speeches of the world.... We'll have glory enough BY-AND-BY.'[24] Somewhere Charles Spurgeon made essentially the same point in more epigrammatic fashion: 'Set small store by present rewards; be grateful for earnests by the way, but look for recompensing joy hereafter.'

The apostle Paul was looking for that recompensing joy. His was a future-oriented definition of success in ministry. He did not think that he had fully grasped the knowledge of Christ, but still wanted to 'press on toward the goal to win the prize' (Phil. 3:14). As he went on to write, 'We eagerly await a Savior from there [heaven], the Lord Jesus Christ, who, by the power that enables him to bring everything under his control, will transform our lowly bodies so that they will be like his glorious body. Therefore, my brothers, you whom I love and long for, my joy and crown!' (Phil. 3:20b–4:1a). Paul was trusting in the power of the Holy Spirit, not only for his own glorification, but also for the glorification of the church. This is the ultimate goal and crowning glory of any preaching ministry: to present the elect unto God ready to receive their eternal inheritance. 'For what is our hope, our joy, or the crown in which we will glory in the presence of our Lord Jesus when he comes? Is it not you? Indeed, you are our glory and joy' (1 Thess. 1:19-20). The exaltation of a pastoral ministry, which is rarely glimpsed in this life, will only be fully displayed at the Second Coming, when God will reveal his Son in the risen church. When – somehow – we attain to that resurrection, we will know Christ's power to the fullest measure.

NOTES

1 The author wishes to acknowledge Adam Brice, George Cottenden, Richard Gaffin, Jr., Randall Grossman, Stephen Smallman, Craig Troxel, and Tim Trumper for their improvements to this essay.

2 John Murray, *Redemption – Accomplished and Applied* (Grand Rapids, MI: Eerdmans, 1955), 161, 165.

3 John Calvin, *Institutes of the Christian Religion*, trans. by Ford Lewis Battles, 2 vols, Library of Christian Classics 20-21 (Philadelphia: Westminster, 1960), III.i.3.

4 Calvin, *Institutes*, III.i-ii.

5 Calvin, *Institutes*, III.ii.24.

6 Calvin, *Institutes*, II.xii.3.

7 See Theodore Beza, *A Briefe and Pithie Summe of the Christian Faith*, trans. by R. F. (London, 1563), IV.12; Hieronymus Zanchius, *Opera Theologica* (Geneva, 1605), 8:503-508.

8 To give just two examples, the English Puritan Thomas Case in *The Morning Exercise Methodized* (London, 1660) and the Scottish Presbyterian Thomas Boston in *Human Nature in its Fourfold State* (Edinburgh, 1720) both organize their teaching on salvation around the doctrine of union with Christ. See also Walter Marshall, *The Gospel-Mystery of Sanctification* (London, 1962).

9 Gordon Stevens Wakefield, *Puritan Devotion: Its Place in the Development of Christian Piety* (London: Epworth, 1957), 5.

10 John Preston, *The Breast-Plate of Faith and Love* (London, 1630), 43-44.

11 Paul Bayne, *An Entire Commentary upon the Whole Epistle of the Apostle Paul to the Ephesians* (London, 1642), 509.

12 Archibald Alexander, 'Col. 1:27, 'Christ in you the hope of glory',' quoted in W. Andrew Hoffecker, *Piety and the Princeton Theologians* (Phillipsburg, NJ: Presbyterian and Reformed, 1981), 34.

13 There is a similar movement from death to resurrection in Romans 5–6 and Colossians 2–3.

14 Sinclair B. Ferguson, *Let's Study Philippians* (Edinburgh: Banner of Truth, 1997), 81.

15 Here we speak of experiential and not of incarnational union. Christ's union with us in our human nature is also richly significant for pastoral theology, but that is a subject for another essay.

16 Stu Weber, 'Tour of Duty,' *Leadership* (17.2), 30.

17 Martin Luther, *Luther's Works*, ed. by Jaroslav Pelikan (St. Louis: Concordia, 1955–58), 12:220-21.

18 Thomas a Kempis, *The Imitation of Christ*, trans. by Ronald Knox and Michael Oakley (New York: Sheed and Ward, 1959), 76-77.

19 See Scott J. Hafemann's compelling dissertation, *Suffering and the Spirit: An Exegetical Study of II Cor. 2:14–3:3 within the Context of the Corinthian Correspondence*, Wissenschaftliche Untersuchungen zum Neuen Testament, Reihe 2, 19 (Tubingen: J. C. B. Mohr, 1986).

20 George Whitefield, *Works* (London, 1771), 4:306.

21 William Still, *Dying to Live* (Fearn, Ross-shire: Christian Focus, 1991), 136.

22 Hughes Oliphant Old, *The Reading and Preaching the Scriptures in the Worship of the Christian Church*, 7 vols (Grand Rapids, MI: Eerdmans, 1998-), 1:202.

23 The story is recounted in John R. W. Stott, *Between Two Worlds: The Art of Preaching in the Twentieth Century* (Grand Rapids, MI: Eerdmans, 1982), 334.

24 Richard Sibbes, *Works of Richard Sibbes*, ed. by Alexander Grant, 7 vols (1862-64; repr. Edinburgh: Banner of Truth, 1973), 1:xxiii-xxiv.

PRACTICAL CALVINISM

Grace, Sonship and Missions

Ronald E. Lutz, John V. Yenchko

In a simple but profound question, the apostle Paul asks the Galatians, 'What happened to all your joy?' (Gal. 4:15). These were people of God who had lost their sense of blessing and enthusiasm in the gospel of Jesus Christ (Gal. 1:6). They had begun with great zeal. Their passion for the gospel was blazing and their willingness to sacrifice for the cause of Christ was extraordinary (Gal. 4:15). But now they are in grave spiritual peril. Something has happened. Paul is perplexed. Those who started strong in the gospel have taken a dangerous and deadly detour.

As Paul seeks to diagnose and explain their problem, he writes that they have somehow embraced the 'children of the slave woman'; they are pursuing the way of the covenant of Sinai that bears children who are slaves – like Hagar. They have lost their sense of the covenant of grace, and somehow are tempted to forget that they, like Isaac, are children of the promise – children of the Jerusalem that is above. How could such a thing happen? Paul attributes it to the fact that they 'want to be under the law' (Gal. 4:21). Until they correct this grave theological error and its practical implications for their spiritual lives, Paul despairs that any fruit will be born from their ministry.

The Galatians are not alone. Throughout the ages and even today, the church flirts with these 'children of the slave woman' and joins in their seductive dance of legalism and formalism. The whisper comes: 'Observe the law and you will live.' For this is what the law taught: 'The man who does these things will live by them' (Gal. 3:12; Lev. 18:5). And so those within the church betray their birthright and enter into a life of unlimited obligation, for it is written, 'Cursed is everyone who does not continue to do everything written in the book of the law' (Gal. 3:10; Deut. 7:26). They do not realize the deadliness of this dance. It will not only rob them of their joy, but will ultimately leave them cursed, since 'all who rely on observing the law are under a curse' (Gal. 3:10a; cf. 1:8-9).

The missionary (pastor, Sunday School teacher, campus worker, etc.) who engages in this dance and pursues this detour becomes joyless. He goes through the motions of ministry, but his heart is cold to the message he brings. His passion for evangelism wanes and his tears for the lost dry up. Those who follow such a leader try to march to the moralistic beat of his drum, trying harder to be 'nice' Christians, but they lack the gospel's promised power to love others and overcome sin. Meanwhile, the missionary's wife becomes angry and bitter because their life of sacrifice does not seem to inspire their followers. Beneath her outward expression of social grace grows a critical, uncharitable, and condemning heart.

How many people in the ministry and in leadership within the church should properly be asked, 'What happened to all your joy?' The inevitable pressures, challenges and disappointments of ministry in the local church and on the mission field are often compounded by a drift toward formalism, moralism, powerlessness and discouragement of the soul, resulting in a disappearance of joy and power in the gospel.

What is the antidote? Practical Calvinism.

The way out of the deadly dance of legalism, formalism and moralism (as well as antinomianism) is to rekindle in our hearts the great doctrines of grace: justification by faith, adoption, sanctification by faith, total depravity, the law/gospel distinction as classically understood, all accompanied by a deep appropriation of the present value of the blood of Christ and his ongoing mediatorial work. We need a full apprehension of our 'legal rights and our personal delights' in Christ. That is to say, we must repeatedly rekindle an apprehension of the legal benefits of our union with Christ (Gal. 4:4, 5), the personal delights we have in our sonship through the indwelling Holy Spirit (Gal. 4:6, 7) and our hope of coming glory when Jesus appears.

This conviction, of course, is not new. It has been understood by many teachers of practical Calvinism. Archibald Alexander, a professor at Princeton Theological Seminary, wrote in 1845:

> It seems desirable to ascertain, as precisely as we can, the reasons why Christians commonly are of so diminutive a stature and of such feeble strength in their religion....
>
> First, there is a defect in our belief in the freeness of divine grace. To exercise unshaken confidence in the doctrine of gratuitous pardon is one of the most difficult things in the world; and to preach this doctrine fully without verging towards antinomianism is no easy task, and is therefore seldom done. But Christians cannot but be lean and feeble when deprived of their proper nutriment. It is by faith that the spiritual life is made to grow; and the doctrine of free grace, without any mixture of human merit, is the only true object of faith. Christians are too much inclined to depend on themselves, and not to derive their life entirely from Christ.
>
> There is a spurious legal religion, which may flourish without the practical belief in the absolute freeness of divine grace, but it possesses none of the characteristics of the Christian's life. It is found to exist in the rankest growth, in systems of religion which are utterly false. But even when the true doctrine is acknowledged in theory, often it is not practically felt and acted on. The new convert lives upon his frames rather than on Christ, while the older Christian is still found struggling in his own strength and, failing in his expectations of success, he becomes discouraged first, and then he sinks into a gloomy despondency, or becomes in a measure careless. At that point the spirit of the world comes with resistless force. Here, I am persuaded, is the root of the evil; and until religious teachers inculcate clearly, fully, and practically, the grace of God as manifested in the gospel, we shall have no vigorous growth of piety among professing Christians.[1]

We agree with Archibald Alexander. We fear that many Christians and Christian workers (including ourselves) are of 'diminutive stature and feeble strength' because of defects in our belief in the freeness of divine grace. We have often observed formalistic, moralistic and neonomian religion that fails 'to exercise unshaken confidence in the doctrine of gratuitous pardon' and thus circles back and conforms to the religion of 'the slave woman' (Gal. 4:24, 25). The church is thus led by joyless missionaries and taskmasters in the pulpit, with converts who become just like them.

When we discover this in ourselves and observe it in defeated missionaries, frustrated church planters, guilty church members or self-righteous taskmasters, what do we do? How do we counsel? What will reinvigorate the missionary fire? What will unleash tears for the lost? What will inspire a love of holiness?

The answer is practical Calvinism, the need to 'preach the gospel to ourselves' and live out the implications of the truths that we are justified, adopted and united to Christ.

Every day, the believer must grow in his confidence that through union with Jesus Christ, he is righteous, loved, accepted and forgiven. Why is this daily affirmation so critical? Because each day the flesh rises up and seeks to minimize the extent and nature of sin. It seeks to justify itself in a variety of ways – including good theology, a record of good works, and achieving the praise of men. For that reason, all people in ministry need daily reminders of the implications of their justification and adoption, in living dependency on the Father's promise of the Spirit. Practically speaking, we suggest (though this is certainly not exhaustive) that all people involved in missions, pastoral ministry and evangelism regularly embrace and apply the following biblical lessons:

I. Our Life Must be a Life of Faith

In order to experience spiritual power, we must answer the question, 'How does what belongs to Christ become ours?' The Bible teaches that we are grafted into Christ by faith and we continue to receive the blessings of our union with him by faith (1 Cor. 6:11; Rom. 8:15; 2 Thess. 2:13). 'Preaching the gospel to yourself' simply means to live by faith, to fix your eyes on Jesus and what he has done for you, and is doing in you (Phil. 2:13, Eph. 3:20). We must examine our hearts and lives to see if we join the apostle Paul in his testimony: 'The life I now live, I live by faith in the Son of God, who loved me and gave himself for me' (Gal. 2: 20). Paul reminds us that Christ dwells in our hearts by faith (Eph. 3:17) and that we live the Christian life the same way we began it: by grace through faith (Col. 2:6). It is by faith that we receive the grace to live. It is by faith that we run the race before us (Heb. 12:1,2), resist the devil (Jas. 4:7) and overcome the world (1 John 5:4). Charles Hodge wrote of the ongoing life of faith: 'The faith by which a believer lives, is not specifically different in its nature or object from the faith required of every man in order to his salvation. The life of faith is only the continued repetition ... of those exercises by which we first receive Christ, in all his fullness and in all his offices, as our God and Savior.'[2]

II. 'The Way Up is Down'

'God opposes the proud but gives grace to the humble' (1 Pet. 5:5). The Christian life is one of repentance. Repentance should be a lifestyle, as Martin Luther reminds us when he stated in the first of his Ninety-Five theses: 'When our Lord and master, Jesus Christ, said, "repent", he meant that the entire life of believers should be one of repentance.' The law of God as traditionally understood has three uses. But the 'second use', which serves the purpose of bringing man under conviction of sin and of making him conscious of his inability to meet the demands of the law, becomes a tutor to lead men to Christ – not just once, but every day throughout his Christian life. Steve Smallman writes: 'I firmly believe in the third use of the law, as refined through the lens of the New Testament. But it struck me after ... listening to Jack Miller that my approach had been to think of the second use as ending once we become believers. But once we become believers, and the Spirit is bearing witness in our hearts to the holiness of God and the depth of his righteous requirements, the law becomes vastly more powerful in our lives than before we believed. So if we preach the law to Christians without also pointing them to Christ as the only true law keeper, we are placing people under a greater burden than they had before coming to Christ. In other words, we preachers need to know how to preach the gospel to believers.'[3]

As C. John (Jack) Miller[4] used to say, 'Cheer up, you are worse than you think.' Any missionary who does not acknowledge this reality and live a life of humble repentance through daily self-examination and confession of sin will soon find his heart tempted to cling to self-justification. When we do not rest in the sufficiency of our justification in Christ, various forms of self-justification are the only alternatives. When we fail to go to Christ daily with our guilt and sin, we are tempted to turn to religious formalism, moralism and legalism. That is why it is entirely possible to theoretically affirm Christ-centered, Reformed theology and yet be functionally legalistic and self-righteous. The human heart is capable of creating an enormous chasm between our 'official' theology and our daily 'functional' theology. This was the point made by Alexander: '... even when the true doctrine is acknowledged in theory, often it is not practically felt and acted on.'

It is essential that those involved in Christian ministry acknowledge and appreciate 'the present value of the blood of Christ.' The apostle John writes, 'But if anybody does sin, we have one who speaks to the Father in our defense – Jesus Christ, the righteous one. He is the atoning sacrifice for our sins, and not only for ours but also for the sins of the whole world' (1 John 2:1-2). When this is regularly apprehended, it leads to humility in a pastor, church planter or missionary. When someone asks him, 'How are you doing?' he should think, 'Not bad for someone who deserves hell!' Rather than being a 'superior talking head,' he is continually humbled and revived by the gospel. He now presents himself as one beggar who says to another beggar, 'I know where to get bread. Come with me and let's get some together.'

The person who has a growing awareness of his sin before God will be well-positioned to rightly understand and embrace the riches of the gospel. We once heard Dr. Cornelius Van Til say, 'The longer I am a Christian, the more I know I am an unworthy sinner.' He then hastened to add that his awareness of and delight in the abundant grace of God in the gospel had also grown with each passing year. Rejoicing in the blessing of our justification and adoption in Christ will not be divorced from a growing awareness of our sin. On the contrary, the gospel will give us the security and freedom in Christ to ask him to search our hearts and expose our sin (Ps. 139:23, 24). The Christian who is growing in grace will grow in self-understanding, seeing the 'sin beneath the sin,' the idols of the heart, and false gospels he clings to. He will repent of his 'righteousness.' As one Puritan said, 'Even our tears of repentance need to be washed in the blood of the Lamb.'

A. W. Tozer spoke of the paradoxical nature of the believer: 'He goes down to get up. If he refuses to go down he is already down, but when he starts down he is on his way up. He is strongest when he is weakest and weakest when he is strong.... He may be and often is highest when he feels lowest, and most sinless when he is most conscious of sin.'[5]

III. We embrace our 'legal rights'

This refers to the forensic nature of the gospel. Note the language of Galatians 4:4, 5: 'But when the time had fully come, God sent his Son, born of a woman, born under *law*, to *redeem* those under *law*, that we might *receive* the *full rights* of sons....' The Westminster Shorter Catechism rightly defines justification as an act (a forensic, legal, complete act) that irreversibly changes our relationship to God. 'Justification is an act of God's free grace, wherein he pardoneth all our sins, and accepteth us as righteous in his sight, only for the righteousness of Christ imputed to us, and received by faith alone.' (Question 33)

We live in a day when much corrupt theology discounts and even denies the legal aspect of the gospel. This corrupt theology minimizes the holiness of God and the utter sinfulness of sin; ignores or denies the necessity of the blood atonement; forgets the covenantal nature of God's relationship with men and the curse sanctions associated with violations and transgressions of his law. In so doing, the realities of justification by faith alone are marginalized in the Christian's life. This spiritually deadly trend ultimately leads to a denial of the sufficiency of the atonement, robbing Christ of the glory he deserves for his atoning work. Furthermore, it robs the missionary/pastor/evangelist of his compelling reason to preach the cross of Christ. If men and women are not guilty sinners who need the substitutionary work of Christ, then the urgency of the mission evaporates.

The *Heidelberg Catechism* asks in Question 60: *'How are you right with God?'*

Answer: Only by true faith in Jesus Christ. Even though my conscience accuses me of having grievously sinned against all of God's commandments and of never having kept any of them, and even though I am still inclined toward all evil, nevertheless, without my deserving it at all, out of sheer grace, God grants and credits to me the perfect satisfaction, righteousness, and holiness of Christ, as if I had never sinned nor been a sinner, as if I had been as perfectly obedient as Christ was obedient for me. All I need to do is to accept this gift of God with a believing heart.

This is critical to Christian ministry because the tender heart that seeks after God will experience an awareness of sin. (Even the person who clings to various forms of self-justification and denial is aware of sin. Those responses are his faulty coping mechanisms.) This is necessary for our walk with Christ. Repentance must follow. But, we must ask, why do so many pastors and Christian workers seem to have so little power to deal with sin? Why are so many missionaries and pastors joyless, sad, and doubting? Thomas Brooks, reflecting upon Satan's devices, writes, 'The first device that Satan hath to keep souls in a sad, doubting, and questioning condition, is, by causing them to ... mind their sins more than their Savior; yea, so to mind their sins as to forget, yea, to neglect their Savior. Their eyes are so fixed upon their disease, that they cannot see the remedy, though it be near; and they do so muse upon their debts, that they have neither mind nor heart to think of their Surety.'[6]

The Christian leader must be able to sing 'Arise, my soul, arise, shake off thy guilty fears, the bleeding sacrifice in my behalf appears. Before the throne my surety stands. Before the throne my surety stands. My name is written on his hands.' Robert Murray McCheyne, the Scottish preacher, said that for every one look at our sin, we need to take ten looks at Christ.

Richard Lovelace summarizes the need for a daily appropriation of the truth of justification, reminding ourselves of our legal standing in Christ.

> Only a fraction of the present body of professing Christians are solidly appropriating the justifying work of Christ in their lives. Many have so light an apprehension of God's holiness and of the extent and guilt of their sin that consciously they see little need for justification, although below the surface of their lives they are deeply guilt-ridden and insecure. Many others have a theoretical commitment to this doctrine, but in their day-to-day existence they rely on their sanctification for justification ... drawing their assurance of acceptance with God from their sincerity, their past experience of conversion, their recent religious performance or the relative infrequency of their conscious, willful disobedience. Few know enough to start each day with a thoroughgoing stand upon Luther's platform: you are accepted, looking outward in faith and claiming the wholly alien righteousness of Christ as the only ground for acceptance, relaxing in that quality of trust which will produce increasing sanctification as faith is active in love and gratitude.[7]

These are two truths: First, that you are more sinful, wicked, selfish and messed up than you could possibly imagine – but second, that in Christ you are more loved, forgiven, cherished and valued than you would ever dare to dream. We need to accept the bad news first and realize that the longer we are Christians, the more we will see of our sin. But as we do, it is meant to drive us to the immeasurable love of Christ again and again (Eph. 3:14-21).

IV. We embrace our 'personal delights', which flow from our relationship with God.

Note the language of Galatians 4:6-7: '... because you are sons, God sent the Spirit of his Son into our hearts, the Spirit who calls out, 'Abba, Father'. So you are no longer a slave, but a son; and since you are a son, God has made you also an heir.'

While the doctrine of adoption is precious to our theological tradition, its practical implications must work their way into the life and ministry of every Christian. In many ways, the primary question is this: do we really enjoy God as the Westminster Shorter Catechism, Question 1, calls us to do? God completely forgives us because of his love and legally adopts us out of his love. We are under his favor and then he gives us the Spirit of favor – the Spirit of sonship.

This is intended to have many implications for life and ministry. Many have been inspired by the life of George Mueller and the many wonderful answers to prayer that highlighted his ministry. But the greatness of George Mueller was rooted in the fact that he delighted in his heavenly Father. His motivation for life and ministry was reinvigorated each morning as he approached the Lord in prayer to prepare his heart and offer his life for a day that would glorify him. George Mueller wrote:

> The point is this: I saw more clearly than ever, that the first great and primary business to which I ought to attend every day was, to have my soul happy in the Lord. The first thing to be concerned about was not, how much I might serve the Lord, how I might glorify the Lord; but how I might get my soul into a happy state, and how my inner man might be nourished. For I might seek to set the truth before the unconverted, I might seek to benefit believers, I might seek to relieve the distressed, I might in other ways seek to behave myself as it becomes a child of God in this world; and yet, not being happy in the Lord, and not be nourished and strengthened in my inner man day by day, all this might not be attended to in a right spirit. [8]

The whole point of Mueller's ministry was to get Christian people to enjoy God. Out of his personal delight in 'Abba Father,' he overflowed with grace and self-forgetting love and hope.

Some people acknowledge that the realities of grace, a delight in God, joy, and free forgiveness are necessary to withstand the posture of the legalist. But they wonder if those truths will, at the same time, fail to speak to the serious spiritual issues of license and antinomianism in our day. It is possible to fall off both sides of a horse! It is true that the doctrines of grace can be abused in the direction of antinomianism. Paul himself seemed to deal with this problem regularly; it may be argued that if the gospel and the lavishness of grace are properly preached, this problem *will* arise in the hearts of some listeners and will need to be addressed. Nevertheless, we contend that sonship theology's strengths more than compensate for these difficulties. Indeed, it is most effective in speaking to the relativistic and antinomian mindset of our day for a number of reasons.

First, the doctrines of grace are only truly understood in the context of the awesome holiness of God. No one can truly understand grace unless he trembles before the justice of God and grieves over the 'exceeding sinfulness of sin.' The life of repentance and the eager embrace of the blessings of the cross and of sonship should never be divorced from the experience of Isaiah, who is 'undone' before the Thrice Holy God (Isa. 6:1-8). These truths will be properly applied to relativism and antinomianism in connection with teaching on the holiness of God that exposes the depth of our sin.

Second, as Walter Marshall wrote long ago, 'we must first receive the comforts of the gospel, that we may be able to sincerely perform the duties of the law.'[9]
The point he makes is this: true obedience from the heart will flow from gratitude as we rest in the riches of God's grace. 'No sin can be crucified either in heart or life, unless it be first pardoned in conscience.'[10] As the first question of the Heidelberg Catechism makes clear, one can only say that he is 'wholeheartedly willing and ready from now on to live for him' *after* he says, 'I am not my own, but belong – body and soul, in life and in death – to my faithful Savior Jesus Christ who has fully paid for all my sins with his precious blood, and has set me free from the tyranny of the devil.' Rightly understood, this calls for a radical paradigm shift. Out of overwhelming gratitude for what Christ has done for me, I give myself totally to him and his will for my life. He defines what is right and wrong. He is Lord of every area of my life.

Third, we must preach the gospel of sheer grace against legalism if we are to reach a deeply antinomian culture. Tim Keller writes, 'First, it [the gospel of grace] renews Christians' joy and wonder in their relationship with God, making them far more effective and attractive witnesses. But secondly, liberal, secular 'Sadducees' must see the pulpit distinguishing between moralism and real gospel Christianity so they can see that what they rejected in their youth wasn't the real thing. Non-Christians will always hear gospel presentations as just appeals to become moral and religious – unless in your preaching you use the good news of grace on legalism.'

Keller goes on to explain the total Lordship of Christ to antinomian listeners, saying, 'If you were saved by your works, there would be a limit to what God could ask of you – you'd have some "rights". But if you're saved by grace, there is no limit to your allegiance to him.' The point is that liberal secular people are considerably more open even to this bad news once they have seen how incredibly comforting the gospel is for people 'inside' the faith and how deadly it is to the moralistic, proud attitudes they so hate in religious people.[11]

All of this leads to an amazing miracle .... self-forgetting, for legalists and antinomians alike. Missionaries, pastors and Christian workers have a lot to worry about. There is much in their lives (fightings and fears .... within and without) that promotes anxiety. What can bring freedom from the massive self- preoccupation that characterizes so many people in ministry?

These truths will produce daily growth in holiness and obedience. When the apostle Paul refers to the gospel as the 'power of God for the salvation of everyone who believes' (Rom. 1:16), he is not simply referring to our initial conversion. The power of God for everyone who believes is a comprehensive way of describing the work of the gospel to transform the believer throughout his entire spiritual journey. We cannot simply preach the gospel to the lost and then give a 'to-do' list to the believer. We cannot allow the Christian life to become Nike Christianity – 'Just Do It!' But neither is the Christian life one of passivity – 'Let go and let God!' The application of the rich truths of the gospel to our hearts will produce living and active faith in Jesus Christ. It will produce a heart reliance that expresses itself in obedience and love. This is the 'obedience that comes from faith' that Paul describes in Romans 1:5. The comforts of the gospel will produce thankful obedience.[12]

Jack Miller observed that many leaders and potential leaders were characterized by spiritual powerlessness and weakness that belied their message. They did not incarnate the truth of the message they presented. Even those who had experienced dramatic, life-changing encounters with the gospel often drifted into formalism and moralism. He saw that many who thoroughly embraced Reformed theology seemed unable to draw personal strength from it for bold, sacrificial ministry. His observation was similar to that of John Newton: 'Calvinism was one of the worst of systems preached theoretically, but one of the best preached practically.'[13]

Jack Miller sought to promote a daily appropriation of grace that would empower ministry. The vision was intimately connected with a burden to see the Great Commission fulfilled. The conviction was that many believers live without a daily awareness of the power of the gospel, the love of God, the power of the cross. Many believers live as functional orphans, alienated and distant from the Lord. They try to cope with their problems through a performance-based Christianity, which ultimately saps the spiritual strength from their lives. The resulting negative fruit includes hypocrisy, division, strife, interpersonal distance, cover-ups, and gossip. Richard Lovelace comments on these dynamics.

> Christians who are no longer sure that God loves and accepts them in Jesus, apart from their present spiritual achievements, are subconsciously radically insecure persons – much less secure than non-Christians, because they have too much light to rest easily under the constant bulletins they receive from their Christian environment about the holiness of God and the righteousness they are supposed to have. Their insecurity shows itself in pride, a fierce defensive assertion of their own righteousness and defensive criticism of others.[14]

Through honesty, confession and repentance as a lifestyle, believers found power and grace in Christ on a daily basis. The vision was to see people empowered by the gospel, set free from sin, self-absorption and guilt. The end result would be repentance from self-centered living, and active daily service of Christ. As this message was preached, dramatic stories began to emerge, especially among pastors and missionaries who had lost their first love and drifted into self-righteousness. Many of these were burned out because of 'performance' – based Christianity and laboring under tremendous guilt. They were proud and arrogant. But the gospel set them free in Christ, free to serve him and to fulfill the Great Commission. The gospel compelled them outward, with boldness and compassion.

The rediscovery of the gospel in the life of the believer has profound implications for the way we present the gospel to unbelievers. Evangelistic ineffectiveness among evangelicals is often related to a conviction that the unbeliever needs an entirely different message from the believer. When that is the case, the believer tends to share the gospel message from a position of superiority and even condescension. However, when we recognize that we both need to hear the same message, a profound change can take place in the heart of the believer and in the atmosphere of the church. When the church culture is saturated with and shaped by the gospel, believers can relate to each other as fellow sinners and strugglers, honestly helping each other apply the grace of God to our lives. We can then welcome unbelievers into that context, showing them how the gospel is at work in our lives and inviting them to join us in tasting the goodness of the Lord.

Our burden is to cultivate in ourselves and our colleagues what Jack Miller called 'a vision of grace so big that it will cause us to give up churchly passivity for bold witnessing activity.'[15] This kind of 'practical Calvinism' produces people of God who are consumed by the gospel. Jack Miller describes such Christians who

> had extraordinary power in evangelism and renewal. They followed an omnipotent Christ, the divine warrior, and He anointed them with His missionary presence. But this power was poured out on those who knew that they were inherently powerless without a constant dependence upon the working of God's grace in their lives... Such men grew into giants on the earth. Though once they were crippled by guilt, Christ cleansed and healed them. He had spoken an authoritative, compelling word of forgiveness to their souls. So, of course, they knew that He could speak the same word of forgiving grace to others through their preaching. God had done great things for them; He could do great things for others.'[16]

We believe the Lord continues to do it in our day. To God be the glory!

NOTES

1. Archibald Alexander, *Thoughts on Religious Experience* (London: The Banner of Truth Trust, originally published 1845), pages 165,166

2. Charles Hodge, *Systematic Theology*, vol. III (Grand Rapids, Michigan: William B. Eerdmans, 1970), page 102.

3. Stephen Smallman, *Sonship Theology: Blessing or Bane? Secured by Christ's Finished Work: Children Not Slaves* (PCA News.com, 2001) pages 3-4.

4. C. John Miller – pastor, author, founder and director of World Harvest Mission

5. A. W. Tozer, *That Incredible Christian* (Harrisburg, Pennsylvania: Christian Publications, 1964), page 12.

6. Thomas Brooks, *Precious Remedies for Satan's Devices* (London: Banner of Truth Trust, originally published 1652), pages 142-147.

7. Richard Lovelace, *Dynamics of Spiritual Life* (Downers Grove, Illinois: InterVarsity Press, 1979), page 101.

8. Quoted in John Piper, *Desiring God* (Portland, Oregon. Multnomah Press, 1986), page 127.

9. Walter Marshall, *The Gospel Mystery of Sanctification* (Grand Rapids, Michigan. Reformation Heritage, 1999. Originally published 1692), page 102

10. Robert Haldane, *Exposition of the Epistle to the Romans* (London: The Banner of Truth Trust, 1958; originally published 1842), page 253.

11. Timothy Keller, *Sonship Theology: Blessing or Bane?* (PCAnews.com, 01/30/2001, comment 70).

12. See Neil Williams, *The Theology of Sonship*, World Harvest Mission, 2001.

13. *The Autobiography of William Jay*, ed. George Redford and John Angell James (London: Banner of Truth, 1974), page 569.

14. Lovelace, page 212.

15. C. John Miller, *Powerful Evangelism for the Powerless* (Phillipsburg, New Jersey: P & R Publishing, 1997), page 2.

16. Miller, pages 4-5.

SUFFERING IN JAMES

Dan G. McCartney

O f all the books of the NT, the Epistle of James is generically the closest to Jewish wisdom literature.[1] Wisdom literature is concerned with the pragmatic questions of *how* to live, and how to understand life, which for the Christian means how to live the life of faith. One of the great questions of wisdom literature is how to deal with suffering, and the experience of suffering causes people to yearn for understanding and wisdom. It is not surprising therefore that James is concerned with Christian suffering. Yet James is not interested in either suffering or wisdom for their own sake. In James the search for wisdom is closely linked with faith. It is James' concern that his hearers evince genuine faith that drives his letter (1:3,6; 2:1,5,14-26; 5:15), and suffering is of interest because it calls forth faith.

In this concern with suffering, James resembles 1 Peter. Both letters address the existential concern of why Christians are suffering, and both link suffering to the deepening of faith. But they deal with it in very distinct ways. 1 Peter, rather like Isaiah (and in dependence on Isaiah), links the suffering of the faithful with the redemptive-historical event of the suffering of the Servant of the Lord (Christ), thus giving the Christian's suffering a theological meaning. Suffering becomes an experiential outworking of the believer's union with Christ. But James has only the slightest traces of this. His focus is, rather like Daniel and the later wisdom literature, on the promise of eschatological reversal and the theme of suffering as opportunity to show faith. For this reason, James has no emphasis on 'suffering for the name' as 1 Peter does. It is not suffering itself, but the Christian's faithful response to suffering, that is of interest to James.

Surprisingly little has been written on the subject of suffering in James. This may be because the subject of suffering only comes up more or less explicitly in the opening exhortation (1:1-12) and part of the closing exhortations (5:7-11). Yet wisdom literature frequently uses *inclusio* (placing a feature at the beginning and the ending of a text) as a defining device. One can see it, for example, in Job, where chapter 1 and chapter 41 frame the long poetic narrative and give it direction. Likewise Matthew, the Gospel most influenced by Jewish wisdom genre (and the Gospel with the closest affinities with James[2]), begins and ends with a reference to 'God with us' (1:23, 28:20) in order to give focus to that Gospel. So here the Christian response to suffering as the framing subject of James appears to be a significant feature of the epistle.

James' treatment of suffering can be described as having three main interests. First, suffering is a characteristic trait of the people of God. Second, suffering is one of the 'trials' or tests that are a means to achieving Christian 'perfection' or maturity. Third, suffering is a call to faithful living, both in response to one's own suffering, and in response to the suffering of others.

Suffering is a Characteristic Trait of God's People

The reference in the first verse of James to the recipients as *diaspora*, whether or not the term here in James implies a strictly Jewish audience, already emphasizes the suffering character of the people of God, as those who are scattered in the world. It may hint as well at the fact that the scattering/sowing is for the benefit of the world, since scattering God's people also scatters the seed of the word which they carry (the theme of word as seed is certainly in 1:18 and 1:21).[3] James thus shares with other NT writers the notion that the suffering of believers benefits others.

James also shares the NT conviction that the eschatological reversal has begun. More on this later, but here note that the community of faith is the community of those who endure in suffering.[4] The people of humility are the people who will be exalted (4:10, 1:9-10).[5] The notion of the community of faith as the suffering community has roots in OT. For example Ps 86:1 uses 'the poor' as equivalent to the pious. The Qumran community regarded itself as the community of the poor (1QH 2:5; 1QpHab 12:3,6,10; 4QpPs37 2:9, 3:10). Possibly James also regarded the Christian community as 'the poor.' (2:5, 1:9 cf. Luke 6:20). But economic poverty is not James' main concern. Where the economically 'poor man' is mentioned, he is not the believer but the person whom the believer is enjoined to treat with respect (2:2-6).[6] Likewise, while it is certainly true that James has some very harsh words for the rich in 5:1-6, which is almost as excoriating as the conviction in 1 Enoch 94-105 that the rich are as a class bound for perdition, the concern is not the fact that they are rich, but that they fail to act responsibly with their wealth, and even oppress the poor. It is because economic and social responsibility are indispensable to faith (2:15-16), that James is concerned with such responsibilities. James is concerned about the genuineness of his readers' faith. Although the community may have had both rich and poor in it, James' concern is therefore not with the political dimensions of social justice, but with brotherliness in the church and the believer's active compassion for those who suffer. Economic poverty, or wealth for that matter, is viewed as another 'test' for the Christian, an opportunity to demonstrate faith by being ever cognizant of the eschatological reversal found in the gospel.[7] And this brings us to the second dimension of suffering in James.

Suffering is one of the Trials that are a Means to Christian Maturity.

There is no notion in James of suffering itself being redemptive, either for the sufferer himself or for someone else. Rather it is the fortitude in the trial that is given positive theological value in James.[8] Again, this is somewhat different than 1 Peter, who focuses heavily on Christ's suffering as redemptive, and the believer's suffering in doing good is a means of identification with Christ. Endurance in 1 Peter is enjoined because of what *suffering* does in the believer, uniting him to Christ's suffering. James rather regards *endurance* as the primary thing that functions in the believer's life, and suffering is mostly seen as an opportunity to let endurance do its job of 'perfecting' or maturing the believer.

This too is more along the lines of wisdom literature (cf. 2 Apoc Bar 52:5-6, Sir 2:1, Wis 3:4f.). Suffering was a test that gave one an opportunity to heroically endure, like Abraham (Jub 19:8) or Joseph (TestJos 2:7) or Job (TestJob 4:5-6). Joy, too is associated with suffering in wisdom thinking. Sir 40:20 locates joy in wisdom, the path of which involves discipline and testing (cf. Sir 4:27).[9] James, in line with this tradition, states (1:2) that trials are to be regarded as all joy. Though James later gives further reasons for joy in testing (v. 12), here he indicates that testings are to be regarded as occasion for joy because they are opportunity to endure and prove faith-keeping, and because they lead to wisdom. Again, in James it is not the suffering itself that produces maturity, but rather the faithful endurance within the trial. To put it succinctly, the Christian who endures is the Christian who matures.

James expresses this notion in a *sorites*, a sequence of causal links, in 1:3-4: trials (*peirasmoi*) are the means of testing (*dokimion*)[10] which provide opportunity for patient endurance (*hypomone*) which leads to perfection or maturity (*teleiotes*). James regards suffering then as something to be rejoiced in, because it moves one toward the eschatological goal of completion or perfection. The completeness or maturity (*teleiotes*) of the believer is simply being what God intends one to be, being all that a human being should be, achieving the goal or purpose (*telos*) of his life. The adjective form (*teleios*) when used of humans typically refers to their being 'full-grown' or mature, though in certain contexts it can mean 'perfect.' Reflected here is Jesus' command that his disciples 'be perfect' (Matt. 5:48) which gets echoed throughout the NT (1 Cor. 14:20, Col. 4:12, cf. 1 Pet. 1:16). Endurance under pressure is a means of growth. As the body builders like to say: 'No pain, no gain'. James' combination of *teleios* with another word for 'complete' (*holokleros*) may imply another dimension to the imagery, that of sacrifice. Offerings that in the OT were acceptable to God had to be perfect and whole, i.e. without defect. Though James is not speaking in a cultic context here, this may very well have evoked the notion of believers as, to use Paul's language, 'living sacrifices, holy and acceptable to God' (Rom. 12:1; cf. 1 Pet. 2:5). And James joins Peter and Paul in attesting to the fact that somehow trials are a necessary part of the preparation of believers.

Along similar lines, James' concern that his hearers be 'not lacking in anything', or being fully equipped may also carry forward the priestly notion of proper investiture and preparation. This phrase might, however, be more closely associated with military imagery, of having a full panoply of armament. Since endurance was the prime virtue of a soldier, this certainly fits. Whatever the particulars of the image in James' mind, the meaning is clear: the strengthening of endurance through trials is an important aspect of Christian life, and without it the Christian is ill-equipped for service to God, whether that service be viewed in military, athletic, or priestly imagery (all of which are used in the NT at one point or another).

The sorites of verses 3-4 is echoed in another sorites which leads to life in 1:12: endurance of trials (*hypomone peirasmon*) is the proof (*dokimos*) which results in the crown of life.[11] Opposite this stands a *sorites* of death in 1:13-15: testing –> desire –> sin –> death. Again this shows that it is not the trial itself that produces maturity and life, for a trial can also result in failure to endure, in giving in to the desire that gives birth to sin and leads to death. Rather it is faithful endurance in the trial that leads to life.

The life that is in view is the 'crown of life', the victor's crown that comes at the end of the race.[12] James 5:1-11 puts it in a more clearly eschatological framework. In concord with later Jewish wisdom literature, James sees the final solution to the problem of evil in eschatology, specifically the 'eschatological reversal,' whereby the proud will be brought low and the lowly will be lifted up. The rich who oppress the poor in 5:1-6 are harshly warned of the coming wrath, and in fact their future judgment is described as something already in place ('your wealth has rotted and moths have eaten your clothes; your silver and gold are corroded'). On the other hand those who suffer in verses 7-11 are encouraged to remember to wait patiently for the coming of the Lord, as the prophets did.[13]

The eschatological dimension is another reason why the enduring of trials may be counted as joy – they are an indication of the nearness of the eschaton. At least it is a reflection of the biblical hope already found in Psalm 126:5: 'those who have sown with tears shall reap with rejoicing.'

What are these 'trials' that we are supposed to count as joy? What kind of 'trials' or 'testing' is involved here?[14] The Greek word *peirasmoi* can mean either 'tests' in the general sense, or the specific kinds of tests rendered in English as 'temptations'. James appears to use the word in both senses. The context of verse 2 makes it clear that James is thinking of the various pressures that are often applied against believers which threaten their well-being and obedience,[15] which may very well cause believers to doubt the sovereignty of God in their lives. But it would not work to translate here as 'temptations'. The injunction of James is here to 'think differently', knowing that when faith is tested, it is proven by the test, and becomes purer and stronger as a result, and this is cause for joy.

The meaning of the word seems to be somewhat different in 1:12-15. The context here demands the sense of 'tempt to evil'. God does not tempt to evil, because he is not tempted by evil. God is 'untemptable' and untestable because that which makes a trial a trial is the evil desire within the person being tested (the pressure to sin comes from within).

Nevertheless, these two senses are not unrelated. Testing by suffering (which is an opportunity to endure) can turn into testing (tempting) to evil, such as being quick to wrath (cf. v. 20) brought on by impatience when faced with testing. But put positively, circumstances of suffering are also opportunities for endurance, or to put it as James does in 4:7, for resisting the devil. It is one's response to the *peirasmoi*, the 'patient endurance,' not the *peirasmoi* themselves, that according to James does the work of maturing. Further, the 'testing' in view is not just physical suffering, nor is it only eschatological tribulation; it is any kind of testing,[16] such as being confronted with the suffering of others (see below), or the need to control the tongue (ch. 3).

Thus James' exhortation is to let patience have its perfect work, or as Dibelius[17] puts it, 'let endurance do its work of perfecting' – i.e. its work which leads to 'perfection' or maturity. Trials and testing have a purpose, and the faithful one should not defeat that purpose by *im*patience, by giving in to wrath, or by abandoning obedience for the sake of comfort.

Suffering calls Forth Faithful Living

The third way James deals with suffering is to note that suffering is a call to faithful living. Adamson[18] points out that in James testing is eschatological, and eschatology is bound up with ethics in James. Suffering is therefore connected with ethics, because suffering drives one to eschatology.[19]

The response demanded of one's own suffering is patient endurance. This exhortation to patience is eschatologically motivated. James compares it to a farmer's patience: 'Be patient, then, brothers, until the Lord's coming. See how the farmer waits for the land to yield its valuable crop and how patient he is for the autumn and spring rains' (5:7). It is because those who cause suffering now will receive it back again (5:4-5) at the parousia of the Lord (5:8-9) that the sufferer now waits patiently. The response of the prophets, and especially Job, to suffering provides the paradigm for believers to be patient in suffering (5:10-11).[20]

But James is even more interested in how the Christian responds to the suffering of others. Because a Christian is a sufferer, he or she is expected to respond to the suffering of others as a fellow sufferer. Hence he even goes so far as to say that true religion[21] is to care for sufferers (1:27). That is to say that, because real faith (2:14-17) is faith in God's exalting the humble, the works that proceed from true faith will involve showing mercy to those who suffer.

Of particular concern to James are the truly destitute (symbolized by 'orphans and widows', who in that social environment were often the most marginalized and powerless people). These are the 'humble' who will be exalted (1:9). The church is the community that anticipates the eschatological reversal by caring for and respecting the poor.

Therefore James is furious with those who show favoritism to the rich. Such favoritism is a major offense for two reasons: 1) it violates the law of love, and belies the character of God as one who cares about the poor (note that the context of the law of love in Leviticus 19 specifically condemns partiality [Lev. 19:15])[22], and 2) such partiality belies the eschatological nature of the community, which ought to echo God's exaltation of the poor. This is the remarkable point of James 2:1-13, that the poor are not just to be pitied, they are to be *respected*.[23] This is quite difficult for most of us who are not poor. Suffering, especially poverty and destitution, makes a person repulsive in the eyes of most, which of course increases the suffering.

Yet the eschatological reversal of the gospel means that it is precisely those who suffer who are to rejoice in trials; it is those who are poor who are rich in faith; it is those who are humble who will be exalted. 'Perfection' and wholeness in the gospel runs counter to the world's notion of wholeness. As Elsa Tamez points out, 'For people today, perfection is linked to success, competition, excelling at the expense of others. For James it is the opposite; for him it is to attend to the needy in order to be consistent with what we believe and what we read in the Bible.'[24] I would only add that this is not just 'for people today'. The world's view of *teleiotes*, the *goal* or *telos* of worldly life and worldly wisdom (3:15), has always been 'success' and the achievement of domination. But the 'wisdom from above' is good behavior in a humble wisdom (3:13).

Finally, suffering calls forth prayer, both by the sufferer and for the sufferer. In 5:13 James tells his hearers: 'Is any one among you suffering? Let him pray' (RSV). 5:14 expands this responsibility of prayer not just to the sufferer but to the church leaders, for whom this is a major calling. In this writer's opinion, the anointing of the sick here commanded is not the establishment of some sacrament of unction, nor is it simply medicinal anointing; it is symbolic of the anointing with the oil of gladness. Isaiah 61:3 is one of the great prophecies that speak of the messianic 'eschatological reversal' texts, where we are told that one of the things the messiah has been anointed for is to 'provide for those who grieve in Zion – to bestow on them a crown of beauty instead of ashes, the oil of gladness instead of mourning, and a garment of praise instead of a spirit of despair' (NIV). It is once again as in 1:2 linking suffering with joy. Sickness, just like other forms of suffering, is a trial, and trials are opportunities for endurance, which leads to maturity.

Conclusion

James' concern with suffering stems from his concern with genuine faith. Suffering is a test of faith, demonstrating both whether one really has it, and what kind of faith it really is. Faith does not show favoritism, and especially does not despise those who suffer from poverty, or any other kind of suffering. Faith, when it encounters the suffering of others, does not simply utter pious wishes of health; it rather looks to the interests of the sufferers, such as widows and orphans. Faith, when it encounters one's own suffering or other form of testing, does not doubt (is not double-minded);[25] it rather waits patiently for the coming of the Lord.

NOTES

A large part of the life of faith is one's attitude toward things in life and his or her response to events. We often can do little to control our environment and the things that happen to us, but we can control the way we think about it, and how we react to it. Knowing how to interpret events and actions is a large part of wisdom, and the faithful attitude of the Christian is one of joy, even when suffering.

1. See my article, 'The Wisdom of James the Just' in *SBJT 4:3* (Fall 2000) 52-64.
2. The relationship is often noted. See the similarities noted in detail in F. Mussner, *Der Jakobusbrief* (HThK XIII/1; Freiburg, 1975) 48-50. P. Hartin (*James and the Q Sayings of Jesus* [JSNTSup; Sheffield: Sheffield Academic Press, 1991]) closely examines these similarities and concludes that Matthew and James came from a common environment and had access to a similar form of 'Q.'
3. F. J. A. Hort, *The Epistle of James: The Greek Text with Introduction, Commentary as Far as Chapter IV Verse 7, and Additional Notes* (London: Macmillan, 1909) 3, regards *diaspora* in James as strictly a reference to the scattering, unconnected with the

sowing of the word in the world, because although such an idea does exist in the OT, it never uses the word group *zera'* (sow; seed) in such connections. However the high level of relationship of James to the synoptic teaching would suggest otherwise, since Jesus in the gospels frequently uses the sowing imagery to refer to the dissemination of the word in the world.

4. James is concerned with individual response to suffering, but his main interest is in the suffering of the community, or the behavior of individual believers as that behavior affects the community.

5. There is some debate as to whether the wealthy man of 1:10 is being addressed as a Christian who should rejoice in the fact that his wealth is temporary, or as a reprobate person who simply is being told to mourn because he will suffer destruction. Whatever answer is given, James' main focus is of course on the eschatological reversal, and consequently a different way of looking at suffering and poverty.

6. Both 'the poor' and 'the rich' are treated in James in the third person. The 'you' of James are those who react in certain ways to the poor and the rich. There is a diatribe against 'you rich' (probably rhetorical) but there is no corresponding commendation or any kind of address to 'you poor'. R. Bauckham (*James: Wisdom of James, Disciple of Jesus the Sage* [New York: Routledge, 1999] 188) therefore argues that at least the bulk of James' hearers were ordinary working class people, who in relation to modern western standards were indeed poor, but who in their own society were not destitute. They had the wherewithal to help the truly poor, the destitute in need of basic means of survival such as food and blankets.

7. Most modern commentators regard the 'rich man' of 1:10 as the generalized outsider or unbeliever who will be utterly destroyed, and who simply stands in contrast to the humble believer of verse 9. They point to the negative presentation of the wealthy in 5:1-6 as oppressors, and their characterization in 2:6 as 'those who drag you into court,' and argue that James does not envision any of his Christian readers as being wealthy. In my opinion, however, as well as that of most older commentators, this problematic passage is not simply a blanket curse upon the rich, but is addressing actual wealthy Christians, exhorting them to remember that their riches are transitory, and to exhibit humility instead of pride in their wealth, as 4:10 and 4:16 enjoin. What would be the point of the warnings and exhortations of 4:13-17 unless there were some actual merchants in the group being addressed?

8. The term for 'endurance' is a common one in Greek moral literature, especially among the Stoics. There it refers to the patient endurance of whatever comes, without allowing distress to influence one's convictions, thinking or lifestyle (cf. F. Hauck, *TDNT* IV:582). Endurance is a particularly desirable characteristic of a soldier. James, like Paul, has taken the term and applied it to the Christian's faithfulness in staying the course in the face of opposition. It is therefore not a little related to the biblical notion of faith.

9. The connection between wisdom and enduring trials is found elsewhere in the NT as well (cf. esp. 1 Pet 1:6 and 4:12f.).

10. *Dokimion* here means not the process but the instrument that is used for testing, as in the LXX of Proverbs 27:21, where the furnace is a *dokimion* for silver and gold (Hort, *James*, 5). Thus it is not the same as its use in 1 Peter 1, where it means 'genuineness' (cf. P. H. Davids, *Epistle of James* [Grand Rapids: Eerdmans, 1982] 68.).

11. We can compare both of them to a similar *sorites* in Romans 5:3-5, though there it is hope that stands at the end of the list rather than 'perfection': *thlipsis –> hypomone –> dokime–> elpis*. In both cases the treatment of suffering is driven by christological eschatology. This is one of the many surprising points of contact between James and Paul's letters which suggest that perhaps the book of Acts is after all accurately portraying

things when it presents Paul and the Jerusalem church as ultimately harmonious, but Paul goes on to add the dimension of the Holy Spirit: 'Hope does not disappoint because the love of God is poured out in our hearts through the Holy Spirit that is given to us.' James on the other hand, with the possible (and in my view unlikely) exception of 4:5, never mentions the Holy Spirit.

12. Could this 'crown' of life be the crown of true wisdom, as in Prov 4:9? This would comport well with the wisdom from above that is to be sought in chap. 3. But here the image seems more to be the gift of life which happens at the end of the story, not the wisdom which enables one to live in the middle of the story.

13. This is quite different from taking things into their own hands, which is perhaps why James, for all its denunciations of wealth and interest in social justice, is virtually ignored by the so called liberation theologians.

14. Many commentators attempt to answer the question whether these 'trials' or testings are particular and real sufferings that the original hearers were experiencing. Understanding James' meaning does not require this to be answered. All believers eventually experience trials of some sort, and at such times these encouragements apply.

15. R. P. Martin, *James* (Waco: Word, 1988) 15.

16. A. Chester, 'The Theology of James,' *The Theology of the Letters of James, Peter, and Jude* (ed. A. &. R. P. M. Chester; Cambridge: Cambridge Univ. Press, 1994) 31.

17. M. Dibelius, *James: A Commentary on the Epistle of James* (Hermeneia; ed. revised by H. Greeven; trans. Michael A Williams; Philadelphia: Fortress, 1975) 74.

18. J. B. Adamson, *James: The Man and His Message* (Grand Rapids: Eerdmans, 1989) 308-16.

19. See also A. Chester, 'The Theology of James', 16-17, 30-31.

20. Anyone who has read the book of Job may want to object to this example, since Job was hardly a model of what we typically regard as patience. But this example may clue us in to the fact that true patience as James uses the term is not passive acceptance, but an unremitting appeal to God for help, and the certain hope of eventual vindication. Cf. Martin, *James*, 16.

21. The term used here for 'religion,' (*threskeia*) means not one's overall faith commitments, but religious practice, acts of piety, or cultic activity. By 'true religion' therefore James does not mean 'the essence of true Christian faith' but 'the essence of true Christian religious activity.'

22. The love command of Lev. 19:18 is shared throughout the NT as definitive for Christian life. Its widespread use as the basis of ethics is probably due to the fact that it was originally promulgated by Jesus himself (Mark 12:29ff and parallels). James even calls it the 'royal law' (cf. S. Laws, *A Commentary on the Epistle of James* [San Francisco: Harper & Row, 1980] 107-09), probably because it was given by the king, or because it pertains to the kingdom of God. James' point is that showing favoritism violates the most basic ethic of God, and hence violates the whole law.

23. Is there any evil more endemic to the church today than the tendency to favor the rich and disrespect the poor?

24. E. Tamez, The Scandalous Message of James: Faith Without Works is Dead (New York: Crossroad, 1990) 86f.

25. The 'doubting' in view in 1:6 is not the search-for-understanding kind of doubt, but rather the double-mindedness of the fence-sitter, who is, as James says, tossed about like a wave of the sea. The one who vacillates in his or her commitment and/or behavior does not have true faith.

BIBLICAL COUNSELING AND PRACTICAL CALVINISM

Jay E. Adams

It is my privilege and pleasure to participate in producing this Festschrift in honor of Dr. Clair Davis. Clair, a good friend, would be happy with the topic given to me: 'Biblical Counseling and Practical Calvinism'. Clair always had more of a leaning to the practical than most of the other faculty I have known.

My title 'Biblical Counseling and Practical Calvinism' means that counseling must be Calvinistic to be biblical and practical. I heartily affirm both of those claims. There are, of course, those who would dispute that statement. I shall not argue the case for practical Calvinism being biblical in this place,[1] but shall merely attempt to demonstrate the fact.

Biblical Counseling is Calvinistic

The fundamental principle of Calvinism is that God is sovereign. The fundamental principle of biblical counseling is that God, not the counselor, changes people in ways that please Him. The two principles mesh much better than a hand in a glove. All else in the Calvinistic system grows out of the fact that God *is* sovereign. Few Christians of any stripe, when pressed, will dispute God's sovereignty. Yet, when it comes down to it, only the Calvinist defines sovereignty in a way that preserves it. Others make man more than he is and God less than He is.

In Calvinistic thought, sovereignty means that from all eternity God decreed everything that ever has or will come to pass. This biblical doctrine is expressly taught in Ephesians 1:11 where we read,

> In Him we were chosen as His inheritance, being predestined according to the purpose of the One Who is operating everything in agreement with the counsel of His will.[2]

In this statement it is also clear that God providentially works in history to bring about His purposes without any flaws or glitches.[3] To be able to plan all things and see to it that all things happen according to that plan is sovereignty.

The sovereignty of God is the basis for Christian counseling. If we could never be sure of God's promises because He is learning and reacting to man – as process theology (recently revived) teaches – we would have no reason to expect that the counsel that we give will hold true. It could change tomorrow with the One Who may have changed His mind today. In fact, counseling might not even need to be biblical, since the Bible would run the risk of becoming outmoded by new, innovative thinking on God's part!

Christian counselees who ask, 'Why did this have to happen to me?' (one of the questions most frequently asked of counselors) need a rock solid answer. They need to know that, no matter how serious the problem that led to the question, God is in absolute control. It is because Romans 8:28 is the promise of the sovereign God, Who does not change His mind, that Christians have been known to bear up under the most trying circumstances. That is practical Calvinism.

While through tears and pain the believer may have difficulty seeing *how* the promise is true, he can at least understand that somehow trials 'work together' to make him more like Christ (*cf.* Rom. 8:29). And he can begin to bring his faith to bear in the trial to see that this end is achieved. God plans all things for His glory and the believer's good. That is the assurance that sovereignty lends to counseling.

A counselor who doubts that God is sovereignly bringing about all events (including tragedies) for the good of those who love Him, will be stumped by the question. He is likely, therefore, to revert to mysticism, agnosticism or the like: 'It will all come out well, somehow,' or 'No one knows how there can be evil in a good God's world.'[4] But such responses are worse than unhelpful – they only confuse and engender more doubt. On the contrary, Calvinistic counselors will firmly affirm that God is in charge and that in His time and way, He will work *even this* out for His honor and the counselee's blessing.

Because God's sovereignty extends to 'everything,' (Eph. 1:11) it extends to salvation. The facts that the famous 'Five Points of Calvinism' systematize, bear significantly upon counseling. While there is not ample space to develop the relationship of those facts and counseling adequately, I should like to mention at least a few ways in which this is so.

Take the fact of total depravity.[5] What teaching could be more practical in counseling? Adam's sin plunged us all (Christ excepted) into guilt and corruption. The former is dealt with by God's act of justification, the latter by His act of regeneration which makes sanctification possible. Sanctification is gradual, halting, spotty and irregular. Clair, in his inimitable way, once illustrated the process of sanctification by saying that if you wished to graph it, it would look like someone praying with a yoyo while ascending a flight of stairs.

Biblical Counseling is Practical

Of what practical value are these truths to the biblical counselor? Since every aspect of man has been affected by sin, there are noetic effects of sin in all of us. Man errs, makes wrong decisions and views life from a distorted perspective. God once put it this way, 'My thoughts are not your thoughts, neither are your ways My ways' (Isa. 55:8, Berkeley). When he attempts to correct his wrong ways by wrong thinking, the ways he adopts lead him into more and more unrighteousness, a phenomenon that is well known to all biblical counselors. Those who believe that there is some aspect of man to which they may appeal will tend to address his problems by offering human wisdom and even recommend counseling by unbelieving practitioners. They know, as Paul taught Galatians 6:1, that believers should be 'restored' only by 'those who have the Spirit'. Truly Christian counselors are biblical precisely because they know that it takes the Spirit working using His Word to replace 'depraved' thinking with godly thinking that will lead to godly ways. Likewise, they refuse to incorporate the theories of depraved men into their counseling practice.

Because 'biblical' counselors believe in progressive

sanctification, they reject those all-at-once plans of escalating to a 'higher plane' by following some manmade recipe. They know that the 'flesh' must be put off gradually as it is replaced by biblical alternatives. They will settle for nothing less than change that God's Spirit produces, knowing that all other change is useless.[6] They view counseling not as some important thing in itself but consider it an aspect of the sanctification process. When the process of sanctification is impeded by a log jam, the counselor's task is to break the log jam so that the process may continue unabated. Remedial counseling, therefore, is largely an emergency measure. This eminently practical view of counseling grows out of the Calvinistic interpretation of the Scriptures.

Because they believe that man has been affected adversely in all aspects of his being, biblical counselors work closely with physicians, recognizing that the inner spiritual side of man (variously styled 'heart, spirit or soul') and the outer physical (body or flesh) interact and influence one another.

Unconditional election is a truth that strikes at the heart of man's problem with sin. When Adam sinned, it was in response to an appeal to become like God. Pride and sinful ambition certainly was involved at the core of his rebellion. Ever since, biblical counselors have had to deal with pride. It lies in the background of nearly every counseling difficulty.

Now the fact of unconditional election stands over against human pride. When God elected Israel as a nation, He drove home the unconditional nature of His choice:

> It was not because you were greater in numbers than any other nation that the Lord fastened His affection upon you and chose you; for you were the least of all peoples. No, it was because the Lord loved you and on account of His oath which He had sworn to your fathers ...' (Deut. 7:7, 8a).

And the oath, and that covenant to which it belonged, were also unconditional. God did not choose the fathers because of anything exceptional in them, but out of His own sovereign plan and purposes. The same is true of all those elected to salvation today (Rom. 9:11-13[7]). God's own sovereign choice flows from Him alone and is dependent upon nothing else (Eph. 1:4, 5, 11). Indeed, everything within us would seem to have militated against the choice. Paul says that it was 'when we were weak ... while we were still sinners ... while we were enemies' that Christ died for us, the ungodly, who are now reconciled by His death (Rom. 5:6, 8, 10).

Pride, as Proverbs 13:10; 16:18 warns, lies somewhere behind all 'strife' and 'goes before destruction'. Husbands and wives, business associates and members of the same congregation contend with one another out of pride, as every biblical counselor knows. He will search it out and meet it with the Calvinistic teaching of the unconditional election of God's own. He will seek instead to foster humility that accords with God's dictum in 1 Peter 5:5, knowing that 'God opposes the proud but helps the humble'. He will not be swayed by the faddish views of those who promote self-esteem teaching. He knows that such humanistic teaching results only in greater pride and selfishness.[8] Rather, he will help counselees to make a sober evaluation of themselves, stressing that they must 'not think more highly' of themselves than they ought to (Rom. 12:3). After all, they were chosen not because they were more lovely, more loving or more loveable than others, but solely because of the grace and mercy of God. Beliefs other than Calvinistic ones, tend to minimize the grace of God at some point or other and tend to maximize human initiative.

Due to divorces, death of a spouse and otherwise, many counselees are lonely. They find it difficult to make new friends. They long for companionship. The truth of limited atonement, properly ministered by a caring counselor, can meet that need as no other doctrine can. It teaches that not only did Christ's death satisfy the Father, but, by His appeasing sacrifice, the Father demonstrated His electing love for individuals. There is One Who loved them *individually* from all eternity. Jesus did not die for some faceless abstraction like 'mankind'. The believer, with all truth, may say, 'He died for *me*.[9]' Luther, more a Calvinist than many present-day Lutherans at this point, commenting on verse one of the twenty-third Psalm once said, 'Thank God for personal pronouns!' In his loneliness at the castle, he could find fellowship with the One Who died for him.[10] The believer knows that 'there is One Who sticks closer than a brother' (Prov. 18:24), and that He will never leave him or forsake him (Heb. 13:5). It is this marvelous truth that Calvinistic counselors have at their fingertips, ever ready to use to comfort and cheer lonely counselees.

Because there are those who think that they have to come to

the Father in their own strength and power, but who fear they do not have the power to do so, the truth of irresistible grace helps immeasurably. Jesus said, 'When I am lifted up from the earth, I will draw all sorts of people to Myself' (John 12:32). They do not come on their own initiative; He draws them. They have no initiative until He, by His Spirit, gives them initiative. There is no excuse for lingering when the gospel call goes forth, like so many in Puritanism did, 'preparing' and waiting for some special 'sensibility' that the Spirit was at work. On the contrary, they ought to reach out with the hand of faith and receive the great salvation that was wrought for them. The very desire for it and the will to believe are themselves given to the elect by the Spirit, Who makes them anxious to be drawn, ready and able to believe. That at no point does our salvation depend on us is a cheering doctrine, the principles of which extend to all the requirements for living a life pleasing to God. Anything good in us, anything worthwhile that we achieve, is due to the grace of God working in us. Listen to this great counseling passage: 'It is God Who is producing in you both the willingness and the ability to please Him' (Phil. 2:13). *You* do it, but by His wisdom and strength – not by yours! You *pursue* the fruit of the Spirit, but when it grows, you must call it *His* fruit.[11] From beginning to end, all that a believer achieves is the result of the gracious work of the Spirit Who dwells within and energizes him to do good works. This is most encouraging to counselees who recognize their own sin and their utter inability to accomplish what they want to accomplish in their own strength.

Finally, the teaching that it is by God's grace that saints persevere in believing and, therefore, can never be lost, is truly comforting. This is especially true for those who, apart from this biblical understanding, would spend much of their lives focusing on themselves and their future destiny, often doing so in agony, as some do who disbelieve this doctrine. The most astute of those who think that Christians may apostatize and overthrow their faith, after trying in vain to 'keep themselves in the faith' soon recognize the impossibility of attempting to do this and give up, often in despair, abandoning themselves to godless living and its consequences.

The Calvinistic counselor takes his counselee to 1 Peter 1:3-5 where he reads about the 'living hope'[12] God provides for His own. What is it? Listen to Peter when he describes that hope. He tells the Christian that it is an incorruptible, unspotted and unfading inheritance that has been kept in the heavens for you who are guarded by God's power through faith that is ready to be revealed in the last time.

Carefully examined, among other things, these verses teach that 1) nothing can go wrong with the inheritance and 2) nothing can go wrong with the heir. Thus the hope is assured. How useful this, and many other passages that teach the perseverance of the saints are! One wonders how any counselor may counsel effectively who does not believe this biblical teaching.

So, from this very brief glimpse at how Calvinistic teaching is both biblical and practical in pursuing the work of Christian counseling, you can begin to see that when it is set forth only abstractly, Calvinism may seem dry and sterile, as many have charged. But it was never intended to be represented that way. The system must be applied in all of its richness and wonder to struggling saints from the pulpit, in the counseling room and by the fireside in the home. Then, and then alone, does it come alive, throbbing with life. Then, and then alone, in all of its flaming brilliance it warms the hearts of those who properly understand it. Calvin's symbol of the faith as a flame in the hand says it all.

NOTES

1. In my view, Calvinism is really biblical Christianity spelled out in systematic form.
2. All New Testament quotations are from *The Christian Counselor's New Testament*. Timeless Texts (Huntersville) 1994.
3. N.B., He is now '*operating* everything *in agreement with* the counsel of His will'. What He wills to come to pass, he works to bring to pass!
4. For more on this see my book, *The Grand Demonstration* (now distributed by Timeless Texts).
5. Total depravity means man is corrupt in all his parts; not that he is as bad as he might be.
6. They will knowingly counsel no one but believers. God has not called counselors to move people from one lifestyle that is displeasing to God to another that is equally displeasing to Him (cf. Romans 8:8: 'Those who are in the flesh *cannot* please God' [emphasis mine]). Until converted, unbelievers cannot think or do those things that God requires. Therefore, biblical counselors evangelize unbelievers rather than counseling them.
7. See *The Grand Demonstration* for an exposition of Romans 9.
8. See my book, *The Biblical View of Self-esteem, Self-love and Self-Image*.
9. Cf. Galatians 2:20.
10. Cf. I John 1:5-7.
11. See my book, *A Theology of Christian Counseling*, p. 250 ff. for a full discussion of this matter.
12. Hope, in the Bible, means 'confident expectation' of something that God has promised and, therefore, is certain. It is not the hope-so 'hope' that we use the word 'hope' to express today.

.

CALVINISM AND CONTEMPORARY CHRISTIAN COUNSELING

David Powlison

Like most former students of Clair Davis, I delight in his extraordinary ability to turn a phrase and tell a story. By a flash of wit or contemporary allusion, he takes some knotted, obscure, and ancient debate and breaks it open as comprehensible, significant, and relevant. Some currently vexed question – some occasion for today's unruly passions, for factions and hostile caricature – appears from a higher vantage point, in brighter light, with wider horizons. Clair, ever the historian-pastor, would thereby call us to greater humility, to more appreciation for fellow Christians, to a more comprehensive vision, to wiser passions. He would never *tell* us that he was pastoring us; he just did history that way.

I vividly remember the opening sentences of Dr. Davis's medieval church history course. 'Sure, Christians are always interested in having an *integrated world and life view*. So all you seminary-types are studying presuppositionalism, reading Van Til, Schaeffer, and Kuyper. You want every square inch to be under Christ's lordship. You want to think Christianly to the very edge of the universe. You want to entertain no brute facts. That's great. Of course, the church had an integrated world and life view for *a thousand years* ... [pause] ... We call it the Dark Ages.' And we were off to the races: intrigued, chastened, ready to learn both how the church gets it right and how the church gets it wrong, both then and now.

Clair would tell history with large-souled sympathy for his subjects. Medieval Christians were not all ignoramuses, heretics, and embarrassments, like a skeleton in our closet. Jesus Christ's kingdom rule in His people shone amid the oddities and archaisms of medieval church, just as amid the all too familiar oddities and modernisms of our churches. True faith did not leapfrog from the apostles to the Reformation to us. Anselm, Bernard, Aquinas, Wycliffe, and the rest, though they are dead, they still speak to the questions that exercise us now. Sure, they got some things flat wrong and completely missed other things that we've learned are crucial. But Clair taught us to appreciate what they got right and to disagree humbly. By his example, he reproved our tendency to disagree arrogantly and irritably. He reminded us that we, too, will get some things wrong and won't even see things that our wiser successors will learn are crucial and glorious.

I remember how Clair characterized some late-1970s debate (the issue now forgotten!) that exercised the Westminster Seminary community. He commented, 'So-and-so is too far to the "left", and such-and-such too far to the "right", and I'm just the old mugwump in the middle.' But that mugwump was no middle-of-the-road relativist or compromiser. He managed a rare trick for a historian: to see and describe both sides fairly, without being cynical or indifferent to the importance of the issues, and then to take a stand. Historical mindedness did not sap committedness. All the while he evidenced that characteristic grace of the best historians: forbearance – even pleasure! – amid the foibles and lurchings of real-time, real-people historical process.

I've never forgotten how Clair the Calvinist sized up the furor over 'charismania' during those days: 'To all appearances, charismatics and Calvinists are miles apart, polar opposites. But really, they're the poles of a *horseshoe* magnet. They're opposites, but only an inch apart. If charismatics would stop and think, and if Calvinists would lighten up and get a life, you could squeeze the two poles together and they'd touch.' He went on to trace commonalities that threaded through all the differences. Clair's own ministry with Pentecostals in Germany bears witness to his vision that the Reformed faith ought to be expressed in ways that adorn our doctrine. He viewed truth as a gift to be taken out to where it's needed, not a possession to hoard and cosset within sectarian walls.

Clair was and is a 'Calvinist' of a particularly vigorous sort, in which gracious, life-giving truth in Christ generates gracious, lived-out practice in Christians. He taught about and cared about piety, counseling, evangelism, ecumenism, worship, church order, politics, and social action, as well as theological formulation. This article on 'counseling' is appropriate, given his interests. Again, to quote Clair, '*Good* practical theology is the hope of orthodoxy today.' Clair Davis is a historian who believes that history is not only what happened but also what's happening. To that end, we look at Calvinism in relationship to contemporary Christian counseling.

The 'Christian Counseling' World

For starters, most of the Christian counseling world is not Calvinistic. Most often, 'Christian counseling' consists of lightly reworked versions of secular theories and practices, embedded in a professional fee-for-service structure indistinguishable from the mental health system. Though practitioners of a Christianized psychotherapy sincerely profess Christian faith, they too-often ignore basic implications of biblical faith: e.g., the scope and purposes of the Word of God, the essentially religious-covenantal character of human experience, God's sovereignty in suffering, the restless depravity but genuine redeemability of the human heart, a presuppositional critique of unbelieving thought-praxis systems, the centrality of the church in God's purposes, the significance of Jesus Christ for the human condition, the dynamics of conversion and progressive sanctification, and so forth. Most Christian counseling is relatively a-theological, and thereby highly theological: conducted from within the gaze and intentions of largely secular world views, rather than from within God's gaze and intentions.

When the 'Christian' aspect is emphasized, Christian counseling usually expresses typically Arminian pieties, operating within a religious sector of 'spiritual' matters: 'salvation,' devotional life, casting out demons, mystical leadings of the Spirit, creedal profession of classic doctrines, churchly activity. Often an implicit or explicit trichotomous view of man distributes 'spiritual' issues to the church, bodily problems to medical science, and psychological matters (cognition, emotion, volition, motivation, relationships, change process: all the interesting stuff, what the Bible is about!) to the modern psychologies. Thus Meier New Life Clinics, the largest Christian mental health company, has routinely given all its patients antidepressant medication (body), psychotherapy and self-help (soul), and Bible studies (spirit), in the name of ministering to the whole person in a Christian way.

Most Christian counseling contains little of the 'world view' thinking characteristic of Calvinism. It is not uncommon for views of human nature derived from humanistic psychology (psychocentric 'needs for love, self-esteem, and achievement'), from cognitive psychology (a stoic analytic where 'irrational self-talk produces negative emotions'), or from temperament theory (adaptations of Myers-Briggs or other temperament tests) to be imported uncritically. Diagnostic constructs are then overlaid with semi-Christian contents: 'Jesus meets your need for self-esteem'; 'Change your self-talk to, "I am fearfully and wonderfully made" and "God doesn't make junk", so you won't feel down on yourself"; 'Timothy was an example of the Phlegmatic type because he was timid....' Secular psychologies set the key, rhythm, and melody, and Christian faith only adds a few grace notes to the composition.

An ambiguously defined, non-Calvinist version of 'common grace and/or general revelation' (the terms are often used interchangeably and as a catch-all) provides the rationale for importing the concepts, practices, and professional structures of the modern psychologies into professing Christian contexts. Van Til described and criticized 'The popular notion of common grace [which says that there is] a neutral field of operation between Christians and non-Christians' (*Common Grace and the Gospel*, p. 24). That 'popular notion' has largely defined the point of view and agenda of the Evangelical psychotherapy movement that has dominated seminaries, Christian colleges and graduate schools, the Christian publishing industry, and the Christian counseling culture since the early 1970s. Under the banner of 'integrating Christianity and Psychology' (or 'Theology and Psychology'), the notion that personality theories, psychotherapies, psychological research, and mental health professions are epistemologically neutral, scientific-medical activities has deeply permeated Evangelical culture.

But along the way, the distinctive perspectives of the Calvinistic world view have not been without voice and effect. A number of sociologists, historians, culture critics, theologians, and pastors have critiqued the ideas and practices of the evangelical psychotherapeutic culture from a broadly or a specifically Calvinist point of view: James Hunter, George Marsden, Os Guinness, David Wells, Jay Adams, Ed Welch, myself, and others. And the positive development of a modern Calvinist pastoral theology of counseling has a history going back to the late 1960s.[1] Christian faith has its own distinctive 'psychology,' our own take on human nature and the cure for what ails us. The Faith's psychology distinctively differs from the environing psychological faiths. Particularly since about 1990, this notion has gained currency. What gaze and intentions drive the Faith's psychology? Here the Calvinist outlook comes into its own with its insight into Scripture as God's self-revelation of how He sees and does things. The mind of Christ restructures our mind, and the practice of Christ redirects our practice.

Scripture and this Thing called 'Counseling'

'The Bible is alive, it speaks to me; it has feet, it runs after me; it has hands, it lays hold on me.' So said Martin Luther, and Calvinists agree. And surely that Bible speaks at every turn to the question of how to fix what is wrong with us. Counseling (as the Bible teaches us to think about it and do it) ought to be about face-to-face, your-name-on-it ministries of Word and deed. It is the interpersonal, personalizing part of the *cura animarum*: curing souls by name and caring for souls in the particulars. Conversational ministry operates in the mode of interactive dialogue, not proclamatory monologue. In a Shakespeare play, as in life, some scenes contain a soliloquy, but most scenes occur in give-and-take dialogue. We sometimes forget that the Bible is the same. For example, in the Gospels, scenes in which Jesus holds a conversation far outnumber scenes in which He teaches or preaches. And His teaching-preaching events often either arise from a conversation or lead to a conversation.

Public ministry (preaching, teaching, worship, Lord's supper, modeling) gives hearers generally applicable truths applied to *somebody else's specifics*. Bible exposition, other stories and illustrations, even anecdotes about yourself, all these give hearers truth-in-application to other people's lives, that the Holy Spirit and their own conscience might make it up close and personal. Necessarily, the public Word does not apply truth to hearers by name or identify particulars of their lives. The sermon does not say, 'Susie Schnorkeltube, I know it's hard to be neglected, and you're still feeling the anguish of your Mom's death, but why are you scowling at your husband, Humperdink, and gossiping about him to various and sundry persons in your neighborhood and prayer group? In His mercy, Jesus Christ comforts, reproves, and changes you.'[2]

But interpersonal ministry (daily conversation, counseling, discipleship, friendship, family, small group, diaconal aid, visitation, mentoring) happens and thrives in names and particulars, in knowing and being known. The pastoral conversation, after hearing well, says, 'Susie, I know....' You can lovingly speak with Susie and Humperdink about the what-happened-he-said-she-said-and-then-what-happened-next, and so tailor redemptive words and deeds to *their specifics*. Conversational ministry, whether casual or by appointment, ought to express the gaze and intentions of Christ, just as public ministry does. All ministries of grace and truth seek to thread the metanarrative of redemptive history into the narratives of individual lives.

Often pastoral counseling is literally pastoral: one of the parties is the designated shepherd and mentor (whether wise or foolish in content, skilled or clumsy in conversation). But most counseling (whether wise or foolish) is essentially a deprofessionalized, everyday affair. Its scope is as wide as 'the tongue', 'one-anothering', and 'encourage one another daily'. Its depth and intricacy plunge as deep as 'the madness in our hearts' and 'the afflictions of the afflicted'. Its duration is 'as long as it is called Today', ending only on the Day when our race is run and, seeing Jesus face-to-face, we become as He is in holiness and joy. A good pastor's ministry of the Word ought to be increasingly skillful and faithful in both proclamation and conversation. A good sheep's ministry of the Word ought to be increasingly skillful and faithful in conversation.

One sometimes hears well-intended statements such as, 'If people would sit under good, faithful preaching of the Word and have a consistent and meaningful personal devotional life, they wouldn't need counseling.' That does contain a partial truth, but it gets things exactly wrong. Good preaching and devotional life will create a community of vigorous mutual counseling arising from vital relationships with God, per Ephesians 3:14–5:2, Hebrews 3:12-14, 4:12-5:3, and 10:19-25. The publicly-proclaimed Word and the privately-pursued Word are intended to become the interpersonally-conversed Word. Publicly, privately, and interpersonally, the ministry of Word-and-deed ought to communicate a single vision of the human condition and the Redeemer Jesus Christ.

What is that human condition? Who is that Redeemer and what is He about? The *Heidelberg Catechism* builds its doctrine of the Christian life on coming to know 'how great my sin and misery are, how I am set free from all my sins and misery, and how I am to thank God for such deliverance.' The Lord's self-witness to His people throughout redemptive history always has this dual thrust: He delivers from *sin* and He delivers from *sufferings*. That's what 'counseling' ought to be about because it's what life is about and what all ministry ought to be about. The problem, 'evil,' is both moral and situational (Eccles. 9:3). We love perversely and do what is perverse; we experience what is painful and confusing. The solution, God's character, words, and deeds – His goodness, lovingkindness, peace, righteousness, mercy, justice, wrath, truth, and glory – remedies both moral and situational evils. So the 'paths of righteousness' into which our Lord leads His sheep are paths where *every* wrong is made right: both the evils we do and the evils that beset us. YHWH provides the sacrificial lamb in place of sinners (justifying righteousness). YHWH instructs sinners in the way (sanctifying righteousness). YHWH provides refuge from enemies, exposure of liars, food for the hungry, and healing for the sick (world-made-sane-and-delightful righteousness). YHWH will right every wrong (glorifying righteousness).

The Triune God works a comprehensive recreation. This story (or some other, misleading, and powerless story) is the stuff of every counseling transaction. *Our Father* forgives the sins of the guilty. He delivers us from the master sins by which Everyman betrays love of God: pride, unbelief and misbelief, fear of man, autonomy, idolatry, and inordinate desire. He delivers us from the derivative sins by which Everyman betrays love of neighbor: anger, lust, avarice, envy, gluttony, sloth, and the rest. This same Father also provides daily bread for the hungry: the seed and fruit tree, the soil, sun, rain, and season; the teeming flock, herd, fish, birds, and game; the wages, salaries, and sales. *Our Lord Jesus Christ* calls us to awaken, to repent, believe, and serve the good King. This good King also raises the dead, lifts up the downcast, and protects the helpless. *Our Holy Spirit* hand-delivers all these goods to us, every good and perfect gift. And so Christ's servants, led by the Holy Spirit, deal gently with the ignorant and wayward. And Christ's servants, led by the Holy Spirit, deal generously with the oppressed, poor, frail, and disabled. The God and Father of our Lord Jesus Christ has done, is doing, and will do all it takes to deliver us from our sins and miseries.

That's what grace and truth are about. That's what ministry is (ought to be) about. That's what counseling is (ought to be) about.

It's a package-deal, a set of complementary glories. But God's people have a hard time keeping *all* the pieces on the table, while seizing hold of the *particular* piece most needed in this or that situation. Why do we find it so hard to minister wisely?

The Unbalancing Act of Good Practical Theology

Part of our difficulty arises from the essential nature of ministry. Application always particularizes truth to hearer and situation. Wise ministry always 'unbalances' truth in order to achieve specific relevance. Ministry is selective. It anecdotalizes, metaphorizes, and personalizes truth to cases. The whole Bible operates this way, never functioning like a systematic theology text. When Paul writes to believers in Galatia, he says, 'False teachers beset you, and you lurch from legalistic religion to licentious indulgence. Remember: faith in Christ receives the Spirit, and works out into love for others.' When James writes to Messiah-trusting members of the Diaspora, he says, 'General life hardships of poverty and sickness beset you, and you too easily play the proud fool. Watch how you talk to and treat others, and always seek the grace that God gives the humble.' When Peter writes to disciples in northern Asia Minor, he says, 'Painful oppression and unfairness beset you, and you are tempted to waver and retaliate. Entrust your lives to your faithful Creator, in light of your incorruptible inheritance in Christ. Do what is right, and use your gifts well, because He will bring you through to glory.' Paul, James, and Peter addressed somewhat different people, facing somewhat different challenges, tempted to somewhat different sins, needing to hear somewhat different truths from and about the Lord, needing to practice somewhat different wisdoms.

Systematic theology traces the deep-structure commonalities in Paul, James, and Peter: the simultaneous operation of vertical and horizontal dimensions, the gift-quality of grace, the *summa* of theology proper and soteriology, the significance of situation, the process quality of Christian experience, etc. But practical theology never talks and acts that way. Ministry never can (never should!) try to say it all at once, 1 to 10 and A to Z. The Bible never does. Truth always comes selected and adapted. So, for example, while Psalms express (and nurture in us) the many moods of an honest relationship with God, Proverbs distill (and exhort in us) the visible fruits of skillfully godly ways to talk, work, sell, make love, use money, raise kids. Psalms are written by people being mistreated; Proverbs are written to people being misled. Ministry works with those sorts of differences. The Bible is a book of case studies in practical theology, teaching what we also must do.

Just as good preaching and counseling 'unbalance' truth to address cases, so good systematic theology 'flattens' truth for the sake of comprehensiveness and coherence.[3] Systematics studies practical theology: the Bible along with current cases, questions, views, practices, and applications. It sums up, abridges, abstracts, rearranges, depersonalizes, and rebalances truth. It excises the names, narrative, experience, dialogue, geography, weather, and culture. The stuff of life-lived and practical theology ends up on the cutting room floor. By so doing, when understood and used rightly, systematics helps to nurture appropriate flexibility in ministry, and guards against exaggeration or minimizing, against axe-grinding, lacunae, and outright error. It guards us against making a one-size-fits-all practical theology out of our best insights, our most successful cases, and our typical experiences. Wisdom demands both balanced reflection and unbalanced applications. But it's hard to do both. On the one hand, 'unbalancing' can veer into imbalance: the miNISter's emPHAsis on a difFERent sylLABle. At worst, it can plunge into outright error: NIS, PHA, FER, or LAB forget their context and erase all else, producing the juggernaut of a faulty system. On the other hand, 'balance' can languish into tidy irrelevance, making no bold bid for the heart's loyalty, and offering no timely care for the sheep's condition. Fruitful ministry manages to keep all the pieces on the table, while seizing hold of today's particularly appropriate piece.

The prayers of Paul in Philippians 1, Colossians 1, and Ephesians 1 and 3 are unto this end. They have two major foci, both of which teach holy unbalances and holy balance to dance in step. First, 'Lord, give us ever more intelligent and affectionate faith' ('affectionate' in the old sense: love, know, trust, fear, delight, hope, need, obey, seek, serve, rejoice, honor, and the rest, all the verbs by which we relate to our God). Wise faith selects from a full quiver of options. Second, 'Lord, give us ever more intelligent and sincere love.' Wise love cares to step into *this* situation, knows how to love *this* person, and practices a lifestyle that is in it for good with diverse people. Wise love selects from a full quiver of options.

Conclusion
Wise Calvinism is the hope of counseling. *Practical* Calvinism! The varied wisdoms necessary for curing what needs curing come into their own via a world view and *modus operandi* that operates in

terms of the Lord of heaven and earth. Theocentricity, *coram Deo*, the Five Points, the *solas*, and the rest will prove to be the redemption of counseling. They glorify the Christ who speaks and acts for our redemption. Whatever of the Redeemer's character is communicable attribute and whatever of the mind of Christ is communicable truth will become the church's character and mind sooner and later. May more and more of it be sooner! On the flip side, 'Good practical theology is the hope of orthodoxy today.' We can put a sharper point on Clair Davis's generality: wise counseling is the hope of Calvinism today (one significant part of hope). May we each and all practice our faith in ways that increasingly adorn our profession.

NOTES

1. For an introduction to this history, see my Ph.D. dissertation, *Competent to Counsel?: The History of a Conservative Protestant Antipsychiatry Movement* (University of Pennsylvania, 1996).
2. Baptism and end-state church discipline are the only places where public ministries of the Word name names and particulars.
3. I am indebted to Rev. James Petty for the gist of this idea.

PART III

ANECDOTES FROM THE MINISTRY AND TEACHING CAREER OF DR. DAVIS

CLAIR DAVIS AS TEACHER

Anonymous Remembrances

When I took Modern Age with Dr. Clair Davis, he was able to vividly portray past conflicts of the church. I knew what the issues were, I could feel the force of both sides of the argument, and I understood history! However, at times I wouldn't have a clue as to whom we were talking about, what part of the world we were in, or when it all happened. At those times I would raise my hand in class and ask, 'Who is this now? What century are we talking?' I also wrote down what I thought were memorable quotes on the top of my note pages. Here they are: (**Editor's Note:** *The following have been systematically grouped to reflect a 'historical theology' of Clair Davis maxims and aphorisms.*)

Personal Revelation:
1. 'I had the Puritan conversion experience. I also had it six times.'
2. 'I think I'd rather have engineers around me than New-Age people.'
3. 'I'm so old I can remember when no one had a philosophy of ministry.'

Wisdom Literature:
1. 'An opera combines the world's greatest music with the world's raunchiest plots.'
2. 'People who spend a lot of money on their wedding tend to stay married longer.'
3. 'Anything in the gray area is pious advice.'

Systematic Theology:
1. 'Scratch an antinomian and you get a Lutheran, scratch a neonomian and you get an Anabaptist.'
2. Definition of Unitarianism: 'The Fatherhood of God, the Brotherhood of man, in the neighborhood of Boston.'
3. 'Hegelian definition of a leader: see where the crowd is going, then run and get ahead of them.'
4. 'Remember Marxism? We had it up until about a year ago.'
5. 'At root, if you are not a Calvinist, you are an Atheist.'

Practical Theology:
1. 'More people die in bed than anywhere else – so stay out of bed!'
2. 'God loves you from all eternity, not just in terms of what you might someday amount to.'
3. 'See how many show up in the morning, and you know who loves the church; see how many show up in the evening, and you know who loves the pastor; see how many show up in the week, and you know who loves the Lord!'
4. 'The Gospel is for Christians, too.'
5. 'The key man in the local church is the bus mechanic, or the print shop man, or the radio station operator...'

Presbyterian Church History:
1. 'About the meanest thing you can do to someone in the 19th century was to cut off his horse's tail. When a fly comes, she'll get a bit ornery.'
2. 'There's no way of getting around it – Presbyterians have a way of splitting.'
3. 'There are too many denominations! The only solution is to start another one!'
4. 'I'd prefer that everyone be a Presbyterian. I guess I'll settle for everyone being a Presbyterian without being aware of it.'

* * *

Tim Lane

In the summer of 1987, I began my four-year 'sprint' to attain a Masters of Divinity Degree at Westminster Theological Seminary. Part of that training involved a systematic theology class covering the Doctrine of Man as well as two church history classes; one covering the Medieval period and another on the Modern period. These three classes seemed to stand apart from the other classes that I took while at WTS! Dr. Clair Davis taught each of these classes. In stark contrast to most of my other classes, Dr. Davis' classes were seemingly non-linear and incredibly humorous! It was the only time while at WTS I remember enjoying feeling confused! Short vignettes of church history were combined with humorous contemporary anecdotes that held the class for a solid sixty minutes, even for those of us who piled up on the back row. Dr. Davis' anecdotes were the subject of conversation as we left class and throughout the week. No one seemed to know what import they had on the content of the class, and at the time we didn't seem to mind. Dr Davis' classes seemed to be a brief respite between Dr. Gaffin's systematic theology classes and Hebrew. Then the time for exams arrived. That is when it all hit. I can recall pouring over my notes from class, trying to make sense of it all. That is when the non-linear became very linear. The carefully woven themes began to appear. One theme, in particular, was glaringly apparent. It was the theme of the obscuring and rediscovering of the Gospel of grace! Over and over again, Dr. Davis had artfully taken us down a vivid path highlighting the destructive impact of moralism only to bring us back to the wonderful rediscovery of the Gospel and its impact on the Church. It became clearer, as I worked through my notes, that all of the modern anecdotes were simply contemporary examples of the same. A few years later, Dr. Davis played a key part in my installation as pastor of Clemson Presbyterian Church in 1995. In his charge, he spoke about Christ. I count it a privilege and honor to have had Dr. Davis as a professor and friend. I have a great deal of gratitude for him. Without realizing it at the time, he was making every moment count by teaching me about Christ who is the head and source of life for His Church!

* * *

Alan Lee

What a joy to know that you and others are preparing a special festschrift for a very, very special man, Dr. Clair Davis. And what a privilege to be asked if I've got a 'Clair Davis Story' which might be included in this volume. I do – and I share it with deep gratitude for ever meeting this humble man and much praise to God for the awesome evidence of His wonderful work in him…

Back in the late '70s and early '80s, the seminary was doing its best to start a unique extension campus in south Florida. Dr. James

Hurley was its director, its students were all third or fourth year M.Div. students who'd relocated to Florida from the Philadelphia campus, and its classes were held at an imposing church building in Miami proper. Westminster professors flew in on a regular schedule to teach two-week sessions of the classes which were otherwise taught over the space of four months up north. The pace of their instruction, the reading assignments and the course load were grueling. And, invariable, the weather outside of our airless classroom was beautiful: 'Come!' it always seemed to say to the students and recently transplanted professors, 'Come outside and play!' We never did, though. The reasonable dutifulness of our professors always prevailed over student appeals for extended recesses, and so we remained indoors and studied.

Well, the schedule eventually called for Clair to make his way to Florida in order to teach his Modern Church course. He arrived in early May, just when the weather was at its sub-tropical best and the students were at their antsy, end-of-the-school-year worst. Temperature, ocean breezes and brilliant blue skies not withstanding, our Modern Church class began like all of the classes before it: With Clair lecturing to drowsy students in our cheerless classroom. Even his folksy, funny and right-on anecdotes couldn't keep us attentive; more than a few of us were caught nodding off that first morning and afternoon.

His class didn't end like all the rest, however. Rick Downs, now pastoring in New England, spoke up for his classmates on day two and proposed an idea which must have touched Clair's generous heart: 'Forget these extended breaks, Dr. Davis!' Rick declared. 'Why don't we just hold our classes at the beach? It's only a few miles away. We could accomplish everything there that we're trying to accomplish here and enjoy the gift of God's creation while we're at it!' Clair asked a few questions, thought it over and then pronounced his decision in his Clair Davis way: 'Fair enough. We'll meet at the beach tomorrow.' And so we did.

Early the next morning, Clair and his class showed up at the beach as arranged. Clair stood with his back to the beach, the natural 'front' of his outdoor classroom, while we students sat on picnic table benches facing the beach and – none of us had anticipated this – a constant parade of bikini-clad Florida women. Every time one of us looked up from his notebook to look at Clair, there was another woman walking across our range of vision just behind him. Finally, the time came for the class to take a break, and Clair dismissed us to a quick dip in the ocean. When we returned to resume our study of Modern Church History, Clair was standing on the other side of the picnic tables so that we had to sit with our backs to the beach to attend to him, while he was facing it. Asked why the switch, he deadpanned, 'Well, none of you were falling asleep this morning, but none of you were taking notes either.' To Clair's credit, let it be noted: He completed his intended number of lectures!

* * *

Joseph V. Novenson – Written earlier during Dr. Davis' hospitalization for cancer.

I have learned to love Christ's Bride as I have studied church history with you. And, I have learned to love her with all her warts and wrinkles. You have both taught me and modeled before me one very wonderful truth in particular.

Some of God's most precious servants have been given a limp for their life. Jacob wrestled with God until he limped away. He left the presence of God blessed as a wounded victor. He won the fight by God's choice, but limped for the rest of his life. Both the victory and the wound spoke of those things that God gives to some of His dearest and most precious servants. He both blesses and causes struggle so that the heart that holds the great blessing may do so with tender hands. I do not know and would not presume to say that I know what God is up to in your life. I am not saying that everything I've just said about Jacob is true about you personally. But I do know that you are one of the most insightful, kind, humble, gracious, merciful, creative and sensitive scholars I have known. And although I have not spent hours with you, from a perspective of watching both near and far and listening to people speak about you, I am bold to say that with a measure of confidence; having given you so many gifts, Jesus would be thoroughly consistent to ask that you carry those gifts with a slight limp in order that greater glory may come to the blessed King and perhaps ... I can say only perhaps...that may be one of the things He has done with the physical struggles and illness you have faced in recent years.

I write with two agendas. First, I thank you for teaching me church history and allowing me to behold a legion of wounded warriors. Second, my heart's cry is to seek to be a small encouragement to someone I admire and respect very much for modeling and serving Christ with a limp.

I number myself among those who have learned from your walking with a limp. You welcome others like me to the army of the Savior's wounded warriors...your life welcomes us all to the platoon of the poverty stricken who are kept by the King...your life, your words, your scholarship, and even your physical limitations are a warm welcome to the marching band who always plays slightly out of tune, but who always plays the notes of praise for the Savior. I am simply playing my broken little clarinet by your side and I am honored to do so because you taught me much about this tune of grace. Clair, you are a trophy of grace and a treasure to know.

* * *

Joseph 'Skip' Ryan
In our Medieval Church History course in 1974, Clair would begin each class with the same question immediately after his opening prayer. The question was intended to remind us of the theological and pastoral problems which led to the necessity of the Reformation. The question was, 'So, how do you get saved?' But one morning, Clair forgot to pray and launched directly into the familiar question. There was a kind of stunned incredulity in the room since the usual routine of prayer had been overlooked. Monty Ledford, a charmingly boisterous student, interrupted Clair as he began to define his familiar question once again in terms of the failure of the medieval consensus. Monty broke the tension of that awkward moment by yelling out from the back of the room, 'How do you get saved if you don't pray?' For the first and only time in my memory, Clair was caught flatfooted without a witty response. He recovered though, laughed his jerky-cough laugh and launched into an eloquent prayer of confession for his forgetfulness.

* * *

George C. Scipione
I always believed that Clair Davis was not only a fantastic teacher but one of the funniest original stand-up comedians of all times. Certainly in theological circles, there is none better. He has an uncanny wisdom, wit and winsome delivery. His keen abilities come to the fore whether alone or in tandem with another. I think he and Jay Adams were Westminster Seminary's answer to Super Chicken and Fred. Perhaps a non-classroom example will suffice.

Almost every year while I attended Westminster Theological Seminary, 1967-1972, there was an annual student/faculty stunt night. The faculty and students would, good naturedly of course, poke fun at each other. Dr. Davis was given a monologue on his experience as a student at WTS. By the time he finished, our sides hurt and our eyes burned with tears. His deadpan delivery of clever observations, etc. were pithy and powerful. He started us off with his attempts to find the campus after arriving at the local train station. He tried to get directions from all sorts of people. Of course no one, not even a policeman, could help. But he did get directions from the local bartender! He had us weeping through three years of struggles – how we could relate – only to end with the granddaddy. Each semester, the faculty would put off definitive answers to questions until the next semester. Obviously, the last semester would be the equivalent of the discovery of the holy grail! But alas, that semester finally came, and he received the biggest bibliography ever written, and had to find the answers on his own! A sweet love for Jesus and 'sweet subtlety in thought' come from a unique servant of Christ. Thank God for gifts like him.

* * *

Mike Sherret

I'll never forget Clair lecturing in Middle Ages. First class, first key question raised (as he loved to teach by raising questions): 'Why study the Middle Ages? Pope's got all the money!' And this followed by his own laughter. Another question raised sometime later: 'What do you do with a heretic? You streeetch him a little!' Again, followed by his laughter, which was worth the price of admission.

During Modern Age Clair taught a lot of things. What sticks in my mind? The time he wove into the lecture the fact that his son at UVA was witnessing to his Jewish friend, and that person's salvation seemed as important to Clair as anything he had planned to teach in lectures.

* * *

Gordon Woolard

It is a privilege for me to write a short note in honor of Clair Davis. He is among my most admired and appreciated professors. I absolutely loved his sense of humor. It made church history so much more human and real. One thing I remember vividly took place outside the classroom. Clair and Lynn were willing to take an evening out of their busy lives to go to a movie with my wife, Marilyn, and me. Although I was the student and he was the professor we went out almost as though it was a double date. After the movie we went back to his home to talk about the film and other cultural media. It was a thrill for a young couple to be taken seriously by an older couple, (and a professor to boot!) Thank you, Clair and Lynn.

CLAIR DAVIS AS COLLEAGUE

John Frame

Newly arrived on the Westminster faculty in 1968, I was asked to teach the systematic theology course Doctrine of God (Theology Proper) that Clair had taught the year before. I asked if he had any advice for a green theologian. He mused to the effect that the Doctrine of God is a strange locus; everything in it could as easily be taught somewhere else in the curriculum. That comment shook up my thinking. Yes, Clair was right: Predestination can be taught under soteriology, rather than theology proper. The acts of God, miracle, providence, and creation, are as much biblical theology as systematic theology. The persons of the Trinity can be discussed under Christology and Pneumatology. The attributes of God can be discussed in connection with his mighty acts; for in Scripture it is God's mighty acts that move people to speak (in praise) of his attributes. So I have come to present the Doctrine of God from many angles, 'multi-perceptively', as we say.

I never had Clair as a teacher, but many times his seemingly off-hand (actually well thought out) observations have pushed me out of my comfort zone, perhaps even more so since my departure from Philadelphia. His views of theological and denominational traditions, the relation of the Reformed faith to Evangelicalism, and the primacy of evangelism, have been especially formative. I mention Clair often as a church historian who is not locked into traditionalist ways of thinking, but who mines our tradition for new possibilities of Christian life and witness. And Clair has humbled me often by his preaching and godly example. May the Lord continue richly to bless his study and witness!

★ ★ ★

Robert B. Strimple

Any friend of Clair Davis, when asked to provide a recollection of his outstanding traits, is bound to list very near the top his dry wit, his infectious laugh, and his readiness to see the humor in most every situation. But the first remembrances that come to my mind are not of our good times together one-on-one but rather of certain times when we enjoyed the special camaraderie of the Westminster Seminary faculty during the 1970s. [I myself lost that when I was asked to 'go west' to California in 1979 to see a Westminster campus established there.] One such occasion arose when our faculty received an invitation from the faculty of Biblical Theological Seminary in Hatfield, Pennsylvania, to play them in a volleyball match on their campus. Well, we had never played volleyball together. Most of us had never played to game very much *apart* from one another either for that matter! But this was a challenge we could not refuse. The gauntlet had been thrown down and had to be taken up. So Clair Davis, Dick Gaffin, Ray Dillard, I, and one or two others all piled into Jay Adam's huge green station wagon and headed off to the Hatfield gym. Now, the fact that Biblical seminary *had* a gym should have been a warning to us, of course. As we learned later when we arrived, their seminary faculty had organized a team to play against student teams in a seminary intramural volleyball league that year, had already played almost a full season, and had done well enough to encourage them to issue our faculty to invitation. *Our* approach to preparation for the big match was a little different – and was so typical of the scholarly Westminster approach to everything. Clair Davis, as chairman of the faculty, had bought a book! *How to Play Winning Volleyball.* So as we drove to our first and last volleyball game together each of us took a turn reading aloud a chapter of our book: 'How to Serve'...'How to Receive'...'How to Dig'... 'How to Set'... 'How to Spike'... Need I report the outcome? Words cannot do justice to the awkward ineptness of our play.. Readers who knew this bookish bunch can paint their own mental pictures of our stumbling and bumbling effort. I shall spare weaker souls the agony. Suffice it to say that I cannot remember our scoring a point. Thankfully, no one was hurt.

★ ★ ★

Robert B. Strimple

Some of the happiest hours I spent with Clair Davis on the Westminster Seminary faculty in the 1970s were in the cramped space that passed for the 'faculty lunchroom' just off the stairwell on the second floor of the Stevenson Library. Clair told us more newly-arrived faculty members that when he had first joined the faculty from Wheaton College he discovered that each of his faculty colleagues ate his bag lunch alone behind the closed door of his library study. But Clair was too social an animal for that and urged us all to join him at lunchtime. It was one of his best faculty chairman decisions. How fondly I remember those lunches lightening and brightening the academic day. Rarely were the conversation topics matters of earnest theological of ecclesiastical concern, but that's what was needed at this mid-day break. As memories begin to fade, there are few of those topics that I can actually recall. There is one, but dare I share such an 'inside ' anecdote and risk tarnish forever the reputation of these Presbyterian ministers?... Most subjects that we took up were pretty well 'milked' of their fun after one lunchtime. But there was one that I recall becoming an ongoing discussion that lasted several days. The 'regulars' in this lunch club were Clair Davis, Ray Dillard, Jay Adams, Dick Gaffin, Norman Shepherd, and I, and others who would join us from time to time. As ordained Presbyterian ministers, we were all called upon quite often, especially during the summer months, to serve as supply preachers in congregations not only in Pennsylvania but also in New Jersey, New York, Delaware, and Maryland. Since many of us were also into camping with our families, we were familiar with the Mobil travel Guide and how useful it could be in providing multiple star ranking of leading campgrounds and motels, listing the amenities of each. Thus it was only natural, I suppose, that Clair should one day come up with the idea that we should put together a guidebook for Presbyterian Supply Preachers in the Middle Atlantic States. I seem to recall that the lunch group had its best attendance ever during those days when we put our heads together to list all the congregations in which we had preached in the last year or two, and shared from our own experiences the information that every man invited to be supply preacher in one of these churches should know: not only the basics like driving directions, times of services, orders of worship, and is the sanctuary air-conditioned; but also such inside information as what length of sermons in tolerated, which woman in the congregation provided the best fried chicken dinner, and when the session last voted a cost-of-living increase to the honorarium! Well, I guess you had to be there ... but remember: it was all in good fun.

★ ★ ★

An email by Dr. Davis to the Westminster Seminary voting faculty, forwarded by Dr. Will Barker.
(**Editor's Note.** This explanation of the history of the Welsh patron saint, Saint David, and the development of the celebration of Saint David's Day, also includes some interesting autobiographical insights, as Dr. Davis reflects on being a Christian from the Welsh tradition in America. Appropriately, Clair sent it on Saint David's Day, March 1, 2002 at 7:19 am.)

If you were lucky enough to be in Wales on March the first, you would find the country in a festive mood. Every self-respecting man, woman and child would be celebrating St. David's Day in one way or another. But who was St. David, and why is he so important to the Welsh? And just how is St. David's Day celebrated in Wales today?

Well, Saint David, or Dewi Sant, as he is known in the Welsh language, is the patron saint of Wales. He was a Celtic monk, abbot and bishop, who lived in the sixth century. During his life, he was the archbishop of Wales, and he was one of many early saints who helped to spread Christianity among the pagan Celtic tribes of western Britain.

For details of the life of Dewi, we depend mainly on his biographer, Rhigyfarch. He wrote *Buchedd Dewi* (the life of David) in the 11th century. Gerallt Gymro (Giraldus Cambrensis), who wrote a book about his travels through Wales in the 12th century, also gives some information about Dewi's early life. Dewi died in the sixth century, so nearly five hundred years elapsed between his death and the first manuscripts recording his life. As a result, it isn't clear how much of the history of Dewi's life is legend rather than fact.

However, both sources say, so we can be relatively certain, that Dewi was a very gentle person who lived a frugal life. It is claimed that he ate mostly bread and herbs – probably watercress, which was widely used at the time. Despite this supposedly meager diet, it is reported that he was tall and physically strong.

Dewi is said to have been of royal lineage. His father, Sant, was the son of Ceredig, who was prince of Ceredigion, a region in South-West Wales. His mother, Non, was the daughter of a local chieftain. Legend has it that Non was also a niece of King Arthur.

Dewi was born near Capel Non (Non's chapel) on the South-West Wales coast near the present city of Saint Dewi. We know a little about his early life – he was educated in a monastery called Hen Fynyw, his teacher being Paulinus, a blind monk. Dewi stayed there for some years before going forth with a party of followers on his missionary travels.

Dewi travelled far on his missionary journeys through Wales, where he established several churches. He also travelled to the south and west of England and Cornwall as well as Brittany. It is also possible that he visited Ireland. Two friends of his, Saints Padarn and Teilo, are said to have often accompanied him on his journeys, and they once went together on a pilgrimage to Jerusalem to meet the Patriarch.

Dewi is sometimes known, in Welsh, as 'Dewi Ddyfrwr' (David the Water Drinker) and, indeed, water was an important part of his life – he is said to have drunk nothing else. Sometimes, as a self-imposed penance, he would stand up to his neck in a lake of cold water, reciting Scripture. Little wonder, then, that some authors have seen Dewi as an early Puritan!

He founded a monastery at Glyn Rhosyn (Rose Vale) on the banks of the small river Alun where the cathedral city of St. David stands today. The monastic brotherhood that Dewi founded was very strict, the brothers having to work very hard besides praying and celebrating masses. They had to get up very early in the morning for prayers and afterwards work very hard to help maintain life at the monastery, cultivating the land and even pulling the plough. Many crafts were followed – beekeeping, in particular, was very important. The monks had to keep themselves fed as well as the many pilgrims and travellers who needed lodgings. They also had to feed and clothe the poor and needy in their neighbourhood.

There are many stories regarding Dewi's life. It is said that he once rose a youth from death, and milestones during his life were marked by the appearance of springs of water. These events are arguably more apocryphal than factual, but are so well known to Welsh-speaking schoolchildren that it is worth mentioning them here.

Perhaps the most well-known story regarding Dewi's life is said to have taken place at the Synod of Llanddewi Brefi. They were to decide whether Dewi was to be Archbishop. A great crowd gathered at the synod, and when Dewi stood up to speak, one of the congregation shouted, 'We won't be able to see or hear him'. At that instant the ground rose till everyone could see and hear Dewi. Unsurprisingly, it was decided, very shortly afterwards, that Dewi would be the Archbishop...

It is claimed that Dewi lived for over 100 years, and it is generally accepted that he died in 589. His last words to his followers were in a sermon on the previous Sunday. Rhigyfarch transcribes these as 'Be joyful, and keep your faith and your creed. Do the little things that you have seen me do and heard about. I will walk the path that our fathers have trod before us.' 'Do the little things' ('Gwnewch y pethau bychain') is today a very well-known phrase in Welsh, and has proved an inspiration to many. On a Tuesday, the first of March, in the year 589, the monastery is said to have been 'filled with angels as Christ received his soul'.

Dewi's body was buried in the grounds of his own monastery, where the Cathedral of St. David now stands. After his death, his influence spread far and wide – first through Britain, along what was left of the Roman roads, and by sea to Cornwall and Brittany.

St David's Day, as celebrated today, dates back to 1120, when Dewi was canonised by Pope Callactus the Second, and March 1st was included in the Church calendar. After Dewi's canonisation, many pilgrimages were made to St. David's, and it was reported that two pilgrimages there equalled one to Rome, and three pilgrimages one to Jerusalem. March 1st was celebrated until the Reformation as a holy day. Many churches are dedicated to Dewi, and some to his mother Non.

It is not certain how much of the history of St. David is fact and how much is mere speculation. At the end of 1996, though, bones were found in St. David's Cathedral which, it is claimed, could be those of Dewi himself. These will soon be taken for radio-carbon dating to the same units that dated the Turin Shroud. So a whole new light could soon be cast on Dewi's life...

I thought the above might give you extra meaning for the day. *Clair*

The above account isn't bad, but omits the fact that in that famous sermon when the ground pushed up so folks could hear and see him (I can identify), the whole point was the rejection of Pelagianism. (Pelagius may have been named Morgan, a Welsh monk himself).

My parents were third-generation Americans, but knew no English until they started school. Welsh was the medium for private communication on the party line. The local baseball team didn't use signs-the coaches just talked Welsh to the players. I knew enough Welsh to call our dog.

My great-grandfather, John R. Daniel, was a farmer-preacher in the old church just east of Randolph WI, where he is buried. Some of his sermons have been translated and are very good. Referring to Hebrews, we seek a better city, he said, remember how in Wales we looked forward to being in America. My mother's family lived in Cambria WI (Latin for Wales).

My father's grandfather came to IA seeking his own land and religious freedom, the right not to pay tithes to the Anglicans. The custom was that one paid in person to the priest, and the priest responded with a glass of liquor. Vaughn Davis was a teetotaler and also frugal, so he brought a bottle with him for the priest's booze, which he later put into his horse medicine.

Everyone was in the Calvinistic Methodist Church, sometimes-called in NY the Whitefield Methodist Church. (The Welsh around here, [Welsh Road, Bryn Mawr, Bryn Athyn] were Quakers).

The creed was essentially the WCF with some additions, notably a chapter on the Good Conscience next to the Assurance chapter. There were congregational elements, with members being received and disciplined by the congregation itself; the mid-week meeting could not be led by the minister, but was a congregational affair. Welsh churches had the reputation of being very emotional but doctrinally frothy. Most global revivals began in Wales; since no one could read the sermons, all the Chinese knew in 1904 was that in Wales there was a revival so they had one too, with their own theology and methods (I was adviser here of a dissertation on revival in China in the early 20th century). The most intriguing revival began with the preacher coming to the platform, not saying a word, praying for a long time, standing up and raising his arms, pausing, then saying, 'Glory!' That was enough.

In 1920 the Calvinist Methodists (CMs) joined the Presbyterian Church (at our Academy of Music), since the Welsh were so dumb that they thought they were primarily Methodists and were hence transferring to the Methodist Church when they moved to a town where there was no CM church (most places). That plan of union affirmed the Welsh right to continue their own mission board, since all contributions to missions are free-will offerings. (How in the world the historians on Machen's team missed that in 1934 is beyond me. A student of mine did a ThM at Princeton on the Machen trial, so I fed him that. His adviser Loetscher had never heard of it and said it was a special Welsh right, not a general Presbyterian principle. Anyone, including Machen, can find it in five minutes by looking in the index to the Digest of GA actions under foreign missions).

CM's went to Ripon College and Princeton Theological Seminary. In the early 50's I was pre-enrolled at Princeton. When I wrote canceling that, saying I was going to Westminster Theological Seminary, the admissions officer, a distant relative of mine, wrote me telling me I was abandoning my Welsh heritage of warm passionate Christianity for the icy deadness at WTS.

When I teach on March 1, I have usually worn the biggest leek I could find, which went into the soup in the evening. Now you know much more than you wanted to know about St. David's Day. Aware that my time in your precious proximity must be winding down, I thought you'd like to know. *DCD*

CLAIR DAVIS AS PRESBYTER

Dominic A. Aquila

One of my first recollections of Clair Davis was his address before the General Synod of the Reformed Presbyterian Church, Evangelical Synod in 1975 on the Plan of Union between the Orthodox Presbyterian Church and the RPCES. He was characteristically incisive in evaluating both churches – and equally humorous in his anecdotal reminiscences. While a number of speakers from both churches were giving predictions about dire consequences if the union should be approved, Clair argued from church history that perhaps both sides were equally wrong in their concerns. What I recall more than his defense of the Union was his genuine love for the Church that was exuded throughout his remarks. That was a lesson in itself for me.

★ ★ ★

Frank Breische

I did not know Clair Davis as a teacher. I did know him as a parishioner and as a friend. Clair came to Wheaton College when I was ministering at Bethel Presbyterian Church. He and Lynn became members of the congregation and, more importantly to me, friends of the Breisches. Lynn and Dort really brought our two families together, but the friendship that I developed with Clair was one that I valued and cherished and still do.

A number of incidents reflect for me the kind of friend that Clair is. Some Sunday mornings, as Clair was leaving church, he'd suggest that we have coffee the next morning. I knew what that meant; something I had said something that didn't register well with Clair, and he wanted to discuss it. I think that I usually convinced him that my presentation of the gospel might be semantically unusual but was doctrinally acceptable, but that may be the rosy glow of ancient memory. I am sure that any minister would benefit from the kind of careful listener that Clair was; I certainly did.

I recall the morning when I was at Geneva Hospital, some 10 to 15 miles west of Wheaton, waiting while Dort gave birth to our youngest child, Sue. I hadn't been waiting too long when Clair showed up. We sat on the front porch of the hospital, which was in a converted house, and watched the sun come up. I certainly don't recall what we talked about, but his presence with me was an unexpected benefit of our friendship and those hours we spent together drew me even closer to him.

There was a time when I was in trouble with my presbytery because of my views about the Christian Sabbath. It was a long process, which went on year after year. Time and again I had to defend myself, first at Presbytery and later at General Assembly. During that time Clair was my confidant, my supporter and my advisor. I wasn't always smart enough to take his advice, but I always considered it and I appreciated it deeply. His historical background was helpful, but his personal support and friendship was even more important. The old saying, 'A friend in need is a friend indeed', was proved true again.

So when I think of Clair, I think first of all of a dear friend. And to that friend, Dort and I want to extend our very best wishes on his retirement from teaching at Westminster but not, I'm sure, from teaching and supporting people in many ways. God bless you, Clair and Lynn!

* * *

Rick Buddemeier

1. He was not aware of an age but of all time.
In 1973, we were gathered in a 'prayer meeting for the nations', and someone asked what places we should pray for. Clair glanced off to one side, accessing his archive in a snatch, and shot out –

Germany. That night we prayed for renewal in Germany and asked God to send workers into a field that had once been the source of much harvest. Twenty-five years later Clair was asked to fly to Germany to preach and teach. He called me up and said, 'Hey, remember we had a little prayer meeting a number of years ago, and we were each asked to name a country we'd like to pray for?' (Why does Clair always say 'Hey, remember...?' when he really means 'You probably forgot and it's my job to help you remember') I did, vaguely. 'I guess, if we wait around long enough and pay enough attention, God will use even folks like us to answer our own prayers.' This was, of course, the last sentence in a detailed historical analysis – the last sentence in a race through his archive, ending with a personal application. It was a teaching 'aware of all time' and happily presented by a man who sees himself and helps us see ourselves embedded in the plans of our sovereign God.

2. I was on the verge of becoming a missionary, concerned about my qualifications and my call. We were sitting by the pool and Clair was musing on the nature of preaching. We talked about a few theorists and a few practitioners and about how he'd listened to too much preaching. He knew my condition, but it was a few months before I realized he was addressing me: 'You know, you say to yourself, 'Now that wasn't a bad sermon, but I think maybe I could do better' – and maybe you should.'

★ ★ ★

Andree Seu

1. Many years ago, when New Life Church met at Friends meetinghouse in Jenkintown, after, Dr. Davis had preached one Sunday the floor was opened up for prayers. A number of people spoke out in prayer, and I was one of them, a prayer whose particulars I don't remember except that it was thinly disguised self-pity and unbelief. When prayer time was closed, I opened my eyes to see Dr. Davis standing inches from my face. He looked me in the eye and said only, 'Most of the world's work is done by people who don't feel good.' Then he walked away. Immediately I was aware that a prophet had spoken to me. His remark was more sobering and helpful than many commiserations.

2. When Dr. Davis was ill and at Holy Redeemer Hospital with cancer, my husband and I came to see him, and Young

started massaging his feet (I was mildly embarrassed). Only two years later the tables were turned and it was Young in the hospital with cancer, and Dr. Davis and Lynn came to see him. And this time Dr. Davis massaged his feet.

3. Regrettably, I never took any of Dr. Davis' church history courses when I was at Westminster 22 years ago. But whatever church history I know, I know from listening to the cassette tapes of those courses in recent years, as I went jogging night after night when the kids were in bed.

PART IV

REPRESENTATIVE BIBLIOGRAPHY OF DR. DAVIS' PUBLISHED ARTICLES

A REPRESENTATIVE
BIBLIOGRAPHY
FOR D. CLAIR DAVIS

'Future Pastors and Modern Problems' *Presbyterian Guardian* 25:10-11 1956

Review of **The Inextinguishable Blaze** by A.S. Wood *Westminster Theological Journal* 25: 49-51 1962

Review of **The Growing Storm** by G.S.M. Walker *Westminster Theological Journal* 26:65-66 1963

Review of **Roman Hellenism and The New Testament** by F.C. Grant *Westminster Theological Journal* 26:167-169 1964

Review of **The Reformation** by W.C. Robinson *Westminster Theological Journal* 27:191-192 1965

Review of **The Formation of Historical Theology** by P.C. Hodgson *Westminster Theological Journal* 29: 233-236 1967

'Using the State for Sectarian Ends' *Christianity Today* 11:8-10 1967

'Creedal Changes and Subscription to the System of Doctrine' *Presbyterian Guardian* 36:45-47 1967

Review of **The Theology of Martin Luther** by P. Althaus *Westminster Theological Journal* 30:103-106 1967

Review of **Christ for Us in the Theology of Dietrich Bonhoeffer** by J. A. Phillips *Westminster Theological Journal* 31:94-98 1968

'In the Meantime' *Presbyterian Guardian* 38:48-50 1969

'He Tells It – Warts and All' *Presbyterian Guardian* 41:38-39 1972

Review of **A History of Fundamentalism in America** by G. W. Dollar *Westminster Theological Journal* 36:397-398 1974

'Kids and the Gospel' *Journal of Pastoral Practice* 1:1:65-67 1977

'Revival or Renewal?' *Journal of Pastoral Practice* 1:2:69-71 1977

'The Altar Call' *Journal of Pastoral Practice* 2:2:57-59 1978

'Presbyterian Roots' *Journal of Pastoral Practice* 3:3:75 1979

'The Evangelism Newspaper' *Journal of Pastoral Practice* 3:3:76-77 1979

'Slow Kids Need a Fast Church' *Journal of Pastoral Practice* 3:3:78-79 1979

'The Task of Church History: Answering the Threat of Historicism' *Westminster Theological Journal* 41:221-227 1979

'Evangelicals and The Presbyterian Tradition: An Alternative Perspective' *Westminster Theological Journal* 42:152-156 1979

'The OPC at a Glance' *New Horizons* 1:5:4 1980

'The Reformed Church of Germany: Calvinists as an Influential Minority' in **John Calvin: His Influence in the Western World**, ed. W. Stanford Reid Grand Rapids: Zondervan 123-138 1982

'Children and Church Membership' *New Horizons* 4:6:20 1983

'Defenders of the Faith' *New Horizons* 5:1:1 1984

'Who Knows More about Trouble than You Do?" *Presbyterian Journal* 43:16:17 1984

'Thank God It's Monday' *Presbyterian Journal* 43:18:9 1984

'The Spirit is No Spook' *Presbyterian Journal* 43:27:9 1984

'Enjoy, Enjoy' *Presbyterian Journal* 43:30:11 1984

'Jesus Keeps it Simple' *Presbyterian Journal* 43:45:10 1985

'Springtime with Jesus' *Presbyterian Journal* 43:50:16 1985

'Special Salvation' *Presbyterian Journal* 45:3:22 1986

'Personal Salvation' *Presbyterian Journal* 45:5:19 1986

'Irresistible Salvatnn" *Presbyterian Journal* 45:8:20 1986

'Persevering Salvation' *Presbyterian Journal* 45:9:22 1986

'What's so Good About Being a Calvinist?' *Presbyterian Journal* 45:11:21 1986

'Come, O Come, Immanuel' *Presbyterian Journal* 45:12:23 1986

'Machen and Liberalism' in **Pressing Toward the Mark: Essays Commemorating Fifty Years of the Orthodox Presbyterian Church,** eds. C.G. Dennison and R.C. Gamble Philadelphia: Committee for the Historian of the OPC 33-51 1986

'Growing Up on Your Knees' *Presbyterian Journal* 45:15:22 1987

'The Last Word' *Presbyterian Journal* 45:16:22 1987

'Covenant-Keeping 200 Years Later' *New Horizons* 8:8:15 1987

'Personal Salvation' (reprint) *Presbyterian Network* 1:1:22-23 1987

Review of **Modern American Religion, Vol. 1: The Irony of It All, 1892–1919** by M.E. Marty *Eternity Magazine* 38:6:40-41 1987
Review of **One Nation Under God: Christian Faith and Political Action in America** by Mark Noll
Eternity Magazine 39:10:47-48 1988

'Counseling in Hope' *Journal of Pastoral Practice* 9:3:5-10 1988

'Irresistible Salvation' (reprint) *Presbyterian Network* 1:4:22-23 1988

'As the World Shifts and Grows, So Does the Church" *Westminster Point of Contact* 4:4 1988

'Persevering Salvation" (reprint) *Presbyterian Network* 1:2:17-18 1988

'Total Salvation" *Presbyterian Network* 1:3:21-22 1988

'Inerrancy and Westminster Calvinism" in **Inerrancy and Hermaneutic** ed. Harvie M. Conn Grand Rapids: Baker 35-46 1988

'Mercersberg Theology" in **New Dictionary of Theology** Downers Grove, IL InterVarsity Press, 421-422 1988

'Nominalism" in **New Dictionary of Theology** Downers Grove, IL InterVarsity Press 471-472 1988

'A Response to the Woman's Role" *PCA Messenger* 13:2:25 1989

'The Love of God and Evangelism" *PCA Messenger* 13:5:8-9 1989

'A Challenge to Theonomy" in **Theonomy: A Reformed Critique,** eds. William S. Barker and W. Robert Godfrey Grand Rapids: Zondervan, 389-402 1990

'Gospel Politics in a Changing World" *Westminster Bulletin* 29:3:6 1990

'Talking for Jesus" *Presbyterian Network* 2:3:22-23 1990

'Presbyterians and Theonomy" *Presbyterian Network* 5:4:3-4 1992

'Presbytery Examinations" *Presbyterian Witness* 7:1:13 1993

'How Did the Church in Rome Become Roman Catholicism?" in: **Roman Catholicism: Evangelical Protestants Analyze What Divides and Unites Us,** ed. John Armstrong Chicago: Moody 45-64 1994

'What Do PCA Folks Say?" *Equip for Ministry* 1:3:7-8 1995

'How do Our Choices and Their Consequences Relate to God's Plan in our Lives?" *Journal of Biblical Counseling* 19:2:57 2001

SCRIPTURE INDEX

PERSONS INDEX

96, 179, 304, 308, 318, 320, 322, 326, 357, 496, 508, 510, 512-13, 515-18, 522, 524, 526
California 23, 510, 516
Wheaton College, Illinois 22-3, 517, 523
Wheeler, Barbara 366
Whitefield, George 132, 144, 235, 360-1, 454
Whitefield Methodist Church 521
Whitgift, John 155
William of Orange, King of England 221-5
William of Ockham
See Occam, William
Williams, D.H. 66
Williams, Roger 185

Williamson, W. Jack 320
Wilson-Kastner, Patricia 270, 274, 276-7
Winslow, Ola 235-6, 239, 244, 262-4
Winthrop, John 185
Woolard, Gordon 513
Woolley, Paul 22-4
Wycliffe, John 75, 142, 496

Yale University 234
Yannaris, Christos 66

Zanchi, Girolamo 190, 447
Zechariah 101
Zeller, Winifried 396, 411
Zurich 150-1, 153-4, 158-60
Zwingli, Ulrich 131, 134

SUBJECT INDEX

joy 49, 108, 196, 205,
243, 259, 261, 271,
273, 418, 448, 454,
461, 463-4, 471, 473,
479-81, 484, 500
judaism 156, 295
judgment 32, 84-5, 92-3, 106,
117, 124, 126, 190,
196-7, 199, 249, 418-
19, 447, 450, 481
day of 205, 354, 418
Last Judgment 196, 417
seat of 107, 119, 195
justice of God 76, 79, 82, 85,
89, 91-3, 109, 186-8,
239, 248, 253-7, 287,
472, 501
social justice 479, 486
*Justice of God in the
Damnation of Sinners*
(J.Edwards) 234, 252,
261
justification 32, 57, 83-4, 103,
108, 126, 135-7, 140,
143, 173, 176, 191-2,
194-6, 199, 239-40,
267, 400, 420, 434-9,
441-2, 446, 466-70, 489
justification by faith
84, 92, 134-6, 239-40,
242, 247, 252, 322,
436-7, 464, 469

Kingdom of God 14, 70,
102-6, 109, 234, 240,
245, 260, 262, 288,
394-5, 400, 413, 453,
486, 496

Laity 141-4, 312, 319-20,
325, 364

last things 417, 419-20
See also eschatology
law 14, 175, 218, 220, 331
canon law 73
church law 215, 333
of God 79-80, 82-3,
89, 98-100, 102, 107-
8, 124, 136, 143, 173-
4, 192-5, 200, 202,
204, 252-3, 276, 399,
416, 421-2, 448, 463-
4, 467-9, 472, 482, 486
leadership (of the church) 18,
56, 74, 110, 144, 153,
159, 215, 307, 311,
324-5, 364, 450, 464
League of Evangelical
Students 304
legalism 464, 467, 473
liberalism (theological) 237,
275, 288, 297, 302-5,
357, 361, 366-9, 384
liberals 289, 365-6, 369
life eternal 45, 60, 103, 105,
107, 136, 167, 186,
191-3, 195-6, 203,
273-4, 431, 449, 458
everlasting 177-8, 189
limited atonement *See*
atonement
liturgy 55-7, 66, 92, 152, 227,
358, 360-1
Loci Communes See
Common Places
logic 164-5
Lord's Day *See* Sabbath
Lord's Supper 72-3, 123, 135,
139, 147, 156, 244,
393-4, 397, 459, 499
lordship 275, 495
love, God's 15, 28, 32, 36, 45,

Mathew Henry's Unpublished Sermons on
The Covenant of Grace
Edited Allan Harman

Fifty years ago Allan Harman was given a small, well-worn book of handwritten sermon notes. It was clear that what he had was Matthew Henry's own handwritten notes, from a series of sermons he preached to his Chester congregation during 1691 and 1692. Harman knew these sermons needed to reach a wider audience and started turned these long forgotten sermons into what you hold in your hand today – a revealing, and deeply spiritual work that allows us to read Matthew Henry on that most fundamental of doctrines – God's promise of unmerited favour to mankind. Harman filled in the shorthand gaps, added footnotes to help with passages obscure to our contemporary ears and translated the Greek, Hebrew and Latin quotes. He also provides a biographical introduction to help us picture Henry and see the context in which these sermons were preached.

Matthew Henry's delightfully clear style is evident throughout the text and provides succinct, memorable quotations, that will stay with you.

'He studied the Scriptures intently (All but four of the Biblical Books are referred to) and organised his material methodically. Constantly he illustrates, not be lengthy stories but by phrases and references which crystallize his points... I can testify to the blessing they have been to me.'

Allan Harman

Allan Harman is a Research Professor at the Presbyterian Theological College, Melbourne.

ISBN 1 85792 796 6

Treatises on the Sacraments
Calvin's Tracts translated by Henry Beveridge
John Calvin

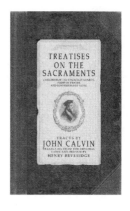

Countless analyses and critiques of Calvin's work have been released over the centuries, and a huge number of Churches and denominations hold to Calvin's teaching to varying degrees. Calvin's name is thrown about in theological discussions covering a broad spectrum, we may know the Calvinist's view, but what does Calvin himself say?

One of the key issues that led to the reformation and the birth of Protestantism was Rome's treatment of the Lord's Supper. This is the main subject of this collection of Calvin's tracts. Calvin and the Reformers believed the Catholic Mass was founded on a grave error that urgently needed to be corrected. According to Rome's doctrine of transubstantiation the bread and wine supernaturally became Christ's body and blood. Calvin on the other hand held that they were symbolic and to say otherwise bordered on idolatry and diminished Christ's once for all sacrifice on the cross. This key point of difference remains to this day and Calvin's writings have become a starting point from which Reformed Theologians have gone on to defend and develop the Protestant stance.

This unedited collection of sermons allows you to read John Calvin's own ideas on issues relating to the sacraments, catechisms, forms of prayer and confessions of faith.

Extensive Introduction by Joel R. Beeke

ISBN 1 85792 725 7

Christian Focus Publications

publishes books for all ages

Our mission statement -

STAYING FAITHFUL
In dependence upon God we seek to help make his infallible word,
the Bible, relevant. Our aim is to ensure that the Lord Jesus Christ
is presented as the only hope to obtain forgiveness of sin, live a
useful life and look forward to heaven with him.

REACHING OUT
Christ's last command requires us to reach out to our world with
his gospel. We seek to help fulfill that by publishing books that
point people towards Jesus and help them to develop a Christ-like
maturity. We aim to equip all levels of readers for life, work ministry
and mission.

Books in our adult range are published in three imprints.

Christian Focus contains popular works including
biographies, commentaries, basic doctrine, and Christian
living. Our children's books are also published in this
imprint.

Mentor focuses on books written at a level suitable for Bible
College and seminary students, pastors, and other serious
readers; the imprint includes commentaries, doctrinal
studies, examination of current issues, and church history.

Christian Heritage contains classic writings from the past.

For a free catalogue of all our titles, please write to
Christian Focus Publications, Ltd
Geanies House, Fearn,
Ross-shire, IV20 1TW, Scotland, United Kingdom
info@christianfocus.com

For details of our titles visit us on our website
www.christianfocus.com

Above: 1943 (age 10) at family home in Washington, Iowa
Below: Circa 1951 with family in Washington, Iowa (age 18) three aunts in center - parents on far right

Above: 1953 college graduation photo
Below: 1959 Göettingen during doctoral studies

Above: 1963 when teaching at Olivet College
Below: Circa 1985 at Westminster Theological Seminary

A Survey of the Order of the Causes of Salvation and Damnation
By William Perkins (1558-1602)

A Survey or Table declaring the order of the causes of salvation and damnation according to God's word. It may be in stead of an ocular Catechism to them which can not read, for by the pointing of the fingers, they may sensibly perceive the chief points of religion, and the order of them

Editor's Note: This classic chart by Perkins, often called the "father of English Puritanism," is presented here without change except for minor spelling and vocabulary modification to reflect contemporary usage. Perkins' presentation is remarkable in that it simultaneously seeks to order the sovereign decrees of God, and to join with them the practical duties of human responsibility in the individual's salvation. The Classic chart can be found in *Introduction to Puritan Theology: A Reader*, Edward Hindson, ed. Foreword by James I. Packer (Grand Rapids: Baker

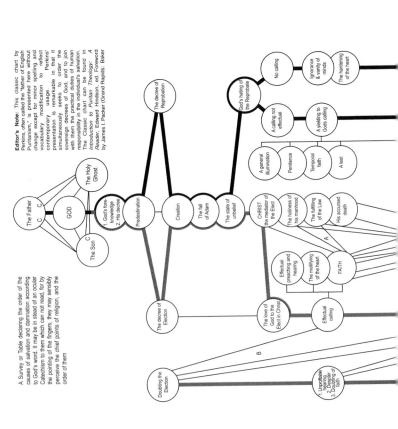

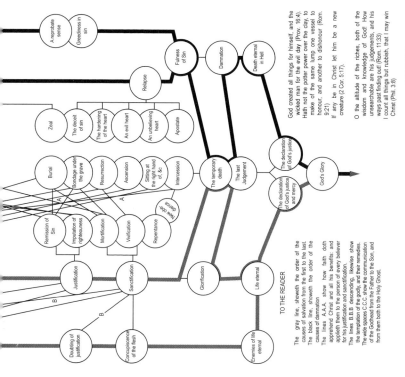

God created all things for himself, and the wicked man for the evil day (Prov. 16:4).
Hath not the potter power over the clay, to make of the same lump one vessel to honour, and another to dishonour (Rom. 9:21).
If any be in Christ let him be a new creature (2 Cor. 5:17).

O the altitude of the riches, both of the wisdom and knowledge of God! How unsearchable are his judgements, and his ways past finding out! (Rom. 11:33).
I count all things but rubbish, that I may win Christ (Phil. 3:8)

Ignatius saying,
My love is crucified.

TO THE READER

The gray line, showeth the order of the causes of salvation from the first to the last.
The black line, showeth the order of the causes of damnation
The lines A.A.A. show how faith doth apprehend Christ and all his benefits; and applieth them to the person of every believer for his justification and sanctification.
The lines B.B.B descending, likewise show the temptation of the godly, and their remedies.
The wide spaces C.C.C. show the communication of the Godhead from the Father to the Son, and from them both to the Holy Ghost.

The Sum of All Christianity
By Theodore Beza (1519-1605)

The Sum of all Christianity, or the description and distribution of the cause of the salvation of the elect and of the destruction of the reprobate, collected from the sacred writings.

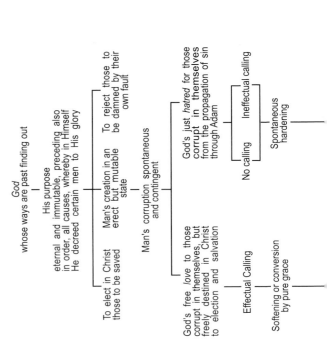

582

Editor's note: This theological chart by Beza, the successor to John Calvin in Geneva, is presented here essentially without change. It represents one of the earliest attempts by a Reformed theologian to order the sovereign decrees of God. From the idea of logically ordering God's decrees, the theological phrase "ordo salutis" or the "order of salvation" has come into common use in Reformed theology. Reformed theology continues to debate whether Beza's order is correct biblically speaking, and in some instances, whether the Bible even allows an ordering of the decrees at all. Beza's "Sum" can be found in Heinrich Heppe, *Reformed Dogmatics: Set Out and Illustrated from the Sources*, revised and edited by Ernst Bizer, trans. by G. T. Thomson (Grand Rapids: Baker Book House, 1978), pp. 147-48.

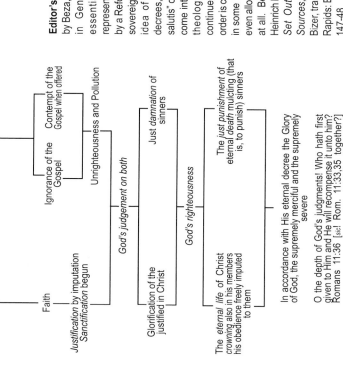

Ignorance of the Gospel — Contempt of the Gospel when offered

Unrighteousness and Pollution

God's judgement on both

Just *damnation* of sinners

Glorification of the justified in Christ

God's righteousness

The *just punishment* of eternal *death* mulcting (that is, to punish) sinners

Faith

Justification by imputation
Sanctification begun

The *eternal life* of Christ *crowning* also in his members his obedience freely imputed to them

In accordance with His eternal decree the Glory of God, the supremely merciful and the supremely severe

O the depth of God's judgments! Who hath first given to Him and He will recompense it unto him? Romans 11:36 [sic] Rom. 11:33,35 together?]